TOYOTA | COROLLA
1988-97 REPAIR MANUAL

CHILTON'S

Deleted

President	Dean F. Morgantini, S.A.E.
Vice President–Finance	Barry L. Beck
Vice President–Sales	Glenn D. Potere
Executive Editor	Kevin M. G. Maher
Production Manager	Ben Greisler, S.A.E.
Project Managers	Michael Abraham, George B. Heinrich III, S.A.E., Will Kessler, A.S.E., S.A.E., Richard Schwartz
Schematics Editor	Christopher G. Ritchie
Editor	Dawn M. Hoch, S.A.E.

CHILTON™ Automotive Books
PUBLISHED BY **W. G. NICHOLS, INC.**

Manufactured in USA
© 1998 W. G. Nichols
1020 Andrew Drive
West Chester, PA 19380
ISBN 0-8019-8827-6
Library of Congress Catalog Card No. 97-78113
1234567890 7654321098

Contents

Contents

SAFETY NOTICE

Proper service and repair procedures are vital to the safe, reliable operation of all motor vehicles, as well as the personal safety of those performing repairs. This manual outlines procedures for servicing and repairing vehicles using safe, effective methods. The procedures contain many NOTES, CAUTIONS and WARNINGS which should be followed, along with standard procedures, to eliminate the possibility of personal injury or improper service which could damage the vehicle or compromise its safety.

It is important to note that repair procedures and techniques, tools and parts for servicing motor vehicles, as well as the skill and experience of the individual performing the work, vary widely. It is not possible to anticipate all of the conceivable ways or conditions under which vehicles may be serviced, or to provide cautions as to all possible hazards that may result. Standard and accepted safety precautions and equipment should be used during cutting, grinding, chiseling, prying, or any other process that can cause material removal or projectiles.

Some procedures require the use of tools specially designed for a specific purpose. Before substituting another tool or procedure, you must be completely satisfied that neither your personal safety, nor the performance of the vehicle, will be endangered.

Although information in this manual is based on industry sources and is complete as possible at the time of publication, the possibility exists that some vehicle manufacturers made later changes which could not be included here. While striving for total accuracy, NP/Chilton cannot assume responsibility for any errors, changes or omissions that may occur in the compilation of this data.

PART NUMBERS

Part numbers listed in this reference are not recommendations by Chilton for any product brand name. They are references that can be used with interchange manuals and aftermarket supplier catalogs to locate each brand supplier's discrete part number.

SPECIAL TOOLS

Special tools are recommended by the vehicle manufacturer to perform their specific job. Use has been kept to a minimum, but, where absolutely necessary, they are referred to in the text by the part number of the tool manufacturer. These tools can be purchased, under the appropriate part number, from your local dealer or regional distributor, or an equivalent tool can be purchased locally from a tool supplier or parts outlet. Before substituting any tool for the one recommended, read the SAFETY NOTICE at the top of this page.

ACKNOWLEDGMENTS

NP/Chilton expresses appreciation to Toyota Motor Co. for their generous assistance.

A special thanks to the fine companies who supported the production of this book. Hand tools, supplied by Craftsman, were used during all phases of vehicle teardown and photography. A Rotary lift, the largest automobile lift manufacturer in the world offering the biggest variety of surface and inground lifts available, was also used.

1

GENERAL INFORMATION AND MAINTENANCE

HOW TO USE THIS BOOK

Chilton's Total Car Care manual for the Toyota Corolla is intended to help you learn more about the inner workings of your vehicle while saving you money on its upkeep and operation.

The beginning of the book will likely be referred to the most, since that is where you will find information for maintenance and tune-up. The other sections deal with the more complex systems of your vehicle. Operating systems from engine through brakes are covered to the extent that the average do-it-yourselfer becomes mechanically involved. This book will not explain such things as rebuilding a differential for the simple reason that the expertise required and the investment in special tools make this task uneconomical. It will, however, give you detailed instructions to help you change your own brake pads and shoes, replace spark plugs, and perform many more jobs that can save you money, give you personal satisfaction and help you avoid expensive problems.

A secondary purpose of this book is a reference for owners who want to understand their vehicle and/or their mechanics better. In this case, no tools at all are required.

Where to Begin

Before removing any bolts, read through the entire procedure. This will give you the overall view of what tools and supplies will be required. There is nothing more frustrating than having to walk to the bus stop on Monday morning because you were short one bolt on Sunday afternoon. So read ahead and plan ahead. Each operation should be approached logically and all procedures thoroughly understood before attempting any work.

All sections contain adjustments, maintenance, removal and installation procedures, and in some cases, repair or overhaul procedures. When repair is not considered practical, we tell you how to remove the part and then how to install the new or rebuilt replacement. In this way, you at least save the labor costs. Backyard repair of some components is just not practical.

Avoiding Trouble

Many procedures in this book require you to "label and disconnect . . ." a group of lines, hoses or wires. Don't be lulled into thinking you can remember where everything goes—you won't. If you hook up vacuum or fuel lines incorrectly, the vehicle will run poorly, if at all. If you hook up electrical wiring incorrectly, you may instantly learn a very expensive lesson.

You don't need to know the official or engineering name for each hose or line. A piece of masking tape on the hose and a piece on its fitting will allow you to assign your own label such as the letter A or a short name. As long as you remember your own code, the lines can be reconnected by matching similar letters or names. Do remember that tape will dissolve in gasoline or other fluids; if a component is to be washed or cleaned, use another method of identification. A permanent felt-tipped marker can be very handy for marking metal parts. Remove any tape or paper labels after assembly.

Maintenance or Repair?

It's necessary to mention the difference between maintenance and repair. Maintenance includes routine inspections, adjustments, and replacement of parts which show signs of normal wear. Maintenance compensates for wear or deterioration. Repair implies that something has broken or is not working. A need for repair is often caused by lack of maintenance. Example: draining and refilling the automatic transmission fluid is maintenance recommended by the manufacturer at specific mileage intervals. Failure to do this can ruin the transmission/transaxle, requiring very expensive repairs. While no maintenance program can prevent items from breaking or wearing out, a general rule can be stated: MAINTENANCE IS CHEAPER THAN REPAIR.

Two basic mechanic's rules should be mentioned here. First, whenever the left side of the vehicle or engine is referred to, it is meant to specify the driver's side. Conversely, the right side of the vehicle means the passenger's side. Second, most screws and bolts are removed by turning counterclockwise, and tightened by turning clockwise.

Safety is always the most important rule. Constantly be aware of the dangers involved in working on an automobile and take the proper precautions. See the information in this section regarding SERVICING YOUR VEHICLE SAFELY and the SAFETY NOTICE on the acknowledgment page.

Avoiding the Most Common Mistakes

Pay attention to the instructions provided. There are 3 common mistakes in mechanical work:

1. Incorrect order of assembly, disassembly or adjustment. When taking something apart or putting it together, performing steps in the wrong order usually just costs you extra time; however, it CAN break something. Read the entire procedure before beginning disassembly. Perform everything in the order in which the instructions say you should, even if you can't immediately see a reason for it. When you're taking apart something that is very intricate, you might want to draw a picture of how it looks when assembled at one point in order to make sure you get everything back in its proper position. We will supply exploded views whenever possible. When making adjustments, perform them in the proper order; often, one adjustment affects another, and you cannot expect even satisfactory results unless each adjustment is made only when it cannot be changed by any other.

2. Overtorquing (or undertorquing). While it is more common for overtorquing to cause damage, undertorquing may allow a fastener to vibrate loose causing serious damage. Especially when dealing with aluminum parts, pay attention to torque specifications and utilize a torque wrench in assembly. If a torque figure is not available, remember that if you are using the right tool to perform the job, you will probably not have to strain yourself to get a fastener tight enough. The pitch of most threads is so slight that the tension you put on the wrench will be multiplied many times in actual force on what you are tightening. A good example of how critical torque is can be seen in the case of spark plug installation, especially where you are putting the plug into an aluminum cylinder head. Too little torque can fail to crush the gasket, causing leakage of combustion gases and consequent overheating of the plug and engine parts. Too much torque can damage the threads or distort the plug, changing the spark gap.

There are many commercial products available for ensuring that fasteners won't come loose, even if they are not torqued just right (a very common brand is Loctite®). If you're worried about getting something together tight enough to hold, but loose enough to avoid mechanical damage during assembly, one of these products might offer substantial insurance. Before choosing a threadlocking compound, read the label on the package and make sure the product is compatible with the materials, fluids, etc. involved.

3. Crossthreading. This occurs when a part such as a bolt is screwed into a nut or casting at the wrong angle and forced. Crossthreading is more likely to occur if access is difficult. It helps to clean and lubricate fasteners, then to start threading with the part to be installed positioned straight in. Then, start the bolt, spark plug, etc. with your fingers. If you encounter resistance, unscrew the part and start over again at a different angle until it can be inserted and turned several times without much effort. Keep in mind that many parts, especially spark plugs, have tapered threads, so that gentle turning will automatically bring the part you're threading to the proper angle, but only if you don't force it or resist a change in angle. Don't put a wrench on the part until it's been tightened a couple of turns by hand. If you suddenly encounter resistance, and the part has not seated fully, don't force it. Pull it back out to make sure it's clean and threading properly.

Always take your time and be patient; once you have some experience, working on your vehicle may well become an enjoyable hobby.

TOOLS AND EQUIPMENT

▶ **See Figures 1 thru 15**

Naturally, without the proper tools and equipment it is impossible to properly service your vehicle. It would also be virtually impossible to catalog every tool that you would need to perform all of the operations in this book. Of course, It would be unwise for the amateur to rush out and buy an expensive set of tools on the theory that he/she may need one or more of them at some time.

The best approach is to proceed slowly, gathering a good quality set of those tools that are used most frequently. Don't be misled by the low cost of bargain tools. It is far better to spend a little more for better quality. Forged wrenches, 6 or 12-point sockets and fine tooth ratchets are by far preferable to their less expensive counterparts. As any good mechanic can tell you, there are few worse experiences than trying to work on a vehicle with bad tools. Your monetary savings will be far outweighed by frustration and mangled knuckles.

Begin accumulating those tools that are used most frequently: those associated with routine maintenance and tune-up. In addition to the normal assortment of screwdrivers and pliers, you should have the following tools:

• Wrenches/sockets and combination open end/box end wrenches in sizes from ⅛–¾ in. or 3mm–19mm (depending on whether your vehicle uses standard or metric fasteners) and a ¹³⁄₁₆ in. or ⅝ in. spark plug socket (depending on plug type).

➡**If possible, buy various length socket drive extensions. Universal-joint and wobble extensions can be extremely useful, but be careful when using them, as they can change the amount of torque applied to the socket.**

• Jackstands for support.
• Oil filter wrench.
• Spout or funnel for pouring fluids.
• Grease gun for chassis lubrication (unless your vehicle is not equipped with any grease fittings—for details, please refer to information on Fluids and Lubricants found later in this section).
• Hydrometer for checking the battery (unless equipped with a sealed, maintenance-free battery).
• A container for draining oil and other fluids.
• Rags for wiping up the inevitable mess.

In addition to the above items there are several others that are not absolutely necessary, but handy to have around. These include Oil Dry® (or an equivalent oil absorbent gravel—such as cat litter) and the usual supply of lubricants, antifreeze and fluids, although these can be purchased as needed. This is a basic list for routine maintenance, but only your personal needs and desire can accurately determine your list of tools.

After performing a few projects on the vehicle, you'll be amazed at the other tools and non-tools on your workbench. Some useful household items

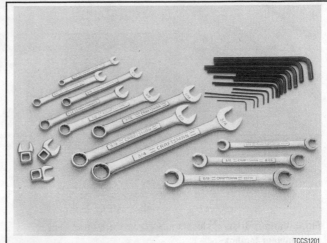
Fig. 2 In addition to ratchets, a good set of wrenches and hex keys will be necessary

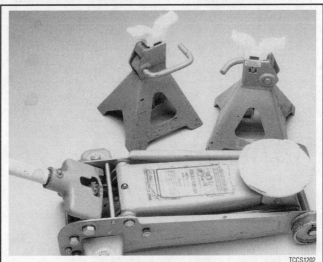
Fig. 3 A hydraulic floor jack and a set of jackstands are essential for lifting and supporting the vehicle

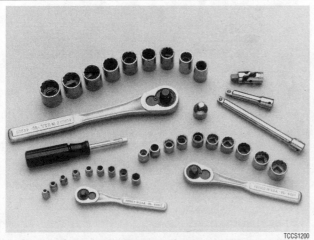
Fig. 1 All but the most basic procedures will require an assortment of ratchets and sockets

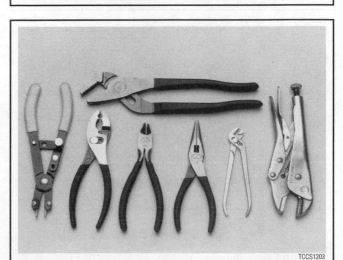
Fig. 4 An assortment of pliers, grippers and cutters will be handy for old rusted parts and stripped bolt heads

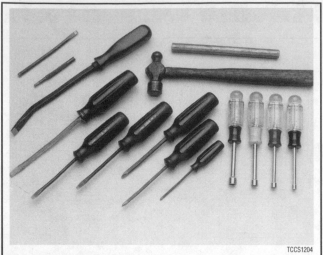

Fig. 5 Various drivers, chisels and prybars are great tools to have in your toolbox

TCCS1204

Fig. 8 A few inexpensive lubrication tools will make maintenance easier

TCCS1210

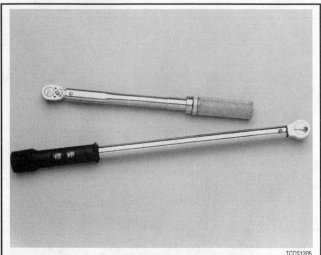

Fig. 6 Many repairs will require the use of a torque wrench to assure the components are properly fastened

TCCS1205

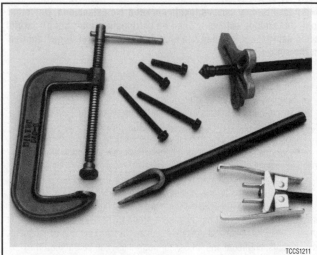

Fig. 9 Various pullers, clamps and separator tools are needed for many larger, more complicated repairs

TCCS1211

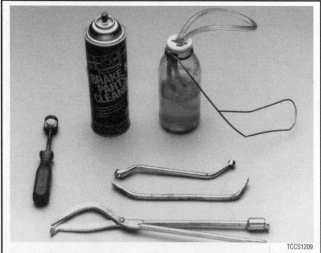

Fig. 7 Although not always necessary, using specialized brake tools will save time

TCCS1209

Fig. 10 A variety of tools and gauges should be used for spark plug gapping and installation

TCCS1212

are: a large turkey baster or siphon, empty coffee cans and ice trays (to store parts), ball of twine, electrical tape for wiring, small rolls of colored tape for tagging lines or hoses, markers and pens, a note pad, golf tees (for plugging vacuum lines), metal coat hangers or a roll of mechanics's wire (to hold things out of the way), dental pick or similar long, pointed probe, a strong magnet, and a small mirror (to see into recesses and under manifolds).

A more advanced set of tools, suitable for tune-up work, can be drawn up easily. While the tools are slightly more sophisticated, they need not be outrageously expensive. There are several inexpensive tach/dwell meters on the market that are every bit as good for the average mechanic as a professional model. Just be sure that it goes to a least 1200–1500 rpm on the

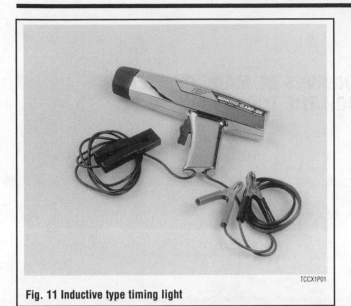

Fig. 11 Inductive type timing light

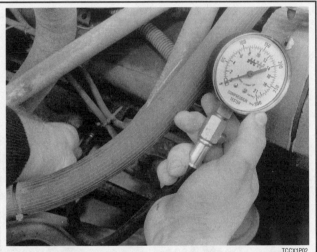

Fig. 12 A screw-in type compression gauge is recommended for compression testing

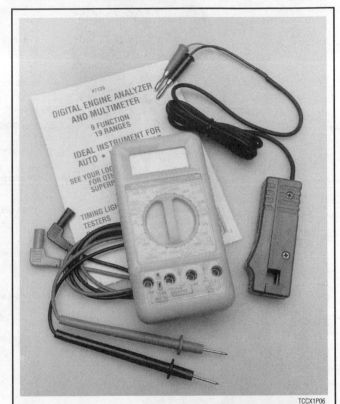

Fig. 14 Most modern automotive multimeters incorporate many helpful features

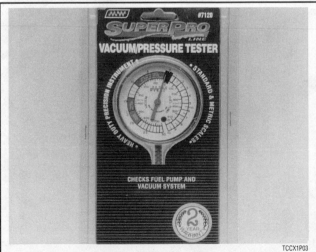

Fig. 13 A vacuum/pressure tester is necessary for many testing procedures

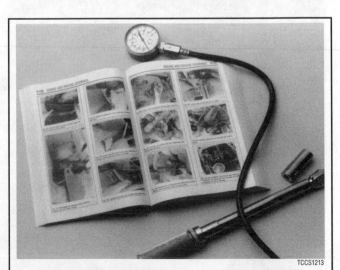

Fig. 15 Proper information is vital, so always have a Chilton Total Car Care manual handy

TCCA1AC1

tach scale and that it works on 4, 6 and 8-cylinder engines. (If you have one or more vehicles with a diesel engine, a special tachometer is required since diesels don't use spark plug ignition systems). The key to these purchases is to make them with an eye towards adaptability and wide range. A basic list of tune-up tools could include:

- Tach/dwell meter.
- Spark plug wrench and gapping tool.
- Feeler gauges for valve or point adjustment. (Even if your vehicle does not use points or require valve adjustments, a feeler gauge is helpful for many repair/overhaul procedures).

A tachometer/dwell meter will ensure accurate tune-up work on vehicles without electronic ignition. The choice of a timing light should be made carefully. A light which works on the DC current supplied by the vehicle's battery is the best choice; it should have a xenon tube for brightness. On any vehicle with an electronic ignition system, a timing light with an inductive pickup that clamps around the No. 1 spark plug cable is preferred.

In addition to these basic tools, there are several other tools and gauges you may find useful. These include:

- Compression gauge. The screw-in type is slower to use, but eliminates the possibility of a faulty reading due to escaping pressure.
- Manifold vacuum gauge.
- 12V test light.
- A combination volt/ohmmeter

- Induction Ammeter. This is used for determining whether or not there is current in a wire. These are handy for use if a wire is broken somewhere in a wiring harness.

As a final note, you will probably find a torque wrench necessary for all but the most basic work. The beam type models are perfectly adequate, although the newer click types (breakaway) are easier to use. The click type torque wrenches tend to be more expensive. Also keep in mind that all types of torque wrenches should be periodically checked and/or recalibrated. You will have to decide for yourself which better fits your purpose.

Special Tools

Normally, the use of special factory tools is avoided for repair procedures, since these are not readily available for the do-it-yourself mechanic. When it is possible to perform the job with more commonly available tools, it will be pointed out, but occasionally, a special tool was designed to perform a specific function and should be used. Before substituting another tool, you should be convinced that neither your safety nor the performance of the vehicle will be compromised.

Special tools can usually be purchased from an automotive parts store or from your dealer. In some cases special tools may be available directly from the tool manufacturer.

SERVICING YOUR VEHICLE SAFELY

▶ **See Figures 16, 17, 18 and 19**

It is virtually impossible to anticipate all of the hazards involved with automotive maintenance and service, but care and common sense will prevent most accidents.

The rules of safety for mechanics range from "don't smoke around gasoline," to "use the proper tool(s) for the job." The trick to avoiding injuries is to develop safe work habits and to take every possible precaution.

Do's

- Do keep a fire extinguisher and first aid kit handy.
- Do wear safety glasses or goggles when cutting, drilling, grinding or prying, even if you have 20–20 vision. If you wear glasses for the sake of vision, wear safety goggles over your regular glasses.
- Do shield your eyes whenever you work around the battery. Batteries contain sulfuric acid. In case of contact with the eyes or skin, flush the area with water or a

mixture of water and baking soda, then seek immediate medical attention.

- Do use safety stands (jackstands) for any undervehicle service. Jacks are for raising vehicles; jackstands are for making sure the vehicle stays raised until you want it to come down. Whenever the vehicle is raised, block the wheels remaining on the ground and set the parking brake.
- Do use adequate ventilation when working with any chemicals or hazardous materials. Like carbon monoxide, the asbestos dust resulting from some brake lining wear can be hazardous in sufficient quantities.
- Do disconnect the negative battery cable when working on the electrical system. The secondary ignition system contains EXTREMELY HIGH VOLTAGE. In some cases it can even exceed 50,000 volts.
- Do follow manufacturer's directions whenever working with potentially hazardous materials. Most chemicals and fluids are poisonous if taken internally.
- Do properly maintain your tools. Loose hammerheads, mushroomed punches and chisels, frayed or poorly grounded electrical cords, excessively worn screwdrivers, spread wrenches (open end), cracked sockets, slipping ratchets, or faulty droplight sockets can cause accidents.

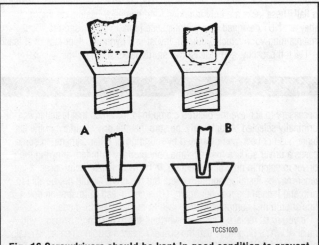

Fig. 16 Screwdrivers should be kept in good condition to prevent injury or damage which could result if the blade slips from the screw

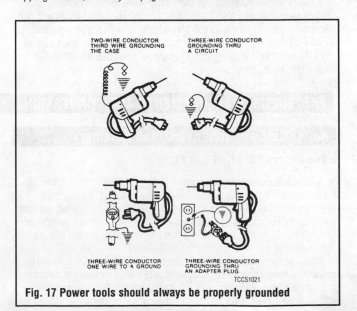

Fig. 17 Power tools should always be properly grounded

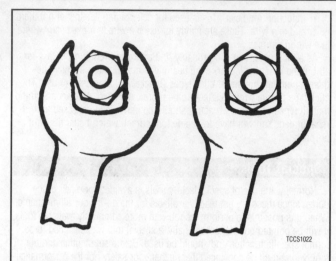

Fig. 18 Using the correct size wrench will help prevent the possibility of rounding off a nut

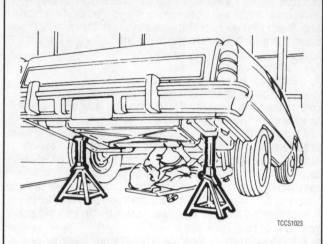

Fig. 19 NEVER work under a vehicle unless it is supported using safety stands (jackstands)

- Likewise, keep your tools clean; a greasy wrench can slip off a bolt head, ruining the bolt and often harming your knuckles in the process.
- Do use the proper size and type of tool for the job at hand. Do select a wrench or socket that fits the nut or bolt. The wrench or socket should sit straight, not cocked.
- Do, when possible, pull on a wrench handle rather than push on it, and adjust your stance to prevent a fall.
- Do be sure that adjustable wrenches are tightly closed on the nut or bolt and pulled so that the force is on the side of the fixed jaw.
- Do strike squarely with a hammer; avoid glancing blows.
- Do set the parking brake and block the drive wheels if the work requires a running engine.

Don'ts

- Don't run the engine in a garage or anywhere else without proper ventilation—EVER! Carbon monoxide is poisonous; it takes a long time to leave the human body and you can build up a deadly supply of it in your system by simply breathing in a little every day. You may not realize you are slowly poisoning yourself. Always use power vents, windows, fans and/or open the garage door.
- Don't work around moving parts while wearing loose clothing. Short sleeves are much safer than long, loose sleeves. Hard-toed shoes with neoprene soles protect your toes and give a better grip on slippery surfaces. Jewelry such as watches, fancy belt buckles, beads or body adornment of any kind is not safe working around a vehicle. Long hair should be tied back under a hat or cap.

- Don't use pockets for toolboxes. A fall or bump can drive a screwdriver deep into your body. Even a rag hanging from your back pocket can wrap around a spinning shaft or fan.
- Don't smoke when working around gasoline, cleaning solvent or other flammable material.
- Don't smoke when working around the battery. When the battery is being charged, it gives off explosive hydrogen gas.
- Don't use gasoline to wash your hands; there are excellent soaps available. Gasoline contains dangerous additives which can enter the body through a cut or through your pores. Gasoline also removes all the natural oils from the skin so that bone dry hands will suck up oil and grease.
- Don't service the air conditioning system unless you are equipped with the necessary tools and training. When liquid or compressed gas refrigerant is released to atmospheric pressure it will absorb heat from whatever it contacts. This will chill or freeze anything it touches. Although refrigerant is normally non-toxic, R-12 becomes a deadly poisonous gas in the presence of an open flame. One good whiff of the vapors from burning refrigerant can be fatal.
- Don't use screwdrivers for anything other than driving screws! A screwdriver used as an prying tool can snap when you least expect it, causing injuries. At the very least, you'll ruin a good screwdriver.
- Don't use a bumper or emergency jack (that little ratchet, scissors, or pantograph jack supplied with the vehicle) for anything other than changing a flat! These jacks are only intended for emergency use out on the road; they are NOT designed as a maintenance tool. If you are serious about maintaining your vehicle yourself, invest in a hydraulic floor jack of at least a 1½ ton capacity, and at least two sturdy jackstands.

FASTENERS, MEASUREMENTS AND CONVERSIONS

Bolts, Nuts and Other Threaded Retainers

▶ See Figures 20, 21, 22 and 23

Although there are a great variety of fasteners found in the modern car or truck, the most commonly used retainer is the threaded fastener (nuts, bolts, screws, studs, etc). Most threaded retainers may be reused, provided that they are not damaged in use or during the repair. Some retainers (such as stretch bolts or torque prevailing nuts) are designed to deform when tightened or in use and should not be reinstalled.

Whenever possible, we will note any special retainers which should be replaced during a procedure. But you should always inspect the condition of a retainer when it is removed and replace any that show signs of damage. Check all threads for rust or corrosion which can increase the torque

necessary to achieve the desired clamp load for which that fastener was originally selected. Additionally, be sure that the driver surface of the fastener has not been compromised by rounding or other damage. In some cases a driver surface may become only partially rounded, allowing the driver to catch in only one direction. In many of these occurrences, a fastener may be installed and tightened, but the driver would not be able to grip and loosen the fastener again. (This could lead to frustration down the line should that component ever need to be disassembled again).

If you must replace a fastener, whether due to design or damage, you must ALWAYS be sure to use the proper replacement. In all cases, a retainer of the same design, material and strength should be used. Markings on the heads of most bolts will help determine the proper strength of the fastener. The same material, thread and pitch must be selected to assure proper installation and safe operation of the vehicle afterwards.

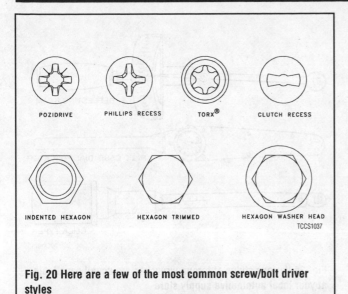

Fig. 20 Here are a few of the most common screw/bolt driver styles

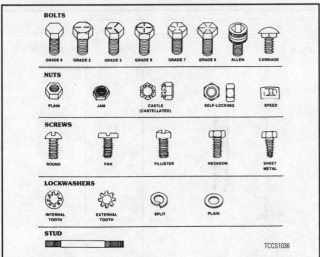

Fig. 21 There are many different types of threaded retainers found on vehicles

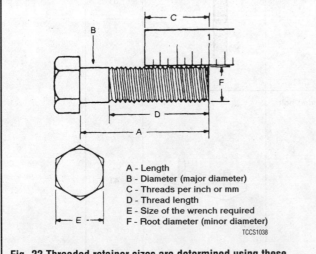

A - Length
B - Diameter (major diameter)
C - Threads per inch or mm
D - Thread length
E - Size of the wrench required
F - Root diameter (minor diameter)

TCCS1038

Fig. 22 Threaded retainer sizes are determined using these measurements

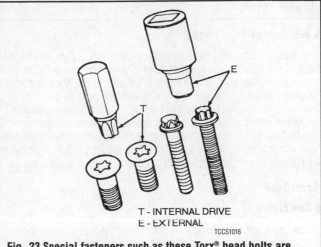

T - INTERNAL DRIVE
E - EXTERNAL

TCCS1016

Fig. 23 Special fasteners such as these Torx® head bolts are used by manufacturers to discourage people from working on vehicles without the proper tools

Thread gauges are available to help measure a bolt or stud's thread. Most automotive and hardware stores keep gauges available to help you select the proper size. In a pinch, you can use another nut or bolt for a thread gauge. If the bolt you are replacing is not too badly damaged, you can select a match by finding another bolt which will thread in its place. If you find a nut which threads properly onto the damaged bolt, then use that nut to help select the replacement bolt. If however, the bolt you are replacing is so badly damaged (broken or drilled out) that its threads cannot be used as a gauge, you might start by looking for another bolt (from the same assembly or a similar location on your vehicle) which will thread into the damaged bolt's mounting. If so, the other bolt can be used to select a nut; the nut can then be used to select the replacement bolt.

In all cases, be absolutely sure you have selected the proper replacement. Don't be shy, you can always ask the store clerk for help.

✳✳ WARNING

Be aware that when you find a bolt with damaged threads, you may also find the nut or drilled hole it was threaded into has also been damaged. If this is the case, you may have to drill and tap the hole, replace the nut or otherwise repair the threads. NEVER try to force a replacement bolt to fit into the damaged threads.

Torque

Torque is defined as the measurement of resistance to turning or rotating. It tends to twist a body about an axis of rotation. A common example of this would be tightening a threaded retainer such as a nut, bolt or screw. Measuring torque is one of the most common ways to help assure that a threaded retainer has been properly fastened.

When tightening a threaded fastener, torque is applied in three distinct areas, the head, the bearing surface and the clamp load. About 50 percent of the measured torque is used in overcoming bearing friction. This is the friction between the bearing surface of the bolt head, screw head or nut face and the base material or washer (the surface on which the fastener is rotating). Approximately 40 percent of the applied torque is used in overcoming thread friction. This leaves only about 10 percent of the applied torque to develop a useful clamp load (the force which holds a joint together). This means that friction can account for as much as 90 percent of the applied torque on a fastener.

TORQUE WRENCHES

▶ **See Figures 24, 25 and 26**

In most applications, a torque wrench can be used to assure proper installation of a fastener. Torque wrenches come in various designs and most automotive supply stores will carry a variety to suit your needs. A torque wrench should be used any time we supply a specific torque value for a fastener. A torque wrench can also be used if you are following the general guidelines in the accompanying charts. Keep in mind that because there is no worldwide standardization of fasteners, the charts are a general guideline and should be used with caution. Again, the general rule of "if you are using the right tool for the job, you should not have to strain to tighten a fastener" applies here.

Beam Type

▶ **See Figure 27**

The beam type torque wrench is one of the most popular types. It consists of a pointer attached to the head that runs the length of the flexible beam (shaft) to a scale located near the handle. As the wrench is pulled, the beam bends and the pointer indicates the torque using the scale.

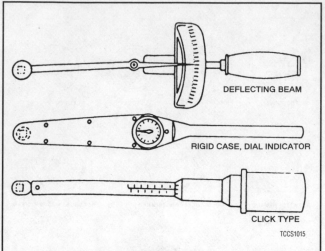

TCCS1015

Fig. 24 Various styles of torque wrenches are usually available at your local automotive supply store

	Mark		Class		Mark	Class
Hexagon head bolt	Bolt head No.	4— 5— 6— 7— 8— 9— 10— 11—	4T 5T 6T 7T 8T 9T 10T 11T	Stud bolt	No mark	4T
		No mark	4T			
Hexagon flange bolt w/ washer hexagon bolt		No mark	4T		Grooved	6T
Hexagon head bolt		Two protruding lines	5T			
Hexagon flange bolt w/ washer hexagon bolt		Two protruding lines	6T	Welded bolt		
Hexagon head bolt		Three protruding lines	7T			4T
Hexagon head bolt		Four protruding lines	8T			

TCCS1240

Fig. 25 Determining bolt strength of metric fasteners—NOTE: this is a typical bolt marking system, but there is not a worldwide standard

Class	Diameter mm	Pitch mm	Specified torque					
			Hexagon head bolt			Hexagon flange bolt		
			N·m	kgf·cm	ft·lbf	N·m	kgf·cm	ft·lbf
4T	6	1	5	55	48 in.·lbf	6	60	52 in.·lbf
	8	1.25	12.5	130	9	14	145	10
	10	1.25	26	260	19	29	290	21
	12	1.25	47	480	35	53	540	39
	14	1.5	74	760	55	84	850	61
	16	1.5	115	1,150	83	—	—	—
5T	6	1	6.5	65	56 in.·lbf	7.5	75	65 in.·lbf
	8	1.25	15.5	160	12	17.5	175	13
	10	1.25	32	330	24	36	360	26
	12	1.25	59	600	43	65	670	48
	14	1.5	91	930	67	100	1,050	76
	16	1.5	140	1,400	101	—	—	—
6T	6	1	8	80	69 in.·lbf	9	90	78 in.·lbf
	8	1.25	19	195	14	21	210	15
	10	1.25	39	400	29	44	440	32
	12	1.25	71	730	53	80	810	59
	14	1.5	110	1,100	80	125	1,250	90
	16	1.5	170	1,750	127	—	—	—
7T	6	1	10.5	110	8	12	120	9
	8	1.25	25	260	19	28	290	21
	10	1.25	52	530	38	58	590	43
	12	1.25	95	970	70	105	1,050	76
	14	1.5	145	1,500	108	165	1,700	123
	16	1.5	230	2,300	166	—	—	—
8T	8	1.25	29	300	22	33	330	24
	10	1.25	61	620	45	68	690	50
	12	1.25	110	1,100	80	120	1,250	90
9T	8	1.25	34	340	25	37	380	27
	10	1.25	70	710	51	78	790	57
	12	1.25	125	1,300	94	140	1,450	105
10T	8	1.25	38	390	28	42	430	31
	10	1.25	78	800	58	88	890	64
	12	1.25	140	1,450	105	155	1,600	116
11T	8	1.25	42	430	31	47	480	35
	10	1.25	87	890	64	97	990	72
	12	1.25	155	1,600	116	175	1,800	130

TCCS1241

Fig. 26 Typical bolt torques for metric fasteners—WARNING: use only as a guide

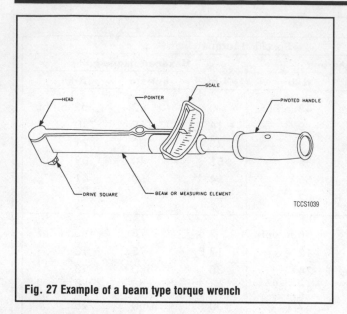

Fig. 27 Example of a beam type torque wrench

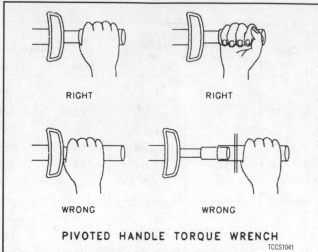

Fig. 29 Torque wrenches with pivoting heads must be grasped and used properly to prevent an incorrect reading

Click (Breakaway) Type

♦ See Figure 28

Another popular design of torque wrench is the click type. To use the click type wrench you pre-adjust it to a torque setting. Once the torque is reached, the wrench has a reflex signaling feature that causes a momentary breakaway of the torque wrench body, sending an impulse to the operator's hand.

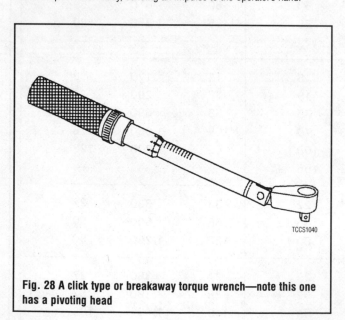

Fig. 28 A click type or breakaway torque wrench—note this one has a pivoting head

Pivot Head Type

♦ See Figure 29

Some torque wrenches (usually of the click type) may be equipped with a pivot head which can allow it to be used in areas of limited access. BUT, it must be used properly. To hold a pivot head wrench, grasp the handle lightly, and as you pull on the handle, it should be floated on the pivot point. If the handle comes in contact with the yoke extension during the process of pulling, there is a very good chance the torque readings will be inaccurate because this could alter the wrench loading point. The design of the handle is usually such as to make it inconvenient to deliberately misuse the wrench.

➡ It should be mentioned that the use of any U-joint, wobble or extension will have an effect on the torque readings, no matter what

type of wrench you are using. For the most accurate readings, install the socket directly on the wrench driver. If necessary, straight extensions (which hold a socket directly under the wrench driver) will have the least effect on the torque reading. Avoid any extension that alters the length of the wrench from the handle to the head/driving point (such as a crow's foot). U-joint or Wobble extensions can greatly affect the readings; avoid their use at all times.

Rigid Case (Direct Reading)

♦ See Figure 30

A rigid case or direct reading torque wrench is equipped with a dial indicator to show torque values. One advantage of these wrenches is that they can be held at any position on the wrench without affecting accuracy. These wrenches are often preferred because they tend to be compact, easy to read and have a great degree of accuracy.

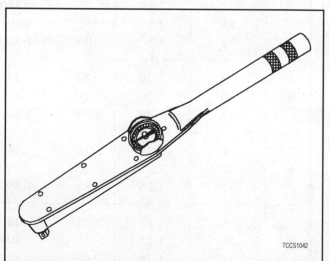

Fig. 30 The rigid case (direct reading) torque wrench uses a dial indicator to show torque

TORQUE ANGLE METERS

♦ See Figure 31

Because the frictional characteristics of each fastener or threaded hole will vary, clamp loads which are based strictly on torque will vary as well.

In most applications, this variance is not significant enough to cause worry. But, in certain applications, a manufacturer's engineers may determine that more precise clamp loads are necessary (such is the case with many aluminum cylinder heads). In these cases, a torque angle method of installation would be specified. When installing fasteners which are torque angle tightened, a predetermined seating torque and standard torque wrench are usually used first to remove any compliance from the joint. The fastener is then tightened the specified additional portion of a turn measured in degrees. A torque angle gauge (mechanical protractor) is used for these applications.

Standard and Metric Measurements

▶ See Figure 32

Throughout this manual, specifications are given to help you determine the condition of various components on your vehicle, or to assist you in their installation. Some of the most common measurements include length (in. or cm/mm), torque (ft. lbs., inch lbs. or Nm) and pressure (psi, in. Hg, kPa or mm Hg). In most cases, we strive to provide the proper measurement as determined by the manufacturer's engineers.

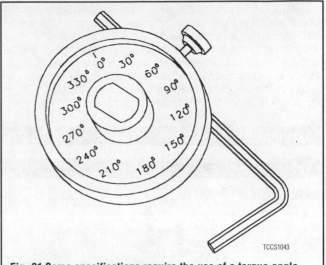

Fig. 31 Some specifications require the use of a torque angle meter (mechanical protractor)

CONVERSION FACTORS

LENGTH–DISTANCE

Inches (in.)	x 25.4	= Millimeters (mm)	x .0394	= Inches
Feet (ft.)	x .305	= Meters (m)	x 3.281	= Feet
Miles	x 1.609	= Kilometers (km)	x .0621	— Miles

VOLUME

Cubic Inches (in3)	x 16.387	= Cubic Centimeters	x .061	= in3
IMP Pints (IMP pt.)	x .568	= Liters (L)	x 1.76	— IMP pt.
IMP Quarts (IMP qt.)	x 1.137	= Liters (L)	x .88	= IMP qt.
IMP Gallons (IMP gal.)	x 4.546	= Liters (L)	x .22	= IMP gal.
IMP Quarts (IMP qt.)	x 1.201	= US Quarts (US qt.)	x .833	= IMP qt.
IMP Gallons (IMP gal.)	x 1.201	= US Gallons (US gal.)	x .833	= IMP gal.
Fl. Ounces	x 29.573	= Milliliters	x .034	= Ounces
US Pints (US pt.)	x .473	= Liters (L)	x 2.113	= Pints
US Quarts (US qt.)	x .946	= Liters (L)	x 1.057	= Quarts
US Gallons (US gal.)	x 3.785	= Liters (L)	x .264	= Gallons

MASS–WEIGHT

Ounces (oz.)	x 28.35	= Grams (g)	x .035	= Ounces
Pounds (lb.)	x .454	= Kilograms (kg)	x 2.205	= Pounds

PRESSURE

Pounds Per Sq. In. (psi)	x 6.895	= Kilopascals (kPa)	x .145	= psi
Inches of Mercury (Hg)	x .4912	= psi	x 2.036	= Hg
Inches of Mercury (Hg)	x 3.377	= Kilopascals (kPa)	x .2961	= Hg
Inches of Water (H$_2$O)	x .07355	= Inches of Mercury	x 13.783	= H$_2$O
Inches of Water (H$_2$O)	x .03613	= psi	x 27.684	= H$_2$O
Inches of Water (H$_2$O)	x .248	= Kilopascals (kPa)	x 4.026	= H$_2$O

TORQUE

Pounds–Force Inches (in–lb)	x .113	= Newton Meters (N·m)	x 8.85	= in–lb
Pounds–Force Feet (ft–lb)	x 1.356	= Newton Meters (N·m)	x .738	= ft–lb

VELOCITY

Miles Per Hour (MPH)	x 1.609	= Kilometers Per Hour (KPH)	x .621	= MPH

POWER

Horsepower (Hp)	x .745	= Kilowatts	x 1.34	= Horsepower

FUEL CONSUMPTION*

Miles Per Gallon IMP (MPG)	x .354	= Kilometers Per Liter (Km/L)
Kilometers Per Liter (Km/L)	x 2.352	= IMP MPG
Miles Per Gallon US (MPG)	x .425	= Kilometers Per Liter (Km/L)
Kilometers Per Liter (Km/L)	x 2.352	= US MPG

*It is common to covert from miles per gallon (mpg) to liters/100 kilometers (1/100 km), where mpg (IMP) x 1/100 km = 282 and mpg (US) x 1/100 km = 235.

TEMPERATURE

Degree Fahrenheit (°F)	= (°C x 1.8) + 32
Degree Celsius (°C)	= (°F – 32) x .56

TCCS1044

Fig. 32 Standard and metric conversion factors chart

Though, in some cases, that value may not be conveniently measured with what is available in your toolbox. Luckily, many of the measuring devices which are available today will have two scales so the Standard or Metric measurements may easily be taken. If any of the various measuring tools which are available to you do not contain the same scale as listed in the specifications, use the accompanying conversion factors to determine the proper value.

The conversion factor chart is used by taking the given specification and multiplying it by the necessary conversion factor. For instance, looking at the first line, if you have a measurement in inches such as "free-play should be 2 in." but your ruler reads only in millimeters, multiply 2 in. by the conversion factor of 25.4 to get the metric equivalent of 50.8mm. Likewise, if the specification was given only in a Metric measurement, for example in Newton Meters (Nm), then look at the center column first. If the measurement is 100 Nm, multiply it by the conversion factor of 0.738 to get 73.8 ft. lbs.

SERIAL NUMBER IDENTIFICATION

Vehicle

▶ **See Figures 33, 34 and 35**

All models have the vehicle identification number stamped on a plate attached to the left side of the instrument panel. The plate is visible by looking through the windshield from the outside.

Some Corolla's also have the VIN stamped into the metal of the outer face of the right front frame rail. The number also appears on the Certification Label attached to the left door pillar.

The serial number consists of a series of 17 digits including the six digit serial or production number. The first three digits are the World Manufacturer Identification number. The next five digits are the Vehicle Description Section. The remaining nine digits are the production numbers including various codes on body style, trim level (base, luxury, etc.) and safety equipment or other information.

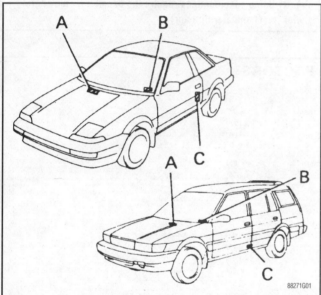

Fig. 33 Serial number identification plate locations on most models

The VIN number is stamped on the firewall to identifiy each model

VEHICLE IDENTIFICATION CHART

Engine Code							Model Year	
Code	Liters	Cu. In. (cc)	Cyl.	Fuel Sys.	Eng. Mfg.		Code	Year
4A-F	1.6	97 (1587)	4	2-BBL	Toyota		J	1988
4A-FE	1.6	97 (1587)	4	MFI	Toyota		K	1989
4A-GE	1.6	97 (1587)	4	MFI	Toyota		L	1990
7A-FE	1.8	107 (1762)	4	MFI	Toyota		M	1991
							N	1992
							P	1993
							R	1994
							S	1995
							T	1996
							U	1997

88271C02

Example

	1		2				Check Digit	3							
Digit	1	2	3	4	5	6	7	8	9	10	11	12	13	14	15	16	17
Example	1	N	X	A	E	0	4	B	7	R	Z	0	0	0	0	0	1

Manufacturer, Make and Type

	Code	Manufacturer	Make	Type
1st - 3rd Digits	1NX	New United Motor Manufacturing, Inc., CA, U.S.A. ‡	Toyota	Passenger Car
	2T1	Toyota Motor Manufacturing, Canada ‡‡	Toyota	Passenger Car

‡ Vehicles are assembled by New United Motor Manufacturing, Inc., CA, U.S.A., but marketed by Toyota.
‡‡ Vehicles are assembled by Toyota Motor Manufacturing, Canada but marketed by Toyota.

Vehicle Description Section (VDS)

		Code	Description
4th Digit	Engine Type	‡‡‡ A	4A-FE 7A-FE
5th Digit	Line	E	Corolla
6th Digit	Model Designation	0	AE101L AE102L
7th Digit	Series (Grade)	0 4 7 9	LE STD DX DX
8th Digit	Body Type & Restraint System	B	4 Door Sedan with Manual Belt and Air Bag

88271G10

Fig. 34 Common serial number identification information—1994 shown

‡‡‡: As for Corolla, engine types are identified as follows:

Engine Type \ Digit	4th Digit	7th Digit
4A-FE	A	4 or 7
7A-FE	A	0 or 9

Vehicle Model Year, Plant of Manufacture and Serial Number

		Code	Description
10th Digit	Vehicle Model Year	R	1994 Model
11th Digit	Plant of Manufacture	Z C	Fremont (CA) Canada
12th - 17th Digit	Serial Number	000001 thru 999999	-----

88271G11

Fig. 35 Common serial number identification information (continued)—1994 shown

Engine

♦ **See Figure 36**

Each engine is referred to by both its family designation, such as 4A-FE, and its production or serial number. The serial number can be important when ordering parts. Certain changes may have been made during production of the engine; different parts will be required if the engine was assembled before or after the change date. Generally, parts stores and dealers list this data in their catalogs, so have the engine number handy when you go.

It's a good idea to record the engine number while the vehicle is new. Jotting it inside the cover of the owner's manual or similar easy-to-find location will prevent having to scrape many years of grime off the engine when the number is finally needed.

The engine serial number consists of an engine series identification number, followed by a 6–digit production number.

Transaxle

The manual and automatic transaxle identification number is stamped on the assembly housing.

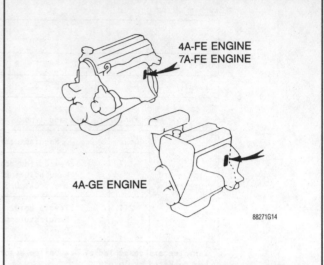

Fig. 36 Common engine serial number identification locations

ENGINE IDENTIFICATION

Year	Model	Engine Displacement Liters (cc)	Engine Series (ID/VIN)	Fuel System	No. of Cylinders	Engine Type
1988	Corolla	1.6 (1587)	4A-F	2-BBL	L4	DOHC
	Corolla	1.6 (1587)	4A-FE	MFI	L4	DOHC
	Corolla	1.6 (1587)	4A-GE	MFI	L4	DOHC
1989	Corolla	1.6 (1587)	4A-F	2-BBL	L4	DOHC
	Corolla	1.6 (1587)	4A-FE	MFI	L4	DOHC
	Corolla	1.6 (1587)	4A-GE	MFI	L4	DOHC
1990	Corolla	1.6 (1587)	4A-FE	MFI	L4	DOHC
	Corolla	1.6 (1587)	4A-GE	MFI	L4	DOHC
1991	Corolla	1.6 (1587)	4A-FE	MFI	L4	DOHC
	Corolla	1.6 (1587)	4A-GE	MFI	L4	DOHC
1992	Corolla	1.6 (1587)	4A-FE	MFI	L4	DOHC
1993	Corolla	1.6 (1587)	4AF-E	MFI	L4	DOHC
	Corolla	1.8 (1762)	7A-FE	MFI	L4	DOHC
1994	Corolla	1.6 (1587)	4AF-E	MFI	L4	DOHC
	Corolla	1.8 (1762)	7A-FE	MFI	L4	DOHC
1995	Corolla	1.6 (1587)	4AF-E	MFI	L4	DOHC
	Corolla	1.8 (1762)	7A-FE	MFI	L4	DOHC
1996	Corolla	1.6 (1587)	4AF-E	MFI	L4	DOHC
	Corolla	1.8 (1762)	7A-FE	MFI	L4	DOHC
1997	Corolla	1.6 (1587)	4AF-E	MFI	L4	DOHC
	Corolla	1.8 (1762)	7A-FE	MFI	L4	DOHC

2-BBL: Two barrel carburetor
MFI: Multiport Injection
DOHC: Dual Over head Cam

88271C01

GENERAL ENGINE SPECIFICATIONS

Year	Engine ID/VIN	Engine Displacement Liters (cc)	Fuel System Type	Net Horsepower @ rpm	Net Torque @ rpm (ft. lbs.)	Bore x Stroke (in.)	Compression Ratio	Oil Pressure
1988	4A-F	1.6 (1587)	2-BBL	102 @ 5800	101 @ 4800	3.19 x 3.03	9.5:1	36-71
	4A-FE	1.6 (1587)	MFI	102 @ 5800	101 @ 4800	3.19 x 3.03	9.5:1	36-71
	4A-GE	1.6 (1587)	MFI	130 @ 6800	102 @ 5800	3.19 x 3.03	9.5:1	36-71
1989	4A-F	1.6 (1587)	2-BBL	102 @ 5800	101 @ 4800	3.19 x 3.03	9.5:1	36-71
	4A-FE	1.6 (1587)	MFI	102 @ 5800	101 @ 4800	3.19 x 3.03	9.5:1	36-71
	4A-GE	1.6 (1587)	MFI	130 @ 6800	102 @ 5800	3.19 x 3.03	9.5:1	36-71
1990	4A-FE	1.6 (1587)	MFI	102 @ 5800	101 @ 4800	3.19 x 3.03	9.5:1	36-71
	4A-GE	1.6 (1587)	MFI	130 @ 6800	102 @ 5800	3.19 x 3.03	9.5:1	36-71
1991	4A-FE	1.6 (1587)	MFI	102 @ 5800	101 @ 4800	3.19 x 3.03	9.5:1	36-71
	4A-GE	1.6 (1587)	MFI	130 @ 6800	105 @ 6000	3.19 x 3.03	9.5:1	36-71
1992	4A-FE	1.6 (1587)	MFI	102 @ 5800	101 @ 4800	3.19 x 3.03	9.5:1	36-71
1993	4AF-E	1.6 (1587)	MFI	102 @ 5800	100 @ 4800	3.19 x 3.03	9.5:1	36-71
	7A-FE	1.8 (1762)	MFI	115 @ 5600	115 @ 2800	3.19 x 3.36	9.5:1	36-71
1994	4AF-E	1.6 (1587)	MFI	102 @ 5800	100 @ 4800	3.19 x 3.03	9.5:1	36-71
	7A-FE	1.8 (1762)	MFI	115 @ 5600	115 @ 2800	3.19 x 3.36	9.5:1	36-71
1995	4AF-E	1.6 (1587)	MFI	105 @ 5800	100 @ 4800	3.19 x 3.03	9.5:1	36-71
	7A-FE	1.8 (1762)	MFI	105 @ 5200	117 @ 2800	3.19 x 3.36	9.5:1	36-71
1996	4AF-E	1.6 (1587)	MFI	100 @ 5600	105 @ 4400	3.19 x 3.03	9.5:1	36-71
	7A-FE	1.8 (1762)	MFI	105 @ 5200	117 @ 2800	3.19 x 3.36	9.5:1	36-71
1997	4AF-E	1.6 (1587)	MFI	100 @ 5600	105 @ 4400	3.19 x 3.03	9.5:1	36-71
	7A-FE	1.8 (1762)	MFI	105 @ 5200	117 @ 2800	3.19 x 3.36	9.5:1	36-71

88273C24

ROUTINE MAINTENANCE AND TUNE-UP

Proper maintenance and tune-up is the key to long and trouble-free vehicle life, and the work can yield its own rewards. Studies have shown that a properly tuned and maintained vehicle can achieve better gas mileage than an out-of-tune vehicle. As a conscientious owner and driver, set aside a Saturday morning, say once a month, to check or replace items which could cause major problems later. Keep your own personal log to jot down which services you performed, how much the parts cost you, the date, and the exact odometer reading at the time. Keep all receipts for such items as engine oil and filters, so that they may be referred to in case of related problems or to determine operating expenses. As a do-it-yourselfer, these receipts are the only proof you have that the required maintenance was performed. In the event of a warranty problem, these receipts will be invaluable.

The literature provided with your vehicle when it was originally delivered includes the factory recommended maintenance schedule. If you no longer have this literature, replacement copies are usually available from the dealer. A maintenance schedule is provided later in this section, in case you do not have the factory literature.

These checks and inspections can be done either by yourself a reputable shop, or the Toyota dealer.

Here are a few of the scheduled maintenance items that need to be checked frequently:

OUTSIDE THE VEHICLE
• Tire pressure—use a gauge to check the pressure
• Tire surfaces and lug nuts—check the tread depth and ensure all the lug nuts are in place
• Tire rotation—rotate every 6200 miles (1000 km)
• Fluid leaks—check the underneath for leaks of any kind
• Doors and the engine hood—check the latches ensuring they are securing properly

INSIDE THE VEHICLE
• Lights—make sure all the lights are in working order
• Reminder indicators—ensue all the warning lights and buzzers function properly
• Horn—toot the horn to make sure it works when needed
• Seats—be aware of any adjuster problems, a moving seat while you're driving is dangerous
• Seat belts—are they all working properly
• Accelerator pedal—check for smooth operation
• Clutch pedal—check for smooth operation and free-play
• Brake pedal—check for smooth operation and free-play
• Brakes—in a safe location, check for any brake pull

IN THE ENGINE COMPARTMENT
• Washer fluid—check the fluid level
• Engine coolant level—make sure the level is between the FULL and LOW marks
• Battery—if you have a maintenance battery, check the electrolyte levels
• Brake and clutch fluid levels—have the levels near the upper line of the reservoirs
• Engine oil level—with the engine **OFF**, check fluid level on the dipstick
• Power steering fluid—the level should be between HOT and COLD
• Exhaust system—visually check for cracks, holes and loose supports. Be aware of a sudden noise change in the exhaust

Along with these maintenance items, a tune-up is also part of this. A tune-up is not what it used to be years ago where you need to replace the spark plugs every 7500 miles (12,000 km). These days you can replace the plugs on some vehicles every 48,000 miles (77,000 km) or even 100,000 miles (160,900 km).

MAINTENANCE COMPONENT LOCATIONS

1. Spark plug wire
2. Radiator cap
3. Distributor
4. Coolant reservoir
5. Windshield washer reservoir
6. Battery
7. Radiator
8. Brake master cylinder reservoir
9. Fuel filter
10. Air cleaner
11. Engine oil fill cap
12. Automatic transaxle dipstick
13. Radiator hose
14. Fuse block

88271P51

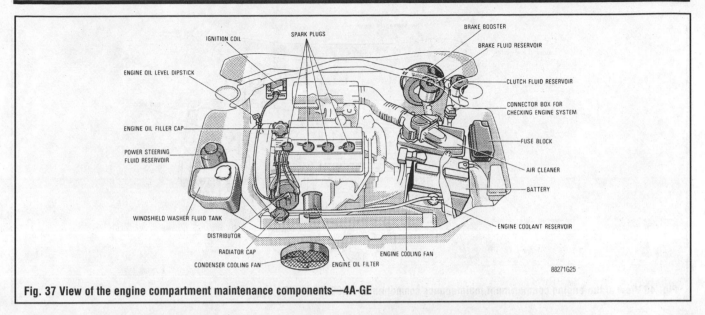

Fig. 37 View of the engine compartment maintenance components—4A-GE

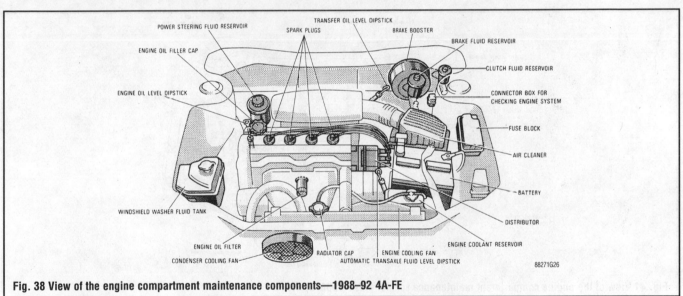

Fig. 38 View of the engine compartment maintenance components—1988–92 4A-FE

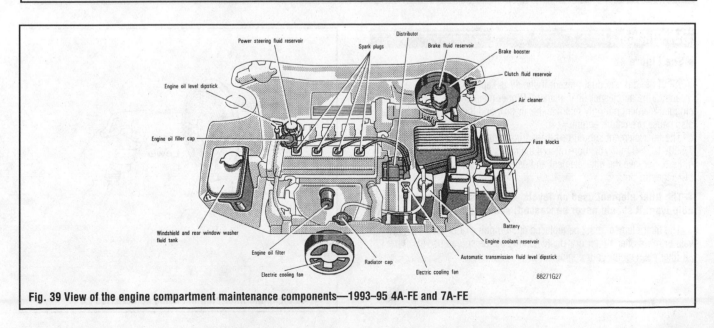

Fig. 39 View of the engine compartment maintenance components—1993–95 4A-FE and 7A-FE

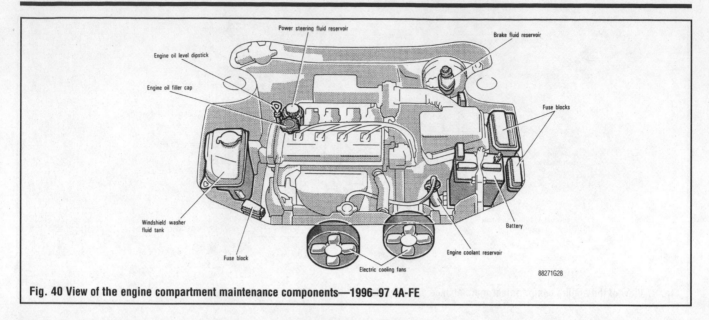

Fig. 40 View of the engine compartment maintenance components—1996–97 4A-FE

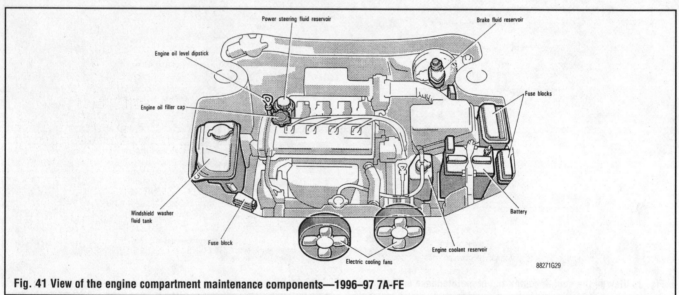

Fig. 41 View of the engine compartment maintenance components—1996–97 7A-FE

Air Cleaner

▶ **See Figure 42**

All of the dirt and dust present in the air is kept out of the engine by means of the air cleaner filter element. Proper maintenance is vital, as a clogged element not only restricts the air flow and thus the power, but can also cause premature engine wear.

The filter element should be cleaned/inspected every 6 months or 7,500–10,000 miles or more often if the car is driven under dry, dusty conditions. Remove the filter element and using low pressure compressed air, blow the dirt out.

➡**The filter element used on Toyota vehicles is of the dry, disposable type. It should never be washed, soaked or oiled.**

The filter element must be replaced at 36 months or 30,000 mile intervals or more often under dry, dusty conditions. Be sure to use the correct air filter element for your engine.

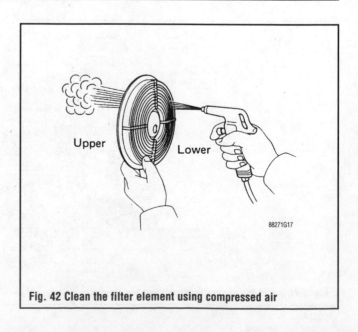

Fig. 42 Clean the filter element using compressed air

REMOVAL & INSTALLATION

♦ **See Figures 43 and 44**

The air filter element should be replaced at the recommended intervals shown in the Maintenance Intervals chart later in this section. If your car is operated under severely dusty conditions or severe operating conditions, more frequent changes will certainly be necessary. Inspect the element at least twice a year. Early spring and early fall are always good times for inspection. Remove the element and check for any perforations or tears in the filter. Check the cleaner housing for signs of dirt or dust that may have leaked through the filter element or in through the snorkel tube. Shine a bright light on one side of the element and look through the filter at the light. If no glow of light can be seen through the element material, replace the filter. If holes in the filter element are apparent or signs of dirt seepage through the filter are evident, replace the filter.

1. Disconnect all hoses, ducts and vacuum tubes which would block removal of the top of the air cleaner assembly.

2. For round air cleaner housings, remove the top cover wing nut and grommet, if present. Most models will also use three or four side clips to further secure the top of the assembly. Pull the wire tab and release the clip. Remove the cover and lift out the filter element.

Unclasp the air cleaner lid from the housing on carbureted models

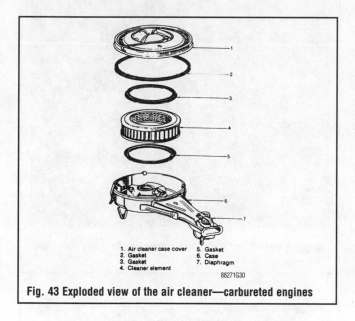

1. Air cleaner case cover
2. Gasket
3. Gasket
4. Cleaner element
5. Gasket
6. Case
7. Diaphragm

88271G30

Fig. 43 Exploded view of the air cleaner—carbureted engines

Remove the wingnut from the top of the cleaner assembly

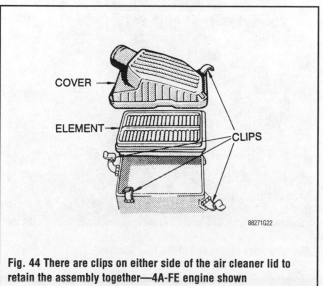

COVER

ELEMENT

CLIPS

88271G22

Fig. 44 There are clips on either side of the air cleaner lid to retain the assembly together—4A-FE engine shown

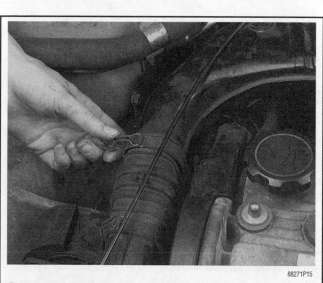

Separate the air cleaner hose from the snorkle

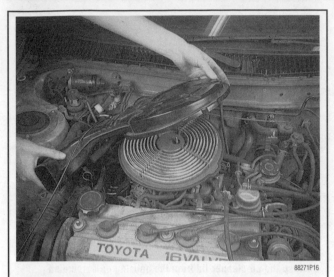

Lift the air cleaner lid, then . . .

. . . remove the air filter from the housing

3. On fuel injected engines, simply release the clips holding the top of the air box and lift the lid. Note that some of these clips may be in close quarters against bodywork or other components; don't pry or force the clips.

4. Remove the filter element. Clean or replace as needed. Wipe clean all surfaces of the air cleaner housing and cover. Check the condition of the mounting gasket and replace it if it appears worn or broken.

To install:

5. Reposition the filter element in the case and install the cover, being careful not to overtighten the wingnut(s). On round-style cleaners (carbureted engines), be certain that the arrows on the cover lid and the snorkel match up properly. The lid of the air cleaner housing must be correctly installed and fit snugly. Air leaks around the top can cause air to bypass the filter and allow dirt into the engine.

➡ Filter elements on fuel injected engines have a TOP and BOTTOM side, be sure they are inserted correctly.

6. Connect all hoses, duct work and vacuum lines.

➡ Never operate the engine without the air filter element in place.

Fuel Filter

The filter should be inspected for external damage and/or leakage at least once a year. The fuel filter should be changed only as necessary. Toyota Motor Corporation recommends replacing the carbureted fuel filters at 15,000 miles and 30,000 miles on fuel injected models.

➡ Fuel lines and connections, fuel tank vapor vent system hoses and fuel tank bands should be inspected every 60,000 miles or every 36 months. The fuel tank cap gasket should be replaced 60,000 miles or every 72 months.

REMOVAL & INSTALLATION

Carbureted Engines

The fuel filter on carbureted engines is a plastic cylinder with two ports for the fuel. It is usually located in the engine compartment near the charcoal canister.

Grasp the clamps and slide them up the hose slightly above the filter ends

Slide the hose off the end of the fuel filter end

Be careful when removing the filter, some fuel may spill out if not held upright

1. Using a pair of pliers, expand the hose clamp on one side of the filter, and slide the clamp further down the hose, past the point to which the filter pipe extends. Remove the other clamp in the same manner.
2. Grasp the hoses near the ends and twist them gently to pull them free from the filter pipe.
3. Pull the filter from the clip and discard.

To install:
4. Install the new filter into the clip. The arrow must point towards the hose that runs to the carburetor.
5. Push the hoses onto the filter pipes, then slide the clamps back into position.
6. Start the engine and check for leaks.

Fuel Injected Engines

1988–92 MODELS

◆ See Figures 45, 46 and 47

The fuel filters on injected engines are a metal cylinder which is located in the engine compartment. You may find it under the injection manifold on some models. Each model varies.
1. Unbolt the retaining screws and remove the protective shield from the fuel filter.

2. Place a pan under the delivery pipe to catch the dripping fuel and SLOWLY loosen the union bolt to bleed off the fuel pressure. The fuel system is under pressure. Release pressure slowly and contain spillage. Observe "no smoking/no open flame precautions".
3. Remove the union bolt and drain the remaining fuel.
4. Disconnect and plug the inlet line.
5. Unbolt and remove the fuel filter.

To install:

➡When tightening the fuel line bolts to the fuel filter, you must use a torque wrench. The tightening torque is very important, as under or over tightening may cause fuel leakage. Insure that there is no fuel line interference and that there is sufficient space between the fuel lines and other components.

6. Coat the flare unit, union nut and all bolt threads with engine oil.
7. Hand-tighten the inlet line to the fuel filter.
8. Install the fuel filter and then tighten the inlet line nut to 22 ft. lbs. (29 Nm).
9. Reconnect the delivery pipe using new gaskets and then tighten the union bolt to 22 ft. lbs. (29 Nm).
10. Run the engine for a short period and check for any fuel leaks.
11. Install the protective shield.

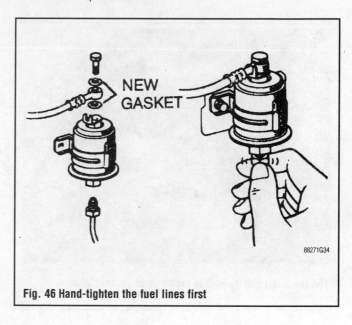

Fig. 46 Hand-tighten the fuel lines first

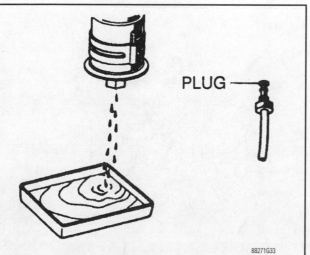

Fig. 45 Place a pan under the delivery pipe to catch the dripping fuel

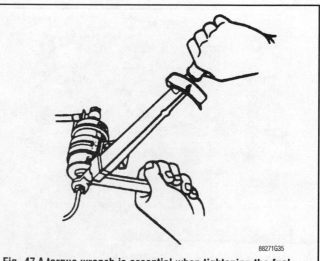

Fig. 47 A torque wrench is essential when tightening the fuel lines to the filter

1993–97 MODELS

◆ **See Figures 48 thru 55**

1. Turn the ignition switch to the **LOCK** position. Disconnect the negative battery cable and wait at least 90 seconds before proceeding with working on the fuel system. This will depressureize the fuel system.

✳✳ CAUTION

Failure to depressurise the fuel system could cause personal injury.

2. Disconnect the Intake Air Temperature (IAT) sensor wiring.
3. Loosen the air cleaner hose clamp bolt, the disconnect the four air cleaner cap clips.
4. Spearate the air cleaner hose from the throttle body, and remove the air cleaner cap together with the air cleaner hose.
5. Disconnect the EVAP canister hose from the charcoal canister.
6. Remove the charcoal canister from the bracket.
7. Place a suitable container or shop towel under the fuel filter. Remove the union bolt and two gaskets, then slowly disconnect the fuel inlet hose from the fuel filter outlet.

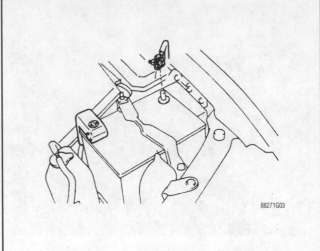

Fig. 49 Disconnect the negative battery cable prior to all fuel system repairs

The fuel filter can be hard to locate on some fuel injected engines

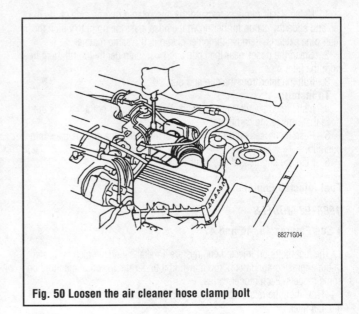

Fig. 50 Loosen the air cleaner hose clamp bolt

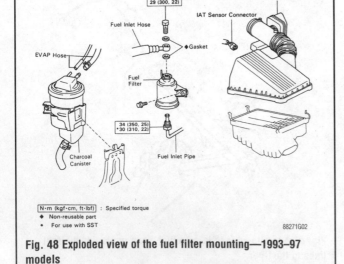

Fig. 48 Exploded view of the fuel filter mounting—1993–97 models

Fig. 51 Remove both EVAP hoses from the charcoal canister

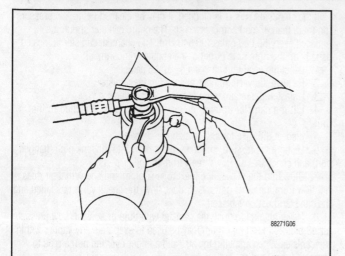

Fig. 52 Remove the union bolt and two gaskets from the fuel fil-ter, then disconnect the inlet hose from the filter

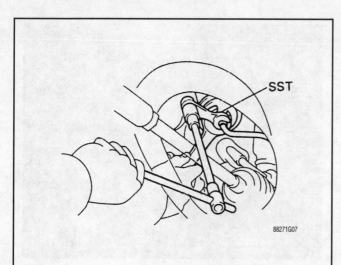

Fig. 53 Using a special tool, disconnect the inlet pipe from the fuel filter

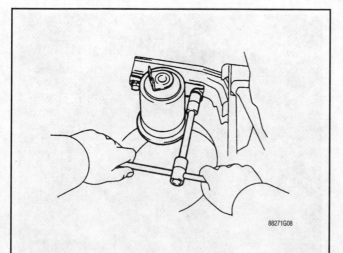

Fig. 54 Remove the two filter mounting bolts, then separate the filter from the vehicle

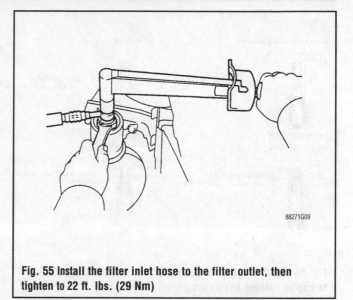

Fig. 55 Install the filter inlet hose to the filter outlet, then tighten to 22 ft. lbs. (29 Nm)

8. Using a special wrench 09631–22020 or equivalent, disconnect the inlet pipe from the fuel filter. Remove the two bolts and the filter from the vehicle.

To install:

9. Install the fuel filter with the two bolts and tighten them to 43 inch lbs. (5 Nm).

10. Using the special wrench 09631–22020 or equivalent, connect the inlet pipe to the fuel filter. Tighten to 22 ft. lbs. (30 Nm). Using a torque wrench, tighten with a fulcrum length of 11.81 inch (30cm). Install the fuel inlet hose to the filter outlet using new gaskets and union bolt. Tighten to 22 ft. lbs. 30 Nm).

11. Install the charcoal canister to the bracket. Connect the two EVAP hoses to the canister.

12. Connect the air cleaner hose to the throttle body. Install the air cleaner cap together with the air cleaner hose.

13. Attach the IAT sensor wiring.

14. Connect the negative battery cable. Start the engine and check for leaks. Reset any various digital equipment such as radio memory and the clock if necessary.

PCV Valve

REMOVAL & INSTALLATION

◆ See Figures 56 and 57

The PCV valve regulates crankcase ventilation during various engine operating conditions. Inspect the PCV valve system every 60,000 miles or every 36 months. Toyota Motor Corporation recommends replacing the PCV valve every 15,000 miles.

1. Check the ventilation hoses for leaks or clogging. Clean or replace as necessary.

2. Locate the PCV valve in the valve cover and pull it out.

3. If the PCV valve failed testing, it will require replacement.

4. Installation is in the reverse order of removal procedure. Replace ventilation hose and clamp if necessary.

Evaporative Canister

SERVICING

◆ See Figure 58

Check the evaporation control system every 15,000 miles (24,000 km). Check the fuel and vapor lines and the vacuum hoses for proper connections and correct routing, as well as condition. Replace clogged, damaged or deteriorated parts as necessary.

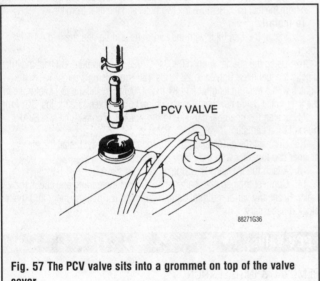

Fig. 56 The PCV valve regulates crankcase ventilation according to engine running conditions

If the charcoal canister is clogged, it may be cleaned using low pressure (no more than 43 psi) compressed air. The entire canister should be replaced every 60,000 miles (96,540 km). The charcoal canister is located usually on the right or left front of the engine compartment.

1. Label the vacuum lines leading to the canister.
2. Remove the vacuum lines attached to the canister.
3. Unfasten the retaining bolts from the canister.
4. Lift the canister up and remove the lower hose attached to the unit.
5. Inspect the case for any cracking or damage.
6. Using low pressure compressed air, blow into the tank pipe (flanged end) and check that air flows freely from the other ports.
7. Blow into the purge pipe (next to tank pipe) and check that air does not flow from the other ports. If air does flow, the check valve has failed and the canister must be replaced.
8. Never attempt to flush the canister with fluid or solvent. Low pressure air 43 psi (294 kPa) maximum may be used to evaporate any vapors within the canister. When applying the air, hold a finger over the purge pipe to force all the air out the bottom port.
9. No carbon should come out of the filter at any time. Loose charcoal is a sign of internal failure in the canister.

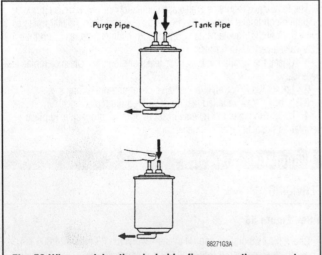

Fig. 57 The PCV valve sits into a grommet on top of the valve cover

When removing the charcoal canister, disconnect any harnesses in the way

Fig. 58 When applying the air, hold a finger over the purge pipe to force all the air out the bottom port

A solenoid may need to be removed to access the canister

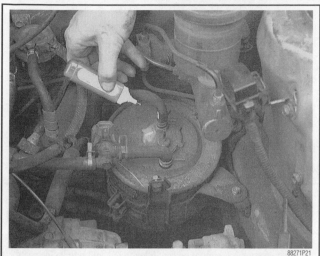

Always label the hoses prevent mixing them up during installation

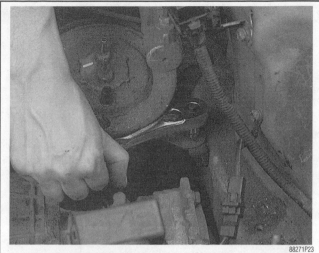

Remove the mounting bolts retaining the canister to the frame rail

Remove the small hose first . . .

Lift the unit from the engine and remove the lower hose from the canister

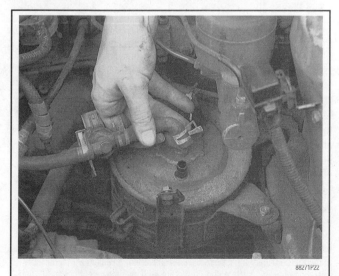

. . . then pull off the two hoses from the top of the canister

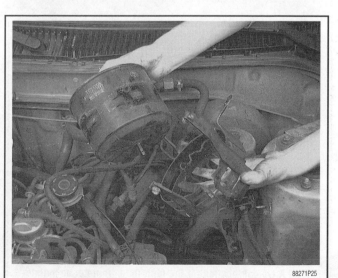

Next, pull the canister from its mounting bracket

Battery

PRECAUTIONS

➡On models with an airbag, wait at least 90 seconds from the time that the ignition switch is turned to the LOCK position and the battery is disconnected before performing any further work.

Always use caution when working on or near the battery. Never allow a tool to bridge the gap between the negative and positive battery terminals. Also, be careful not to allow a tool to provide a ground between the positive cable/terminal and any metal component on the vehicle. Either of these conditions will cause a short circuit, leading to sparks and possible personal injury.

Do not smoke, have an open flame or create sparks near a battery; the gases contained in the battery are very explosive and, if ignited, could cause severe injury or death.

All batteries, regardless of type, should be carefully secured by a battery hold-down device. If this is not done, the battery terminals or casing may crack from stress applied to the battery during vehicle operation. A battery which is not secured may allow acid to leak out, making it discharge faster; such leaking corrosive acid can also eat away at components under the hood.

Always visually inspect the battery case for cracks, leakage and corrosion. A white corrosive substance on the battery case or on nearby components would indicate a leaking or cracked battery. If the battery is cracked, it should be replaced immediately.

GENERAL MAINTENANCE

♦ See Figure 59

A battery that is not sealed must be checked periodically for electrolyte level. You cannot add water to a sealed maintenance-free battery (though not all maintenance-free batteries are sealed); however, a sealed battery must also be checked for proper electrolyte level, as indicated by the color of the built-in hydrometer "eye."

Always keep the battery cables and terminals free of corrosion. Check these components about once a year. Refer to the removal, installation and cleaning procedures outlined in this section.

Keep the top of the battery clean, as a film of dirt can help completely discharge a battery that is not used for long periods. A solution of baking soda and water may be used for cleaning, but be careful to flush this off with clear water. DO NOT let any of the solution into the filler holes. Baking soda neutralizes battery acid and will de-activate a battery cell.

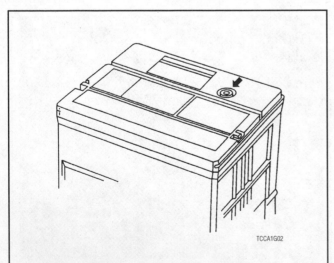

TCCA1G02

Fig. 59 A typical location for the built-in hydrometer on maintenance-free batteries

Batteries in vehicles which are not operated on a regular basis can fall victim to parasitic loads (small current drains which are constantly drawing current from the battery). Normal parasitic loads may drain a battery on a vehicle that is in storage and not used for 6–8 weeks. Vehicles that have additional accessories such as a cellular phone, an alarm system or other devices that increase parasitic load may discharge a battery sooner. If the vehicle is to be stored for 6–8 weeks in a secure area and the alarm system, if present, is not necessary, the negative battery cable should be disconnected at the onset of storage to protect the battery charge.

Remember that constantly discharging and recharging will shorten battery life. Take care not to allow a battery to be needlessly discharged.

BATTERY FLUID

Check the battery electrolyte level at least once a month, or more often in hot weather or during periods of extended vehicle operation. On non-sealed batteries, the level can be checked either through the case on translucent batteries or by removing the cell caps on opaque-cased types. The electrolyte level in each cell should be kept filled to the split ring inside each cell, or the line marked on the outside of the case.

If the level is low, add only distilled water through the opening until the level is correct. Each cell is separate from the others, so each must be checked and filled individually. Distilled water should be used, because the chemicals and minerals found in most drinking water are harmful to the battery and could significantly shorten its life.

If water is added in freezing weather, the vehicle should be driven several miles to allow the water to mix with the electrolyte. Otherwise, the battery could freeze.

Although some maintenance-free batteries have removable cell caps for access to the electrolyte, the electrolyte condition and level on all sealed maintenance-free batteries must be checked using the built-in hydrometer "eye." The exact type of eye varies between battery manufacturers, but most apply a sticker to the battery itself explaining the possible readings. When in doubt, refer to the battery manufacturer's instructions to interpret battery condition using the built-in hydrometer.

➡Although the readings from built-in hydrometers found in sealed batteries may vary, a green eye usually indicates a properly charged battery with sufficient fluid level. A dark eye is normally an indicator of a battery with sufficient fluid, but one which may be low in charge. And a light or yellow eye is usually an indication that electrolyte supply has dropped below the necessary level for battery (and hydrometer) operation. In this last case, sealed batteries with an insufficient electrolyte level must usually be discarded.

Checking the Specific Gravity

♦ See Figure 60

A hydrometer is required to check the specific gravity on all batteries that are not maintenance-free. On batteries that are maintenance-free, the specific gravity is checked by observing the built-in hydrometer "eye" on the top of the battery case. Check with your battery's manufacturer for proper interpretation of its built-in hydrometer readings.

❊❊ CAUTION

Battery electrolyte contains sulfuric acid. If you should splash any on your skin or in your eyes, flush the affected area with plenty of clear water. If it lands in your eyes, get medical help immediately.

The fluid (sulfuric acid solution) contained in the battery cells will tell you many things about the condition of the battery. Because the cell plates must be kept submerged below the fluid level in order to operate, maintaining the fluid level is extremely important. And, because the specific gravity of the acid is an indication of electrical charge, testing the fluid can be an aid in determining if the battery must be replaced. A battery in a vehicle with a properly operating charging system should require little maintenance, but careful, periodic inspection should reveal problems before they leave you stranded.

On non-maintenance-free batteries, the fluid level can be checked through the case on translucent models; the cell caps must be removed on other models

As stated earlier, the specific gravity of a battery's electrolyte level can be used as an indication of battery charge. At least once a year, check the specific gravity of the battery. It should be between 1.20 and 1.26 on the gravity scale. Most auto supply stores carry a variety of inexpensive battery testing hydrometers. These can be used on any non-sealed battery to test the specific gravity in each cell.

The battery testing hydrometer has a squeeze bulb at one end and a nozzle at the other. Battery electrolyte is sucked into the hydrometer until the float is lifted from its seat. The specific gravity is then read by noting the position of the float. If gravity is low in one or more cells, the battery should be slowly charged and checked again to see if the gravity has come up. Generally, if after charging, the specific gravity between any two cells varies more than 50 points (0.50), the battery should be replaced, as it can no longer produce sufficient voltage to guarantee proper operation.

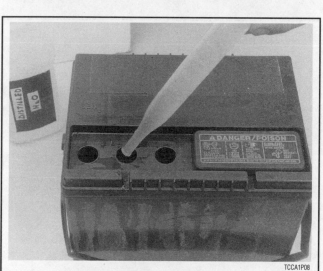

If the fluid level is low, add only distilled water through the opening until the level is correct

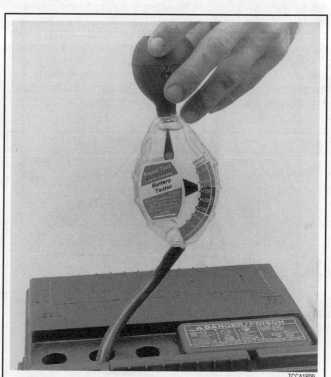

Check the specific gravity of the battery's electrolyte with a hydrometer

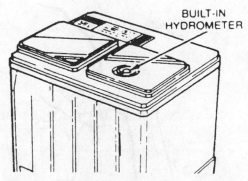

Location of indicator on sealed battery

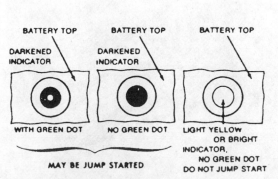

Check the appearance of the charge indicator on top of the battery before attempting a jump start; if it's not green or dark, do not jump start the car

Fig. 60 A typical sealed (maintenance-free) battery with a built-in hydrometer—NOTE that the hydrometer eye may vary between battery manufacturers; always refer to the battery's label

CABLES

▶ **See Figures 61, 62, 63, 64 and 65**

Once a year (or as necessary), the battery terminals and the cable clamps should be cleaned. Loosen the clamps and remove the cables, negative cable first. On batteries with posts on top, the use of a puller specially made for this purpose is recommended. These are inexpensive and available in most auto parts stores. Side terminal battery cables are secured with a small bolt.

Clean the cable clamps and the battery terminal with a wire brush, until all corrosion, grease, etc., is removed and the metal is shiny. It is especially important to clean the inside of the clamp thoroughly (an old knife is useful here), since a small deposit of foreign material or oxidation there will prevent a sound electrical connection and inhibit either starting or charging. Special tools are available for cleaning these parts, one type for conventional top post batteries and another type for side terminal batteries. It is also a good idea to apply some dielectric grease to the terminal, as this will aid in the prevention of corrosion.

After the clamps and terminals are clean, reinstall the cables, negative cable last; DO NOT hammer the clamps onto battery posts. Tighten the clamps securely, but do not distort them. Give the clamps and terminals a thin external coating of grease after installation, to retard corrosion.

Fig. 63 Place the tool over the battery posts and twist to clean until the metal is shiny

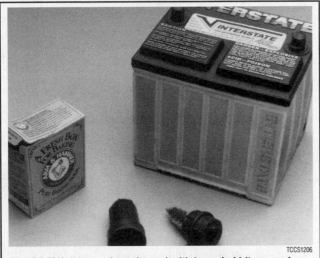

Fig. 61 Maintenance is performed with household items and with special tools like this post cleaner

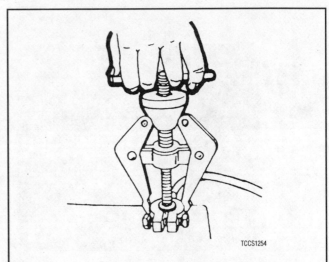

Fig. 64 A special tool is available to pull the clamp from the post

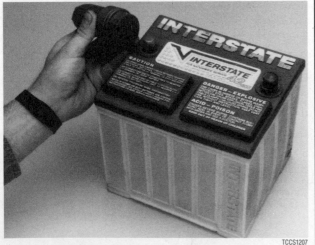

Fig. 62 The underside of this special battery tool has a wire brush to clean post terminals

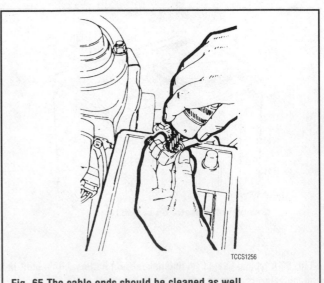

Fig. 65 The cable ends should be cleaned as well

Check the cables at the same time that the terminals are cleaned. If the cable insulation is cracked or broken, or if the ends are frayed, the cable should be replaced with a new cable of the same length and gauge.

CHARGING

❊❊ CAUTION

The chemical reaction which takes place in all batteries generates explosive hydrogen gas. A spark can cause the battery to explode and splash acid. To avoid serious personal injury, be sure there is proper ventilation and take appropriate fire safety precautions when connecting, disconnecting, or charging a battery and when using jumper cables.

A battery should be charged at a slow rate to keep the plates inside from getting too hot. However, if some maintenance-free batteries are allowed to discharge until they are almost "dead," they may have to be charged at a high rate to bring them back to "life." Always follow the charger manufacturer's instructions on charging the battery.

REPLACEMENT

When it becomes necessary to replace the battery, select one with an amperage rating equal to or greater than the battery originally installed. Deterioration and just plain aging of the battery cables, starter motor, and associated wires makes the battery's job harder in successive years. The slow increase in electrical resistance over time makes it prudent to install a new battery with a greater capacity than the old.

Belts

INSPECTION

▶ **See Figures 66 thru 71**

Check the condition of the drive belts and check and adjust the belt tension every 15,000 miles (24,000 km).

Inspect the belts for signs of glazing or cracking. A glazed belt will be perfectly smooth from slippage, while a good belt will have a slight texture of fabric visible. Cracks will generally start at the inner edge of the belt and run outward. All worn or damaged drive belts should be replaced immediately. It is best to replace all drive belts at one time, as a preventive maintenance measure, during this service operation.

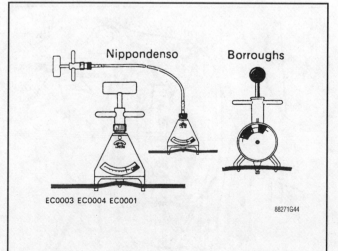

Fig. 66 Types of belt tension gauges used for checking belt tension

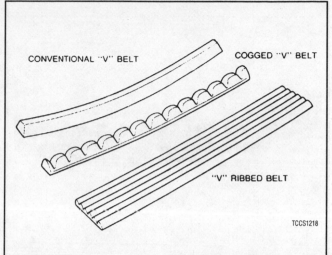

Fig. 67 There are typically 3 types of accessory drive belts found on vehicles today

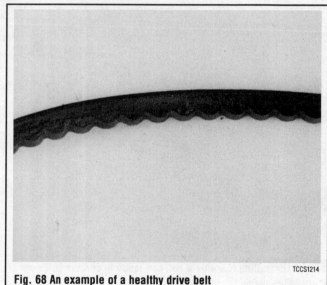

Fig. 68 An example of a healthy drive belt

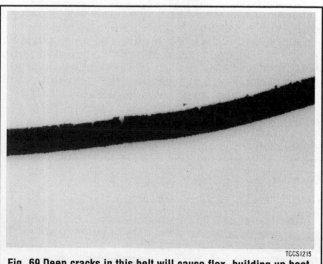

Fig. 69 Deep cracks in this belt will cause flex, building up heat that will eventually lead to belt failure

Fig. 70 The cover of this belt is worn, exposing the critical reinforcing cords to excessive wear

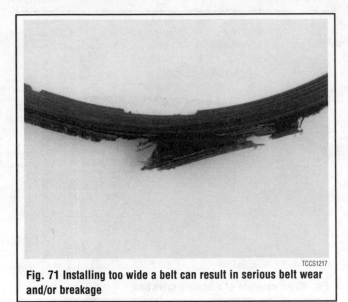

Fig. 71 Installing too wide a belt can result in serious belt wear and/or breakage

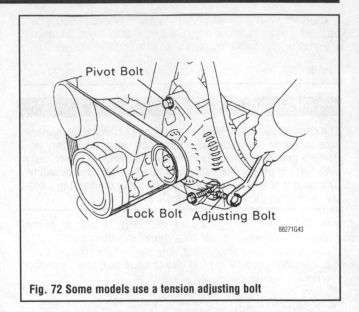

Fig. 72 Some models use a tension adjusting bolt

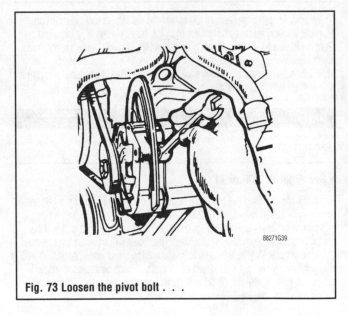

Fig. 73 Loosen the pivot bolt . . .

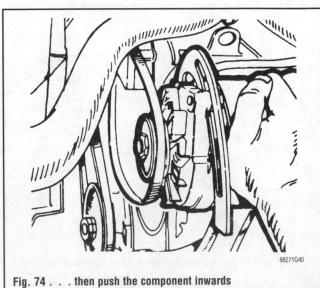

Fig. 74 . . . then push the component inwards

Belt tension does not refer to play or droop. by placing your thumb midway between the two pulleys, it should be possible to depress the belt ¼–½ in. (6–13mm). If any of the belts can be depressed more than this, or cannot be depressed this much, adjust the tension. While this is an inaccurate test, it provides a quick reference. Inadequate tension will always result in slippage or wear, while excessive tension will damage pulley bearings and cause belts to fray and crack. A belt should be tight enough to perform without slipping or squealing.

It is not a bad idea to replace all belts at 60,000 miles (96,000km) regardless of there condition.

ADJUSTMENT

Alternator

▶ See Figures 72, 73, 74, 75 and 76

To adjust the tension of the alternator drive belt on all models, loosen the pivot and mounting bolts on the alternator. Using a wooden hammer handle, a broomstick or your hand, move the alternator one way or the other until the proper tension is achieved. Do not use a screwdriver or any other metal device such as a pry bar, as a lever. Tighten the mounting bolts securely, run the engine about a minute, stop the engine then recheck the belt tension.

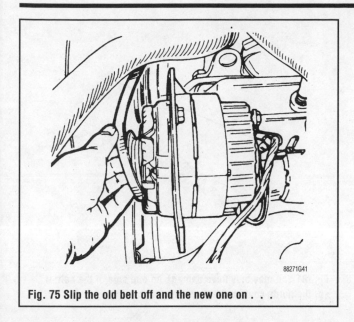

Fig. 75 Slip the old belt off and the new one on . . .

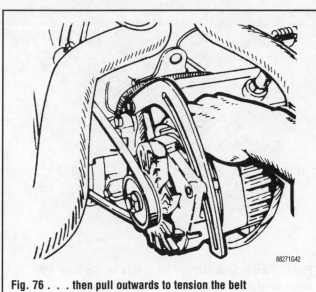

Fig. 76 . . . then pull outwards to tension the belt

Air Conditioning Compressor

A/C compressor (always use caution when working near the A/C compressor) belt tension can be adjusted by turning the tension adjusting bolt which is located on the compressor tensioner bracket. Turn the bolt clockwise to tighten the belt and counterclockwise to loosen it.

Power Steering Pump

Tension on the power steering belt is adjusted by means of an idler pulley (some models may use just a lower adjusting bracket setup—similar to alternator adjustment service procedure). Loosen the lock bolt and turn the adjusting bolt on the idler pulley until the desired tension is felt and then tighten the lock bolt.

REMOVAL & INSTALLATION

On some engines the washer reservoir tank may need to be removed first. If a belt must be replaced, the driven unit must be loosened and moved to its extreme loosest position, generally by moving it toward the center of the motor. After removing the old belt, check the pulleys for dirt or built-up material which could affect belt contact. Carefully install the new

belt, remembering that it is new and unused—it may appear to be just a little too small to fit over the pulley flanges. Fit the belt over the largest pulley (usually the crankshaft pulley at the bottom center of the motor) first, then work on the smaller one(s). Gentle pressure in the direction of rotation is helpful. Some belts run around a third or idler pulley, which acts as an additional pivot in the belt's path. It may be possible to loosen the idler pulley as well as the main component, making your job much easier. Depending on which belt(s) you are changing, it may be necessary to loosen or remove other interfering belts to get at the one(s) you want.

When buying replacement belts, remember that the fit is critical according to the length of the belt, the width of the belt, the depth of the belt and the angle or profile of the V shape (always match up old belt with new belt if possible). The belt shape should exactly match the shape of the pulley; belts that are not an exact match can cause noise, slippage and premature failure.

After the new belt is installed, draw tension on it by moving the driven unit away from the motor and tighten its mounting bolts. This is sometimes a three- or four-handed job; you may find an assistant helpful. Make sure that all the bolts you loosened get retightened and that any other loosened belts also have the correct tension. A new belt can be expected to stretch a bit after installation so be prepared to re-adjust your new belt.

➡ **After installing a new belt, run the engine for about 5 minutes and then recheck the belt tension.**

Timing Belts

INSPECTION

▶ **See Figures 77 thru 85**

The 1988–97 Corolla engines utilizes a timing belt to drive the camshaft from the crankshaft's turning motion and to maintain proper valve timing. Manufacturers schedule periodic timing belt replacement to assure optimum engine performance, to make sure the motorist is never stranded should the belt break (as the engine will stop instantly) and to prevent the possibility of severe internal engine damage should the belt break.

Although these engines are interference motors (it is not listed by the manufacturer as a motor whose valves might contact the pistons if the camshaft was rotated separately from the crankshaft) the first 2 reasons for periodic replacement still apply. Toyota does recommend replacement of the timing belt at 60,000 miles (96,000 km) on vehicles idled for extensive periods of time or for models driven long distances at low speeds.

Whether or not you decide to replace it, you would be wise to check it periodically to make sure it has not become damaged or worn. Generally

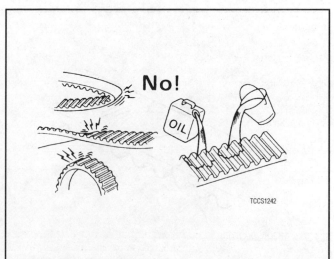

Fig. 77 Do not bend, twist or turn the timing belt inside out. Never allow oil, water or steam to contact the belt

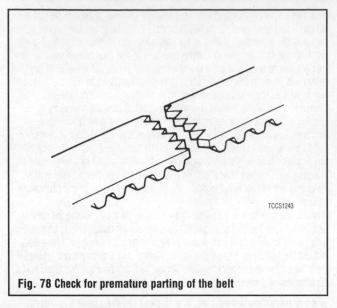

Fig. 78 Check for premature parting of the belt

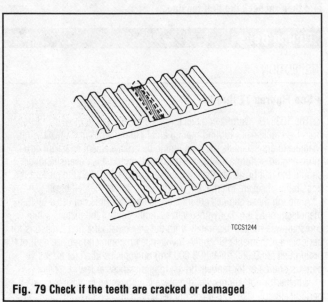

Fig. 79 Check if the teeth are cracked or damaged

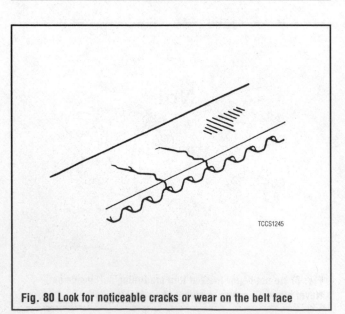

Fig. 80 Look for noticeable cracks or wear on the belt face

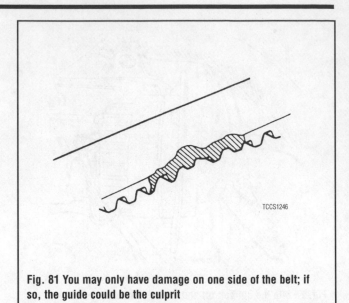

Fig. 81 You may only have damage on one side of the belt; if so, the guide could be the culprit

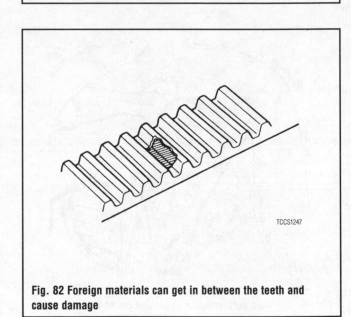

Fig. 82 Foreign materials can get in between the teeth and cause damage

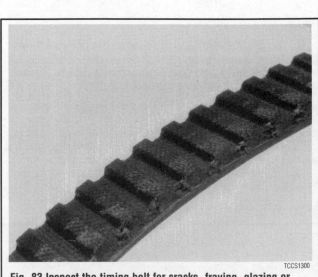

Fig. 83 Inspect the timing belt for cracks, fraying, glazing or damage of any kind

Fig. 84 Damage on only one side of the timing belt may indicate a faulty guide

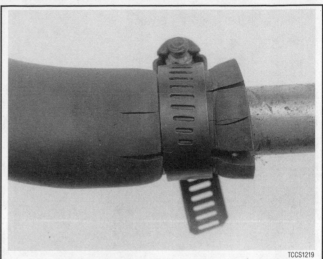

Fig. 86 The cracks developing along this hose are a result of age-related hardening

Fig. 85 ALWAYS replace the timing belt at the interval specified by the manufacturer

Fig. 87 A hose clamp that is too tight can cause older hoses to separate and tear on either side of the clamp

speaking, a severely damaged belt will show as engine performance would drop dramatically, but a damaged belt (which could give out suddenly) may not give as much warning. In general, any time the engine timing cover(s) is(are) removed you should inspect the belt for premature parting, severe cracks or missing teeth. Also, an access plug is provided in the upper portion of the timing cover so that camshaft timing can be checked without cover removal. If timing is found to be off, cover removal and further belt inspection or replacement is necessary.

Hoses

INSPECTION

▶ **See Figures 86, 87, 88 and 89**

Upper and lower radiator hoses along with the heater hoses should be checked for deterioration, leaks and loose hose clamps at least every 15,000 miles (24,000 km). It is also wise to check the hoses periodically in early spring and at the beginning of the fall or winter when you are performing other maintenance. A quick visual inspection could discover a weakened hose which might have left you stranded if it had remained unrepaired.

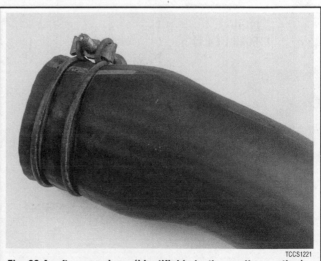

Fig. 88 A soft spongy hose (identifiable by the swollen section) will eventually burst and should be replaced

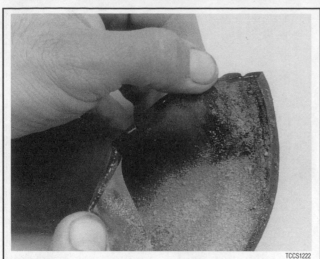

TCCS1222

Fig. 89 Hoses are likely to deteriorate from the inside if the cooling system is not periodically flushed

Whenever you are checking the hoses, make sure the engine and cooling system are cold. Visually inspect for cracking, rotting or collapsed hoses, and replace as necessary. Run your hand along the length of the hose. If a weak or swollen spot is noted when squeezing the hose wall, the hose should be replaced.

REMOVAL & INSTALLATION

▶ See Figure 90

1. Remove the radiator pressure cap.

❋❋ CAUTION

Never remove the pressure cap while the engine is running, or personal injury from scalding hot coolant or steam may result. If possible, wait until the engine has cooled to remove the pressure cap. If this is not possible, wrap a thick cloth around the pressure cap and turn it slowly to the stop. Step back while the pressure is released from the cooling system. When you are sure all the pressure has been released, use the cloth to turn and remove the cap.

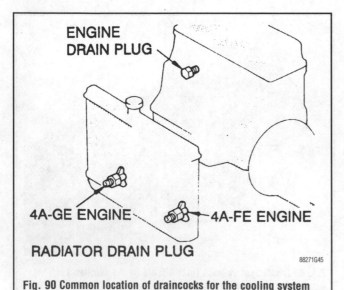

ENGINE DRAIN PLUG

4A-GE ENGINE — 4A-FE ENGINE

RADIATOR DRAIN PLUG

88271G45

Fig. 90 Common location of draincocks for the cooling system

2. Position a clean container under the radiator and/or engine draincock or plug, then open the drain and allow the cooling system to drain to an appropriate level. For some upper hoses, only a little coolant must be drained. To remove hoses positioned lower on the engine, such as a lower radiator hose, the entire cooling system must be emptied.

❋❋ CAUTION

When draining coolant, keep in mind that cats and dogs are attracted by ethylene glycol antifreeze, and are quite likely to drink any that is left in an uncovered container or in puddles on the ground. This will prove fatal in sufficient quantity. Always drain coolant into a sealable container. Coolant may be reused unless it is contaminated or several years old.

3. Loosen the hose clamps at each end of the hose requiring replacement. Clamps are usually either of the spring tension type (which require pliers to squeeze the tabs and loosen) or of the screw tension type (which require screw or hex drivers to loosen). Pull the clamps back on the hose away from the connection.

4. Twist, pull and slide the hose off the fitting, taking care not to damage the neck of the component from which the hose is being removed.

➡If the hose is stuck at the connection, do not try to insert a screwdriver or other sharp tool under the hose end in an effort to free it, as the connection and/or hose may become damaged. Heater connections especially may be easily damaged by such a procedure. If the hose is to be replaced, use a single-edged razor blade to make a slice along the portion of the hose which is stuck on the connection, perpendicular to the end of the hose. Do not cut deep so as to prevent damaging the connection. The hose can then be peeled from the connection and discarded.

5. Clean both hose mounting connections. Inspect the condition of the hose clamps and replace them, if necessary.

To install:

6. Dip the ends of the new hose into clean engine coolant to ease installation.

7. Slide the clamps over the replacement hose, then slide the hose ends over the connections into position.

8. Position and secure the clamps at least ¼ in. (6.35mm) from the ends of the hose. Make sure they are located beyond the raised bead of the connector.

9. Close the radiator or engine drains and properly refill the cooling system with the clean drained engine coolant or a suitable mixture of ethylene glycol coolant and water.

10. If available, install a pressure tester and check for leaks. If a pressure tester is not available, run the engine until normal operating temperature is reached (allowing the system to naturally pressurize), then check for leaks.

❋❋ CAUTION

If you are checking for leaks with the system at normal operating temperature, BE EXTREMELY CAREFUL not to touch any moving or hot engine parts. Once temperature has been reached, shut the engine OFF, and check for leaks around the hose fittings and connections which were removed earlier.

CV-Boots

INSPECTION

▶ See Figures 91 and 92

The CV (Constant Velocity) boots should be checked for damage each time the oil is changed and any other time the vehicle is raised for service. These boots keep water, grime, dirt and other damaging matter from entering the CV-joints. Any of these could cause early CV-joint failure which can be expensive to repair. Heavy grease thrown around the inside of the front wheel(s) and on

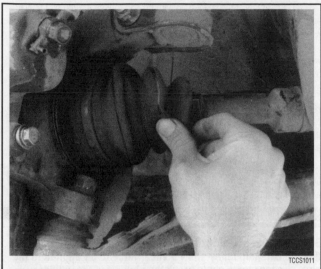

Fig. 91 CV-boots must be inspected periodically for damage

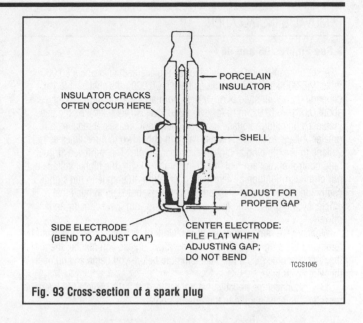

Fig. 93 Cross-section of a spark plug

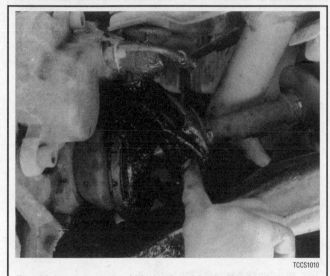

Fig. 92 A torn boot should be replaced immediately

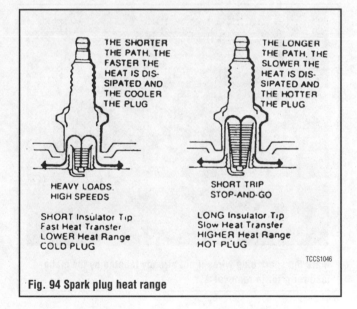

Fig. 94 Spark plug heat range

the brake caliper/drum can be an indication of a torn boot. Thoroughly check the boots for missing clamps and tears. If the boot is damaged, it should be replaced immediately. Please refer to Section 7 for procedures.

Spark Plugs

▶ See Figure 93 and 94

A typical spark plug consists of a metal shell surrounding a ceramic insulator. A metal electrode extends downward through the center of the insulator and protrudes a small distance. Located at the end of the plug and attached to the side of the outer metal shell is the side electrode. The side electrode bends in at a 90° angle so that its tip is just past and parallel to the tip of the center electrode. The distance between these two electrodes (measured in thousandths of an inch or hundredths of a millimeter) is called the spark plug gap.

The spark plug does not produce a spark but instead provides a gap across which the current can arc. The coil produces anywhere from 20,000 to 50,000 volts (depending on the type and application) which travels through the wires to the spark plugs. The current passes along the center electrode and jumps the gap to the side electrode, and in doing so, ignites the air/fuel mixture in the combustion chamber.

SPARK PLUG HEAT RANGE

Spark plug heat range is the ability of the plug to dissipate heat. The longer the insulator (or the farther it extends into the engine), the hotter the plug will operate; the shorter the insulator (the closer the electrode is to the block's cooling passages) the cooler it will operate. A plug that absorbs little heat and remains too cool will quickly accumulate deposits of oil and carbon since it is not hot enough to burn them off. This leads to plug fouling and consequently to misfiring. A plug that absorbs too much heat will have no deposits but, due to the excessive heat, the electrodes will burn away quickly and might possibly lead to preignition or other ignition problems. Preignition takes place when plug tips get so hot that they glow sufficiently to ignite the air/fuel mixture before the actual spark occurs. This early ignition will usually cause a pinging during low speeds and heavy loads.

The general rule of thumb for choosing the correct heat range when picking a spark plug is: if most of your driving is long distance, high speed travel, use a colder plug; if most of your driving is stop and go, use a hotter plug. Original equipment plugs are generally a good compromise between the 2 styles and most people never have the need to change their plugs from the factory-recommended heat range.

REMOVAL & INSTALLATION

♦ See Figures 95 and 96

A set of spark plugs usually requires replacement after about 30,000 miles (48,000 km), platinum plugs have a 60,000 mile change interval, depending on your style of driving. In normal operation plug gap increases about 0.001 in. (0.025mm) for every 2500 miles (4000 km). As the gap increases, the plug's voltage requirement also increases. It requires a greater voltage to jump the wider gap and about two to three times as much voltage to fire the plug at high speeds than at idle. The improved air/fuel ratio control of modern fuel injection combined with the higher voltage output of modern ignition systems will often allow an engine to run significantly longer on a set of standard spark plugs, but keep in mind that efficiency will drop as the gap widdens (along with fuel economy and power).

When you're removing spark plugs, work on one at a time. Don't start by removing the plug wires all at once, because, unless you number them, they may become mixed up. Take a minute before you begin and number the wires with tape.

1. Disconnect the negative battery cable, and if the vehicle has been run recently, allow the engine to thoroughly cool.

2. Carefully twist the spark plug wire boot to loosen it, then pull upward and remove the boot from the plug. Be sure to pull on the boot and not on the wire, otherwise the connector located inside the boot may become separated.

3. Using compressed air, blow any water or debris from the spark plug well to assure that no harmful contaminants are allowed to enter the combustion chamber when the spark plug is removed. If compressed air is not available, use a rag or a brush to clean the area.

➡Remove the spark plugs when the engine is cold, if possible, to prevent damage to the threads. If removal of the plugs is difficult, apply a few drops of penetrating oil or silicone spray to the area around the base of the plug, and allow it a few minutes to work.

4. Using a spark plug socket that is equipped with a rubber insert to properly hold the plug, turn the spark plug counterclockwise to loosen and remove the spark plug from the bore.

❊❊ WARNING

Be sure not to use a flexible extension on the socket. Use of a flexible extension may allow a shear force to be applied to the plug. A shear force could break the plug off in the cylinder head, leading to costly and frustrating repairs.

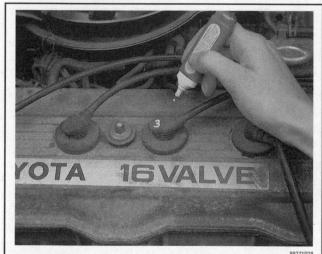

Mark the spark plug wires if not already labeled by the manufacturer prior to removal

88271P28

Use an extension to reach the spark plug

88271P30

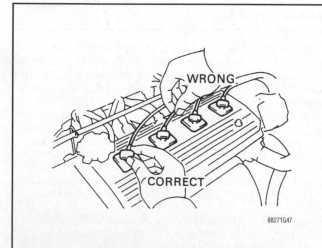

Fig. 95 Twist and remove the plug wires correctly or damage to the wires can occur

88271G47

Be careful not to drop the plug out of the socket

88271P31

To install:

5. Inspect the spark plug boot for tears or damage. If a damaged boot is found, the spark plug wire must be replaced.

6. Using a wire feeler gauge, check and adjust the spark plug gap. When using a gauge, the proper size should pass between the electrodes with a slight drag. The next larger size should not be able to pass while the next smaller size should pass freely.

7. Carefully thread the plug into the bore by hand. If resistance is felt before the plug is almost completely threaded, back the plug out and begin threading again. In small, hard to reach areas, an old spark plug wire and boot could be used as a threading tool. The boot will hold the plug while you twist the end of the wire and the wire is supple enough to twist before it would allow the plug to crossthread.

> ※ **WARNING**
>
> **Do not use the spark plug socket to thread the plugs. Always carefully thread the plug by hand or using an old plug wire to prevent the possibility of crossthreading and damaging the cylinder head bore.**

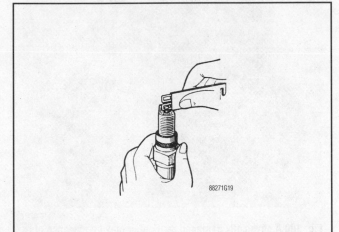

Fig. 96 If adjusting the gap, bend only the base of the ground electrode, do not touch the tip

After the plug is installed, reinsert the spark plug wire. Make sure it enegages

8. Carefully tighten the spark plug. If the plug you are installing is equipped with a crush washer, seat the plug, then tighten about ¼ turn to crush the washer. If you are installing a tapered seat plug, tighten the plug to specifications provided by the vehicle or plug manufacturer.

9. Apply a small amount of silicone dielectric compound to the end of the spark plug lead or inside the spark plug boot to prevent sticking, then install the boot to the spark plug and push until it clicks into place. The click may be felt or heard, then gently pull back on the boot to assure proper contact.

INSPECTION & GAPPING

▶ **See Figures 97 thru 107**

Check the plugs for deposits and wear. If they are not going to be replaced, clean the plugs thoroughly. Remember that any kind of deposit will decrease the efficiency of the plug. Plugs can be cleaned on a spark plug cleaning machine, which can sometimes be found in service stations, or you can do an acceptable job of cleaning with a stiff brush. If the plugs are cleaned, the electrodes must be filed flat. Use an ignition points file, not an emery board or the like, which will leave deposits. The electrodes must be filed perfectly flat with sharp edges; rounded edges reduce the spark plug voltage by as much as 50%.

Check spark plug gap before installation. The ground electrode (the L-shaped one connected to the body of the plug) must be parallel to the center electrode and the specified size wire gauge (please refer to the Tune-Up Specifications chart for details) must pass between the electrodes with a slight drag.

➡ **On platinum spark plug applications DO NOT use a wire brush for cleaning spark plugs. NEVER attempt to adjust gap/clean used platinum spark plugs. Platinum spark plugs should be replaced every 60,000 miles (95,000 km).**

Fig. 97 A normally worn spark plug should have light tan or gray deposits on the firing tip

Always check the gap on new plugs as they are not always set correctly at the factory. Do not use a flat feeler gauge when measuring the gap on a used plug, because the reading may be inaccurate. A round-wire type gapping tool is the best way to check the gap. The correct gauge should pass through the electrode gap with a slight drag. If you're in doubt, try one size smaller and one larger. The smaller gauge should go through easily, while the larger one shouldn't go through at all. Wire gapping tools usually have a bending tool attached. Use that to adjust the side electrode until the proper distance is obtained. Absolutely never attempt to bend the center electrode. Also, be careful not to bend the side electrode too far or too often as it may weaken and break off within the engine, requiring removal of the cylinder head to retrieve it.

TCCS2136

Fig. 98 A carbon fouled plug, identified by soft, sooty, black deposits, may indicate an improperly tuned vehicle. Check the air cleaner, ignition components and engine control system

TCCS2137

Fig. 100 A physically damaged spark plug may be evidence of severe detonation in that cylinder. Watch that cylinder carefully between services, as a continued detonation will not only damage the plug, but could also damage the engine

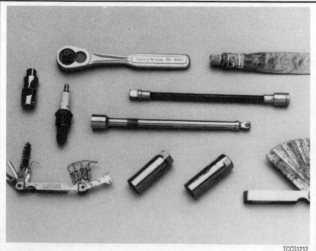

TCCS1212

Fig. 99 A variety of tools and gauges are needed for spark plug service

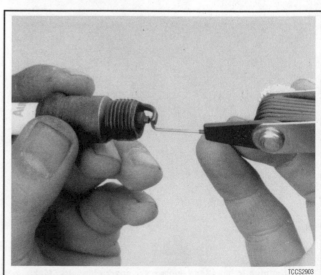

TCCS2903

Fig. 101 Checking the spark plug gap with a feeler gauge

TCCS2138

Fig. 102 An oil fouled spark plug indicates an engine with worn piston rings and/or bad valve seals allowing excessive oil to enter the chamber

TCCS2139

Fig. 104 This spark plug has been left in the engine too long, as evidenced by the extreme gap—Plugs with such an extreme gap can cause misfiring and stumbling accompanied by a noticeable lack of power

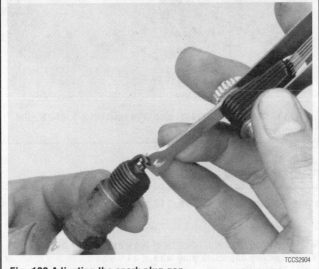

TCCS2904

Fig. 103 Adjusting the spark plug gap

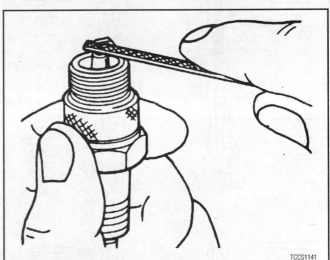

TCCS1141

Fig. 105 If the standard plug is in good condition, the electrode may be filed flat—CAUTION: do not file platinum plugs

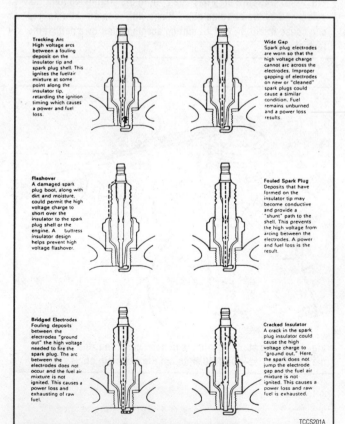

Fig. 106 A bridged or almost bridged spark plug, identified by a build-up between the electrodes caused by excessive carbon or oil build-up on the plug

Tracking Arc
High voltage arcs between a fouling deposit on the insulator tip and spark plug shell. This ignites the fuel/air mixture at some point along the insulator tip, retarding the ignition timing which causes a power and fuel loss.

Wide Gap
Spark plug electrodes are worn so that the high voltage charge cannot arc across the electrodes. Improper gapping of electrodes on new or "cleaned" spark plugs could cause a similar condition. Fuel remains unburned and a power loss results.

Flashover
A damaged spark plug boot, along with dirt and moisture, could permit the high voltage charge to short over the insulator to the spark plug shell or the engine. A buttress insulator design helps prevent high voltage flashover.

Fouled Spark Plug
Deposits that have formed on the insulator tip may become conductive and provide a "shunt" path to the shell. This prevents the high voltage from arcing between the electrodes. A power and fuel loss is the result.

Bridged Electrodes
Fouling deposits between the electrodes "ground out" the high voltage needed to fire the spark plug. The arc between the electrodes does not occur and the fuel air mixture is not ignited. This causes a power loss and exhausting of raw fuel.

Cracked Insulator
A crack in the spark plug insulator could cause the high voltage charge to "ground out." Here, the spark does not jump the electrode gap and the fuel air mixture is not ignited. This causes a power loss and raw fuel is exhausted.

Fig. 107 Used spark plugs which show damage may indicate engine problems

Spark Plug Wires

TESTING

♦ See Figure 108

At every tune-up, visually inspect the spark plug cables for burns, cuts, or breaks in the insulation. Check the boots and the nipples on the distributor cap and coil. Replace any damaged wiring.

Every 30,000 miles or so, the resistance of the wires may be checked with an ohmmeter. Wires with excessive resistance will cause misfiring, and may make the engine difficult to start in damp weather. Generally the useful life of the cables is 30,000–50,000 miles.

To check resistance, remove the distributor cap, leaving the wires attached. Connect one lead of an ohmmeter to an electrode within the cap; connect the other lead to the corresponding spark plug terminal (remove it from the plug for this test). Replace any wire which shows a resistance over 25,000 ohms per wire.

It should be remembered that resistance is also a function of length; the longer the cable, the greater the resistance. Thus, if the cables on your car are longer than the factory originals, resistance will be higher, quite possibly outside these limits.

When installing new spark plug wires (cables), replace them ONE AT A TIME to avoid mix-ups. Start by replacing the longest one first. Install the boot firmly over the spark plug. Route the wire over the same path as the original. Insert the nipple firmly into the tower on the cap or the coil.

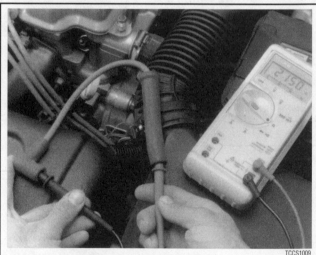

Fig. 108 Checking individual plug wire resistance with a digital ohmmeter

REMOVAL & INSTALLATION

♦ See Figures 109, 110, 111, 112 and 113

1. Disconnect the negative battery cable.

➡If there is no tape around to label the wires. It may be a good idea to remove one spark plug wire at a time so not to mix them up during installation.

2. Label and disconnect the wires from each spark plug one at a time.

3. Remove the spark plug wires from the distributor cap. On some models you may need to use a flat bladed tool to lift up the lock claw and disconnect the holder from the cap. Separate the wires at the grommet.

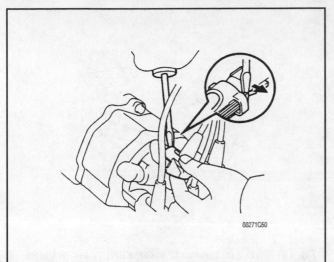

Fig. 109 Lift up the lock claw and disconnect the holder from the distributor cap

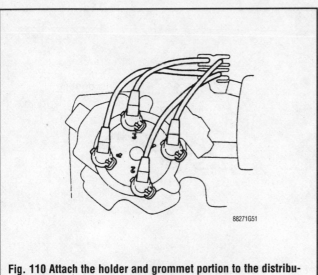

Fig. 110 Attach the holder and grommet portion to the distributor cap

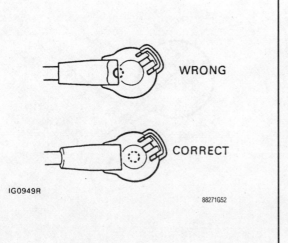

Fig. 111 Holder installation to the grommet and cap is important

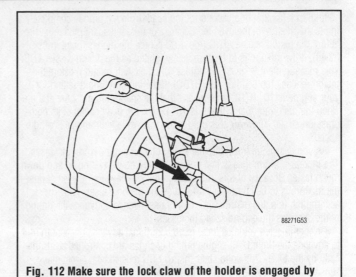

Fig. 112 Make sure the lock claw of the holder is engaged by lightly pulling the holder

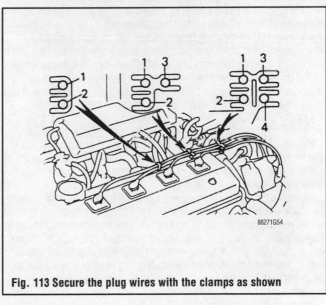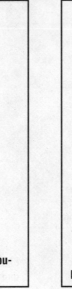

Fig. 113 Secure the plug wires with the clamps as shown

✳✳ WARNING

Do not pull on the plug wires to remove them, this may damage the conductor inside.

4. Pull the plug wires from the retaining clamps.
To install:
5. Attach the holder and grommet portion to the distributor cap. Make sure that the holder is installed correctly to the grommet and cap.
6. Check that the lock claw of the holder is engaged by lightly pulling on the holder.
7. Secure the wires with the clamps as shown.

Ignition Timing

GENERAL INFORMATION

Ignition timing is the measurement (in degrees) of crankshaft position at the instant the spark plug fires. Ignition timing is adjusted by loosening the distributor locking device and turning the distributor in the engine.

It takes a fraction of a second for the spark from the plug to completely ignite the mixture in the cylinder. Because of this, the spark plug must fire before the piston reaches TDC (top dead center, the highest point in its travel), if the mixture is to be completely ignited as the piston passes TDC. This measurement is given in degrees (of crankshaft rotation) before the piston reaches top dead center (BTDC). If the ignition timing setting for your engine is 10° BTDC, this means that the spark plug must fire at a time when the piston for that cylinder is 10° before top dead center of its compression stroke. However, this only holds true while your engine is at idle speed.

As you accelerate from idle, the speed of your engine (rpm) increases. The increase in rpm means that the pistons are now traveling up and down much faster. Because of this, the spark plugs will have to fire even sooner if the mixture is to be completely ignited as the piston passes TDC. To accomplish this, the distributor incorporates means to advance the timing of the spark as the engine speed increases.

On fuel injected vehicles there is no centrifugal advance or vacuum unit to advance the timing. All engine timing changes are controlled electronically by the ECU. This solid state "brain" ECU receives data from many sensors and commands changes in spark timing based on immediate driving conditions. This instant response allows the engine to be kept at peak performance and economy throughout the driving cycle. Basic timing and idle speed can still be checked and adjusted on these engines.

If the ignition timing is set too far advanced (BTDC), the ignition and expansion of the air/fuel mixture in the cylinder will try to force the piston down while it is still traveling upward. This causes engine ping, a sound which resembles marbles being dropped into an empty tin can. If the ignition timing is too far retarded (after, or ATDC), the piston will have already started down on the power stroke when the air/fuel mixture ignites and expands. This will cause the piston to be forced down only a portion of its travel. This results in poor engine performance and lack of power.

Ignition timing adjustment is checked with a timing light. This instrument is connected to the number one (No. 1) spark plug of the engine. The timing light flashes every time an electrical current is sent from the distributor through the No. 1 spark plug wire to the spark plug. The crankshaft pulley and the front cover of the engine are marked with a timing pointer and a timing scale.

When the timing pointer is aligned with the 0 mark on the timing scale, the piston in the No. 1 cylinder is at TDC of it compression stroke. With the engine running, and the timing light aimed at the timing pointer and timing scale, the stroboscopic (periodic) flashes from the timing light will allow you to check the ignition timing setting of the engine. The timing light flashes every time the spark plug in the No. 1 cylinder of the engine fires. Since the flash from the timing light makes the crankshaft pulley seem to stand still for a moment, you will be able to read the exact position of the piston in the No. 1 cylinder on the timing scale on the front of the engine.

If you're buying a timing light, make sure the unit you select is rated for electronic or solid-state ignitions. Generally, these lights have two wires which connect to the battery with alligator clips and a third wire which connects to the No. 1 plug wire. The best lights have an inductive pick-up on the third wire; this allows you to simply clip the small box over the wire. Older lights may require the removal of the plug wire and the installation of an in-line adapter. Since the spark plugs in the twin-cam engines are in deep wells, rigging the adapter can be difficult. Buy quality the first time and the tool will give lasting results and ease of use.

INSPECTION & ADJUSTMENT

Carbureted Engines

▶ See Figures 114, 115, 116, 117 and 118

1. Warm-up the engine, then turn the ignition OFF. Connect a tachometer to both battery terminals and to the service connector coming from the distributor.

2. Clean off the timing marks. The marks are on the crankshaft pulley and timing cover. The timing notches in the crankshaft pulley are normally marked at the factory with red or white paint. You may want to retouch them

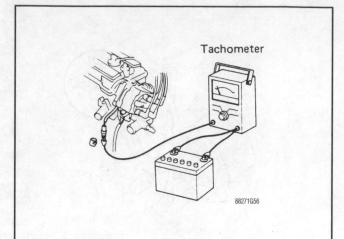

Fig. 114 Attach a tachometer to both the battery and terminals of the service connector coming from the distributor—1988–89 models

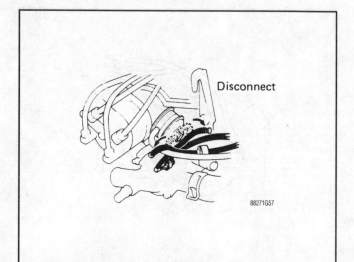

Fig. 115 Disconnect the vacuum line(s) from the distributor vacuum unit

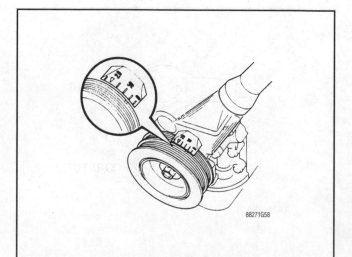

Fig. 116 With the engine idling, use a timing light to check the timing

if they are dark, using chalk or paint. Fluorescent (dayglow) paint is excellent for this purpose. You might have to bump the engine around with the starter (just touch the key to the **START** position very briefly) to find the pulley marks.

3. Connect a timing light according to the manufacturer's instructions.

4. Disconnect the vacuum line(s) from the distributor vacuum unit. Clamp or plug the line(s); golf tees are excellent for this job. Any vacuum leak will make the engine run poorly.

5. Be sure that the all wires are clear of the fan and moving belts, pulleys etc. Start the engine.

❊❊ CAUTION

Keep fingers, clothes, tools, hair, and wiring leads clear of the all moving parts. Be sure that you are running the engine in a well ventilated area.

6. Allow the engine to run at idle speed with the gear shift in Neutral (manual) and Park (P) with automatic transmission. Use the tachometer to check idle speed and adjust the idle if necessary. Idle speed is 750 rpm with a manual transmission or 850 rpm with an automatic transmission.

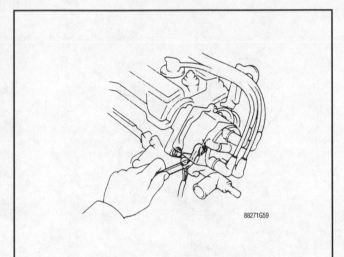

Fig. 117 If necessary, loosen the distributor bolts and turn the distributor, then recheck the timing

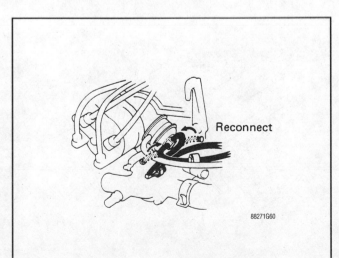

Fig. 118 Reconnect the vacuum line(s) to the distributor vacuum unit

❊❊ CAUTION

Be sure that the parking brake is set and that the front wheels are blocked to prevent the vehicle from rolling.

7. Point the timing light at the marks indicated in the chart and illustrations. With the engine at idle, timing should be at the specification given on the "Tune-Up Specifications" chart.

8. If the timing is not at the specification, loosen the pinch bolt (hold-down bolt) at the base of the distributor just enough so that the distributor can be turned. Turn the distributor to advance or retard the timing as required. Once the proper marks are seen to align, timing is correct. Tighten the hold-down bolt.

➡**Remember that you are using metal tools on a running engine. Watch out for moving parts and don't touch any of the spark plug wires with the wrench.**

9. Recheck the timing. Stop the engine; disconnect the tachometer and timing light.

Fuel Injected Engines

1988–95 MODELS

◗ **See Figures 119 thru 124**

This service procedure is for setting base ignition timing. Refer to underhood emission sticker for any additional service procedure steps and/or specifications.

These engines require a tachometer hook-up to the check connector—see illustrations. NEVER allow the tachometer terminal to become grounded; severe and expensive damage can occur to the coil and/or igniter.

Some tachometers are not compatible with this ignition system, confirm the compatibility of your unit before using.

1. Warm the engine to normal operating temperature. Turn off all electrical accessories. Do not attempt to check timing specification or idle speed on a cold engine.

2. Connect a tachometer (connect the tachometer (+) terminal to the terminal IG- of the check connector) and check the engine idle speed to be sure it is within the specification given in the Tune-Up Specifications chart or underhood emission sticker.

3. Remove the cap on the diagnostic check connector. Using a small jumper wire or Special Service Tool SST 09843-18020, short terminals TE1 (test terminal No. 1) and E1 (earth-ground) together.

4. If the timing marks are difficult to see, shut the engine **OFF** and use a dab of paint or chalk to make them more visible.

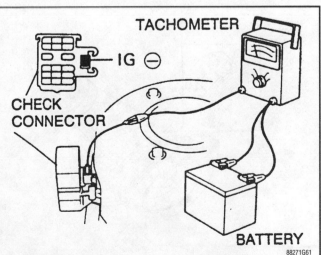

Fig. 119 Attach the tachometer to the battery and check connector terminals

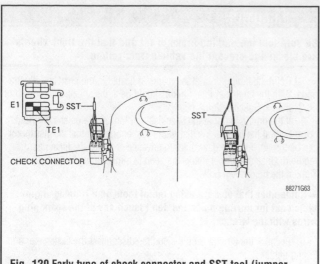

Fig. 120 Early type of check connector and SST tool (jumper wire) for base timing adjustment

5. Connect a timing light according to the manufacturer's instructions.

6. Start the engine and use the timing light to observe the timing marks. With the jumper wire in the check connector the timing should be to specifications (refer to underhood emission sticker as necessary) with the engine fully warmed up (at correct idle speed) and the transmission in correct position. If the timing is not correct, loosen the bolts at the distributor just enough so that the distributor can be turned. Turn the distributor to advance or retard the timing as required. Once the proper marks are seen to align with the timing light, timing is correct.

7. Without changing the position of the distributor, tighten the distributor bolts and double check the timing with the light (check idle speed as necessary).

8. Disconnect the jumper wire or Special Service Tool (SST) at the diagnostic check connector.

➡**This jumper will be used repeatedly during diagnostics in later sections. Take the time to make a proper jumper with correct terminals or probes. It's a valuable special tool for very low cost.**

9. Refer to the underhood emission sticker for timing specification and any additional service procedure steps. If necessary, repeat the timing adjustment procedure.

10. Shut the engine **OFF** and disconnect all test equipment. Roadtest the vehicle for proper operation.

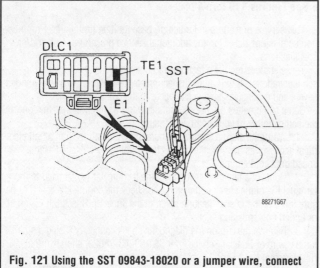

Fig. 121 Using the SST 09843-18020 or a jumper wire, connect terminals TE1 and E1 of the DLC1 (also used on OBD-II)

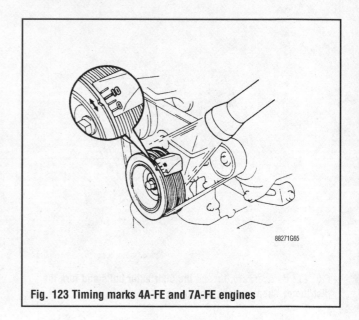

Fig. 123 Timing marks 4A-FE and 7A-FE engines

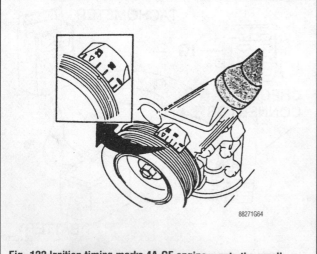

Fig. 122 Ignition timing marks 4A-GE engine—note the small notch on the pulley, this is the mark to align with the degree scale

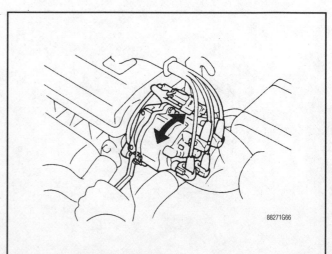

Fig. 124 If necessary, loosen the 2 mounting bolts and turn the distributor to adjust the timing

1996–97 MODELS

♦ See Figures 121, 125 and 126

➡Toyota's hand-held tester or an equivalent OBD-II scan tool must be used for this procedure.

1. Warm the engine to normal operating temperature.
2. Connect an OBD-II compliant scan tool to the DLC3 located under the dash on the driver's side. Refer to Section 4 for more information.
3. Connect the timing light to the engine.
4. Using SST 09843-18020 or its equivalent jumper wire, connect terminals TE1 and E1 of the DLC1 under the hood.
5. After the engine speed is kept at about 1000–1500 rpm for 5 seconds, check that it returns to idle speed.
6. Check the ignition timing, the reading should be 10° BTDC at idle.
7. On 4A-FE engines, if adjustment is necessary, loosen the 2 hold-down bolts, and adjust by turning the IIA. Tighten the hold-down bolts to 14 ft. lbs. (20 Nm), and recheck the ignition timing.
8. Remove the jumper wire from the DLC1.
9. Recheck the timing, the mark ranges from 5°–15° BTDC at idle.
10. Disconnect the scan tool.
11. Disconnect the timing light.

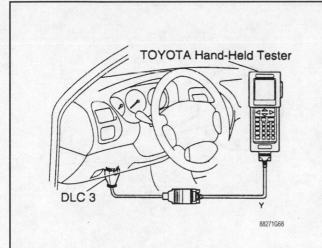

Fig. 125 Connect an OBD-II scan tool to the DLC3 located under the driver's side of the dash

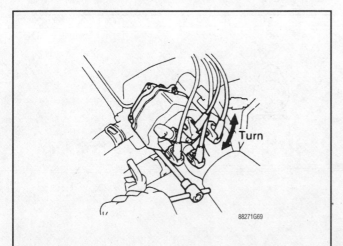

Fig. 126 Loosen the hold-down bolts and rotate the distributor to adjust

Valve Lash

GENERAL INFORMATION

➡Check and adjust the valve clearance every 60,000 miles or 72 months.

Valve clearance is one factor which determines how far the intake and exhaust valves will open into the cylinder. If the valve clearance is too large, part of the lift of the camshaft will be used up in removing the excessive clearance, thus the valves will not be opened far enough. This condition has two effects, the valve train components will emit a tapping noise as they take up the excessive clearance, and the engine will perform poorly, since the less the intake valve opens, the smaller the amount of air/fuel mixture that will be admitted to the cylinders. The less the exhaust valves open, the greater the back-pressure in the cylinder which prevents the proper air/fuel mixture from entering the cylinder.

If the valve clearance is too small, the intake and exhaust valves will not fully seat on the cylinder head when they close. When a valve seats on the cylinder head it does two things, it seals the combustion chamber so none of the gases in the cylinder can escape and it cools itself by transferring some of the heat it absorbed from the combustion process through the cylinder head and into the engine cooling system. Therefore, if the valve clearance is too small, the engine will run poorly due to gases escaping from the combustion chamber, and the valves will overheat and warp since they cannot transfer heat unless they are touching the seat in the cylinder head.

ADJUSTMENT

1988–92 Models

♦ See Figures 127 thru 134

➡The use of the correct special tools or their equivalent is REQUIRED for this procedure. The valve adjustment requires removal of the adjusting shims (Tool kit J–37141 available from Kent-Moore Tool or a Toyota equivalent No. 09248–55010) and accurate measurement of the shims with a micrometer. A selection of replacement shims (refer to parts department of your Toyota dealer) is also required. Do not attempt this procedure if you are not equipped with the proper tools. Valves on these engines are adjusted with the engine cold. Do not attempt adjustment if the engine has been run within the previous 4 hours. An overnight cooling period is recommended.

1. Remove the spark plug wires from the valve cover.
2. Remove the valve cover following procedures discussed in Section 3.
3. Turn the crankshaft to align the groove in the crankshaft pulley with the **0** mark on the timing belt cover. Removing the spark plugs makes this easier, but is not required.
4. Check that the lifters on No.1 cylinder are loose and those on No.4 are tight. If not, turn the crankshaft pulley one full revolution (360°).
5. Using the feeler gauge, measure the clearance on the valves in the positions shown in the diagram labeled First Pass. Make a written record of any measurements which are not within specification.
6. Rotate the crankshaft pulley one full turn (360°) and check the clearance on the other valves. The positions are shown on the diagram labeled Second Pass. Any measurements not within specification should be added to your written record.
   - Intake clearance COLD: 0.006–0.010 in. (0.15–0.25mm)
   - Exhaust clearance COLD: 0.008–0.012 in. (0.20–0.30mm)
   - Intake clearance HOT: 0.008–0.012 in. (0.20–0.30mm)
   - Exhaust clearance HOT: 0.010–0.014 in. (0.26–0.36mm)
7. For ANY given valve needing adjustment:
   a. Turn the crankshaft pulley until the camshaft lobe points upward over the valve. This takes the tension off the valve and spring.

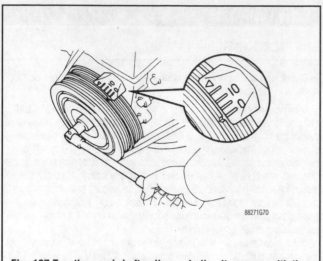

Fig. 127 Turn the crankshaft pulley and align its groove with the timing mark 0

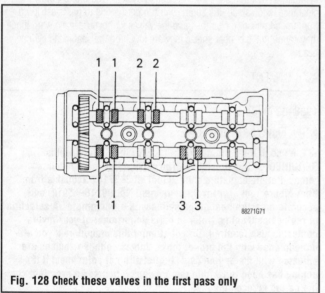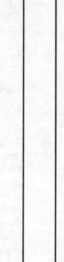

Fig. 128 Check these valves in the first pass only

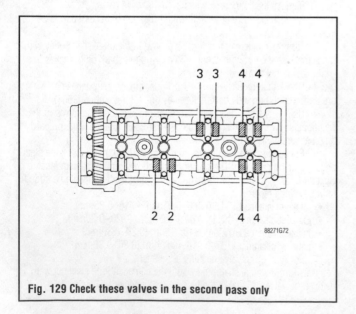

Fig. 129 Check these valves in the second pass only

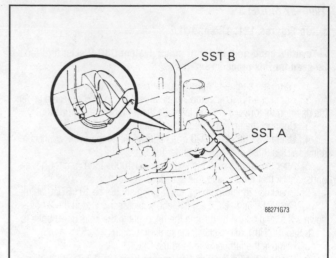

Fig. 130 Press down the valve lifter with SST-A and hold the lifter down with SST-B

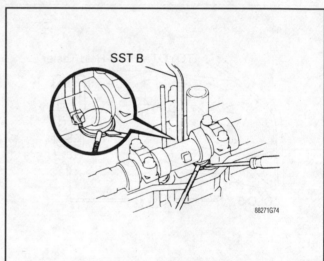

Fig. 131 Remove the adjusting shim with a flatbladed tool and a magnetic finger

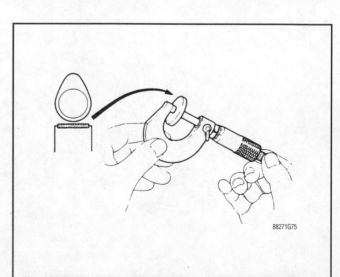

Fig. 132 Using a micrometer, measure the removed adjusting shim size

Adjusting Shim Selection Chart

Intake

Measured Clearance (mm)	Installed Shim Thickness (mm)																																												
	2.500	2.525	2.550	2.575	2.600	2.620	2.640	2.650	2.660	2.680	2.700	2.720	2.740	2.750	2.760	2.780	2.800	2.820	2.840	2.850	2.860	2.880	2.900	2.920	2.940	2.950	2.960	2.980	3.000	3.020	3.040	3.050	3.060	3.080	3.100	3.120	3.140	3.150	3.160	3.180	3.200	3.225	3.250	3.275	3.300
0.000 — 0.009										02	02	04	04	04	04	06	06	08	08	08	08	10	10	12	12	12	12	14	14	16	16	16	16	18	18	20	20	20	20	22	22	24	24	26	26
0.010 — 0.025									02	02	02	04	04	04	06	06	06	08	08	08	10	10	10	12	12	12	14	14	14	16	16	16	18	18	18	20	20	20	22	22	22	24	24	26	26
0.026 — 0.029								02	02	02	04	04	04	06	06	06	08	08	08	10	10	10	12	12	12	14	14	14	16	16	16	18	18	18	20	20	20	22	22	22	24	24	26	26	28
0.030 — 0.040							02	02	02	02	04	04	04	06	06	06	08	08	08	10	10	10	12	12	12	14	14	14	16	16	16	18	18	18	20	20	20	22	22	22	24	24	26	26	28
0.041 — 0.050							02	02	02	02	04	04	06	06	06	06	08	08	10	10	10	10	12	12	14	14	14	14	16	16	18	18	18	18	20	20	22	22	22	22	24	24	26	26	28
0.051 — 0.070						02	02	02	02	04	04	06	06	06	06	08	08	10	10	10	10	12	12	14	14	14	14	16	16	18	18	18	18	20	20	22	22	22	22	24	24	26	26	28	28
0.071 — 0.075					02	02	02	02	04	04	04	06	06	06	08	08	08	10	10	10	12	12	12	14	14	14	16	16	16	18	18	18	20	20	20	22	22	22	24	24	24	26	26	28	28
0.076 — 0.090					02	02	02	04	04	04	06	06	06	08	08	08	10	10	10	12	12	12	14	14	14	16	16	16	18	18	18	20	20	20	22	22	22	24	24	24	26	26	28	28	30
0.091 — 0.100					02	02	04	04	04	04	06	06	08	08	08	08	10	10	12	12	12	12	14	14	16	16	16	16	18	18	20	20	20	20	22	22	24	24	24	24	26	26	28	28	30
0.101 — 0.120				02	02	02	04	04	04	06	06	06	08	08	08	10	10	10	12	12	12	14	14	14	16	16	16	18	18	18	20	20	20	22	22	22	24	24	24	26	26	28	28	30	30
0.121 — 0.125			02	02	02	04	04	04	06	06	06	08	08	08	10	10	10	12	12	12	14	14	14	16	16	16	18	18	18	20	20	20	22	22	22	24	24	24	26	26	26	28	28	30	30
0.126 — 0.140			02	02	04	04	04	06	06	06	08	08	08	10	10	10	12	12	12	14	14	14	16	16	16	18	18	18	20	20	20	22	22	22	24	24	24	26	26	26	28	28	30	30	32
0.141 — 0.149			02	02	04	04	06	06	06	06	08	08	10	10	10	10	12	12	14	14	14	14	16	16	18	18	18	18	20	20	22	22	22	22	24	24	26	26	26	26	28	28	30	30	32
0.150 — 0.250																																													
0.251 — 0.270	04	06	06	08	08	10	10	10	10	12	12	14	14	14	14	16	16	18	18	18	18	20	20	22	22	22	22	24	24	26	26	26	26	28	28	30	30	30	30	32	32	34	34		
0.271 — 0.275	04	06	06	08	08	10	10	10	12	12	12	14	14	14	16	16	16	18	18	18	20	20	20	22	22	22	24	24	24	26	26	26	28	28	28	30	30	30	32	32	32	34	34		
0.276 — 0.290	06	06	08	08	10	10	10	12	12	12	14	14	14	16	16	16	18	18	18	20	20	20	22	22	22	24	24	24	26	26	26	28	28	28	30	30	30	32	32	32	34	34			
0.291 — 0.300	06	06	08	08	10	10	12	12	12	12	14	14	16	16	16	16	18	18	20	20	20	20	22	22	24	24	24	24	26	26	28	28	28	28	30	30	32	32	32	32	34	34			
0.301 — 0.320	06	08	08	10	10	12	12	12	12	14	14	16	16	16	16	18	18	20	20	20	20	22	22	24	24	24	24	26	26	28	28	28	28	30	30	32	32	32	32	34	34				
0.321 — 0.325	06	08	08	10	10	12	12	12	14	14	24	16	16	16	18	18	18	20	20	20	22	22	22	24	24	24	26	26	26	28	28	28	30	30	30	32	32	32	34	34	34				
0.326 — 0.340	08	08	10	10	12	12	12	14	14	24	16	16	16	18	18	18	20	20	20	22	22	22	24	24	24	26	26	26	28	28	28	30	30	30	32	32	32	34	34	34					
0.341 — 0.350	08	08	10	10	12	12	14	14	14	14	16	16	18	18	18	18	20	20	22	22	22	22	24	24	26	26	26	26	28	28	30	30	30	30	32	32	34	34	34						
0.351 — 0.370	08	10	10	12	12	14	14	14	14	16	16	18	18	18	18	20	20	22	22	22	22	24	24	26	26	26	26	28	28	30	30	30	30	32	32	34	34	34	34						
0.371 — 0.375	08	10	10	12	12	14	14	14	16	16	16	18	18	18	20	20	20	22	22	22	24	24	24	26	26	26	28	28	28	30	30	30	32	32	32	34	34	34							
0.376 — 0.390	10	10	12	12	14	14	14	16	16	16	18	18	18	20	20	20	22	22	22	24	24	24	26	26	26	28	28	28	30	30	30	32	32	32	34	34	34								
0.391 — 0.400	10	10	12	12	14	14	16	16	16	16	18	18	20	20	20	20	22	22	24	24	24	24	26	26	28	28	28	28	30	30	32	32	32	32	34	34									
0.401 — 0.420	10	12	12	14	14	16	16	16	16	18	18	20	20	20	20	22	22	24	24	24	24	26	26	28	28	28	28	30	30	32	32	32	32	34	34										
0.421 — 0.425	10	12	12	14	14	16	16	16	18	18	18	20	20	20	22	22	22	24	24	24	26	26	26	28	28	28	30	30	30	32	32	32	34	34	34										
0.426 — 0.440	12	12	14	14	16	16	16	18	18	18	20	20	20	22	22	22	24	24	24	26	26	26	28	28	28	30	30	30	32	32	32	34	34	34											
0.441 — 0.450	12	12	14	14	16	16	18	18	18	18	20	20	22	22	22	22	24	24	26	26	26	26	28	28	30	30	30	30	32	32	34	34	34	34											
0.451 — 0.470	12	14	14	16	16	18	18	18	18	20	20	22	22	22	22	24	24	26	26	26	26	28	28	30	30	30	30	32	32	34	34	34	34												
0.471 — 0.475	12	14	14	16	16	18	18	18	20	20	20	22	22	22	24	24	24	26	26	26	28	28	28	30	30	30	32	32	32	34	34	34													
0.476 — 0.490	14	14	16	16	18	18	18	20	20	20	22	22	22	24	24	24	26	26	26	28	28	28	30	30	30	32	32	32	34	34	34														
0.491 — 0.500	14	14	16	16	18	18	20	20	20	20	22	22	24	24	24	24	26	26	28	28	28	28	30	30	32	32	32	32	34	34															
0.501 — 0.520	14	16	16	18	18	20	20	20	20	22	22	24	24	24	24	26	26	28	28	28	28	30	30	32	32	32	32	34	34																
0.521 — 0.525	14	16	16	18	18	20	20	20	22	22	22	24	24	24	26	26	26	28	28	28	30	30	30	32	32	32	34	34	34																
0.526 — 0.540	16	16	18	18	20	20	20	22	22	22	24	24	24	26	26	26	28	28	28	30	30	30	32	32	32	34	34	34																	
0.541 — 0.550	16	16	18	18	20	20	22	22	22	22	24	24	26	26	26	26	28	28	30	30	30	30	32	32	34	34	34	34																	
0.551 — 0.570	16	18	18	20	20	22	22	22	22	24	24	26	26	26	26	28	28	30	30	30	30	32	32	34	34	34	34																		
0.571 — 0.575	16	18	18	20	20	22	22	22	24	24	24	26	26	26	28	28	28	30	30	30	32	32	32	34	34	34																			
0.575 — 0.590	18	18	20	20	22	22	22	24	24	24	26	26	26	28	28	28	30	30	30	32	32	32	34	34	34																				
0.591 — 0.600	18	18	20	20	22	22	24	24	24	24	26	26	28	28	28	28	30	30	32	32	32	32	34	34																					
0.601 — 0.620	18	20	20	22	22	24	24	24	24	26	26	28	28	28	28	30	30	32	32	32	32	34	34																						
0.621 — 0.625	18	20	20	22	22	24	24	24	26	26	26	28	28	28	30	30	30	32	32	32	34	34	34																						
0.626 — 0.640	20	20	22	22	24	24	24	26	26	26	28	28	28	30	30	30	32	32	32	34	34	34																							
0.641 — 0.650	20	20	22	22	24	24	26	26	26	26	28	28	30	30	30	30	32	32	34	34	34	34																							
0.651 — 0.670	20	22	22	24	24	26	26	26	26	28	28	30	30	30	30	32	32	34	34	34	34																								
0.671 — 0.675	20	22	22	24	24	26	26	26	28	28	28	30	30	30	32	32	32	34	34	34																									
0.676 — 0.690	22	22	24	24	26	26	26	28	28	28	30	30	30	32	32	32	34	34	34																										
0.691 — 0.700	22	22	24	24	26	26	28	28	28	28	30	30	32	32	32	32	34	34																											
0.701 — 0.720	22	24	24	26	26	28	28	28	28	30	30	32	32	32	32	34	34																												
0.721 — 0.725	22	24	24	26	26	28	28	28	30	30	30	32	32	32	34	34	34																												
0.726 — 0.740	24	24	26	26	28	28	28	30	30	30	32	32	32	34	34	34																													
0.741 — 0.750	24	24	26	26	28	28	30	30	30	30	32	32	34	34	34																														
0.751 — 0.770	24	26	26	28	28	30	30	30	30	32	32	34	34	34	34																														
0.771 — 0.775	24	26	26	28	28	30	30	30	32	32	32	34	34	34																															
0.776 — 0.790	26	26	28	28	30	30	30	32	32	32	34	34	34																																
0.791 — 0.800	26	26	28	28	30	30	32	32	32	32	34	34																																	
0.801 — 0.820	26	28	28	30	30	32	32	32	32	34	34																																		
0.821 — 0.825	26	28	28	30	30	32	32	32	34	34	34																																		
0.826 — 0.840	28	28	30	30	32	32	32	34	34	34																																			
0.841 — 0.850	28	28	30	30	32	32	34	34	34	34																																			
0.851 — 0.870	28	30	30	32	32	34	34	34	34																																				
0.871 — 0.875	28	30	30	32	32	34	34	34																																					
0.876 — 0.890	30	30	32	32	34	34	34																																						
0.891 — 0.900	30	30	32	32	34	34																																							
0.901 — 0.925	30	32	32	34	34																																								
0.926 — 0.950	32	32	34	34																																									
0.951 — 0.975	32	34	34																																										
0.976 — 1.000	34	34																																											
1.001 — 1.025	34																																												

Shim thickness mm (in.)

Shim No.	Thickness	Shim No.	Thickness
02	2.500 (0.0984)	20	2.950 (0.1161)
04	2.550 (0.1004)	22	3.000 (0.1181)
06	2.600 (0.1024)	24	3.050 (0.1201)
08	2.650 (0.1043)	26	3.100 (0.1220)
10	2.700 (0.1063)	28	3.150 (0.1240)
12	2.750 (0.1083)	30	3.200 (0.1260)
14	2.800 (0.1102)	32	3.250 (0.1280)
16	2.850 (0.1122)	34	3.300 (0.1299)
18	2.900 (0.1142)		

Intake valve clearance (cold):
0.15 — 0.25 mm (0.06 — 0.010 in.)

Exampie: **A 2.800 mm shim is installed and the measured clearance is 0.450 mm. Replace the 2.800 mm shim with shim No. 24 (3.050 mm).**

88271G77

Fig. 133 Shim selection chart—intake

Adjusting Shim Selection Chart

Exhaust

Installed Shim Thickness (mm)

Column headers (Installed Shim Thickness, mm): 2.500, 2.525, 2.550, 2.575, 2.600, 2.620, 2.640, 2.650, 2.660, 2.680, 2.700, 2.720, 2.740, 2.750, 2.760, 2.780, 2.800, 2.820, 2.840, 2.850, 2.860, 2.880, 2.900, 2.920, 2.940, 2.950, 2.960, 2.980, 3.000, 3.020, 3.040, 3.050, 3.060, 3.080, 3.100, 3.120, 3.140, 3.150, 3.160, 3.180, 3.200, 3.225, 3.250, 3.275, 3.300

Measured Clearance (mm) ranges (row labels):

Measured Clearance (mm)
0.000 — 0.009
0.010 — 0.025
0.026 — 0.040
0.041 — 0.050
0.051 — 0.070
0.071 — 0.090
0.091 — 0.100
0.101 — 0.120
0.121 — 0.140
0.141 — 0.150
0.151 — 0.170
0.171 — 0.190
0.191 — 0.199
0.200 — 0.300
0.301 — 0.320
0.321 — 0.325
0.326 — 0.340
0.341 — 0.350
0.351 — 0.370
0.371 — 0.375
0.376 — 0.390
0.391 — 0.400
0.401 — 0.420
0.421 — 0.425
0.426 — 0.440
0.441 — 0.450
0.451 — 0.470
0.471 — 0.475
0.476 — 0.490
0.491 — 0.500
0.501 — 0.520
0.521 — 0.525
0.526 — 0.540
0.541 — 0.550
0.551 — 0.570
0.571 — 0.575
0.576 — 0.590
0.591 — 0.600
0.601 — 0.620
0.621 — 0.625
0.626 — 0.640
0.641 — 0.650
0.651 — 0.670
0.671 — 0.675
0.676 — 0.690
0.691 — 0.700
0.701 — 0.720
0.721 — 0.725
0.726 — 0.740
0.741 — 0.750
0.751 — 0.770
0.771 — 0.775
0.776 — 0.790
0.791 — 0.800
0.801 — 0.820
0.821 — 0.825
0.826 — 0.840
0.841 — 0.850
0.851 — 0.870
0.871 — 0.875
0.876 — 0.890
0.891 — 0.900
0.901 — 0.925
0.926 — 0.950
0.951 — 0.975
0.976 — 1.000
1.025 — 1.001
1.026 — 1.050
1.051 — 1.075

Shim thickness — mm (in.)

Shim No.	Thickness	Shim No.	Thickness
02	2.500 (0.0984)	20	2.950 (0.1161)
04	2.550 (0.1004)	22	3.000 (0.1181)
06	2.600 (0.1024)	24	3.050 (0.1201)
08	2.650 (0.1043)	26	3.100 (0.1220)
10	2.700 (0.1063)	28	3.150 (0.1240)
12	2.750 (0.1083)	30	3.200 (0.1260)
14	2.800 (0.1102)	32	3.250 (0.1280)
16	2.850 (0.1122)	34	3.300 (0.1299)
18	2.900 (0.1142)		

Exhaust valve clearance (cold):
  0.20 — 0.30 mm (0.008 — 0.012 in.)

Example: A 2.800 mm shim is installed
and the measured clearance
is 0.450 mm.
Replace the 2.800 mm shim
with shim No. 22 (3.000 mm).

88271G78

Fig. 134 Shim selection chart—exhaust

b. Using the forked tool (SST-A), press the valve lifter downward and hold it there. Some tool kits require a second tool for holding the lifter in place (SST-B), allowing the first to be removed.

c. Using small magnetic tools, remove the adjusting shim from the top of the lifter.

d. Use the micrometer and measure the thickness of the shim removed. Determine the thickness of the new shim using the formula below or the selection charts. For the purposes of the following formula, T = Thickness of the old shim; A = Valve clearance measured; N = Thickness of the new shim

• Intake side (camshaft nearest intake manifold): N = T + (A - 0.20mm (0.008 in.))

• Exhaust side (camshaft nearest exhaust manifold): N = T + (A - 0.25mm (0.010 in.)

8. Select a shim closest to the calculated thickness. Use the lifter depressor tool to press down the lifter and install the shim. Shims are available in 17 sizes from 0.0984–0.1299 in. (2.50mm–3.30mm). The standard increment is 0.0020 in. (0.05mm).

9. Repeat steps a through e for each valve needing adjustment.

10. Reinstall the valve cover, following the procedures outlined in Section 3.

11. Install the spark plug wires.

12. Check and adjust the timing and idle speed, following the procedures outlined in this section. Road test the vehicle for proper operation.

1993–97 Models

▶ See Figures 135 thru 149

➡Inspect and adjust the valve clearance while the engine is cold.

1. Remove the spark plug wires from the valve cover.

2. Remove the valve cover and gasket as described in Section 3.

3. Set the No. 1 cylinder to TDC by turning the crankshaft pulley and align its groove with the timing mark "0" of the No. 1 timing cover. Check that the hole of the camshaft timing pulley is aligned with the timing mark of the bearing cap. If not, turn the crankshaft one revolution (360°).

4. To inspect the valve clearance, check only the valves indicated.

a. Using a thickness gage, measure the clearance between the valve lifter and camshaft. Record the out-of-specification valve clearance measurements. They will be used later to determine the required replacement adjusting shim.

• Intake COLD: 0.006–0.010 in. (0.15–0.25mm)

• Exhaust COLD: 0.010–0.014 in. 90.25–0.35mm)

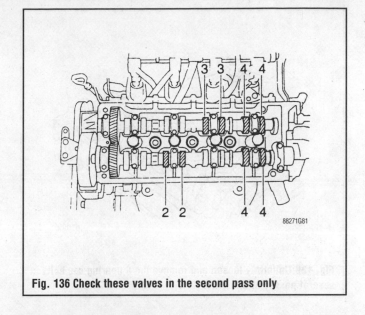

Fig. 136 Check these valves in the second pass only

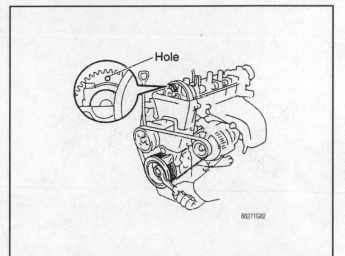

Fig. 137 Turn the crankshaft pulley so that the hole in the sub-gear (which sets the sub-gear to the camshaft drive gear) comes up

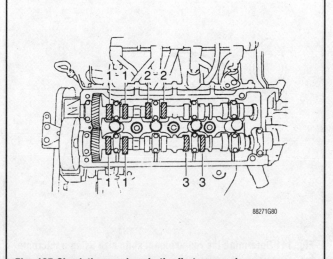

Fig. 135 Check these valves in the first pass only

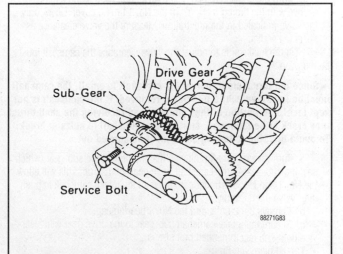

Fig. 138 Secure the sub-gear to the driven gear with a service bolt

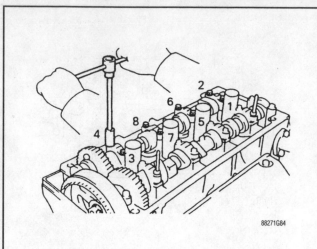

Fig. 139 Uniformly loosen and remove the 8 bearing cap bolts in several passes in this order

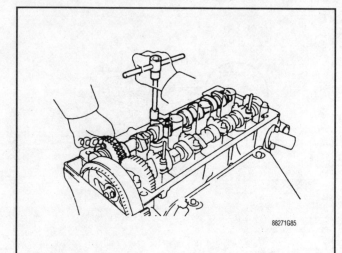

Fig. 140 Alternately loosen the camshaft cap bolts with the camshaft gear pulled up if necessary

b. Turn the crankshaft pulley one revolution (360°) and align its groove with the timing mark "0" of the No. 1 timing cover. Check only the valve indicated in the illustration. Measure the valve clearance as specified earlier.

5. On the intake side to adjust the valve clearance the camshaft must be removed.

➥ Since the thrust clearance of the camshaft is small, the camshaft must be kept level while it is being removed. If the camshaft is not kept level, the portion of the cylinder head receiving the shaft thrust may crack or be damaged, causing the camshaft to seize or break. To avoid this, the following steps must be carried out.

a. Turn the crankshaft pulley so that the hole in the sub-gear (which sets the sub-gear to the camshaft drive gear) comes up. This will allow the No. 1 and No. 3 cylinder cam lobes of the intake camshaft to push their valve lifters evenly.

b. Remove the 2 bolts and the No. 1 bearing cap.

c. Secure the intake camshaft sub-gear to the drive gear with a service bolt. The recommended bolt size is:

- Thread diameter: 6mm
- Thread pitch: 1.0mm
- Bolt length: 0.63–0.79 in. (16–20mm)

➥ When removing the camshaft, make sure that the torsional spring force of the sub-gear has been eliminated by the previous operation.

d. Uniformilly loosen and remove the 8 bearing cap bolts in several passes, in the sequence shown in the illustration.

e. Remove the 4 bearing caps and camshaft.

➥ If the camshaft is not being lifted out straight and level, reinstall the No. 3 bearing cap with the 2 bolts. Then alternately loosen and remove the bearing cap bolts with the camshaft gear pulled up.

✱✱ WARNING

Do not pry on or attempt to force the camshaft with a tool or other object.

6. Remove the adjusting shim with a small flat bladed tool.

7. Determine the replacement adjusting shim size by following the formula or charts.

a. Using a micrometer, measure the thickness of the removed shim. Calculate the thickness of a new shim so that the valve clearance comes within the specified value.

- T: Thickness of the remove shim
- A: Measured value of clearance
- N: Thickness of the new shim
- Intake: N= T + (A - 0.008 in. (0.20mm))

b. Select a new shim with a thickness as close as possible to calculate value. The shims are available in 16 sizes in increments of 0.0020 in. (0.05mm). They range from 1.0039 in. (2.55mm to 0.1299 in. (3.30mm).

8. Install the new adjusting shim by placing the shim on the valve lifter.

9. Install the intake camshaft.

➥ Since the thrust clearance of the camshaft is small, the camshaft must be kept level while it is being removed. If the camshaft is not kept level, the portion of the cylinder head receiving the shaft thrust may crack or be damaged, causing the camshaft to seize or break. To avoid this, the following steps must be carried out.

a. Turn the crankshaft pulley, set the exhaust camshaft so that the knock pin is slightly above the top of the cylinder head. Apply multi purpose grease to the thrust portion of the camshaft.

b. engage the intake camshaft gear to the exhaust camshaft gear by matching the assembly installation mark on each gear.

➥ There are also timing marks (for TDC) on each gear. DO NOT use these marks.

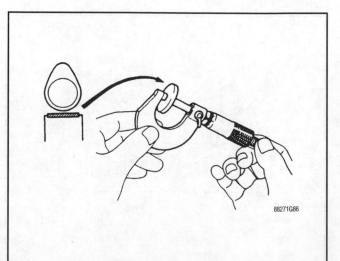

Fig. 141 Determine the replacement shim size using a micrometer

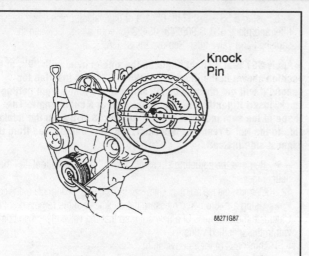

Fig. 142 Set the exhaust camshaft so that the knock pin is slightly above the top of the cylinder head

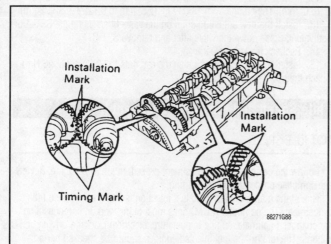

Fig. 143 Engage the intake camshaft gear to the exhaust gear by matching the installation marks on each gear

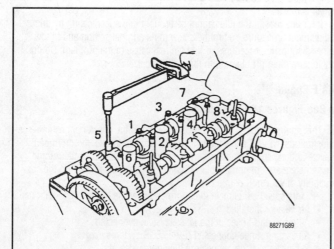

Fig. 144 Install and tighten uniformly the 8 bearing cap bolts in several passes in this order

c. Roll down the intake camshaft onto the bearing journals while engaging gears with each other. The angle allows the No. 1 and No. 3 cylinder cam lobes of the intake camshaft to push their valve lifters evenly.

d. Install the 4 bearing caps in their proper locations. Apply a light coat of engine oil on the threads and under the heads of the bearing cap bolts.

e. Install and uniformly tighten the 8 bearing cap bolts in several passes, in the sequence shown to 9 ft. lbs. (13 Nm).

f. Remove the service bolt. Install the No. 1 bearing cap with the arrow mark facing forward.

➡**If the No. 1 bearing cap does not fit properly, push the camshaft gear backwards by prying apart the cylinder head and camshaft gear with a flat bladed tool.**

g. Apply a light coat of engine oil on the threads and under the heads of the bearing cap bolts. Install and alternately tighten the bearing cap bolts in several passes to 9 ft. lbs. (13 Nm).

10. Recheck the valve clearance.

11. To adjust the exhaust valve clearance, turn the crankshaft so that the cam lobe of the camshaft on the adjusting valve is upward.

a. Positon the notch of the valve lifter facing the front of the vehicle.

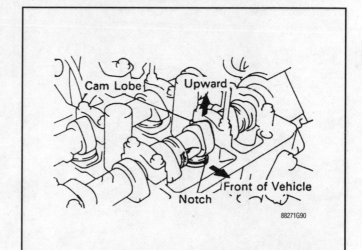

Fig. 145 Turn the crankshaft so the cam lobe of the camshaft on the adjusting valve is upward, be sure the notch faces the front

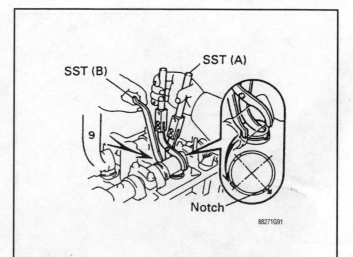

Fig. 146 Use SST-A to press down the valve lifter, then place SST-B between the camshaft and lifter

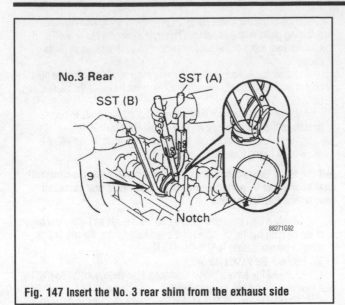

Fig. 147 Insert the No. 3 rear shim from the exhaust side

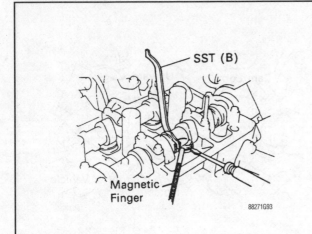

Fig. 148 Remove the shim with a flatbladed tool and a magnetic finger

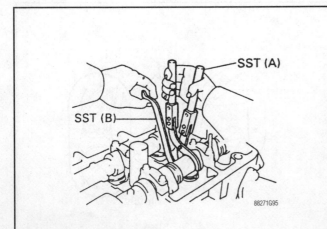

Fig. 149 Install the new adjusting shim on the valve lifter using SST-A or equivalent

b. using a SST-A (09248–05410) or equivalent, press down the valve lifter and place SST-B 909248–05420 (or equivalent), between the camshaft and valve lifter. Remove the SST-A.

➡**Apply SST-B at a slight angle on the side marked with "9", at the position shown in the illustration. When SST-B is inserted too deeply, it will get pinched by the shim. To prevent it from getting stuck, insert it gently from the intake side at a slight angle. The shape of the cam makes it difficult to insert SST-B from the intake side to the No. 3 rear. For this shim, it is best approached from the exhaust side instead.**

c. Remove the adjusting shim with a small flat bladed tool and magnetic finger.

12. Determine the replacement shim size by following the formula or the chart.

a. Using a micrometer, measure the thickness of the removed shim. Calculate the thickness of a new shim so that the valve clearance comes within the specified value.
- T: Thickness of the remove shim
- A: Measured value of clearance
- N: Thickness of the new shim
- Intake: N= T + (A - 0.008 in. (0.20mm))

b. Select a new shim with a thickness as close as possible to calculate value. The shims are available in 16 sizes in increments of 0.0020 in. (0.05mm). They range from 1.0039 in. (2.55mm to 0.1299 in. (3.30mm).

13. Install the new adjusting shim on the valve lifter. Using the SST-A or equivalent, press down the valve lifter and remove SST-B.

14. Recheck the valve clearance.

15. Install the valve cover. Tighten the cap nuts to 52 inch lbs. 96 Nm). Attach the spark plug wires.

Idle Speed and Mixture Adjustment

HOT IDLE SPEED

Follow the correct service adjustment procedure for your engine. Review the complete procedure before starting.

One of the merits of electronic fuel injection is that it requires so little adjustment. The computer (ECM) does most of the work in compensating for changes in climate, engine temperature, electrical load and driving conditions. The idle on the fuel injected engines should be checked periodically (15,000 miles or 24 months) but not adjusted unless out of specifications by more than 50 rpm.

The idle speed adjusting screw is located on the side of the throttle body. You can find the throttle body by following the accelerator cable to its end. The adjusting screw may have a cap over it. If so, pop the cap off with a small screwdriver.

If for any reason the idle cannot be brought into specification by this adjustment procedure, return the screw to its original setting and follow other diagnostic procedures to find the real cause of the problem. Do not try to cure other problems with this adjustment.

4A-F Engine

▶ See Figures 150 thru 155

This engine requires a tachometer hook-up to the check connector—see illustrations. NEVER allow the tachometer terminal to become grounded; severe and expensive damage can occur to the coil and/or igniter. Some tachometers are not compatible with this ignition system, confirm the compatibility of your unit before using.

1. Idle speed adjustment is performed under the following conditions:
- Air cleaner installed
- All pipes and hoses of the intake system connected
- All vacuum lines connected (EVAP, EGR systems ect.)
- EFI system wiring connectors fully plugged
- Engine at normal operating temperature
- Accesories switched off
- Transmission in "N" range

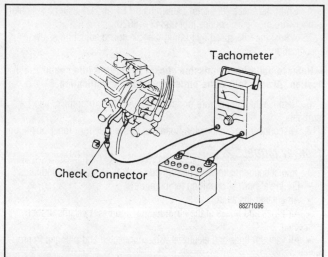

Fig. 150 Attach the tachometer positive terminal to the check connector at the distributor

2. Connect the tachometer to the engine. Remove the rubber cap and connect the tachometer positive terminal to the check connector at the distributor (IIA).

3. Set the idle speed by turning the IDLE SPEED adjusting screw. Speed is 650 rpm for manual transmission and 750 rpm's for automatic transmissions.

➡**Make adjustments with the engine cooling fan OFF. Leave the tachometer connected for further adjustments.**

4. To adjust the fast idle speed, shut the engine **OFF** and remove the air cleaner.

5. Plug the AS hose to prevent leakage of the exhaust gases, and plug the HIC hose and ASV hose (California models) to prevent rough idling.

6. Disconnect the hose from the TVSV M port and plug the M port. This will shut off the choke opener and EGR system.

7. Set the fast idle cam. while holding the throttle valve slightly open, pull up the fast idle cam and hold it closed as you release the throttle valve.

➡**Check that the fast idle cam is set at the 1 step.**

8. Start the engine, but DO NOT touch the accelerator pedal.

9. Set the fast idles speed by turning the fast idle adjustment screw. Speed should be at 3000 rpm's.

10. Install the air cleaner.

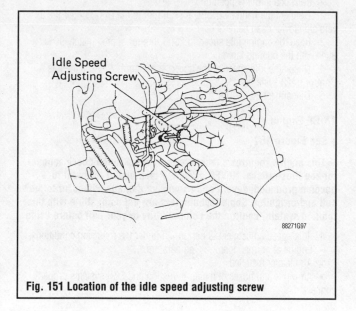

Fig. 151 Location of the idle speed adjusting screw

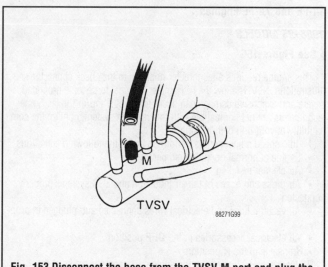

Fig. 153 Disconnect the hose from the TVSV M port and plug the port

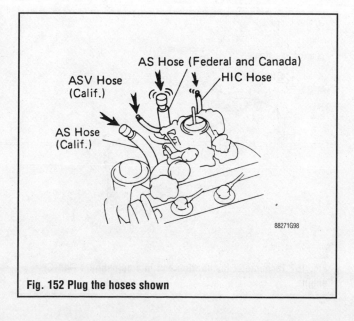

Fig. 152 Plug the hoses shown

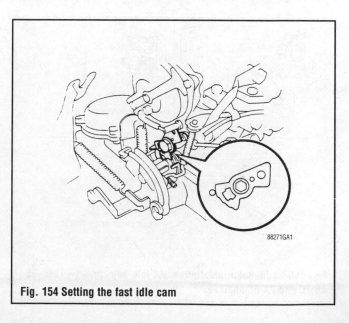

Fig. 154 Setting the fast idle cam

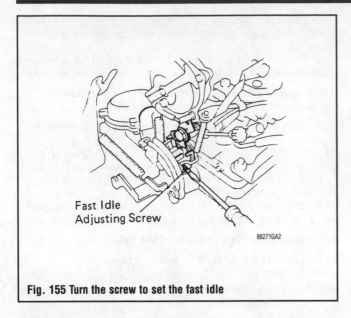

Fig. 155 Turn the screw to set the fast idle

4A-FE and 7A-FE Engines

1988–95 MODELS

▶ See Figure 156

This engine requires a tachometer hook-up to the check connector-see illustrations. NEVER allow the tachometer terminal to become grounded; severe and expensive damage can occur to the coil and/or igniter. Some tachometers are not compatible with this ignition system, confirm the compatibility of your unit before using.

1. Idle speed adjustment is performed under the following conditions:
- Engine at normal operating temperature
- Air cleaner installed
- Air pipes and hoses of the air induction and EGR systems properly connected
- All vacuum lines and electrical wires connected and plugged in properly
- All electrical accessories in the **OFF** position
- Transaxle in the **N** position

2. Connect a tachometer to the engine. Connect the probe of the tachometer to terminal IG- of the check connector.

3. Run the engine at 2500 rpm for 90 seconds.

4. Short the check connector at terminals **TE1** and **E1** using a suitable jumper wire or special service tool 09843–18020.

5. Adjust the idle speed by turning the idle speed adjusting screw to specification.

➡Refer to underhood emission sticker to confirm idle speed specification. Always follow the emission sticker specification.

6. Remove the jumper wire or special service tool from the connector terminals.

7. Disconnect the tachometer. Road test the vehicle for proper operation.

1996–97 MODELS

1. Idle speed adjustment is performed under the following conditions:
- Engine at normal operating temperature.
- Air cleaner installed.
- Air pipes and hoses of the air induction and EGR systems properly connected.
- All vacuum lines and electrical wires connected and plugged in properly.
- SFI system wiring connectors fully plugged
- All electrical accessories in the **OFF** position.
- Ignition timing set correctly
- Transaxle in the **N** position.

2. Connect the hand held OBD II scan tool to the DLC3 under the drivers side lower dash panel.

3. Race the engine idle speed to 2500 rpm for approximately 90 seconds with the cooling fan off.

4. Check the idle speed. If the speed is not correct, check the Idle Air Control (IAC) system.

5. Disconnect the OBD II scan tool.

4A-GE Engine

▶ See Figure 157

➡This engine requires a tachometer hook-up to the check connector-see illustrations. NEVER allow the tachometer terminal to become grounded; severe and expensive damage can occur to the coil and/or igniter. Some tachometers are not compatible with this ignition system, confirm the compatibility of your unit before using.

1. Idle speed adjustment is performed under the following conditions:
- Engine at normal operating temperature.
- Air cleaner installed.
- Air pipes and hoses of the air induction and EGR systems properly connected.

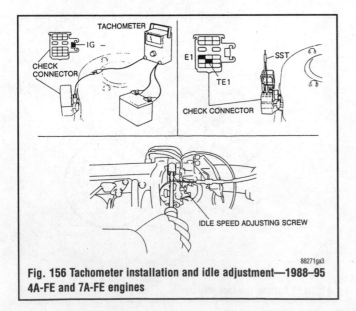

Fig. 156 Tachometer installation and idle adjustment—1988–95 4A-FE and 7A-FE engines

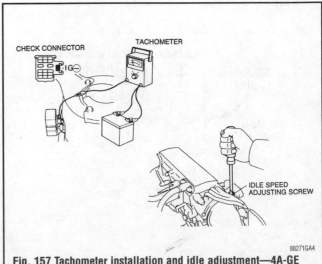

Fig. 157 Tachometer installation and idle adjustment—4A-GE engine

• All vacuum lines and electrical wires connected and plugged in properly.
• All electrical accessories in the **OFF** position.
• Transaxle in the **N** position.
2. Connect a tachometer to the engine. Connect the probe of the tachometer to terminal IG- of the check connector.
3. Run the engine at 2500 rpm for 2 minutes.
4. Adjust the idle speed by turning the idle speed adjusting screw to specification.

➡**Refer to underhood emission sticker to confirm idle speed specification. Always follow the emission sticker specification.**

5. Disconnect the tachometer. Road test the vehicle for proper operation.

MIXTURE

The air/fuel ratio burned within the engine is controlled by the ECM, based on information delivered by the various sensors on the engine. It is not adjustable as a routine maintenance item. The easiest way to check the air/fuel mixture is to put the car through a tailpipe emissions test. Whether or not this is required in your area, it's a good way of putting numbers on the combustion efficiency of the engine. The engine can only burn so much fuel; if too much is being delivered, it will show up on the test as unburned hydrocarbons (HC).

Putting the car through this test once a year from the time it is newly acquired can provide an excellent baseline for diagnosing future problems.

Air Conditioning System

SYSTEM SERVICE & REPAIR

➡**It is recommended that the A/C system be serviced by an EPA Section 609 certified automotive technician utilizing a refrigerant recovery/recycling machine.**

The do-it-yourselfer should not service his/her own vehicle's A/C system for many reasons, including legal concerns, personal injury, environmental damage and cost. The following are some of the reasons why you may decide not to service your own vehicle's A/C system.

According to the U.S. Clean Air Act, it is a federal crime to service or repair (involving the refrigerant) a Motor Vehicle Air Conditioning (MVAC) system for money without being EPA certified. It is also illegal to vent R-12 and R-134a refrigerants into the atmosphere. Selling or distributing A/C system refrigerant (in a container which contains less than 20 pounds of refrigerant) to any person who is not EPA 609 certified is also not allowed by law.

State and/or local laws may be more strict than the federal regulations, so be sure to check with your state and/or local authorities for further information. For further federal information on the legality of servicing your A/C system, call the EPA Stratospheric Ozone Hotline.

➡**Federal law dictates that a fine of up to $25,000 may be leveled on people convicted of venting refrigerant into the atmosphere. Additionally, the EPA may pay up to $10,000 for information or services leading to a criminal conviction of the violation of these laws.**

GASOLINE ENGINE TUNE-UP SPECIFICATIONS

Year	Engine ID/VIN	Engine Displacement Liters (cc)	Spark Plugs Gap (in.)	Ignition Timing (deg.) MT	AT	Fuel Pump (psi)	Idle Speed (rpm) MT	AT	Valve Clearance In.	Ex.
1988	4A-F	1.6 (1587)	0.31	10B	10B	38-44	750	750	0.006-0.010	0.008-0.012
	4A-FE	1.6 (1587)	0.31	10B	10B	38-44	750	750	0.006-0.010	0.008-0.012
	4A-GE	1.6 (1587)	0.31	10B	10B	38-44	800	800	0.006-0.010	0.008-0.012
1989	4A-F	1.6 (1587)	0.31	10B	10B	38-44	750	750	0.006-0.010	0.008-0.012
	4A-FE	1.6 (1587)	0.31	10B	10B	38-44	750	750	0.006-0.010	0.008-0.012
	4A-GE	1.6 (1587)	0.31	10B	10B	38-44	800	800	0.006-0.010	0.008-0.012
1990	4A-FE	1.6 (1587)	0.31	10B	10B	38-44	750	750	0.006-0.010	0.008-0.012
	4A-GE	1.6 (1587)	0.31	10B	10B	38-44	800	800	0.006-0.010	0.008-0.012
1991	4A-FE	1.6 (1587)	0.31	10B	10B	38-44	750	750	0.006-0.010	0.008-0.012
	4A-GE	1.6 (1587)	0.31	10B	10B	38-44	800	800	0.006-0.010	0.008-0.012
1992	4A-FE	1.6 (1587)	0.31	10B	10B	38-44	750	750	0.006-0.010	0.008-0.012
1993	4AF-E	1.6 (1587)	0.31	10B	10B	38-44	750	750	0.006-0.010	0.010-0.014
	7A-FE	1.8 (1762)	0.31	10B	10B	38-44	800	800	0.006-0.010	0.010-0.014
1994	4AF-E	1.6 (1587)	0.31	10B	10B	38-44	750	750	0.006-0.010	0.010-0.014
	7A-FE	1.8 (1762)	0.31	10B	10B	38-44	800	800	0.006-0.010	0.010-0.014
1995	4AF-E	1.6 (1587)	0.31	10B	10B	38-44	750	750	0.006-0.010	0.010-0.014
	7A-FE	1.8 (1762)	0.31	10B	10B	38-44	800	800	0.006-0.010	0.010-0.014
1996	4AF-E	1.6 (1587)	0.31	10B	10B	38-44	750	750	0.006-0.010	0.010-0.014
	7A-FE	1.8 (1762)	0.31	10B	10B	38-44	800	800	0.006-0.010	0.010-0.014
1997	4AF-E	1.6 (1587)	0.31	10B	10B	38-44	750	750	0.006-0.010	0.010-0.014
	7A-FE	1.8 (1762)	0.31	10B	10B	38-44	800	800	0.006-0.010	0.010-0.014

88271C04

When servicing an A/C system you run the risk of handling or coming in contact with refrigerant, which may result in skin or eye irritation or frostbite. Although low in toxicity (due to chemical stability), inhalation of concentrated refrigerant fumes is dangerous and can result in death; cases of fatal cardiac arrhythmia have been reported in people accidentally subjected to high levels of refrigerant. Some early symptoms include loss of concentration and drowsiness.

➡**Generally, the limit for exposure is lower for R-134a than it is for R-12. Exceptional care must be practiced when handling R-134a.**

Also, refrigerants can decompose at high temperatures (near gas heaters or open flame), which may result in hydrofluoric acid, hydrochloric acid and phosgene (a fatal nerve gas).

R-12 refrigerant can damage the environment because it is a Chlorofluorocarbon (CFC), which has been proven to add to ozone layer depletion, leading to increasing levels of UV radiation. UV radiation has been linked with an increase in skin cancer, suppression of the human immune system, an increase in cataracts, damage to crops, damage to aquatic organisms, an increase in ground-level ozone, and increased global warming.

R-134a refrigerant is a greenhouse gas which, if allowed to vent into the atmosphere, will contribute to global warming (the Greenhouse Effect).

It is usually more economically feasible to have a certified MVAC automotive technician perform A/C system service on your vehicle. Some possible reasons for this are as follows:
- While it is illegal to service an A/C system without the proper equipment, the home mechanic would have to purchase an expensive refrigerant recovery/recycling machine to service his/her own vehicle.
- Since only a certified person may purchase refrigerant—according to the Clean Air Act, there are specific restrictions on selling or distributing A/C system refrigerant—it is legally impossible (unless certified) for the home mechanic to service his/her own vehicle. Procuring refrigerant in an illegal fashion exposes one to the risk of paying a $25,000 fine to the EPA.

R-12 Refrigerant Conversion

If your vehicle still uses R-12 refrigerant, one way to save A/C system costs down the road is to investigate the possibility of having your system converted to R-134a. The older R-12 systems can be easily converted to R-134a refrigerant by a certified automotive technician by installing a few new components and changing the system oil.

The cost of R-12 is steadily rising and will continue to increase, because it is no longer imported or manufactured in the United States. Therefore, it is often possible to have an R-12 system converted to R-134a and recharged for less than it would cost to just charge the system with R-12.

If you are interested in having your system converted, contact local automotive service stations for more details and information.

PREVENTIVE MAINTENANCE

◆ **See Figures 158 and 159**

Although the A/C system should not be serviced by the do-it-yourselfer, preventive maintenance can be practiced and A/C system inspections can be performed to help maintain the efficiency of the vehicle's A/C system. For preventive maintenance, perform the following:
- The easiest and most important preventive maintenance for your A/C system is to be sure that it is used on a regular basis. Running the system for five minutes each month (no matter what the season) will help ensure that the seals and all internal components remain lubricated.

➡**Some newer vehicles automatically operate the A/C system compressor whenever the windshield defroster is activated. When running, the compressor lubricates the A/C system components; therefore, the A/C system would not need to be operated each month.**

- In order to prevent heater core freeze-up during A/C operation, it is necessary to maintain proper antifreeze protection. Use a hand-held coolant tester (hydrometer) to periodically check the condition of the antifreeze in your engine's cooling system.

Fig. 158 A coolant tester can be used to determine the freezing and boiling levels of the coolant in your vehicle

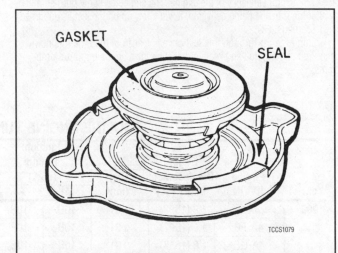

Fig. 159 To ensure efficient cooling system operation, inspect the radiator cap gasket and seal

➡**Antifreeze should not be used longer than the manufacturer specifies.**

- For efficient operation of an air conditioned vehicle's cooling system, the radiator cap should have a holding pressure which meets manufacturer's specifications. A cap which fails to hold these pressures should be replaced.
- Any obstruction of or damage to the condenser configuration will restrict air flow which is essential to its efficient operation. It is, therefore, a good rule to keep this unit clean and in proper physical shape.

➡**Bug screens which are mounted in front of the condenser (unless they are original equipment) are regarded as obstructions.**

- The condensation drain tube expels any water which accumulates on the bottom of the evaporator housing into the engine compartment. If this tube is obstructed, the air conditioning performance can be restricted and condensation buildup can spill over onto the vehicle's floor.

SYSTEM INSPECTION

◆ **See Figure 160**

Although the A/C system should not be serviced by the do-it-yourselfer, preventive maintenance can be practiced and A/C system inspections can be performed to help maintain the efficiency of the vehicle's A/C system. For A/C system inspection, perform the following:

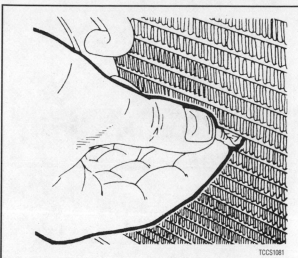

Fig. 160 Periodically remove any debris from the condenser and radiator fins

The easiest and often most important check for the air conditioning system consists of a visual inspection of the system components. Visually inspect the air conditioning system for refrigerant leaks, damaged compressor clutch, abnormal compressor drive belt tension and/or condition, plugged evaporator drain tube, blocked condenser fins, disconnected or broken wires, blown fuses, corroded connections and poor insulation.

A refrigerant leak will usually appear as an oily residue at the leakage point in the system. The oily residue soon picks up dust or dirt particles from the surrounding air and appears greasy. Through time, this will build up and appear to be a heavy dirt impregnated grease.

For a thorough visual and operational inspection, check the following:

• Check the surface of the radiator and condenser for dirt, leaves or other material which might block air flow.

• Check for kinks in hoses and lines. Check the system for leaks.

• Make sure the drive belt is properly tensioned. When the air conditioning is operating, make sure the drive belt is free of noise or slippage.

• Make sure the blower motor operates at all appropriate positions, then check for distribution of the air from all outlets with the blower on **HIGH** or **MAX**.

➡ **Keep in mind that under conditions of high humidity, air discharged from the A/C vents may not feel as cold as expected, even if the system is working properly. This is because vaporized moisture in humid air retains heat more effectively than dry air, thereby making humid air more difficult to cool.**

• Make sure the air passage selection lever is operating correctly. Start the engine and warm it to normal operating temperature, then make sure the temperature selection lever is operating correctly.

Windshield Wipers

ELEMENT (REFILL) CARE & REPLACEMENT

▶ **See Figures 161 thru 170**

For maximum effectiveness and longest element life, the windshield and wiper blades should be kept clean. Dirt, tree sap, road tar and so on will cause streaking, smearing and blade deterioration if left on the glass. It is advisable to wash the windshield carefully with a commercial glass cleaner at least once a month. Wipe off the rubber blades with the wet rag afterwards. Do not attempt to move wipers across the windshield by hand; damage to the motor and drive mechanism will result.

To inspect and/or replace the wiper blade elements, place the wiper switch in the **LOW** speed position and the ignition switch in the **ACC** position. When the wiper blades are approximately vertical on the windshield, turn the ignition switch to **OFF**.

Examine the wiper blade elements. If they are found to be cracked, broken or torn, they should be replaced immediately. Replacement intervals will vary with usage, although ozone deterioration usually limits element life to about one year. If the wiper pattern is smeared or streaked, or if the blade chatters across the glass, the elements should be replaced. It is easiest and most sensible to replace the elements in pairs.

If your vehicle is equipped with aftermarket blades, there are several different types of refills and your vehicle might have any kind. Aftermarket blades and arms rarely use the exact same type blade or refill as the original equipment. Here are some typical aftermarket blades; not all may be available for your vehicle:

The Anco® type uses a release button that is pushed down to allow the refill to slide out of the yoke jaws. The new refill slides back into the frame and locks in place.

Some Trico® refills are removed by locating where the metal backing strip or the refill is wider. Insert a small screwdriver blade between the frame and metal backing strip. Press down to release the refill from the retaining tab.

Other types of Trico® refills have two metal tabs which are unlocked by squeezing them together. The rubber filler can then be withdrawn from the frame jaws. A new refill is installed by inserting the refill into the front frame jaws and sliding it rearward to engage the remaining frame jaws. There are usually four jaws; be certain when installing that the refill is engaged in all of them. At the end of its travel, the tabs will lock into place on the front jaws of the wiper blade frame.

Another type of refill is made from polycarbonate. The refill has a simple locking device at one end which flexes downward out of the groove into which the jaws of the holder fit, allowing easy release. By sliding the new refill through all the jaws and pushing through the slight resistance when it reaches the end of its travel, the refill will lock into position.

To replace the Tridon® refill, it is necessary to remove the wiper blade. This refill has a plastic backing strip with a notch about 1 in. (25mm) from the end. Hold the blade (frame) on a hard surface so that the frame is tightly bowed. Grip the tip of the backing strip and pull up while twisting counterclockwise. The backing strip will snap out of the retaining tab. Do this for the remaining tabs until the refill is free of the blade. The length of these refills is molded into the end and they should be replaced with identical types.

Regardless of the type of refill used, be sure to follow the part manufacturer's instructions closely. Make sure that all of the frame jaws are engaged as the refill is pushed into place and locked. If the metal blade holder and frame are allowed to touch the glass during wiper operation, the glass will be scratched.

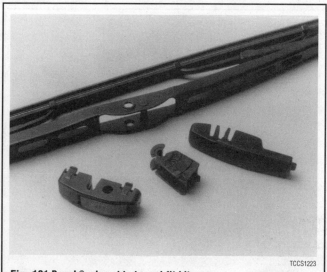

Fig. 161 Bosch® wiper blade and fit kit

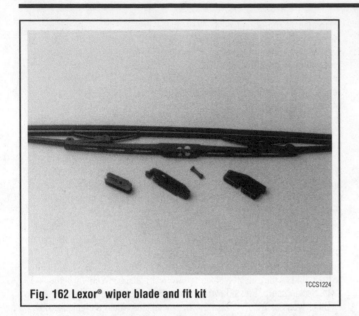

Fig. 162 Lexor® wiper blade and fit kit

TCCS1224

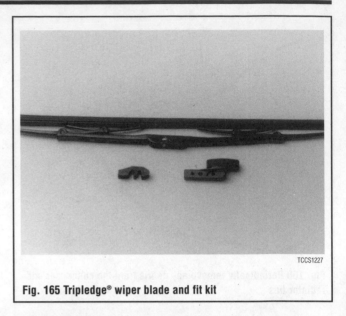

Fig. 165 Tripledge® wiper blade and fit kit

TCCS1227

Fig. 163 Pylon® wiper blade and adaptor

TCCS1225

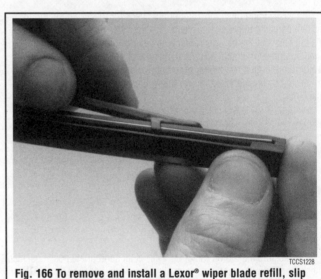

Fig. 166 To remove and install a Lexor® wiper blade refill, slip out the old insert and slide in a new one

TCCS1228

Fig. 164 Trico® wiper blade and fit kit

TCCS1226

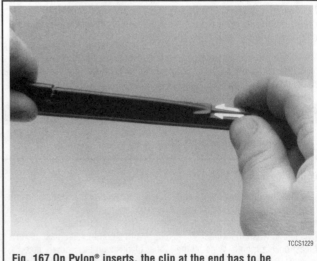

Fig. 167 On Pylon® inserts, the clip at the end has to be removed prior to sliding the insert off

TCCS1229

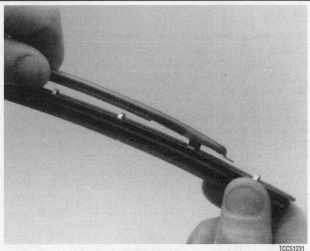

Fig. 168 On Trico® wiper blades, the tab at the end of the blade must be turned up . . .

TCCS1230

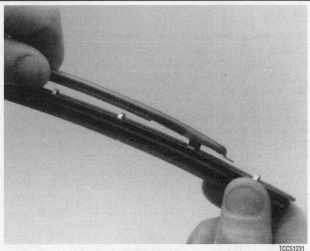

Fig. 169 . . . then the insert can be removed. After installing the replacement insert, bend the tab back

TCCS1231

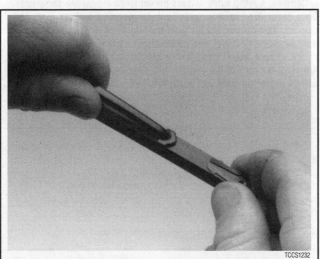

Fig. 170 The Tripledge® wiper blade insert is removed and installed using a securing clip

TCCS1232

Tires and Wheels

Common sense and good driving habits will afford maximum tire life. Fast starts, sudden stops and hard cornering are hard on tires and will shorten their useful life span. Make sure that you don't overload the vehicle or run with incorrect pressure in the tires. Both of these practices will increase tread wear.

➡**For optimum tire life, keep the tires properly inflated, rotate them often and have the wheel alignment checked periodically.**

Inspect your tires frequently. Be especially careful to watch for bubbles in the tread or sidewall, deep cuts or underinflation. Replace any tires with bubbles in the sidewall. If cuts are so deep that they penetrate to the cords, discard the tire. Any cut in the sidewall of a radial tire renders it unsafe. Also look for uneven tread wear patterns that may indicate the front end is out of alignment or that the tires are out of balance.

TIRE ROTATION

▶ **See Figures 171, 172 and 173**

Tires must be rotated periodically to equalize wear patterns that vary with a tire's position on the vehicle. Tires will also wear in an uneven way as the front steering/suspension system wears to the point where the alignment should be reset.

Rotating the tires will ensure maximum life for the tires as a set, so you will not have to discard a tire early due to wear on only part of the tread. Regular rotation is required to equalize wear.

When rotating "unidirectional tires," make sure that they always roll in the same direction. This means that a tire used on the left side of the vehicle must not be switched to the right side and vice-versa. Such tires should only be rotated front-to-rear or rear-to-front, while always remaining on the same side of the vehicle. These tires are marked on the sidewall as to the direction of rotation; observe the marks when reinstalling the tire(s).

Some styled or "mag" wheels may have different offsets front to rear. In these cases, the rear wheels must not be used up front and vice-versa. Furthermore, if these wheels are equipped with unidirectional tires, they cannot be rotated unless the tire is remounted for the proper direction of rotation.

➡**The compact or space-saver spare is strictly for emergency use. It must never be included in the tire rotation or placed on the vehicle for everyday use.**

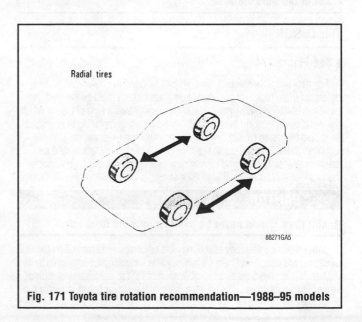

Radial tires

88271GA5

Fig. 171 Toyota tire rotation recommendation—1988–95 models

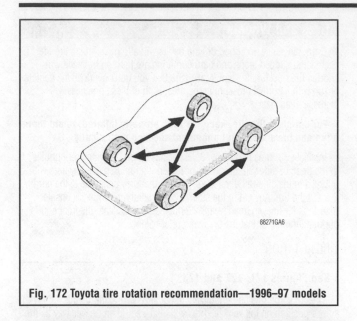

Fig. 172 Toyota tire rotation recommendation—1996–97 models

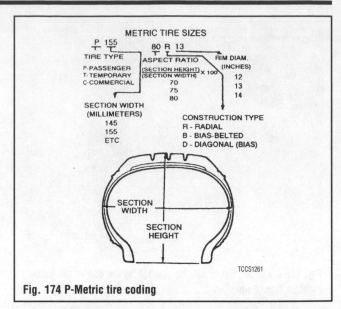

Fig. 174 P-Metric tire coding

Fig. 173 Unidirectional tires are identifiable by sidewall arrows and/or the word "rotation"

TIRE DESIGN

▶ See Figure 174

For maximum satisfaction, tires should be used in sets of four. Mixing of different types (radial, bias-belted, fiberglass belted) must be avoided. In most cases, the vehicle manufacturer has designated a type of tire on which the vehicle will perform best. Your first choice when replacing tires should be to use the same type of tire that the manufacturer recommends.

When radial tires are used, tire sizes and wheel diameters should be selected to maintain ground clearance and tire load capacity equivalent to the original specified tire. Radial tires should always be used in sets of four.

✳✳ CAUTION

Radial tires should never be used on only the front axle.

When selecting tires, pay attention to the original size as marked on the tire. Most tires are described using an industry size code sometimes referred to as P-Metric. This allows the exact identification of the tire specifications, regardless of the manufacturer. If selecting a different tire size or brand, remember to check the installed tire for any sign of interference with the body or suspension while the vehicle is stopping, turning sharply or heavily loaded.

Snow Tires

Good radial tires can produce a big advantage in slippery weather, but in snow, a street radial tire does not have sufficient tread to provide traction and control. The small grooves of a street tire quickly pack with snow and the tire behaves like a billiard ball on a marble floor. The more open, chunky tread of a snow tire will self-clean as the tire turns, providing much better grip on snowy surfaces.

To satisfy municipalities requiring snow tires during weather emergencies, most snow tires carry either an M + S designation after the tire size stamped on the sidewall, or the designation "all-season." In general, no change in tire size is necessary when buying snow tires.

Most manufacturers strongly recommend the use of 4 snow tires on their vehicles for reasons of stability. If snow tires are fitted only to the drive wheels, the opposite end of the vehicle may become very unstable when braking or turning on slippery surfaces. This instability can lead to unpleasant endings if the driver can't counteract the slide in time.

Note that snow tires, whether 2 or 4, will affect vehicle handling in all non-snow situations. The stiffer, heavier snow tires will noticeably change the turning and braking characteristics of the vehicle. Once the snow tires are installed, you must re-learn the behavior of the vehicle and drive accordingly.

➡**Consider buying extra wheels on which to mount the snow tires. Once done, the "snow wheels" can be installed and removed as needed. This eliminates the potential damage to tires or wheels from seasonal removal and installation. Even if your vehicle has styled wheels, see if inexpensive steel wheels are available. Although the look of the vehicle will change, the expensive wheels will be protected from salt, curb hits and pothole damage.**

TIRE STORAGE

If they are mounted on wheels, store the tires at proper inflation pressure. All tires should be kept in a cool, dry place. If they are stored in the garage or basement, do not let them stand on a concrete floor; set them on strips of wood, a mat or a large stack of newspaper. Keeping them away from direct moisture is of paramount importance. Tires should not be stored upright, but in a flat position.

INFLATION & INSPECTION

▶ See Figures 175 thru 182

The importance of proper tire inflation cannot be overemphasized. A tire employs air as part of its structure. It is designed around the sup-

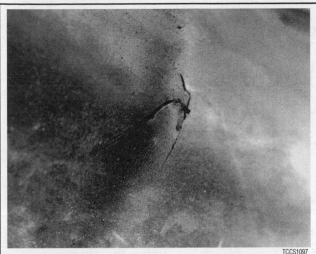

Fig. 175 Tires should be checked frequently for any sign of puncture or damage

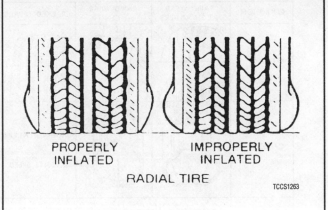

Fig. 178 Radial tires have a characteristic sidewall bulge; don't try to measure pressure by looking at the tire. Use a quality air pressure gauge

Fig. 176 Tires with deep cuts, or cuts which show bulging should be replaced immediately

porting strength of the air at a specified pressure. For this reason, improper inflation drastically reduces the tire's ability to perform as intended. A tire will lose some air in day-to-day use; having to add a few pounds of air periodically is not necessarily a sign of a leaking tire.

Two items should be a permanent fixture in every glove compartment: an accurate tire pressure gauge and a tread depth gauge. Check the tire pressure (including the spare) regularly with a pocket type gauge. Too often, the gauge on the end of the air hose at your corner garage is not accurate because it suffers too much abuse. Always check tire pressure when the tires are cold, as pressure increases with temperature. If you must move the vehicle to check the tire inflation, do not drive more than a mile before checking. A cold tire is generally one that has not been driven for more than three hours.

A plate or sticker is normally provided somewhere in the vehicle (door post, hood, tailgate or trunk lid) which shows the proper pressure for the tires. Never counteract excessive pressure build-up by bleeding off air pressure (letting some air out). This will cause the tire to run hotter and wear quicker.

❊❊❊ CAUTION

Never exceed the maximum tire pressure embossed on the tire! This is the pressure to be used when the tire is at maximum loading, but it is rarely the correct pressure for everyday driving. Consult the owner's manual or the tire pressure sticker for the correct tire pressure.

Once you've maintained the correct tire pressures for several weeks, you'll be familiar with the vehicle's braking and handling personality. Slight adjustments in tire pressures can fine-tune these characteristics, but never change the cold pressure specification by more than 2 psi. A slightly softer tire pressure will give a softer ride but also yield lower fuel mileage. A slightly harder tire will give crisper dry road handling but can cause skidding on wet surfaces. Unless you're fully attuned to the vehicle, stick to the recommended inflation pressures.

All tires made since 1968 have built-in tread wear indicator bars that show up as ½ in. (13mm) wide smooth bands across the tire when 1/16 in. (1.5mm) of tread remains. The appearance of tread wear indicators means that the tires should be replaced. In fact, many states have laws prohibiting the use of tires with less than this amount of tread.

You can check your own tread depth with an inexpensive gauge or by using a Lincoln head penny. Slip the Lincoln penny (with Lincoln's head upside-down) into several tread grooves. If you can see the top of Lincoln's

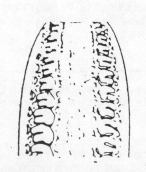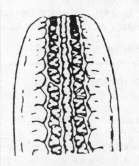

- DRIVE WHEEL HEAVY ACCELERATION
- OVERINFLATION

- HARD CORNERING
- UNDERINFLATION
- LACK OF ROTATION

Fig. 177 Examples of inflation-related tire wear patterns

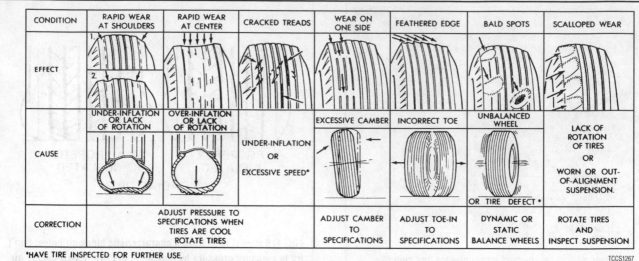

CONDITION	RAPID WEAR AT SHOULDERS	RAPID WEAR AT CENTER	CRACKED TREADS	WEAR ON ONE SIDE	FEATHERED EDGE	BALD SPOTS	SCALLOPED WEAR
EFFECT							
CAUSE	UNDER-INFLATION OR LACK OF ROTATION	OVER-INFLATION OR LACK OF ROTATION	UNDER-INFLATION OR EXCESSIVE SPEED*	EXCESSIVE CAMBER	INCORRECT TOE	UNBALANCED WHEEL OR TIRE DEFECT*	LACK OF ROTATION OF TIRES OR WORN OR OUT-OF-ALIGNMENT SUSPENSION.
CORRECTION	ADJUST PRESSURE TO SPECIFICATIONS WHEN TIRES ARE COOL ROTATE TIRES			ADJUST CAMBER TO SPECIFICATIONS	ADJUST TOE-IN TO SPECIFICATIONS	DYNAMIC OR STATIC BALANCE WHEELS	ROTATE TIRES AND INSPECT SUSPENSION

*HAVE TIRE INSPECTED FOR FURTHER USE.

TCCS1267

Fig. 179 Common tire wear patterns and causes

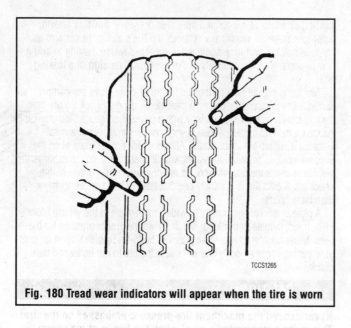

Fig. 180 Tread wear indicators will appear when the tire is worn

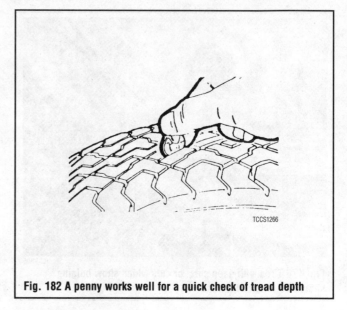

Fig. 182 A penny works well for a quick check of tread depth

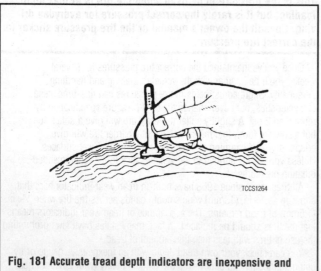

Fig. 181 Accurate tread depth indicators are inexpensive and handy

head in 2 adjacent grooves, the tire has less than 1/16 in. (1.5mm) tread left and should be replaced. You can measure snow tires in the same manner by using the "tails" side of the Lincoln penny. If you can see the top of the Lincoln memorial, it's time to replace the snow tire(s).

CARE OF SPECIAL WHEELS

If you have invested money in magnesium, aluminum alloy or sport wheels, special precautions should be taken to make sure your investment is not wasted and that your special wheels look good for the life of the vehicle.

Special wheels are easily damaged and/or scratched. Occasionally check the rims for cracking, impact damage or air leaks. If any of these are found, replace the wheel. But in order to prevent this type of damage and the costly replacement of a special wheel, observe the following precautions:

• Use extra care not to damage the wheels during removal, installation, balancing, etc. After removal of the wheels from the vehicle, place them on a mat or other protective surface. If they are to be stored for any length of time, support them on strips of wood. Never store tires and wheels upright; the tread may develop flat spots.

- When driving, watch for hazards; it doesn't take much to crack a wheel.
- When washing, use a mild soap or non-abrasive dish detergent (keeping in mind that detergent tends to remove wax). Avoid cleansers with abrasives or the use of hard brushes. There are many cleaners and polishes for special wheels.

- If possible, remove the wheels during the winter. Salt and sand used for snow removal can severely damage the finish of a wheel.
- Make certain the recommended lug nut torque is never exceeded or the wheel may crack. Never use snow chains on special wheels; severe scratching will occur.

FLUIDS AND LUBRICANTS

Fluid Disposal

Used fluids such as engine oil, transmission fluid, antifreeze and brake fluid are hazardous wastes and must be disposed of properly. Before draining any fluids, consult with your local authorities; in many areas waste oil, etc. is being accepted as a part of recycling programs. A number of service stations and auto parts stores are also accepting waste fluids for recycling.

Be sure of the recycling center's policies before draining any fluids, as many will not accept different fluids that have been mixed together.

Oil and Fuel Recommendations

OIL

▶ See Figures 183 and 184

The SAE (Society of Automotive Engineers) grade number indicates the viscosity of the engine oil; its resistance to flow at a given temperature. The lower the SAE grade number, the lighter the oil. For example, the mono-grade oils begin with SAE 5 weight, which is a thin, light oil, and continue in viscosity up to SAE 80 or 90 weight, which are heavy gear lubricants. These oils are also known as "straight weight", meaning they are of a single viscosity, and do not vary with engine temperature.

Multi-viscosity oils offer the important advantage of being adaptable to temperature extremes. These oils have designations such as 10W–40, 20W–50, etc. The "10W–40" means that in winter (the "W" in the designation) the oil acts like a thin 10 weight oil, allowing the engine to spin easily when cold and offering rapid lubrication. Once the engine has warmed up, however, the oil acts like a straight 40 weight, maintaining good lubrication and protection for the engine's internal components. A 20W–50 oil would therefore be slightly heavier than and not as ideal in cold weather as the 10W–40, but would offer better protection at higher rpm and temperatures because when warm it acts like a 50 weight oil. Whichever oil viscosity you choose when changing the oil, make sure you are anticipating the temperatures your engine will be operating in until the oil is changed again. Refer to the oil viscosity chart for oil recommendations according to temperature.

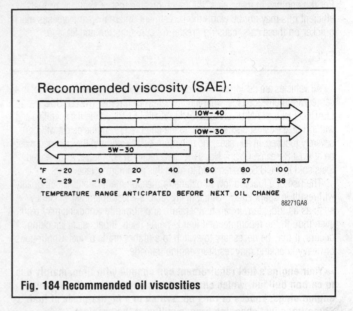

Fig. 184 Recommended oil viscosities

The API (American Petroleum Institute) designation indicates the classification of engine oil used under certain given operating conditions. Only oils designated for use "Service SG" or greater should be used. Oils of the SG type perform a variety of functions inside the engine in addition to the basic function as a lubricant. Through a balanced system of metallic detergents and polymeric dispersants, the oil prevents the formation of high and low temperature deposits and also keeps sludge and particles of dirt in suspension. Acids, particularly sulfuric acid, as well as other by-products of combustion, are neutralized. Both the SAE grade number and the API designation bottle be found on the oil can. For recommended oil viscosities, refer to the chart.

SYNTHETIC OIL

There are many excellent synthetic and fuel-efficient oils currently available that can provide better gas mileage, longer service life, and in some cases better engine protection. These benefits do not come without a few hitches, however, the main one being the price of synthetic oils, which is three or four times the price per quart of conventional oil.

Synthetic oil is not for every car and every type of driving, so you should consider your engine's condition and your type of driving. Also, check your car's warranty conditions regarding the use of synthetic oils.

Both brand new engines and older, high mileage engines are the wrong candidates for synthetic oil. The synthetic oils are so slippery that they can prevent the proper break-in of new engines; most manufacturer's recommend that you wait until the engine is properly broken in—5,000 miles (8,046km)—before using synthetic oil. Older engines with wear have a different problem with synthetics: they use (consume during operation) more oil as they age. Slippery synthetic oils get past these worn parts easily. If your engine is using conventional oil, it will use synthetics much faster. If your car is leaking oil past old seals you'll have a much greater leak problem with synthetics.

Consider your type of driving. If most of your accumulated mileage is high speed, highway type driving, the more expensive synthetic oils may be of benefit. Extended highway driving gives the engine a chance to warm up, accumulating less acids in the oil and putting less stress on the engine

Fig. 183 Look for the API oil identification label when choosing your engine oil

over the long run. Under these conditions, the oil change interval can be extended (as long as your oil filter can last the extended life of the oil) up to the advertised mileage claims of the synthetics. Cars with synthetic oils may show increased fuel economy in highway driving, due to less internal friction. However, many automotive experts agree that 50,000 miles (80,465km) is too long to keep any oil in your engine.

Cars used under harder circumstances, such as stop-and-go, city type driving, short trips, or extended idling, should be serviced more frequently. For the engines in these cars, the much greater cost of synthetic or fuel-efficient oils may not be worth the investment. Internal wear increases much quicker on these cars, causing greater oil consumption and leakage.

FUEL

All vehicles are designed to run on unleaded fuel. The use of leaded fuel in a car requiring unleaded fuel will plug the catalytic converter (NEVER USE LEADED FUEL IN AN UNLEADED FUEL VEHICLE), rendering it inoperative and will increase exhaust back-pressure to the point where engine output will be severely reduced. In all cases, the minimum octane rating of the fuel used must be at least Research Octane No. 91 (octane rating 87) or higher. All unleaded fuels sold in the U.S. are required to meet this minimum octane rating.

The use of a fuel too low in octane (a measurement of anti-knock quality) will result in spark knock. Since many factors affect operating efficiency, such as altitude, terrain, air temperature and humidity, knocking may result even though the recommended fuel is being used. If persistent knocking occurs, it may be necessary to switch to a higher grade of fuel. Continuous or heavy knocking may result in engine damage.

➥**Your engine's fuel requirement can change with time, mainly due to carbon buildup, which changes the compression ratio. If your engine pings, knocks or runs on, switch to a higher grade of fuel. Sometimes just changing brands will cure the problem.**

OPERATION IN FOREIGN COUNTRIES

If you plan to drive your car outside the United States or Canada, there is a possibility that fuels will be too low in anti-knock quality and could produce engine damage. It is wise to consult with local authorities upon arrival in a foreign country to determine the best fuels available.

Engine

OIL LEVEL CHECK

✳✳ CAUTION

Prolonged and repeated skin contact with used engine oil, with no effort to remove the oil, may be harmful. Always follow these simple precautions when handling used motor oil.

• Avoid prolonged skin contact with used motor oil.
• Remove oil from skin by washing thoroughly with soap and water or waterless hand cleaner. Do not use gasoline, thinners or other solvents.
• Avoid prolonged skin contact with oil-soaked clothing. Every time you stop for fuel, check the engine oil as follows:
1. Park the car on level ground.
2. When checking the oil level it is best for the engine to be at operating temperature, although checking the oil immediately after stopping will lead to a false reading. Wait a few minutes after turning off the engine to allow the oil to drain back into the crankcase.
3. Open the hood and locate the dipstick. Pull the dipstick from its tube, wipe it clean and reinsert it.
4. Pull the dipstick out again and, holding it horizontally, read the oil level. The oil should be between the **F** and **L** or high and low marks on the dipstick. If the oil is below the **L** or low mark, add oil of the proper viscosity through the capped opening on the top of the valve (cylinder head) cover.

On some models, the engine oil dipstick is marked

88271P61

5. Replace the dipstick and check the oil level again after adding any oil. Be careful not to overfill the crankcase. Approximately 1 quart (0.9L) of oil will raise the level from the **L** or low mark to the **F** or high mark. Excess oil will generally be consumed at an accelerated rate.

OIL & FILTER CHANGE

▶ **See Figures 185, 186 and 187**

The oil and filter should be changed every 7500 miles (12,000 km).

✳✳ CAUTION

Prolonged and repeated skin contact with used engine oil, with no effort to remove the oil, may cause skin cancer. Always follow these simple precautions when handling used motor oil:

• Avoid prolonged skin contact with used motor oil.
• Remove oil from skin by washing thoroughly with soap and water or waterless hand cleaner. Do not use gasoline, thinners or other solvents.
• Avoid prolonged skin contact with oil-soaked clothing.
The oil drain plug is located on the bottom, rear of the oil pan (bottom of the engine, underneath the car). The oil filter is located on the side of the engine.

The mileage figures given are the Toyota recommended intervals assuming normal driving and conditions. Normal driving requires that the vehicle be driven far enough to warm up the oil; usually this is about 10 miles (16 km) or so. If your everyday use is shorter than this (one way), your use qualifies as severe duty.

Severe duty includes dusty, polluted or off-road conditions, as well as stop-and-go short haul uses. Regularly towing a trailer also puts the truck in this category, as does constant operation with a near capacity load. Change the oil and filter at ½ the normal interval. Half of 7500 equals 3250 miles (5229 km); round it down to the easily remembered 3000 mile (5000 km) interval. For some owners, that may be once a month; for others, it may be six months.

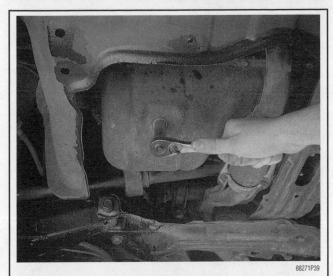

Loosen the oil drain plug in a counterclockwise direction

Always drain the oil after the engine has been running long enough to bring it to normal operating temperature. Hot oil will flow easier and more contaminants will be removed along with the oil than if it were drained cold. To change the oil and filter:

1. Run the engine until it reaches normal operating temperature.
2. Remove the oil filler cap this will allow the oil to drain easier.
3. Jack up the front of the car and support it on safety stands.
4. Slide a drain pan of at least 6 quarts capacity under the oil pan.
5. Loosen the drain plug with a wrench. Turn the plug out by hand. By keeping an inward pressure on the plug as you unscrew it, oil won't escape past the threads and you can remove it without being burned by hot oil.
6. Allow the oil to drain completely and then install the drain plug. Don't overtighten the plug, or you'll be buying a new pan or a replacement plug for stripped threads.
7. On some models it will be necessary to remove the engine under cover to access the oil filter.
8. Using a filter wrench, remove the oil filter. Keep in mind that it's holding about one quart of dirty, hot oil. Make certain the old gasket comes off with the filter and is not stuck to the block.
9. Empty the old filter into the drain pan and dispose of the filter.
10. Using a clean rag, wipe off the filter adapter on the engine block. Be sure that the rag doesn't leave any lint which could clog an oil passage.

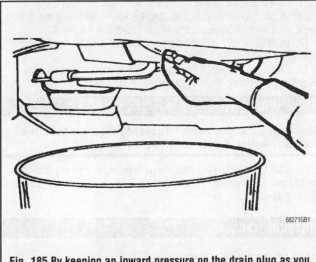

Fig. 185 By keeping an inward pressure on the drain plug as you unscrew it, the oil won't escape past the threads

To access the oil filter on some models, you must remove the engine undercover

Allow the engine oil to drain completely out of the oil pan

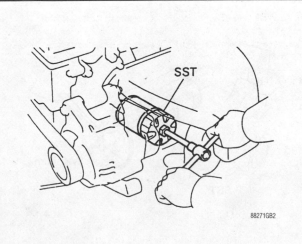

Fig. 186 Special adapters are availble to remove the oil filter

Before installing a new oil filter, lightly coat the rubber gasket with clean oil

TCCS1901

Add oil through the valve (cylinder head) cover only

88271P62

Fill the filter with oil and install it by hand

88271P41

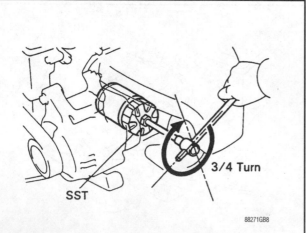

3/4 Turn

SST

88271GB8

Fig. 187 To seat the filter, use the wrench and tighten the filter an additional ¾ turn

11. Coat the rubber gasket on the filter with fresh oil. Spin it onto the engine by hand; when the gasket touches the adapter surface give it another ½–¾ turn. No more, or you'll squash the gasket and it will leak.

12. Refill the engine with the correct amount of fresh oil through the valve cover. See the "Capacities" chart.

13. Check the oil level on the dipstick. It is normal for the level to be a bit above the full mark. Start the engine and allow it to idle for a few minutes.

❋❋ WARNING

Do not run the engine above idle speed until it has built up oil pressure, indicated when the oil light goes out.

14. Shut **OFF** the engine, allow the oil to drain for a minute, and check the oil level. Check around the filter and drain plug for any leaks, and correct as necessary.

Manual Transaxle

FLUID RECOMMENDATIONS

The manual transaxles use API GL–4 or GL–5 (oil grade) which is SAE 75W-90 or SAE 80W-90 (viscosity).
- 1988–92 2WD—GL–4 or GL–5
- 1988–92 4WD—E50 or GL–5
- 1993—GL–3, GL–4 or GL–5
- 1994–97—GL–4 or GL–5

LEVEL CHECK

▶ **See Figures 188, 189, 190 and 191**

The oil in the manual transaxle should be checked at least every 15,000 miles or 24 months. If vehicle is operated under severe conditions change the manual transaxle oil at this service interval.

1. With the car parked on a level surface, remove the filler plug from the side of the transaxle housing. The left side engine under cover may need to be removed to check the fluid level.

2. If the lubricant begins to trickle out of the hole, there is enough. Otherwise, carefully insert your finger (watch out for sharp threads) and check to see if the oil is up to the edge of the hole.

3. If not, add oil through the hole until the level is at the edge of the hole. Most gear lubricants come in a plastic squeeze bottle with a nozzle, making additions simple.

4. Replace the filler plug and engine cover if removed.

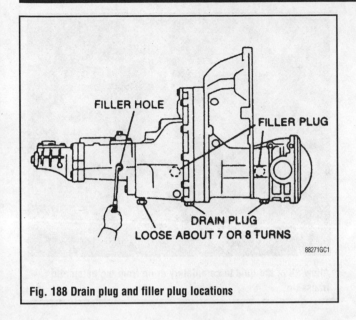

Fig. 188 Drain plug and filler plug locations

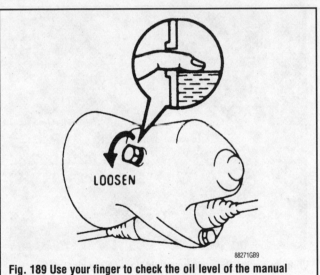

Fig. 189 Use your finger to check the oil level of the manual transaxle

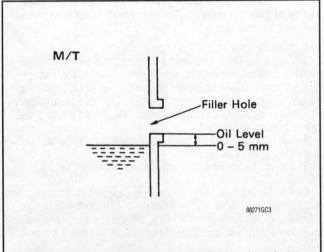

Fig. 190 The oil level should come within 0.20 in. (5mm) of the bottom edge of the filler hole

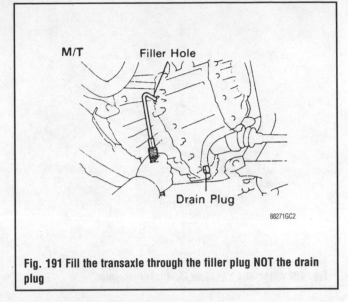

Fig. 191 Fill the transaxle through the filler plug NOT the drain plug

DRAIN & REFILL

▶ **See Figures 188 and 191**

1. Raise and safely support the vehicle as necessary. The oil must be hot before it is drained. If the car is driven until the engine is at normal operating temperature, the oil should be hot enough.
2. Remove the left side engine under cover.
3. Remove the filler plug to provide a vent.
4. The drain plug is on the bottom of the transaxle. Place a large container underneath the transaxle and remove the plug.
5. Allow the oil to drain completely. Clean off the plug and replace it. Tighten it until it is just snug.
6. Fill the transaxle with the proper oil till it runs out of the filler hole. This usually comes in a plastic squeeze bottle or use a kitchen baster to squirt the oil in. Refer to the Capacities Chart for the proper amount of oil to add.
7. The oil level should come up to the top of the filler hole.
8. Replace the filler plug. Install the engine cover if it was removed.
9. Drive the car for a few minutes, stop, and check for any leaks.

Automatic Transaxle

FLUID RECOMMENDATIONS

All vehicles equipped with automatic transaxles use Dexron®II or Dexron III automatic transaxle fluid except All-Trac/4WD models which use Toyota automatic transaxle fluid type T or equivalent.
- 1988–92 2WD—Dexron II or Dexron III
- 1988–92 4WD—Type T
- 1993–97—Dexton II or Dexron III

LEVEL CHECK

▶ **See Figure 192**

The oil in the automatic transaxle should be checked at least every 15,000 miles or 24 months. If vehicle is operated under severe conditions change the automatic transaxle oil at this service interval.

The fluid level should be checked only when the transaxle is HOT (normal operating temperature). The transaxle is considered hot after about 20 miles of highway driving.

1. Park the car on a level surface with the engine idling. Shift the transaxle into **N** or **P** and set the parking brake.

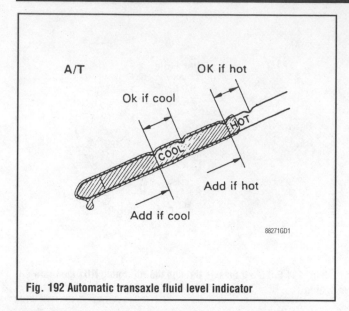

Fig. 192 Automatic transaxle fluid level indicator

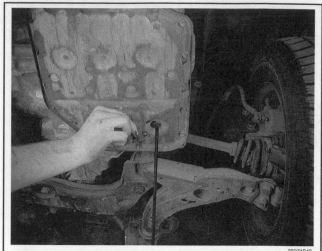

Allow all of the fluid to completely drain from the automatic transaxle

2. Remove the dipstick, wipe it clean and reinsert it firmly. Be sure that it has been pushed all the way in. Remove the dipstick and check the fluid level while holding it horizontally. With the engine running, the fluid level should be between the second and third notches on the dipstick.

3. If the fluid level is below the second notch, add the required type of transaxle fluid until the proper level is reached. This is easily done with the aid of a funnel. Check the level often as you are filling the transaxle. Be extremely careful not to overfill it. Overfilling will cause slippage, seal damage and overheating. Approximately one pint (0.47L) of transaxle fluid will raise the level from one notch to the other.

The fluid on the dipstick should always be a bright red color. If it is discolored (brown or black), or smells burnt, serious transaxle troubles, probably due to overheating, should be suspected. The transaxle should be inspected by a qualified service (ASE certified) technician to locate the cause of the burnt fluid.

DRAIN & REFILL

The automatic transaxle has a drain plug so you can remove the plug, drain the fluid, replace the plug and then refill the transaxle.

1. Raise and safely support the vehicle as necessary. Remove the plug and gasket if equipped, then drain the fluid into a large pan.

With the engine OFF, add new fluid through the dipstick tube using a funnel

➡Some transaxles use a metal gasket and others a fiber gasket. The metal gasket is reusable. The fiber gasket is not to be reused and must be replaced.

2. Install the drain plug and gasket if equipped.

3. It is a good idea to measure the amount of fluid drained from the transaxle to determine the correct amount of fresh fluid to add. This is because some parts of the transaxle may not drain completely and using the dry refill amount specified in the Capacities Chart could lead to overfilling. Fluid is added only through the dipstick tube. Always use the proper type automatic transaxle fluid.

4. Add automatic transaxle fluid (vehicle must be on a level surface when refilling) to the correct level.

5. Replace the dipstick after filling. Start the engine and allow it to idle. DO NOT race the engine.

6. After the engine has idled for a few minutes, shift the transaxle slowly through the gears (always hold your foot on the brake pedal) and then return it to **P**. With the engine still idling, check the fluid level on the dipstick. If necessary, add more fluid to raise the level to where it is supposed to be.

7. Check the drain plug for transaxle fluid leakage. Dispose of used oil properly. Do not throw it in the trash or pour it on the ground.

Loosen the automatic transaxle drain plug

PAN & FILTER SERVICE

▶ See Figures 193 and 194

The automatic transaxle filter should be changed every time the transaxle fluid is change. Always replace the transaxle pan gasket when oil pan is removed. Note location of all transaxle oil filter (strainer) retaining bolts. Always torque all transaxle oil pan retaining bolts in progressive steps.

➡This service operation should be performed with the engine and transaxle COLD.

1. Raise and safely support the vehicle as necessary. Remove the plug and drain the fluid. When the fluid stops coming out of the drain hole, loosen the pan retaining screws until the pan can be pulled down at one corner. If the pan is stuck, tap the edges lightly with a plastic mallet to loosen it; Don't pry it or wedge a screwdriver into the seam. Lower the corner of the pan and allow the remaining fluid to drain out.

2. After the pan has drained completely, remove the pan retaining screws and then remove the pan and gasket.

3. Clean the pan thoroughly and allow it to air dry. If you wipe it out with a rag you run the risk of leaving bits of lint in the pan which will clog the tiny hydraulic passages in the transaxle.

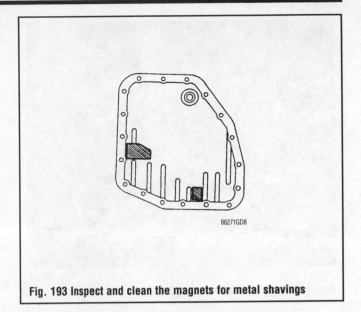

Fig. 193 Inspect and clean the magnets for metal shavings

Remove the pan retaining bolts after draining the system

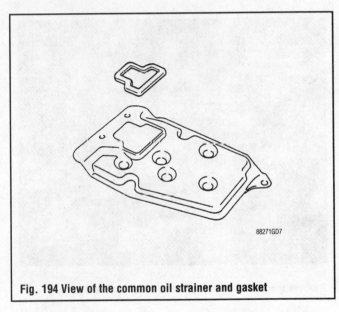

Fig. 194 View of the common oil strainer and gasket

4. With the pan removed, the transaxle filter (strainer) is visible. The filter should be changed any time the transaxle oil is drained. Remove the bolts holding the filter and remove the filter and gasket if so equipped.

➡Some filter retaining bolts are different lengths and MUST BE reinstalled in their correct locations. Take great care not to interchange them.

5. Clean the mating surfaces for the oil pan and the filter; make sure all traces of the old gasket material is removed.

6. Install the new strainer assembly (some models use a gasket under the oil strainer). Install the retaining bolts in their correct locations and tighten evenly.

7. Install the pan (magnets in the correct location in oil pan if so equipped) using a new gasket and tighten the retaining bolts in progressive steps to 45–60 inch lbs.

8. Install the drain plug.

9. It is a good idea to measure the amount of fluid drained from the transaxle to determine the correct amount of fresh fluid to be added. This is because some parts of the transaxle may not drain completely. Do not overfill the transaxle assembly.

10. With the engine **OFF**, add new automatic transaxle fluid through the dipstick tube to the correct level. Refer to the Capacities Chart at the end of Section 1 as necessary.

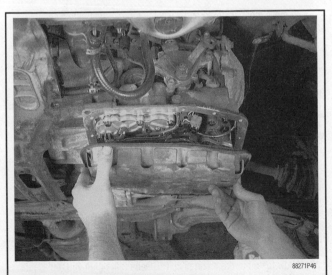

Lower the transaxle pan to access the strainer

Remove the oil strainer mounting bolts and gasket

Remove the strainer and replace or clean as needed

11. Start the engine (always hold your foot on the brake) and shift the gear selector into all positions, allowing each gear to engage momentarily. Shift into **P**. DO NOT race the engine!

12. With the engine idling, check the fluid level. Add fluid up to correct level on the dipstick.

13. Check the transaxle oil pan and drain plug for oil leakage. Dispose of used oil properly. Do not throw it in the trash or pour it on the ground.

Transfer Case

FLUID RECOMMENDATIONS

All 4WD vehicles use API GL–5 hypoid type gear oil (oil grade) SAE 80W–90 (viscosity).

LEVEL CHECK

▶ **See Figure 195**

The oil in the transfer case should be replaced every 15,000 miles (24,000 km).

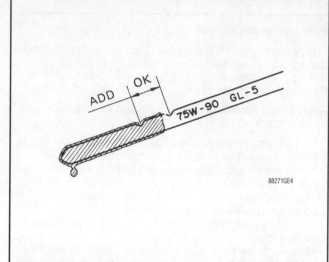

Fig. 195 Check the oil level on the dipstick for the transfer case

➡ **If the vehicle has just been driven for a long period of time at a high speed or in city traffic in hot weather, or if the vehicle has been pulling a trailer, an accurate oil level can not be obtained. Check the level after 5 minuets or more.**

1. Pull the dipstick out and wipe it clean.

2. Reinsert the dipstick then push it in as far as possible. Pull the dipstick out and look at the oil level. If the level is different on the front and reverse sides of the dipstick, read the level which is lower.

3. If the level is low add multi purpose gear oil. Add fluid through the dipstick tube using a funnel to bring the level within range.

✳✳ WARNING

Avoid overfilling, it may cause transfer damage.

4. After add the oil, drive the vehicle for more than 30 seconds and recheck the oil level. Top off if necessary.

DRAIN & REFILL

Automatic

1. Remove the lower plug and allow the fluid to drain into a suitable container.

2. Reinstall the drain plug and tighten securely.

3. Add new oil through the filler tube, use API GL–5 hypoid type gear oil (oil grade) SAE 80W–90 (viscosity).

4. Check that the fluid level is between the land **F** marks on the dipstick.

➡ **Do not overfill.**

Manual

The front transfer unit is part of the transaxel on all manual vehicles

1. Raise and safely support the vehicle as necessary. The oil must be hot before it is drained. If the car is driven until the engine is at normal operating temperature, the oil should be hot enough.

2. Remove the left side engine under cover.

3. Remove the filler plug to provide a vent.

4. The drain plug is on the bottom of the transfer. Place a large container underneath the transfer and remove the plug.

5. Allow the oil to drain completely. Clean off the plug and replace it. Tighten it until it is just snug.

6. Fill the transfer case with the proper oil till it runs out of the filler hole. This usually comes in a plastic squeeze bottle or use a kitchen baster to squirt the oil in. Refer to the Capacities Chart for the proper amount of oil to add.

7. The oil level should come up to the top of the filler hole.

8. Replace the filler plug. Install the engine cover if it was removed.

9. Drive the car for a few minutes, stop, and check for any leaks.

Front Differential

FLUID RECOMMENDATIONS

All front differentials in the 3 speed automatics (A131L) use Dexron II.

DRAIN & REFILL

▶ See Figures 196, 197 and 198

➡ Only the 3 speed automatic (A131L) transaxles have a separate front differential unit.

1. Loosen the filler plug for the differential.

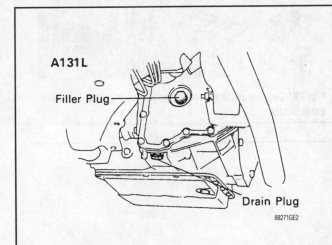

Fig. 196 A 10mm hexagon wrench will be needed to loosen and remove the drain plug on the differential

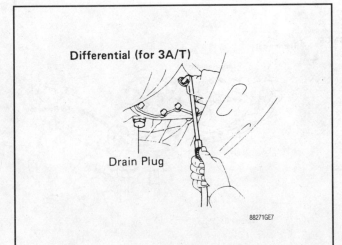

Fig. 197 Add fresh fluid through the differential fill hole on the A131L automatic transaxle models

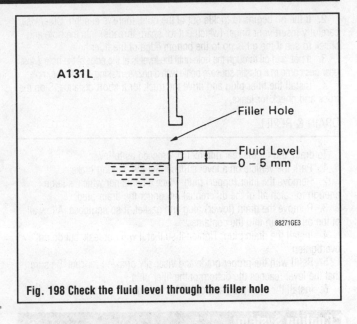

Fig. 198 Check the fluid level through the filler hole

2. To remove the plug from the differential on A131L models, use a 10mm hexagon wrench.

3. Reinstall and securely tighten the plug.

4. Add new oil (Dexron II) through the filler hole till it begins to runout then tighten the plug.

Rear Differential

FLUID RECOMMENDATIONS

All rear differentials in the 4WD models use API GL–4 (oil grade) which is SAE 80W-90 (viscosity).

LEVEL CHECK

▶ See Figure 199

This rear differential applies to 4WD models only.

1. With the vehicle parked on a level surface, remove the filler plug from the back of the differential.

➡ The plug on the bottom is the drain plug.

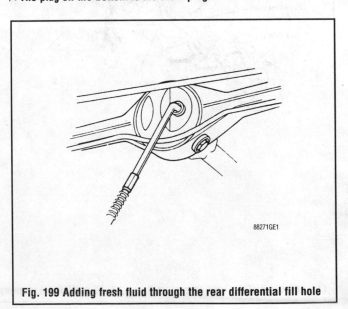

Fig. 199 Adding fresh fluid through the rear differential fill hole

2. If the oil begins to trickle out of the hole, there is enough. Otherwise, carefully insert your finger (watch out for sharp threads) into the hole and check to see if the oil is up to the bottom edge of the filler hole.

3. If not, add oil through the hole until the level is at the edge of the hole. Most gear oils come in a plastic squeeze bottle with a nozzle, making additions simple.

4. Install the filler plug and drive the truck for a short distance. Stop the truck and check for leaks.

DRAIN & REFILL

To drain and fill the rear differential, proceed as follows:

1. Park the vehicle on a level surface. Set the parking brake.

2. Remove the filler (upper) plug. Place a container which is large enough to catch all of the differential oil, under the drain plug.

3. Remove the drain (lower) plug and gasket, if so equipped. Allow all of the oil to drain into the container.

4. Install the drain plug. Tighten it so that it will not leak, but do not overtighten.

5. Refill with the proper grade and viscosity of axle lubricant. Be sure that the level reaches the bottom of the filler plug.

6. Install the filler plug and check for leakage.

Cooling System

▶ **See Figure 200**

FLUID RECOMMENDATIONS

The correct coolant is any permanent, high quality ethylene glycol antifreeze mixed in a 50/50 concentration with water. This mixture gives the best combination of antifreeze and anti-boil characteristics within the engine.

LEVEL CHECK

▶ **See Figures 201 and 202**

❋❋ CAUTION

Always allow the car to sit and cool for an hour or so (longer is better) before removing the radiator cap. To avoid injury when working on a warm engine, cover the radiator cap

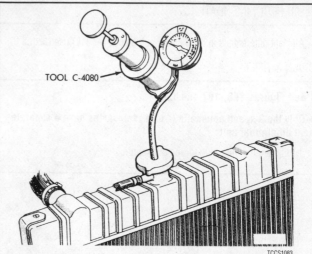

TCCS1083

Fig. 201 Cooling systems should be pressure tested for leaks periodically

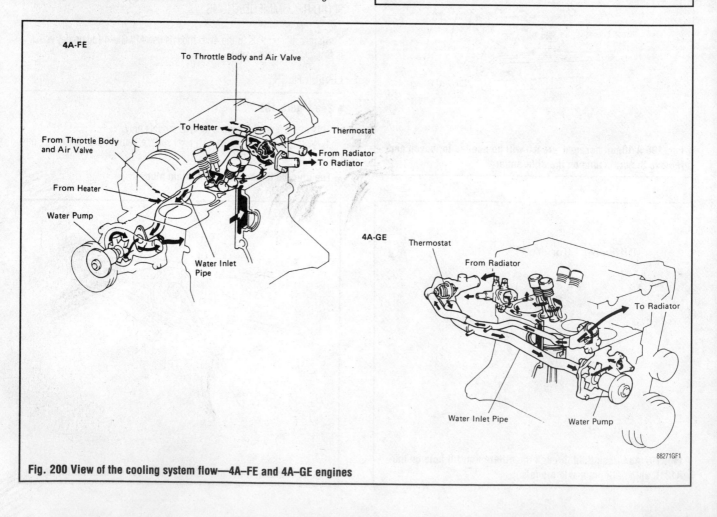

88271GF1

Fig. 200 View of the cooling system flow—4A–FE and 4A–GE engines

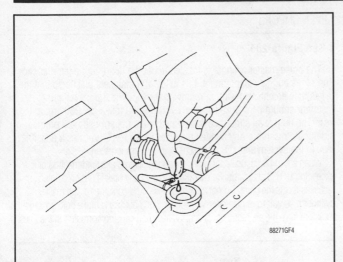

Fig. 202 On a COLD engine, place your finger in the radiator opening and check for oil and rust deposits

with a thick cloth and turn it slowly counterclockwise until the pressure begins to escape. After the pressure is completely removed, remove the cap. Never remove the cap until the pressure is gone. There should be no excessive rust deposits around the radiator cap or filler tube. The coolant should be free from any oil. On a COLD engine, place your finger in the coolant and check for oil or rust deposits.

It's best to check the coolant level when the engine is COLD. The radiator coolant level should be between the LOW and the FULL lines on the expansion tank when the engine is cold. If low, check for leakage and add coolant up to the FULL line but do not overfill.

➡ Check the freeze protection rating of the antifreeze at least once a year or as necessary with a suitable antifreeze tester.

DRAIN & REFILL

◗ See Figures 203 and 204

The engine coolant should be changed for the fist time at 45,000 miles (72,000 km) or 36 months which ever comes first. After the initial change

Toyota recommends the coolant be changed every 30,000 miles (48,000 km) or 2 years. Replacing the coolant is necessary to remove the scale, rust and chemical by-products which build up in the system.

1. Draining the cooling system is always done with the engine **COLD**.
2. Remove the radiator cap.
3. Position the drain pan under the draincock on the bottom of the radiator. Additionally, some engines have a draincock on the side of the engine block, near the oil filter. This should be opened to aid in draining the cooling system completely. If for some reason the radiator draincock can't be used, you can loosen and remove the lower radiator hose at its joint to the radiator.

✹✹ CAUTION

When draining the coolant, keep in mind that cats and dogs are attracted by the ethylene glycol antifreeze, and are quite likely to drink any that is left in an uncovered container or in puddles on the ground. This will prove fatal in sufficient quantity. Always drain the coolant into a sealable container. Coolant should be reused unless it is contaminated or several years old.

Removing the engine undercover may be required to access the draincock on the radiator

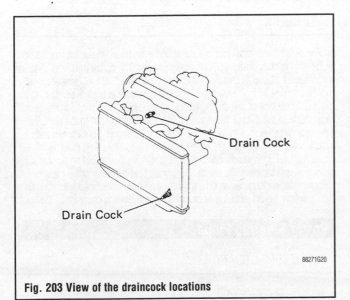

Fig. 203 View of the draincock locations

Drain Cock

Drain Cock

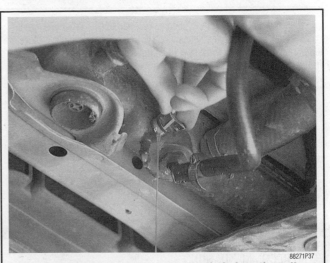

Turn the draincock to allow the coolant to drain from the radiator

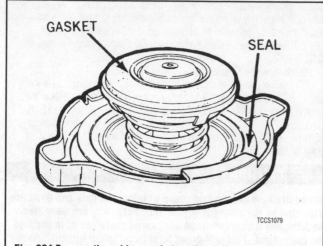

Fig. 204 Be sure the rubber gasket on the radiator cap has a tight seal

4. If the lower hose is to be used as the drain, loosen the clamp on the hose and slide it back so it's out of the way. Gently break the grip of the hose on its fitting by twisting or prying with a suitable tool. Do not exert too much force or you will damage the radiator fitting. Remove the hose end from the radiator and direct the hose into the drain pan. You now have fluid running from both the hose and the radiator.

5. When the system stops draining, close both draincocks as necessary.

6. Using a funnel if necessary, fill the radiator with a 50/50 solution of antifreeze and water. Allow time for the fluid to run through the hoses and into the engine.

7. Fill the radiator to just below the filler neck. With the radiator cap off, start the engine and let it idle; this will circulate the coolant and begin to eliminate air in the system. Top up the radiator as the level drops.

8. When the level is reasonably stable, shut the engine **OFF**, and replace the radiator cap. Fill the expansion tank to the correct level and cap the expansion tank.

9. Drive the car for 10 or 15 minutes; the temperature gauge should be fully within the normal operating range. It is helpful to set the heater to its hottest setting while driving—this circulates the coolant throughout the entire system and helps eliminate air bubbles.

10. After the engine has cooled (2–3 hours), check the level in the radiator and the expansion tank, adding coolant as necessary.

FLUSHING THE COOLING SYSTEM

Proceed with draining the system as outlined above. When the system has drained, reconnect any hoses close to the radiator draincock. Move the temperature control for the heater to its hottest position; this allows the heater core to be flushed as well. Using a garden hose or bucket, fill the radiator and allow the water to run out the engine drain cock. Continue until the water runs clear. Be sure to clean the expansion tank as well.

If the system is badly contaminated with rust or scale, you can use a commercial flushing solution to clean it out. Follow the manufacturer's instructions. Some causes of rust are air in the system, failure to change the coolant regularly, use of excessively hard or soft water, and/or failure to use the correct mix of antifreeze and water.

After the system has been flushed, continue with the refill procedures outlined above. Check the condition of the radiator cap and its gasket, replacing the radiator cap as necessary.

Brake Master Cylinder

FLUID RECOMMENDATIONS

All vehicles use DOT 3 or SAE J1703 brake fluid.

LEVEL CHECK

▶ **See Figure 205**

The brake master cylinder is located under the hood, in the left rear section of the engine compartment. It is made of translucent plastic so that the levels may be checked without removing the top. The fluid level in the reservoir should be checked at least every 15,000 miles (24,000km) or 1 year. The fluid level should be maintained at the uppermost mark on the side of the reservoir. Any sudden decrease in the level indicates a possible leak in the system and should be checked out immediately.

When adding fluid, use only fresh, uncontaminated brake fluid meeting or exceeding DOT 3 standards. Be careful not to spill any brake fluid on painted surfaces, as it eats the paint. Do not allow the brake fluid container or the master cylinder reservoir to remain open any longer than necessary; brake fluid absorbs moisture from the air, reducing its effectiveness and causing corrosion in the lines.

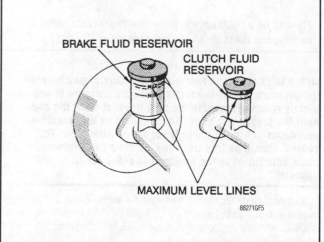

Fig. 205 The brake master and clutch master cylinders are next to each other in the engine compartment

Clutch Master Cylinder

FLUID RECOMMENDATIONS

All vehicles use DOT 3 or SAE J1703 brake fluid.

LEVEL CHECK

The clutch master cylinder is located under the hood, in the left rear section of the engine compartment near the brake master. The clutch master is made of a translucent plastic so that the levels may be checked without removing the top. The fluid level in the reservoir should be checked at least every 15,000 miles (24,000 km) or 1 year. The fluid level should be maintained at the uppermost mark on the side of the reservoir. Any sudden decrease in the level indicates a possible leak in the system and should be checked out immediately.

When adding fluid, use only fresh, uncontaminated brake fluid meeting or exceeding DOT 3 standards. Be careful not to spill any brake fluid on painted surfaces, as it eats the paint. Do not allow the brake fluid container or the master cylinder reservoir to remain open any longer than necessary; brake fluid absorbs moisture from the air, reducing its effectiveness and causing corrosion in the lines.

Power Steering Pump

FLUID RECOMMENDATIONS

All vehicles use Dexron®II or III type automatic transmission fluid.

LEVEL CHECK

♦ See Figures 206 and 207

The fluid level in the power steering reservoir should be checked at least every 15,000 miles (24,000 km) or 1 year. The vehicle should be parked on level ground, with the engine warm and running at normal idle. If the level is low, add Dexron®II or III type ATF until the proper level is achieved. The air cleaner lid may need to be removed on some models to access the power steering fluid reservoir cap.

Some models may have a reservoir with markings on the outside of the reservoir and others the cap has a built-in dipstick.

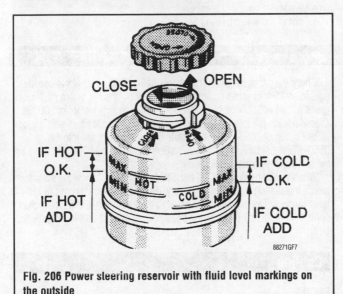

Fig. 206 Power steering reservoir with fluid level markings on the outside

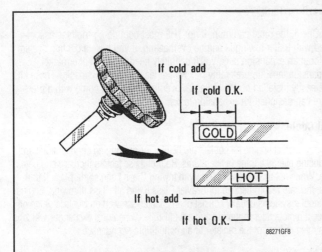

Fig. 207 Some power steering pumps have the fluid level markings on the cap

Chassis Greasing

Chassis greasing is not required on the front wheel drive Corollas.

Body Lubrication

There is no set period recommended by Toyota for body lubrication. However, it is a good idea to lubricate the following body points at least

Always use a funnel to fill the power steering reservoir to keep from spilling any fluid

once a year, especially in the fall before cold weather. **Lubricate with engine oil:**
- Door lock latches
- Door lock rollers
- Door, hood and hinge pivots **Lubricate with Lubriplate:**
- Trunk lid latch and hinge
- Glove box door latch
- Front seat slides **Lubricate with silicone spray:**
- All rubber weather stripping
- Hood stops

When finished lubricating a body part, be sure that all the excess lubricant has been wiped off, especially in the areas of the car which may come in contact with clothing.

Wheel Bearings

REPACKING

➡**Sodium based grease is not compatible with lithium based grease. Read the package labels and be careful not to mix the two types. If there is any doubt as to the type of grease used, completely clean the old grease from the bearing and hub before replacing.**

Before handling the bearings, there are a few things that you should remember to do and not to do.
DO the following:
- Remove all outside dirt from the housing before exposing the bearing.
- Treat a used bearing as gently as you would a new one.
- Work with clean tools in clean surroundings.
- Use clean, dry gloves, or at least clean, dry hands.
- Clean solvents and flushing fluids are a must.
- Use clean paper when laying out the bearings to dry.
- Protect disassembled bearings from rust and dirt. Cover them up.
- Use clean, lint-free rags to wipe the bearings.
- Keep the bearings in oil-proof paper when they are to be stored or are not in use.
- Clean the inside of the housing before replacing the bearing.

Do NOT do the following:
- Do not work in dirty surroundings.
- Do not use dirty, chipped or damaged tools.
- Do not work on wooden work benches or use wooden mallets.
- Do not handle bearings with dirty or moist hands.
- Do not use gasoline for cleaning. Use a safe solvent.
- Do not spin dry bearings with compressed air. They will be damaged.

- Do not use cotton waste or dirty cloths to wipe bearings.
- Do not scratch or nick bearing surfaces.
- Do not allow the bearing to come in contact with dirt or rust at any time.

The rear wheel bearings require periodic maintenance. Use a suitable premium high melting point grease. Long fiber type greases must not be used. This service is recommended every 20,000 miles (32,000 km or 2 years.

➥**For information on Wheel Bearing removal and installation, refer to Section 8 of this manual.**

1. Remove the wheel bearing.
2. Clean all parts in a non-flammable solvent and let them air dry.

➥**Only use lint-free rags to dry the bearings. Never spin-dry a bearing with compressed air, as this will damage the rollers.**

3. Check for excessive wear and damage. Replace the bearing as necessary.

➥**Packing wheel bearings with grease is best accomplished by using a wheel bearing packer (available at most automotive parts stores).**

4. If a wheel bearing packer is not available, the bearings may be packed by hand.
   a. Place a "healthy" glob of grease in the palm of one hand.
   b. Force the edge of the bearing into the grease so that the grease fills the space between the rollers and the bearing cage.
   c. Keep rotating the bearing while continuing to push the grease through.
   d. Continue until the grease is forced out the other side of the bearing.
5. Place the packed bearing on a clean surface and cover it until it is time for installation.
6. Install the wheel bearing.

TRAILER TOWING

♦ **See Figure 208**

General Recommendations

Your vehicle was primarily designed to carry passengers and cargo. It is important to remember that towing a trailer will place additional loads on your vehicles engine, drivetrain, steering, braking and other systems. However, if you decide to tow a trailer, using the prior equipment is a must.

Local laws may require specific equipment such as trailer brakes or fender mounted mirrors. Check your local laws.

Trailer Weight

The weight of the trailer is the most important factor. A good weight-to-horsepower ratio is about 35:1, 35 lbs. of Gross Combined Weight (GCW) for every horsepower your engine develops. Multiply the engine's rated horsepower by 35 and subtract the weight of the vehicle passengers and luggage. The number remaining is the approximate ideal maximum weight you should tow, although a numerically higher axle ratio can help compensate for heavier weight.

Hitch (Tongue) Weight

Calculate the hitch weight in order to select a proper hitch. The weight of the hitch is usually 9–11% of the trailer gross weight and should be measured with the trailer loaded. Hitches fall into various categories: those that mount on the frame and rear bumper, the bolt-on type, or the weld-on distribution type used for larger trailers. Axle mounted or clamp-on bumper hitches should never be used.

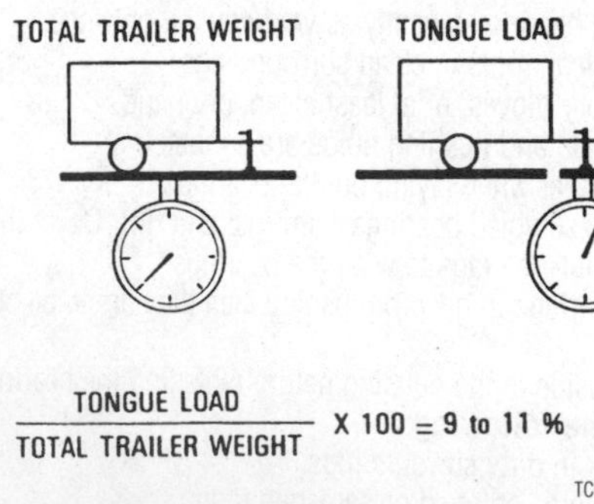

Check the gross weight rating of your trailer. Tongue weight is usually figured as 10% of gross trailer weight. Therefore, a trailer with a maximum gross weight of 2000 lbs. will have a maximum tongue weight of 200 lbs. Class I trailers fall into this category. Class II trailers are those with a gross weight rating of 2000–3000 lbs., while Class III trailers fall into the 3500–6000 lbs. category. Class IV trailers are those over 6000 lbs. and are for use with fifth wheel trucks, only.

When you've determined the hitch that you'll need, follow the manufacturer's installation instructions, exactly, especially when it comes to fastener torques. The hitch will subjected to a lot of stress and good hitches come with hardened bolts. Never substitute an inferior bolt for a hardened bolt.

Cooling

ENGINE

Overflow Tank

One of the most common, if not THE most common, problems associated with trailer towing is engine overheating. If you have a cooling system without an expansion tank, you'll definitely need to get an aftermarket expansion tank kit, preferably one with at least a 2 quart capacity. These kits are easily installed on the radiator's overflow hose, and come with a pressure cap designed for expansion tanks.

Oil Cooler

Aftermarket engine oil coolers are helpful for prolonging engine oil life and reducing overall engine temperatures. Both of these factors increase engine life. While not absolutely necessary in towing Class I and some Class II trailers, they are recommended for heavier Class II and all Class III towing. Engine oil cooler systems usually consist of an adapter, screwed on in place of the oil filter, a remote filter mounting and a multi-tube, finned heat exchanger, which is mounted in front of the radiator or air conditioning condenser.

TRANSAXLE

An automatic transaxle is usually recommended for trailer towing. Modern automatics have proven reliable and, of course, easy to operate, in trailer towing. The increased load of a trailer, however, causes an increase in the temperature of the automatic transaxle fluid. Heat is the worst enemy of an automatic transaxle. As the temperature of the fluid increases, the life of the fluid decreases.

It is essential, therefore, that you install an automatic transaxle cooler. The cooler, which consists of a multi-tube, finned heat exchanger, is usually installed in front of the radiator or air conditioning compressor, and hooked in-line with the transaxle cooler tank inlet line. Follow the cooler manufacturer's installation instructions.

TOTAL TRAILER WEIGHT   TONGUE LOAD

$$\frac{TONGUE\ LOAD}{TOTAL\ TRAILER\ WEIGHT} \times 100 = 9\ to\ 11\ \%$$

TCCS1005

Fig. 208 Calculating proper tongue weight for your trailer

Select a cooler of at least adequate capacity, based upon the combined gross weights of the vehicle and trailer.

Cooler manufacturers recommend that you use an aftermarket cooler in addition to, and not instead of, the present cooling tank in your radiator. If you do want to use it in place of the radiator cooling tank, get a cooler at least two sizes larger than normally necessary.

➡A transaxle cooler can, sometimes, cause slow or harsh shifting in the transaxle during cold weather, until the fluid has a chance to come up to normal operating temperature. Some coolers can be purchased with or retrofitted with a temperature bypass valve which will allow fluid flow through the cooler only when the fluid has reached above a certain operating temperature.

Handling A Trailer

Towing a trailer with ease and safety requires a certain amount of experience. It's a good idea to learn the feel of a trailer by practicing turning, stopping and backing in an open area such as an empty parking lot.

JUMP STARTING A DEAD BATTERY

▶ See Figure 209

Whenever a vehicle is jump started, precautions must be followed in order to prevent the possibility of personal injury. Remember that batteries contain a small amount of explosive hydrogen gas which is a by-product of battery charging. Sparks should always be avoided when working around batteries, especially when attaching jumper cables. To minimize the possibility of accidental sparks, follow the procedure carefully.

✷✷ CAUTION

NEVER hook the batteries up in a series circuit or the entire electrical system will go up in smoke, including the starter!

Vehicles equipped with a diesel engine may utilize two 12 volt batteries. If so, the batteries are connected in a parallel circuit (positive terminal to positive terminal, negative terminal to negative terminal). Hooking the batteries up in parallel circuit increases battery cranking power without increasing total battery voltage output. Output remains at 12 volts. On the other hand, hooking two 12 volt batteries up in a series circuit (positive terminal to negative terminal, positive terminal to negative terminal) increases total battery output to 24 volts (12 volts plus 12 volts).

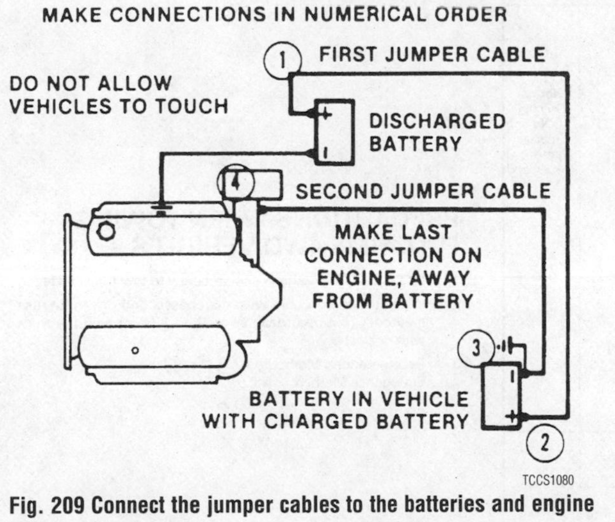

Fig. 209 Connect the jumper cables to the batteries and engine in the order shown

Jump Starting Precautions

- Be sure that both batteries are of the same voltage. Vehicles covered by this manual and most vehicles on the road today utilize a 12 volt charging system.
- Be sure that both batteries are of the same polarity (have the same terminal, in most cases NEGATIVE grounded).
- Be sure that the vehicles are not touching or a short could occur.
- On serviceable batteries, be sure the vent cap holes are not obstructed.
- Do not smoke or allow sparks anywhere near the batteries.
- In cold weather, make sure the battery electrolyte is not frozen. This can occur more readily in a battery that has been in a state of discharge.
- Do not allow electrolyte to contact your skin or clothing.

Jump Starting Procedure

1. Make sure that the voltages of the 2 batteries are the same. Most batteries and charging systems are of the 12 volt variety.
2. Pull the jumping vehicle (with the good battery) into a position so the jumper cables can reach the dead battery and that vehicle's engine. Make sure that the vehicles do NOT touch.
3. Place the transmissions/transaxles of both vehicles in **Neutral** (MT) or **P** (AT), as applicable, then firmly set their parking brakes.

➡If necessary for safety reasons, the hazard lights on both vehicles may be operated throughout the entire procedure without significantly increasing the difficulty of jumping the dead battery.

4. Turn all lights and accessories OFF on both vehicles. Make sure the ignition switches on both vehicles are turned to the **OFF** position.
5. Cover the battery cell caps with a rag, but do not cover the terminals.
6. Make sure the terminals on both batteries are clean and free of corrosion or proper electrical connection will be impeded. If necessary, clean the battery terminals before proceeding.
7. Identify the positive (+) and negative (-) terminals on both batteries.
8. Connect the first jumper cable to the positive (+) terminal of the dead battery, then connect the other end of that cable to the positive (+) terminal of the booster (good) battery.
9. Connect one end of the other jumper cable to the negative (-) terminal on the booster battery and the final cable clamp to an engine bolt head, alternator bracket or other solid, metallic point on the engine with the dead battery. Try to pick a ground on the engine that is positioned away from the battery in order to minimize the possibility of the 2 clamps touching should one loosen during the procedure. DO NOT connect this clamp to the negative (-) terminal of the bad battery.

✷✷ CAUTION

Be very careful to keep the jumper cables away from moving parts (cooling fan, belts, etc.) on both engines.

10. Check to make sure that the cables are routed away from any moving parts, then start the donor vehicle's engine. Run the engine at moderate speed for several minutes to allow the dead battery a chance to receive some initial charge.
11. With the donor vehicle's engine still running slightly above idle, try to start the vehicle with the dead battery. Crank the engine for no more than 10 seconds at a time and let the starter cool for at least 20 seconds between tries. If the vehicle does not start in 3 tries, it is likely that something else is also wrong or that the battery needs additional time to charge.
12. Once the vehicle is started, allow it to run at idle for a few seconds to make sure that it is operating properly.
13. Turn ON the headlights, heater blower and, if equipped, the rear defroster of both vehicles in order to reduce the severity of voltage spikes

and subsequent risk of damage to the vehicles' electrical systems when the cables are disconnected. This step is especially important to any vehicle equipped with computer control modules.

14. Carefully disconnect the cables in the reverse order of connection. Start with the negative cable that is attached to the engine ground, then the negative cable on the donor battery. Disconnect the positive cable from the donor battery and finally, disconnect the positive cable from the formerly dead battery. Be careful when disconnecting the cables from the positive terminals not to allow the alligator clips to touch any metal on either vehicle or a short and sparks will occur.

TOWING THE VEHICLE

♦ **See Figures 210 and 211**

The absolute best way to have the car towed or transported is on a flatbed or rollback transporter. These units are becoming more common and are very useful for moving disabled vehicles quickly. Most vehicles have lower bodywork and undertrays which can be easily damaged by the sling of a conventional tow truck; an operator unfamiliar with your particular model can cause severe damage to the suspension or drive line by hooking up chains and J-hooks incorrectly.

If a flatbed is not available (you should specifically request one), the car may be towed by a hoist or conventional tow vehicle. Front wheel drive cars with automatic transaxle must be towed with the drive wheels off the ground. FWD cars with a manual transaxle can be towed with either end up in the air or with all four wheels on the ground. You need only remember that the transaxle must be in neutral, the parking brake must be off and the ignition switch must be in the **ACC** position. The steering column lock is not strong enough to hold the front wheels straight under towing.

The Corolla All-Trac vehicle presents its own towing problems. Since the front and rear wheels are connected through the drive system, all four wheels must be considered in the towing arrangement. If a flatbed is not available, the All-Trac should be towed with the front end elevated. As the

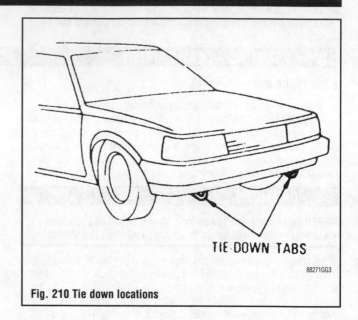

Fig. 210 Tie down locations

Type of Transaxle / Towing Method	Manual Transaxle			Automatic Transaxle			
	Parking Brake	T/M Shift Lever Position	Center Diff.	Parking Brake	T/M Shift Lever Position	Center Diff. Control Switch	Mode Select Lever on Transaxle
① Flat Bed Truck	Applied	1st Gear	Free or Lock (Center Differential Control Switch "ON" or "OFF")	Applied	"P" range	"AUTO" or "OFF"	Free (Normal Driving) No Special Operation Necessary
② Sling-Type Tow Truck with Dollies							
③ Sling-Type Two Truck (Front wheels must be able to rotate freely)	Released	Neutral	Free (Center Differential Control Switch "OFF")	Release	"N" range	"OFF"	↑
④ Towing with a Rope	Released	Neutral	Free (Center Differential Control Switch "OFF")	Released	"N" range	"OFF"	↑

NOTE: Do not tow the vehicle at a speed faster than 18 mph (30 km/h) or a distance greater than 50 miles (80 km).

PRECAUTIONS WHEN TOWING FULL-TIME 4WD VEHICLES

1. Use one of the methods shown below to tow the vehicle.

2. When there is trouble with the chassis and drivetrain, use method ① (flat bed truck) or method ② (sling type toe truck with dollies).

3. Recommended Methods: No. ①, ② or ③
   Emergency Method: No. ④

NOTE: Do not use any towing methods other than those shown above.
For example, the towing method shown below is dangerous, so do not use it.

During towing with this towing method, there is a danger of the drivetrain heating up and causing breakdown, or of the front wheels flying off the dolly.

Fig. 211 Towing procedures for 4WD models

rear wheels roll on the ground, the front wheels will turn. They must be clear of the hoist and sling equipment. If the vehicle cannot be towed front-end-up, both ends must be elevated, using a set of dolly wheels.

Most vehicles have conveniently located tie-down hooks at the front of the vehicle. These make ideal locations to secure a rope or chain for towing the car or extracting it from an off-road excursion. The vehicle may only be towed on hard surfaced roads and only in a normal or forward direction.

A driver must be in the towed vehicle to control it. Before towing, the parking brake must be released and the transaxle put in neutral. Do NOT flat tow the vehicle if the brakes, steering, axles, suspension or drive line is damaged. If the engine is not running, the power assists for the steering and brakes will not be operating. Steering and braking will require more time and much more effort without the assist.

JACKING

▶ See Figure 212

Your vehicle was supplied with a jack for emergency road repairs. This jack is fine for changing a flat tire or other short term procedures not requiring you to go beneath the vehicle. If it is used in an emergency situation, carefully follow the instructions provided either with the jack or in your owner's manual. Do not attempt to use the jack on any portions of the vehicle other than specified by the vehicle manufacturer. Always block the diagonally opposite wheel when using a jack.

A more convenient way of jacking is the use of a garage or floor jack. You may use the floor jack to raise the vehicle and place stands on the jacking points under the vehicle.

Never place the jack under the radiator, engine or transmission components. Severe and expensive damage will result when the jack is raised. Additionally, never jack under the floorpan or bodywork; the metal will deform.

Whenever you plan to work under the vehicle, you must support it on jackstands or ramps. Never use cinder blocks or stacks of wood to support the vehicle, even if you're only going to be under it for a few minutes. Never crawl under the vehicle when it is supported only by the tire-changing jack or other floor jack.

➡**Always position a block of wood or small rubber pad on top of the jack or jackstand to protect the lifting point's finish when lifting or supporting the vehicle.**

88271P32

Jacking point on the rear of the vehicle using a hydraulic jack

88271P34

Place the hydraulic jack under the crossmember raise the front of the vehicle

88271P33

Always use saftey stands to support the vehicle

88271P35

Place the saftey stands on both sides of the car

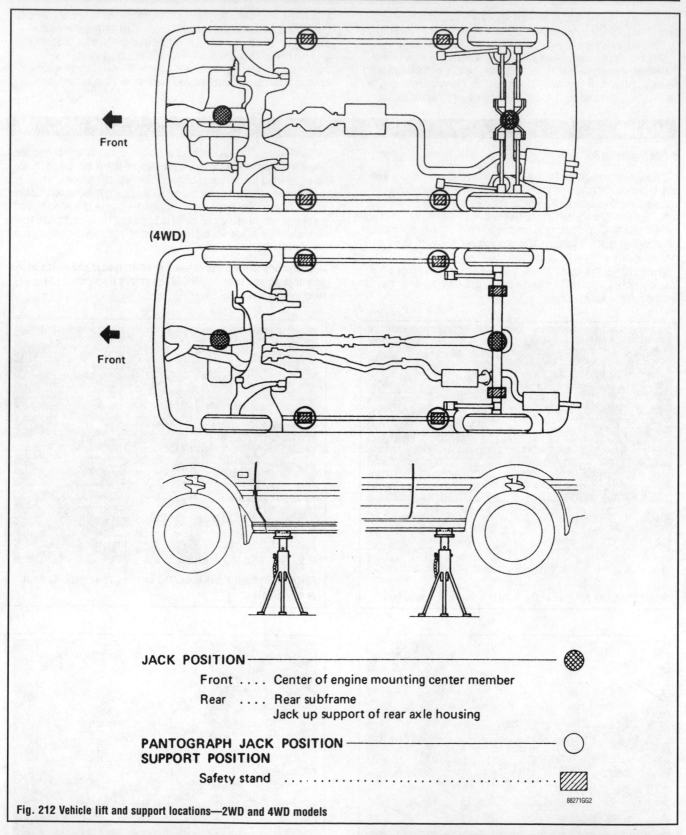

JACK POSITION
Front .... Center of engine mounting center member
Rear .... Rear subframe
Jack up support of rear axle housing

PANTOGRAPH JACK POSITION
SUPPORT POSITION
Safety stand ....

88271GG2

Fig. 212 Vehicle lift and support locations—2WD and 4WD models

Small hydraulic, screw, or scissors jacks are satisfactory for raising the vehicle. Drive-on trestles or ramps are also a handy and safe way to both raise and support the vehicle. Be careful though, some ramps may be too steep to drive your vehicle onto without scraping the front bottom panels. Never support the vehicle on any suspension member (unless specifically instructed to do so by a repair manual) or by an underbody panel.

Jacking Precautions

The following safety points cannot be overemphasized:
• Always block the opposite wheel or wheels to keep the vehicle from rolling off the jack.
• When raising the front of the vehicle, firmly apply the parking brake.

• When the drive wheels are to remain on the ground, leave the vehicle in gear to help prevent it from rolling.

• Always use jackstands to support the vehicle when you are working underneath. Place the stands beneath the vehicle's jacking brackets. Before climbing underneath, rock the vehicle a bit to make sure it is firmly supported.

(4A-F ENGINE) MAINTENANCE SCHEDULE

Maintenance operations: A = Check and adjust if necessary;
R = Replace, change or lubricate;
I = Inspect and correct or replace if necessary

NORMAL CONDITION SCHEDULE

System	Service interval (Odometer reading or months, whichever comes first) / Maintenance items	Maintenance services beyond 60,000 miles (96,000 km) should be performed at the same intervals shown in each maintenance schedule.					
	Miles x 1,000	10	20	30	40	50	60
	Km x 1,000	16	32	48	64	80	96
	Months	12	24	36	48	60	72
ENGINE	Valve clearance						A
	Drive belts(1)						I
	Engine oil and oil filter*	R	R	R	R	R	R
	Engine coolant(2)						R
	Exhaust pipes and mountings			I			I
FUEL	Idle speed and fast idle speed(3)			A			
	Throttle positioner system(3)			A			
	Air filter*			R			R
	Fuel lines and connections			I			I
	Fuel tank cap gasket						R
IGNITION	Spark plugs**			R			R
EVAP	Charcoal canister						I
BRAKES	Brake linings and drums		I		I		I
	Brake pads and discs		I		I		I
	Brake line pipes and hoses		I		I		I
CHASSIS	Steering linkage		I		I		I
	Drive shaft boots		I		I		I
	Ball joints and dust covers		I		I		I
	Automatic transaxle, manual transaxle, differential and steering gear housing oil		I		I		I
	Bolts and nuts on chassis and body		I		I		I

Maintenance services indicated by a start (★) or asterisk (*) are required under the terms of the Emission Control Systems Warranty. See Owner's Guide or Warranty Booklet for complete warranty information.

    ★ For vehicles sold in California

    * For vehicles sold outside California

NOTE:

(1)   After 60,000 miles (96,000 km) or 72 months, inspect every 10,000 miles (16,000 km) or 12 months.

(2)   After 60,000 miles (96,000 km) or 72 months, replace every 30,000 miles (48,000 km) or 36 months.

(3)   After 30,000 miles (48,000 km) or 36 months, adjustment is not necessary.

88271C15

(4A-F ENGINE) MAINTENANCE SCHEDULE

Maintenance operations: A = Check and adjust if necessary;
R = Replace, change or lubricate;
I = Inspect and correct or replace if necessary

Follow the severe condition schedule if vehicle is operated mainly under one or more of the following severe conditions.

- Towing a trailer, using a camper or car top carrier.
- Repeat short trips less than 5 miles (8 km) and outside temperatures remain below freezing.
- Extensive idling and/or low speed driving for a long distance such as police, taxi or door-to-door delivery use.
- Operating on dusty, rough, muddy or salt spread roads.

SEVERE CONDITION SCHEDULE

System	Service interval / Maintenance items	Miles x 1,000: 5	10	15	20	25	30	35	40	45	50	55	60
		Km x 1,000: 8	16	24	32	40	48	56	64	72	80	88	96
		Months: 6	12	18	24	30	36	42	48	54	60	66	72
ENGINE	Timing belt												R (1)
	Valve clearance						A						A
	Drive belts(2)						I						I
	Engine oil and oil filter*	R	R	R	R	R	R	R	R	R	R	R	R
	Engine coolant(3)												R
	Exhaust pipes and mountings		I				I			I			I
FUEL	Idle speed and fast idle speed(4)						A						
	Throttle positioner system(4)						A						
	Air filter*(5)	I	I	I	I	I	R	I	I	I	I	I	R
	Fuel lines and connections						I						I
	Fuel tank cap gasket												R
IGNITION	Spark plugs**						R						R
EVAP	Charcoal canister												I
BRAKES	Brake linings and drums		I		I		I		I		I		I
	Brake pads and discs		I		I		I		I		I		I
	Brake line pipes and hoses				I				I				I
CHASSIS	Steering linkage(6)		I		I		I		I		I		I
	Drive shaft boots		I		I		I		I		I		I
	Ball joints and dust covers		I		I		I		I		I		I
	Automatic transaxle, manual transaxle, differential and steering gear housing oil(7)				R				R				R
	Bolts and nuts on chassis and body(6)		I		I		I		I		I		I

Maintenance services beyond 60,000 miles (96,000 km) should be performed at the same intervals shown in each maintenance schedule.

Maintenance services indicated by a star (★) or asterisk (*) are required under the terms of the Emission Control Systems Warranty. See Owner's Guide or Warranty Booklet for complete warranty information.

   ★ For vehicles sold in California
   * For vehicles sold outside California

NOTE:
(1) For the vehicles frequently idled for extensive periods and/or driven for long distance at low speeds such as taxi, police and door-to-door delivery, it is recommended to change at 60,000 miles (96,000 km).
(2) After 60,000 miles (96,000 km) or 72 months, inspect every 10,000 miles (16,000 km) or 12 months.
(3) After 60,000 miles (96,000 km) or 72 months, replace every 30,000 miles (48,000 km) or 36 months.
(4) After 30,000 miles (48,000 km) or 36 months, adjustment is not necessary.
(5) Applicable when operating mainly on dusty roads. If not, follow the normal condition schedule.
(6) Applicable when operating mainly on rough and/or muddy roads. If not follow the normal condition schedule.
(7) For the steering gear housing, inspect for oil leakage only.

MAINTENANCE SCHEDULE—EXCEPT 4AF ENGINE

SCHEDULE A

CONDITIONS:
- Towing a trailer, using a camper or car top carrier.
- Repeated short trips less than 5 miles (8 km) and outside temperatures remain below freezing.
- Extensive idling and/or low speed driving for a long distance such as police, taxi or door-to-door delivery use.
- Operating on dusty, rough, muddy or salt spread roads.

Maintenance operation:
A = Check and adjust if necessary;
R = Replace, change or lubricate;
I = Inspect and correct or replace if necessary

Maintenance services beyond 60,000 miles (96,000 km) should continue to be performed at the same intervals shown for each maintenance schedule.

System	Maintenance items	3.75 / 6	7.5 / 12	11.25 / 18	15 / 24	18.75 / 30	22.5 / 36	26.25 / 42	30 / 48	33.75 / 54	37.5 / 60	41.25 / 66	45 / 72	48.75 / 78	52.5 / 84	56.25 / 90	60 / 96	Months
	(Miles ×1,000 / km ×1,000)																	—
ENGINE	Timing belt (1)																R	
	Valve clearance																A	A: Every 72 months
	Drive belt																I	I: First period, 60,000 miles (96,000 km) or 72 months. I: After that every 7,500 miles (12,000 km) or 12 months
	Engine oil and oil filter ★	R	R	R	R	R	R	R	R	R	R	R	R	R	R	R	R	R: Every 6 months
	Engine coolant												R					R: First period, 45,000 miles (72,000 km) or 36 months. R: After that every 30,000 miles (48,000 km) or 24 months
	Exhaust pipes and mountings				I				I				I				I	I: Every 24 months
FUEL	Idle speed		A				A				A				A			A: First period, 7,500 miles (12,000 km) or 12 months, second period 15,000 miles (24,000 km) or 24 months. A: After that every 15,000 miles (24,000 km) or 24 months
	Air filter (2) ★				I		R		I				R				I	I: Every 6 months; R: Every 36 months
	Fuel lines and connections (3)						I						I					I: Every 36 months
	Fuel tank cap gasket																R	R: Every 72 months
IGNITION	Spark plugs ★ *								R								R	R: Every 36 months
EVAP	Charcoal canister																I	I: Every 72 months
BRAKES	Brake lining and drums (4)		I		I		I		I		I		I		I		I	I: Every 12 months
	Brake pads and discs (Front and rear)		I		I		I		I		I		I		I		I	I: Every 12 months
	Brake line pipes and hoses				I				I				I				I	I: Every 24 months
CHASSIS	Steering linkage		I		I		I		I		I		I		I		I	I: Every 12 months
	Drive shaft boots		I		I		I		I		I		I		I		I	I: Every 12 months
	Ball joints and dust covers		I		I		I		I		I		I		I		I	I: Every 12 months
	Manual transaxle, automatic transaxle, transfer and differential				R				R				R				R	R: Every 24 months
	Steering gear housing oil (5)				I				I				I				I	I: Every 24 months
	Bolts and nuts on chassis and body (6)		I		I		I		I		I		I		I		I	I: Every 12 months

Maintenance services indicated by a star (★) or asterisk (*) are required under the terms of the Emission Control Systems Warranty. See Owner's Guide or Warranty Booklet for complete warranty information.

★ For vehicles sold in California
* For vehicles sold outside California

(1) Applicable to vehicles operated under coditions of extensive idling and/or low speed driving for long distances such as police, taxi or door-to-door delivery use.
(2) Applicable when operating mainly on dusty road. If not, apply SCHEDULE B.
(3) Includes inspection of fuel tank band and vapor vent system.
(4) Also applicable to lining drum for parking brake.
(5) Check for oil leaks from steering gear housing.
(6) Applicable only when operating mainly on rough, muddy roads. The applicable parts are listed below. For other usage conditions, refer to SCHEDULE B.
- Front and rear suspension member to body
- Strut bar bracket to body bolts
- Bolts for sheet installation

88271C17

MAINTENANCE SCHEDULE—EXCEPT 4AF ENGINE

SCHEDULE B

CONDITIONS: Conditions other than those listed for SCHEDULE A.

Maintenance services beyond 60,000 miles (96,000 km) should continue to be performed at the same intervals shown for each maintenance schedule.

System	Maintenance items	Miles × 1,000: 7.5 / km: 12	15 / 24	22.5 / 36	30 / 48	37.5 / 60	45 / 72	52.5 / 84	60 / 96	Months
ENGINE	Valve clearance								A	A: Every 72 months
	Drive belt									I: First period, 60,000 miles (96,000 km) or 72 months. I: After that every 7,500 miles (12,000 km) or 12 months.
	Engine oil and oil filter ★	R	R	R	R	R	R	R	R	R: Every 12 months
	Engine coolant									R: First period, 45,000 miles (72,000 km) or 36 months. R: After that every 30,000 miles (48,000 km) or 24 months.
	Exhaust pipes and mountings				I				I	I: Every 36 months
FUEL	Idle speed									A: First period. 7,500 miles (12,000 km) or 12 months, second period 15,000 miles (24,000 km) or 24 months A: After that every 15,000 miles (24,000 km) or 24 months
	Air filter ★				R				R	R: Every 36 months
	Fuel lines and connections (1)				I				R	I: Every 36 months
	Fuel tank cap gasket								R	R: Every 72 months
IGNITION	Spark plugs ★ *				R				R	R: Every 36 months
EVAP	Charcoal canister								I	I: Every 72 months
BRAKES	Brake lining and drums (2)		I		I		I		I	I: Every 24 months
	Brake pads and discs (Front and rear)		I		I		I		I	I: Every 24 months
	Brake line pipes and hoses		I		I		I		I	I: Every 24 months
CHASSIS	Steering linkage		I		I		I		I	I: Every 24 months
	Drive shaft boots		I		I		I		I	I: Every 24 months
	Ball joints and dust covers		I		I		I		I	I: Every 24 months
	Manual transaxle, automatic transaxle, transfer and differential(3)		I		I		I		I	I: Every 24 months
	Steering gear housing oil (4)		I		I		I		I	I: Every 24 months
	Bolts and nuts on chassis and body (5)		I		I		I		I	I: Every 24 months

Maintenance services indicated by a star (★) or asterisk (*) are required under the terms of the Emission Control Systems Warranty. See Owner's Guide or Warranty Booklet for complete warranty information.

★ For vehicles sold in California
* For vehicles sold outside California

(1) Includes inspection of fuel tank band and vapor vent system.
(2) Also applicable to lining drum for parking brake.
(3) Check for leakage
(4) Check for oil leaks from steering gear housing.
(5) The applicable parts are listed below.
- Front and rear suspension member to body
- Strut bar bracket to body bolt
- Bolts for sheet installation

8827TC18

CAPACITIES

| Year | Model | Engine ID/VIN | Engine Displacement Liters (cc) | Engine Oil with Filter | Transaxle (qts.) | | | Transfer Case (qts.) | Drive Axle | | Fuel Tank (gal.) | Cooling System (qts.) |
					4-Spd	5-Spd	Auto.		Front (qts.)	Rear (qts.)		
1988	Corolla	4A-F	1.6 (1587)	3.9	-	2.7	③	-	1.5	-	13.2	①
	Corolla	4A-FE	1.6 (1587)	3.4	-	④	③	0.8	1.5	1.2	13.2	②
	Corolla	4A-GE	1.6 (1587)	3.9	-	2.7	③	-	1.5	-	13.2	6.3
1989	Corolla	4A-F	1.6 (1587)	3.9	-	2.7	③	-	1.5	-	13.2	①
	Corolla	4A-FE	1.6 (1587)	3.4	-	④	③	0.8	1.5	1.2	13.2	②
	Corolla	4A-GE	1.6 (1587)	3.9	-	2.7	③	-	1.5	-	13.2	6.3
1990	Corolla	4A-FE	1.6 (1587)	3.4	-	④	③	0.8	1.5	1.2	13.2	②
	Corolla	4A-GE	1.6 (1587)	3.9	-	2.7	③	-	1.5	-	13.2	6.3
1991	Corolla	4A-FE	1.6 (1587)	3.4	-	④	③	0.8	1.5	1.2	13.2	②
	Corolla	4A-GE	1.6 (1587)	3.9	-	2.7	③	-	1.5	-	13.2	6.3
1992	Corolla	4A-FE	1.6 (1587)	3.4	-	④	⑤	0.8	1.5	1.2	13.2	②
1993	Corolla	4AF-E	1.6 (1587)	3.2	-	2.7	③	-	1.5	-	13.2	⑥
	Corolla	7A-FE	1.8 (1762)	3.9	-	2.7	③	-	1.5	-	13.2	⑦
1994	Corolla	4AF-E	1.6 (1587)	3.2	-	2.7	③	-	1.5	-	13.2	⑥
	Corolla	7A-FE	1.8 (1762)	3.9	-	2.7	③	-	1.5	-	13.2	⑦
1995	Corolla	4AF-E	1.6 (1587)	3.2	-	2.7	③	-	1.5	-	13.2	⑧
	Corolla	7A-FE	1.8 (1762)	3.9	-	2.7	③	-	1.5	-	13.2	⑨
1996	Corolla	4AF-E	1.6 (1587)	3.2	-	2.0	③	-	1.5	-	13.2	⑧
	Corolla	7A-FE	1.8 (1762)	3.9	-	2.0	③	-	1.5	-	13.2	⑨
1997	Corolla	4AF-E	1.6 (1587)	3.2	-	2.0	③	-	1.5	-	13.2	⑧
	Corolla	7A-FE	1.8 (1762)	3.9	-	2.0	③	-	1.5	-	13.2	⑨

① Manual transaxle: 5.9 qts.
3 speed Automatic transaxle: 5.8 qts.
4 Speed Automatic transaxle: 6.1 qts.

② 4WD manual: 6.6 qts.
4WD automatic: 6.4 qts.
Except 4WD manual:6.0 qts.
Except 4WD 3speed automatic: 5.8 qts.
Except 4WD 4speed automatic: 6.1 qts.

③ A131L: 2.6 qts.
A240L: 3.3 qts.
A241H: 3.3 qts.

④ Except 4WD: 2.7 qts.
4WD: 5.3 qts.

⑤ 4WD 4 speed: 3.3 qts.
4 speed: 3.3 qts.
3 speed: 2.6 qts.

⑥ Manual: 5.6 qts.
Automatic: 6.2 qts.

⑦ Manual: 5.8 qts.
Automatic: 6.6 qts.

⑧ Nippon Manual: 5.6 qts.
Automatic: 6.2 qts.

⑧ Harrison Manual: 6.3 qts.
Automatic: 6.2 qts.
Toyo Manual: 5.5 qts.

⑨ Nippon Manual: 5.8 qts.
Automatic: 6.6 qts.
Harrison Manual: 6.6 qts.
Automatic: 6.4 qts.

88271C19

ENGLISH TO METRIC CONVERSION: MASS (WEIGHT)

Current **mass** measurement is expressed in pounds and ounces (lbs. & ozs.). The metric unit of mass (or weight) is the kilogram (kg). Even although this table does not show conversion of masses (weights) larger than 15 lbs, it is easy to calculate larger units by following the data immediately below.

To convert ounces (oz.) to grams (g): multiply th number of ozs. by 28
To convert grams (g) to ounces (oz.): multiply the number of grams by .035

To convert pounds (lbs.) to kilograms (kg): multiply the number of lbs. by .45
To convert kilograms (kg) to pounds (lbs.): multiply the number of kilograms by 2.2

lbs	kg	lbs	kg	oz	kg	oz	kg
0.1	0.04	0.9	0.41	0.1	0.003	0.9	0.024
0.2	0.09	1	0.4	0.2	0.005	1	0.03
0.3	0.14	2	0.9	0.3	0.008	2	0.06
0.4	0.18	3	1.4	0.4	0.011	3	0.08
0.5	0.23	4	1.8	0.5	0.014	4	0.11
0.6	0.27	5	2.3	0.6	0.017	5	0.14
0.7	0.32	10	4.5	0.7	0.020	10	0.28
0.8	0.36	15	6.8	0.8	0.023	15	0.42

ENGLISH TO METRIC CONVERSION: TEMPERATURE

To convert Fahrenheit (°F) to Celsius (°C): take number of °F and subtract 32; multiply result by 5; divide result by 9

To convert Celsius (°C) to Fahrenheit (°F): take number of °C and multiply by 9; divide result by 5; add 32 to total

Fahrenheit (F)	Celsius (C)			Fahrenheit (F)	Celsius (C)			Fahrenheit (F)	Celsius (C)		
°F	°C	°C	°F	°F	°C	°C	°F	°F	°C	°C	°F
−40	−40	−38	−36.4	80	26.7	18	64.4	215	101.7	80	176
−35	−37.2	−36	−32.8	85	29.4	20	68	220	104.4	85	185
−30	−34.4	−34	−29.2	90	32.2	22	71.6	225	107.2	90	194
−25	−31.7	−32	−25.6	95	35.0	24	75.2	230	110.0	95	202
−20	−28.9	−30	−22	100	37.8	26	78.8	235	112.8	100	212
−15	−26.1	−28	−18.4	105	40.6	28	82.4	240	115.6	105	221
−10	−23.3	−26	−14.8	110	43.3	30	86	245	118.3	110	230
−5	−20.6	−24	−11.2	115	46.1	32	89.6	250	121.1	115	239
0	−17.8	−22	−7.6	120	48.9	34	93.2	255	123.9	120	248
1	−17.2	−20	−4	125	51.7	36	96.8	260	126.6	125	257
2	−16.7	−18	−0.4	130	54.4	38	100.4	265	129.4	130	266
3	−16.1	−16	3.2	135	57.2	40	104	270	132.2	135	275
4	−15.6	−14	6.8	140	60.0	42	107.6	275	135.0	140	284
5	−15.0	−12	10.4	145	62.8	44	112.2	280	137.8	145	293
10	−12.2	−10	14	150	65.6	46	114.8	285	140.6	150	302
15	−9.4	−8	17.6	155	68.3	48	118.4	290	143.3	155	311
20	−6.7	−6	21.2	160	71.1	50	122	295	146.1	160	320
25	−3.9	−4	24.8	165	73.9	52	125.6	300	148.9	165	329
30	−1.1	−2	28.4	170	76.7	54	129.2	305	151.7	170	338
35	1.7	0	32	175	79.4	56	132.8	310	154.4	175	347
40	4.4	2	35.6	180	82.2	58	136.4	315	157.2	180	356
45	7.2	4	39.2	185	85.0	60	140	320	160.0	185	365
50	10.0	6	42.8	190	87.8	62	143.6	325	162.8	190	374
55	12.8	8	46.4	195	90.6	64	147.2	330	165.6	195	383
60	15.6	10	50	200	93.3	66	150.8	335	168.3	200	392
65	18.3	12	53.6	205	96.1	68	154.4	340	171.1	205	401
70	21.1	14	57.2	210	98.9	70	158	345	173.9	210	410
75	23.9	16	60.8	212	100.0	75	167	350	176.7	215	414

TCCS1C01

ENGLISH TO METRIC CONVERSION: LENGTH

To convert inches (ins.) to millimeters (mm): multiply number of inches by 25.4

To convert millimeters (mm) to inches (ins.): multiply number of millimeters by .04

Inches		Decimals	Milli-meters	Inches to millimeters inches	mm	Inches		Decimals	Milli-meters	Inches to millimeters inches	mm
	1/64	0.051625	0.3969	0.0001	0.00254		33/64	0.515625	13.0969	0.6	15.24
1/32		0.03125	0.7937	0.0002	0.00508	17/32		0.53125	13.4937	0.7	17.78
	3/64	0.046875	1.1906	0.0003	0.00762		35/64	0.546875	13.8906	0.8	20.32
1/16		0.0625	1.5875	0.0004	0.01016	9/16		0.5625	14.2875	0.9	22.86
	5/64	0.078125	1.9844	0.0005	0.01270		37/64	0.578125	14.6844	1	25.4
3/32		0.09375	2.3812	0.0006	0.01524	19/32		0.59375	15.0812	2	50.8
	7/64	0.109375	2.7781	0.0007	0.01778		39/64	0.609375	15.4781	3	76.2
1/8		0.125	3.1750	0.0008	0.02032	5/8		0.625	15.8750	4	101.6
	9/64	0.140625	3.5719	0.0009	0.02286		41/64	0.640625	16.2719	5	127.0
5/32		0.15625	3.9687	0.001	0.0254	21/32		0.65625	16.6687	6	152.4
	11/64	0.171875	4.3656	0.002	0.0508		43/64	0.671875	17.0656	7	177.8
3/16		0.1875	4.7625	0.003	0.0762	11/16		0.6875	17.4625	8	203.2
	13/64	0.203125	5.1594	0.004	0.1016		45/64	0.703125	17.8594	9	228.6
7/32		0.21875	5.5562	0.005	0.1270	23/32		0.71875	18.2562	10	254.0
	15/64	0.234375	5.9531	0.006	0.1524		47/64	0.734375	18.6531	11	279.4
1/4		0.25	6.3500	0.007	0.1778	3/4		0.75	19.0500	12	304.8
	17/64	0.265625	6.7469	0.008	0.2032		49/64	0.765625	19.4469	13	330.2
9/32		0.28125	7.1437	0.009	0.2286	25/32		0.78125	19.8437	14	355.6
	19/64	0.296875	7.5406	0.01	0.254		51/64	0.796875	20.2406	15	381.0
5/16		0.3125	7.9375	0.02	0.508	13/16		0.8125	20.6375	16	406.4
	21/64	0.328125	8.3344	0.03	0.762		53/64	0.828125	21.0344	17	431.8
11/32		0.34375	8.7312	0.04	1.016	27/32		0.84375	21.4312	18	457.2
	23/64	0.359375	9.1281	0.05	1.270		55/64	0.859375	21.8281	19	482.6
3/8		0.375	9.5250	0.06	1.524	7/8		0.875	22.2250	20	508.0
	25/64	0.390625	9.9219	0.07	1.778		57/64	0.890625	22.6219	21	533.4
13/32		0.40625	10.3187	0.08	2.032	29/32		0.90625	23.0187	22	558.8
	27/64	0.421875	10.7156	0.09	2.286		59/64	0.921875	23.4156	23	584.2
7/16		0.4375	11.1125	0.1	2.54	15/16		0.9375	23.8125	24	609.6
	29/64	0.453125	11.5094	0.2	5.08		61/64	0.953125	24.2094	25	635.0
15/32		0.46875	11.9062	0.3	7.62	31/32		0.96875	24.6062	26	660.4
	31/64	0.484375	12.3031	0.4	10.16		63/64	0.984375	25.0031	27	690.6
1/2		0.5	12.7000	0.5	12.70						

ENGLISH TO METRIC CONVERSION: TORQUE

To convert foot-pounds (ft. lbs.) to Newton-meters: multiply the number of ft. lbs. by 1.3

To convert inch-pounds (in. lbs.) to Newton-meters: multiply the number of in. lbs. by .11

in lbs	N-m	in lbs	N-m	in lbs	N-m	in lbs	N-m	in lbs	N-m
0.1	0.01	1	0.11	10	1.13	19	2.15	28	3.16
0.2	0.02	2	0.23	11	1.24	20	2.26	29	3.28
0.3	0.03	3	0.34	12	1.36	21	2.37	30	3.39
0.4	0.04	4	0.45	13	1.47	22	2.49	31	3.50
0.5	0.06	5	0.56	14	1.58	23	2.60	32	3.62
0.6	0.07	6	0.68	15	1.70	24	2.71	33	3.73
0.7	0.08	7	0.78	16	1.81	25	2.82	34	3.84
0.8	0.09	8	0.90	17	1.92	26	2.94	35	3.95
0.9	0.10	9	1.02	18	2.03	27	3.05	36	4.0

TCCS1C02

ENGLISH TO METRIC CONVERSION: TORQUE

Torque is now expressed as either foot-pounds (ft./lbs.) or inch-pounds (in./lbs.). The metric measurement unit for torque is the Newton-meter (Nm). This unit—the Nm—will be used for all SI metric torque references, both the present ft./lbs. and in./lbs.

ft lbs	N-m	ft lbs	N-m	ft lbs	N-m	ft lbs	N-m
0.1	0.1	33	44.7	74	100.3	115	155.9
0.2	0.3	34	46.1	75	101.7	116	157.3
0.3	0.4	35	47.4	76	103.0	117	158.6
0.4	0.5	36	48.8	77	104.4	118	160.0
0.5	0.7	37	50.7	78	105.8	119	161.3
0.6	0.8	38	51.5	79	107.1	120	162.7
0.7	1.0	39	52.9	80	108.5	121	164.0
0.8	1.1	40	54.2	81	109.8	122	165.4
0.9	1.2	41	55.6	82	111.2	123	166.8
1	1.3	42	56.9	83	112.5	124	168.1
2	2.7	43	58.3	84	113.9	125	169.5
3	4.1	44	59.7	85	115.2	126	170.8
4	5.4	45	61.0	86	116.6	127	172.2
5	6.8	46	62.4	87	118.0	128	173.5
6	8.1	47	63.7	88	119.3	129	174.9
7	9.5	48	65.1	89	120.7	130	176.2
8	10.8	49	66.4	90	122.0	131	177.6
9	12.2	50	67.8	91	123.4	132	179.0
10	13.6	51	69.2	92	124.7	133	180.3
11	14.9	52	70.5	93	126.1	134	181.7
12	16.3	53	71.9	94	127.4	135	183.0
13	17.6	54	73.2	95	128.8	136	184.4
14	18.9	55	74.6	96	130.2	137	185.7
15	20.3	56	75.9	97	131.5	138	187.1
16	21.7	57	77.3	98	132.9	139	188.5
17	23.0	58	78.6	99	134.2	140	189.8
18	24.4	59	80.0	100	135.6	141	191.2
19	25.8	60	81.4	101	136.9	142	192.5
20	27.1	61	82.7	102	138.3	143	193.9
21	28.5	62	84.1	103	139.6	144	195.2
22	29.8	63	85.4	104	141.0	145	196.6
23	31.2	64	86.8	105	142.4	146	198.0
24	32.5	65	88.1	106	143.7	147	199.3
25	33.9	66	89.5	107	145.1	148	200.7
26	35.2	67	90.8	108	146.4	149	202.0
27	36.6	68	92.2	109	147.8	150	203.4
28	38.0	69	93.6	110	149.1	151	204.7
29	39.3	70	94.9	111	150.5	152	206.1
30	40.7	71	96.3	112	151.8	153	207.4
31	42.0	72	97.6	113	153.2	154	208.8
32	43.4	73	99.0	114	154.6	155	210.2

TCCS1C03

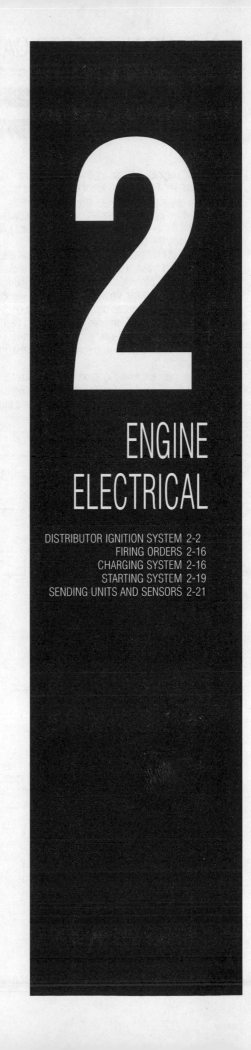

DISTRIBUTOR IGNITION SYSTEM

General Information

♦ **See Figure 1**

The 4A-GE engines are equipped with the Electronic Spark Advance (ESA) system. The Electronic Control Unit (ECU) is programmed with data for optimum ignition timing under any and all operating conditions. Using the data provided by the sensors which monitor the various engine functions (rpm, intake air volume, engine temperature ect.) the ECU triggers the spark at precisely the right instant.

The Integrated Ignition Assembly (IIA) is a typical electronic ignition system. There are two types of this system used on Corollas. On the 4A-F engines, the major components consist of an integral ignition coil, signal generator (pick-up), igniter, vacuum and governor weight advance system and a rotor and distributor cap distribution system.

On the 4A-FE and 7A-FE engines equipped with the IIA system the major components consist of an integral ignition coil, igniter, pick-up coils, condenser (on some models), IIA wire (on some models), rotor and distributor cap.

Service on these electronic ignition systems consists of inspection of the distributor cap, rotor and the ignition wires, replacing them as necessary. In addition, the air gap between the signal rotor and the projection on the pickup coil should be checked periodically.

PRECAUTIONS

• Do not leave the ignition switch on for more than 10 minutes if the engine will not start.

• With a tachometer connected to the system, connect the test probe of the tachometer to the positive terminal to: the service connector at the distributor.

• As some tachometers are not compatible with this ignition system, confirm the compatibility of your unit before using.

• Never allow the tachometer terminal to touch ground as this could damage the igniter and/or the ignition coil.

• Do not disconnect the battery when the engine is running.

• Check that the igniter is properly grounded to the body.

Diagnosis and Testing

If ignition problems or a no start condition are encountered, first perform an "On Vehicle Inspection Spark Test". Check that spark occurs, if no spark occurs, follow the correct diagnostic flow chart (engine and year) and necessary service procedures.

SPARK TEST

4A-F, 4A-FE and 7A-FE Engines

♦ **See Figures 2, 3, 4 and 5**

1. Tag and disconnect the spark plug wires from the spark plugs.
2. Remove the spark plugs and install the spark plug wires to each spark plug.
3. Ground (do not hold spark plug) the spark plug; check if spark occurs while engine is being cranked.

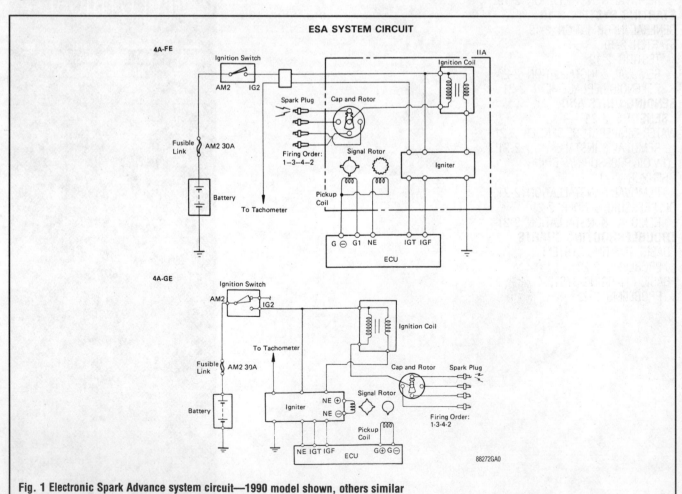

Fig. 1 Electronic Spark Advance system circuit—1990 model shown, others similar

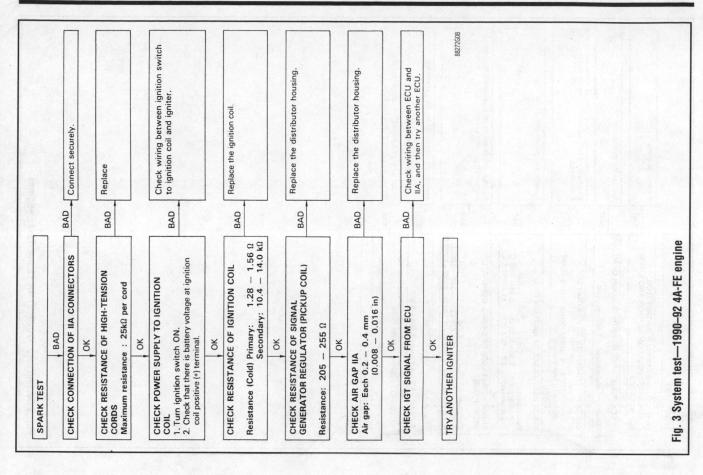

Fig. 3 System test—1990-92 4A-FE engine

88272G08

SPARK TEST		
↓ BAD		
CHECK CONNECTION OF IIA CONNECTORS	BAD →	Connect securely.
↓ OK		
CHECK RESISTANCE OF HIGH-TENSION CORDS Maximum resistance : 25kΩ per cord	BAD →	Replace
↓ OK		
CHECK POWER SUPPLY TO IGNITION COIL 1. Turn ignition switch ON. 2. Check that there is battery voltage at ignition coil positive (+) terminal.	BAD →	Check wiring between ignition switch to ignition coil and igniter.
↓ OK		
CHECK RESISTANCE OF IGNITION COIL Resistance (Cold) Primary: 1.28 — 1.56 Ω Secondary: 10.4 — 14.0 kΩ	BAD →	Replace the ignition coil.
↓ OK		
CHECK RESISTANCE OF SIGNAL GENERATOR REGULATOR (PICKUP COIL) Resistance: 205 — 255 Ω	BAD →	Replace the distributor housing.
↓ OK		
CHECK AIR GAP IIA Air gap: Each 0.2 — 0.4 mm (0.008 — 0.016 in)	BAD →	Replace the distributor housing.
↓ OK		
CHECK IGT SIGNAL FROM ECU	BAD →	Check wiring between ECU and IIA, and then try another ECU.
↓ OK		
TRY ANOTHER IGNITER		

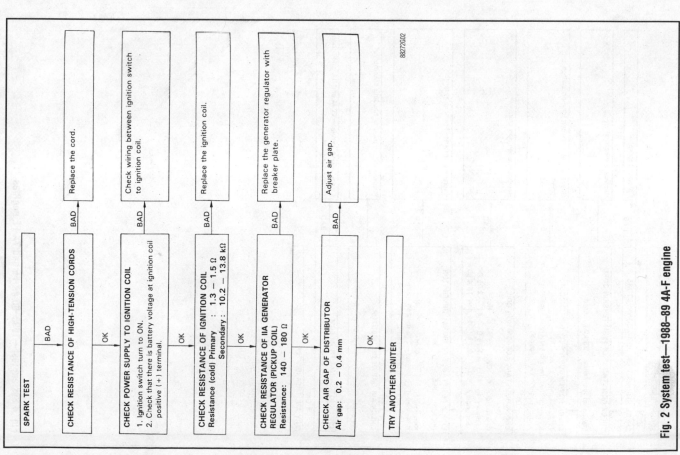

Fig. 2 System test—1988-89 4A-F engine

88272G02

SPARK TEST		
↓ BAD		
CHECK RESISTANCE OF HIGH-TENSION CORDS	BAD →	Replace the cord.
↓ OK		
CHECK POWER SUPPLY TO IGNITION COIL 1. Ignition switch turn to ON. 2. Check that there is battery voltage at ignition coil positive (+) terminal.	BAD →	Check wiring between ignition switch to ignition coil.
↓ OK		
CHECK RESISTANCE OF IGNITION COIL Resistance (cold) Primary : 1.3 — 1.5 Ω Secondary : 10.2 — 13.8 kΩ	BAD →	Replace the ignition coil.
↓ OK		
CHECK RESISTANCE OF IIA GENERATOR REGULATOR (PICKUP COIL) Resistance: 140 — 180 Ω	BAD →	Replace the generator regulator with breaker plate.
↓ OK		
CHECK AIR GAP OF DISTRIBUTOR Air gap: 0.2 — 0.4 mm	BAD →	Adjust air gap.
↓ OK		
TRY ANOTHER IGNITER		

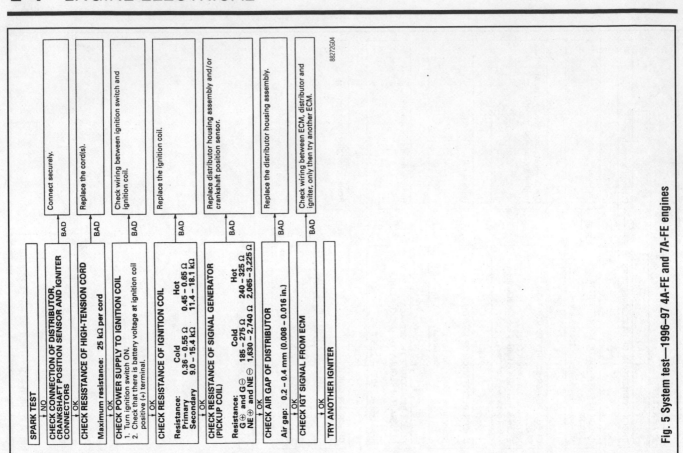

SPARK TEST →NO→ **CHECK CONNECTION OF DISTRIBUTOR, CRANKSHAFT POSITION SENSOR AND IGNITER CONNECTORS** —BAD→ Connect securely.

↓OK

CHECK RESISTANCE OF HIGH-TENSION CORD —BAD→ Replace the cord(s).

Maximum resistance: 25 kΩ per cord

↓OK

CHECK POWER SUPPLY TO IGNITION COIL
1. Turn ignition switch ON.
2. Check that there is battery voltage at ignition coil positive (+) terminal.
—BAD→ Check wiring between ignition switch and ignition coil.

↓OK

CHECK RESISTANCE OF IGNITION COIL —BAD→ Replace the ignition coil.

Resistance:	Cold	Hot
Primary	0.36 – 0.55 Ω	0.45 – 0.65 Ω
Secondary	9.0 – 15.4 kΩ	11.4 – 18.1 kΩ

↓OK

CHECK RESISTANCE OF SIGNAL GENERATOR (PICKUP COIL) —BAD→ Replace distributor housing assembly and/or crankshaft position sensor.

Resistance:	Cold	Hot
G ⊕ and G ⊖	185 – 275 Ω	240 – 325 Ω
NE ⊕ and NE ⊖	1,630 – 2,740 Ω	2,065 – 3,225 Ω

↓OK

CHECK AIR GAP OF DISTRIBUTOR —BAD→ Replace the distributor housing assembly.

Air gap: 0.2 – 0.4 mm (0.008 – 0.016 in.)

↓OK

CHECK IGT SIGNAL FROM ECM —BAD→ Check wiring between ECM, distributor and igniter, only then try another ECM.

↓OK

TRY ANOTHER IGNITER

88272604

Fig. 5 System test—1996–97 4A-FE and 7A-FE engines

SPARK TEST →NO→ **CHECK CONNECTION OF IIA CONNECTORS** —BAD→ Connect securely.

↓OK

CHECK RESISTANCE OF HIGH-TENSION CORD —BAD→ Replace the cord(s).

Maximum resistance: 25 kΩ per cord

↓OK

CHECK POWER SUPPLY TO IGNITION COIL
1. Turn ignition switch ON.
2. Check that there is battery voltage at ignition coil positive (+) terminal.
—BAD→ Check wiring between ignition switch and ignition coil.

↓OK

CHECK RESISTANCE OF IGNITION COIL —BAD→ Replace the ignition coil.

Resistance:	Cold	Hot
Primary	1.11 – 1.75 Ω	1.41 – 2.05 Ω
Secondary	9.0 – 15.7 kΩ	11.4 – 18.4 kΩ

↓OK

CHECK RESISTANCE OF SIGNAL GENERATOR (PICKUP COIL) —BAD→ Replace distributor housing assembly.

Resistance:	Cold	Hot
G ⊕ and G ⊖	185 – 275 Ω	240 – 325 Ω
NE ⊕ and NE ⊖	370 – 550 Ω	475 – 650 Ω

↓OK

CHECK AIR GAP OF DISTRIBUTOR —BAD→ Replace the distributor housing assembly.

Air gap: 0.2 – 0.4 mm (0.008 – 0.016 in.)

↓OK

CHECK IGT SIGNAL FROM ECM —BAD→ Check wiring between ECM and IIA, only then try another ECM.

↓OK

TRY ANOTHER IGNITER

88272603

Fig. 4 System test—1993–95 4A-FE and 7A-FE engines

➡ Crank the engine for no more than 2 seconds at a time to prevent flooding the engine with gasoline.

4. If good spark does not occur, follow the correct diagnostic flow chart (engine and year) and necessary service procedures.

4A-GE Engines

♦ See Figures 6 and 7

1. On 4A-GE engine disconnect the coil wire from distributor. Hold the coil wire end about ½ inch from a good body ground; check if spark occurs while engine is being cranked.

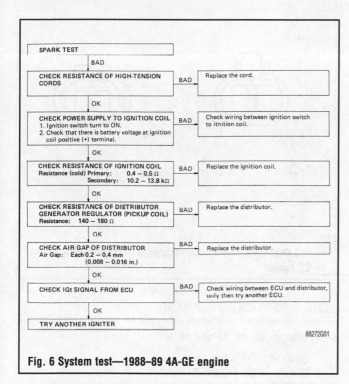

Fig. 6 System test—1988–89 4A-GE engine

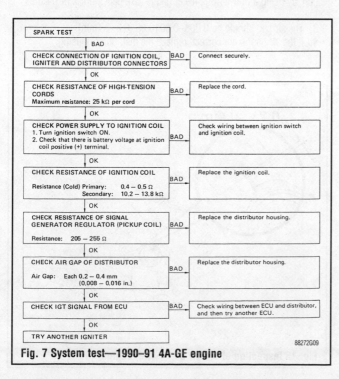

Fig. 7 System test—1990–91 4A-GE engine

➡ Crank the engine for no more than 2 seconds at a time to prevent flooding the engine with gasoline.

2. If good spark does not occur, follow the correct diagnostic flow chart (engine and year) and necessary service procedures.

SIGNAL GENERATOR (PICK-UP) RESISTANCE TEST

4A-F Engines

♦ See Figure 8

1. Using a suitable ohmmeter, check the resistance of the signal generator.
2. Pick up coil resistance should be 140–180 ohms.
3. If the resistance is not correct, replace the pick-up coil.

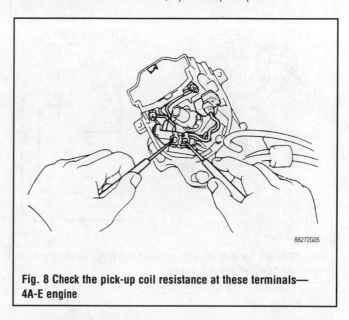

Fig. 8 Check the pick-up coil resistance at these terminals—4A-E engine

4A-FE and 7A-FE Engines

1988–92 MODELS

♦ See Figure 9

1. Using a suitable ohmmeter, check the resistance between terminals G1 and G- and NE and G- of the signal generator.

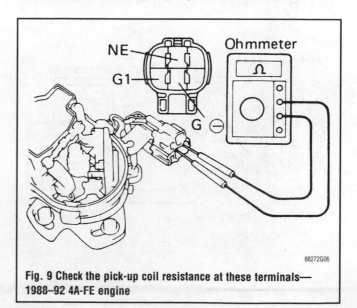

Fig. 9 Check the pick-up coil resistance at these terminals—1988–92 4A-FE engine

2. The signal generator (pick-up coil) resistance cold should be 205–255 ohms.

3. If the resistance is not correct, replace the distributor housing.

1993–95 MODELS

▶ See Figure 10

1. Using a suitable ohmmeter, check the resistance between terminals G+ and G– and NE+ and NE– of the signal generator.

2. The signal generator (pick-up coil) resistance cold should be 185–275 ohms on G+ and G–; and 370–550 ohms cold on NE+ and NE–. Check the chart for reference.

3. If the resistance is not correct, replace the distributor housing.

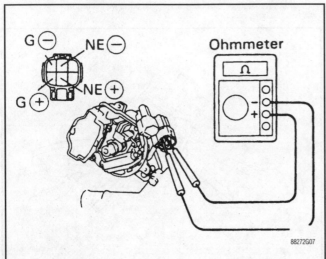

Fig. 10 Check the pick-up coil resistance at these terminals— 1993–95 4A-FE and 7A-FE engines

1996–97 MODELS

▶ See Figure 11

1. Using a suitable ohmmeter, check the resistance between terminals G+ and G– and NE+ and NE– of the signal generator.

2. The signal generator (pick-up coil) resistance cold should be 185–275 ohms on G+ and G–; and 1630–2740 ohms cold on NE+ and NE–. Check the chart for reference.

3. If the resistance is not correct, replace the distributor housing.

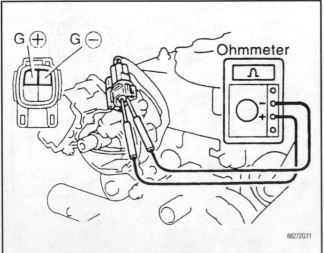

Fig. 11 Check the pick-up coil resistance at these terminals— 1996–97 4A-FE and 7A-FE engines

4A-GE Engine

▶ See Figure 12

1. Using a suitable ohmmeter, check the resistance of the two signal generators between terminals G+ and G– and NE+ and NE– of the signal generator.

2. The signal generators resistance should be 1988–89; 140–180 ohms. and on 1991 models; 205–255 ohms.

3. If the resistance is not correct, replace the distributor housing.

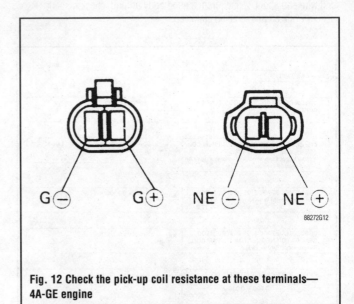

Fig. 12 Check the pick-up coil resistance at these terminals— 4A-GE engine

SIGNAL GENERATOR AIR GAP INSPECTION

▶ See Figures 13, 14, 15 and 16

1. Remove the distributor cap.

2. Measure the gap between the signal rotor and the pick-up coil projection, by using a non-ferrous feeler gauge (use paper, brass or plastic gauge).

3. The air gap should be 0.008–0.0016 in. (0.2–0.4mm).

4. If the air gap is not correct, replace the distributor housing.

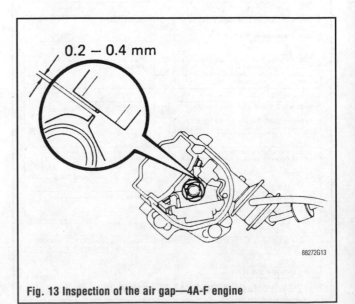

Fig. 13 Inspection of the air gap—4A-F engine

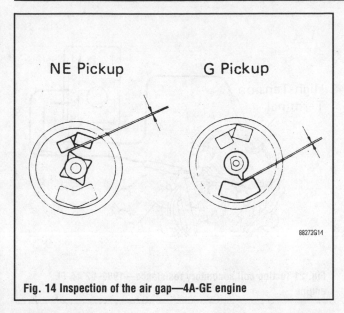

Fig. 14 Inspection of the air gap—4A-GE engine

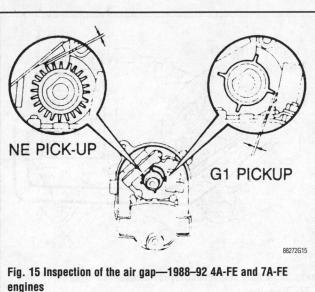

Fig. 15 Inspection of the air gap—1988–92 4A-FE and 7A-FE engines

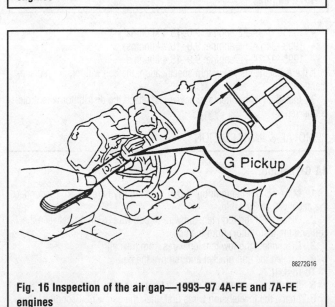

Fig. 16 Inspection of the air gap—1993–97 4A-FE and 7A-FE engines

Ignition Coil

TESTING

Primary Resistance

◆ See Figures 17, 18 and 19

➡This test requires the use of an ohmmeter. When using this tool, make sure the scale is set properly for the range of resistance you expect to encounter during the test. Always perform these tests with the ignition OFF.

1. Label and disconnect the spark plug wire leading to the ignition coil. On all models except the 4A-GE engine, remove the distributor cap, rotor and dust cover. If equipped, disconnect the distributor wiring.

2. Using an ohmmeter, check the resistance between the positive (+) and the negative (-) terminals on the coil. The resistance COLD should be:

- 1988–91 4A-GE engine: 0.4–0.5 ohms
- 1988–89 4A-F engine: 1.3–1.5 ohms
- 1988–92 4A-FE engine: 1.25–1.56 ohms
- 1992–95 4A-FE engine: 1.11–1.75 ohms

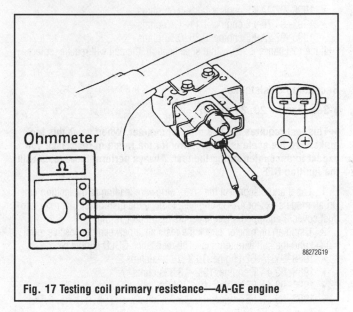

Fig. 17 Testing coil primary resistance—4A-GE engine

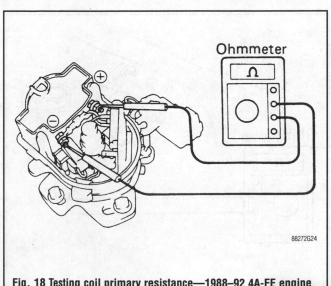

Fig. 18 Testing coil primary resistance—1988–92 4A-FE engine

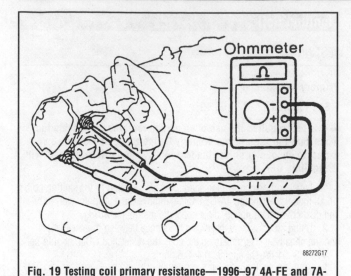

Fig. 19 Testing coil primary resistance—1996–97 4A-FE and 7A-FE engines

- 1996–97 4A-FE engine: 0.36–0.55 ohms
- 1993–94 7A-FE engine: 1.11–1.75 ohms
- 1995–97 7A-FE engine: 0.36–0.55 ohms

If the resistance is not within specification, the coil will require replacement.

Secondary Resistance

♦ See Figures 20, 21 and 22

➡This test requires the use of an ohmmeter. When using this tool, make sure the scale is set properly for the range of resistance you expect to encounter during the test. Always perform these tests with the ignition OFF.

1. Label and disconnect the spark plug wire leading to the ignition coil. On all models except 4A-GE engines, remove the distributor cap, rotor and dust cover. If equipped, disconnect the distributor wiring.

2. Using an ohmmeter, check the resistance between the positive terminal (+) and the coil wire terminal. The resistance COLD should be:
- 1988–91 4A-GE engine: 10.2–13.8 kilohms
- 1988–89 4A-F engine: 10.2–13.8 kilohms
- 1990–92 4A-FE engine: 10.4–14.0 kilohms
- 1992–95 4A-FE engine: 9.0–15.7 kilohms

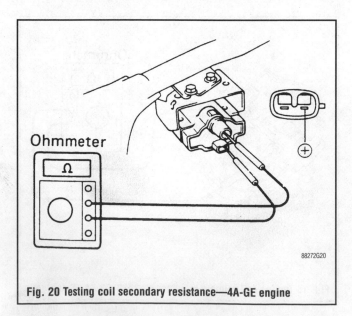

Fig. 20 Testing coil secondary resistance—4A-GE engine

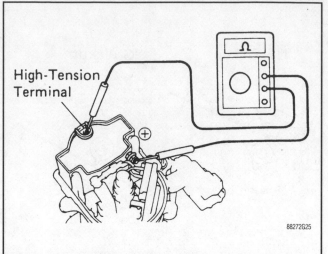

Fig. 21 Testing coil secondary resistance—1988–92 4A-FE engine

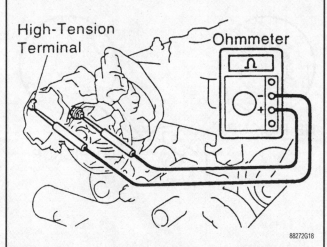

Fig. 22 Testing coil secondary resistance—1996–97 4A-FE and 7A-FE engines

- 1995–97 4A-FE engine: 9.0–15.4 kilohms
- 1993–94 7A-FE engine: 9.0–15.7 kilohms
- 1995–97 7A-FE engine: 9.0–15.4 kilohms

If the resistance is not within specification, the coil will require replacement.

3. Install all components removed and attach the distributor wire if disconnected.

REMOVAL & INSTALLATION

4A-GE Engine

1. Make certain the ignition is **OFF** and the key is removed. Disconnect the negative battery cable.

2. Disconnect the high tension wire or coil wire (running between the coil and the distributor) from the coil.

3. Disconnect the low tension wires from the coil.

4. Loosen the coil bracket and remove the coil.

To install:

5. Install the new coil and securely tighten the bracket.

6. Attach the low tension wires first, then the coil wire. Reconnect the battery cable.

7. Reset any various digital equipment such as radio memory and the clock if necessary.

Except 4A-GE Engine

◆ **See Figures 23 thru 34**

The internal coil found within the distributor on the 4A-F, 4A-FE and 7A-FE engines can be changed without removing the distributor (a selection of various short screwdrivers may be required for access to the screws) but it is recommended to remove the distributor and then replace the coil assembly.

1. Disconnect the negative battery cable.
2. Disconnect the distributor wiring.
3. Disconnect the vacuum advance hoses (if equipped).
4. Label and disconnect the plug wires from the distributor.
5. Remove the hold-down bolts and pull out the distributor.
6. Remove the distributor rotor with O-ring. Discard the O-ring.
7. Remove the dust cover over the distributor components and remove the dust cover over the ignition coil.

➡**Note position and routing of all internal distributor assembly wiring.**

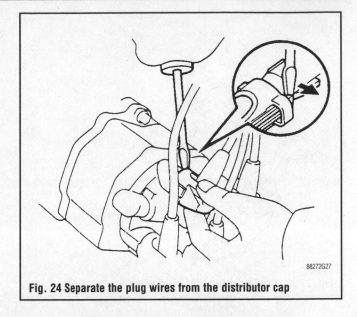
Fig. 24 Separate the plug wires from the distributor cap

The ignition coil is located inside the distributor cap dust cover

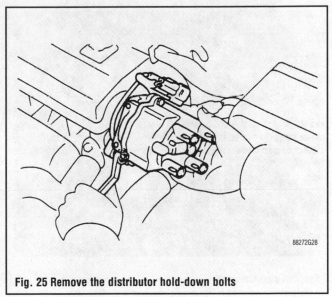
Fig. 25 Remove the distributor hold-down bolts

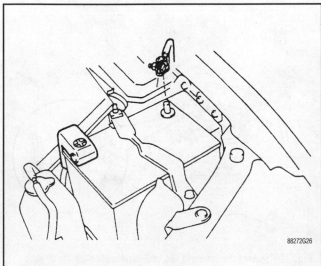
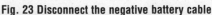
Fig. 23 Disconnect the negative battery cable

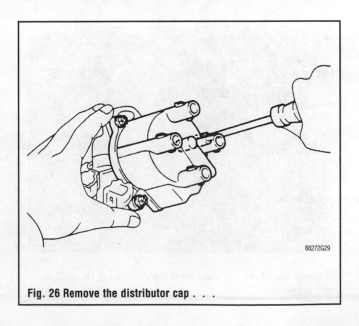
Fig. 26 Remove the distributor cap . . .

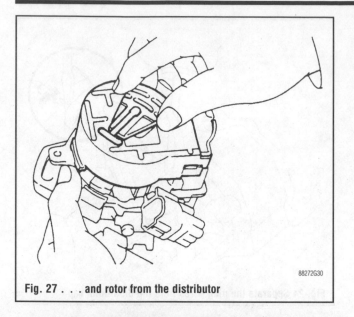

Fig. 27 . . . and rotor from the distributor

88272G30

Remove the 4 screws retaining the coil to the distributor

88272P11

Pull the dust cover off

88272P09

Remove the ignition coil from the distributor housing

88272P12

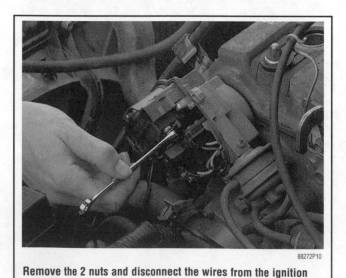

Remove the 2 nuts and disconnect the wires from the ignition coil terminals

88272P10

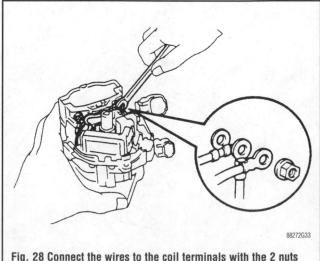

Fig. 28 Connect the wires to the coil terminals with the 2 nuts as shown

88272G33

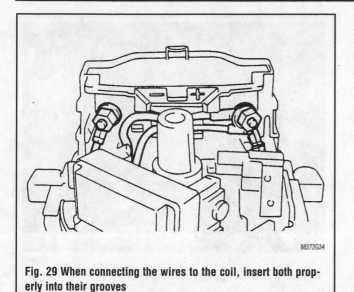

Fig. 29 When connecting the wires to the coil, insert both properly into their grooves

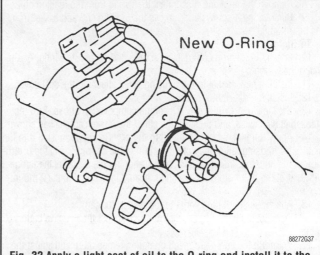

Fig. 32 Apply a light coat of oil to the O-ring and install it to the end of the distributor assembly

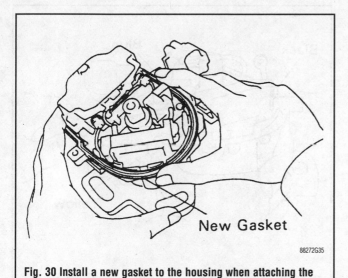

Fig. 30 Install a new gasket to the housing when attaching the duct cover

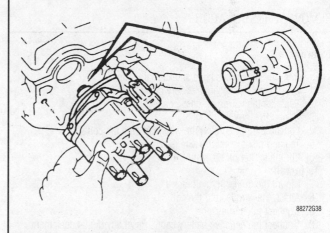

Fig. 33 Insert the distributor, aligning the center of the flange with the bolt hole on the cylinder head

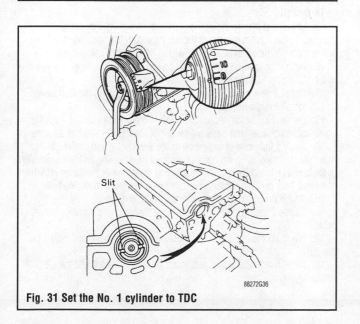

Fig. 31 Set the No. 1 cylinder to TDC

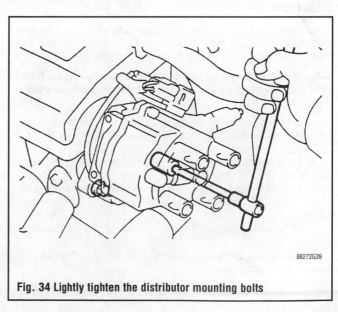

Fig. 34 Lightly tighten the distributor mounting bolts

8. Remove the nuts and disconnect the wiring from the ignition coil.

9. Remove the 4 screws and remove the ignition coil and gasket from the distributor.

To install:

10. Install the ignition coil, gasket, screws and secure its wiring. Again, watch the wiring positions.

11. Install a new gasket to the housing when attaching the dust cover.

12. Install the distributor rotor.

13. Set the No. 1 cylinder to TDC of the compression stroke. Turn the crankshaft clockwise, and position the slit of the intake camshaft as shown.

14. Apply a light coat of engine oil to the new O-ring and install it to the distributor housing. align the cutout portion of the coupling with the protrusion of the housing. Insert the distributor, aligning the center of the flange with that of the bolt hole on the cylinder head. Lightly tighten the 2 mounting bolts.

15. Attach the spark plug wires to the distributor cap.

16. Connect the wiring to the distributor. Connect the negative battery cable.

17. Warm up the engine to reach operating temperature and adjust the timing.

18. Reset any digital equipment such as radio memory and the clock if necessary.

Igniter (Ignition Module)

REMOVAL & INSTALLATION

External

Only the 4A-GE engines have an external igniter.

1. Disconnect the negative battery cable.
2. Separate the wiring harness connections.
3. Unbolt the igniter.
4. Loosen the nut holding the wire lead onto the coil.
5. Tag and disconnect the wire lead.
6. Lift the igniter off its mount.

To install:

7. Mount the igniter to the bracket.
8. Attach the wire lead to the coil.
9. Connect the harness.
10. Connect the negative battery cable. Reset any digital equipment such as radio memory and the clock if necessary.

Internal

▶ **See Figure 35**

The igniter is not applicable to all Corolla models. All 4A-F engines have an ignitor inside the distributor assembly. The 4A-FE engines also have an internal igniter from 1988–1995 as do the 7A-FE engines from 1993 to 1994.

➡**Review the complete service procedure before this repair. Note position, color of wire and routing of all internal distributor assembly wiring.**

1. Disconnect the negative battery cable.
2. Remove the distributor as outlined.
3. Remove the distributor rotor.
4. Remove the dust cover over the distributor components and remove the dust cover over the ignition coil.
5. Remove the nuts and disconnect the wiring from the ignition coil.
6. Remove the screws retaining the ignition coil and gasket from the distributor.
7. At the igniter terminals, disconnect the wiring from the attaching points.
8. Loosen and remove the two screws holding the igniter, then pull it from the distributor.

Remove the two screws retaining the igniter inside the distributor

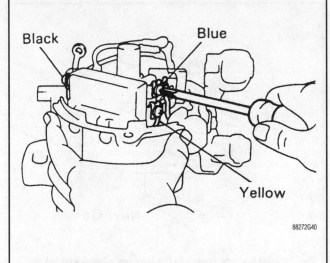

Fig. 35 Be sure to attach the proper wires to the terminals

To install:

9. Install and secure the igniter, connect its wiring. Pay particular attention to the correct routing of the wiring within the housing. There is one correct position only; any other wiring placements risk damage.

10. Install the ignition coil, gasket, screws and secure its wiring. Again, watch the wiring positions.

11. Install a new gasket to the housing when attaching the dust cover.

12. Install the distributor rotor.

13. Set the No. 1 cylinder to TDC of the compression stroke. Turn the crankshaft clockwise, and position the slit of the intake camshaft as shown.

14. Apply a light coat of engine oil to the new O-ring and install it to the distributor housing. align the cutout portion of the coupling with the protrusion of the housing. Insert the distributor, aligning the center of the flange with that of the bolt hole on the cylinder head. Lightly tighten the 2 mounting bolts.

15. Attach the spark plug wires to the distributor cap.

16. Connect the wiring to the distributor. Connect the negative battery cable.

17. Warm up the engine to reach operating temperature and adjust the timing.

18. Reset any digital equipment such as radio memory and the clock if necessary.

Distributor

REMOVAL

♦ See Figures 36, 37, 38, 39 and 40

➡Once the distributor is removed, the engine should NOT be turned or moved out of position. Should this occur, please refer to the engine rotated installation procedure.

1. Disconnect the negative battery cable.
2. Disconnect the distributor wire(s) at its harness.
3. On the 4A-F engines, disconnect the vacuum advance hoses.

➡**On some models the distributor wires are part of the cap and can not be separated.**

4. Remove the distributor cap. Label and disconnect the wires from the cap. On some engines it will be necessary to use a flat bladed tool to lift up the lock claw and disconnect the holder from the cap.

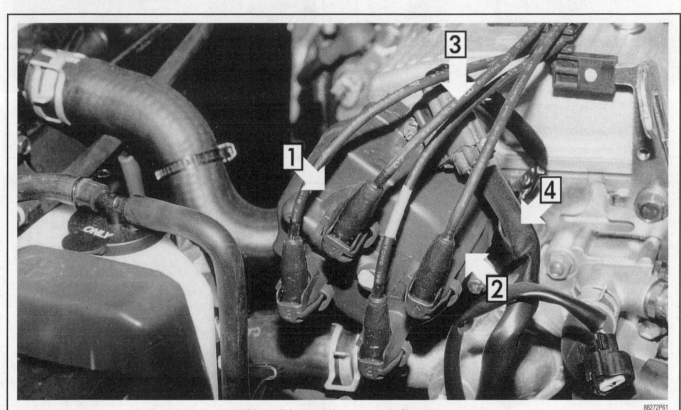

1. Internal ignition coil (under cap)
2. Distributor cap
3. Plug wires
4. Distributor wiring harness

Distributor components—4A-F engine

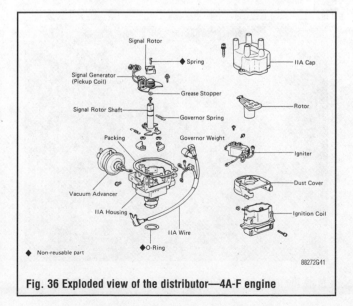

Fig. 36 Exploded view of the distributor—4A-F engine

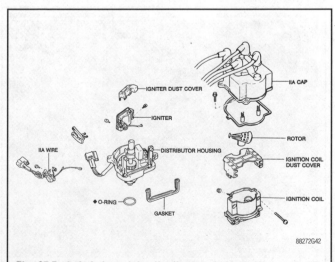

Fig. 37 Exploded view of the distributor—1993 4A-FE and 7A-FE engines

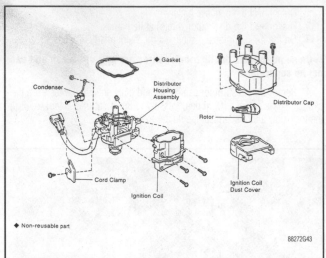

Fig. 38 Exploded view of the distributor—1996–97 4A-FE and 7A-FE engines

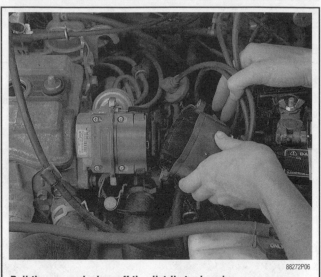

Pull the cap and wires off the distributor housing

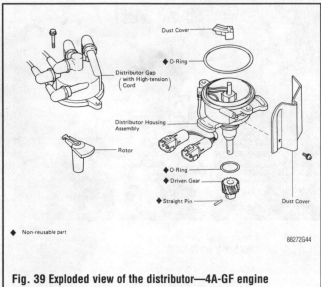

Fig. 39 Exploded view of the distributor—4A-GF engine

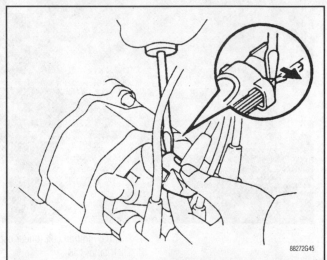

Fig. 40 On some engines, use a flat bladed tool to lift up the lock claw to disconnect the holder from the distributor cap

Loosen the screws holding the cap onto the housing

Mark the position of the rotor relative to the distributor housing

Label and remove all vacuum hoses attached to the advance on the distributor if equipped

If necessary, remove the rotor

Remove the distributor hold-down bolts before pulling the unit from the engine

Pull the distributor straight out from the engine

5. Carefully note the position of the distributor rotor relative to the distributor housing (also note position of distributor to the engine assembly); a mark made on the casing/housing will be necessary for reassembly. Use a marker or tape so the mark doesn't rub off during handling of the case/housing.

6. Remove the distributor hold-down bolts.

7. Carefully pull the distributor from the engine assembly. Remove the O-ring from the distributor shaft.

INSTALLATION

Engine Not Rotated

1. Install a new O-ring with lightly coated engine oil onto the distributor shaft.

2. If the engine has not been moved out of position, align the rotor with the mark you made earlier and reinstall the distributor, aligning the mark made for distributor housing to engine assembly. Position it carefully and make sure the drive gear engages properly within the engine.

3. Install the hold-down bolts.

4. Install the distributor cap.

5. Install the wiring to the distributor. On the 4A-F engine, attach the vacuum hoses.

6. Connect the negative battery cable.

7. Warm up the engine to reach operating temperature and adjust the timing.

Engine Rotated

If the engine has been cranked, dismantled or the timing otherwise lost while the distributor was out, proceed as follows:

1. Remove the No.1 spark plug.

2. Place your finger over the spark plug hole and rotate the crankshaft clockwise to TDC (Top Dead Center). Watch the timing marks on the pulley; as they approach the ZERO point, you should feel pressure (compression) on your finger. If not, turn the crankshaft another full rotation and line up the timing marks.

➡The spark plugs are in deep wells; use a screwdriver or equivalent to fill the hole and feel the compression.

3. Temporarily install the rotor in the distributor without the dust cover, if equipped. Turn the distributor shaft so that the rotor is pointing toward the No. 1 terminal in the distributor cap. On the 4A-GE engine, align the drilled mark on the driven gear with the groove of the housing. On the 4A-F, 4A-FE and 7A-FE engines, align the cutout of the coupling with the line of the housing.

4. Align the matchmarks on the distributor body and the engine block which were made during removal. Install the distributor in the block by rotating it slightly (no more than one gear tooth in either direction) until the driven gear (lubricate drive gear with clean engine oil) meshes with the drive.

5. Temporarily tighten the distributor hold-down bolts.

6. Remove the rotor and install the dust cover, if equipped. Replace the rotor and the distributor cap.

7. Reconnect all electrical wiring and vacuum hoses if equipped. Install the No. 1 spark plug and all plug wires if necessary.

8. Warm the engine and check ignition timing. Tighten the distributor hold-down bolts.

FIRING ORDERS

▶ **See Figures 41 and 42**

➡**To avoid confusion, remove and tag the spark plug wires one at a time, for replacement.**

If a distributor is not keyed for installation with only one orientation, it could have been removed previously and rewired. The resultant wiring would hold the correct firing order, but could change the relative placement of the plug towers in relation to the engine. For this reason it is imperative that you label all wires before disconnecting any of them. Also, before removal, compare the current wiring with the accompanying illustrations. If the current wiring does not match, make notes in your book to reflect how your engine is wired.

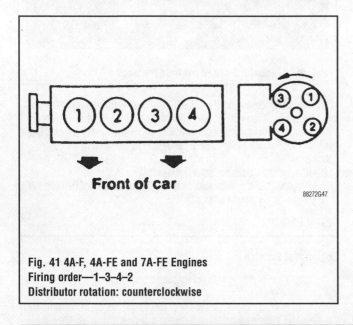

Fig. 41 4A-F, 4A-FE and 7A-FE Engines
Firing order—1–3–4–2
Distributor rotation: counterclockwise

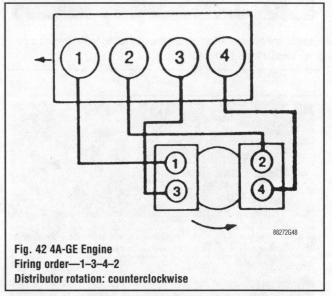

Fig. 42 4A-GE Engine
Firing order—1–3–4–2
Distributor rotation: counterclockwise

CHARGING SYSTEM

General Information

The automobile charging system provides electrical power for operation of the vehicle's ignition and all the electrical accessories. The battery serves as an electrical surge or storage tank, storing (in chemical form) the energy originally produced by the engine-driven alternator. The system also provides a means of regulating alternator output to protect the battery from being overcharged and to avoid excessive voltage to the accessories.

The vehicle's alternator is driven mechanically, through belts, by the engine crankshaft. It consists of two coils of fine wire, one stationary (the stator), and one movable (the rotor). The rotor may also be known as the armature, and consists of fine wire wrapped around an iron core which is mounted on a shaft. The electricity which flows through the two coils of wire (provided initially be the battery in some cases) creates an intense magnetic field around both the rotor and stator, and the interaction between the two fields creates voltage, allowing the alternator to power the accessories and charge the battery.

Almost all vehicles today use alternators because they are more efficient, can be rotated at higher speeds, and have fewer brush problems. In an alternator, the field rotates while all the current produced passes only through the stator windings. The brushes bear against continuous slip rings rather than a commutator. This causes the current produced to periodically reverse the direction of its flow, very similar to the power supply to your house. Diodes (electrical one-way switches) block the flow of current from traveling in the wrong direction. A series of diodes is wired together to permit the alternating flow of the stator to be converted to a pulsating, but unidirectional flow at the alternator output. This inverter circuit switches the AC current unusable by the vehicle to the standard DC or direct current. The alternator's field is wired in series with the voltage regulator.

The voltage regulator is contained within the alternator. Simply described, it consists of solid-state components whose job it is to limit the output of the alternator to usable levels. Excess output can damage the battery and overvoltage can destroy electrical components.

Alternator Precautions

Several precautions must be observed with alternator equipped vehicles to avoid damaging the unit. They are as follows:

1. If the battery is removed or disconnected for any reason, make sure that it is reconnected with the correct polarity. Reversing the battery connections may result in damage to the one-way rectifiers.

2. When utilizing a booster battery as a starting aid, always connect it as follows: positive to positive, and negative (booster battery) to a good ground on the engine of the car being started.

3. Never use a fast charger as a booster to start a car with an alternator.

4. When servicing the battery with a fast charger, always disconnect the car battery cables.

5. Never attempt to polarize an alternator.

6. Never apply more than 12 volts when attempting to jump start the vehicle.

7. Do not short across or ground any of the terminals on the alternator.

8. Never disconnect the alternator or the battery with the engine running.

9. Always disconnect the battery terminals when performing any service on the electrical system.

10. Disconnect the battery ground cable if arc welding (such as body repair) is to be done on any part of the car.

Noise from an alternator may be caused by a loose drive pulley, a loose belt, loose mounting bolts, worn or dirty bearings or worn internal parts. A high frequency whine that is heard at high engine speed or full alternator output is acceptable and should not be considered a sign of alternator failure.

Alternator

TESTING

1. Make sure the battery terminals are not loose or corroded. Check the fusible link for continuity.

2. Inspect the drive belt for excessive wear. Check the drive belt tension. If necessary adjust the drive belt.

3. Check the following fuses for continuity: ENGINE, CHARGE, IGN fuses.

4. Visually check alternator wiring and listen for abnormal noises.

5. Check that the discharge warning light comes ON when the ignition switch is turned **ON**. Start the engine. Check that the warning light goes out.

6. Check the charging circuit WITHOUT A LOAD. Connect a battery/alternator tester according to the manufacturer's instructions.

7. Check the charging circuit WITH A LOAD (turn on high beams and heater fan). Connect a battery/alternator tester according to the manufacturer's instructions.

8. Replace the necessary parts. Recheck the charging system. The standard amperage with a load on the system should be 30 amps. If a battery is fully charged, sometimes the indication will be less than 30 amps.

REMOVAL & INSTALLATION

▶ **See Figures 43 thru 48**

➡Toyota installs different types of alternators on the Corolla models. One is the Delco and the other is Nippondenso. The Delco models are not to be disassembled. The Nippondenso models are built slightly different depending on the plant your vehicle was produced at; US or Canada. Find out which type your vehicle has before proceeding with disassembly.

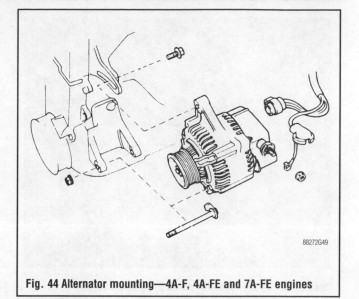
Fig. 44 Alternator mounting—4A-F, 4A-FE and 7A-FE engines

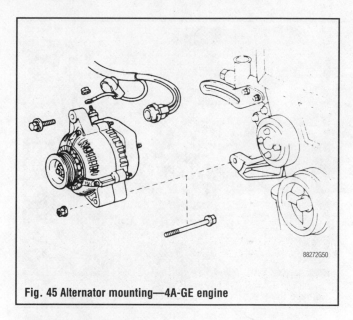
Fig. 45 Alternator mounting—4A-GE engine

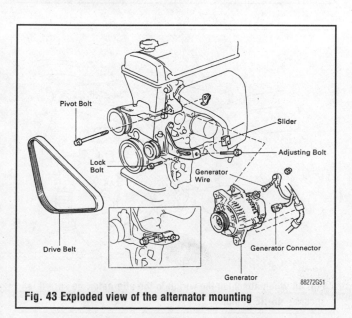
Fig. 43 Exploded view of the alternator mounting

Loosen the pivot and adjusting bolts

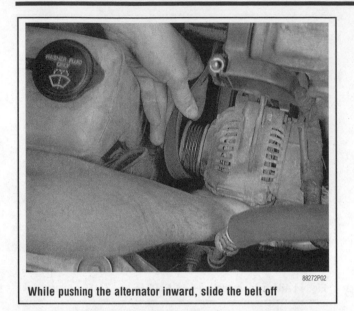

While pushing the alternator inward, slide the belt off

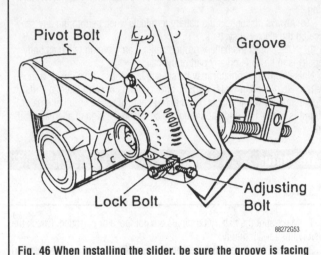

Fig. 46 When installing the slider, be sure the groove is facing in the direction shown

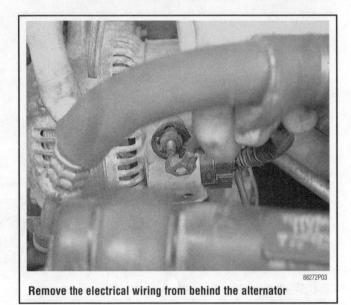

Remove the electrical wiring from behind the alternator

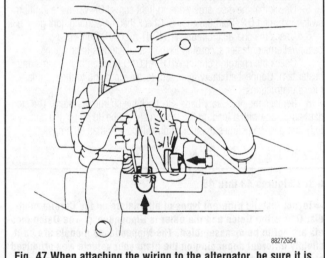

Fig. 47 When attaching the wiring to the alternator, be sure it is secure—except 4A-GE engine

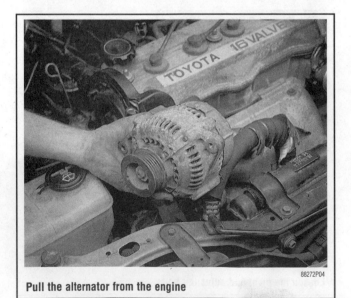

Pull the alternator from the engine

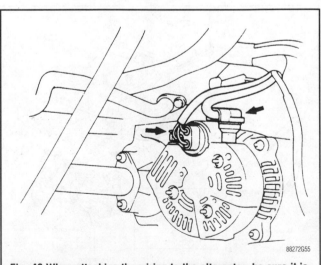

Fig. 48 When attaching the wiring to the alternator, be sure it is secure—4A-GE engine

1. Disconnect the negative battery cable.

➡**Failure to disconnect the battery can cause personal injury and damage to the car. If a tool is accidentally shorted at the alternator, it can become hot enough to cause a serious burn. It may be necessary to remove the gravel shield and work from underneath the car in order to gain access to the alternator retaining bolts.**

2. Disconnect the electrical wiring from the alternator.
3. Loosen the adjusting lock bolt (lower bolt) and pivot (upper) bolt. Remove the drive belt. It may be necessary to remove other belts for access.
4. Remove the lower bolt first, support the alternator and remove the upper pivot bolt. Remove the alternator from the car.
5. Installation is the reverse of the removal procedure. When reinstalling, remember to leave the bolts finger tight so that the belt may be adjusted to the correct tension.

➡**When installing the slider, be sure the groove is facing in the direction shown.**

STARTING SYSTEM

General Information

The battery is the first link in the chain of mechanisms which work together to provide cranking of the automobile engine. In most modern cars, the battery is a lead/acid electrochemical device consisting of six 2 volt subsections (cells) connected in series so the unit is capable of producing approximately 12 volts of electrical power. Each subsection consists of a series of positive and negative plates held a short distance apart in a solution of sulfuric acid and water.

The two types of plates are of dissimilar metals. This causes a chemical reaction to be set up, and it is this reaction which produces current flow from the battery when its positive and negative terminals are connected to an electrical appliance such as a lamp or motor. The continued transfer of electrons would eventually convert the sulfuric acid to water, and make the two plates identical in chemical composition. As electrical energy is removed from the battery, its voltage output tends to drop. Thus, measuring battery voltage and battery electrolyte composition are two ways of checking the ability of the unit to supply power. During the starting of the engine, electrical energy is removed from the battery. However, if the charging circuit is in good condition and the operating conditions are normal, the power removed from the battery will be replaced by the generator (or alternator) which will force electrons back through the battery, reversing the normal flow, and restoring the battery to its original chemical state.

The battery and starting motor are linked by very heavy electrical cables designed to minimize resistance to the flow of current. Generally, the major power supply cable that leaves the battery goes directly to the starter, while other electrical system needs are supplied by a smaller cable. During starter operation, power flows from the battery to the starter and is grounded through the car's frame and the battery's negative ground strap.

The starting motor is a specially designed, direct current electric motor capable of producing a very great amount of power for its size. One thing that allows the motor to produce a great deal of power is its tremendous rotating speed. It drives the engine through a tiny pinion gear (attached to the starter's armature), which drives the very large flywheel ring gear at a greatly reduced speed. Another factor allowing it to produce so much power is that only intermittent operation is required of it. Thus, little allowance for air circulation is required, and the windings can be built into a very small space.

The starter solenoid is a magnetic device which employs the small current supplied by the start circuit of the ignition switch. This magnetic action moves a plunger which mechanically engages the starter and closes the heavy switch connecting it to the battery. The starting switch circuit con-

6. Make sure that the electrical plugs and connectors are properly seated and secure in their mounts. Adjust belt tension and tighten all necessary hardware. Tighten the pivot bolt to 45 ft. lbs. (61 Nm) and the lock bolt to 14 ft. lbs. (19 Nm).
7. Reconnect the negative battery cable.
8. Reset any digital equipment such as radio memory and the clock if necessary.

Regulator

REMOVAL & INSTALLATION

The voltage regulator is contained within the alternator. It is an Integrated Circuit (IC) type. If the regulator is defective, replace the alternator with a new or rebuilt unit.

sists of the starting switch contained within the ignition switch, a transmission neutral safety switch or clutch pedal switch, and the wiring necessary to connect these in series with the starter solenoid or relay.

The pinion, a small gear, is mounted to a one-way drive clutch. This clutch is splined to the starter armature shaft. When the ignition switch is moved to the **START** position, the solenoid plunger slides the pinion toward the flywheel ring gear via a collar and spring. If the teeth on the pinion and flywheel match properly, the pinion will engage the flywheel immediately. If the gear teeth butt one another, the spring will be compressed and will force the gears to mesh as soon as the starter turns far enough to allow them to do so. As the solenoid plunger reaches the end of its travel, it closes the contacts that connect the battery and starter and then the engine is cranked.

As soon as the engine starts, the flywheel ring gear begins turning fast enough to drive the pinion at an extremely high rate of speed. At this point, the one-way clutch begins allowing the pinion to spin faster than the starter shaft so that the starter will not operate at excessive speed. When the ignition switch is released from the starter position, the solenoid is de-energized, and a spring pulls the gear out of mesh interrupting the current flow to the starter.

Some starters employ a separate relay, mounted away from the starter, to switch the motor and solenoid current on and off. The relay replaces the solenoid electrical switch, but does not eliminate the need for a solenoid mounted on the starter used to mechanically engage the starter drive gears. The relay is used to reduce the amount of current the starting switch must carry.

Starter

TESTING

✳✳ WARNING

This tests must be performed within 3 to 5 seconds to avoid burning out the starter.

Pull-in

♦ **See Figure 49**

Disconnect the field coil lead from the terminal C. Connect the battery to the solenoid switch as shown. See if the clutch pinion gear movement is outward. If the gear does not move perform the hold-in test.

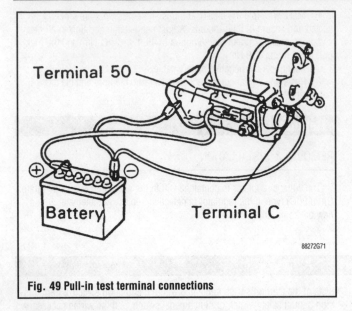

Fig. 49 Pull-in test terminal connections

Hold-in

▶ **See Figure 50**

Attach the battery to the starter as shown and with the clutch pinion gear out, disconnect the negative lead from terminal C. Check to make sure the pinion gear stays in the outward position. If the clutch gear returns inwards, perform the clutch pinion gear return test.

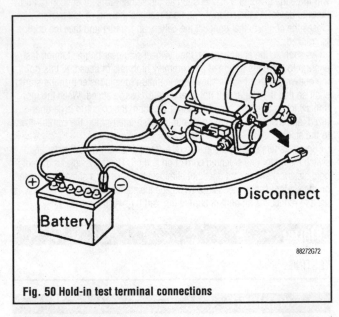

Fig. 50 Hold-in test terminal connections

Clutch Pinion Gear Return

▶ **See Figure 51**

Disconnect the negative lead from the solenoid body. Check the clutch pinion gear returns inward. If not perform the no-load test.

No-load

▶ **See Figure 52**

Attach a battery and ammeter to the starter. Check that the starter rotates smoothly and steadily with the pinion gear moving out. Check the ammeter shows the correct current. 90 amps or less at 11.5 volts. If not replace the starter.

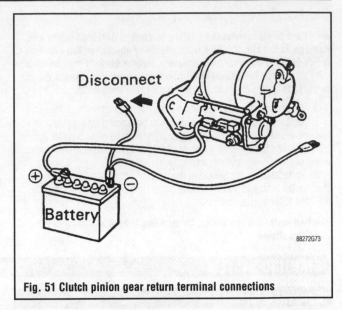

Fig. 51 Clutch pinion gear return terminal connections

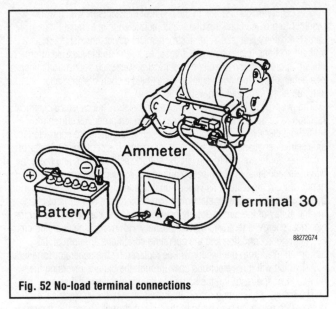

Fig. 52 No-load terminal connections

REMOVAL & INSTALLATION

4A-F, 4A-FE and 7A-FE Engines

1. Disconnect the negative battery cable.
2. Remove the air cleaner assembly (with hose).
3. Disconnect all the wiring from the starter terminals.
4. Remove the starter mounting bolts. Remove the starter.

To install:

5. Attach the connector to the terminal on the solenoid switch. Connect the cable from the battery to the starter and secure with the nut.
6. Place the starter in the flywheel bellhousing, tighten the mounting bolts to 29 ft. lbs. (39 Nm).
7. Install the air cleaner assembly.
8. Connect the negative battery cable.
9. Check the starter for proper operation.

4A-GE Engine

1. Disconnect the negative battery cable. Remove the both engine under covers.

2. Remove the front exhaust pipe.

3. Remove the electric cooling fan.

4. Disconnect all the wiring from the starter terminals.

5. Remove the starter mounting bolts. Remove the starter.

To install:

6. Attach the connector to the terminal on the starter solenoid. Connect the cable from the battery to the terminal on the switch and secure with the nut to 29 ft. lbs. (39 Nm).

7. Install the electric cooling fan.

8. Install the front exhaust pipe.

9. Install the left and right engine under covers.

10. Connect the negative battery cable.

11. Check that the starter works properly.

SOLENOID REPLACEMENT

The starter solenoid (magnetic switch) is an integral part of the starter assembly.

1. Remove the starter from the car. Remove the heat insulator from the starter assembly, if equipped.

2. Disconnect the wire lead from the magnetic switch terminal.

3. Remove the two long, through bolts holding the field frame to the magnetic switch. Pull out the field frame with the armature from the magnetic switch.

4. On 1.0kw starters, remove the felt seal. On 1.4kw starters, remove the O-ring.

5. To remove the starter housing from the magnetic switch assembly:

   a. On 1.0 kw starters, remove the two screws and the starter housing with the idler gear and clutch assembly.

   b. On 1.4kw units, remove the two screws and the starter housing with the pinion gear, idler and clutch assembly.

To install:

6. If necessary, install the gears and clutch assembly to the starter housing. Apply grease to the gear and clutch assemblies and:

   a. On 1.0kw starters, place the clutch assembly, idler gear and bearing in the starter housing.

   b. On 1.4kw starters, place the clutch assembly, idler gear, bearing and pinion gear in the starter housing.

7. Insert the spring into the clutch shaft hole and place the starter housing onto the magnetic switch. Install the two screws.

8. On 1.0kw units, install the felt seal on the armature shaft. On 1.4kw units, install the O-ring on the field frame.

9. Install the field frame with the armature onto the magnetic switch assembly and install the two through bolts.

➡**There is a protrusion or tab on each part; make sure you line them up correctly.**

10. Connect the wire to the terminal on the magnetic switch. Install the heat insulator, if equipped.

11. Reinstall the starter on the vehicle. Check starter system for proper operation.

SENDING UNITS AND SENSORS

Water Temperature Sender

REMOVAL & INSTALLATION

➡**The water temperature sender usually threads into the thermostat housing.**

1. Disconnect the negative battery cable.

2. Drain the cooling system.

3. Disconnect the electrical wiring from the sensor.

4. Carefully unscrew the sensor from the engine.

To install:

5. Place a piece of Teflon tape around the sensor threads and screw the unit securely into the engine.

6. Attach the wiring to the sensor.

7. Fill the cooling system.

8. Connect the negative battery cable.

9. Start the engine and top off the cooling system if necessary.

10. Reset any digital equipment such as radio memory and the clock if necessary.

Low Oil Pressure Warning Sensor

REMOVAL & INSTALLATION

1. Disconnect the negative battery cable.

2. Separate the electrical connector from the sensor.

3. Remove the sensor from the engine.

To install:

4. Place a small amount of clean engine oil on the threads of the sensor and carefully insert and secure the unit.

5. Attach the electrical wiring to the sensor.

6. Connect the negative battery cable. Check the oil level and add fluid as needed.

7. Reset any digital equipment such as radio memory and the clock if necessary.

Oil Pressure Sender

REMOVAL & INSTALLATION

1. Disconnect the negative battery cable.

2. Disconnect the electrical wiring from the oil pressure sender.

3. Remove the oil pressure sender from the engine.

To install:

4. Place a small amount of clean engine oil on the threads of the sensor and carefully insert and secure the unit.

5. Attach the electrical wiring to the sensor.

6. Connect the negative battery cable. Check the oil level and add fluid as needed.

7. Reset any digital equipment such as radio memory and the clock if necessary.

Troubleshooting Basic Starting System Problems

Problem	Cause	Solution
Starter motor rotates engine slowly	• Battery charge low or battery defective	• Charge or replace battery
	• Defective circuit between battery and starter motor	• Clean and tighten, or replace cables
	• Low load current	• Bench-test starter motor. Inspect for worn brushes and weak brush springs.
	• High load current	• Bench-test starter motor. Check engine for friction, drag or coolant in cylinders. Check ring gear-to-pinion gear clearance.
Starter motor will not rotate engine	• Battery charge low or battery defective	• Charge or replace battery
	• Faulty solenoid	• Check solenoid ground. Repair or replace as necessary.
	• Damaged drive pinion gear or ring gear	• Replace damaged gear(s)
	• Starter motor engagement weak	• Bench-test starter motor
	• Starter motor rotates slowly with high load current	• Inspect drive yoke pull-down and point gap, check for worn end bushings, check ring gear clearance
	• Engine seized	• Repair engine
Starter motor drive will not engage (solenoid known to be good)	• Defective contact point assembly	• Repair or replace contact point assembly
	• Inadequate contact point assembly ground	• Repair connection at ground screw
	• Defective hold-in coil	• Replace field winding assembly
Starter motor drive will not disengage	• Starter motor loose on flywheel housing	• Tighten mounting bolts
	• Worn drive end busing	• Replace bushing
	• Damaged ring gear teeth	• Replace ring gear or driveplate
	• Drive yoke return spring broken or missing	• Replace spring
Starter motor drive disengages prematurely	• Weak drive assembly thrust spring	• Replace drive mechanism
	• Hold-in coil defective	• Replace field winding assembly
Low load current	• Worn brushes	• Replace brushes
	• Weak brush springs	• Replace springs

TCCS2C01

Troubleshooting Basic Charging System Problems

Problem	Cause	Solution
Noisy alternator	• Loose mountings	• Tighten mounting bolts
	• Loose drive pulley	• Tighten pulley
	• Worn bearings	• Replace alternator
	• Brush noise	• Replace alternator
	• Internal circuits shorted (High pitched whine)	• Replace alternator
Squeal when starting engine or accelerating	• Glazed or loose belt	• Replace or adjust belt
Indicator light remains on or ammeter indicates discharge (engine running)	• Broken belt	• Install belt
	• Broken or disconnected wires	• Repair or connect wiring
	• Internal alternator problems	• Replace alternator
	• Defective voltage regulator	• Replace voltage regulator/alternator
Car light bulbs continually burn out— battery needs water continually	• Alternator/regulator overcharging	• Replace voltage regulator/alternator
Car lights flare on acceleration	• Battery low	• Charge or replace battery
	• Internal alternator/regulator problems	• Replace alternator/regulator
Low voltage output (alternator light flickers continually or ammeter needle wanders)	• Loose or worn belt	• Replace or adjust belt
	• Dirty or corroded connections	• Clean or replace connections
	• Internal alternator/regulator problems	• Replace alternator/regulator

TCCS2C02

3

ENGINE AND ENGINE OVERHAUL

4A-F ENGINE SPECIFICATIONS

Description	English	Metric
Compression pressure		
STD	191 psi	1320 kPa
Limit	142 psi	981 kPa
differential of pressure between each cylinder	14 psi or less	98 kPa or less
Idler Pulley tension spring		
Free length	1.512 inch	38.4mm
Installed tension at 1.976 inch (50.2mm)	8.4 lb.	38 N
Cylinder head		
Head surface warpage limit	0.0020 inch	0.05mm
Manifold surface warpage limit	0.0039 inch	0.10mm
Cylinder head thickness	3.75 inch	95.3mm
Valve seat		
refacing angle	30, 45, 60 degrees	30, 45, 60 degrees
contacting angle	45 degrees	45 degrees
contacting width	0.039-0.055 inch	1.0-1.4mm
Spark plug tube protrusion height	1835-1866 inch	46.6-47.4mm
Valve guide bushing		
Inner diameter	0.2366-0.2374 inch	6.01-6.03mm
Outer diameter		
STD	0.4331-0.431 inch	11.000-11.027mm
O/S	0.4350-0.4361 inch	11.050-11.077mm
Protrusion height	0.500-0.516 inch	12.7-13.1mm
Valve		
Overall length		
STD		
intake	3.6004 inch	91.45mm
exhaust	3.6181 inch	91.90mm
Limit		
intake	3.5807 inch	90.95mm
exhaust	3.5984 inch	91.40mm
Valve face angle	45.5 degrees	45.5 degrees
Stem diameter		
intake	0.2350-002356 inch	5.970-5.985mm
exhaust	0.2348-0.2354 inch	5.965-5.980mm
Valve head edge thickness	0.039 inch	1.0mm
Valve spring		
Free length	1.724 inch	43.8 mm
Installed length	1.366 inch	34.7mm
Installed load		
STD	155 N	34.8 lb
Limit	143 N	32.2 lb
Squareness	0.098 inch	2.5 kg

88273C25

4A-F ENGINE SPECIFICATIONS

Description	English	Metric
Valve lifter		
Outer diameter	1.1014-1.1018 inch	27.975-27.985mm
ilner diameter	1.1024-1.1032 inch	28.000-28.021mm
Lifter-to-head oil clearance		
STD	0.0006-0.0018 inch	0.015-0.046mm
Limit	0.0039 inch	0.10mm
Intake and exhaust manifolds		
Surface warpage		
intake	0.008 inch	0.2mm
exhaust	0.012 inch	0.3mm
Camshaft		
Thrust clearance		
intake	0.0012-0.0033 inch	0.030-0.085mm
exhaust	0.0014-0.0035 inch	0.035-0.090mm
Journal oil clearance		
STD	0.0014-0.0028 inch	0.035-0.072mm
Limit	0.0039 inch	0.10mm
Journal diameter		
exhaust No. 1	0.9822-0.9829 inch	24.949-24.965mm
others	0.9035-0.9041 inch	22.949-22.965mm
Circle runout	0.0016 inch	0.04mm
Cam lobe height		
STD		
intake	1.3862-1.3902 inch	35.21-35.31mm
exhaust	1.3744-1.3783 inch	34.91-35.01mm
Limit		
intake	1.3457 inch	34.81mm
exhaust	1.3587 inch	34.51mm
Camshaft gear spring end free distance	0.6732-0.6890 inch	17.1-17.5mm
Camshaft gear backlash		
STD	0.0008-0.0079 inch	0.020-0.200mm
Limit	0.0188 inch	0.30mm
Cylinder block		
Cylinder head surface warpage	0.0020 inch	0.05mm
Cylinder bore wear	0.008 inch	0.2mm
Difference of bore between cylinder	0.0020 inch	0.050mm
Taper and out-of-round	0.0008 inch	0.02mm
Piston and Ring		
Piston diameter		
STD	3.1862-3.1874 inch	80.93-80.96mm
O/S 0.50	3.2059-3.2071 inch	81.43-81.46mm
Piston to cylinder clearance	0.0024-0.0031 inch	0.06-0.08mm
Piston ring end gap		
No. 1 STD	0.0098-0.0138 inch	0.25-0.35mm
Limit	0.0421 inch	1.07mm

88273C26

4A-F ENGINE SPECIFICATIONS

Description	English	Metric
Piston and Ring (continued)		
Piston ring end gap		
No. 2 STD	0.0059-0.0118 inch	0.15-0.30mm
Limit	0.0402 inch	1.02mm
oil STD	0.0039-0.0236 inch	0.10-0.60mm
Limit	0.0638 inch	1.62mm
Ring-to-ring groove clearance		
No. 1	0.0016-0.0031 inch	0.04-0.08mm
No. 2	0.0012-0.0028 inch	0.03-0.07mm
Connecting rod and bearing		
Thrust clearance		
STD	0.0059-0.0098 inch	0.15-0.25mm
Limit	0.0118 inch	0.30mm
Connecting rod bearing center wall thickness		
STD No. 1	0.0585-0.0587 inch	1.486-1.490mm
No. 2	0.0587-0.0588 inch	1.490-1.494mm
No. 3	0.0588-0.0590 inch	1.494-1.498mm
U/S 0.25	0.0633-0.0635 inch	1.607-1.613mm
Bearing oil clearance		
STD	0.0008-0.0020 inch	0.020-0.051mm
Limit	0.0031 inch	0.08mm
Rod bend	0.0020 inch	0.05mm
Rod twist	0.0020 inch	0.05mm
Crankshaft		
Thrust clearance		
STD	0.0008-0.0087 inch	0.02-0.22mm
Limit	0.0118 inch	0.30mm
Thrust washer thickness	0.0961-0.0980 inch	2.440-2.490mm
Main journal oil clearance		
STD	0.0006-0.0013 inch	0.015-0.033mm
U/S 0.25	0.0005-0.0021 inch	0.013-0.053mm
Limit	0.0039 inch	0.10mm
Main journal diameter		
STD	1.8891-1.8898 inch	47.982-48.000mm
Main journal finished diameter		
U/S 0.25	1.8797-1.8801 inch	47.745-47.755mm
Main bearing wall thickness		
STD No. 1	0.0788-0.0789 inch	2.002-2.005mm
No. 2	0.0789-0.0791 inch	2.005-2.008mm
No. 3	0.0791-0.0792 inch	2.008-2.011mm
No. 4	0.0792-0.0793 inch	2.011-2.014mm
No. 5	0.0793-0.0794 inch	2.014-2.017mm
U/S 0.25	0.0835-0.0837 inch	2.121-2.127mm
Crank pin diameter	1.5742-1.5748 inch	39.985-40.000mm
Crank pin finished diameter U/S 0.25	1.5648-1.5652 inch	39.745-39.755mm

88273C27

4A-F ENGINE SPECIFICATIONS

Description	English	Metric
Crankshaft (continued)		
Circle runout limit	0.0024 inch	0.06mm
Main journal taper and out-of-round limit	0.0008 inch	0.02mm
Crank pin journal taper and out-of-round limit	0.0008 inch	0.02mm

88273C28

1988-92 4A-FE ENGINE SPECIFICATIONS

Description	English	Metric
Compression pressure		
STD	191 psi	1320 kPa
Limit	142 psi	981 kPa
Differential of pressure between each cylinder	14 psi or less	98 kPa or less
Idler Pulley tension spring		
Free length	1.512 inch	38.4mm
Installed tension at 1.976 inch (50.2mm)	7.9-8.8 lbf.	35-39 N
Cylinder head		
Head surface warpage limit	0.0020 inch	0.05mm
Manifold surface warpage limit	0.0039 inch	0.10mm
Valve seat		
refacing angle	30, 45, 60 degrees	30, 45, 60 degrees
contacting angle	45 degrees	45 degrees
contacting width	0.047-0.063 inch	1.2-1.6mm
Spark plug tube protrusion height	1843-1874 inch	46.8-47.6mm
Valve guide bushing		
Inner diameter	0.2366-0.2374 inch	6.01-6.03mm
Outer diameter		
STD	0.4331-0.431 inch	11.000-11.027mm
O/S	0.4350-0.4361 inch	11.050-11.077mm
Protrusion height	0.500-0.516 inch	12.7-13.1mm
Valve		
Overall length		
STD		
intake	3.6004 inch	91.45mm
exhaust	3.6181 inch	91.90mm
Limit		
intake	3.5807 inch	90.95mm
exhaust	3.5984 inch	91.40mm
Valve face angle	44.5 degrees	44.5 degrees
Stem diameter		
intake	0.2350-002356 inch	5.970-5.985mm
exhaust	0.2348-0.2354 inch	5.965-5.980mm
Valve head margin thickness		
1988-91	0.039 inch	1.0mm
1992	0.020 inch	0.5mm
Valve spring		
Free length	1.724 inch	43.8 mm
Installed length	1.366 inch	34.7mm
Installed load		
STD	155 N	34.8 lb
Limit	143 N	32.2 lb
Squareness	0.075 inch	2.0 kg

88273C29

1988-92 4A-FE ENGINE SPECIFICATIONS

Description	English	Metric
Valve lifter		
Outer diameter	1.1014-1.1018 inch	27.975-27.985mm
Inner diameter	1.1026-1.1034 inch	28.005-28.026mm
Lifter-to-head oil clearance		
STD	0.0008-0.0020 inch	0.020-0.051mm
Limit 1988-91	0.0039 inch	0.10mm
1992	0.0028 inch	0.07mm
Intake and exhaust manifolds		
Surface warpage		
intake	0.0079 inch	0.2mm
exhaust	0.0118 inch	0.3mm
Camshaft		
Thrust clearance		
intake	0.0012-0.0033 inch	0.030-0.085mm
exhaust	0.0014-0.0035 inch	0.035-0.090mm
Journal oil clearance		
STD	0.0014-0.0028 inch	0.035-0.072mm
Limit	0.0039 inch	0.10mm
Journal diameter		
exhaust No. 1	0.9822-0.9829 inch	24.949-24.965mm
others	0.9035-0.9041 inch	22.949-22.965mm
Circle runout	0.0016 inch	0.04mm
Cam lobe height		
STD		
intake	1.3862-1.3902 inch	35.21-35.31mm
exhaust	1.3744-1.3783 inch	34.91-35.01mm
Limit		
intake	1.3705 inch	34.81mm
exhaust	1.3587 inch	34.51mm
Camshaft gear spring end free distance	0.6732-0.6890 inch	17.1-17.5mm
Camshaft gear backlash		
STD	0.0008-0.0079 inch	0.020-0.200mm
Limit	0.0188 inch	0.30mm
Cylinder block		
Cylinder head surface warpage	0.0020 inch	0.05mm
Cylinder bore wear	0.008 inch	0.2mm
Difference of bore between cylinder	0.0020 inch	0.050mm
Taper and out-of-round	0.0008 inch	0.02mm
Piston and Ring		
Piston diameter		
STD Mark 1	3.1862-3.1866 inch	80.93-80.96mm
Mark 2	3.1866-3.1870 inch	80.94-80.95mm
Mark 3	3.1870-3.1874 inch	80.95-80.96mm
O/S 0.50	3.2059-3.2071 inch	81.43-81.46mm
Piston to cylinder clearance	0.0024-0.0031 inch	0.06-0.08mm
Piston ring end gap		
No. 1 STD	0.0098-0.0177 inch	0.25-0.45mm
Limit	0.0413 inch	1.05mm

88273C30

1988-92 4A-FE ENGINE SPECIFICATIONS

Description			English	Metric
Piston and Ring (continued)				
Piston ring end gap				
No. 2	STD		0.0059-0.0157 inch	0.15-0.40mm
	Limit		0.0394 inch	1.00mm
oil	STD		0.0039-0.0276 inch	0.10-0.70mm
	Limit		0.0512 inch	1.30mm
Ring-to-ring groove clearance				
No. 1			0.0016-0.0031 inch	0.04-0.08mm
No. 2			0.0012-0.0028 inch	0.03-0.07mm
Connecting rod and bearing				
Thrust clearance				
STD			0.0059-0.0098 inch	0.15-0.25mm
Limit			0.0118 inch	0.30mm
Connecting rod bearing center wall thickness				
STD	No. 1		0.0585-0.0587 inch	1.486-1.490mm
	No. 2		0.0587-0.0588 inch	1.490-1.494mm
	No. 3		0.0588-0.0590 inch	1.494-1.498mm
	U/S 0.25		0.0633-0.0635 inch	1.607-1.613mm
Bearing oil clearance				
STD			0.0008-0.0020 inch	0.020-0.051mm
Limit			0.0031 inch	0.08mm
Rod bend			0.0020 inch	0.05mm
Rod twist			0.0020 inch	0.05mm
Crankshaft				
Thrust clearance				
STD			0.0008-0.0087 inch	0.02-0.22mm
Limit			0.0118 inch	0.30mm
Thrust washer thickness			0.0961-0.0980 inch	2.440-2.490mm
Main journal oil clearance				
STD			0.0006-0.0013 inch	0.015-0.033mm
U/S 0.25			0.0007-0.0022 inch	0.013-0.056mm
Limit			0.0039 inch	0.10mm
Main journal diameter				
STD			1.8891-1.8898 inch	47.982-48.000mm
Main journal finished diameter				
U/S 0.25			1.8797-1.8801 inch	47.745-47.755mm
Main bearing wall thickness				
STD	No. 1		0.0788-0.0789 inch	2.002-2.005mm
	No. 2		0.0789-0.0791 inch	2.005-2.008mm
	No. 3		0.0791-0.0792 inch	2.008-2.011mm
	No. 4		0.0792-0.0793 inch	2.011-2.014mm
	No. 5		0.0793-0.0794 inch	2.014-2.017mm
	U/S 0.25		0.0835-0.0837 inch	2.121-2.127mm
Crank pin diameter			1.5742-1.5748 inch	39.985-40.000mm
Crank pin finished diameter U/S 0.25			1.5648-1.5652 inch	39.745-39.755mm

88273C31

1988-92 4A-FE ENGINE SPECIFICATIONS

Description	English	Metric
Crankshaft (continued)		
Circle runout limit	0.0024 inch	0.06mm
Main journal taper and out-of-round limit	0.0008 inch	0.02mm
Crank pin journal taper and out-of-round limit	0.0008 inch	0.02mm

88273C32

1993-97 4A-FE AND 7A-FE ENGINE SPECIFICATIONS

Description	English	Metric
Compression pressure		
STD	191 psi	1320 kPa
Limit	142 psi	981 kPa
Differential of pressure between each cylinder	14 psi or less	98 kPa or less
Idler Pulley tension spring		
Free length	1.390 inch	35.3mm
Installed tension at 1.976 inch (50.2mm)	7.9-8.8 lbf.	35-39 N
Cylinder head		
Head surface warpage limit	0.0020 inch	0.05mm
Manifold surface warpage limit	0.0039 inch	0.10mm
Valve seat		
refacing angle 1993-95	30, 45, 75 degrees	30, 45, 75 degrees
refacing angle 1996-97	30, 45, 60 degrees	30, 45, 60 degrees
contacting angle	45 degrees	45 degrees
contacting width	0.039-0.055 inch	1.0-1.4mm
Valve guide bushing		
Inner diameter	0.2366-0.2374 inch	6.01-6.03mm
Outer diameter		
1993-95		
STD	0.4331-0.4342 inch	11.000-11.027mm
O/S	0.4350-0.4361 inch	11.050-11.077mm
1996-97		
STD	0.4350-0.4354 inch	11.048-11.059mm
O/S	0.4369-0.4374 inch	11.098-11.109mm
Valve		
Overall length		
STD		
intake 1993-94	3.6004 inch	91.45mm
intake 1995	3.4429 inch	87.45
exhaust	3.4583 inch	87.84mm
Limit		
intake 1993-94	3.5807 inch	90.95mm
intake 1995	3.4232 inch	86.95mm
exhaust	3.4390 inch	87.35mm
Valve face angle	44.5 degrees	44.5 degrees
Stem diameter		
intake	0.2350-002356 inch	5.970-5.985mm
exhaust	0.2348-0.2354 inch	5.965-5.980mm
Valve head margin thickness		
STD	0.031-0.047 inch	0.8-1.2mm
Limit	0.020 inch	0.5mm
Valve spring		
Free length		
1993-95 4A-FE	1.520 inch	38.6 mm
7A-FE	1.669 inch	42.4mm
1996-97	1.669 inch	42.4mm
Installed load	157-174 N	35.5-39.0 lbf

88273C33

1993-97 4A-FE AND 7A-FE ENGINE SPECIFICATIONS

Description	English	Metric
Valve lifter		
Outer diameter	1.2191-1.2195 inch	30.966-30.976mm
Inner diameter	1.2205-1.2215 inch	31.000-31.025mm
Lifter-to-head oil clearance		
STD	0.0009-0.0023 inch	0.024-0.059mm
Limit	0.0028 inch	0.07mm
Intake and exhaust manifolds		
Surface warpage		
intake	0.0079 inch	0.2mm
exhaust	0.0118 inch	0.3mm
Camshaft		
Thrust clearance		
intake	0.0012-0.0033 inch	0.030-0.085mm
exhaust	0.0014-0.0035 inch	0.035-0.090mm
Journal oil clearance		
STD	0.0014-0.0028 inch	0.035-0.072mm
Limit	0.0039 inch	0.10mm
Journal diameter	0.9822-0.9829 inch	24.949-24.965mm
Circle runout	0.0016 inch	0.04mm
Cam lobe height		
STD 1993-95		
intake 4A-FE	1.6500-1.6539 inch	41.91-42.01mm
intake 7A-FE	1.6421-1.6461 inch	41.71-41.81mm
1996-97		
intake	1.6421-1.6461 inch	41.71-41.81mm
exhaust	1.6520-1.6560 inch	41.96-42.06mm
Limit 1993-95		
intake 4A-FE	1.6339 inch	41.50mm
intake 7A-FE	1.6260 inch	41.30mm
1996-97		
intake	1.6260 inch	41.30mm
exhaust	1.6358 inch	41.55mm
Camshaft gear spring end free distance	0.669-0.693 inch	17.0-17.6mm
Camshaft gear backlash		
STD	0.0008-0.0079 inch	0.020-0.200mm
Limit	0.0188 inch	0.30mm
Cylinder block		
Cylinder head surface warpage limit	0.0020 inch	0.05mm
Cylinder bore diameter STD		
Mark 1	3.1890-3.1894 inch	81.000-81.010mm
Mark 2	3.1894-3.1898 inch	81-010-81.020mm
Mark 3	3.1898-3.1902 inch	81.020-81.030mm
Piston and Ring		
Piston diameter		
STD Mark 1	3.1852-3.1856 inch	80.93-80.96mm
Mark 2	3.1856-3.1860 inch	80.94-80.95mm
Mark 3	3.1860-3.1864 inch	80.95-80.96mm

88273C34

1993-97 4A-FE AND 7A-FE ENGINE SPECIFICATIONS

Description			English	Metric
Piston diameter (continued)				
	O/S 0.50		3.2049-3.2061 inch	81.43-81.46mm
Piston to cylinder clearance STD			0.0033-0.0041 inch	0.06-0.08mm
Piston ring end gap				
	No. 1	STD	0.0098-0.0138 inch	0.25-0.35mm
		Limit	0.0413 inch	1.05mm
	No. 2	STD	0.0138-0.0197 inch	0.350-0.500mm
		Limit	0.0472 inch	1.20mm
	oil	STD	0.0039-0.0157 inch	0.100-0.400mm
		Limit	0.0413 inch	1.05mm
Ring-to-ring groove clearance				
	No. 1	1993-95	0.0003-0.0031 inch	0.008-0.080mm
	No. 1	1996-97	0.0018-0.0033 inch	0.045-0.085mm
	No. 2		0.0012-0.0028 inch	0.03-0.07mm
Connecting rod and bearing				
Thrust clearance				
	STD		0.0059-0.0098 inch	0.15-0.25mm
	Limit		0.0118 inch	0.30mm
Connecting rod bearing center wall thickness				
	STD	No. 1	0.0585-0.0587 inch	1.486-1.490mm
		No. 2	0.0587-0.0588 inch	1.490-1.494mm
		No. 3	0.0588-0.0590 inch	1.494-1.498mm
Connecting rod oil clearance (4A-FE)				
	STD (STD)		0.0008-0.0020 inch	0.020-0.051mm
	STD (U/S 0.25)		0.0007-0.0026 inch	0.019-0.065mm
	Limit		0.0031 inch	0.08mm
Connecting rod oil clearance (7A-FE)				
	STD (STD)		0.0008-0.0017 inch	0.020-0.044mm
	STD (U/S 0.25)		0.0007-0.0022 inch	0.019-0.058mm
	Limit		0.0031 inch	0.08mm
Rod bend			0.0020 inch	0.05mm
Rod twist			0.0020 inch	0.05mm
Crankshaft				
Thrust clearance				
	STD		0.0008-0.0087 inch	0.02-0.22mm
	Limit		0.0118 inch	0.30mm
Thrust washer thickness			0.0961-0.0980 inch	2.440-2.490mm
Main journal oil clearance				
	STD		0.0006-0.0013 inch	0.015-0.033mm
	U/S 0.25		0.0007-0.0022 inch	0.013-0.056mm
	Limit		0.0039 inch	0.10mm
Main journal diameter				
	STD		1.8891-1.8898 inch	47.982-48.000mm
Main bearing wall thickness				
	STD	No. 1	0.0788-0.0789 inch	2.002-2.005mm
		No. 2	0.0789-0.0791 inch	2.005-2.008mm

1993-97 4A-FE AND 7A-FE ENGINE SPECIFICATIONS

Description	English	Metric
Main bearing wall thickness (continued)		
STD No. 3	0.0791-0.0792 inch	2.008-2.011mm
No. 4	0.0792-0.0793 inch	2.011-2.014mm
No. 5	0.0793-0.0794 inch	2.014-2.017mm
Crank pin diameter		
4A-FE	1.5742-1.5748 inch	39.985-40.000mm
7A-FE	1.8891-1.8898 inch	47.988-48.000mm
Crankshaft (continued)		
Circle runout limit	0.0012 inch	0.03mm
Main journal taper and out-of-round limit	0.0002 inch	0.005mm
Crank pin journal taper and out-of-round limit	0.0002 inch	0.005mm

88273C36

4A-GE ENGINE SPECIFICATIONS

Description	English	Metric
Compression pressure		
STD	190 psi	1314 kPa
Limit	142 psi	981 kPa
Differential of pressure between each cylinder	14 psi or less	98 kPa or less
Idler Pulley tension spring		
Free length	1.713 inch	43.5mm
Installed tension at 1.976 inch (50.2mm)	20.9-23.1 lbf.	93-103 N
Cylinder head		
Cylinder block warpage limit	0.0020 inch	0.05mm
Intake manifold warpage limit	0.0020 inch	0.05mm
Exhaust manifold warpage limit	0.0039 inch	0.10mm
Valve seat		
refacing angle	30, 45, 60 degrees	30, 45, 60 degrees
contacting angle	45 degrees	45 degrees
contacting width	0.039-0.055 inch	1.0-1.4mm
Valve guide bushing		
Inner diameter	0.2366-0.2374 inch	6.01-6.03mm
Outer diameter		
STD	0.4344-0.4348 inch	11.033-11.044mm
O/S	0.4363-0.4368 inch	11.083-11.094mm
Valve		
Overall length		
STD		
intake	3.9213 inch	99.60mm
exhaust	3.9272 inch	99.75mm
Limit		
intake	3.9016 inch	99.10mm
exhaust	3.9075 inch	99.25mm
Valve face angle	44.5 degrees	44.5 degrees
Stem diameter		
intake	0.2350-002356 inch	5.970-5.985mm
exhaust	0.2348-0.2354 inch	5.965-5.980mm
Valve head margin thickness		
STD	0.031-0.047 inch	0.8-1.2mm
Limit	0.020 inch	0.5mm
Valve spring		
Free length	1.6177 inch	41.09mm
Installed load		
STD	160 N	35.9 lb
Limit	143 N	32.2 lb
Squareness	0.071 inch	1.8mm

88273C37

4A-GE ENGINE SPECIFICATIONS

Description	English	Metric
Valve lifter		
Outer diameter	1.1014-1.1018 inch	27.975-27.985mm
Inner diameter	1.1026-1.1034 inch	28.005-28.026mm
Lifter-to-head oil clearance		
STD	0.0005-0.0018 inch	0.015-0.046mm
Limit	0.0039 inch	0.10mm
Intake and exhaust manifolds		
Surface warpage		
intake	0.0020 inch	0.05mm
exhaust	0.0118 inch	0.30mm
Camshaft		
Thrust clearance		
STD	0.0031-0.0075 inch	0.080-0.190mm
Limit	0.0118 inch	0.035-0.090mm
Journal oil clearance		
STD	0.0014-0.0028 inch	0.035-0.072mm
Limit	0.0039 inch	0.10mm
Journal diameter		
exhaust No. 1	1.0610-1.0616 inch	26.949-26.965mm
Circle runout	0.0016 inch	0.04mm
Cam lobe height		
STD	1.3823-1.3980 inch	35.419-35.510mm
Limit	1.3862 inch	35.21mm
Cylinder block		
Cylinder head surface warpage	0.0020 inch	0.05mm
Cylinder bore wear	0.008 inch	0.2mm
Difference of bore between cylinder	0.0020 inch	0.050mm
Taper and out-of-round	0.0008 inch	0.02mm
Piston and Ring		
Piston diameter		
STD Mark 1	3.1846-3.1850 inch	80.89-80.90mm
Mark 2	3.1850-3.1854 inch	80.90-80.91mm
Mark 3	3.1854-3.1858 inch	80.91-80.92mm
O/S 0.50	3.2043-3.2055 inch	81.39-81.42mm
Piston to cylinder clearance	0.0039-0.0047 inch	0.10-0.12mm
Piston ring end gap		
STD No. 1	0.0098-0.0185 inch	0.25-0.47mm
Limit	0.0421 inch	1.07mm

88273C38

4A-GE ENGINE SPECIFICATIONS

Description	English	Metric
Piston and Ring (continued)		
Piston ring end gap		
STD No. 2	0.0079-0.0165 inch	0.20-0.42mm
Limit	0.0402 inch	1.02mm
STD Oil	0.0059-0.0205 inch	0.15-0.52mm
Limit	0.0441 inch	1.12mm
Ring-to-ring groove clearance		
No. 1	0.0012-0.0031 inch	0.03-0.08mm
No. 2	0.0012-0.0028 inch	0.03-0.07mm
Connecting rod and bearing		
Thrust clearance		
STD	0.0059-0.0098 inch	0.15-0.25mm
Limit	0.0118 inch	0.30mm
Connecting rod bearing center wall thickness		
STD No. 1	0.0585-0.0587 inch	1.486-1.490mm
No. 2	0.0587-0.0588 inch	1.490-1.494mm
No. 3	0.0588-0.0590 inch	1.494-1.498mm
U/S 0.25	0.0633-0.0635 inch	1.607-1.613mm
Bearing oil clearance		
STD	0.0008-0.0020 inch	0.020-0.051mm
Limit	0.0031 inch	0.08mm
Rod bend	0.0012 inch	0.03mm
Rod twist	0.0020 inch	0.05mm
Crankshaft		
Thrust clearance		
STD	0.0008-0.0087 inch	0.02-0.22mm
Limit	0.0118 inch	0.30mm
Thrust washer thickness	0.0961-0.0980 inch	2.440-2.490mm
Main journal oil clearance		
STD	0.0006-0.0013 inch	0.015-0.033mm
U/S 0.25	0.0007-0.0022 inch	0.013-0.056mm
Limit	0.0039 inch	0.10mm
Main journal diameter		
STD	1.8891-1.8898 inch	47.982-48.000mm
Main journal finished diameter		
U/S 0.25	1.8797-1.8801 inch	47.745-47.755mm
Main bearing wall thickness		
STD No. 1	0.0788-0.0789 inch	2.002-2.005mm
No. 2	0.0789-0.0791 inch	2.005-2.008mm
No. 3	0.0791-0.0792 inch	2.008-2.011mm
No. 4	0.0792-0.0793 inch	2.011-2.014mm
No. 5	0.0793-0.0794 inch	2.014-2.017mm
U/S 0.25	0.0835-0.0837 inch	2.121-2.127mm
Crank pin diameter	1.6529-1.6535 inch	41.985-42.000mm
Crank pin finished diameter U/S 0.25	1.6435-1.6439 inch	41.745-41.755mm
Circle runout limit	0.0024 inch	0.06mm
Main journal taper and out-of-round limit	0.0008 inch	0.02mm
Crank pin journal taper and out-of-round limit	0.0008 inch	0.02mm

88273C39

ENGINE MECHANICAL

Engine

REMOVAL & INSTALLATION

In the process of removing the engine, you will come across a number of steps which call for the removal of a separate component or system, such as "disconnect the exhaust system" or "remove the radiator." In most instances, a detailed removal procedure can be found elsewhere in this manual.

It is virtually impossible to list each individual wire and hose which must be disconnected, simply because so many different model and engine combinations have been manufactured. Careful observation and common sense are the best possible approaches to any repair procedure.

Removal and installation of the engine can be made easier if you follow these basic points:

- If you have to drain any of the fluids, use a suitable container.
- Always tag any wires or hoses and, if possible, the components they came from before disconnecting them.
- Because there are so many bolts and fasteners involved, store and label the retainers from components separately in muffin pans, jars or coffee cans. This will prevent confusion during installation.
- After unbolting the transmission or transaxle, always make sure it is properly supported.
- If it is necessary to disconnect the air conditioning system, have this service performed by a qualified technician using a recovery/recycling station. If the system does not have to be disconnected, unbolt the compressor and set it aside.
- When unbolting the engine mounts, always make sure the engine is properly supported. When removing the engine, make sure that any lifting devices are properly attached to the engine. It is recommended that if your engine is supplied with lifting hooks, your lifting apparatus be attached to them.
- Lift the engine from its compartment slowly, checking that no hoses, wires or other components are still connected.
- After the engine is clear of the compartment, place it on an engine stand or workbench.
- After the engine has been removed, you can perform a partial or full teardown of the engine using the procedures outlined in this manual.

4A-F Engine

1. Disconnect the negative battery cable.
2. Remove the battery.
3. Remove the hood (mark the hood hinges for correct installation). Have a helper assist you and be careful not to damage the painted bodywork.
4. Remove the engine under covers.
5. Drain the cooling system, engine and transaxle fluids.
6. Removwe the air cleaner and flexible hose.
7. Remove the coolant reservoir tank, radiator and fan.
8. If equipped with an automatic, disconnect the accelerator and throttle cables at the carburetor.
9. Label and disconnect all electrical wiring and vacuum lines necessary to remove the engine.
10. Disconnect the fuel lines at the fuel pump. Plug the lines.
11. Disconnect the heater hoses at the water inlet housing.
12. Remove the power steering pump and set aside with the lines still attached.
13. Remove the air conditioning compressor and set it aside with the refrigerant lines still attached.
14. Disconnect the speedometer cable from the transaxle.
15. On manual transaxles, remove the slave cylinder and set aside with the hydraulic lines still attached.

16. Disconnect the shift control cables.
17. Raise and support the vehicle.
18. Remove the 2 nuts from the flange then, disconnect the exhaust pipe from the exhaust manifold.
19. Disconnect the halfshafts at the transaxle.
20. Remove the 2 hole covers, then remove the front, center and rear engine mounts from the center crossmember. Remove the bolts, insulators and center member.
21. Attach a suitable hoisting device to the lifting brackets on the engine.
22. Remove the bolts and mounting stay. Remove the bolt, nuts and the through-bolt. Next pull out the right side engine mount. Remove the bolts retaining the left mounting stay. Unbolt and remove the left engine mount bracket from the transaxle.
23. Inspect and make sure all components are disconnected and labeled. Lift the engine/transaxle assembly out of the vehicle.

To install:

24. Install the engine in the reverse order of removal paying particular attention to the following.
25. Before reinstalling the engine in the car, several components must be reattached or connected. Install the transaxle to the engine (if separated); tighten the 12mm bolts to 47 ft. lbs. (64 Nm) and the 10mm bolts to 34 ft. lbs. (46 Nm). Tighten all other components to the following specifications:

- Starter mounting bolts—29 ft. lbs. (39 Nm)
- Right motor mount and through bolt—58 ft. lbs. (78 Nm).
- Engine mounting automatics—38 ft. lbs. (52 Nm)
- Engine mounting bracket-to-transaxle—45 ft. lbs. (61 Nm)
- Engine mounting stay LH—15 ft. lbs. (21 Nm)
- Engine mounting LH-to-transaxle manual—38 ft. lbs. (52 Nm)
- Engine mounting stay RH—31 ft. lbs. (42 Nm)
- Engine mounting RH-to-engine manual-nut—38 ft. lbs. (52 Nm)
- Engine mounting RH-to-engine manual bolt—47 ft. lbs. (64 Nm)
- Engine mounting bolt front—35 ft. lbs. (48 Nm)
- Engine mounting bolt center—38 ft. lbs. (52 Nm)
- Engine mounting bolt rear—42 ft. lbs. (57 Nm)
- Engine front and rear mounting bolts—58 ft. lbs. (78 Nm)
- Power steering pump pulley bolt—28 ft. lbs. (38 Nm)
- Exhaust pipe-to-manifold—46 ft. lbs. (62 Nm)

26. Fill the transaxle with the correct amount of oil, and fill the engine with oil.
27. Fill the cooling system with the proper amount of fluid.
28. Double check all installation items, paying particular attention to loose hoses or hanging wires, untightened nuts, poor routing of hoses and wires (too tight or rubbing) and tools left in the engine area.
29. Connect the negative battery cable.
30. Start the engine and allow it to reach normal operating temperature. Check carefully for leaks. Shut the engine **OFF**.
31. Raise the front end of the car, support on jackstands and install the splash shields below the car.
32. Lower the car to the ground. With your helper, install the hood and adjust it for proper fit and latching. Road test the vehicle for proper operation.

4A-FE and 7A-FE Engines

▶ **See Figures 1 thru 18**

1. Remove the hood (mark the hood hinges for correct installation). Have a helper assist you and be careful not to damage the painted bodywork.

➡ **The fuel system is under pressure. Release pressure slowly and contain spillage. Observe no smoking/no open flame precautions. Have a Class B-C (dry powder) fire extinguisher within arm's reach at all times.**

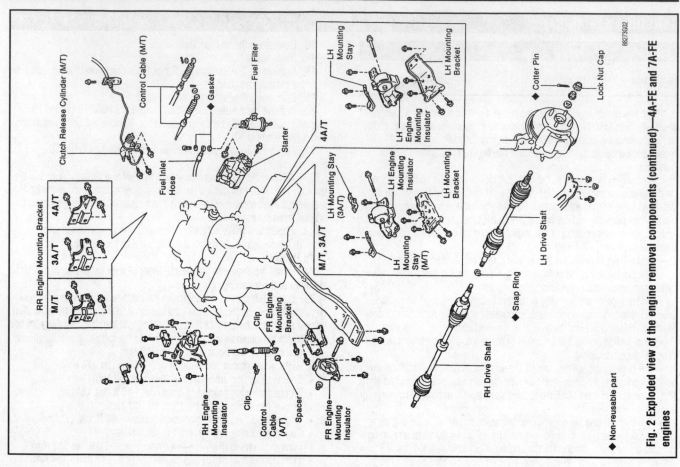

Fig. 2 Exploded view of the engine removal components (continued)—4A-FE and 7A-FE engines

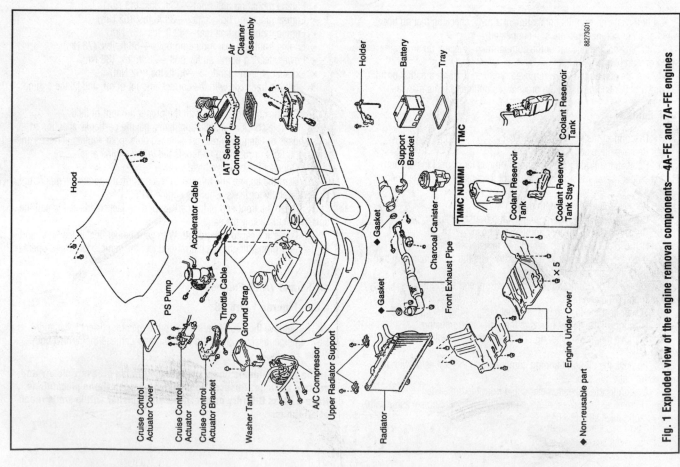

Fig. 1 Exploded view of the engine removal components—4A-FE and 7A-FE engines

2. Relieve the fuel system pressure. Disconnect the negative battery
cable, then the positive battery cable and remove the battery.

3. Raise the vehicle and safely support it on jackstands.

4. Remove the left and right splash shields.

5. Drain the engine oil and the transmission oil.

6. Drain the engine coolant.

7. Disconnect the accelerator cable from the bracket. On automatics
disconnect the throttle cable from the accelerator bracket.

8. Remove the air cleaner hose and the air cleaner assembly.

9. Remove the coolant reservoir. Remove the radiator and fan assembly.

10. Remove the washer reservoir tank.

11. Disconnect and remove the cruise control actuator.

12. Label and disconnect the main engine wiring harness from its
related sensors and switches.

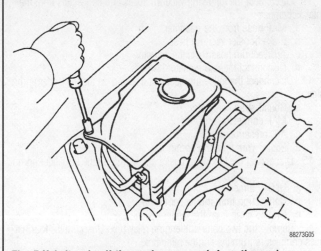

Fig. 5 Unbolt and pull the washer reservoir from the engine
compartment—4A-FE and 7A-FE engines

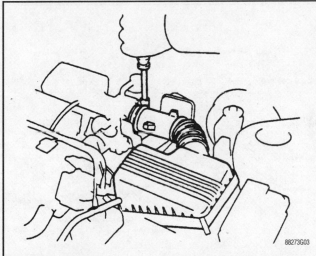

Fig. 3 Unbolt and remove the air cleaner assembly—4A-FE and
7A-FE engines

Fig. 6 Disconnect the hose and remove the charcoal canister
from the bracket—4A-FE and 7A-FE engines

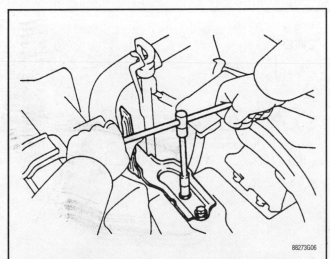

Fig. 4 Remove the bolts retaining the coolant reservoir stay—
4A-FE and 7A-FE engines

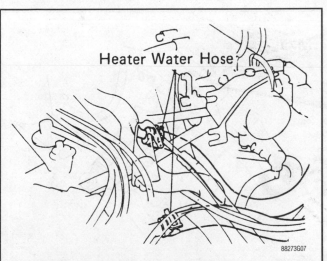

Fig. 7 Disconnect the heater hoses from the water inlet housing
and pipe—4A-FE and 7A-FE engines

13. Disconnect the following vacuum hoses and connectors from the intake chamber:
   a. MAP hose from the gas filter
   b. Brake booster vacuum hose
   c. A/C vacuum hose from the actuator
   d. Disconnect the A/C actuator harness
14. Disconnect the following hoses and wiring on the RH fender apron side:
   a. Gound strap connector
   b. MAP connector
   c. A/C pressure switch
   d. Engine wire from the apron
15. Disconnect the following hoses and wiring on the LH fender apron side:
   a. DLC1 connector
   b. Connection from the fender apron
   c. Ground strap from the fender apron
16. Remove the two bolts and engine relay box. Unsecure the four harness connectors from the engine relay box.
17. Remove the charcoal canister.
18. Disconnect the heater hoses.
19. Carefully disconnect the fuel inlet and return lines.

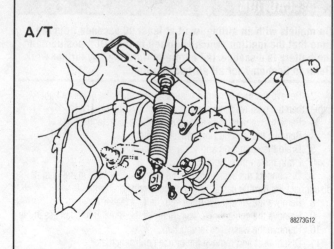

Fig. 10 On automatic transaxles, disconnect the control cable from the shift ever—4A-FE and 7A-FE engines

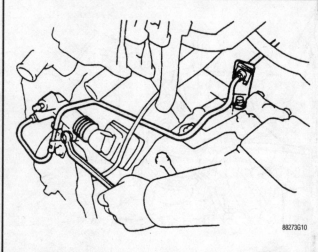

Fig. 8 Unbolt and set aside the slave cylinder, DO NOT disconnect the hydraulic lines—4A-FE and 7A-FE engines

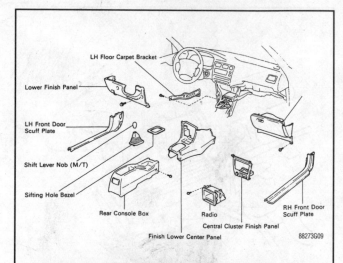

Fig. 11 Exploded view of the removal components in the cabin—4A-FE and 7A-FE engines

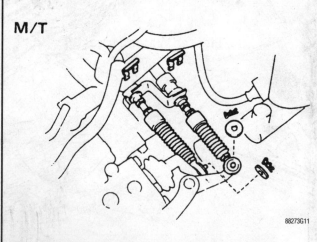

Fig. 9 On manual transaxles, disconnect the shift control cables—4A-FE and 7A-FE engines

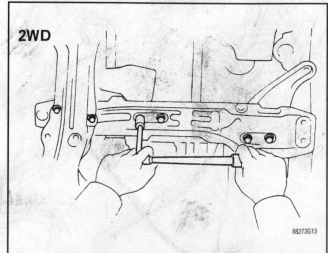

Fig. 12 Removing the 2WD center member mounting—4A-FE and 7A-FE engines

20. If equipped with manual transaxle, unbolt the clutch slave cylinder from the bell housing and move the cylinder out of the way. Don't disconnect any lines or hoses. Disconnect the shift control cables by removing the two clips, the washers and retainers.

21. On automatics, disconnect the control cable from the shift lever by unsecuring the clip and retainer.

22. Disconnect the engine wiring from the cabin. Remove both door scuff plates, the lower panel with glove box door, radio, center console cluster finish panel, rear console box and detach any associated wiring. Disconnect the wiring from the ECU and pull the harness out through the cowl panel.

23. Loosen the power steering pump mounting bolt and through bolt. Remove the drive belt.

24. Remove the four bolts holding the air conditioner compressor and remove the compressor. DO NOT loosen or remove any lines or hoses. Move the compressor out of the way and hang it from a piece of stiff wire.

25. Disconnect the speedometer cable from the transaxle.

26. Disconnect the oxygen sensor. Remove the two bolts from the exhaust pipe flange and separate the pipe from the exhaust manifold.

27. Raise the car and support it safely on jackstands.

28. On 4WD models, disconnect the oil cooler hoses.

29. Remove the nuts and bolts and separate the halfshafts from the transaxle.

30. On 4WD models, disconnect the propeller shaft.

31. Remove the through bolt from the rear transaxle mount.

32. Remove the nuts from the center transaxle mount and the rear mount.

33. Lower the vehicle to the ground and attach the lifting equipment to the brackets on the engine. Take tension on the hoist line or chain just enough to support the engine but no more. Hang the engine wires and hoses on the chain or cable.

34. Remove the three exhaust hanger bracket nuts and the hanger. Remove the two center crossmember-to-main crossmember bolts. Remove the three center crossmember-to-radiator support bolts.

✳✳ CAUTION

Support the crossmembers with a jack or jackstands when loosening the bolts. The pieces are heavy and could fall on you.

35. On 4WD models, remove the eight crossmember-to-body bolts, then remove the two bolts holding the control arm brackets to the underbody. Remove the two center mount-to-transaxle bolts and remove the mount. Carefully lower the center mount and crossmember and remove from under the car.

36. At the left engine mount, remove the three bolts and the bracket, then remove the bolt, two nuts, through bolt and mounting. Remove the three bolts and the air cleaner bracket.

37. Loosen and remove the five bolts and disconnect the mounting bracket from the transaxle bracket. Remove the through bolt and mounting.

38. Carefully and slowly raise the engine and transaxle assembly out of the car. Tilt the transaxle down to clear the right engine mount. Be careful not to hit the steering gear housing. Make sure the engine is clear of all wiring, lines and hoses.

39. Support the engine assembly on a suitable stand; do not allow it to remain on the hoist for any length of time.

40. With the engine properly supported, disconnect the reverse light switch and the neutral safety switch (automatic transaxle).

41. Remove the rear end cover plate.

42. If equipped with automatic transaxle, remove the 6 torque converter mounting bolts.

43. Remove the starter.

44. Support the transaxle, remove the retaining bolts in the case and remove the transaxle from the engine. Pull the unit straight off the engine; do not allow it to hang partially removed on the shaft. Keep the automatic transaxle level; if it tilts forward the converter may fall off.

To install:

45. Before reinstalling the engine in the vehicle, several components must be reattached or connected.

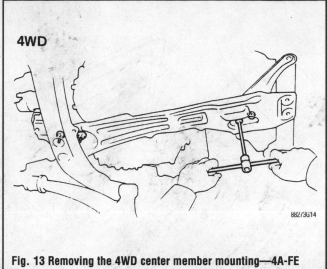

Fig. 13 Removing the 4WD center member mounting—4A-FE engine

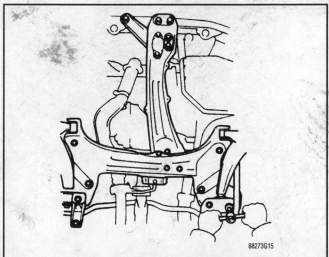

Fig. 14 4WD front suspension crossmember mounting—4A-FE engine

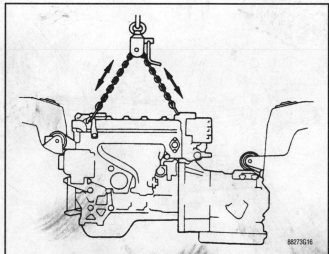

Fig. 15 Carefully attach a chain hoist to the engine hangers and lift the assembly out—4A-FE and 7A-FE engines

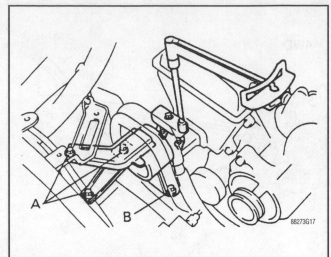

Fig. 16 Tighten the RH insulator-to-body and bracket bolts—1993–95 4A-FE and 7A-FE engines

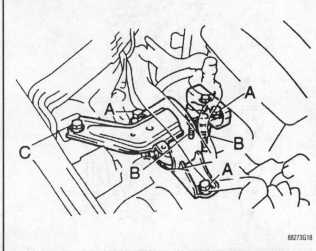

Fig. 17 Tighten the RH insulator-to-body and bracket bolts—1996–97 4A-FE and 7A-FE engines

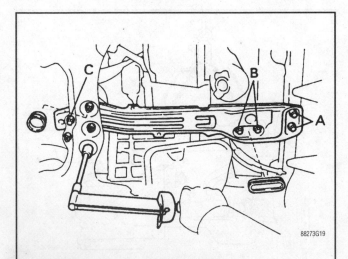

Fig. 18 Tighten the bolts retaining the center member to the body—4A-FE and 7A-FE engines

46. Attach the chain hoist or lift apparatus to the engine and lower it into the engine compartment.

➡**Tilt the transaxle downward and lower the engine to clear the left motor mount. As before, be careful not to hit the power steering housing (rack) or the throttle position sensor.**

47. Level the engine and align each mount with its bracket. Installation is the reverse of removal for engine installation. Tighten the components to the following specifications on 1988–92 models:
- RH mounting insulator-to-engine bracket bolt—47 ft. lbs. (64 Nm)
- RH mounting insulator-to-engine bracket nut—38 ft. lbs. (52 Nm)
- RH insulator-to-body bracket—64 ft. lbs. (87 Nm)
- LH insulator-to-transaxle case bracket—35 ft. lbs. (48 Nm)
- RH mounting stay—31 ft. lbs. (42 Nm)
- LH mounting stay—15 ft. lbs. (21 Nm)
- Engine center member front and rear mounting bolt—64 ft. lbs. (87 Nm)
- Engine center member 5 bolts—45 ft. lbs. (61 Nm)
- 4WD front crossmember lower control arm—152 ft. lbs. (206 Nm)
- 4WD front crossmember rear bolt—94 ft. lbs. (127 Nm)
- Front mounting-to-member—35 ft. lbs. (48 Nm)
- Center (2WD) mounting-to-center—38 ft. lbs. (52 Nm)
- Rear (2WD) mounting-to-member—38 ft. lbs. (52 Nm)
- Rear (4WD) mounting-to-member—42 ft. lbs. (57 Nm)
- Front pipe-to-exhaust manifold—46 ft. lbs. (62 Nm)

48. Tighten the components to the following specifications on 1993–97 models:
- Front engine mounting bracket—57 ft. lbs. (77 Nm)
- LH mounting bracket—38 ft. lbs. (52 Nm)
- LH insulator-to-bracket—41 ft. lbs. (56 Nm)
- LH insulator through-bolt—64 ft. lbs. (87 Nm)
- LH stay—15 ft. lbs. (21 Nm)
- RH insulator-to-body and bracket (A)—47 ft. lbs. (64 Nm)
- RH insulator-to-body and bracket (B)—38 ft. lbs. (52 Nm)
- RH insulator-to-body and bracket (C)—19 ft. lbs. (25 Nm)
- Engine mounting center member-to-body (A)—45 ft. lbs. (61 Nm)
- Engine mounting center member-to-body (B)—47 ft. lbs. (64 Nm)
- Engine mounting center member-to-body (C)—35 ft. lbs. (48 Nm)
- Engine mounting center member-to-body nut—42 ft. lbs. (57 Nm)
- Front mounting insulator-to-bracket—64 ft. lbs. (87 Nm)
- Fuel inlet hose—22 ft. lbs. (29 Nm)

49. Install the battery. Connect the positive cable to the starter terminal, then to the battery. DO NOT connect the negative battery cable at this time.

50. Fill the transmission with the correct amount of fluid.

51. Refill the engine coolant.

52. Fill the engine with the correct amount of oil.

53. Double check all installation items, paying particular attention to loose hoses or hanging wires, untightened nuts, poor routing of hoses and wires (too tight or rubbing) and tools left in the engine area.

54. Connect the negative battery cable. Start the engine and allow it to idle. As the engine warms up, shift the automatic transmission into each gear range allowing it to engage momentarily. After each gear has been selected, put the shifter in PARK and check the transmission fluid level.

55. Shut the engine **OFF** and check the engine area carefully for leaks, particularly around any line or hose which was disconnected during removal.

56. Raise and support the front end of the car on jackstands. Replace the left and right splash shields and lower the vehicle.

57. With the help of an assistant, reinstall the hood. Adjust the hood for proper fit and latching. Road test the vehicle for proper operation.

4A-GE Engine

▶ See Figures 19, 20, 21, 22 and 23

1. Relieve the fuel system pressure. Disconnect the negative battery cable.

2. With a helper remove the hood (mark hood hinges for correct installation) from the car. Use care not to damage the paint finish on the vehicle.

3. Drain the engine oil.
4. Drain the cooling system.
5. Drain the transaxle oil.
6. Remove the air cleaner assembly.
7. Remove the coolant reservoir tank and remove the PCV hose.
8. Label and remove the heater hoses from the water inlet housing.
9. Label and disconnect the fuel inlet hose from the fuel filter.

➡ **The fuel system is under pressure. Release pressure slowly and contain spillage. Observe no smoking/no open flame precautions. Have a Class B-C (dry powder) fire extinguisher within arm's reach at all times.**

10. Disconnect the heater and air hoses from the air valve.
11. Remove the fuel return hose from the pressure regulator.
12. If equipped with a manual transaxle, remove the slave cylinder from the housing. Loosen the mounting bolts and move the cylinder out of the way but do not loosen or remove the fluid hose running to the cylinder.
13. Disconnect the vacuum hose running to the charcoal canister.
14. Disconnect the shift control cable, the speedometer cable (at the transaxle) and the accelerator cable (at the throttle body).
15. If equipped with cruise control, disconnect the cables. Remove the cruise control actuator by:
   a. Disconnecting the vacuum hose.
   b. Removing the cover and the 3 bolts.
   c. Disconnecting the actuator wiring and removing the actuator.
16. Remove the ignition coil.
17. Remove the main engine wiring harness in the following steps:
   a. From inside the car, remove the right side cowl (kick) panel.
   b. Disconnect the wiring harness at junction block 4.
   c. Remove the cover over the Electronic Control Module (ECM) and carefully disconnect the ECM plugs.
   d. Pull the main wiring harness into the engine compartment.
18. Disconnect the wiring at the number 2 junction block in the engine compartment.
19. Remove the engine and transaxle ground straps.
20. Disconnect the washer valve harness.
21. Remove the wiring at the cruise control vacuum pump harness and the vacuum switch connector.
22. Remove the hose from the brake vacuum booster.
23. Depending on equipment, remove the air conditioning compressor and/or the power steering pump. Note that the units are to be removed from their mounts and placed out of the way— DO NOT disconnect hoses and lines from the units.
   a. Remove the power steering pump pulley nut.
   b. Loosen the idler pulley adjusting and pulley bolts.

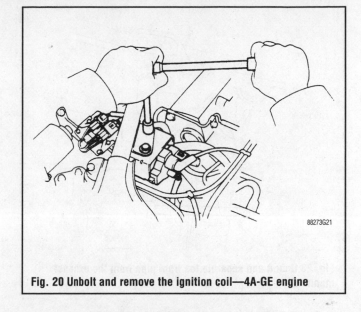

Fig. 20 Unbolt and remove the ignition coil—4A-GE engine

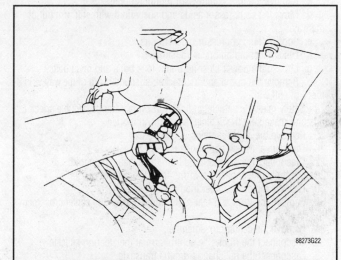

Fig. 21 Pull the engine wiring through the cowl panel—95 4A-FE and 7A-FE engines

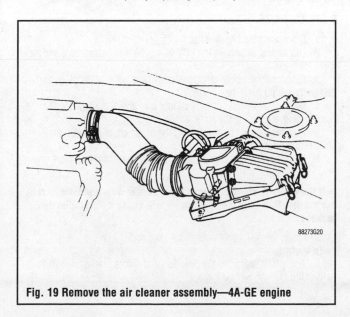

Fig. 19 Remove the air cleaner assembly—4A-GE engine

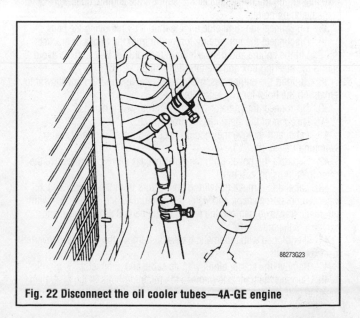

Fig. 22 Disconnect the oil cooler tubes—4A-GE engine

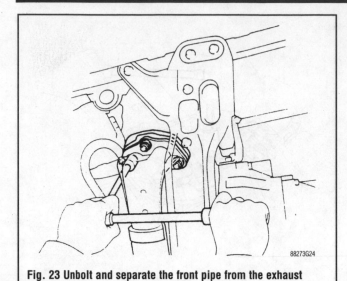

Fig. 23 Unbolt and separate the front pipe from the exhaust manifold

c. Remove the four compressor mounting bolts.

d. Move the compressor aside and suspend it with stiff wire out of the way.

e. Loosen the compressor bracket bolts.

f. Disconnect the oil pressure harness.

g. Loosen the power steering pump lock bolts and pivot bolts.

h. Remove the pump and its bracket; suspend it out of the way with a piece of stiff wire.

24. Safely raise the vehicle and support on jackstands. Double check the stands and make sure the vehicle is solidly supported.

25. Remove the splash shields under the car.

26. Disconnect the oil cooler hoses.

27. Disconnect the exhaust pipe from the exhaust manifold.

28. Carefully disconnect the wiring from the oxygen sensor.

29. Remove the cover under the flywheel.

30. Remove the front and rear motor mounts from the center crossmember.

31. Remove the center crossmember.

32. Disconnect the right side control arm at the steering knuckle.

33. Disconnect the halfshafts from the transaxle.

34. Lower the vehicle to the ground. Install the engine hoist to the lifting bracket on the engine. Hang the engine wires and hoses on the lift chain. Take tension on the hoist sufficient to support the engine; double check all hoist attaching points.

35. Disconnect the right side engine mount by removing the bolt.

36. Disconnect the left side motor mount from the transaxle bracket.

37. Lift the engine and transaxle from the vehicle. Be careful to avoid hitting the steering box and the throttle position sensor.

38. Support the engine assembly on a suitable stand; do not allow it to remain on the hoist for any length of time.

39. Disconnect the radiator fan temperature switch harness.

40. Disconnect the start injector time switch.

41. Label and remove the vacuum hoses from the Bimetal Vacuum Switching Valves (BVSV).

42. Separate the hoses from the water bypass valves, then remove the water inlet housing assembly.

43. Label and remove the wiring connectors from the reverse switch, water temperature sensor, and water temperature switch. If equipped with automatic transaxle, remove the wiring to the neutral safety switch and transaxle solenoid.

44. If equipped with automatic transaxle, remove the 6 torque converter-to-flexplate bolts.

45. Remove the starter along with its cable and connector.

46. Support the transaxle, remove the retaining bolts in the case, then separate the transaxle from the engine. Pull the unit straight off the engine;

do not allow it to hang partially removed on the shaft. Keep the automatic transaxle level; if it tilts forward the converter may fall off.

To install:

47. Install the engine in the reverse order of removal paying particular attention to the following.

48. Before reinstalling the engine in the car, several components must be reattached or connected. Install the transaxle to the engine; tighten the 12mm bolts to 47 ft. lbs. (64 Nm) and the 10mm bolts to 34 ft. lbs. (46 Nm). Tighten other components to the following specifications:

- Starter mounting bolts—29 ft. lbs. (39 Nm)
- Right motor mount and through bolt—58 ft. lbs. (78 Nm).
- Engine mounting automatics—38 ft. lbs. (52 Nm)
- Engine mounting bracket-to-transaxle—45 ft. lbs. (61 Nm)
- Engine mounting stay LH—15 ft. lbs. (21 Nm)
- Engine mounting LH-to-transaxle manual—38 ft. lbs. (52 Nm)
- Engine mounting stay RH—31 ft. lbs. (42 Nm)
- Engine mounting RH-to-engine manual-nut—38 ft. lbs. (52 Nm)
- Engine mounting RH-to-engine manual bolt—47 ft. lbs. (64 Nm)
- Engine mounting bolt front—35 ft. lbs. (48 Nm)
- Engine mounting bolt center—38 ft. lbs. (52 Nm)
- Engine mounting bolt rear—42 ft. lbs. (57 Nm)
- Engine rear mounting bolt—64 ft. lbs. (87 Nm)
- Engine front mounting bolt—64 ft. lbs. (87 Nm)
- Power steering pump pulley bolt—28 ft. lbs. (38 Nm)

49. Fill the transaxle with the correct amount of oil, and fill the engine with oil.

50. Fill the cooling system with the proper amount of fluid.

51. Double check all installation items, paying particular attention to loose hoses or hanging wires, untightened nuts, poor routing of hoses and wires (too tight or rubbing) and tools left in the engine area.

52. Connect the negative battery cable.

53. Start the engine and allow it to reach normal operating temperature. Check carefully for leaks. Shut the engine **OFF**.

54. Raise the front end of the car, support on jackstands and install the splash shields below the car.

55. Lower the car to the ground. With your helper, install the hood and adjust it for proper fit and latching. Road test the vehicle for proper operation.

Rocker Arm (Valve) Cover

REMOVAL & INSTALLATION

4A-GE Engine

▶ See Figure 24

1. Disconnect the negative battery cable.

2. Disconnect or remove the PCV valve, the accelerator cable and the wiring harness.

3. Disconnect (mark or label) the spark plug wires at the plugs and detach the wiring to the noise filter.

4. Disconnect the oil pressure sender wire and, if equipped with air conditioning, the wire to the compressor.

5. Remove the four bolts retaining the center cover (between the cam covers) and its gasket.

6. Remove the eight cap nuts, the rubber seals and two valve covers.

➡**If the cover is stuck in place, tap a corner with a plastic or rubber mallet. Don't pry the cover up; it will cause deformation and leakage.**

7. Clean the mating surfaces of the head and the covers.

To install:

8. Apply RTV sealant to the cylinder head before reassembly. This step is REQUIRED to prevent oil leakage.

9. Install the covers with new gaskets. Install the seals and the cap nut,

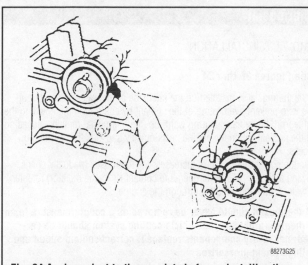

Fig. 24 Apply sealant to these points before reinstalling the valve cover—4A-GE engine

Loosen the three valve cover retaining nuts

making sure everything is properly seated. Tighten the cap nuts in several steps to 9 ft. lbs. (12 Nm).

10. Install the center cover with its gasket .

11. Connect the wiring to the oil pressure sender and the compressor, if equipped.

12. Connect the wiring to the noise filter and install the spark plug wires.

13. Connect, in this order, the wiring harness, the accelerator cable, the PCV valve and the negative battery cable.

14. Start the engine and check for leaks after the engine has warmed up. Minor leaks may be cured by slightly snugging the cover bolts. Any leak that is still present after about a ¼ turn CANNOT be cured by further tightening. Remove the cover again and either reposition or replace the gasket.

4A-F, 4A-FE and 7A-FE Engines

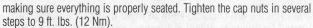 **See Figure 25**

1. Disconnect the negative battery cable.

2. Disconnect the PCV and the vacuum hose.

3. Loosen the engine wiring harness running over the upper timing belt cover for easier access to the valve cover.

Remove the cap nuts and seals, then lift the valve cover off the cylinder head

Twist, then pull the wires from the rocker cover

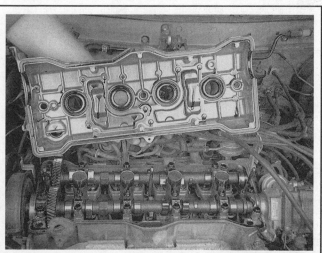

Lift the valve cover off the cylinder head . . .

. . . then remove and discard the old gasket

88273P35

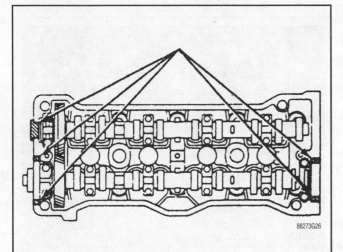

88273G26

Fig. 25 Apply sealant to these points before reinstalling the valve cover—4A-F, 4A-FE and 7A-FE engines

4. Remove the spark plug wires (mark or label) from the spark plugs.

5. Remove the 3 cap nuts, the seals below them and the valve cover.

To install:

6. Clean the mating surfaces of the head and the cover. Install a new gasket before installing the valve cover.

7. Apply RTV sealant to the cylinder head before reassembly. This step is REQUIRED to prevent oil leakage.

8. Install the cover with a new gasket. Install the seals and the cap nut, making sure everything is properly seated. Tighten the cap nuts in steps to 6–9 ft. lbs. (8–12 Nm).

9. Reconnect the spark plug wires and reposition the wiring harness over the timing belt cover.

10. Connect the vacuum hose, the PCV hose and the negative battery cable.

11. Start the engine and check for leaks after the engine has warmed up. Minor leaks may be cured by slightly snugging the cover bolts. Any leak that is still present after about a ¼ turn CANNOT be cured by further tightening. Remove the cover again and either reposition or replace the gasket.

Thermostat

REMOVAL & INSTALLATION

▶ **See Figures 26 thru 34**

The thermostat is installed on the inlet side of the water pump. Its purpose is to prevent overheating of the coolant by controlling the flow into the engine from the radiator. During warm up, the thermostat remains closed so that the coolant within the engine heats quickly and aids the warming up process.

As the coolant temperature increases, the thermostat gradually opens, allowing a supply of lower temperature coolant (from the radiator) to enter the water pump and circulate through the engine.

➡ **A thermostat should never be removed as a countermeasure to an overheating problem. The vehicle cooling system should be serviced, necessary components replaced, correct coolant added and cooling system pressurized.**

1. Drain the cooling system and save the coolant for reuse.

✷✷ CAUTION

When draining the coolant, keep in mind that cats and dogs are attracted by ethylene glycol antifreeze, and are quite likely to drink any that is left in an uncovered container or in puddles on the ground. This will prove fatal in sufficient quantity. Always drain the coolant into a sealable container. Coolant should be reused unless it is contaminated or several years old.

2. Remove the water inlet (disconnect electrical wiring) and remove the thermostat. Carefully observe the positioning of the thermostat within the housing. Clean all mounting surfaces before installation.

To install:

3. On the 4A-FE engine, place the thermostat in the water inlet housing. Install a new gasket to the thermostat and align the jiggle valve of the thermostat as shown in the water inlet housing. The jiggle valve may be set within 10° of either side of the prescribed position (two types of thermostat are used).

4. On the 7A-FE engine, place the thermostat in the water inlet housing. Install a new gasket to the thermostat and align the jiggle valve of the ther-

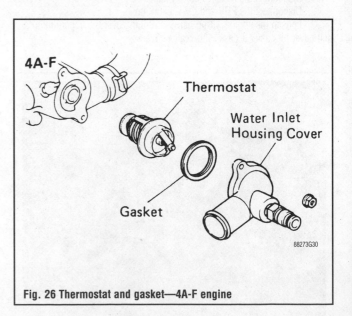

Fig. 26 Thermostat and gasket—4A-F engine

88273G30

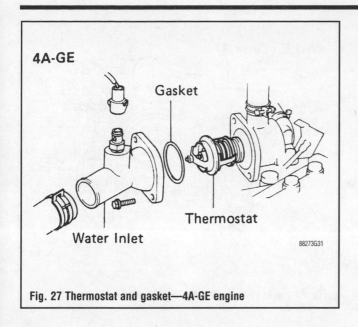

Fig. 27 Thermostat and gasket—4A-GE engine

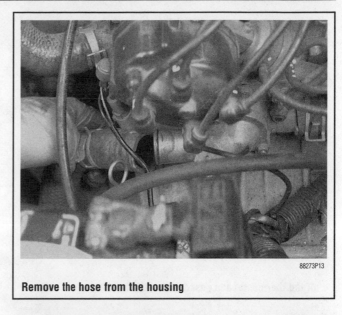

Remove the hose from the housing

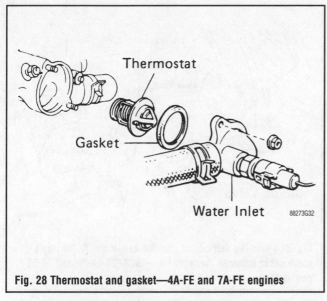

Fig. 28 Thermostat and gasket—4A-FE and 7A-FE engines

Remove the bolts retaining the housing to the cylinder head . . .

Disconnect the sensor wiring from the thermostat housing

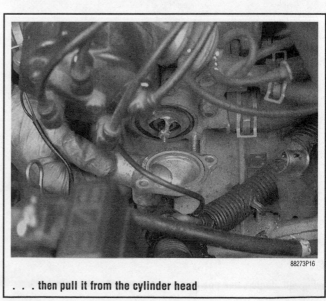

. . . then pull it from the cylinder head

Pull the thermostat and gasket out of the housing

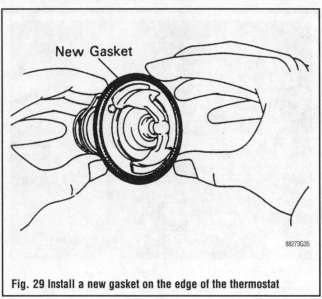

Fig. 29 Install a new gasket on the edge of the thermostat

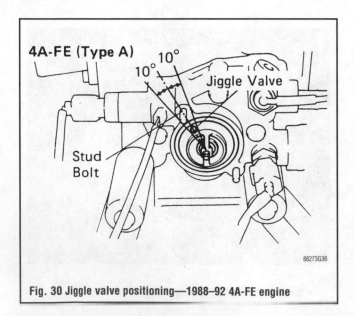

Fig. 30 Jiggle valve positioning—1988–92 4A-FE engine

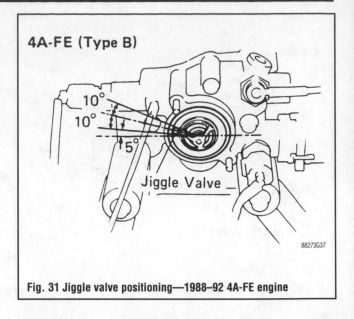

Fig. 31 Jiggle valve positioning—1988–92 4A-FE engine

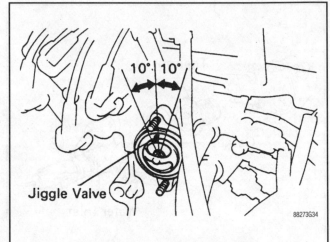

Fig. 32 Place the thermostat into the housing with the jiggle valve set in between these points—1993–97 4A-FE and 7A-FE engines

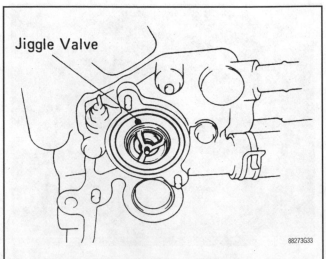

Fig. 33 Align the jiggle valve to seat in this position—4A-F and 4A-GE engines

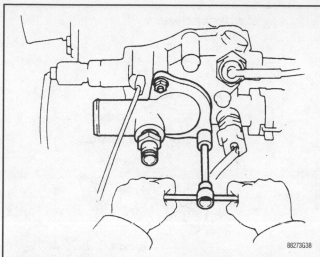

Fig. 34 Tighten the two hold-down bolts or nuts in steps. Do not overtighten these bolts!

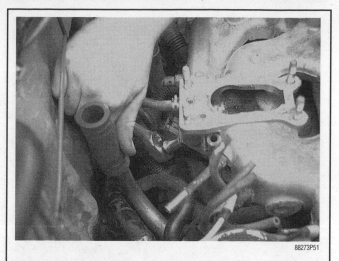

Unbolt and remove the intake manifold stay located in the back of the engine

mostat with the upper side of the stud bolt. The jiggle valve may be set within 10° of either side of the prescribed position.

5. On the 4A-F and 4A-GE engines, place the thermostat in the water inlet housing. Install a new gasket to the thermostat and align the jiggle valve of the thermostat so that it is positioned above the water inlet housing.

6. Install the water inlet (attach electrical wiring). Install the two hold-down bolts or nuts and tighten them to 7 ft. lbs. (9 Nm) (in steps). Do not overtighten these bolts!

7. Refill the cooling system with coolant.

8. Start the engine. During the warm up period, observe the temperature gauge for normal behavior. Also during this period, check the water inlet housing area for any sign of leakage. Remember to check for leaks under both cold and hot conditions.

Intake Manifold

REMOVAL & INSTALLATION

4F-E Engine

➡It is not necessary to remove the carburetor for this procedure. If you do, remember to inspect and replace any new hoses for gaskets.

1. Relieve the fuel pressure. Disconnect the negative battery cable.
2. Remove the air cleaner assembly. Drain the coolant.
3. Tag and remove all wires, hoses or cables in the way of intake manifold removal. Remove the intake manifold stay (bracket).
4. Remove the seven bolts, two nuts, wire clamp, manifold and gasket from the engine. discard the old gasket.

To install:

5. Install a new gasket and place the intake manifold into position. Attach the wire clamp, insert the seven bolts and two nuts. Tighten in steps to 14 ft. lbs. (19 Nm).

6. Install the manifold stay and tighten the top bolt to 14 ft. lbs. (19 Nm) and the bottom bolt to 29 ft. lbs. (39 Nm). Check the vacuum diagram to attach any hoses not sure of during installation.

7. Attach the water hose and connect the PCV hose. Reattach any wiring disconnected.

8. Refill the cooling system with coolant.

9. Start the engine. During the warm up period, observe the temperature gauge for normal behavior. Also during this period, check the water inlet housing area for any sign of leakage. Remember to check for leaks under both cold and hot conditions.

Unbolt the intake manifold (carburetor removed) . . .

. . . then pull the manifold off the cylinder head

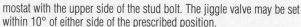

Remember to scrape the gasket from the edge of the manifold and mating surface

4A-GE, 4A-FE and 7A-FE Engines

◆ **See Figures 35, 36, 37, 38 and 39**

➡On the 1993–97 4A-FE and 7A-FE engines, the upper intake air chamber and intake manifold can be separated. A metal gasket is used to improve sealing performance. No cold start injector assembly is used on the 1993–97 vehicles.

1. Relieve the fuel pressure. Disconnect the negative battery cable.
2. Remove the air cleaner assembly. Drain the coolant.
3. Tag and remove all wires, hoses or cables in the way of intake manifold removal. Remove the intake manifold stay (bracket).
4. Remove the cold start injector pipe, if equipped.
5. Disconnect the electrical connectors and remove the fuel delivery pipe (fuel rail) and remove the injectors. During removal, be careful not to drop the injectors.

❊❊❊ CAUTION

The fuel system is under pressure. Release pressure slowly and contain spillage. Observe no smoking/no open flame precautions. Have a Class B-C (dry powder) fire extinguisher within arm's reach at all times.

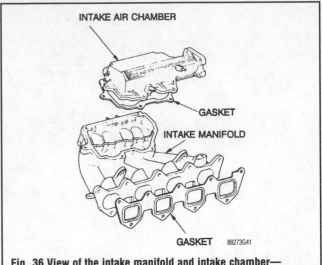

Fig. 36 View of the intake manifold and intake chamber—1993–97 4A-FE and 7A-FE engines

INTAKE AIR CHAMBER
GASKET
INTAKE MANIFOLD
GASKET

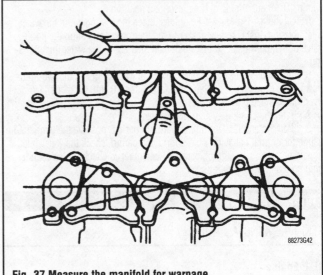

Fig. 37 Measure the manifold for warpage

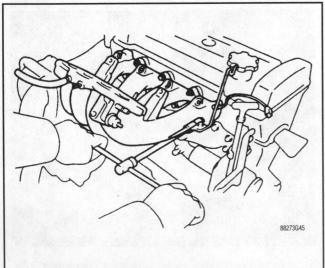

Fig. 35 Removing the intake manifold retaining bolts and nuts

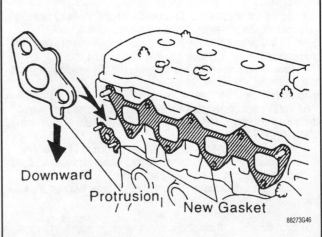

Downward
Protrusion
New Gasket

Fig. 38 The 7A-FE engines utilize an EGR gasket, place into position correctly

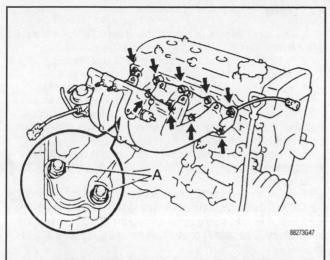

Fig. 39 Tighten the intake manifold bolts to specifications, (A) is a different specification

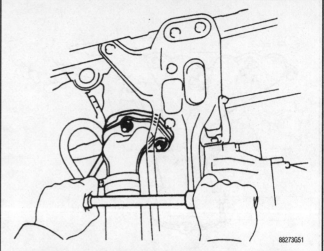

Fig. 40 Remove the three nuts retaining the front pipe to the exhaust manifold—4A-GE engine

6. Remove the intake manifold retaining bolts and nuts. Remove the intake manifold from the vehicle.

7. On some models (usually 7A-FE) the EGR valve will be removed with the intake manifold. Separate the unit from the intake and attach to the new manifold.

To install:

8. Clean the gasket mating surfaces, being careful not to damage them. Check the mating surfaces for warpage with a straightedge. The specification for maximum warpage on the intake manifold is on 4A-FE and 7A-FE engines; 0.0079 in. (0.20 mm) and on 4A-GE engines 0.0020 in. (0.05 mm). If warpage is greater than maximum, replace the manifold.

9. On the 7A-FE engines if the EGR valve was removed, place a new gasket no the cylinder head facing the protrusion downward.

10. Match the old gasket with the new one for an exact match. Use a new gasket when installing the manifold, then tighten the bolts and nuts evenly and in several passes from the center outward. Tighten the bolts to the following:

- Intake manifold; 1988–89—20 ft. lbs. (27 Nm)
- Intake manifold; 1990–94—14 ft. lbs. (19 Nm)
- Intake manifold bolt (A) 1995–97—9 ft. lbs. (13 Nm)
- Intake manifold except (A) 1995–97—14 ft. lbs. (19 Nm)

11. Install the intake manifold stay (bracket) and tighten to specifications.

- Intake manifold stay 1988–89—16 ft. lbs. (22 Nm)
- Intake manifold stay 12mm bolt 1990–97—14 ft. lbs. (19 Nm)
- Intake manifold stay 14mm bolt 1990–97—29 ft. lbs. (39 Nm)

12. Install the cold start injector pipe, if equipped. Tighten the cold start injector union bolt to 18 ft. lbs. (24 Nm).

13. Install all necessary wires, hoses or cables. Install the air cleaner assembly.

14. Refill the cooling system. Connect the negative battery cable. Start the engine. Check for leaks and road test for proper operation.

Exhaust Manifold

REMOVAL & INSTALLATION

4A-GE Engine

▶ **See Figures 40, 41, 42, 43 and 44**

1. Disconnect the negative battery cable. Raise the vehicle and support safely. Remove the right gravel shield from under the vehicle.

2. Remove the front exhaust pipe from the exhaust manifold.

3. Remove the four bolts and two nuts retaining the upper heat insulator. Pull the upper insulator off the vehicle.

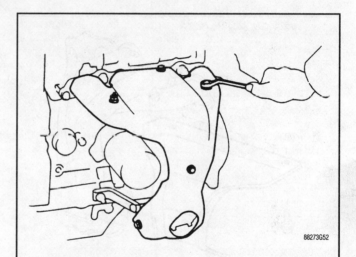

Fig. 41 Unbolt the upper insulator from the exhaust manifold—4A-GE engine

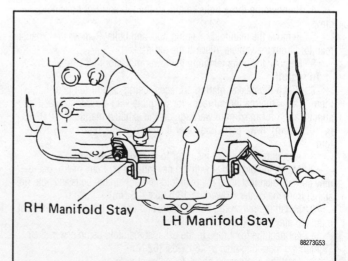

RH Manifold Stay

LH Manifold Stay

Fig. 42 Loosen and remove the manifold stay retaining bolts for both sides—4A-GE engine

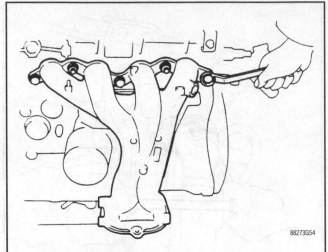

Fig. 43 Unbolt and separate the exhaust manifold from the engine—4A-GE engine

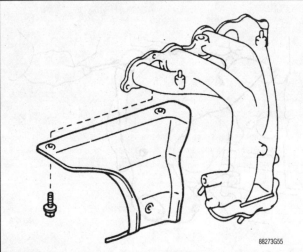

Fig. 44 The lower insulator must be removed from the manifold also—4A-GE engine

4. Remove the three bolts retaining the left and right manifold stays.

5. Remove the manifold retaining nuts and bolts. Remove the exhaust manifold from the vehicle. discard the old gasket.

6. Remove the bolts retaining the lower insulator to the manifold.

To install:

7. Clean the gasket mating surfaces, being careful not to damage them. Check the mating surfaces for warpage with a straightedge. The specification for maximum warpage on the exhaust manifold is 0.0118 in. (0.30 mm). If warpage is greater than maximum, replace the manifold.

8. Attach the lower heat insulator to the exhaust manifold.

9. Match the old gasket with the new one for an exact match. Use a new gasket when installing the manifold and tighten the bolts and nuts (in steps) from the center outward to 18 ft. lbs. (25 Nm).

10. Install the remaining components and tighten left and right exhaust manifold stay bolts to 29 ft. lbs. (39 Nm).

11. connect the front pipe to the exhaust manifold using new gaskets. Tighten the mounting nuts to 46 ft. lbs. (62 Nm).

12. Start the engine and check for exhaust leaks.

4A-F Engine

1. Disconnect the negative battery cable. Raise the vehicle and support safely. Remove the right gravel shield from under the vehicle.

2. Separate the front exhaust pipe from the exhaust manifold.

3. Remove the two bolts and manifold stay from the engine.

4. Remove the air cleaner hose attached to the exhaust manifold.

5. Remove the five bolts and the upper manifold insulator. Disconnect the oxygen sensor wiring. Unsecure the three bolts, two nuts and discard the gasket. Pull off the exhaust manifold. Remove the three bolts retaining the lower manifold insulator.

6. Remove the oxygen sensor and install it into the new manifold. Always use a new gasket.

To install:

7. Clean the gasket mating surfaces, being careful not to damage them. Check the mating surfaces for warpage with a straightedge. The specification for maximum warpage on the exhaust manifold is 0.0039 in. (0.10mm). If warpage is greater than maximum, replace the manifold.

8. Install the lower manifold insulator with the three bolts. Using a new

Remove the two bolts retaining the manifold stay

Pull the hose from the exhaust manifold and air cleaner

Loosen and remove the nuts and bolts retaining the upper insulator to the manifold—4A-F engine

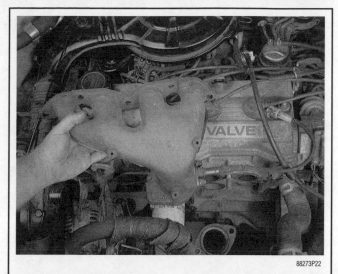

Lift the exhaust manifold off the engine

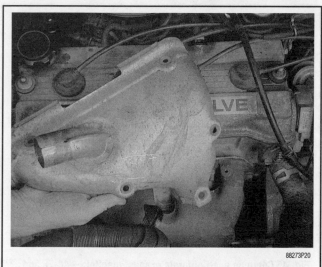

Pull the upper heat shield off of the manifold and set it aside

Discard the exhaust flange gasket . . .

Unbolt the manifold from the cylinder head

. . . and the manifold gasket

Always clean the area of any gasket material

gasket, install the exhaust manifold with the two nuts and three bolts. Tighten the to 18 ft. lbs. (25 Nm).

9. Install the upper manifold insulator with the five mounting bolts. Attach the manifold stay and tighten to 29 ft. lbs. (39 Nm).

10. Attach the front pipe to the exhaust manifold using new gaskets, and tighten the nuts to 46 ft. lbs. (62 Nm).

11. Install any other components removed. Attach the negative battery cable. Lower the vehicle to the ground and check for leaks.

12. Attach the right gravel shield.

4A-FE and 7A-FE Engines

1988–92 MODELS

➡️Only the 4A-FE engine was available on the 1988–92 models. Keep in mind that new nuts may be needed for the front exhaust pipe. Theses nuts are usually not reusable.

1. Disconnect the negative battery cable. Raise the vehicle and support safely. Remove the right gravel shield from under the vehicle.

2. Remove the front exhaust pipe from the exhaust manifold.

3. Remove the upper heat insulator. Remove the manifold stay (bracket).

4. Remove the manifold retaining nuts. Remove the exhaust manifold from the vehicle.

To install:

5. Clean the gasket mating surfaces, being careful not to damage them. Check the mating surfaces for warpage with a straightedge. The specification for maximum warpage on the exhaust manifold is 0.0118 in. (0.30mm). If warpage is greater than maximum, replace the manifold.

6. Match the old gasket with the new for an exact match. Use a new gasket when installing the manifold and tighten the bolts (in steps) from the center outward to 18 ft. lbs. (25 Nm).

7. Install the remaining components and tighten the exhaust manifold stay (bracket) bolts to 29 ft. lbs. (39 Nm). Place new front pipe gaskets into position and tighten the pipe to the manifold to 46 ft. lbs. (62 Nm). New nuts may be needed during installation.

8. Start the engine and check for exhaust leaks.

1993–97 MODELS

▶ See Figures 45 and 46

➡️On the 1993–97 models, the shape of the exhaust manifold was changed to adopt a manifold catalytic converter (TWC) on the California models. On these applications, remove the exhaust manifold assembly, then separate the catalytic converter from the manifold. Keep in mind that new nuts may be needed for the front exhaust pipe. Theses nuts are usually not reusable.

1. Disconnect the negative battery cable. Raise the vehicle and support safely. Remove the right gravel shield from under the vehicle.

2. On California models, separate the TWC from the front pipe. Removing the bolts and support bracket holding the front pipe to the TWC. Discard the front pipe exhaust gaskets.

3. On all other models, remove the nuts securing the front exhaust pipe to the exhaust manifold.
   discard the old exhaust pipe gaskets.

➡️If the oxygen sensor must be removed on models equipped with them in the manifold, never reuse the old gasket. Replace the gasket.

4. To remove the exhaust manifold on all except California models:
   a. Remove the 5 bolts and upper heat insulator.
   b. Remove the 3 bolts and manifold stay.
   c. Remove the 5 nuts, exhaust manifold and gasket. Discard the old gasket.
   d. Remove the 3 bolts and lower heat insulator from the exhaust manifold.

5. To remove the exhaust manifold on California models:
   a. Disconnect the main oxygen sensor connection.
   b. Remove the 4 bolts securing the upper heat insulator.
   c. Remove the 2 bolts and manifold stay.

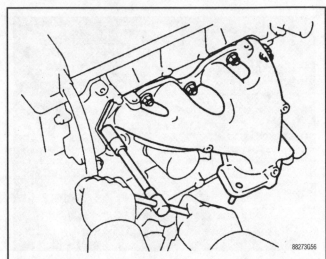

Fig. 45 Common non-California exhaust manifold—4A-FE and 7A-FE engines

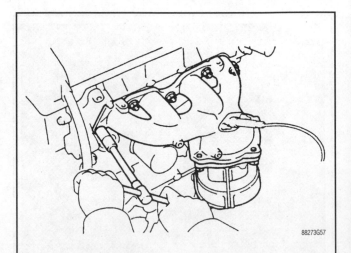

Fig. 46 Exhaust manifold with TWC catalyst attached—4A-FE and 7A-FE engines

d. Remove the 5 nuts, exhaust manifold assembly and gasket. Discard the old gasket.

e. Remove the 3 bolts securing the lower heat insulator to the exhaust manifold.

To install:

6. Clean the gasket mating surfaces, being careful not to damage them. Check the mating surfaces for warpage with a straightedge. The specification for maximum warpage on the exhaust manifold is 0.0039 in. (0.10mm). If warpage is greater than maximum, replace the manifold.

7. Match the old gasket with the new for an exact match. Use a new gasket when installing the manifold.

➡**If the oxygen sensor must be removed on models equipped with them in the manifold, never reuse the old gasket. Replace the gasket.**

8. On California models:

a. Install the lower heat insulator to the manifold with the 3 bolts.

b. Install a new gasket and manifold with the 5 retaining nuts. Uniformly tighten the bolts in several passes to 25 ft. lbs. (34 Nm).

c. Install the manifold stays with the 2 securing bolts. Alternately tighten the bolts to 29 ft. lbs. (39 Nm).

9. On non-California models:

a. Install the lower insulator to the exhaust manifold with the 3 bolts.

b. Install a new gasket and manifold with the 5 retaining nuts. Uniformly tighten the bolts in several passes to 25 ft. lbs. (34 Nm).

c. Install the manifold stay with 3 bolts. Tighten the bolts alternately to 29 ft. lbs. (39 Nm).

d. Install the upper heat shield and tighten the retaining bolts.

10. Attach the front exhaust pipe to the manifold suing new gaskets. Tighten the securing nuts to 46 ft. lbs. (62 Nm). Install and tighten the bolts for the support bracket retaining the pipe to the TWC to 14 ft. lbs. (43 Nm). Connect the oxygen sensor wiring if equipped. Double check all components are secure.

11. Connect the negative battery cable. Lower the vehicle. Start the engine and check for leaks. If none are found install the right gravel shield.

Radiator

REMOVAL & INSTALLATION

▶ See Figures 47, 48 and 49

1. Disconnect the negative battcry cable. Drain the cooling system.

❋❋ CAUTION

When draining the coolant, keep in mind that cats and dogs are attracted by the ethylene glycol antifreeze, and are quite likely to drink any that is left in an uncovered container or in puddles on the ground. This will prove fatal in sufficient quantity. Always drain the coolant into a sealable container. Coolant should be reused unless it is contaminated or several years old.

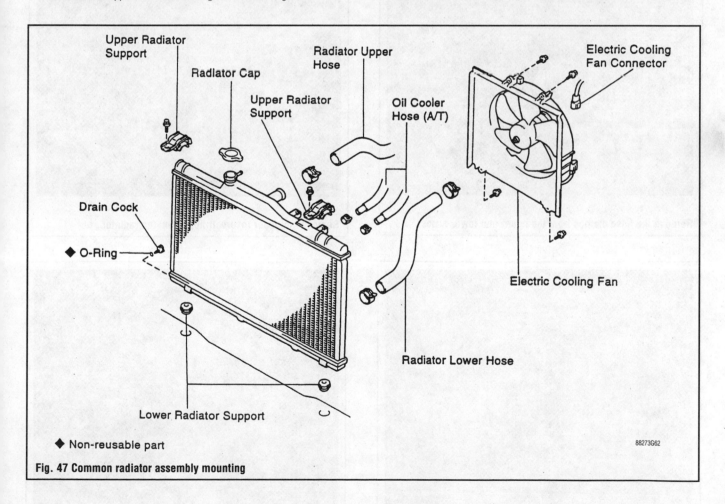

Fig. 47 Common radiator assembly mounting

2. Disconnect the electric cooling fan wiring.

3. Unfasten the clamps and remove the radiator upper and lower hoses.

4. If equipped with an automatic transaxle, disconnect the oil cooler lines (always use a line wrench).

5. Separate the coolant reservoir hose from the radiator. On some models remove the reservoir if necessary.

6. Remove the 2 bolts and two upper supports. Lift out the radiator with the cooling fan attached. Remove the 2 lower supports from the unit. Use care not to damage the radiator fins or the cooling fan.

7. Once out remove the 4 bolts retraining the electric cooling fan assembly to the radiator.

To install:

8. Install the electric cooling fan assembly and secure to the radiator.

9. Place the 2 lower radiator supports in position.

10. Place the radiator/cooling fan assembly in position and install the 2 upper supports with the bolts. Tighten the retaining bolts to 9 ft. lbs. (13 Nm). Make sure that the rubber cushions are not depressed after installation.

11. Reconnect the transaxle oil cooler lines, if equipped.

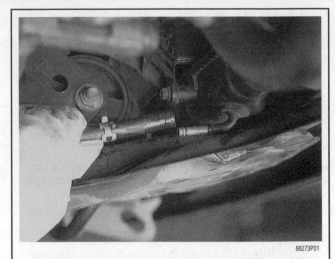

On automatic transaxles, disconnect the oil cooler lines from the radiator

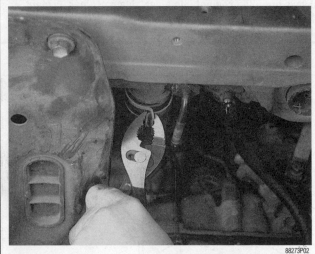

Remove the hose clamps from the upper and lower hoses . . .

Remove the upper reservoir hose from the radiator

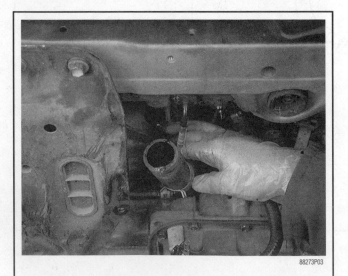

. . . then slide the hoses off the radiator inlet and outlet ports

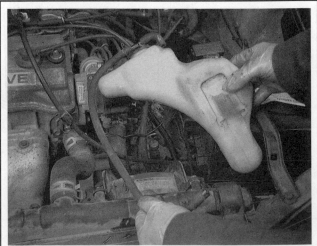

On some models it may be easier if the reservoir is removed

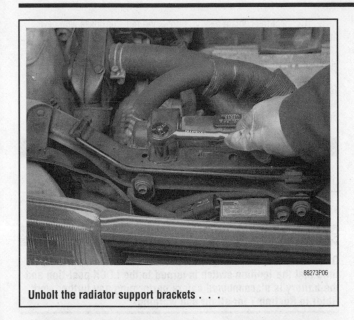

Unbolt the radiator support brackets . . .

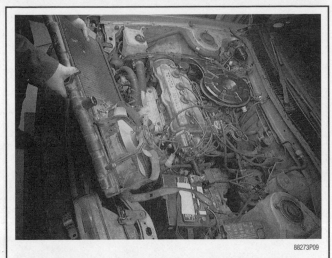

Pull the radiator and cooling fan assembly out of the engine compartment

. . . and remove the brackets from the top of the unit

1. Radiator
2. Cooling fan blade
3. Shroud
4. Cooling fan motor

Unbolt the electric cooling fan from the radiator

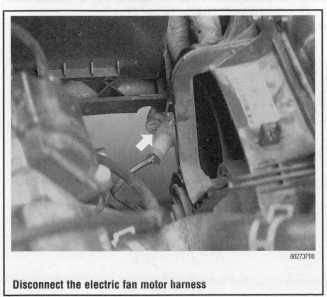

Disconnect the electric fan motor harness

Lift the fan off and install it on the new radiator

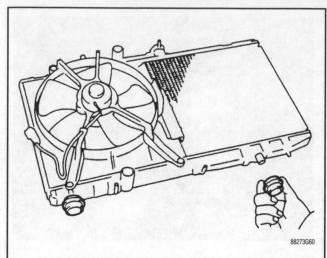

Fig. 48 Place the two lower radiator supports in position on the body of the unit

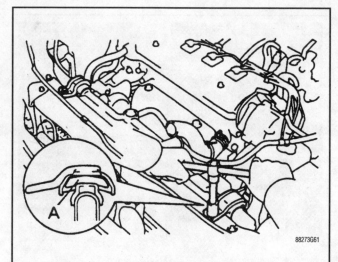

Fig. 49 When tightening the upper supports make sure the cushion is not depressed

12. Connect the coolant reservoir hose and radiator hoses with new hose clamps.

13. Reconnect the electrical wiring for the cooling fan. Connect the negative battery cable.

14. Fill the cooling system. Start the engine, check for coolant leaks. Top off the cooling system as necessary. Check the automatic transaxle fluid level. fill as needed, with the correct type of fluid. Refer to Section 1.

Electric Cooling Fan

REMOVAL & INSTALLATION

◆ See Figures 50 and 51

❋❋ CAUTION

On models with an airbag, wait at least 90 seconds from the time that the ignition switch is turned to the LOCK posi-tion and the battery is disconnected before performing any further work. Refer to Section 7 for all air bag warnings.

1. Disconnect the negative battery cable. Drain the cooling system.

2. Remove the coolant reservoir tank. Disconnect the upper radiator hose from the radiator.

3. Disconnect the electric cooling fan connector. Remove the 4 bolts and remove the cooling fan and shroud as an assembly.

4. Remove the cooling fan motor from the fan shroud, if necessary.

To install:

5. Reattach any components disassembled from the cooling fan assembly if separated. Tighten the cooling fan blade to 55 inch lbs. (6 Nm) and the fan motor to 23 inch lbs. (3 Nm).

6. Secure the cooling fan assembly to the radiator.

7. Attach the upper radiator hose.

8. Connect the negative battery cable. Fill the cooling system. Start the engine and check for proper cooling fan operation. Top off the system as necessary.

TESTING

➡**Always check all fuses and circuit breakers in all junction and relay blocks before troubleshooting the electric cooling fan circuit.**

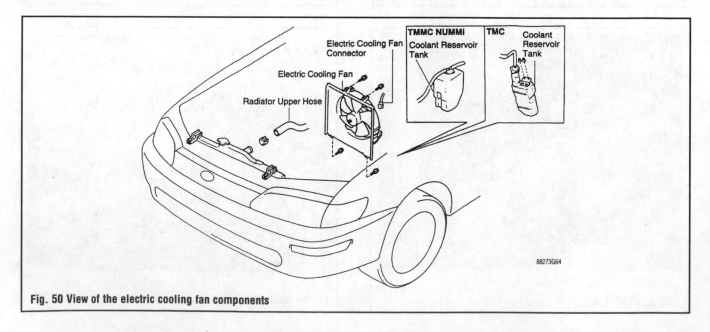

Fig. 50 View of the electric cooling fan components

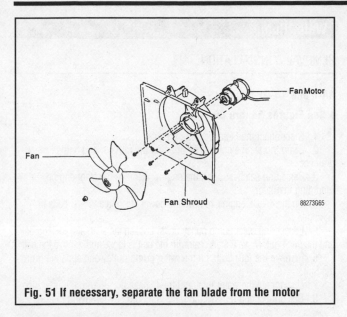

Fig. 51 If necessary, separate the fan blade from the motor

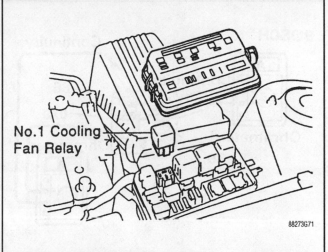

Fig. 53 The cooling fan relay is located in the fuse block in the engine compartment

Engine Coolant Temperature (ECT) Switch

▶ See Figure 52

Inspect the vehicle with the coolant temperature is low, below 83° C (181° F).

1. Turn the ignition **ON**. Check that the cooling fan stops. If not, check the cooling fan relay and electric coolant temperature switch (ECT), then check for a loose connection or severed wire between the cooling fan relay and ECT switch.

2. Disconnect the ECT switch wiring. Check that the cooling fan rotates. If not, inspect the cooling fan relay, engine main relay and fuse. Check for a short circuit between the cooling fan relay and ECT switch. Attach the ECT switch wiring.

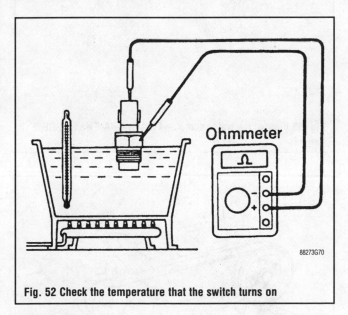

Fig. 52 Check the temperature that the switch turns on

Cooling Fan Relay

NIPPONDENSO

▶ See Figures 53 and 54

1. Using an ohmmeter, check that there is continuity between terminal 1 and terminal 2.

2. Using an ohmmeter, check that there is continuity between terminal 3 and terminal 4.

3. If continuity is not as specified, replace the relay.

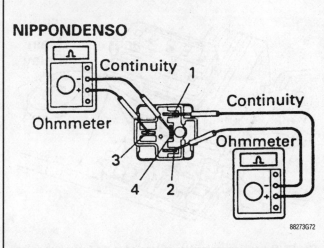

Fig. 54 Using an ohmmeter, check for continuity at the cooling fan relay

BOSCH

▶ See Figure 55

1. Using an ohmmeter, check that there is continuity between terminals 86 and 85.

2. Check that there is continuity between terminals 30 and 87a.

3. If continuity is not as specified, replace the relay.

Main Relay

▶ See Figures 56 and 57

1. Using an ohmmeter, check that there is continuity between terminal 1 and terminal 3.

2. If continuity is not as specified, replace the relay.

3. Next, check that there is continuity between terminal 2 and terminal 4.

4. If continuity is not as specified, replace the relay.

5. Check that there is no continuity between terminal 3 and terminal 5.

6. If continuity is not as specified, replace the relay.

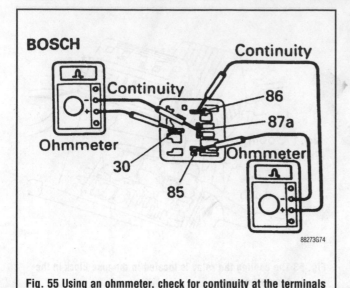

Fig. 55 Using an ohmmeter, check for continuity at the terminals

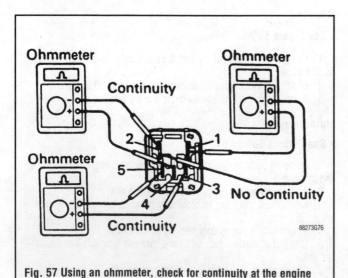

Fig. 56 The engine main relay is located in the fuse block in the engine compartment

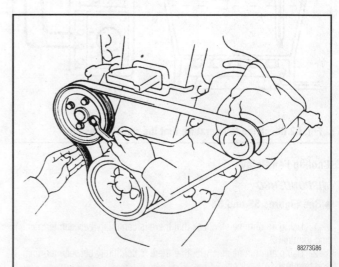

Fig. 57 Using an ohmmeter, check for continuity at the engine main relay

Water Pump

REMOVAL & INSTALLATION

4A-F and 4A-GE Engines

♦ **See Figures 58 thru 66**

1. Disconnect the negative battery cable.
2. Drain the engine coolant by opening the radiator and engine block draincocks.
3. Raise and safely support the engine. Remove the front engine mounting insulator.
4. On the 4A-GE engine, remove the power steering and A/C belts if equipped.
5. Loosen the water pump pulley bolts. Loosen the alternator locking bolt and the pivot nut. Move the alternator till the belt is loose and remove the belt.
6. Remove the four bolts on the water pump pulley and separate from the unit.
7. Disconnect the water inlet and the bypass hoses from the inlet pipe.
8. Disconnect and remove the water inlet pipe by removing the two

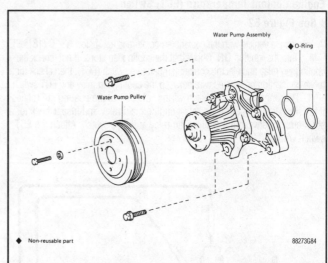

Fig. 58 View of the water pump and pulley—4A-F and 4A-GE engines

Fig. 59 Loosening the water pump pulley bolts—4A-F and 4A-GE engines

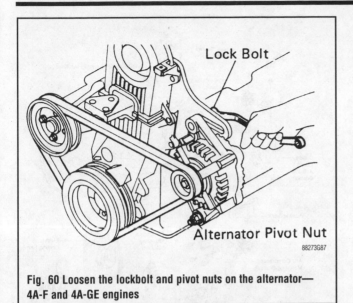

Fig. 60 Loosen the lockbolt and pivot nuts on the alternator—4A-F and 4A-GE engines

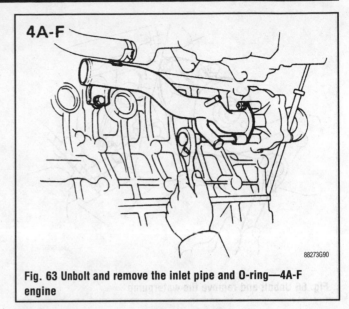

Fig. 63 Unbolt and remove the inlet pipe and O-ring—4A-F engine

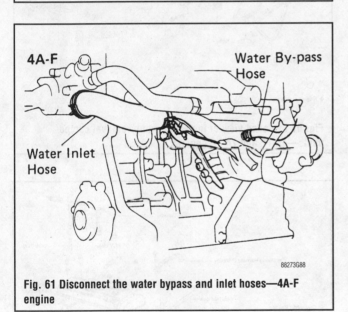

Fig. 61 Disconnect the water bypass and inlet hoses—4A-F engine

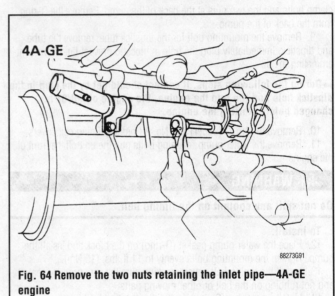

Fig. 64 Remove the two nuts retaining the inlet pipe—4A-GE engine

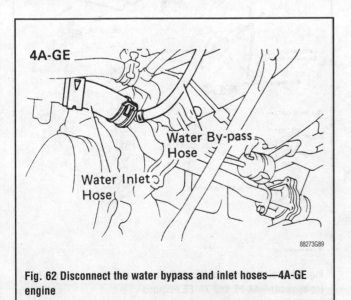

Fig. 62 Disconnect the water bypass and inlet hoses—4A-GE engine

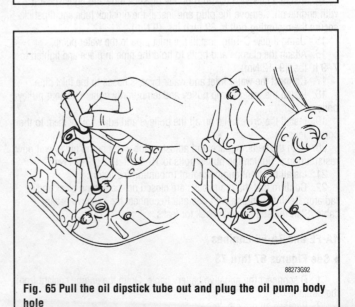

Fig. 65 Pull the oil dipstick tube out and plug the oil pump body hole

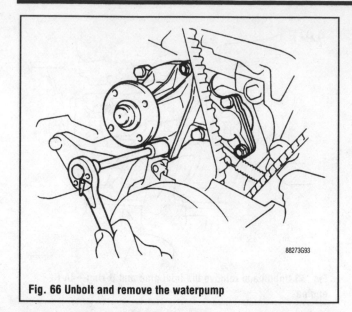

Fig. 66 Unbolt and remove the waterpump

clamp bolts and the two nuts at the back of the pump. Remove the O-ring from the back of the pump.

9. Remove the mounting bolt for the dipstick tube; remove the tube and dipstick. Immediately plug the hole in block to prevent fluid from contaminating the oil.

➡**During the following steps, if coolant should get by the plug in the dipstick hole and run into the engine, the engine oil MUST be changed before starting the engine.**

10. Remove the No. 3 (upper) and No. 2 (middle) timing belt covers.
11. Remove the water pump retaining bolts pull the unit off the front of the engine.

❊❊❊ WARNING

Do not spill any coolant on the timing belt.

To install:

12. Place the water pump gasket (O-ring) on the block and install the pump. Tighten the mounting bolts evenly to 11 ft. lbs. (15 Nm).
13. Install the timing belt covers, making sure they are properly seated and not rubbing on the belt or other moving parts.
14. Install a new seal (O-ring) on the dipstick tube and lightly coat it with engine oil. Remove the plug and install the dipstick tube and dipstick; secure the mounting bolt to 82 inch lbs. (9 Nm).
15. Using a new O-ring, install the inlet pipe to the water pump.
16. Attach the clamps and bolts to hold the pipe in place and tighten to 7–9 ft. lbs. (9–12 Nm).
17. Connect the water inlet and water bypass hoses to the inlet pipe.
18. Install the water pump pulley and temporarily tighten the four pulley bolts.
19. Install the drive belts on all the pulleys and adjust all of them to the correct tension.
20. With the belts in place and adjusted, the water pump pulley will now resist turning. Tighten the pulley bolts to 16–18 ft. lbs. (22–24 Nm).
21. Install the front engine mount (mounting insulator).
22. Confirm that the draincocks are closed on the engine block and radiator. Refill the engine with coolant. Reconnect the negative battery cable. Start the engine and check for leaks.

4A-FE and 7A-FE Engines

◗ **See Figures 67 thru 73**

1. Disconnect the negative battery cable. Drain the engine coolant from the radiator.
2. Remove all drive belts.

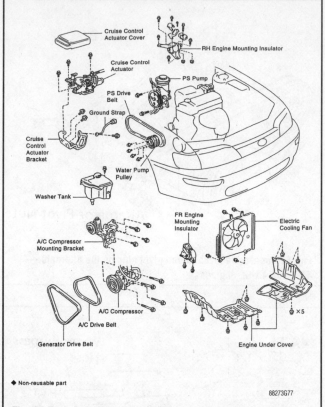

Fig. 67 Exploded view of the water pump removal components—4A-FE and 7A-FE engines

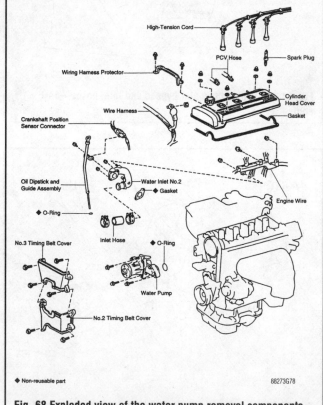

Fig. 68 Exploded view of the water pump removal components (continued)—4A-FE and 7A-FE engines

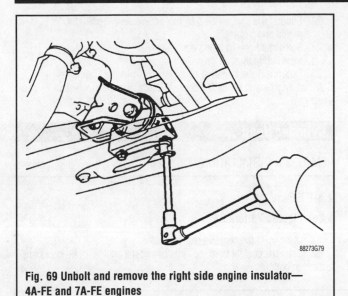

Fig. 69 Unbolt and remove the right side engine insulator—4A-FE and 7A-FE engines

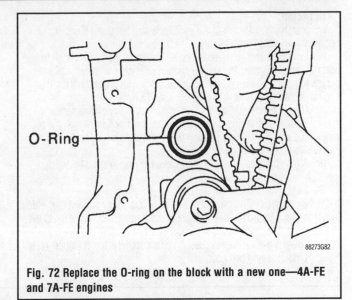

Fig. 72 Replace the O-ring on the block with a new one—4A-FE and 7A-FE engines

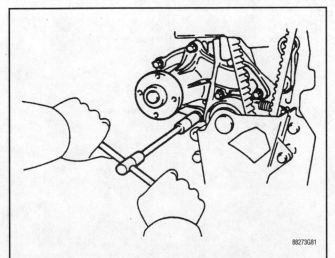

Fig. 70 Access hole to remove the nut and through-bolt for the front engine insulator—4A-FE and 7A-FE engines

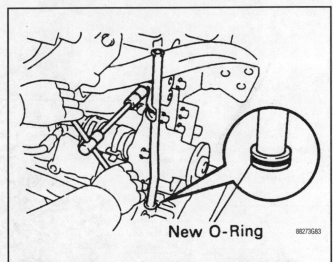

Fig. 73 Don't forget to use a new O-ring on the tube before securing to the engine

Fig. 71 Unbolt and remove the water pump and O-ring—4A-FE and 7A-FE engines

3. Support the engine using suitable equipment.

4. Remove the right engine mount and insulator.

5. Remove the No. 3 (upper) and No. 2 (middle) timing belt covers.

6. If equipped with power steering, raise and safely support the vehicle. Remove the front transaxle mounting insulator. Access the nut and through-bolt, through the hole. Lower the vehicle, remove the cooling fan assembly.

7. Remove the mounting bolt for the dipstick tube; remove the tube and dipstick. Immediately plug the hole in the block to prevent fluid from contaminating the oil.

8. If equipped, disconnect the crankshaft position sensor wiring from the dipstick guide. Remove the mounting bolt and pull out the dipstick guide and gauge. Discard the O-ring on the tube.

9. Disconnect the wiring for the water temperature sensor.

10. Remove the 2 nuts securing the engine coolant pipe to the cylinder block.

11. Loosen the clamp and remove the coolant inlet pipe.

12. Loosen the clamp and remove the coolant inlet hose from the water pump.

13. If equipped with power steering, raise the engine and remove the mounting bolts for the water pump. Remove the water pump and O-ring from the vehicle.

To install:

14. Install a new O-ring to the vehicle. Install the water pump and tighten the retaining bolts evenly to 11 ft. lbs. (15 Nm).

15. Lower the engine if necessary, and connect the coolant hose to the water pump. Reconnect the engine coolant inlet pipe to the vehicle and secure to hose with clamp and secure to block with 2 nuts. Tighten the engine coolant inlet pipe nuts to 11 ft. lbs. (15 Nm).

16. Connect the electrical wiring for the water temperature sensor.

17. Place a new O-ring on the end of the dipstick tube. Install the oil guide tube and tighten the retaining bolt to 84 inch lbs. (9 Nm). Install the oil level indicator to the guide tube.

18. Attach the crankshaft position sensor wiring to the oil dipstick guide, if removed.

19. Install the radiator fan assembly, if necessary.

20. If equipped with power steering, raise and safely support the vehicle. Install the front transaxle mount. Tighten the through bolt nut to 64 ft. lbs. (87 Nm) and 2 mount bolts to 47 ft. lbs. (64 Nm). Install the hole cover.

21. Lower the vehicle (if necessary) and install the No. 3 (upper) and No. 2 (middle) timing belt covers.

22. Support the engine using suitable equipment. Install the right engine mount and insulator.

23. Remove all engine lifting equipment.

24. Install and adjust all drive belts.

25. Reconnect the negative battery cable. Fill the cooling system. Start the engine and check for coolant leaks. Top off the system as necessary.

Cylinder Head

REMOVAL & INSTALLATION

4 A-F Engine

▶ **See Figures 74 thru 93**

1. Disconnect the negative battery cable.
2. Drain the coolant from the radiator and the engine. Drain cocks are located in both.

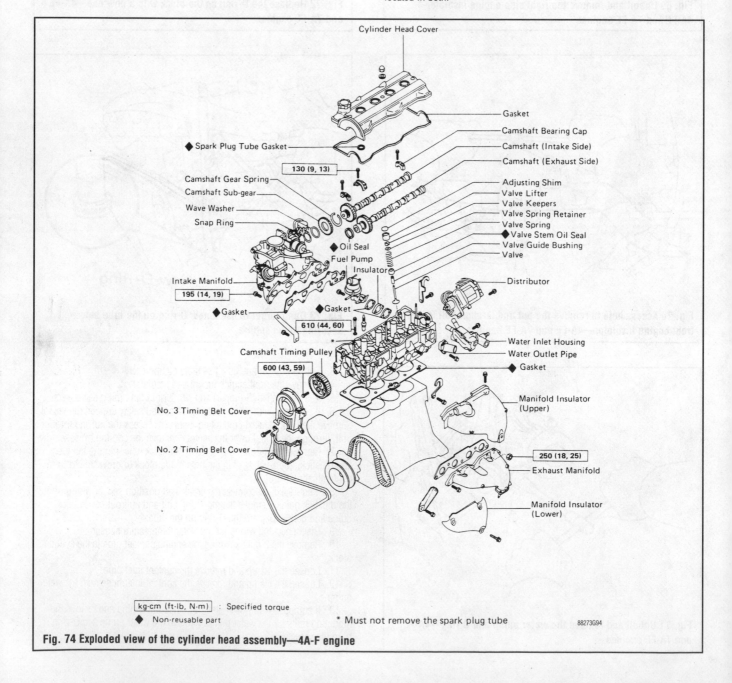

Fig. 74 Exploded view of the cylinder head assembly—4A-F engine

3. Remove the engine under cover. Raising and supporting the vehicle may be required for removal of this component.

4. Remove the nuts holding the front exhaust pipe to the manifold.

5. Remove the air cleaner hose and assembly.

6. Disconnect the accelerator cable and throttle cable for the automatic transaxles.

7. Label and unplug the following connectors:
- Two accelerator connections
- Oil pressure switch
- A/C pressure switch and A/C connector
- EBCV connector
- Carburetor connectors
- CMH connector
- Two vacuum switch connectors
- Water temperature sensor
- EGR gas temperature sensor connector (Calif.)
- IIA connector
- Cooling fan temperature switch
- Oxygen sensor connector

8. Disconnect the following vacuum hoses:
- EBCV vacuum hose
- VSV of A/C vacuum hose

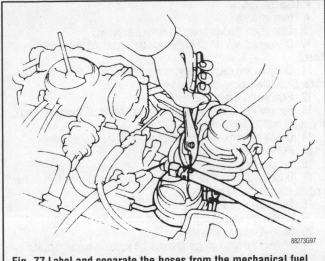

Fig. 77 Label and separate the hoses from the mechanical fuel pump—4A-F engine

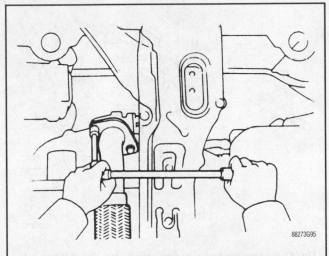

Fig. 75 Unbolt the front exhaust pipe from the manifold—4A-F-E engine

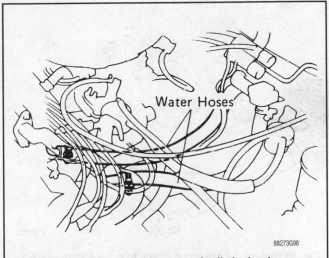

Fig. 78 Disconnect the water bypass and cylinder head rear plate hoses

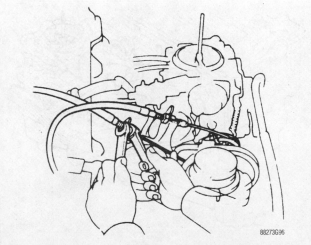

Fig. 76 Disconnect the accelerator and throttle cables from the automatic transaxle

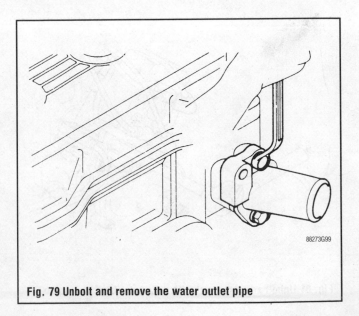

Fig. 79 Unbolt and remove the water outlet pipe

- Charcoal canister
- Power steering

9. Disconnect the fuel hoses from the fuel pump.

10. Disconnect and set off to the side the upper and lower radiator hoses.

11. Unclamp and detach the water hose from the cylinder head rear plate. Disconnect the water by-pass hose.

12. Remove the water outlet pipe.

13. Remove the bolts retaining the exhaust manifold stay, then unbolt the upper manifold insulator.

14. Unbolt and remove the exhaust manifold and lower insulator.

15. Remove the distributor.

16. Remove the water inlet housing.

17. Unbolt and remove the fuel pump, insulator and gaskets from the engine. discard the old gaskets.

18. Remove the intake manifold.

19. Loosen the water pump pulley and remove the drive belt.

20. Remove the air pump stay.

21. Remove the spark plugs. Remove the valve cover, cap nuts and gasket. Discard the old gasket and cap nuts.

22. Unbolt and remove the No. 2 and No. 3 timing belt covers.

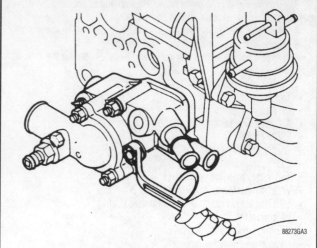

Fig. 82 Remove the nuts and bolt retaining the inlet water housing

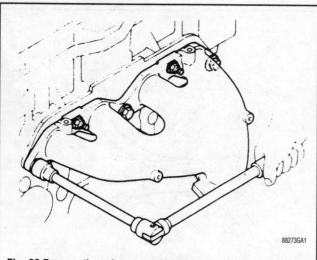

Fig. 80 Remove the exhaust manifold from the engine—4A-F engine

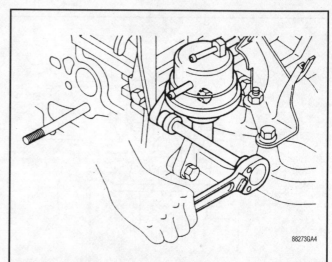

Fig. 83 Remove the fuel pump mounting bolts and pull the unit off the engine, discard the old gaskets

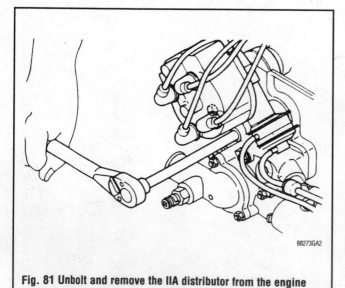

Fig. 81 Unbolt and remove the IIA distributor from the engine

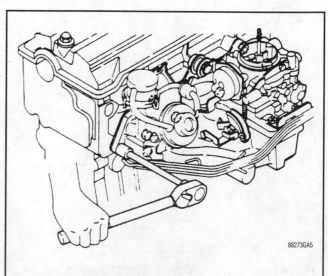

Fig. 84 Unbolt the intake manifold from the cylinder head

23. Set the No. 1 cylinder to TDC of the compression stroke.

24. Remove the No. 3 and No. 2 front covers. Turn the crankshaft pulley and align its groove with the **0** mark on the No. 1 front cover. Check that the camshaft pulley hole aligns with the mark on the No. 1 camshaft bearing cap (exhaust side). If not, rotate the crankshaft 360 degrees until the marks are aligned.

25. Remove the plug from the No. 1 front cover and matchmark the timing belt to the camshaft pulley. Loosen the idler pulley mounting bolt and push the pulley to the left as far as it will go; tighten the bolt. Slide the timing belt off the camshaft pulley and support it so it won't fall into the case.

26. Remove the camshaft pulley and check the camshaft thrust clearance. Remove the camshafts—refer to the necessary service procedures in this section.

27. Gradually loosen the cylinder head mounting bolts in several passes, in the proper sequence. Remove the cylinder head. Discard the old half moons.

To install:

28. Install new half moons into the head. They look similar to a half circle made out of rubber.

29. Place a new cylinder head gasket on the block. be careful of the installation direction.

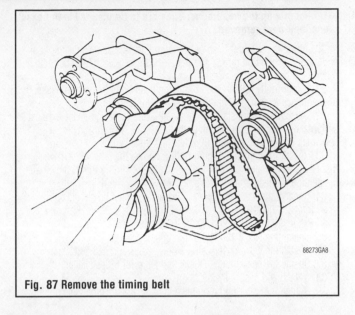

Fig. 87 Remove the timing belt

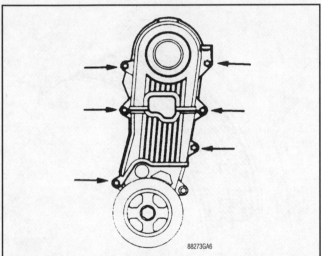

Fig. 85 Remove these retaining bolts from the No. 2 and No. 3 timing bolts

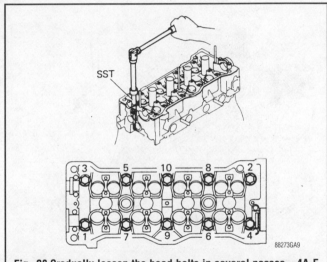

Fig. 88 Gradually loosen the head bolts in several passes—4A-F engine

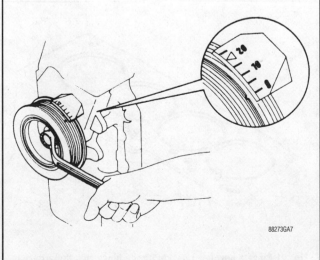

Fig. 86 Set the No. 1 cylinder to TDC of the compression stroke

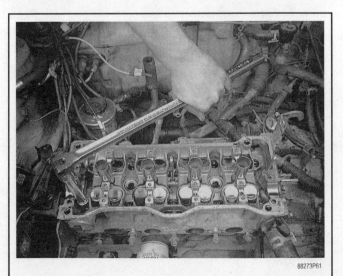

Use a breaker bar to loosen the cylinder head bolts

➡Do not mix up the head bolts. They are to be inserted in the exact place they were removed.

30. Place the cylinder head on top of the gasket. Apply a light coat of engine oil to each bolt thread and under the head of each head bolt. Do not mix up the head bolts.

31. Uniformilly tighten each of the ten head bolts in several passes, in the sequence shown. Tighten them to 44 ft. lbs. (60 Nm).

32. Assembly and install the camshafts. Gradually tighten the exhaust and intake camshaft bearing cap bolts to 9 ft. lbs. (13 Nm) in proper sequence shown in Camshaft Removal and Installation.

33. Install the camshaft timing pulley, tighten the pulley bolt to 43 ft. lbs. (59 Nm). Install the timing belt. Refer to the Timing Belt Removal and Installation procedure later in this section.

34. Inspect the valve clearance. Clearance when cold should be:

- Intake: 0.006–0.010 in. (0.15–0.25mm)
- Exhaust:0.008–0.012 in. (0.20–0.30mm)

35. Install the No. 2 and No. 3 timing belt covers.

36. Install the valve cover using a new gasket and cap nuts.

37. Install the spark plugs. Check the gap prior to installation.

38. Attach and secure the air pump stay.

39. Attach the water pump pulley and place the drive belt into position.

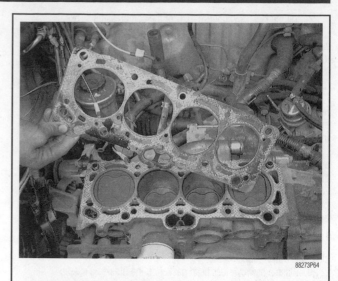

ALWAYS discard all old head gaskets

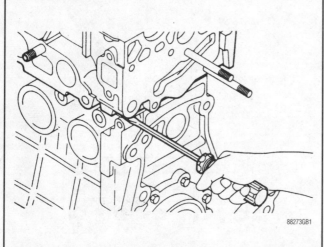

Fig. 89 If the head is difficult to remove, pry between the head and block projection

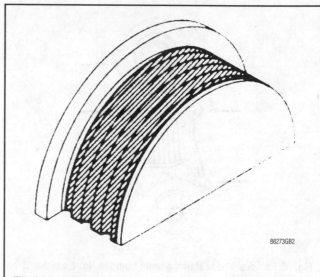

Fig. 90 Install new half moons prior to cylinder head installation

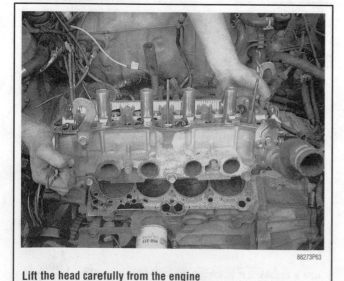

Lift the head carefully from the engine

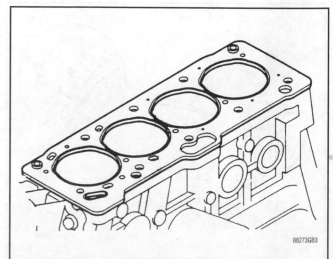

Fig. 91 Place a new head gasket on the block with the arrows in the correct direction—4A-F engine

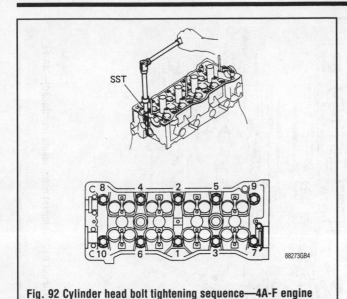

SST

C 8 4 2 5 9

C 10 6 1 3 7

88273GB4

Fig. 92 Cylinder head bolt tightening sequence—4A-F engine

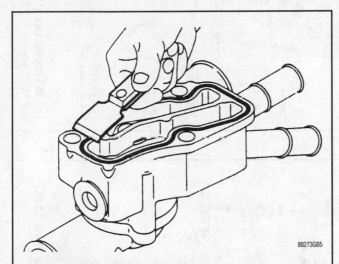

88273GB5

Fig. 93 Remove all old packing material on the inlet housing with a scraper

40. Install the intake manifold sing a new gasket. Tighten the nuts and bolts to 14 ft. lbs. (19 Nm). Install the manifold stay and tighten the upper bolt to 14 ft. lbs. (19 Nm). and the lower bolt to 29 ft. lbs. (39 Nm). Attach the water and PCV hoses.

41. Install the fuel pump using two new gaskets. Place one gasket into position, insulator, another gasket and the pump. Tighten the mounting bolts till secure.

42. When installing the water inlet housing, remove any old packing material first. Be careful not to drop any oil on the contact surfaces of the inlet housing or cylinder head.

    a. Apply sealant 08826–00100 (FIPG) or equivalent to the inlet housing. Avoid applying any excessive amount to the surface. Be especially careful around the oil passages. Components must be assembled within 3 mins. of application. Otherwise the FIPG must be removed and reapplied.

    b. Install the water inlet housing and tighten to 14 ft. lbs. (19 Nm). Attach the two hoses.

43. Install the exhaust manifold. Tighten the manifold nuts and bolts to 18 ft. lbs. (25 Nm) and the stay to 29 ft. lbs. (39 Nm).

44. Install the water outlet pipe. Remove any old packing material. Place new FIPG into position and tighten with bolts to 14 ft. lbs. (19 Nm).

45. Attach the water hoses, one connects to the cylinder head rear plate and the other is a by pass hose.

46. Connect and secure the upper and lower radiator hoses.

47. Attach the fuel pump hoses.

48. Connect the vacuum hoses and wiring that were labeled and disconnected.

49. Attach the accelerator cable and throttle cable for the automatic transaxle.

50. Install the air cleaner hose and air cleaner assembly.

51. Attach the front pipe to the exhaust manifold.

52. Refill the cooling system with coolant. Refer to the Capacities chart.

53. Connect the negative battery cable.

54. Start the engine, top off the cooling system. Check the oil and coolant levels. inspect for leaks.

55. Install the engine undercovers.

56. Check the ignition timing. Timing should be 5° BTDC at 900 rpm. with the transaxle in Neutral with the vacuum advance off.

57. Recheck the coolant and oil levels.

4A-FE and 7A-FE Engines

▶ See Figures 94 thru 100

1. Disconnect the negative battery cable at the battery. Drain the cooling system.

2. Remove the right side engine undercover.

3. Remove the air cleaner and hoses; disconnect the intake air temperature sensor.

4. Disconnect the accelerator and throttle cables at the bracket on vehicles with automatic transaxle.

5. Remove the cruise control actuator cable.

6. If necessary, remove the alternator and the distributor.

7. Disconnect the oxygen sensor wiring at the front pipe. Separate the front pipe from the exhaust manifold.

8. Tag and disconnect all wires, lines and hoses that may interfere with exhaust manifold, intake manifold and cylinder head removal.

9. Remove the 2 mounting bolts and lift out the exhaust manifold stay. Remove the upper manifold insulator and then remove the exhaust manifold.

10. Disconnect the fuel lines. Disconnect the heater hoses at the engine.

11. Disconnect the water hose and the bypass hose at the rear of the cylinder head. Remove the 2 bolts and pull off the water outlet pipe.

12. Disconnect the 2 water hoses at the water inlet (front of head) and then remove the inlet housing.

13. Detach the ground strap connector.

14. Disconnect these hoses from the intake chamber; MAP sensor hose, brake booster hose and air hose from the air pipe.

15. On models with EGR, remove the Vacuum Switching Valve (VSV).

16. Remove the intake manifold stay and the air pipe.

17. If necessary, unbolt and remove the throttle body and the air intake chamber.

18. Disconnect the PCV, fuel return and vacuum sensing hoses.

19. Remove the fuel inlet pipe and the cold start injector pipe (no cold start injector is used on the 1993–97 vehicles). Disconnect the 4 vacuum hoses and then remove the EGR vacuum modulator.

20. Remove the fuel delivery pipe along with the injectors, spacers and insulators.

21. Unbolt the engine wire cover at the intake manifold, then disconnect the wire at the cylinder head.

22. Remove the intake manifold assembly.

23. If necessary, remove the RH engine mounting insulator.

24. If necessary, remove the drive belts and then remove the water pump pulley.

25. Remove the spark plugs, cylinder head cover and semi-circular plug.

26. Remove the No. 3 and No. 2 front covers. Turn the crankshaft pulley and align its groove with the **0** mark on the No. 1 front cover. Check that the camshaft pulley hole aligns with the mark on the No. 1 camshaft bearing cap (exhaust side). If not, rotate the crankshaft 360 degrees until the marks are aligned.

    a. Remove the plug from the No. 1 front cover and matchmark the timing belt to the camshaft pulley. Loosen the idler pulley mounting bolt and push the pulley to the left as far as it will go; tighten the bolt. Slide

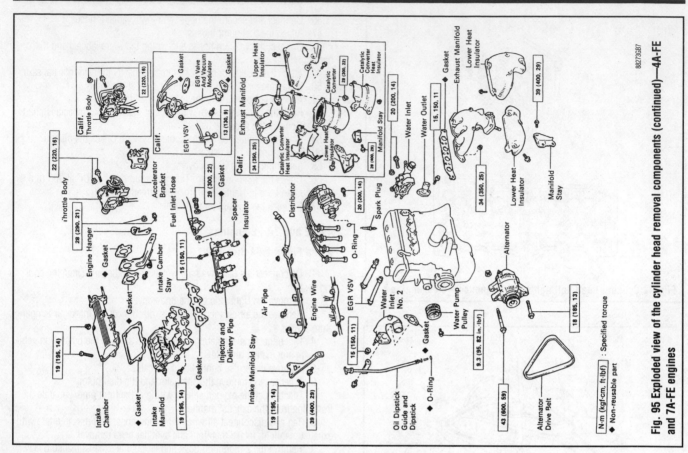

Fig. 95 Exploded view of the cylinder head removal components (continued)—4A-FE and 7A-FE engines

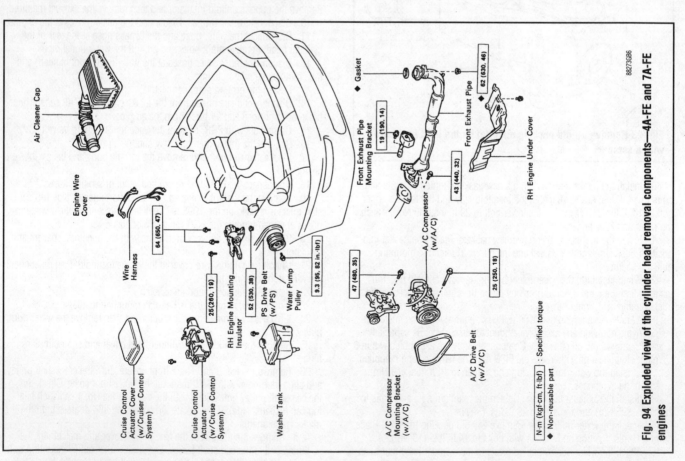

Fig. 94 Exploded view of the cylinder head removal components—4A-FE and 7A-FE engines

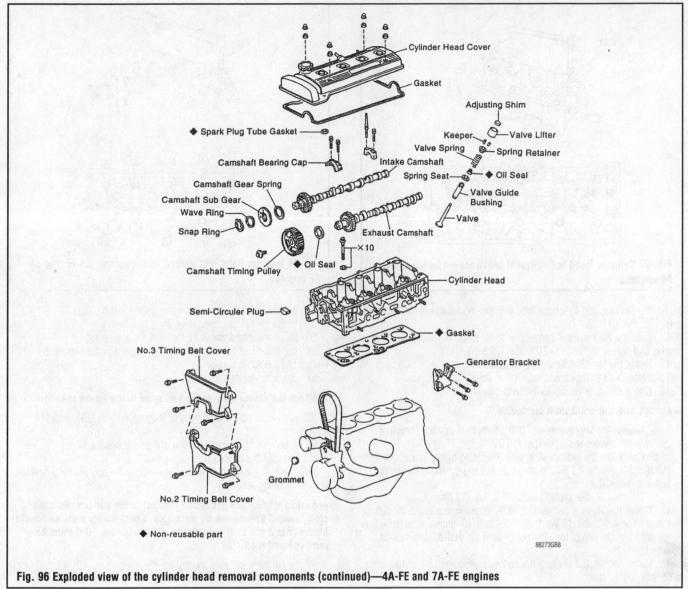

Fig. 96 Exploded view of the cylinder head removal components (continued)—4A-FE and 7A-FE engines

the timing belt off the camshaft pulley and support it so it won't fall into the case.

27. Remove the camshaft timing pulley.

28. Unbolt and remove the alternator bracket and two engine hangers.

29. If necessary, remove the oil dipstick guide and dipstick. Discard the old O-ring from the guide. Disconnect the Crankshaft Position Sensor (CPS) wiring.

30. On some models there is a second water inlet, unbolt and remove.

31. Remove the camshafts—refer to the necessary service procedures in this section.

32. Remove the half moon rubber plug. Discard and replace with a new one.

✳✳✳ WARNING

Cylinder head warpage or cracking could result from removing the bolts in the incorrect order.

33. Gradually loosen the 10 cylinder head mounting bolts in several passes, in the proper sequence. Remove the cylinder head.

➡ **The cylinder head bolts on the intake side of the cylinder head are (A) 3.54 in. (90mm) and the bolts on the exhaust side of the head are (B) 4.25 in. (108mm). Label the bolts to ensure proper installation.**

To install:

34. Clean all the gasket mating surfaces on the cylinder head and block.

35. Position the cylinder head on the block with a new gasket. Lightly coat the cylinder head bolts with engine oil and then install them. On 1988–92 vehicles, tighten the bolts in 3 stages, in the proper sequence. On the final pass, tighten the bolts to 44 ft. lbs. (60 Nm).

36. On the 1993–97 vehicles, coat the head bolts with engine oil and tighten them in several passes, in the sequence shown, to 22 ft. lbs. (29 Nm). Mark the front of each bolt with a dab of paint and then retighten the bolts a further 90° turn. The paint dabs should now all be at a 90° angle to the front of the head. Retighten the bolts one more time a further 90° turn. The paint dabs should now all be pointing toward the rear of the head.

37. Install the camshafts as outlined in this section.

38. Check and adjust the valve clearance. Refer Valve adjustment in Section 1.

39. Install the water inlet No. 2 and tighten the retainers to 11 ft. lbs. (15 Nm). Attach the inlet hose.

40. Install and tighten the engine hangers to 20 ft. lbs. (27 Nm), the fan adjusting bar to 14 ft. lbs. (20 Nm); and the generator bracket to 20 ft. lbs. (26 Nm) if removed.

41. If removed install the oil dipstick, apply a small amount of engine oil to the new O-ring and place on the end of the tube. Insert the dipstick

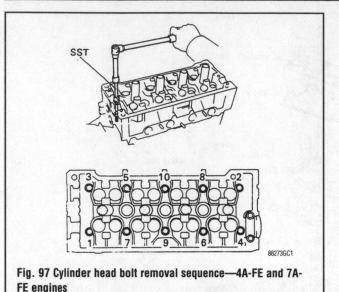

Fig. 97 Cylinder head bolt removal sequence—4A-FE and 7A-FE engines

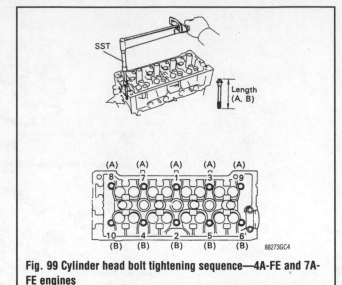

Fig. 99 Cylinder head bolt tightening sequence—4A-FE and 7A-FE engines

gauge into the tube and attach the tube with the mounting bolt and tighten to 82 inch lbs. (9 Nm).

42. Engauge the electrical connection to the CPS. Install the alternator bracket and tighten the bolts to 20 ft. lbs. (26 Nm).

43. Install the camshaft timing pulley and timing belt, refer to Timing Belt and Sprockets Removal and Installation later in this section.

44. Check the valve timing as follows:

➡**Always turn the crankshaft clockwise.**

   a. Loosen the idler pulley bolt half a turn, then turn the crankshaft pulley 2 full revolutions from TDC to TDC.

   b. Check that the pulleys align with the timing marks in the accompanying illustration. If the timing marks do not align, remove the timing belt and reinstall it.

   c. Tighten the idler pulley bolt to 27 ft. lbs. (37 Nm).

45. Check that there is belt tension at the position illustrated, the deflection should be 4.4 ft. lbs. (20N): 0.20–0.24 inch. (5–6mm). If the deflection is not within range, adjust the idler pulley until the desired deflection is achieved.

46. Install the No. 2 and No. 3 timing belt covers and tighten the bolts to 65 inch lbs. (7 Nm).

47. Install the half moon plug, using a lubricant (FIPG).

48. Install the valve cover with a new gasket and cap nuts.

49. Install the RH mounting insulator if removed.

50. Install the intake manifold. Connect the engine wiring.

51. Install the fuel injectors and delivery pipe, air intake chamber and throttle body. Refer to Section 5.

52. attach the air pipe and fuel hose clamp.

➡**Attach the clamp claw of the fuel hose to the intake manifold.**

53. Install the intake manifold stay. If equipped with EGR, install the VSV.

54. Attach the MAP, brake booster and power steering hoses.

55. Engauge the ground strap connector.

56. Clean all gasket material on the water inlet. Apply the FIPG seal to the inlet housing assembly.

➡**Avoid applying any excessive amount to the surface. Be especially careful around the oil passages. Components must be assembled within 3 mins. of application. Otherwise the FIPG must be removed and reapplied.**

57. Install the water inlet and tighten the retainers to 14 ft. lbs. (20 Nm).

58. Install the water outlet. Apply the FIPG seal to the inlet housing assembly and tighten the retainers to 14 ft. lbs. (20 Nm).

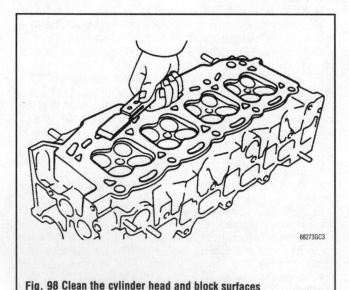

Fig. 98 Clean the cylinder head and block surfaces

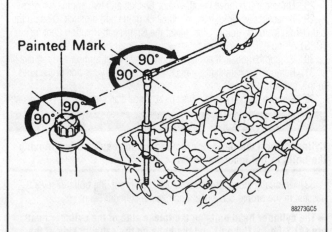

Fig. 100 On the 1993–97 models, tighten the head bolts the last two passes at 90° turns

➡Avoid applying any excessive amount to the surface. Be especially careful around the oil passages. Components must be assembled within 3 mins. of application. Otherwise the FIPG must be removed and reapplied.

59. Install the exhaust manifold and the front exhaust pipe.
60. Install the distributor and alternator.
61. Engage the accelerator cable bracket to the throttle body.
62. Install the air cleaner hose and cap.
63. Connect the negative battery cable.
64. Fill the cooling system. Check the crankcase and transmission. Start the vehicle and check for leaks. Top off the cooling system.
65. Turn the vehicle **OFF** and install the RH engine under cover. Check the ignition timing.
66. Test drive the vehicle to ensure proper operation.
67. Recheck the fluids.

4A-GE Engine

▶ See Figures 101 thru 113

1. Disconnect the negative battery cable. Remove the RH engine undercover. Drain the cooling system and engine oil.
2. Loosen the clamp and then disconnect the air cleaner hose from the throttle body. Disconnect the actuator and accelerator cables from the bracket on the throttle body.
3. If equipped with power steering, remove the power steering pump hoses.
4. Remove the water by-pass hoses.
5. Remove the washer reservoir.
6. Disconnect the brake vacuum hose.
7. If equipped with cruise control, remove the actuator.
8. Remove the upper radiator hose.
9. disconnect the ignition coil wiring. Remove the bolts retaining the coil to the bracket and remove the unit.
10. Disengage the engine wire from the No. 4 timing belt cover. Detach the distributor wires, oil pressure sender gauge wire, and compressor wiring for models with A/C.
11. Unbolt and pull out the distributor.
12. On California models, disconnect the EGR gas temperature sensor connection. Label and separate the hoses from the vacuum pipe. Loosen the bolt and EGR vacuum modulator. Remove the union bolt, four bolts, EGR valve, pipe assembly and gaskets.
13. Separate the front pipe from the exhaust manifold.
14. Unbolt and remove the exhaust manifold.
15. Label and pull the PCV hose from the valve.

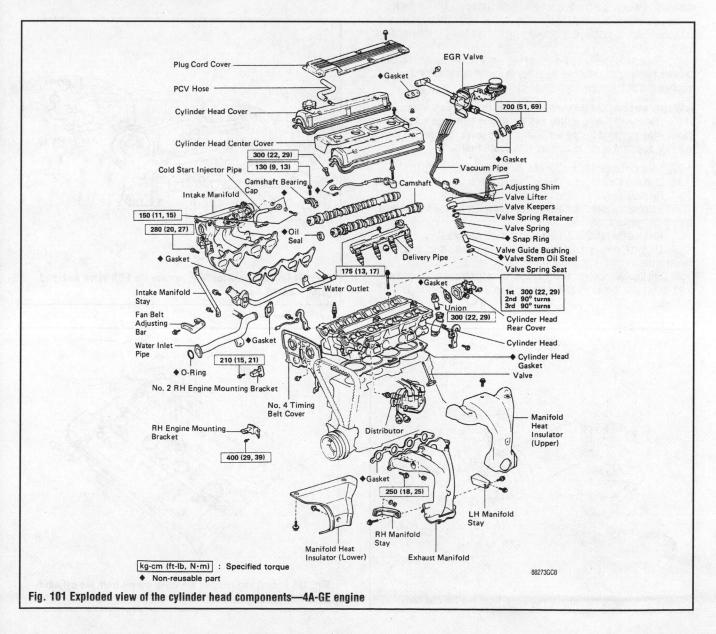

Fig. 101 Exploded view of the cylinder head components—4A-GE engine

16. Remove the cold start injector pipe, delivery pipe and injectors. Refer to Section 5.

17. Remove the No. 1 fuel pipe with gaskets. from the intake manifold and valve cover. Remove the pressure regulator if equipped.

18. Disconnect the No. 2 and No. 3 water by-pass hoses from the auxiliary air valve if equipped.

19. Label and disengage the all engine wiring preventing intake, exhaust manifold, valve cover and cylinder head removal.

20. On models with power steering and/or A/C, remove the drive belts.

21. Loosen the water pump pulley bolts and the alternator drive belt.

22. Remove the water outlet and by-pass pipe. Unbolt the alternator drive belt adjusting bar, water outlet and by-pass assembly. Discard the gaskets.

23. Remove the water inlet pipe.

24. Remove the RH engine mounting insulator.

25. Remove the intake manifold.

26. Unbolt and remove the water pump pulley.

27. Remove the No. 3 and No. 2 timing belt covers. On models with A/C, remove the idler pulley. Remove the seven mounting bolts, cord support plate, No. 2 and No. 3 covers and gaskets. Discard the old gaskets.

28. Remove both valve covers. Discard the old gaskets and cap nuts.

29. Remove the spark plugs.

30. Set the No. 1 cylinder to TDC at the compression stroke. Turn the crankshaft pulley and align its groove with the timing mark "0" of the No. 1 timing belt cover. Check that the lifters on the No. 1 cylinder are loose and the valve lifters on the No. 4 cylinder are tight. If not turn the crankshaft one revolution (360°).

31. Place matchmarks on the timing belt and 2 timing pulleys. Loosen the idler pulley bolts and move the pulley to the left as far as it will go, then retighten the bolt. Remove the timing belt from the camshaft pulleys.

➡**When removing the timing belt, support the belt so the meshing of the crankshaft timing pulley and the timing belt does not shift. Never drop anything inside the timing case cover. Be sure the timing belt does not come in contact with dust or oil.**

32. Lock the camshafts and remove the timing pulleys.

33. Unbolt and remove the RH mounting brackets.

34. Remove the No. 4 timing belt cover.

35. Remove the camshafts. Refer to Camshaft Removal and Installation later in this section.

36. Remove the No. 2 PCV hose from the cylinder head.

37. Loosen the 10 cylinder head bolts gradually in 3 stages, and in the proper order.

38. Lift the cylinder head from the dowels on the block and place the head on wooden blocks on a work bench. Remove the engine hangers and the union.

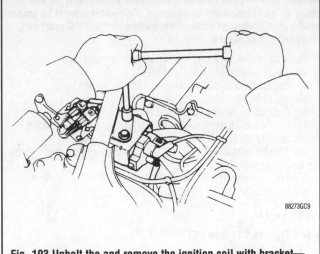

Fig. 103 Unbolt the and remove the ignition coil with bracket—4A-GE engine

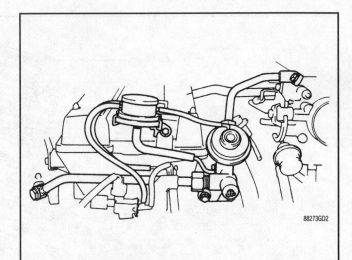

Fig. 104 On California models, remove the EGR valve and modulator—4A-GE engine

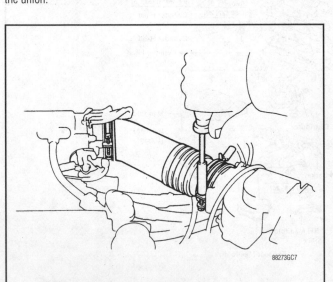

Fig. 102 Remove the air cleaner hose from the throttle body

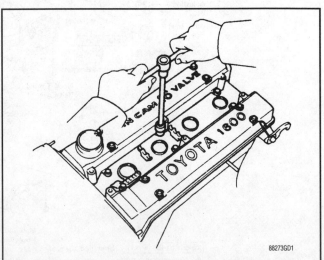

Fig. 105 Unbolt and remove the valve covers from the cylinder head—4A-GE engine

➡The cylinder head bolts on the intake side of the cylinder head are 3.54 in. (90mm) and the bolts on the exhaust side of the head are 4.25 in. (108mm). Label the bolts to ensure proper installation.

To install:

39. Clean all the gasket mating surfaces on the cylinder head and block.

40. Apply LOCTITE 242 on two or three threads of the union. tighten the union to 22 ft. lbs. (29 Nm).

41. Install the engine hangers and ground strap connector, tighten the hangers to 18 ft. lbs. (25 Nm).

42. Position the cylinder head on the block with a new gasket.

43. After coating the head bolts with engine oil, install and tighten the head bolts in several passes, in the sequence shown to 22 ft. lbs. (29 Nm). Mark the front of each bolt with a dab of paint and then retighten the bolts a further 90° turn. The paint dabs should now all be at a 90° angle to the front of the head. Retighten the bolts one more time a further 90° turn. The paint dabs should now all be pointing toward the rear of the head.

44. Connect the PCV hose to the cylinder head. Install the two clamps.

45. Position the camshafts into the cylinder head as described in Camshaft Removal and Installation.

46. Install the No. 4 timing belt cover, tighten the retaining bolts to 82 inch lbs. (9 Nm).

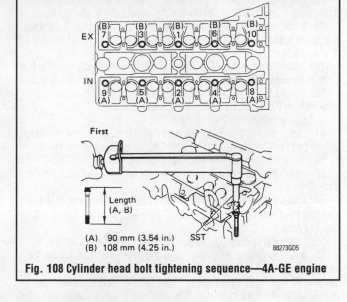

Fig. 108 Cylinder head bolt tightening sequence—4A-GE engine

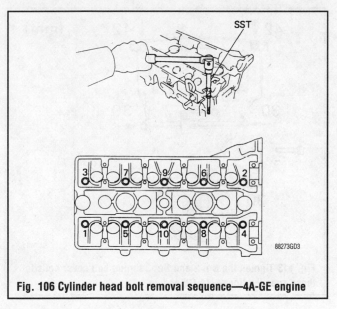

Fig. 106 Cylinder head bolt removal sequence—4A-GE engine

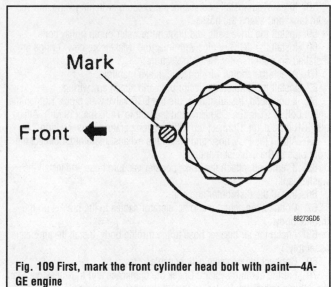

Fig. 109 First, mark the front cylinder head bolt with paint—4A-GE engine

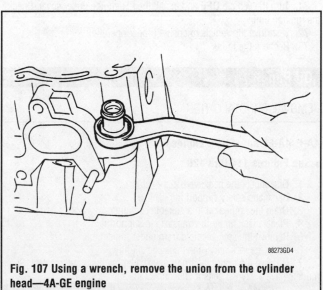

Fig. 107 Using a wrench, remove the union from the cylinder head—4A-GE engine

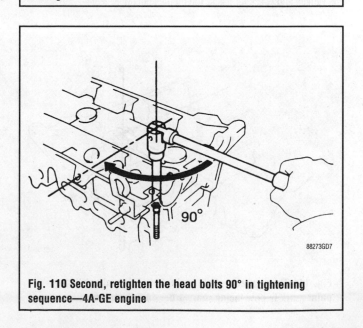

Fig. 110 Second, retighten the head bolts 90° in tightening sequence—4A-GE engine

47. Install the RH mounting brackets, tighten the one bracket with three bolts to 29 ft. lbs. (39 Nm) and the No. 2 bracket to 15 ft. lbs. (21 Nm).

48. Install the camshaft timing pulleys, lock each camshaft and tighten the pulley bolts; 1988–89 models 34 ft. lbs. (47 Nm), 1990–91 models 43 ft. lbs. (59 Nm).

49. Install the timing belt. Check the valve timing and timing belt deflection. Refer to the Timing Belt Removal and Installation procedure later in this section.

50. Inspect the valve clearance. Clearance when cold should be:
- Intake: 0.006–0.010 in. (0.15–0.25mm)
- Exhaust: 0.008–0.012 in. (0.20–0.30mm)

51. Install the No. 2 and No. 3 timing belt covers. Check the illustration as per bolt installation. On models with A/C, install the idler pulley.

52. Temporarily install the water pump pulley.

53. Install the valve covers using a new gaskets and cap nuts. Tighten the valve covers to 9 ft. lbs. (13 Nm).

54. Install the water outlet with the No. 1 by-pass hose. tighten the cylinder head side bolts to 20 ft. lbs. (27 Nm) and the block side to 9 ft. lbs. (13 Nm).

55. Install the spark plugs. Check the gap prior to installation.

56. Install the intake air control valve and intake manifold, tighten the manifold mounting bolts to 20 ft. lbs. (27 Nm). Tighten the stay: 12mm bolts to 16 ft. lbs. (22 Nm) and the 14mm bolts to 29 ft. lbs. (39 Nm).

57. Install the RH engine mounting insulator. Install the water inlet pipe.

58. If removed, install and secure the vacuum switching valve and vacuum tank; and attach the hoses.

59. Install the drive belts and tighten the water pump pulley bolts.

60. Install the delivery pipe with injectors. Make sure new O-rings are installed on each injector. Refer to Section 5.

61. Attach the engine wiring to the intake manifold.

62. Install the cold start injector pipe and attach any wiring.

63. If equipped, install and secure the EGR valve with pipes. Tighten the union bolt to 51 ft. lbs. 969 Nm) and the bolt to 14 ft. lbs. (19 Nm). Attach the EGR modulator. Connect the EGR gas temperature sensor wiring.

64. Attach the PCV hose and install the exhaust manifold. Connect the front pipe to the exhaust manifold.

65. If removed, attach the brake booster vacuum hose and install the washer tank.

66. Install the distributor and coil.

67. Connect the actuator and accelerator cables to the bracket on the throttle body.

68. Attach the air cleaner hose to the throttle body. Install the air cleaner assembly.

69. Connect the negative battery cable.

70. Fill the cooling system. Check the crankcase and transmission. Start the vehicle and check for leaks. Top off the cooling system.

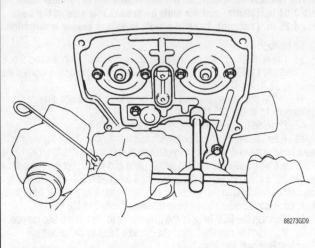

Fig. 112 Install and tighten the No. 4 timing belt cover to 82 inch lbs.—4A-GE engine

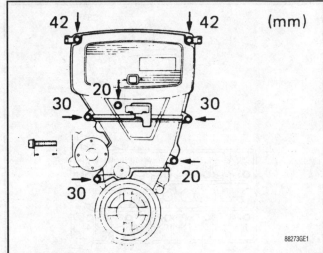

Fig. 113 Tighten the No. 2 and No. 3 timing belt cover bolts to these specifications—4A-GE engine

71. Turn the vehicle **OFF** and install the RH engine under cover. Check the ignition timing.

72. Test drive the vehicle to ensure proper operation.

73. Recheck the fluids.

Oil Pan

REMOVAL & INSTALLATION

4A-F, 4A-FE and 4A-GE Engines

▶ See Figures 114 thru 120

1. Disconnect the negative battery cable.
2. Raise and safely support the vehicle.
3. Drain the engine oil in a suitable container.
4. Place a jack under the transaxle to support it.
5. Remove the splash shield from under the engine.
6. Raise the jack under the transaxle slightly.
7. Remove the front pipe from the exhaust manifold and catalyst. Some models have a oxygen sensor, disconnect the wiring.
8. On the 4A-F and 4A-FE engines, remove the center mounting.

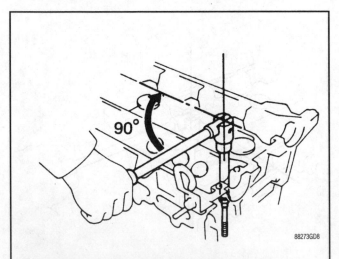

Fig. 111 Third, again retighten the bolts, then check that the paint mark is now facing rearward—4A-GE engine

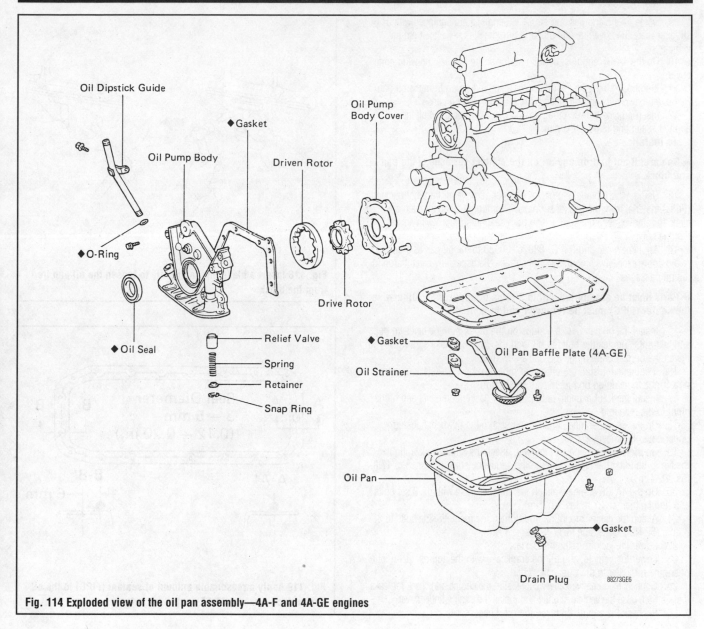

Fig. 114 Exploded view of the oil pan assembly—4A-F and 4A-GE engines

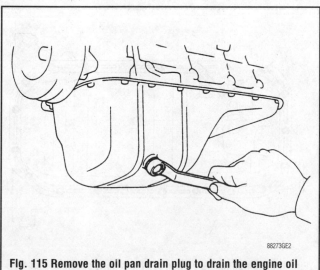

Fig. 115 Remove the oil pan drain plug to drain the engine oil from the crankcase

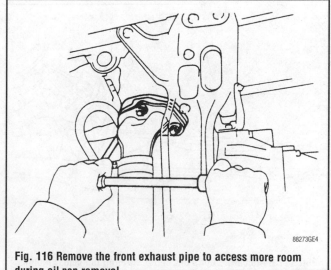

Fig. 116 Remove the front exhaust pipe to access more room during oil pan removal

9. Some 4A-FE engines and all 4A-GE engines are equipped with a stiffener plate. Remove the set bolts and pull the stiffener plate from the vehicle.

10. On the 4A-GE engines, unbolt and lower the flywheel housing under cover.

11. If equipped, remove the oil cooler hose and union from the oil pan. Remove the two nuts and nineteen bolts retaining the oil pan.

12. Insert a blade between the pan and cylinder block, cut off the applied sealer and remove the pan.

To install:

→Be careful not to drop any oil on the contact surfaces of the pan and block.

13. Using a razor blade and gasket scraper, remove all traces of packing (FIPG) material from the gasket surfaces. Thoroughly clean all main surfaces to remove loose material. Clean both sealing surfaces with non-residue solvent.

14. Apply new packing (FIPG) 08826–00080 to the oil pan as shown. Avoid apply excessive amounts to the surface. Be especially careful around the oil passages.

→Parts must be assembled within 3 mins of application. Otherwise, the sealer (FIPG) must be removed and reapplied.

15. Install the oil pan over the studs on the block with the nineteen bolts and two nuts. Tighten the bolts to 43 inch lbs. (5 Nm). Make sure when you install the oil pan drain plug, you use a new gasket.

16. If equipped, install the oil cooler pipe, two new gaskets and union bolt. Tighten the union bolt to 18 ft. lbs. (25 Nm).

17. Install the front exhaust pipe (with new gaskets on either end of the pipe) to the manifold.

18. On the 4A-GE engines, install and secure the flywheel housing under cover if removed.

19. On the 4A-FE engines if removed, attach the stiffener plate. tighten the No. 1 bolt first then the 5 bolts in the sequence shown. Tighten to 17 ft. lbs. (23 Nm).

20. On the 4A-GE engines, attach the stiffener plate with the 3 set bolts and tighten them to 27 ft. lbs. (37 Nm).

21. Attach the center mounting and tighten the member side bolts to 38 ft. lbs. (52 Nm), plate side to 17 ft. lbs. (23 Nm).

22. Lower the jack from the transaxle.

23. Lower the vehicle, and fill the crankcase with the appropriate amount of engine oil. Refer to the Capacities chart.

24. Connect the negative battery cable, start the engine and check for leaks. If all is well, raise the vehicle slightly and install the engine under cover.

25. Recheck the engine oil level, top off if necessary.

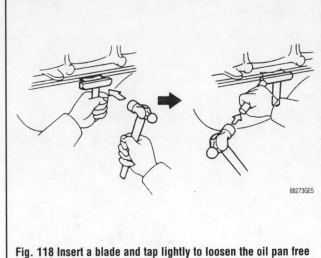

Fig. 118 Insert a blade and tap lightly to loosen the oil pan free from the block

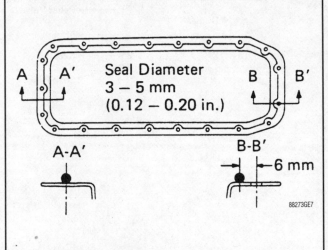

Fig. 119 Apply a reasonable amount of sealant (FIPG) to the oil pan surface—except 7A-FE engine

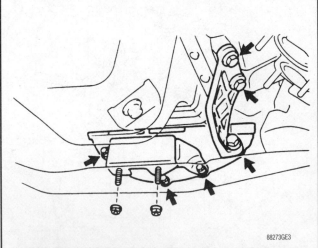

Fig. 117 Remove the bolts and nuts retaining the center mounting—4A-F engine

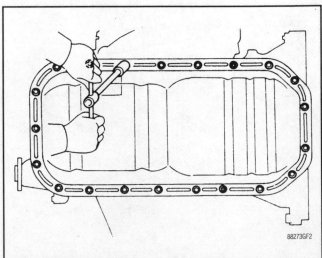

Fig. 120 Tighten the 19 oil pan retaining bolts securely—4A-F, 4A-FE and 4A-GE engines

7A-FE Engine

♦ **See Figures 121 thru 130**

➥On the 1993–97 7A-FE engine, a 2 piece oil pan assembly is used. The No. 1 oil pan (upper) is made of aluminum and the No. 2 oil pan (lower) is made of steel. The upper oil pan section is secured to the cylinder block and the transaxle housing, increasing rigidity.

1. Disconnect the negative battery cable.
2. Raise and safely support the vehicle.
3. Drain the engine oil in a suitable container.
4. Place a jack under the transaxle to support it.
5. Remove the splash shield from under the engine.
6. Raise the jack under the transaxle slightly.
7. Discxonnect the oxygen sensor wiring at the front pipe. Remove the bolts retaining the front pipe to the mounting bracket. Unbolt the support bracket holding the pipe to the catalyst. Remove the nuts and lower the pipe from the engine.
8. Remove the 13 bolts and 2 nuts retaining the No. 2 oil pan. Insert a blade between the pan and the baffle plate. Carefully pry the pan off.
9. To remove the upper (No. 1) oil pan continue.
10. Remove the bolts and nuts retaining the baffle plate.

11. Remove the oil strainer and gasket. Discard the old gasket.
12. Remove the 3 transaxle mounting bolts from the engine rear end plate side. Remove the 6 bolts, the using a 5mm hexagon wrench, remove the 14 bolts securing the No. 1 oil pan. Insert a pry tool between the pan and block and carefully separate the pan from the engine.

To install:

➥Be careful not to drop any oil on the contact surfaces of the pan and block.

13. Using a razor blade and gasket scraper, remove all traces of packing (FIPG) material from the gasket surfaces. Thoroughly clean all mating surfaces to remove loose material. Clean both sealing surfaces with non-residue solvent.
14. Apply new packing (FIPG) 08826–00080 to the No. 1 oil pan as shown. Avoid apply excessive amounts to the surface. Be especially careful around the oil passages.

➥Parts must be assembled within 3 mins of application. Otherwise, the sealer (FIPG) must be removed and reapplied.

15. Using a 5mm hexagon wrench, install the No. 1 oil pan with 14 NEW bolts. Tighten the bolts (A) to 12 ft. lbs. (16 Nm). Install the 6 bolts (B), and tighten them to 69 inch lbs. (8 Nm).

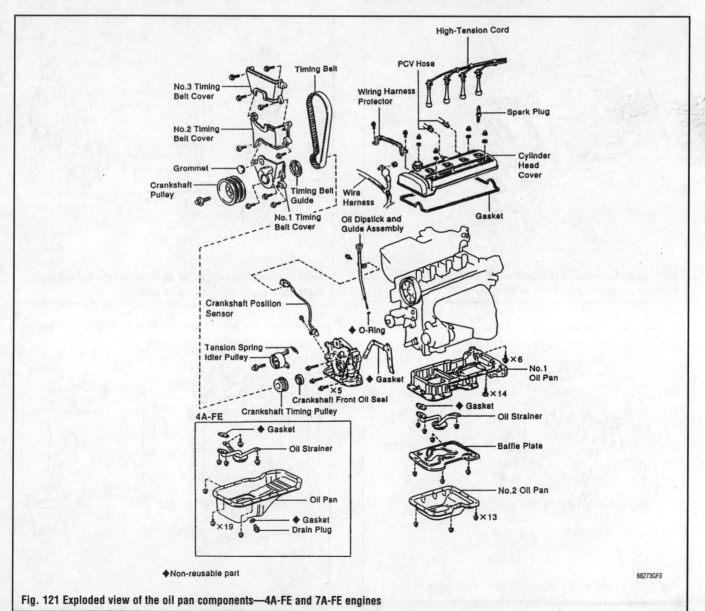

♦Non-reusable part

88273GF3

Fig. 121 Exploded view of the oil pan components—4A-FE and 7A-FE engines

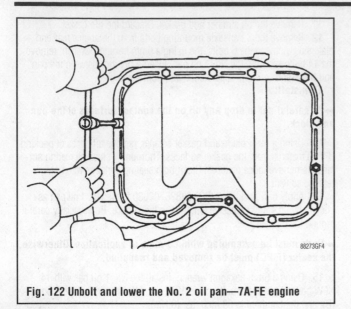

Fig. 122 Unbolt and lower the No. 2 oil pan—7A-FE engine

16. Install and tighten the 3 transaxle mounting bolts to the engine rear end plate side and tighten them to 17 ft. lbs. (23 Nm).

17. Place a new gasket on the oil strainer and tighten the retaining nuts to 82 inch lbs. (9 Nm).

18. Attach the oil pan baffle and tighten the mounting bolts and nuts to 69 inch lbs. (8 Nm).

19. Using a razor blade and gasket scraper, remove all traces of packing (FIPG) material from the gasket surfaces. Thoroughly clean all mating surfaces to remove loose material. Clean both sealing surfaces with non-residue solvent.

20. Apply new packing (FIPG) 08826–00080 to the No. 2 oil pan as shown. Avoid apply excessive amounts to the surface. Be especially careful around the oil passages.

➡**Parts must be assembled within 3 mins of application. Otherwise, the sealer (FIPG) must be removed and reapplied.**

21. Attach the No. 2 oil pan and tighten the 13 bolts and 2 nuts to 43 inch lbs. (5 Nm).

22. Using new gaskets, attach the front exhaust pipe to the manifold and catalyst.

23. Lower the jack from the transaxle.

24. Lower the vehicle, and fill the crankcase with the appropriate amount of engine oil. Refer to the Capacities chart.

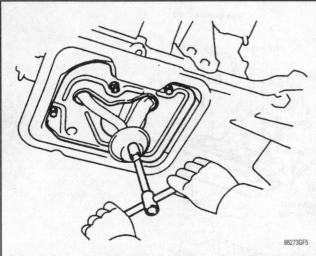

Fig. 123 Remove the 2 bolts, nuts and lower the baffle plate from the upper oil pan—7A-FE engine

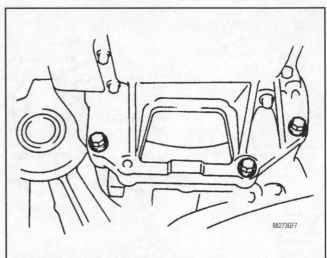

Fig. 125 Unbolt and remove the transaxle mounting from the engine rear end plate side—7A-FE engine

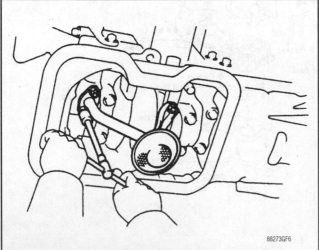

Fig. 124 Remove the oil strainer to access the upper oil pan—7A-FE engine

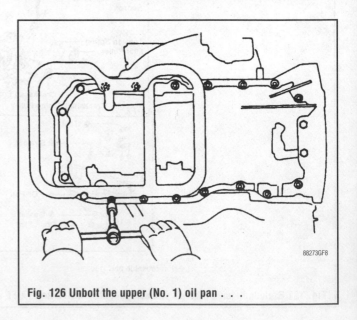

Fig. 126 Unbolt the upper (No. 1) oil pan . . .

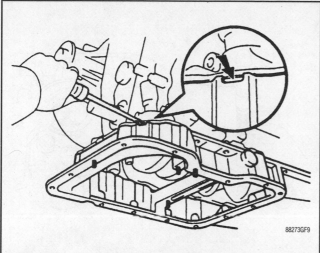

Fig. 127 . . . and pry between the block and pan to remove—7A-FE engine

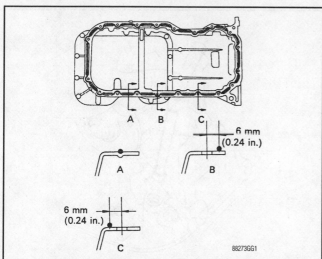

Fig. 128 Apply a reasonable amount of sealant (FIPG) to the No. 1 oil pan surface—7A-FE engine

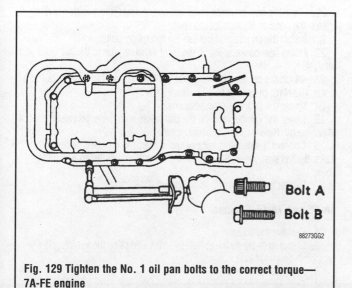

Fig. 129 Tighten the No. 1 oil pan bolts to the correct torque—7A-FE engine

Seal Width 3 – 5 mm

6 mm (0.24 in.)   6 mm (0.24 in.)

Fig. 130 Apply FIPG to the No. 2 oil pan as shown—7A-FE engine

25. Connect the negative battery cable, start the engine and check for leaks. If all is well, raise the vehicle slightly and install the engine under cover.
26. Recheck the engine oil level, top off if necessary.

Oil Pump

REMOVAL & INSTALLATION

➡When repairing or replacing the oil pump assembly, the oil pan and strainer should be removed and cleaned.

4A-F Engine

◗ See Figures 131, 132, 133, 134 and 135

1. Disconnect the negative battery cable.
2. Raise and safely support the vehicle.
3. Drain the engine oil in a suitable container.
4. Place a jack under the transaxle to support it.
5. Remove the splash shield from under the engine.
6. Raise the jack under the transaxle slightly.
7. Unbolt and lower the center mounting.

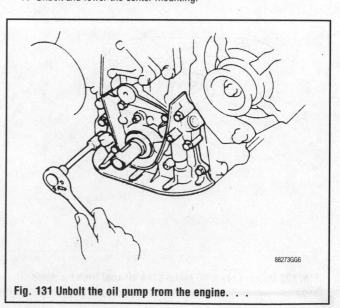

Fig. 131 Unbolt the oil pump from the engine. . .

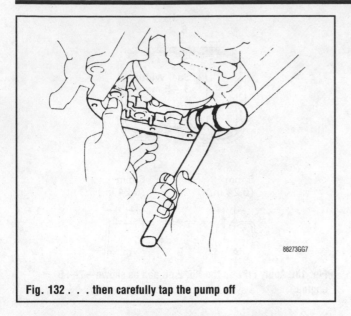

Fig. 132 . . . then carefully tap the pump off

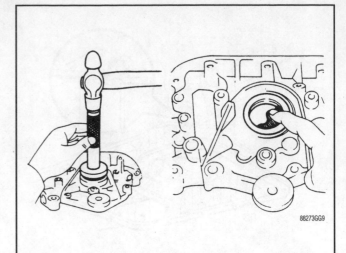

Fig. 134 Apply a small amount of engine oil on the seal, then carefully tap it into the pump body

8. Remove the front pipe from the exhaust manifold and catalyst.

9. Remove the two nuts and nineteen bolts retaining the oil pan.

10. Insert a blade between the pan and cylinder block, cut off the applied sealer and remove the pan.

11. Remove the oil strainer and discard the old gasket.

12. Remove the timing belt, idler pulley and crankshaft timing pulley. Refer to Timing Belt and Sprockets later in this section.

13. Remove the oil dipstick and tube assembly.

14. Unbolt the oil pump, then using a plastic hammer, gently tap on the pump body to loosen.

15. To replace the oil seal, pry the old seal from the pump.

To install:

16. Carefull tap a new seal into the pump body. The seal must be primed with engine oil or mufti purpose grease prior to installation.

17. Place a new gasket on the block, then install the pump with the spline teeth of the drive gear engaged with the large teeth of the crankshaft. Secure with the bolts and tighten to 16 ft. lbs. (21 Nm).

18. To install the dipstick, push in the dipstick guide with a new O-ring coated with a small amount of engine oil. Place the O-ring on the guide. Attach the tube with the mounting bolt and insert the dipstick.

19. Install the crankshaft timing pulley, idler pulley and timing belt. Refer to Timing Belt and Sprockets later in this section.

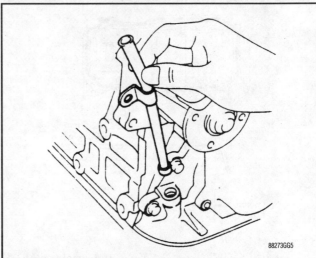

Fig. 135 With a new O-ring, insert the dipstick tube into the engine

20. Place the new oil strainer gasket and strainer into position and tighten the bolts to 82 inch lbs. (9 Nm).

21. Install the oil pan and tighten the mounting bolts.

22. Using new gaskets, attach the front exhaust pipe to the manifold and catalyst.

23. Attach the center mounting and tighten the member side bolts to 38 ft. lbs. (52 Nm), plate side to 17 ft. lbs. (23 Nm).

24. Lower the jack from the transaxle.

25. Lower the vehicle, and fill the crankcase with the appropriate amount of engine oil. Refer to the Capacities chart.

26. Connect the negative battery cable, start the engine and check for leaks. If all is well, raise the vehicle slightly and install the engine under cover.

27. Recheck the engine oil level, top off if necessary.

4A-FE and 7A-FE Engines

1. Remove the hood.

2. Disconnect the negative battery cable and raise the vehicle. Safely support it on jackstands.

3. Drain the engine oil.

4. Remove the engine under covers.

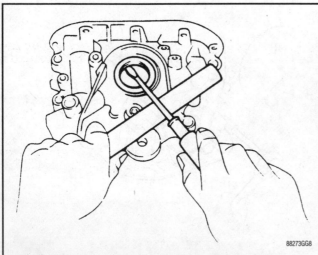

Fig. 133 Using a pry tool, remove the oil seal from the pump body

5. Remove the timing belt. Refer to the Timing Belt Removal and Installation later in this section.

6. Remove the bolt securing the idler pulley and tension spring.

7. Remove the crankshaft timing pulley. Position shop rags to prevent damage to components. If the pulley can not be removed by hand, use two pry tools.

8. On the 7A-FE engines, remove the oil dipstick guide and dipstick. Disconnect the crankshaft position sensor wiring from the guide. Remove the mounting bolt and pull out the guide and gauge. Remove the old O-ring from the guide and discard.

9. Remove the front exhaust pipe. Disconnect the oxygen sensor wiring. Remove the bolts holding the front pipe to the mounting bracket. Unbolt the support bracket retaining the TWC to the front pipe. Remove the nuts and lower the pipe.

10. On the 4A-FE engine, Unbolt the stiffener plate.

11. Remove the oil pan.

12. On the 7A-FE engine, unbolt and remove the oil pan baffle plate.

13. Remove the oil pick-up and strainer assembly.

14. On the 7A-FE engines, remove the No. 1 oil pan.

15. Unbolt the oil pump. On the 7A-FE engines, remove the bolt and the crankshaft position sensor, then the pump retaining bolts and pump. If the unit is secure to the body, use a plastic hammer and tap gently to separate. Discard the gasket.

16. To replace the oil seal, pry the old seal from the pump.

To install:

17. Carefull tap a new seal into the pump body. The seal must be primed with engine oil or mufti purpose grease prior to installation.

18. Place a new gasket on the block, then install the pump with the spline teeth of the oil pump rotor engaged with the large teeth of the crankshaft. Secure with the bolts and tighten to 16 ft. lbs. (21 Nm).

Be sure the long bolt is in the correct position. On the 7A-FE engine, install the crankshaft position sensor.

19. On the 7A-FE engine, install the No. 1 oil pan. Refer to Oil Pan Removal and Installation earlier in this section.

20. Attach the oil strainer using a new gasket and tighten to 82 inch lbs. (9 Nm).

21. Install the oil pan. Refer to Oil pan Removal and Installation earlier in this section.

22. On the 4A-FE engine, attach the stiffener plate and tighten to 17 ft. lbs. (23 Nm).

23. Attach the front pipe. Connect the oxygen sensor wiring if removed.

24. Install the oil dipstick guide and dipstick. Place a new O-ring on the end of the tube. Tighten the dipstick retaining bolt to 82 inch lbs. (9 Nm). On the 7A-FE engines, connect the crankshaft position sensor wiring to the dipstick guide.

25. Insatall the crankshaft timing pulley. Align the pulley set key with the key groove of the pulley. Slide the timing pulley, facing the flange side inward.

26. Temporarily install the idler pulley and tension spring. Do not tighten the bolt yet. Push the pulley as far left as it will go and tighten the bolt.

27. Install the timing belt.

28. Lower the jack from the transaxle.

29. Lower the vehicle, and fill the crankcase with the appropriate amount of engine oil. Refer to the Capacities chart.

30. Connect the negative battery cable, start the engine and check for leaks. If all is well, raise the vehicle slightly and install the engine under cover.

31. Recheck the engine oil level, top off if necessary.

32. Install the hood.

4A-GE Engine

1. Remove the hood.

2. Disconnect the negative battery cable.

3. Drain the engine oil. Make sure the old gasket is discarded, and an new one installed prior to drainplug installation.

4. Remove the timing belt, idler pulley and crankshaft timing pulley.

When removing the RH engine mounting, attach the engine hoist chain to the lifting bracket on the engine and raise the engine slightly.

5. Remove the oil dipstick and tube assembly. Discard the O-ring.

6. Remove the front exhaust pipe from the engine.

7. Remove the stiffener plate from the engine. Unbolt the flywheel housing cover.

8. Remove the oil pan as previously outlined.

9. Remove the oil pick-up and strainer.

10. Remove the oil pan baffle plate.

11. Remove the oil pump retaining bolts. Using a plastic hammer gently tap the edge of the pump to release.

12. To replace the oil seal, pry the old seal from the pump.

To install:

13. Carefull tap a new seal into the pump body. The seal must be primed with engine oil or mufti purpose grease prior to installation.

14. Place a new gasket on the cylinder block, install the oil pump to the block with the spline teeth of the drive gear engaged with the large teeth of the crankshaft. Install and tighten the retaining bolts to 16 ft. lbs. (21 Nm). Make sure the long bolt is in the correct position.

15. To install the baffle plate, using a razor blade and gasket scraper, remove all traces of packing (FIPG) material from the gasket surfaces. Thoroughly clean all main surfaces to remove loose material. Clean both sealing surfaces with non-residue solvent.

16. Apply new packing (FIPG) 08826–00080 to the baffle. Avoid apply excessive amounts to the surface.

➡**Parts must be assembled within 3 mins of application. Otherwise, the sealer (FIPG) must be removed and reapplied.**

17. Install and secure the oil baffle plate.

18. Place a new oil strainer gasket and install the oil strainer with the retaining bolts and nuts. Tighten to 82 inch lbs. (9 Nm).

19. Install the oil pan as described earlier in this section.

20. Install the flywheel housing under cover.

21. Attach the stiffener plate tightening the retaining bolts to 27 ft. lbs. (37 Nm).

22. Install the front exhaust pipe.

23. Install the oil dipstick guide and dipstick. Place a new O-ring on the end of the tube. Tighten the dipstick retaining bolt to 82 inch lbs. (9 Nm).

24. Install the crankshaft timing pulley, idler pulley and timing belt as described later in this section.

25. Lower the jack from the transaxle.

26. Lower the vehicle, and fill the crankcase with the appropriate amount of engine oil. Refer to the Capacities chart.

27. Connect the negative battery cable, start the engine and check for leaks. If all is well, raise the vehicle slightly and install the engine under cover.

28. Recheck the engine oil level, top off if necessary.

29. Install the hood.

Crankshaft Pulley

REMOVAL & INSTALLATION

To remove the crankshaft pulley refer to the "Timing Belt Cover" removal and installation service procedures.

Timing Belt Cover

REMOVAL & INSTALLATION

4A-GE Engine

▶ **See Figures 136, 137, 138, 139 and 140**

1. Disconnect the negative battery cable.

2. Raise the vehicle and safely support it on jackstands.

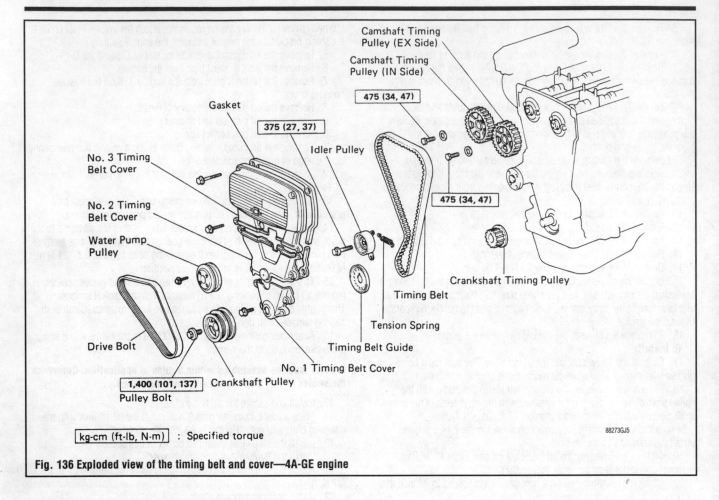

Fig. 136 Exploded view of the timing belt and cover—4A-GE engine

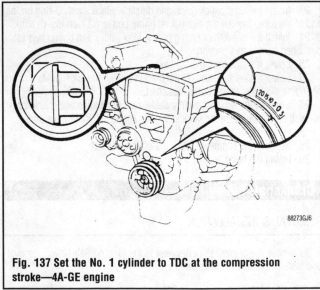

Fig. 137 Set the No. 1 cylinder to TDC at the compression stroke—4A-GE engine

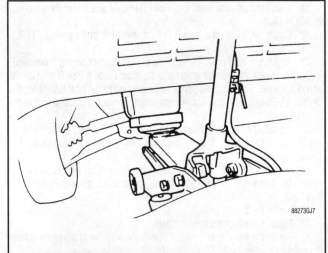

Fig. 138 Support the engine with a jack and piece of wood when removing the RH engine mounting—4A-GE engine

3. Remove the right front wheel.
4. Remove the splash shield from under the car.
5. Drain the coolant into clean containers. Close the draincocks when the system is empty.
6. Lower the car to the ground. Disconnect the accelerator cable and, if equipped, the cruise control cable.
7. Remove the cruise control actuator, if equipped.
8. Remove the washer reservoir.
9. Labvel and disconnect the plug wires. Carefully remove the ignition coil.

10. Disconnect the radiator hose at the water outlet.
11. Remove the power steering drive belt and the alternator drive belt.
12. Remove the spark plugs.
13. Rotate the crankshaft clockwise and set the engine to TDC/compression on No. 1 cylinder. Align the crankshaft marks at zero; look through the oil filler hole and make sure the small hole in the end of the camshaft can be seen.
14. Raise and safely support the vehicle. Disconnect the center engine mount.

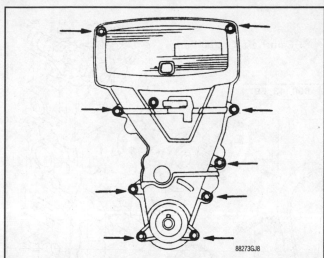

Fig. 139 Remove the 10 timing belt cover retaining bolt—4A-GE engine

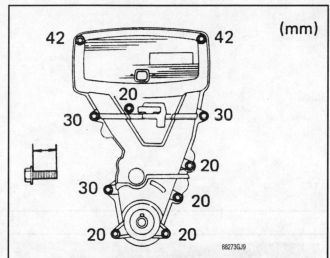

Fig. 140 Install the timing belt cover bolts, make sure the correct length bolts are installed—4A-GE engine

15. Lower the vehicle to the ground.
16. Support the engine either from above or below. Disconnect the right engine mount from the engine.
17. Raise the engine and remove the mount.
18. Unbolt and remove the water pump pulley.
19. Remove the crankshaft pulley.
20. Remove the 10 bolts and pull off the timing belt covers with their gaskets.

➡The bolts are different lengths; they must be returned to their correct location at reassembly. Label or diagram the bolts during removal.

To install:

➡When reinstalling, make certain that the gaskets and their mating surfaces are clean and free from dirt and oil. The gasket itself must be free of cuts and deformations and must fit securely in the grooves of the covers.

21. Install the gaskets to the belt covers. Place No. 1, No. 2 and No. 3 timing belt covers and support plate into position and secure with the 10 mounting bolts. Be careful of bolt placement. Refer to the illustration for placement.
22. Install the crankshaft pulley, again using the counterholding tool. Tighten the bolt to 101 ft. lbs. (137 Nm).
23. Temporarily install the water pump pulley.
24. Raise the engine slightly with a jack. Install the right engine mount. Tighten the nut to 38 ft. lbs. (52 Nm) and the through bolt to 64 ft. lbs. (87 Nm). Attach the RH mounting stay and tighten the three bolts to 31 ft. lbs. (42 Nm). Remove the jack.
25. Install the spark plugs, tighten 13 ft. lbs. (18 Nm) and attach the plug wires. Install the plug cord cover with bolts.
26. Connect the engine wire to the timing belt cover. Attach the following: distributor wiring, oil pressure gauge wiring, ad compressor wiring if equipped with A/C.
27. Install the alternator drive belt and the power steering drive belt. Adjust the belts to the correct tension. Attach the water pump pulley and tighten the four bolts.
28. Connect the radiator hose to the water outlet port.
29. Install the ignition coil.
30. Install the cruise control actuator and the cruise control cable, if equipped.
31. Connect the accelerator cable.
32. Install the washer reservoir tank.
33. Refill the cooling system with the correct amount of anti-freeze and water.
34. Connect the negative battery cable.
35. Start the engine and check for leaks. Allow the engine to warm up and check the work areas carefully for seepage.
36. Install the splash shield under the car. Install the right front wheel.
37. Test drive the vehicle and top off the coolant level if necessary.

4A-F Engine

▶ See Figures 141 and 142

1. Disconnect the negative battery cable.
2. Raise and support the vehicle. Remove the RH wheel and RH engine splash shield.
3. Lower the vehicle slightly and support the one side with jackstands. Remove the air cleaner assembly.
4. Loosen the water pump pulley bolts and slide off the alternator drive belt. Remove all other drive belts including the compressor if equipped. But do not disconnect any A/C lines. Hang the unit with wire to the side. Remove the compressor bracket also.
5. When removing the power steering pump drive belt, swing the pump as far over as possible to remove the belt.
6. On models with A/C, remove the bracket over top of the valve cover and disconnect the harness.
7. Remove the washer fluid reservoir from the engine compartment.
8. Remove the valve cover from the cylinder head. Discard all gaskets.

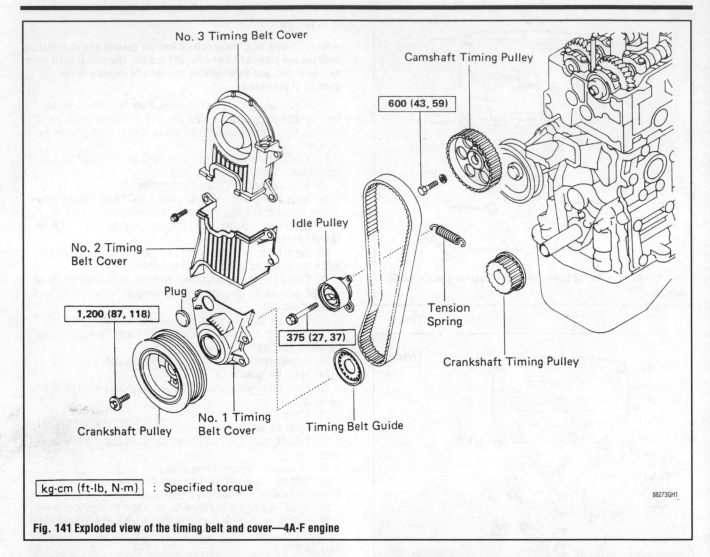

No. 3 Timing Belt Cover

Camshaft Timing Pulley

600 (43, 59)

No. 2 Timing Belt Cover

Idle Pulley

Plug

1,200 (87, 118)

375 (27, 37)

Tension Spring

Crankshaft Timing Pulley

Crankshaft Pulley

No. 1 Timing Belt Cover

Timing Belt Guide

kg-cm (ft-lb, N·m) : Specified torque

Fig. 141 Exploded view of the timing belt and cover—4A-F engine

Remove the drive belts from the engine

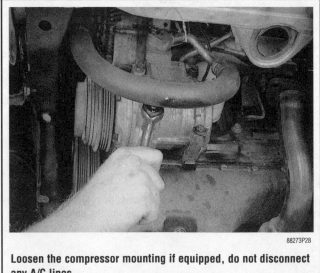

Loosen the compressor mounting if equipped, do not disconnect any A/C lines

Use a piece of wire hang the compressor out of the way

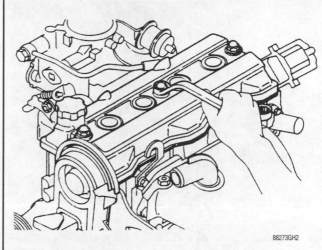

Fig. 142 Remove the valve cover from the cylinder head—except 4A-GE engine

Unbolt and remove the compressor mounting bracket

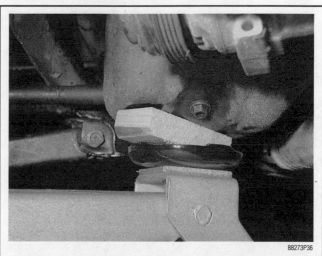

Place a piece of wood with a hydraulic jack under the oil pan and raise the engine on the right side

Remove the A/C bracket that fits over the top of the valve cover and set aside

Remove the upper bolts and bracket of the RH engine mount

A center bolt under the bracket should be removed next

Raise the engine slightly more and remove the water pump pulley

A through-bolt and two nuts located under the mount are removed last

Using a special tool, hold the crankshaft pulley, then remove the pulley bolt—4A-F engine

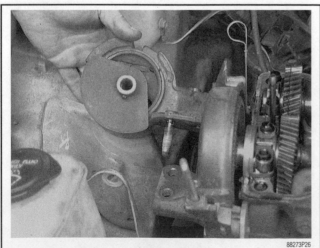

Lift the RH engine mounting off the engine while still supported by the jack

Using a gear puller, remove the pulley—4A-F engine

Loosen the upper timing cover retaining bolts

Pull the upper cover off the front of the engine

Do the same for the other two timing covers—4A-F engine

9. Set the No. 1 cylinder to TDC of the compression stroke.

10. Remove the RH engine mounting insulator. Set the jack to the engine with a piece of wood between the jack and engine. Remove the mounting bolts and stay. Remove the bolt, two nuts, through bolt and RH mounting.

11. Remove the water pump pulley.

➡**When removing the water pump pulley, it may be necessary to raise the engine to slide the pulley off.**

12. Using a special tool, retain the crankshaft pulley, then remove the pulley bolt. Remove the crankshaft pulley.

13. Unbolt the timing belt covers and remove them from the engine.

To install:

➡**When reinstalling, make certain that the gaskets and their mating surfaces are clean and free from dirt and oil. The gasket itself must be free of cuts and deformations and must fit securely in the grooves of the covers.**

14. Attach the timing belt covers, tighten the mounting bolts.

15. Whe installing the crankshaft pulley, apply a light coat of engine oil on the threads and heads under the pulley set bolt. Align the pulley set key with the key groove of the pulley and install. Tighten the mounting bolt to 87 ft. lbs. (118 Nm).

16. Temporarily install the water pump pulley.

17. With the jack still in position, install the RH engine mounting insulator to the engine mounting bracket. Align the RH insulator with the body bracket and secure with the through bolt and nut. Tighten the bolt to 47 ft. lbs. (64 Nm), the nut to 38 ft. lbs. (52 Nm) and the through bolt to 64 ft. lbs. (87 Nm). Attach the RH mounting stay and tighten the bolts to 31 ft. lbs. (42 Nm). Remove the jack.

18. Install the valve cover with a new gasket and cap nuts.

19. Place all drive belts into position and adjust.

20. Tighten the water pump pulley bolt.

21. insatall the air cleaner. RH splash shield and RH wheel.

22. Lower the vehicle, check the fluids levels. Connect the negative battery cable.

23. Test drive the vehicle.

4A-FE and 7A-FE Engines

◆ **See Figures 143 and 144**

1. Disconnect the negative battery cable.
2. Raise the vehicle and safely support it on jackstands.
3. Remove the washer reservoir tank.
4. Remove the right splash shield from under the car.
5. Remove the RH front wheel. Lower the vehicle.
6. Depending on equipment, loosen the air conditioner compressor, the power steering pump and the alternator on their adjusting bolts. Remove the drive belts.
7. Disconnect the harness from the ground wire on the RH fender apron.
8. Support the engine either from above (chain hoist) or below (floor jack and wood block) and remove the through bolt at the right engine mount.
9. Carefully elevate the engine enough to gain access to the water pump pulley.
10. Remove the water pump pulley. Lower the engine to its normal position.
11. Remove the valve cover. Make sure to label all hoses and wiring.
12. Remove the bolts retaining the No. 3 and No. 2 timing belt covers.
13. Remove the crankshaft pulley.
14. Remove the three bolts retaining the (No. 1) lower timing belt cover. Separate the cover from the front of the engine. Remove the timing belt guide.

To install:

15. Install the No. 1 timing cover and tighten the mounting bolts to 65 inch lbs. (7 Nm).

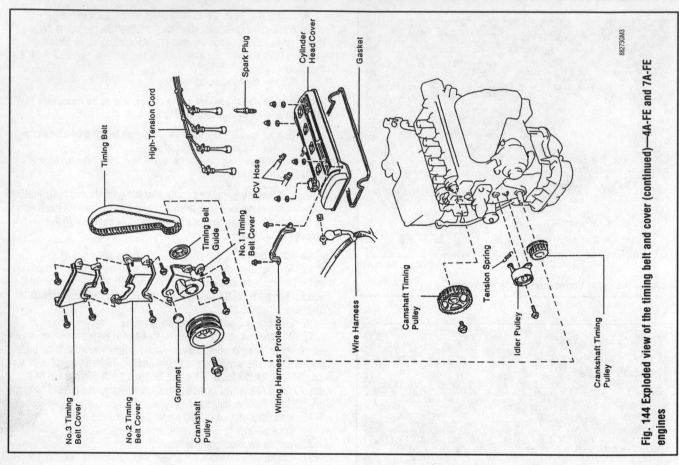

Fig. 144 Exploded view of the timing belt and cover (continued)—4A-FE and 7A-FE engines

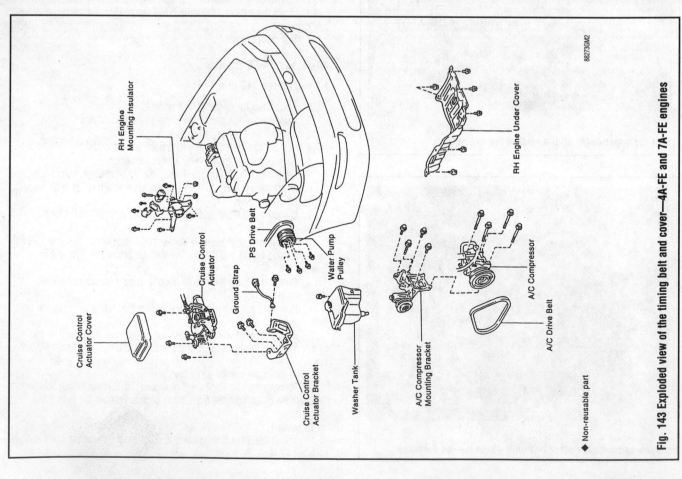

Fig. 143 Exploded view of the timing belt and cover—4A-FE and 7A-FE engines

◆ Non-reusable part

16. Temporoily install the crankshaft pulley, and align its groove with the timing mark "0" of the No. 1 timing belt cover.

17. Install the No. 2 and No. 3 timing belt covers, tighten the bolts to 65 inch lbs. (7 Nm).

18. Install the crankshaft pulley by aligning the set key with the key groove of the pulley, the slide the component on. Tighten the pulley bolt to 87 ft. lbs. (118 Nm).

19. Install the valve cover using new gaskets and cap nuts.

20. Temporarily install the water pump pulley.

21. Install the RH engine mounting insulator. Refer to the Torque Specifications chart at the beginning of this section.

22. Attach the engine ground connection on the RH fender apron.

23. Install and adjust the drive belts.

24. Install the RH engine splash shield, front wheel, cruise control actuator and washer tank.

25. Check the fluid levels, connect the negative battery cable and start the engine. Check for leaks and test drive.

Timing Belt and Sprockets

REMOVAL & INSTALLATION

➡️Timing belts must always be handled carefully and kept completely free of dirt, grease, fluids and lubricants. This includes any accidental contact from spillage. These same precautions apply to the pulleys and contact surfaces on which the belt rides. The belt must never be crimped, twisted or bent. Never use tools to pry or wedge the belt into place. Such actions will damage the structure of the belt and possibly cause breakage. The timing belt should be replaced at 60,000 miles if the vehicle is used for severe service: towing, repeated short trips in cold weather, extended idling or low speed driving for long distances, etc.

4A-GE Engine

▶ See Figures 145 thru 155

1. Disconnect the negative battery cable. Remove the timing belt covers.
2. Remove the timing belt guide from the crankshaft pulley.

➡️If reusing the timing belt, draw a direction arrow on the belt (in the direction of engine revolution), and place matchmarks on the pulleys and belt.

3. Loosen the timing belt idler pulley, move it to the left (to take tension off the belt) and tighten its bolt.
4. Carefully slip the timing belt off the pulleys.

➡️Do not disturb the position of the camshafts or the crankshaft during removal.

5. Remove the idler pulley bolt, pulley and return spring.
6. Remove the crankshaft timing pulley.
7. Remove the PCV hose and the valve cover.
8. Use an adjustable wrench to counterhold the camshaft. Be careful not to damage the cylinder head. Loosen the center bolt in each camshaft pulley and remove the pulley. Label the pulleys and keep them clean.
9. Check the timing belt carefully for any signs of cracking or deterioration. Pay particular attention to the area where each tooth or cog attaches to the backing of the belt. If the belt shows signs of damage, check the contact faces of the pulleys for possible burrs or scratches.
10. Check the idler pulley by holding it in your hand and spinning it. It should rotate freely and quietly. Any sign of grinding or abnormal noise indicates the pulley should be replaced.
11. Check the free length of the tension spring. Correct length is 1.713 inch. (43.5mm) measured at the inside faces of the hooks. A spring which has stretched during use will not apply the correct tension to the pulley; replace the spring.
12. If you can test the tension of the spring, look for 22 lbs. of tension at 50mm of length. If in doubt, replace the spring.

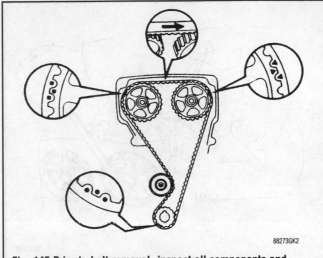

Fig. 145 Prior to belt removal, inspect all components and matchmark for installation—4A-GE engine

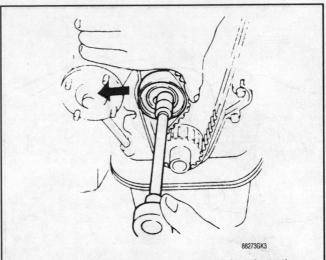

Fig. 146 Loosen the idler pulley bolt and push it as far to the left as it will go, tighten it, remove the belt . . .

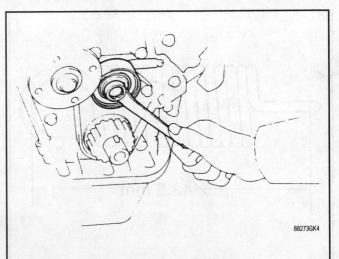

Fig. 147 . . . then remove the idler pulley bolt, pulley, and tension spring—4A-GE engine

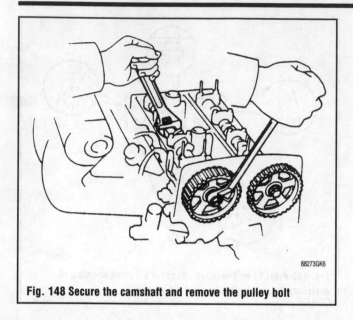

Fig. 148 Secure the camshaft and remove the pulley bolt

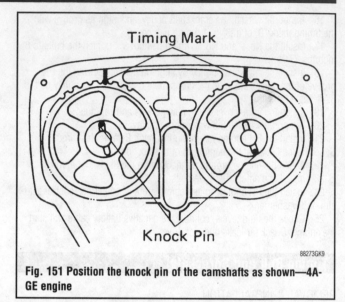

Fig. 151 Position the knock pin of the camshafts as shown—4A-GE engine

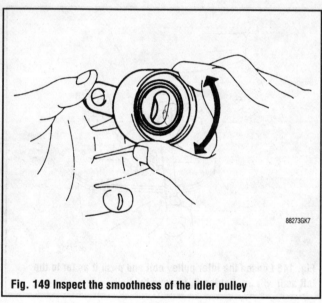

Fig. 149 Inspect the smoothness of the idler pulley

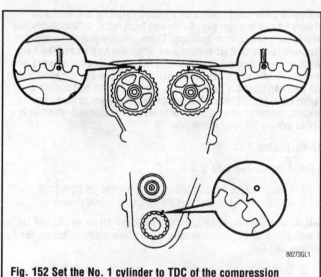

Fig. 152 Set the No. 1 cylinder to TDC of the compression stroke—4A-GE engine

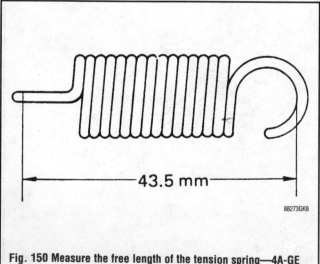

Fig. 150 Measure the free length of the tension spring—4A-GE engine

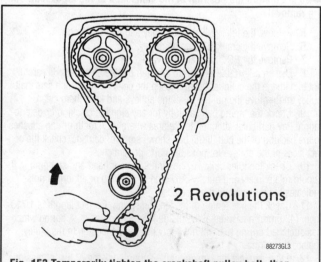

Fig. 153 Temporarily tighten the crankshaft pulley bolt, then turn it 2 revolutions from TDC to TDC—4A-GE engine

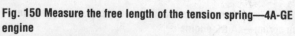

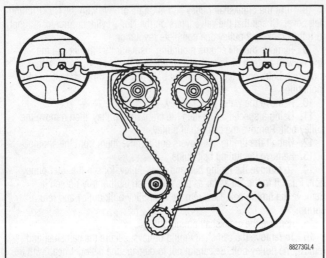

Fig. 154 Check that each pulley aligns with the timing marks—4A-GE engine

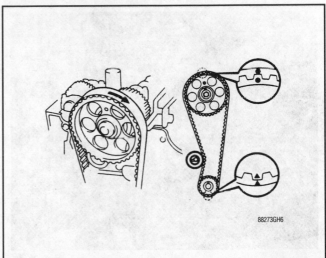

sure (2 kg). If the belt tension is incorrect, readjust it by repeating the previous steps. If the tension is correct, tighten the idler pulley bolt to 27 ft. lbs. (37 Nm).

21. Remove the crankshaft pulley bolt.

22. Install the timing belt guide onto the crankshaft timing pulley. Make sure that the cup side is facing outward.

23. Install the timing belt covers. Refer to the Timing Belt Removal and Installation earlier in this section.

4A-F Engine

▶ **See Figures 156 thru 164**

1. Disconnect the negative battery cable.

2. Raise and support the vehicle. Remove the RH wheel and RH engine splash shield.

3. Lower the vehicle slightly and support the one side with jackstands. Remove the air cleaner assembly.

4. Loosen the water pump pulley bolts and slide off the alternator drive belt. Remove all other drive belts.

5. Remove the spark plugs.

6. Remove the valve cover from the cylinder head. Discard all gaskets.

7. Set the No. 1 cylinder to TDC of the compression stroke.

Fig. 155 Install the timing belt guide onto the crankshaft pulley, cup side facing outward—4A-GE engine

Fig. 156 Draw a direction arrow on the belt (in the direction of revolution) if reusing it—4A-F engine

To install:

13. Align the camshaft knock pin and the pulley. Reinstall the camshaft timing belt pulleys, making sure the pulley fits properly on the shaft and that the timing marks align correctly. Tighten the center bolt on each pulley to 43 ft. lbs.(58 Nm). Be careful not to damage the cylinder head during installation.

14. Before reinstalling the belt, double check that the crank and camshafts are exactly in their correct positions. The alignment marks on the pulleys should align with the cast marks on the head and oil pump.

15. Reinstall the valve covers with new gaskets and attach PCV hose.

16. Install the timing belt idler pulley and its tensioning spring. Move the idler to the left and temporarily tighten its bolt.

17. Carefully observing the matchmarks made earlier, install the timing belt onto the pulleys.

18. Slowly release tension on the idler pulley bolt and allow the idler to take up tension on the timing belt. DO NOT allow the idler to slam into the belt; the belt may become damaged.

19. Temporarily install the crankshaft pulley bolt. Turn the engine clockwise through two complete revolutions, stopping at TDC. Check that each pulley aligns with its marks.

20. Check the tension of the timing belt at a top point halfway between the two camshaft sprockets. The correct deflection is 4mm at 4.4 lbs. pres-

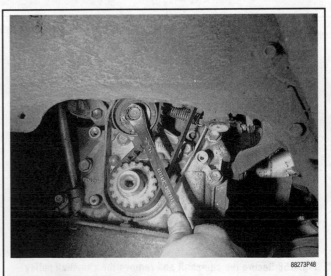

Loosen the idler pulley bolt

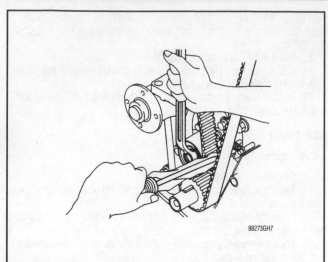

Fig. 157 Push the pulley left as far as it will go, then tighten—4A-F engine

Remove the timing belt from above the engine. Note the direction of the arrow

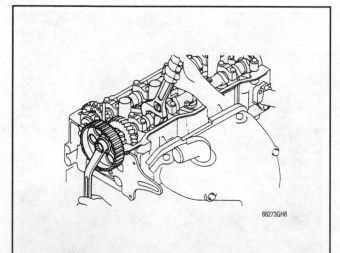

Fig. 158 Secure the camshaft and remove the camshaft pulley bolt—4A-F engine

8. Turn the crankshaft pulley and align its groove with the No. 1 timing belt cover. Check that the valve lifters on the No. 1 cylinder are loose. If not, turn the crankshaft pulley one complete revolution.

9. Remove the RH engine mounting insulator. Set the jack to the engine with a piece of wood between the jack and engine. Remove the mounting bolts and stay. Remove the bolt, two nuts, through bolt and RH mounting.

10. Remove the water pump pulley.

11. Using a special tool, retain the crankshaft pulley, then remove the pulley bolt. Remove the crankshaft pulley.

12. Unbolt the timing belt covers and remove them from the engine.

13. Remove the timing belt guide.

14. To remove the timing belt and idler pulley, loosen the idler pulley bolt. Push it to the left as far as possible, then temporarily tighten it. Remove the timing belt. Now remove the pulley bolt, pulley and return spring.

15. Remove the crankshaft timing pulley.

16. To remove the camshaft timing pulleys, secure the camshaft and remove the pulley bolt. Be careful not to damage the cylinder head with the wrench.

To install:

17. Check the idler pulley by holding it in your hand and spinning it. It should rotate freely and quietly. Any sign of grinding or abnormal noise indicates the pulley should be replaced.

18. Check the free length of the tension spring. Correct length is 1.512 inch. (38.4mm) measured at the inside faces of the hooks. A spring which has stretched during use will not apply the correct tension to the pulley; replace the spring.

➡When reinstalling, make certain that the gaskets and their mating surfaces are clean and free from dirt and oil. The gasket itself must be free of cuts and deformations and must fit securely in the grooves of the covers.

19. Align the camshaft knock pin and camshaft timing pulley. Secure the camshaft and tighten the camshaft timing pulley bolt. Align the bearing cap mark and the center of the small hole on the camshaft timing pulley. Remove any oil or water on the camshaft pulley and keep it clean.

20. Install the camshaft timing pulley and align the TDC marks on the oil pump body and crankshaft timing pulley.

21. Temporarily install the timing belt idler pulley with the mounting bolt. Install the tension spring. Pry the timing belt idler pulley toward the left as far as it will go and temporarily tighten it.

22. Install the timing belt.

23. Check the valve timing and belt tension. Loosen the timing belt idler pulley mounting bolt. Temporarily install the crank pulley bolt and turn the crankcase two revolutions clockwise from TDC to TDC. Check the valve timing. Insure that each pulley aligns with the marks as shown in the illustration.

24. Tighten the timing belt idler pulley bolt to 27 ft. lbs. (37 Nm). Remove the temporarily install cranks pulley bolt.

25. Measure the timing belt deflection at the SIDE point, looking for 0.20–0.24 inch (5–6mm) of deflection at 4.4 pounds of pressure (2 kg). If the deflection is not correct, readjust the idler pulley.

26. Install the timing belt guide facing the cup side outward.

27. Attach the timing belt covers, tighten the mounting bolts.

28. Whe installing the crankshaft pulley, apply a light coat of engine oil on the threads and heads under the pulley set bolt. Align the pulley set key with the key groove of the pulley and install. Tighten the mounting bolt to 87 ft. lbs. (118 Nm).

29. Temporarily install the water pump pulley.

30. With the jack still in position, install the RH engine mounting insulator to the engine mounting bracket. Align the RH insulator with the body bracket and secure with the through bolt and nut. Tighten the bolt to 47 ft. lbs. (64 Nm), the nut to 38 ft. lbs. (52 Nm) and the through bolt to 64 ft. lbs. (87 Nm). Attach the RH mounting stay and tighten the bolts to 31 ft. lbs. (42 Nm). Remove the jack.

31. Insatall the valve cover with a new gasket and cap nuts.

32. Install the spark plugs, tighten them, to 13 ft. lbs. (18 Nm).

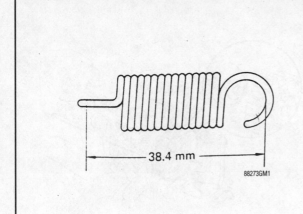

Fig. 159 Measure the free length of the tension spring—4A-F engine

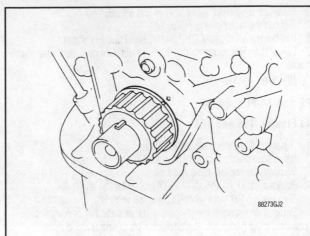

Fig. 162 Align the marks on the oil pump body and crankshaft timing pulley—4A-F engine

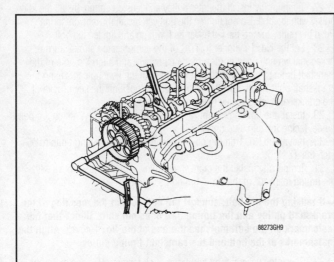

Fig. 160 Secure the camshaft and tighten the pulley bolt—4A-F engine

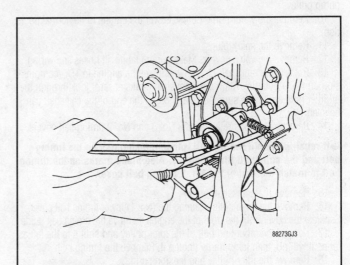

Fig. 163 Install the idler pulley and tension spring, prying the pulley toward the left—4A-F engine

Fig. 161 Align the bearing cap mark and the center small hole on the camshaft timing pulley—4A-F engine

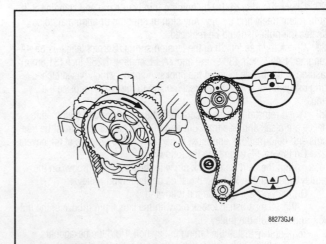

Fig. 164 Install the timing belt. Remember the direction arrow—4A-F engine

33. Place all drive belts into position and adjust.
34. Tighten the water pump pulley bolt.
35. install the air cleaner. RH splash shield and RH wheel.
36. Lower the vehicle, check the fluids levels. Connect the negative battery cable.
37. Test drive the vehicle.

4A-FE and 7A-FE Engines

▶ See Figures 165 and 166

1. Disconnect the negative battery cable.
2. Raise the vehicle and safely support it on jackstands.
3. Remove the washer reservoir tank.
4. Remove the right splash shield from under the car.
5. Remove the RH front wheel. Lower the vehicle.
6. Depending on equipment, loosen the air conditioner compressor, the power steering pump and the alternator on their adjusting bolts. Remove the drive belts.
7. Disconnect the harness from the ground wire on the RH fender apron.
8. Support the engine either from above (chain hoist) or below (floor jack and wood block) and remove the through bolt at the right engine mount.
9. Carefully elevate the engine enough to gain access to the water pump pulley.
10. Remove the water pump pulley. Lower the engine to its normal position.
11. Remove the spark plugs.
12. Remove the valve covers. Make sure to labile all hoses and wiring.
13. Rotate the crankshaft clockwise and set the engine to TDC/compression on No. 1 cylinder. Align the crankshaft marks at zero; look through the oil filler hole and make sure the small hole in the end of the camshaft can be seen.
14. Remove the bolts retaining the No. 3 and No. 2 timing belt covers.

➡If reusing the old timing belt, place matchmarks on the timing belt and the camshaft timing pulley. Also place marks on the timing belt to match the end of the No. 1 timing belt cover.

15. Remove the crankshaft pulley.
16. Remove the three bolts retaining the (No. 1) lower timing belt cover. Separate the cover from the front of the engine. Remove the timing belt guide.
17. Loosen the mounting bolt of the idler pulley and shift it to the left as far as it will go, then temporarily tighten it. Remove the timing belt.
18. Remove the idler pulley and tension spring.
19. To remove the crankshaft pulley, hold the hexagonal head wrench portion of the camshaft with a wrench, then remove the bolt and timing pulley. Be careful not to damage the cylinder head with the wrench.

To install:
20. Check the idler pulley by holding it in your hand and spinning it. It should rotate freely and quietly. Any sign of grinding or abnormal noise indicates the pulley should be replaced.
21. Check the free length of the tension spring. Correct length is on 4A-FE engine; 1.453 inch. (36.9mm) and 7A-FE engine; 1.252 inch (31.8mm) measured at the inside faces of the hooks. A spring which has stretched during use will not apply the correct tension to the pulley; replace the spring.
22. When reinstalling, make certain that the gaskets and their mating surfaces are clean and free from dirt and oil. The gasket itself must be free of cuts and deformations and must fit securely in the grooves of the covers.
23. On the 4A-FE engine do the following:
    a. Align the camshaft knock pin with the knock pin groove on the pulley side with the **K** mark, the slide on the timing pulley.
24. On the 7A-FE engine do the following:
    a. Align the camshaft knock pin with the knock pin groove of the pulley, and slide on the pulley.
25. Temporarily install the timing pulley bolt. Hold the hexagonal wrench head portion of the camshaft with a wrench, then tighten the timing pulley bolt to 43 ft. lbs. (59 Nm).
26. Install the crankshaft pulley. Align the pulley set key with the groove of the pulley. Slide on the timing pulley, facing the flange side inwards.

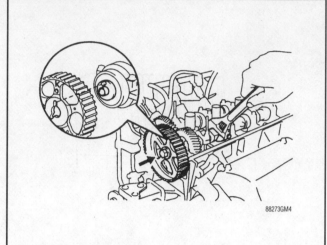

Fig. 165 Align the camshaft knock pin with the groove on the pulley side with the K mark—4A-FE engine

27. Temporarilly install the idler pulley and tension spring. Install the idler pulley with the bolt. Do not tighten the bolt yet. Install the tension spring. Push the pulley toward the left as far as it will go and tighten the bolt.
28. Set the No. 1 cylinder to TDC of the compression stroke. Turn the hexagonal wrench head portion of the camshaft, and align the hole of the camshaft timing pulley with the timing mark of the bearing cap. Using the crankshaft pulley bolt, turn the crankshaft and position the key groove of the crankshaft timing pulley upward.
29. Install the timing belt on the crankshaft timing pulley. Attach the belt guide, facing the cup side outward.
30. Install the No. 1 timing cover and tighten the mounting bolts to 65 inch lbs. (7 Nm).
31. Temporoily install the crankshaft pulley, and align its groove with the timing mark "0" of the No. 1 timing belt cover.

➡If reusing the old belt, support the belt so that the meshing of the crankshaft pulley and the timing belt does not shift. Check that the matchmark on the belt matches the end of the No. 1 cover. Align the matchmarks of the belt and the camshaft timing pulley.

32. Check the valve timing and timing belt tension. Remove the grommet and loosen the timing belt idler pulley mounting bolt.
    a. Turn the crankshaft pulley 2 revolutions clockwise from TDC to TDC.
    b. Check that each pulley aligns with the marks as shown in the illustration. If the timing marks do not align, remove the timing belt and reinstall it. Tighten the timing belt idler mounting bolt to 27 ft. lbs. (37 Nm). Install the grommet and the No. 1 timing belt cover.
33. Measure the timing belt deflection at the SIDE point, looking for 0.20–0.24 inch (5–6mm) of deflection at 4.4 lbs. pressure (2 kg). If the deflection is not correct, readjust the idler pulley.
34. Install the No. 2 and No. 3 timing belt covers, tighten the bolts to 65 inch lbs. (7 Nm).
35. Install the crankshaft pulley by aligning the set key with the key groove of the pulley, the slide the component on. Tighten the pulley bolt to 87 ft. lbs. (118 Nm).
36. Install the valve cover.
37. Install the spark plugs.
38. Temporarily install the water pump pulley.
39. Install the RH engine mounting insulator. Refer to the Torque Specifications chart at the beginning of this section.
40. Attach the engine ground connection on the RH fender apron.
41. Install and adjust the drive belts.
42. Install the RH engine splash shield, front wheel, cruise control actuator and washer tank.
43. Check the fluid levels, connect the negative battery cable and start the engine. Check for leaks and test drive.

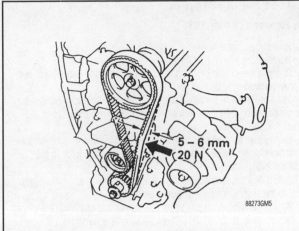

Fig. 166 Inspect the belt deflection at this position—4A-FE and 7A-FE engines

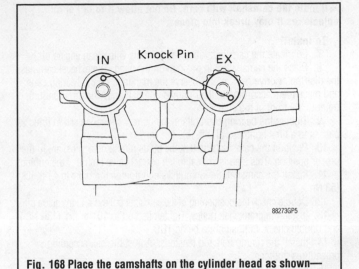

Fig. 168 Place the camshafts on the cylinder head as shown—4A-GE engine

Camshaft and Bearings

REMOVAL & INSTALLATION

➡Camshaft end-play (thrust clearance) must be checked before the cam is removed. Please refer to the "Inspection" section for details of this check.

4A-GE Engine

◆ See Figures 167 thru 172

1. Remove the valve cover and the timing belt covers.
2. Make certain thc engine is set to TDC/compression on No.1 cylinder. Remove the timing belt following procedures outlined earlier in this section.
3. Remove the crankshaft pulley.
4. Remove the camshaft timing belt pulleys.
5. Loosen and remove the camshaft bearing caps in the proper sequence. It is recommended that the bolts be loosened in two or three passes.
6. With the bearing caps removed, the camshaft(s) may be lifted clear of the head. If both cams are to be removed, label them clearly—they are not interchangeable.

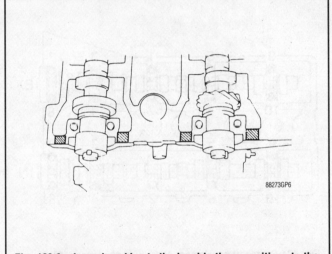

Fig. 169 Apply seal packing to the head in these positions to the head—4A-GE engine

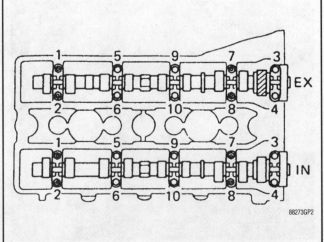

Fig. 167 Camshaft bearing cap loosening sequence—4A-GE engine

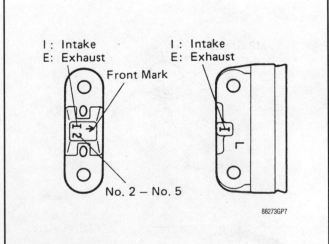

Fig. 170 Each bearing cap has its own number and front mark—4A-GE engine

➡Handle the camshaft with care. Do not allow it to fall or hit objects, as it may break into pieces.

To install:

7. Lubricate the camshaft lobes and journals with clean engine oil.

8. Place the camshaft(s) in position on the head. The exhaust cam has the distributor drive gear on it. Observe the markings on the bearing caps and place them according to their numbered positions. The arrow should point to the front of the engine.

9. Tighten the bearing cap bolts in the correct sequence and in three passes to a final tightness of 9 ft. lbs. (12 Nm).

10. Position the camshafts so that the guide pins (knock pins) are in the proper position. This step is critical to the correct valve timing of the engine.

11. Install the camshaft timing pulleys and tighten the bolts to 43 ft. lbs. (58 Nm).

12. Double check the positioning of the camshaft pulleys and the guide pin.

13. Install the crankshaft pulley. Tighten its bolt to 101 ft. lbs. (136 Nm) and double check its position to be on TDC.

14. Install the timing belt and tensioner. Adjust the belt according to procedures outlined.

15. Install the timing belt covers.

16. Install the valve cover.

4A-F, 4A-FE and 7A-FE Engines

♦ **See Figures 173 thru 183**

1. Remove the valve cover.

2. Remove the timing belt covers.

3. Remove the timing belt and idler pulley following procedures outlined previously in this section.

4. Hold the exhaust camshaft with an adjustable wrench and remove the camshaft timing belt gear. Be careful not to damage the head or the camshaft during this work.

5. Gently turn the camshafts with an adjustable wrench until the service bolt hole in the intake camshaft end gear is straight up or in the "12 o'clock" position.

6. Alternately loosen the bearing cap bolts in the number 1 position (closest to the pulley) intake and exhaust bearing caps.

7. Attach the intake camshaft end gear to the sub gear with a service bolt. The service bolt should be of the following specifications:

- Thread diameter: 0.24 inch (6.0mm)
- Thread pitch: 0.04 inch (1.0mm)
- Bolt length: 0.63–0.79 inch (16–20mm)

8. Uniformly loosen each intake camshaft bearing cap bolt a little at a time and in the correct sequence.

Fig. 171 Camshaft bearing cap tightening sequence—4A-GE engine

Hold the exhaust camshaft with a wrench and remove the belt gear

Fig. 172 Apply multipurpose grease to the new camshaft oil seal lip prior to installation—4A-GE engine

Pull the gear off the end of the exhaust cam carefully

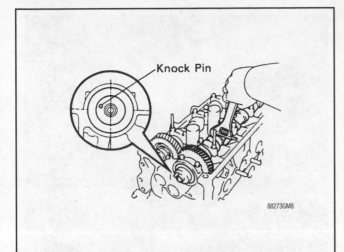

Fig. 173 Set the exhaust camshaft so that the knock pin is slightly above the top of the head—4A-F, 4A-FE and 7A-FE engines

. . . then the intake cap

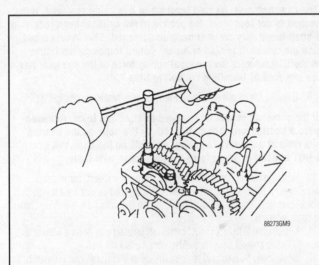

Fig. 174 Remove the 2 bolts and front bearing cap—4A-F, 4A-FE and 7A-FE engines

Secure the intake camshaft sub-gear to the main gear with a service bolt—4A-F, 4A-FE and 7A-FE engines

Loosen the exhaust bearing cap . . .

Fig. 175 Uniformly loosen and remove the 8 intake bearing cap bolts in several passes—4A-F, 4A-FE and 7A-FE engines

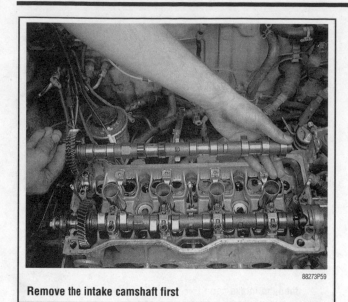

Remove the intake camshaft first

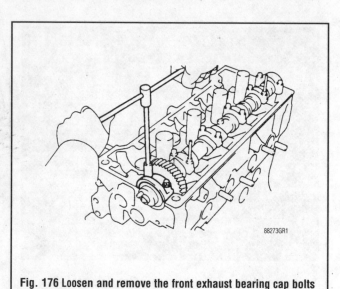

Fig. 176 Loosen and remove the front exhaust bearing cap bolts in several passes—4A-F, 4A-FE and 7A-FE engines

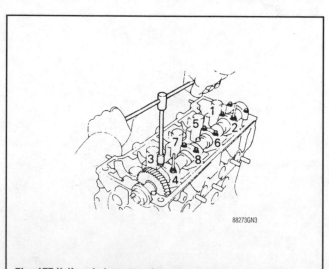

Fig. 177 Uniformly loosen and remove the 8 exhaust bearing cap bolts in several passes—4A-F, 4A-FE and 7A-FE engines

Now remove the exhaust camshaft

➡The camshaft must be held level while it is being removed. If the camshaft is not kept level, the portion of the cylinder head receiving the shaft thrust may crack or become damaged. This in turn could cause the camshaft to bind or break. Before removing the intake camshaft, make sure the torsional spring force of the sub gear has been removed by installing the bolt in Step 7.

9. Remove the bearing caps and remove the intake camshaft.

➡If the camshaft cannot be removed straight and level, retighten the No.3 bearing cap. Alternately loosen the bolts on the bearing cap a little at a time while pulling upwards on the camshaft gear. DO NOT attempt to pry or force the cam loose with tools.

10. With the intake camshaft removed, turn the exhaust camshaft approximately 105°, so that the knock pin in the end is just past the "5 o'clock" position. This puts equal loadings on the camshaft, allowing easier and safer removal.

11. Loosen the 2 front exhaust camshaft bearing cap bolts a little at a time and in the correct sequence. Also remove the oil seal.

12. Uniformily loosen and remove the other 8 exhaust bearing cap bolts in several passes.

➡If the camshaft cannot be removed straight and level, retighten the No. 3 bearing cap. Alternately loosen the bolts on the bearing cap a little at a time while pulling upwards on the camshaft gear. DO NOT attempt to pry or force the cam loose with tools.

13. When reinstalling, remember that the camshafts must be handled carefully and kept straight and level to avoid damage.

To install:

14. Lubricate the camshaft lobes and journals with clean engine oil.

15. Place the exhaust camshaft on the cylinder head so that the cam lobes press evenly on the lifters for cylinders No. 1 and 3. This will put the guide pin in the "just past 5 o'clock" position.

16. Place the bearing caps in position according to the number cast into the cap. The arrow should point towards the pulley end of the engine.

17. Tighten the bearing cap bolts gradually and in the proper sequence to 9 ft. lbs. (13 Nm).

18. Apply multi-purpose grease, to a new exhaust camshaft oil seal.

19. Install the exhaust camshaft oil seal using a suitable tool. Be very careful not to install the seal on a slant or allow it to tilt during installation.

20. Turn the exhaust cam until the cam lobes of No. 4 cylinder press down on their lifters.

21. Hold the intake camshaft next to the exhaust camshaft and engage the gears by matching the alignment marks on each gear.

22. Keeping the gears engaged, roll the intake camshaft down and into its bearing journals.

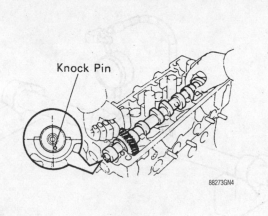

Fig. 178 Place the exhaust camshaft so that the knock pin is located slightly counterclockwise from the vertical axis of the cam—4A-F, 4A-FE and 7A-FE engines

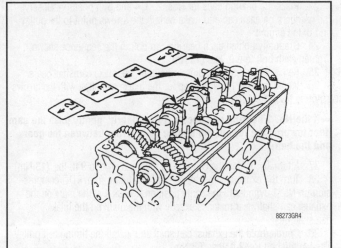

Fig. 181 Intake bearing cap identification—4A-F, 4A-FE and 7A-FE engines

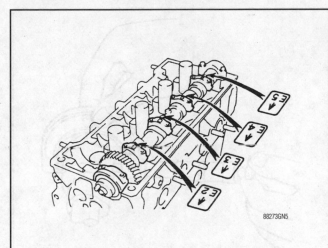

Fig. 179 Install the 5 exhaust bearing caps in their proper locations—4A-F, 4A-FE and 7A-FE engines

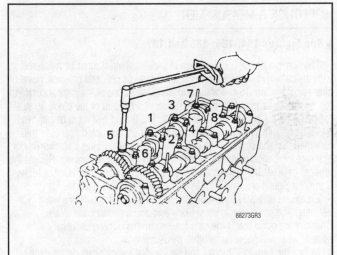

Fig. 182 Tightening sequence for the 8 intake bearing cap bolts—4A-F, 4A-FE and 7A-FE engines

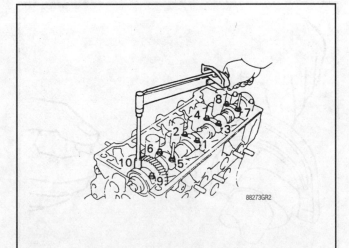

Fig. 180 Uniformly tighten the 10 exhaust bearing cap bolts in several passes—4A-F, 4A-FE and 7A-FE engines

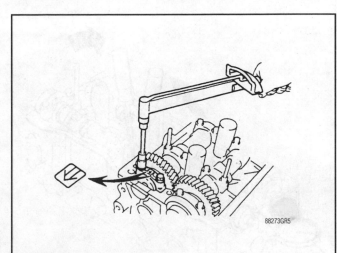

Fig. 183 Install and tighten the No. 1 bearing cap on the intake camshaft—4A-F, 4A-FE and 7A-FE engines

23. Place the bearing caps for Nos. 2, 3, 4 and 5 in position. Observe the numbers on each cap and make certain the arrows point to the pulley end of the engine.

24. Gradually tighten each bearing cap bolt in the sequence shown. Tighten each bolt to 9 ft. lbs. (13 Nm).

25. Remove any retaining pins or bolts in the intake camshaft gears.

26. Install the No. 1 bearing cap for the intake camshaft with the arrows pointing toward the front.

➡️**If the No. 1 bearing cap does not fit properly, gently push the cam gear towards the rear of the engine by levering between the gear and the head.**

27. Alternately tighten the cap bolts a little at a time to 9 ft. lbs. (13 Nm).

28. Turn the exhaust camshaft one full revolution from TDC/compression on No. 1 cylinder to the same position. Check that the mark on the exhaust camshaft gear matches exactly with the mark on the intake camshaft gear.

29. Counterhold the exhaust camshaft and install the timing belt pulley. Tighten the bolt to 43 ft. lbs. (58 Nm).

30. Double check both the crankshaft and camshaft positions, ensuring that they are both set to TDC/compression for No. 1 cylinder.

31. Install the timing belt following the procedures outlined.

32. Install the timing belt covers and the valve cover.

INSPECTION & MEASUREMENT

◆ **See Figures 184, 185, 186 and 187**

The end-play or thrust clearance of the camshaft(s) must be measured with the camshaft installed in the head. It may be checked before removal or after reinstallation. To check the end-play, mount a dial indicator accurate to ten one-thousandths (four decimal places) on the end of the block, so that the tip bears on the end of the camshaft. The timing belt must be removed. It will be necessary to remove the pulleys for unobstructed access to the camshaft. Set the scale on the dial indicator to zero. Using a screwdriver or similar tool, gently lever the camshaft fore-and-aft in its mounts. Record the amount of deflection shown on the gauge and compare this number to the Camshaft Specifications Chart at the beginning of this section.

Excessive end-play may indicate either a worn camshaft or a worn cylinder head; the worn cam is most likely and much cheaper to replace. Chances are good that if the cam is worn in this dimension (axial), substantial wear will show up in other measurements.

Mount the cam in V-blocks and set the dial indicator up on the center bearing journal. Zero the dial and rotate the camshaft. The circular runout should not exceed 0.0016 in. (0.04mm). Excess runout means the camshaft must be replaced.

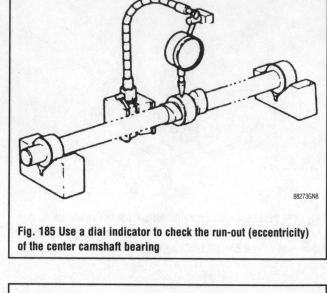

Fig. 185 Use a dial indicator to check the run-out (eccentricity) of the center camshaft bearing

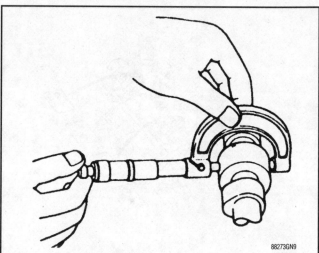

Fig. 186 Use a micrometer to check the camshaft journal diameter

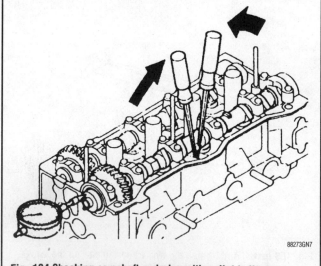

Fig. 184 Checking camshaft end-play with a dial indicator

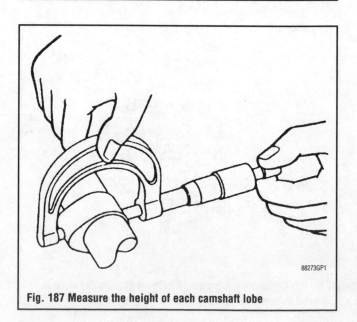

Fig. 187 Measure the height of each camshaft lobe

Using a micrometer or Vernier caliper, measure the diameter of all the journals and the height of all the lobes. Record the readings and compare them to the Camshaft Specifications Chart. Any measurement beyond the stated limits indicates wear and the camshaft must be replaced.

Lobe wear is generally accompanied by scoring or visible metal damage on the lobes. Overhead camshaft engines are very sensitive to proper lubrication with clean, fresh oil. A worn camshaft may be your report card for poor maintenance intervals and late oil changes.

On the twin-cam engines, a new camshaft will require readjusting the valves, so new shims are in order.

The clearance between the camshaft and its journals (bearings) must also be measured. Clean the camshaft, the journals and the bearing caps of any remaining oil and place the camshaft in position on the head. Lay a piece of compressible gauging material (Plastigage® or similar) on top of each journal on the camshaft.

Install the bearing caps in their correct order with the arrows pointing towards the front (pulley end) of the engine. Install the bearing cap bolts and tighten them in three passes to the correct tightness of 9 ft. lbs.

➡**Do not turn the camshaft with the gauging material installed.**

Remove the bearing caps (in the correct order) and measure the gauging material at its widest point by comparing it to the scale provided with the package. Compare these measurements to the Engine Rebuilding Chart in this section. Any measurement beyond specifications indicates wear. If you have already measured the camshaft (or replaced it) and determined it to be usable, excess bearing clearance indicates the need for a new cylinder head.

Remove the camshaft from the head and remove all traces of the gauging material. Check carefully for any small pieces clinging to contact faces.

Engine Core Plugs (Freeze Plugs)

REMOVAL & INSTALLATION

▶ **See Figures 188 and 189**

1. Raise and safely support the vehicle, as required.

✳ CAUTION

When draining coolant, keep in mind that cats and dogs are attracted by ethylene glycol antifreeze, and are quite likely to drink any that is left in an uncovered container or in puddles on the ground. This will prove fatal in sufficient quantity. Always drain coolant into a sealable container. Coolant may be reused unless it is contaminated or several years old.

2. Drain the cooling system. If the freeze plug is located in the cylinder block, it will be necessary to remove the drain plug from the side of the block to make sure all coolant is drained.

3. Drill a ½ in. (13mm) hole in the center of the plug. Remove the plug with a slide hammer or pry it out with a prybar.

➡**Be careful to stop drilling as soon as the bit breaks through the plug to prevent damaging the engine.**

4. Clean all dirt and corrosion from the freeze plug bore. Check the freeze plug bore for damage that would interfere with sealing. If the bore is damaged, the bore will have to be machined for an oversize plug.

To install:

5. Coat the plug bore and the freeze plug sealing surface with water proof sealer.

6. Install cup-type freeze plugs with the flanged edge outward. The plug must be driven in with a tool that does not contact the flange of the plug. If an improper tool is used, the plug sealing edge will be damaged and leakage will result.

7. Expansion-type freeze plugs are installed with the flanged edge inward. The plug must be driven in with a tool that does not contact the crowned portion of the plug. If an improper tool is used, the plug and/or plug bore will be damaged.

8. Replace any drain plugs that were removed and lower the vehicle.

9. Fill the cooling system, start the engine and check for leaks.

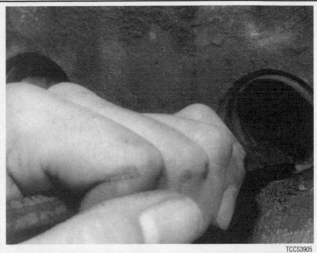

Fig. 188 Using a punch and hammer, the freeze plug can be loosened in the block

Fig. 189 Once the freeze plug has been loosened, it can be removed from the block

Rear Main Seal

REMOVAL & INSTALLATION

▶ **See Figures 190, 191 and 192**

1. Remove the transaxle from the vehicle. Follow procedures outlined in Section 7.

2. If equipped with a manual transaxle, perform the following procedures:

   a. Matchmark the pressure plate and flywheel.

   b. Remove the pressure plate-to-flywheel bolts and the clutch assembly from the vehicle.

   c. Remove the flywheel-to-crankshaft bolts and the flywheel. The flywheel is a moderately heavy component. Handle it carefully and protect it on the workbench.

3. If equipped with an automatic transaxle, perform the following procedures:

   a. Matchmark the flexplate or driveplate and crankshaft.

   b. Remove the torque converter drive plate-to-crankshaft bolts and the torque converter drive plate or flexplate.

4. Remove the bolts holding the rear end plate to the engine and the remove the rear end plate.

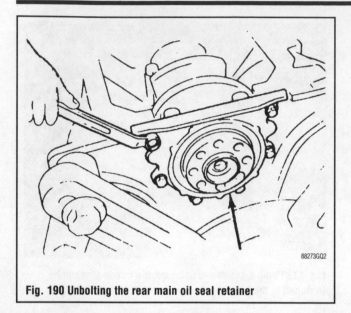

Fig. 190 Unbolting the rear main oil seal retainer

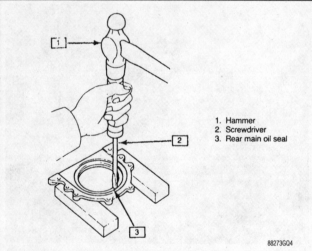

1. Hammer
2. Screwdriver
3. Rear main oil seal

Fig. 191 Removing the rear main oil seal from the retainer— note the supports under the housing

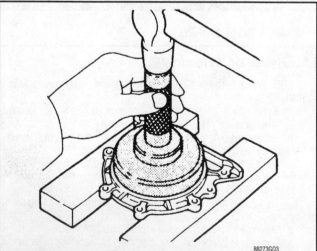

Fig. 192 Tap a new oil seal in until the surface is flush with the seal edge

5. Remove the rear oil seal retainer-to-engine bolts, rear oil seal retainer to oil pan bolts and the rear oil seal retainer.

6. Using a small pry bar, pry the rear oil seal retainer from the mating surfaces.

7. Using a drive punch or a hammer and small screwdriver, drive the oil seal from the rear bearing retainer.

8. Using a putty knife, clean the gasket mounting surfaces. Make certain that the contact surfaces are completely free of oil and foreign matter.

To install:

9. Clean the oil seal mounting surface.

10. Using multi-purpose grease, lubricate the new seal lips.

11. Using a suitable seal installation tool, tap the seal straight into the bore of the retainer.

12. Position a new gasket on the retainer and coat it lightly with gasket sealer. Fit the seal retainer into place on the engine; be careful when installing the oil seal over the crankshaft.

13. Install the six retaining bolts and tighten them to 7 ft. lbs. (84 inch lbs.)

14. Install the rear end plate. Tighten its bolts to 7.5 ft. lbs. (90 inch lbs.).

15. Reinstall either the flexplate (automatic) or the flywheel (manual), carefully observing the matchmarks made earlier. Tighten the flexplate bolts or the flywheel bolts to specifications.

16. Install the clutch disc and pressure plate (manual transaxle).

17. Reinstall the transaxle.

Flywheel and Ring Gear

REMOVAL & INSTALLATION

1. Remove the transaxle, following procedures outlined in Section 7.
2. For cars equipped with automatic transaxle:
   a. Matchmark the driveplate and the crankshaft.
   b. Loosen the retaining bolts a little at a time and in a criss-cross pattern. Support the driveplate as the last bolts are removed and then lift the driveplate away from the engine.
3. For manual transaxle cars:
   a. Matchmark the pressure plate assembly and the flywheel.
   b. Loosen the pressure plate retaining bolts a little at a time and in a criss-cross pattern. Support the pressure plate and clutch assembly as the last bolt is removed and lift them away from the flywheel.
   c. Matchmark the flywheel and crankshaft. Loosen the retaining bolts evenly and in a criss-cross pattern. Support the flywheel during removal of the last bolts and remove the flywheel.
4. Carefully inspect the teeth on the flywheel or driveplate for any signs of wearing or chipping. If anything beyond minimal contact wear is found, replace the unit.

➡Since the flywheel is driven by the starter gear, you would be wise to inspect the starter drive if any wear is found on the flywheel teeth. A worn starter can cause damage to the flywheel.

To install:

5. Place the flywheel or driveplate in position on the crankshaft and make sure the matchmarks align. Install the retaining bolts finger tight.

6. Tighten the bolts in a diagonal pattern and in three passes. Tighten the flywheel bolts (manual) or the driveplate bolts (automatic) to specifications.

7. Install the clutch and pressure plate assembly. Tighten all mounting bolts to specifications.

➡If the clutch appears worn or cracked in any way, replace it with a new disc, pressure plate and release bearing. The slight extra cost of the parts will prevent having to remove the transaxle again later.

8. Reinstall the transaxle assembly. Road test the vehicle for proper operation.

RING GEAR REPLACEMENT

If the ring gear teeth on the driveplate or flywheel are damaged, the unit must be replaced. The ring gear cannot be separated or reinstalled individually.

If a flywheel is replaced on a manual transaxle vehicle, the installation of a new clutch disc, pressure plate and release bearing is highly recommended.

EXHAUST SYSTEM

Inspection

➡Safety glasses should be worn at all times when working on or near the exhaust system. Older exhaust systems will almost always be covered with loose rust particles which will shower you when disturbed. These particles are more than a nuisance and could injure your eye.

❋❋ CAUTION

Do NOT perform exhaust repairs or inspection with the engine or exhaust hot. Allow the system to cool completely before attempting any work. Exhaust systems are noted for sharp edges, flaking metal and rusted bolts. Gloves and eye protection are required. A healthy supply of penetrating oil and rags is highly recommended.

Your vehicle must be raised and supported safely to inspect the exhaust system properly. By placing 4 safety stands under the vehicle for support should provide enough room for you to slide under the vehicle and inspect the system completely. Start the inspection at the exhaust manifold or turbocharger pipe where the header pipe is attached and work your way to the back of the vehicle. On dual exhaust systems, remember to inspect both sides of the vehicle. Check the complete exhaust system for open seams, holes loose connections, or other deterioration which could permit exhaust fumes to seep into the passenger compartment. Inspect all mounting brackets and hangers for deterioration, some models may have rubber O-rings that can be overstretched and non-supportive. These components will need to be replaced if found. It has always been a practice to use a pointed tool to poke up into the exhaust system where the deterioration spots are to see whether or not they crumble. Some models may have heat shield covering certain parts of the exhaust system , it will be necessary to remove these shields to have the exhaust visible for inspection also.

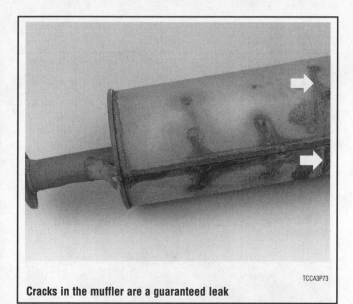
Cracks in the muffler are a guaranteed leak

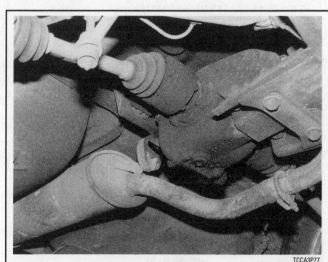
Make sure the exhaust components are not contacting the body or suspension

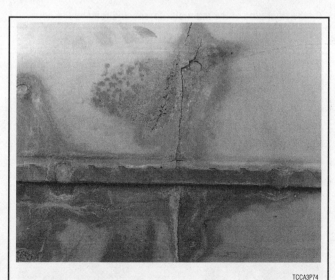
Check the muffler for rotted spot welds and seams

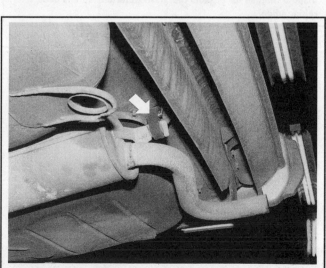
Check for overstreached or torn exhaust hangers

Example of a badly deteriorated exhaust pipe

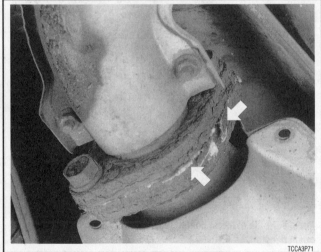

Inspect flanges for gaskets that have deteriorated and need replacement

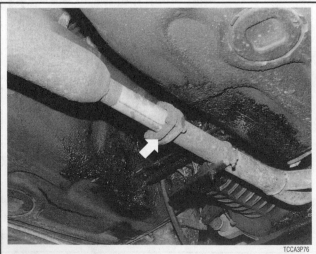

Some systems, like this one, use large O-rings (donuts) in between the flanges

REPLACEMENT

▶ See Figures 193 and 194

There are basically two types of exhaust systems. One is the flange type where the component ends are attached with bolts and a gasket in-between. The other exhaust system is the slip joint type. These components slip into one another using clamps to retain them together.

✳✳ CAUTION

Allow the exhaust system to cool sufficiently before spraying a solvent exhaust fasteners. Some solvents are highly flammable and could ignite when sprayed on hot exhaust components.

Before removing any component of the exhaust system, ALWAYS squirt a liquid rust dissolving agent onto the fasteners for ease of removal. A lot of knuckle skin will be saved by following this rule. It may even be wise to spray the fasteners and allow them to sit overnight.

On the front pipe at the manifold, loosen and remove the bolts

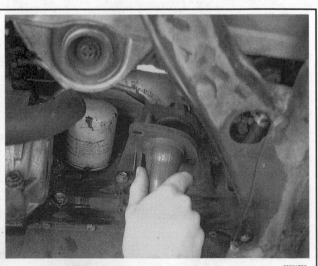

Separate the front pipe from the exhaust manifold

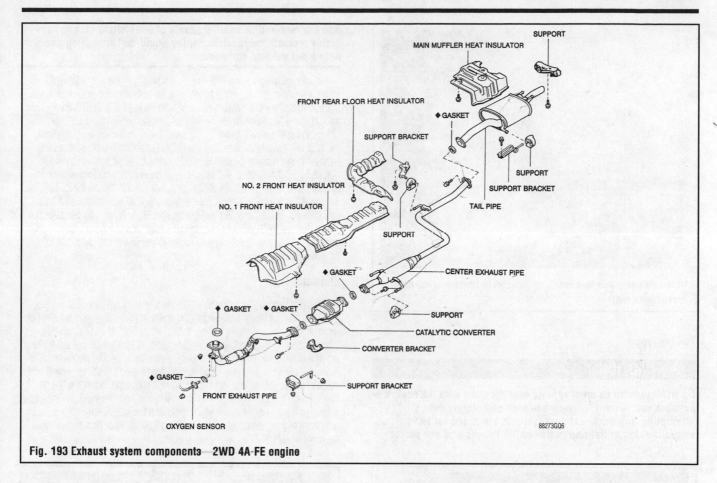

Fig. 193 Exhaust system components—2WD 4A-FE engine

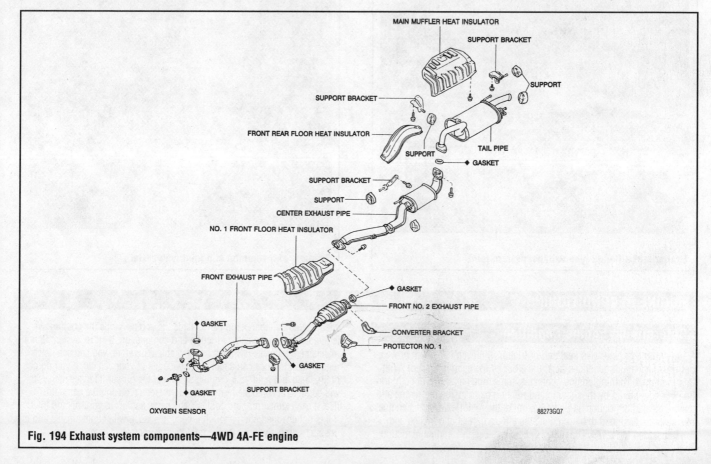

Fig. 194 Exhaust system components—4WD 4A-FE engine

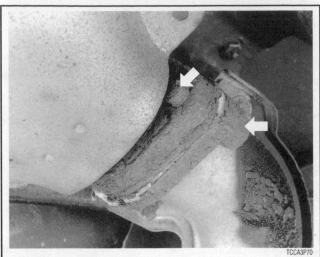

Nuts and bolts will be extremely difficult to remove when deteriorated with rust

Flange Type

Do NOT perform exhaust repairs or inspection with the engine or exhaust hot. Allow the system to cool completely before attempting any work. Exhaust systems are noted for sharp edges, flaking metal and rusted bolts. Gloves and eye protec-

tion are required. A healthy supply of penetrating oil and rags is highly recommended. Never spray liquid rust dissolving agent onto a hot exhaust component.

Before removing any component on a flange type system, ALWAYS squirt a liquid rust dissolving agent onto the fasteners for ease of removal. Start by unbolting the exhaust piece at both ends (if required). When unbolting the headpipe from the manifold, make sure that the bolts are free before trying to remove them. if you snap a stud in the exhaust manifold, the stud will have to be removed with a bolt extractor, which often means removal of the manifold itself. Next, disconnect the component from the mounting; slight twisting and turning may be required to remove the component completely from the vehicle. You may need to tap on the component with a rubber mallet to loosen the component. If all else fails, use a hacksaw to separate the parts. An oxy-acetylene cutting torch may be faster but the sparks are DANGEROUS near the fuel tank, and at the very least, accidents could happen, resulting in damage to the under-car parts, not to mention yourself.

Slip Joint Type

Before removing any component on the slip joint type exhaust system, ALWAYS squirt a liquid rust dissolving agent onto the fasteners for ease of removal. Start by unbolting the exhaust piece at both ends (if required). When unbolting the headpipe from the manifold, make sure that the bolts are free before trying to remove them. if you snap a stud in the exhaust manifold, the stud will have to be removed with a bolt extractor, which often means removal of the manifold itself. Next, remove the mounting U-bolts from around the exhaust pipe you are extracting from the vehicle. Don't be surprised if the U-bolts break while removing the nuts. Loosen the exhaust pipe from any mounting brackets retaining it to the floor pan and separate the components.

Example of a flange type exhaust system joint

Example of a common slip joint type system

ENGINE RECONDITIONING

Determining Engine Condition

Anything that generates heat and/or friction will eventually burn or wear out (ie. a light bulb generates heat, therefore its life span is limited). With this in mind, a running engine generates tremendous amounts of both; friction is encountered by the moving and rotating parts inside the engine and heat is created by friction and combustion of the fuel. However, the engine has systems designed to help reduce the effects of heat and friction and provide added longevity. The oiling system reduces the amount of friction

encountered by the moving parts inside the engine, while the cooling system reduces heat created by friction and combustion. If either system is not maintained, a break-down will be inevitable. Therefore, you can see how regular maintenance can affect the service life of your vehicle. If you do not drain, flush and refill your cooling system at the proper intervals, deposits will begin to accumulate in the radiator, thereby reducing the amount of heat it can extract from the coolant. The same applies to your oil and filter; if it is not changed often enough it becomes laden with contaminates and is unable to properly lubricate the engine. This increases friction and wear.

There are a number of methods for evaluating the condition of your engine. A compression test can reveal the condition of your pistons, piston rings, cylinder bores, head gasket(s), valves and valve seats. An oil pressure test can warn you of possible engine bearing, or oil pump failures. Excessive oil consumption, evidence of oil in the engine air intake area and/or bluish smoke from the tail pipe may indicate worn piston rings, worn valve guides and/or valve seals. As a general rule, an engine that uses no more than one quart of oil every 1000 miles is in good condition. Engines that use one quart of oil or more in less than 1000 miles should first be checked for oil leaks. If any oil leaks are present, have them fixed before determining how much oil is consumed by the engine, especially if blue smoke is not visible at the tail pipe.

COMPRESSION TEST

A noticeable lack of engine power, excessive oil consumption and/or poor fuel mileage measured over an extended period are all indicators of internal engine wear. Worn piston rings, scored or worn cylinder bores, blown head gaskets, sticking or burnt valves, and worn valve seats are all possible culprits. A check of each cylinder's compression will help locate the problem.

➡A screw-in type compression gauge is more accurate than the type you simply hold against the spark plug hole. Although it takes slightly longer to use, it's worth the effort to obtain a more accurate reading.

1. Make sure that the proper amount and viscosity of engine oil is in the crankcase, then ensure the battery is fully charged.
2. Warm-up the engine to normal operating temperature, then shut the engine OFF.
3. Disable the ignition system.
4. Label and disconnect all of the spark plug wires from the plugs.
5. Thoroughly clean the cylinder head area around the spark plug ports, then remove the spark plugs.
6. Set the throttle plate to the fully open (wide-open throttle) position. You can block the accelerator linkage open for this, or you can have an assistant fully depress the accelerator pedal.
7. Install a screw-in type compression gauge into the No. 1 spark plug hole until the fitting is snug.

❊❊ WARNING

Be careful not to crossthread the spark plug hole.

8. According to the tool manufacturer's instructions, connect a remote starting switch to the starting circuit.

TCCS3801

A screw-in type compression gauge is more accurate and easier to use without an assistant

9. With the ignition switch in the OFF position, use the remote starting switch to crank the engine through at least five compression strokes (approximately 5 seconds of cranking) and record the highest reading on the gauge.
10. Repeat the test on each cylinder, cranking the engine approximately the same number of compression strokes and/or time as the first.
11. Compare the highest readings from each cylinder to that of the others. The indicated compression pressures are considered within specifications if the lowest reading cylinder is within 75 percent of the pressure recorded for the highest reading cylinder. For example, if your highest reading cylinder pressure was 150 psi (1034 kPa), then 75 percent of that would be 113 psi (779 kPa). So the lowest reading cylinder should be no less than 113 psi (779 kPa).
12. If a cylinder exhibits an unusually low compression reading, pour a tablespoon of clean engine oil into the cylinder through the spark plug hole and repeat the compression test. If the compression rises after adding oil, it means that the cylinder's piston rings and/or cylinder bore are damaged or worn. If the pressure remains low, the valves may not be seating properly (a valve job is needed), or the head gasket may be blown near that cylinder. If compression in any two adjacent cylinders is low, and if the addition of oil doesn't help raise compression, there is leakage past the head gasket. Oil and coolant in the combustion chamber, combined with blue or constant white smoke from the tail pipe, are symptoms of this problem. However, don't be alarmed by the normal white smoke emitted from the tail pipe during engine warm-up or from cold weather driving. There may be evidence of water droplets on the engine dipstick and/or oil droplets in the cooling system if a head gasket is blown.

OIL PRESSURE TEST

Check for proper oil pressure at the sending unit passage with an externally mounted mechanical oil pressure gauge (as opposed to relying on a factory installed dash-mounted gauge). A tachometer may also be needed, as some specifications may require running the engine at a specific rpm.

1. With the engine cold, locate and remove the oil pressure sending unit.
2. Following the manufacturer's instructions, connect a mechanical oil pressure gauge and, if necessary, a tachometer to the engine.
3. Start the engine and allow it to idle.
4. Check the oil pressure reading when cold and record the number. You may need to run the engine at a specified rpm, so check the specifications chart located earlier in this section.
5. Run the engine until normal operating temperature is reached (upper radiator hose will feel warm).
6. Check the oil pressure reading again with the engine hot and record the number. Turn the engine OFF.
7. Compare your hot oil pressure reading to that given in the chart. If the reading is low, check the cold pressure reading against the chart. If the cold pressure is well above the specification, and the hot reading was lower than the specification, you may have the wrong viscosity oil in the engine. Change the oil, making sure to use the proper grade and quantity, then repeat the test.

Low oil pressure readings could be attributed to internal component wear, pump related problems, a low oil level, or oil viscosity that is too low. High oil pressure readings could be caused by an overfilled crankcase, too high of an oil viscosity or a faulty pressure relief valve.

Buy or Rebuild?

Now that you have determined that your engine is worn out, you must make some decisions. The question of whether or not an engine is worth rebuilding is largely a subjective matter and one of personal worth. Is the engine a popular one, or is it an obsolete model? Are parts available? Will it get acceptable gas mileage once it is rebuilt? Is the car it's being put into worth keeping? Would it be less expensive to buy a new engine, have your engine rebuilt by a pro, rebuild it yourself or buy a used engine from a salvage yard? Or would it be simpler and less expensive to buy another car? If you have considered all these matters and more, and have still decided to rebuild the engine, then it is time to decide how you will rebuild it.

→The editors at Chilton feel that most engine machining should be performed by a professional machine shop. Don't think of it as wasting money, rather, as an assurance that the job has been done right the first time. There are many expensive and specialized tools required to perform such tasks as boring and honing an engine block or having a valve job done on a cylinder head. Even inspecting the parts requires expensive micrometers and gauges to properly measure wear and clearances. Also, a machine shop can deliver to you clean, and ready to assemble parts, saving you time and aggravation. Your maximum savings will come from performing the removal, disassembly, assembly and installation of the engine and purchasing or renting only the tools required to perform the above tasks. Depending on the particular circumstances, you may save 40 to 60 percent of the cost doing these yourself.

A complete rebuild or overhaul of an engine involves replacing all of the moving parts (pistons, rods, crankshaft, camshaft, etc.) with new ones and machining the non-moving wearing surfaces of the block and heads. Unfortunately, this may not be cost effective. For instance, your crankshaft may have been damaged or worn, but it can be machined undersize for a minimal fee.

So, as you can see, you can replace everything inside the engine, but, it is wiser to replace only those parts which are really needed, and, if possible, repair the more expensive ones. Later in this section, we will break the engine down into its two main components: the cylinder head and the engine block. We will discuss each component, and the recommended parts to replace during a rebuild on each.

Engine Overhaul Tips

Most engine overhaul procedures are fairly standard. In addition to specific parts replacement procedures and specifications for your individual engine, this section is also a guide to acceptable rebuilding procedures. Examples of standard rebuilding practice are given and should be used along with specific details concerning your particular engine.

Competent and accurate machine shop services will ensure maximum performance, reliability and engine life. In most instances it is more profitable for the do-it-yourself mechanic to remove, clean and inspect the component, buy the necessary parts and deliver these to a shop for actual machine work.

Much of the assembly work (crankshaft, bearings, piston rods, and other components) is well within the scope of the do-it-yourself mechanic's tools and abilities. You will have to decide for yourself the depth of involvement you desire in an engine repair or rebuild.

TOOLS

The tools required for an engine overhaul or parts replacement will depend on the depth of your involvement. With a few exceptions, they will be the tools found in a mechanic's tool kit (see Section 1 of this manual). More in-depth work will require some or all of the following:
- A dial indicator (reading in thousandths) mounted on a universal base
- Micrometers and telescope gauges
- Jaw and screw-type pullers
- Scraper
- Valve spring compressor
- Ring groove cleaner
- Piston ring expander and compressor
- Ridge reamer
- Cylinder hone or glaze breaker
- Plastigage®
- Engine stand

The use of most of these tools is illustrated in this section. Many can be rented for a one-time use from a local parts jobber or tool supply house specializing in automotive work.

Occasionally, the use of special tools is called for. See the information on Special Tools and the Safety Notice in the front of this book before substituting another tool.

OVERHAUL TIPS

Aluminum has become extremely popular for use in engines, due to its low weight. Observe the following precautions when handling aluminum parts:
- Never hot tank aluminum parts (the caustic hot tank solution will eat the aluminum.
- Remove all aluminum parts (identification tag, etc.) from engine parts prior to the tanking.
- Always coat threads lightly with engine oil or anti-seize compounds before installation, to prevent seizure.
- Never overtighten bolts or spark plugs especially in aluminum threads.

When assembling the engine, any parts that will be exposed to frictional contact must be prelubed to provide lubrication at initial start-up. Any product specifically formulated for this purpose can be used, but engine oil is not recommended as a prelube in most cases.

When semi-permanent (locked, but removable) installation of bolts or nuts is desired, threads should be cleaned and coated with Loctite® or another similar, commercial non-hardening sealant.

CLEANING

Before the engine and its components are inspected, they must be thoroughly cleaned. You will need to remove any engine varnish, oil sludge and/or carbon deposits from all of the components to insure an accurate inspection. A crack in the engine block or cylinder head can easily become overlooked if hidden by a layer of sludge or carbon.

Most of the cleaning process can be carried out with common hand tools and readily available solvents or solutions. Carbon deposits can be chipped away using a hammer and a hard wooden chisel. Old gasket material and varnish or sludge can usually be removed using a scraper and/or cleaning solvent. Extremely stubborn deposits may require the use of a power drill with a wire brush. If using a wire brush, use extreme care around any critical machined surfaces (such as the gasket surfaces, bearing saddles, cylinder bores, etc.). USE OF A WIRE BRUSH IS NOT RECOMMENDED ON ANY ALUMINUM COMPONENTS. Always follow any safety recommendations given by the manufacturer of the tool and/or solvent. You should always wear eye protection during any cleaning process involving scraping, chipping or spraying of solvents.

An alternative to the mess and hassle of cleaning the parts yourself is to drop them off at a local garage or machine shop. They will, more than likely, have the necessary equipment to properly clean all of the parts for a nominal fee.

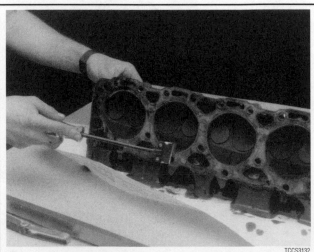

TCCS3132

Use a gasket scraper to remove the old gasket material from the mating surfaces

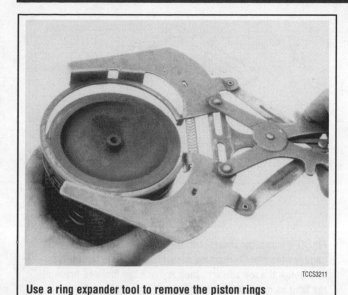

Use a ring expander tool to remove the piston rings

Clean the piston ring grooves using a ring groove cleaner tool, or . . .

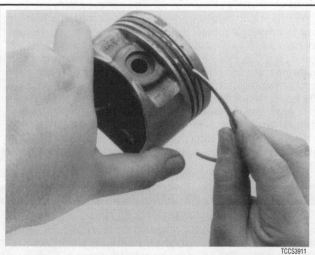

. . . use a piece of an old ring to clean the grooves. Be careful, the ring can be quite sharp

✳✳ CAUTION

Always wear eye protection during any cleaning process involving scraping, chipping or spraying of solvents.

Remove any oil galley plugs, freeze plugs and/or pressed-in bearings and carefully wash and degrease all of the engine components including the fasteners and bolts. Small parts such as the valves, springs, etc., should be placed in a metal basket and allowed to soak. Use pipe cleaner type brushes, and clean all passageways in the components. Use a ring expander and remove the rings from the pistons. Clean the piston ring grooves with a special tool or a piece of broken ring. Scrape the carbon off of the top of the piston. You should never use a wire brush on the pistons. After preparing all of the piston assemblies in this manner, wash and degrease them again.

✳✳ WARNING

Use extreme care when cleaning around the cylinder head valve seats. A mistake or slip may cost you a new seat.

When cleaning the cylinder head, remove carbon from the combustion chamber with the valves installed. This will avoid damaging the valve seats.

REPAIRING DAMAGED THREADS

▶ **See Figures 195, 196, 197, 198 and 199**

Several methods of repairing damaged threads are available. Heli-Coil® (shown here), Keenserts® and Microdot® are among the most widely used. All involve basically the same principle—drilling out stripped threads, tapping the hole and installing a prewound insert—making welding, plugging and oversize fasteners unnecessary.

Two types of thread repair inserts are usually supplied: a standard type for most inch coarse, inch fine, metric course and metric fine thread sizes and a spark lug type to fit most spark plug port sizes. Consult the individual tool manufacturer's catalog to determine exact applications. Typical thread repair kits will contain a selection of prewound threaded inserts, a tap (corresponding to the outside diameter threads of the insert) and an installation tool. Spark plug inserts usually differ because they require a tap equipped with pilot threads and a combined reamer/tap section. Most manufacturers also supply blister-packed thread repair inserts separately in addition to a master kit containing a variety of taps and inserts plus installation tools.

Before attempting to repair a threaded hole, remove any snapped, broken or damaged bolts or studs. Penetrating oil can be used to free frozen threads. The offending item can usually be removed with locking pliers or

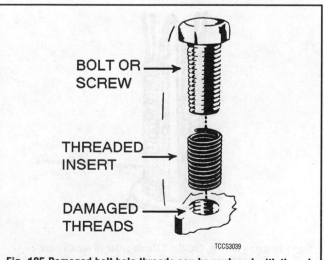

Fig. 195 Damaged bolt hole threads can be replaced with thread repair inserts

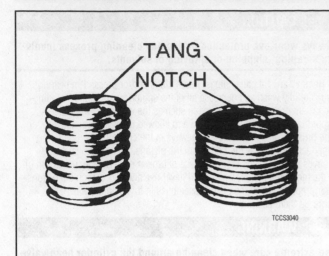

TCCS3040

Fig. 196 Standard thread repair insert (left), and spark plug thread insert

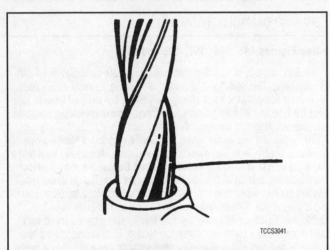

TCCS3041

Fig. 197 Drill out the damaged threads with the specified size bit. Be sure to drill completely through the hole or to the bottom of a blind hole

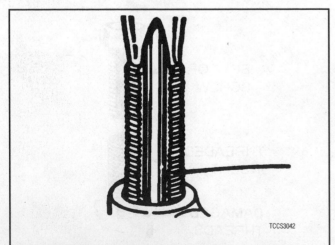

TCCS3042

Fig. 198 Using the kit, tap the hole in order to receive the thread insert. Keep the tap well oiled and back it out frequently to avoid clogging the threads

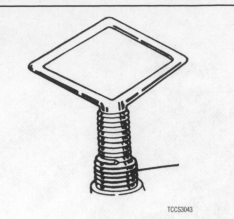

TCCS3043

Fig. 199 Screw the insert onto the installer tool until the tang engages the slot. Thread the insert into the hole until it is ¼–½ turn below the top surface, then remove the tool and break off the tang using a punch

using a screw/stud extractor. After the hole is clear, the thread can be repaired, as shown in the series of accompanying illustrations and in the kit manufacturer's instructions.

Engine Preparation

To properly rebuild an engine, you must first remove it from the vehicle, then disassemble and diagnose it. Ideally you should place your engine on an engine stand. This affords you the best access to the engine components. Follow the manufacturer's directions for using the stand with your particular engine. Remove the flywheel or flexplate before installing the engine to the stand.

Now that you have the engine on a stand, and assuming that you have drained the oil and coolant from the engine, it's time to strip it of all but the necessary components. Before you start disassembling the engine, you may want to take a moment to draw some pictures, or fabricate some labels or containers to mark the locations of various components and the bolts and/or studs which fasten them. Modern day engines use a lot of little brackets and clips which hold wiring harnesses and such, and these holders are often mounted on studs and/or bolts that can be easily mixed up. The manufacturer spent a lot of time and money designing your vehicle, and they wouldn't have wasted any of it by haphazardly placing brackets, clips or fasteners on the vehicle. If it's present when you disassemble it, put it back when you assemble, you will regret not remembering that little bracket which holds a wire harness out of the path of a rotating part.

You should begin by unbolting any accessories still attached to the engine, such as the water pump, power steering pump, alternator, etc. Then, unfasten any manifolds (intake or exhaust) which were not removed during the engine removal procedure. Finally, remove any covers remaining on the engine such as the rocker arm, front or timing cover and oil pan. Some front covers may require the vibration damper and/or crank pulley to be removed beforehand. The idea is to reduce the engine to the bare necessities (cylinder head(s), valve train, engine block, crankshaft, pistons and connecting rods), plus any other `in block' components such as oil pumps, balance shafts and auxiliary shafts.

Finally, remove the cylinder head(s) from the engine block and carefully place on a bench. Disassembly instructions for each component follow later in this section.

Cylinder Head

There are two basic types of cylinder heads used on today's automobiles: the Overhead Valve (OHV) and the Overhead Camshaft (OHC). The latter can also be broken down into two subgroups: the Single Overhead Camshaft (SOHC) and the Dual Overhead Camshaft (DOHC). Generally, if there is only a single camshaft on a head, it is just referred to as an OHC head. Also, an engine with a OHV cylinder head is also known as a pushrod engine.

Most cylinder heads these days are made of an aluminum alloy due to its light weight, durability and heat transfer qualities. However, cast iron was the material of choice in the past, and is still used on many vehicles today. Whether made from aluminum or iron, all cylinder heads have valves and seats. Some use two valves per cylinder, while the more hi-tech engines will utilize a multi-valve configuration using 3, 4 and even 5 valves per cylinder. When the valve contacts the seat, it does so on precision machined surfaces, which seals the combustion chamber. All cylinder heads have a valve guide for each valve. The guide centers the valve to the seat and allows it to move up and down within it. The clearance between the valve and guide can be critical. Too much clearance and the engine may consume oil, lose vacuum and/or damage the seat. Too little, and the valve can stick in the guide causing the engine to run poorly if at all, and possibly causing severe damage. The last component all cylinder heads have are valve springs. The spring holds the valve against its seat. It also returns the valve to this position when the valve has been opened by the valve train or camshaft. The spring is fastened to the valve by a retainer and valve locks (sometimes called keepers). Aluminum heads will also have a valve spring shim to keep the spring from wearing away the aluminum.

An ideal method of rebuilding the cylinder head would involve replacing all of the valves, guides, seats, springs, etc. with new ones. However, depending on how the engine was maintained, often this is not necessary. A major cause of valve, guide and seat wear is an improperly tuned engine. An engine that is running too rich, will often wash the lubricating oil out of the guide with gasoline, causing it to wear rapidly. Conversely, an engine which is running too lean will place higher combustion temperatures on the valves and seats allowing them to wear or even burn. Springs fall victim to the driving habits of the individual. A driver who often runs the engine rpm to the redline will wear out or break the springs faster then one that stays well below it. Unfortunately, mileage takes it toll on all of the parts. Generally, the valves, guides, springs and seats in a cylinder head can be machined and re-used, saving you money. However, if a valve is burnt, it may be wise to replace all of the valves, since they were all operating in the same environment. The same goes for any other component on the cylinder head. Think of it as an insurance policy against future problems related to that component.

Unfortunately, the only way to find out which components need replacing, is to disassemble and carefully check each piece. After the cylinder head(s) are disassembled, thoroughly clean all of the components.

DISASSEMBLY

Whether it is a single or dual overhead camshaft cylinder head, the disassembly procedure is relatively unchanged. One aspect to pay attention to is careful labeling of the parts on the dual camshaft cylinder head. There will be an intake camshaft and followers as well as an exhaust camshaft and followers and they must be labeled as such. In some cases, the components are identical and could easily be installed incorrectly. DO NOT MIX THEM UP! Determining which is which is very simple; the intake camshaft and components are on the same side of the head as was the intake manifold. Conversely, the exhaust camshaft and components are on the same side of the head as was the exhaust manifold.

CUP TYPE CAMSHAFT FOLLOWERS

Most cylinder heads with cup type camshaft followers will have the valve spring, retainer and locks recessed within the follower's bore. You will need a C-clamp style valve spring compressor tool, an OHC spring removal tool (or equivalent) and a small magnet to disassemble the head.

1. If not already removed, remove the camshaft(s) and/or followers. Mark their positions for assembly.

2. Position the cylinder head to allow use of a C-clamp style valve spring compressor tool.

➡️It is preferred to position the cylinder head gasket surface facing you with the valve springs facing the opposite direction and the head laying horizontal.

3. With the OHC spring removal adapter tool positioned inside of the follower bore, compress the valve spring using the C-clamp style valve spring compressor.

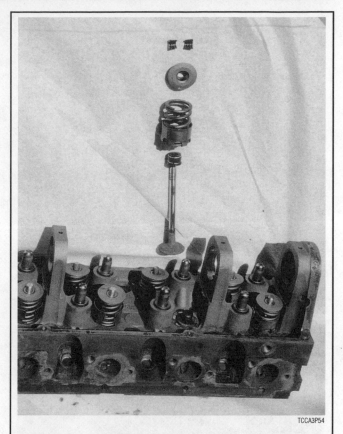

TCCA3P54

Exploded view of a valve, seal, spring, retainer and locks from an OHC cylinder head

TCCA3P02

Example of a multivalve cylinder head. Note how it has 2 intake and 2 exhaust valve ports

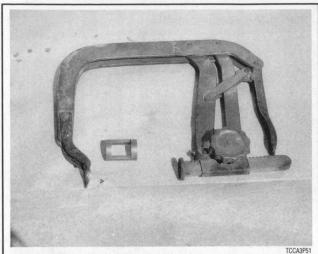

C-clamp type spring compressor and an OHC spring removal tool (center) for cup type followers

Most cup type follower cylinder heads retain the camshaft using bolt-on bearing caps

Position the OHC spring tool in the follower bore, then compress the spring with a C-clamp type tool

4. Remove the valve locks. A small magnetic tool or screwdriver will aid in removal.

5. Release the compressor tool and remove the spring assembly.

6. Withdraw the valve from the cylinder head.

7. If equipped, remove the valve seal.

➡️**Special valve seal removal tools are available. Regular or needle nose type pliers, if used with care, will work just as well. If using ordinary pliers, be sure not to damage the follower bore. The follower and its bore are machined to close tolerances and any damage to the bore will effect this relationship.**

8. If equipped, remove the valve spring shim. A small magnetic tool or screwdriver will aid in removal.

9. Repeat Steps 3 through 8 until all of the valves have been removed.

Rocker Arm Type Camshaft Followers

Most cylinder heads with rocker arm-type camshaft followers are easily disassembled using a standard valve spring compressor. However, certain models may not have enough open space around the spring for the standard tool and may require you to use a C-clamp style compressor tool instead.

1. If not already removed, remove the rocker arms and/or shafts and the camshaft. If applicable, also remove the hydraulic lash adjusters. Mark their positions for assembly.

2. Position the cylinder head to allow access to the valve spring.

3. Use a valve spring compressor tool to relieve the spring tension from the retainer.

➡️**Due to engine varnish, the retainer may stick to the valve locks. A gentle tap with a hammer may help to break it loose.**

4. Remove the valve locks from the valve tip and/or retainer. A small magnet may help in removing the small locks.

5. Lift the valve spring, tool and all, off of the valve stem.

6. If equipped, remove the valve seal. If the seal is difficult to remove with the valve in place, try removing the valve first, then the seal. Follow the steps below for valve removal.

7. Position the head to allow access for withdrawing the valve.

Example of the shaft mounted rocker arms on some OHC heads

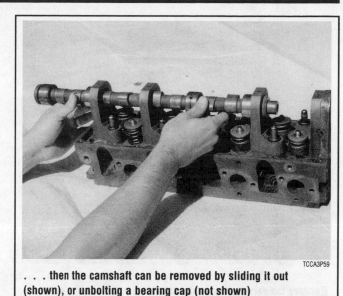

. . . then the camshaft can be removed by sliding it out (shown), or unbolting a bearing cap (not shown)

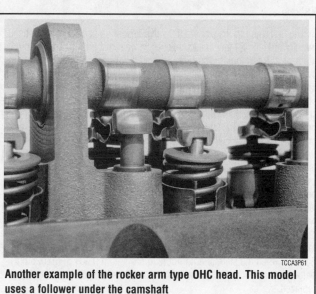

Another example of the rocker arm type OHC head. This model uses a follower under the camshaft

Compress the valve spring . . .

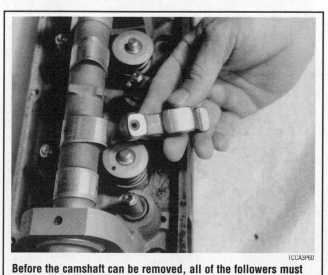

Before the camshaft can be removed, all of the followers must first be removed . . .

. . . then remove the valve locks from the valve stem and spring retainer

Remove the valve spring and retainer from the cylinder head

Remove the valve seal from the guide. Some gentle prying or pliers may help to remove stubborn ones

All aluminum and some cast iron heads will have these valve spring shims. Remove all of them as well

➡Cylinder heads that have seen a lot of miles and/or abuse may have mushroomed the valve lock grove and/or tip, causing difficulty in removal of the valve. If this has happened, use a metal file to carefully remove the high spots around the lock grooves and/or tip. Only file it enough to allow removal.

  8. Remove the valve from the cylinder head.
  9. If equipped, remove the valve spring shim. A small magnetic tool or screwdriver will aid in removal.
  10. Repeat Steps 3 though 9 until all of the valves have been removed.

INSPECTION

Now that all of the cylinder head components are clean, it's time to inspect them for wear and/or damage. To accurately inspect them, you will need some specialized tools:

- A 0–1 inch micrometer for the valves
- A dial indicator or inside diameter gauge for the valve guides
- A spring pressure test gauge

If you do not have access to the proper tools, you may want to bring the components to a shop that does.

Valves

The first thing to inspect are the valve heads. Look closely at the head, margin and face for any cracks, excessive wear or burning. The margin is the best place to look for burning. It should have a squared edge with an even width all around the diameter. When a valve burns, the margin will look melted and the edges rounded. Also inspect the valve head for any signs of tulipping. This will show as a lifting of the edges or dishing in the center of the head and will usually not occur to all of the valves. All of the heads should look the same, any that seem dished more than others are probably bad. Next, inspect the valve lock grooves and valve tips. Check for any burrs around the lock grooves, especially if you had to file them to remove the valve. Valve tips should appear flat, although slight rounding with high mileage engines is normal. Slightly worn valve tips will need to be machined flat. Last, measure the valve stem diameter with the micrometer. Measure the area that rides within the guide, especially towards the tip where most of the wear occurs. Take several measurements along its length and compare them to each other. Wear should be even along the length with little to no taper. If no minimum diameter is given in the specifications, then the stem should not read more than 0.001 in. (0.025mm) below the specification. Any valves that fail these inspections should be replaced.

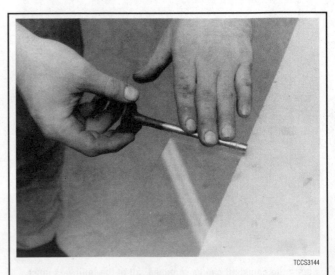

Valve stems may be rolled on a flat surface to check for bends

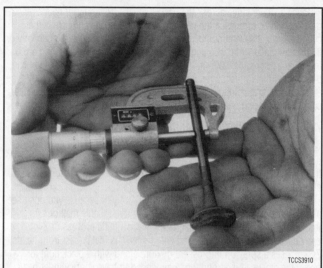

Use a micrometer to check the valve stem diameter

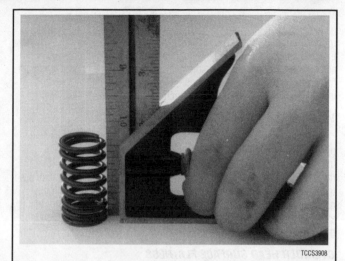

Check the valve spring for squareness on a flat surface; a carpenter's square can be used

Springs, Retainers and Valve Locks

The first thing to check is the most obvious, broken springs. Next check the free length and squareness of each spring. If applicable, insure to distinguish between intake and exhaust springs. Use a ruler and/or carpenters square to measure the length. A carpenters square should be used to check the springs for squareness. If a spring pressure test gauge is available, check each springs rating and compare to the specifications chart. Check the readings against the specifications given. Any springs that fail these inspections should be replaced.

The spring retainers rarely need replacing, however they should still be checked as a precaution. Inspect the spring mating surface and the valve lock retention area for any signs of excessive wear. Also check for any signs of cracking. Replace any retainers that are questionable.

Valve locks should be inspected for excessive wear on the outside contact area as well as on the inner notched surface. Any locks which appear worn or broken and its respective valve should be replaced.

Cylinder Head

There are several things to check on the cylinder head: valve guides, seats, cylinder head surface flatness, cracks and physical damage.

VALVE GUIDES

Now that you know the valves are good, you can use them to check the guides, although a new valve, if available, is preferred. Before you measure anything, look at the guides carefully and inspect them for any cracks, chips or breakage. Also if the guide is a removable style (as in most aluminum heads), check them for any looseness or evidence of movement. All of the guides should appear to be at the same height from the spring seat. If any seem lower (or higher) from another, the guide has moved. Mount a dial indicator onto the spring side of the cylinder head. Lightly oil the valve stem and insert it into the cylinder head. Position the dial indicator against the valve stem near the tip and zero the gauge. Grasp the valve stem and wiggle towards and away from the dial indicator and observe the readings.

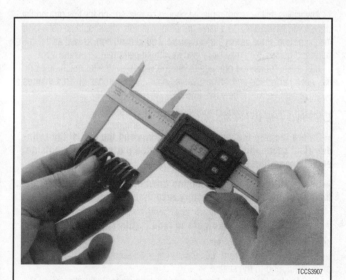

Use a caliper to check the valve spring free-length

A dial gauge may be used to check valve stem-to-guide clearance; read the gauge while moving the valve stem

Mount the dial indicator 90 degrees from the initial point and zero the gauge and again take a reading. Compare the two readings for a out of round condition. Check the readings against the specifications given. An Inside Diameter (I.D.) gauge designed for valve guides will give you an accurate valve guide bore measurement. If the I.D. gauge is used, compare the readings with the specifications given. Any guides that fail these inspections should be replaced or machined.

VALVE SEATS

A visual inspection of the valve seats should show a slightly worn and pitted surface where the valve face contacts the seat. Inspect the seat carefully for severe pitting or cracks. Also, a seat that is badly worn will be recessed into the cylinder head. A severely worn or recessed seat may need to be replaced. All cracked seats must be replaced. A seat concentricity gauge, if available, should be used to check the seat run-out. If run-out exceeds specifications the seat must be machined (if no specification is given use 0.002 in. or 0.051mm).

CYLINDER HEAD SURFACE FLATNESS

After you have cleaned the gasket surface of the cylinder head of any old gasket material, check the head for flatness.

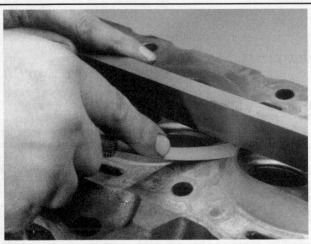

TCCS3919

Check the head for flatness across the center of the head surface using a straightedge and feeler gauge

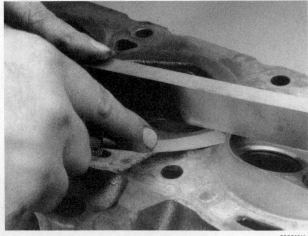

TCCS3918

Checks should also be made along both diagonals of the head surface

Place a straightedge across the gasket surface. Using feeler gauges, determine the clearance at the center of the straightedge and across the cylinder head at several points. Check along the centerline and diagonally on the head surface. If the warpage exceeds 0.003 in. (0.076mm) within a 6.0 in. (15.2cm) span, or 0.006 in. (0.152mm) over the total length of the head, the cylinder head must be resurfaced. After resurfacing the heads of a V-type engine, the intake manifold flange surface should be checked, and if necessary, milled proportionally to allow for the change in its mounting position.

CRACKS AND PHYSICAL DAMAGE

Generally, cracks are limited to the combustion chamber, however, it is not uncommon for the head to crack in a spark plug hole, port, outside of the head or in the valve spring/rocker arm area. The first area to inspect is always the hottest: the exhaust seat/port area.

A visual inspection should be performed, but just because you don't see a crack does not mean it is not there. Some more reliable methods for inspecting for cracks include Magnaflux®, a magnetic process or Zyglo®, a dye penetrant. Magnaflux® is used only on ferrous metal (cast iron) heads. Zyglo® uses a spray on fluorescent mixture along with a black light to reveal the cracks. It is strongly recommended to have your cylinder head checked professionally for cracks, especially if the engine was known to have overheated and/or leaked or consumed coolant. Contact a local shop for availability and pricing of these services.

Physical damage is usually very evident. For example, a broken mounting ear from dropping the head or a bent or broken stud and/or bolt. All of these defects should be fixed or, if unrepairable, the head should be replaced.

Camshaft and Followers

Inspect the camshaft(s) and followers as described earlier in this section.

REFINISHING & REPAIRING

Many of the procedures given for refinishing and repairing the cylinder head components must be performed by a machine shop. Certain steps, if the inspected part is not worn, can be performed yourself inexpensively. However, you spent a lot of time and effort so far, why risk trying to save a couple bucks if you might have to do it all over again?

Valves

Any valves that were not replaced should be refaced and the tips ground flat. Unless you have access to a valve grinding machine, this should be done by a machine shop. If the valves are in extremely good condition, as well as the valve seats and guides, they may be lapped in without performing machine work.

It is a recommended practice to lap the valves even after machine work has been performed and/or new valves have been purchased. This insures a positive seal between the valve and seat.

LAPPING THE VALVES

➡Before lapping the valves to the seats, read the rest of the cylinder head section to insure that any related parts are in acceptable enough condition to continue.

➡Before any valve seat machining and/or lapping can be performed, the guides must be within factory recommended specifications.

1. Invert the cylinder head.
2. Lightly lubricate the valve stems and insert them into the cylinder head in their numbered order.
3. Raise the valve from the seat and apply a small amount of fine lapping compound to the seat.
4. Moisten the suction head of a hand-lapping tool and attach it to the head of the valve.
5. Rotate the tool between the palms of both hands, changing the position of the valve on the valve seat and lifting the tool often to prevent grooving.
6. Lap the valve until a smooth, polished circle is evident on the valve and seat.
7. Remove the tool and the valve. Wipe away all traces of the grinding compound and store the valve to maintain its lapped location.

Do not get the valves out of order after they have been lapped. They must be put back with the same valve seat they were lapped with.

Springs, Retainers and Valve Locks

There is no repair or refinishing possible with the springs, retainers and valve locks. If they are found to be worn or defective, they must be replaced with new (or known good) parts.

Cylinder Head

Most refinishing procedures dealing with the cylinder head must be performed by a machine shop. Read the sections below and review your inspection data to determine whether or not machining is necessary.

VALVE GUIDE

➡ If any machining or replacements are made to the valve guides, the seats must be machined.

Unless the valve guides need machining or replacing, the only service to perform is to thoroughly clean them of any dirt or oil residue.

There are only two types of valve guides used on automobile engines: the replaceable-type (all aluminum heads) and the cast-in integral-type (most cast iron heads). There are four recommended methods for repairing worn guides.
- Knurling
- Inserts
- Reaming oversize
- Replacing

Knurling is a process in which metal is displaced and raised, thereby reducing clearance, giving a true center, and providing oil control. It is the least expensive way of repairing the valve guides. However, it is not necessarily the best, and in some cases, a knurled valve guide will not stand up for more than a short time. It requires a special knurlizer and precision reaming tools to obtain proper clearances. It would not be cost effective to purchase these tools, unless you plan on rebuilding several of the same cylinder head.

Installing a guide insert involves machining the guide to accept a bronze insert. One style is the coil-type which is installed into a threaded guide. Another is the thin-walled insert where the guide is reamed oversize to accept a split-sleeve insert. After the insert is installed, a special tool is then run through the guide to expand the insert, locking it to the guide. The insert is then reamed to the standard size for proper valve clearance.

Reaming for oversize valves restores normal clearances and provides a true valve seat. Most cast-in type guides can be reamed to accept an valve with an oversize stem. The cost factor for this can become quite high as you will need to purchase the reamer and new, oversize stem valves for all guides which were reamed. Oversizes are generally 0.003 to 0.030 in. (0.076 to 0.762mm), with 0.015 in. (0.381mm) being the most common.

To replace cast-in type valve guides, they must be drilled out, then reamed to accept replacement guides. This must be done on a fixture which will allow centering and leveling off of the original valve seat or guide, otherwise a serious guide-to-seat misalignment may occur making it impossible to properly machine the seat.

Replaceable-type guides are pressed into the cylinder head. A hammer and a stepped drift or punch may be used to install and remove the guides. Before removing the guides, measure the protrusion on the spring side of the head and record it for installation. Use the stepped drift to hammer out the old guide from the combustion chamber side of the head. When installing, determine whether or not the guide also seals a water jacket in the head, and if it does, use the recommended sealing agent. If there is no water jacket, grease the valve guide and its bore. Use the stepped drift, and hammer the new guide into the cylinder head from the spring side of the cylinder head. A stack of washers the same thickness as the measured protrusion may help the installation process.

VALVE SEATS

➡ Before any valve seat machining can be performed, the guides must be within factory recommended specifications.

➡ If any machining or replacements were made to the valve guides, the seats must be machined.

If the seats are in good condition, the valves can be lapped to the seats, and the cylinder head assembled. See the valves section for instructions on lapping.

If the valve seats are worn, cracked or damaged, they must be serviced by a machine shop. The valve seat must be perfectly centered to the valve guide, which requires very accurate machining.

CYLINDER HEAD SURFACE

If the cylinder head is warped, it must be machined flat. If the warpage is extremely severe, the head may need to be replaced. In some instances, it may be possible to straighten a warped head enough to allow machining. In either case, contact a professional machine shop for service.

➡ Any OHC cylinder head that shows excessive warpage should have the camshaft bearing journals align bored after the cylinder head has been resurfaced.

Failure to align bore the camshaft bearing journals could result in severe engine damage including but not limited to: valve and piston damage, connecting rod damage, camshaft and/or crankshaft breakage.

CRACKS AND PHYSICAL DAMAGE

Certain cracks can be repaired in both cast iron and aluminum heads. For cast iron, a tapered threaded insert is installed along the length of the crack. Aluminum can also use the tapered inserts, however welding is the preferred method. Some physical damage can be repaired through brazing or welding. Contact a machine shop to get expert advice for your particular dilemma.

ASSEMBLY

The first step for any assembly job is to have a clean area in which to work. Next, thoroughly clean all of the parts and components that are to be assembled. Finally, place all of the components onto a suitable work space and, if necessary, arrange the parts to their respective positions.

Cup Type Camshaft Followers

To install the springs, retainers and valve locks on heads which have these components recessed into the camshaft follower's bore, you will need a small screwdriver-type tool, some clean white grease and a lot of patience. You will also need the C-clamp style spring compressor and the OHC tool used to disassemble the head.

1. Lightly lubricate the valve stems and insert all of the valves into the cylinder head. If possible, maintain their original locations.
2. If equipped, install any valve spring shims which were removed.
3. If equipped, install the new valve seals, keeping the following in mind:
- If the valve seal presses over the guide, lightly lubricate the outer guide surfaces.
- If the seal is an O-ring type, it is installed just after compressing the spring but before the valve locks.
4. Place the valve spring and retainer over the stem.
5. Position the spring compressor and the OHC tool, then compress the spring.
6. Using a small screwdriver as a spatula, fill the valve stem side of the lock with white grease. Use the excess grease on the screwdriver to fasten the lock to the driver.

Once assembled, check the valve clearance and correct as needed

7. Carefully install the valve lock, which is stuck to the end of the screwdriver, to the valve stem then press on it with the screwdriver until the grease squeezes out. The valve lock should now be stuck to the stem.

8. Repeat Steps 6 and 7 for the remaining valve lock.

9. Relieve the spring pressure slowly and insure that neither valve lock becomes dislodged by the retainer.

10. Remove the spring compressor tool.

11. Repeat Steps 2 through 10 until all of the springs have been installed.

12. Install the followers, camshaft(s) and any other components that were removed for disassembly.

Rocker Arm Type Camshaft Followers

1. Lightly lubricate the valve stems and insert all of the valves into the cylinder head. If possible, maintain their original locations.

2. If equipped, install any valve spring shims which were removed.

3. If equipped, install the new valve seals, keeping the following in mind:

• If the valve seal presses over the guide, lightly lubricate the outer guide surfaces.

• If the seal is an O-ring type, it is installed just after compressing the spring but before the valve locks.

4. Place the valve spring and retainer over the stem.

5. Position the spring compressor tool and compress the spring.

6. Assemble the valve locks to the stem.

7. Relieve the spring pressure slowly and insure that neither valve lock becomes dislodged by the retainer.

8. Remove the spring compressor tool.

9. Repeat Steps 2 through 8 until all of the springs have been installed.

10. Install the camshaft(s), rockers, shafts and any other components that were removed for disassembly.

Engine Block

GENERAL INFORMATION

A thorough overhaul or rebuild of an engine block would include replacing the pistons, rings, bearings, timing belt/chain assembly and oil pump. For OHV engines also include a new camshaft and lifters. The block would then have the cylinders bored and honed oversize (or if using removable cylinder sleeves, new sleeves installed) and the crankshaft would be cut undersize to provide new wearing surfaces and perfect clearances. However, your particular engine may not have everything worn out. What if only the

piston rings have worn out and the clearances on everything else are still within factory specifications? Well, you could just replace the rings and put it back together, but this would be a very rare example. Chances are, if one component in your engine is worn, other components are sure to follow, and soon. At the very least, you should always replace the rings, bearings and oil pump. This is what is commonly called a freshen up".

Cylinder Ridge Removal

Because the top piston ring does not travel to the very top of the cylinder, a ridge is built up between the end of the travel and the top of the cylinder bore.

Pushing the piston and connecting rod assembly past the ridge can be difficult, and damage to the piston ring lands could occur. If the ridge is not removed before installing a new piston or not removed at all, piston ring breakage and piston damage may occur.

➡It is always recommended that you remove any cylinder ridges before removing the piston and connecting rod assemblies. If you know that new pistons are going to be installed and the engine block will be bored oversize, you may be able to forego this step. However, some ridges may actually prevent the assemblies from being removed, necessitating its removal.

There are several different types of ridge reamers on the market, none of which are inexpensive. Unless a great deal of engine rebuilding is anticipated, borrow or rent a reamer.

1. Turn the crankshaft until the piston is at the bottom of its travel.

2. Cover the head of the piston with a rag.

3. Follow the tool manufacturers instructions and cut away the ridge, exercising extreme care to avoid cutting too deeply.

4. Remove the ridge reamer, the rag and as many of the cuttings as possible. Continue until all of the cylinder ridges have been removed.

DISASSEMBLY

The engine disassembly instructions following assume that you have the engine mounted on an engine stand. If not, it is easiest to disassemble the engine on a bench or the floor with it resting on the bellhousing or transmission mounting surface. You must be able to access the connecting rod fasteners and turn the crankshaft during disassembly. Also, all engine covers (timing, front, side, oil pan, whatever) should have already been removed. Engines which are seized or locked up may not be able to be completely disassembled, and a core (salvage yard) engine should be purchased.

If not done during the cylinder head removal, remove the timing chain/belt and/or gear/sprocket assembly. Remove the oil pick-up and

Place rubber hose over the connecting rod studs to protect the crankshaft and cylinder bores from damage

pump assembly and, if necessary, the pump drive. If equipped, remove any balance or auxiliary shafts. If necessary, remove the cylinder ridge from the top of the bore. See the cylinder ridge removal procedure earlier in this section.

Rotate the engine over so that the crankshaft is exposed. Use a number punch or scribe and mark each connecting rod with its respective cylinder number. The cylinder closest to the front of the engine is always number 1. However, depending on the engine placement, the front of the engine could either be the flywheel or damper/pulley end. Generally the front of the engine faces the front of the vehicle. Use a number punch or scribe and also mark the main bearing caps from front to rear with the front most cap being number 1 (if there are five caps, mark them 1 through 5, front to rear).

✷✷ WARNING

Take special care when pushing the connecting rod up from the crankshaft because the sharp threads of the rod bolts/studs will score the crankshaft journal. Insure that special plastic caps are installed over them, or cut two pieces of rubber hose to do the same.

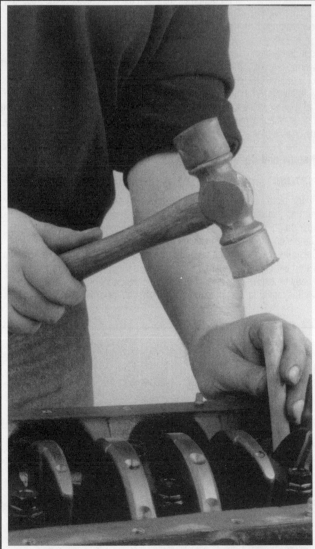

TCCS3804

Carefully tap the piston out of the bore using a wooden dowel

Again, rotate the engine, this time to position the number one cylinder bore (head surface) up. Turn the crankshaft until the number one piston is at the bottom of its travel, this should allow the maximum access to its connecting rod. Remove the number one connecting rods fasteners and cap and place two lengths of rubber hose over the rod bolts/studs to protect the crankshaft from damage. Using a sturdy wooden dowel and a hammer, push the connecting rod up about 1 in. (25mm) from the crankshaft and remove the upper bearing insert. Continue pushing or tapping the connecting rod up until the piston rings are out of the cylinder bore. Remove the piston and rod by hand, put the upper half of the bearing insert back into the rod, install the cap with its bearing insert installed, and hand-tighten the cap fasteners. If the parts are kept in order in this manner, they will not get lost and you will be able to tell which bearings came form what cylinder if any problems are discovered and diagnosis is necessary. Remove all the other piston assemblies in the same manner. On V-style engines, remove all of the pistons from one bank, then reposition the engine with the other cylinder bank head surface up, and remove that banks piston assemblies.

The only remaining component in the engine block should now be the crankshaft. Loosen the main bearing caps evenly until the fasteners can be turned by hand, then remove them and the caps. Remove the crankshaft from the engine block. Thoroughly clean all of the components.

INSPECTION

Now that the engine block and all of its components are clean, it's time to inspect them for wear and/or damage. To accurately inspect them, you will need some specialized tools:
- Two or three separate micrometers to measure the pistons and crankshaft journals
- A dial indicator
- Telescoping gauges for the cylinder bores
- A rod alignment fixture to check for bent connecting rods

If you do not have access to the proper tools, you may want to bring the components to a shop that does.

Generally, you shouldn't expect cracks in the engine block or its components unless it was known to leak, consume or mix engine fluids, it was severely overheated, or there was evidence of bad bearings and/or crankshaft damage. A visual inspection should be performed on all of the components, but just because you don't see a crack does not mean it is not there. Some more reliable methods for inspecting for cracks include Magnaflux®, a magnetic process or Zyglo®, a dye penetrant. Magnaflux® is used only on ferrous metal (cast iron). Zyglo® uses a spray on fluorescent mixture along with a black light to reveal the cracks. It is strongly recommended to have your engine block checked professionally for cracks, especially if the engine was known to have overheated and/or leaked or consumed coolant. Contact a local shop for availability and pricing of these services.

Engine Block

ENGINE BLOCK BEARING ALIGNMENT

Remove the main bearing caps and, if still installed, the main bearing inserts. Inspect all of the main bearing saddles and caps for damage, burrs or high spots. If damage is found, and it is caused from a spun main bearing, the block will need to be align-bored or, if severe enough, replacement. Any burrs or high spots should be carefully removed with a metal file.

Place a straightedge on the bearing saddles, in the engine block, along the centerline of the crankshaft. If any clearance exists between the straightedge and the saddles, the block must be align-bored.

Align-boring consists of machining the main bearing saddles and caps by means of a flycutter that runs through the bearing saddles.

DECK FLATNESS

The top of the engine block where the cylinder head mounts is called the deck. Insure that the deck surface is clean of dirt, carbon deposits and old gasket material. Place a straightedge across the surface of the deck along its centerline and, using feeler gauges, check the clearance along several points. Repeat the checking procedure with the straightedge placed along both diagonals of the deck surface. If the reading exceeds 0.003 in. (0.076mm) within a 6.0 in. (15.2cm) span, or 0.006 in. (0.152mm) over the total length of the deck, it must be machined.

CYLINDER BORES

The cylinder bores house the pistons and are slightly larger than the pistons themselves. A common piston-to-bore clearance is 0.0015–0.0025 in. (0.0381mm–0.0635mm). Inspect and measure the cylinder bores. The bore should be checked for out-of-roundness, taper and size. The results of this inspection will determine whether the cylinder can be used in its existing size and condition, or a rebore to the next oversize is required (or in the case of removable sleeves, have replacements installed).

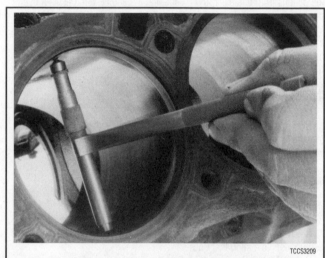

TCCS3209

Use a telescoping gauge to measure the cylinder bore diameter—take several readings within the same bore

The amount of cylinder wall wear is always greater at the top of the cylinder than at the bottom. This wear is known as taper. Any cylinder that has a taper of 0.0012 in. (0.305mm) or more, must be rebored. Measurements are taken at a number of positions in each cylinder: at the top, middle and bottom and at two points at each position; that is, at a point 90 degrees from the crankshaft centerline, as well as a point parallel to the crankshaft centerline. The measurements are made with either a special dial indicator or a telescopic gauge and micrometer. If the necessary precision tools to check the bore are not available, take the block to a machine shop and have them mike it. Also if you don't have the tools to check the cylinder bores, chances are you will not have the necessary devices to check the pistons, connecting rods and crankshaft. Take these components with you and save yourself an extra trip.

For our procedures, we will use a telescopic gauge and a micrometer. You will need one of each, with a measuring range which covers your cylinder bore size.

1. Position the telescopic gauge in the cylinder bore, loosen the gauges lock and allow it to expand.

➡**Your first two readings will be at the top of the cylinder bore, then proceed to the middle and finally the bottom, making a total of six measurements.**

2. Hold the gauge square in the bore, 90 degrees from the crankshaft centerline, and gently tighten the lock. Tilt the gauge back to remove it from the bore.

3. Measure the gauge with the micrometer and record the reading.

4. Again, hold the gauge square in the bore, this time parallel to the crankshaft centerline, and gently tighten the lock. Again, you will tilt the gauge back to remove it from the bore.

5. Measure the gauge with the micrometer and record this reading. The difference between these two readings is the out-of-round measurement of the cylinder.

6. Repeat steps 1 through 5, each time going to the next lower position, until you reach the bottom of the cylinder. Then go to the next cylinder, and continue until all of the cylinders have been measured.

The difference between these measurements will tell you all about the wear in your cylinders. The measurements which were taken 90 degrees from the crankshaft centerline will always reflect the most wear. That is because at this position is where the engine power presses the piston against the cylinder bore the hardest. This is known as thrust wear. Take your top, 90 degree measurement and compare it to your bottom, 90 degree measurement. The difference between them is the taper. When you measure your pistons, you will compare these readings to your piston sizes and determine piston-to-wall clearance.

Crankshaft

Inspect the crankshaft for visible signs of wear or damage. All of the journals should be perfectly round and smooth. Slight scores are normal for a used crankshaft, but you should hardly feel them with your fingernail. When measuring the crankshaft with a micrometer, you will take readings at the front and rear of each journal, then turn the micrometer 90 degrees and take two more readings, front and rear. The difference between the front-to-rear readings is the journal taper and the first-to-90 degree reading is the out-of-round measurement. Generally, there should be no taper or out-of-roundness found, however, up to 0.0005 in. (0.0127mm) for either can be overlooked. Also, the readings should fall within the factory specifications for journal diameters.

If the crankshaft journals fall within specifications, it is recommended that it be polished before being returned to service. Polishing the crankshaft insures that any minor burrs or high spots are smoothed, thereby reducing the chance of scoring the new bearings.

Pistons and Connecting Rods

PISTONS

The piston should be visually inspected for any signs of cracking or burning (caused by hot spots or detonation), and scuffing or excessive wear on the skirts. The wristpin attaches the piston to the connecting rod. The piston should move freely on the wrist pin, both sliding and pivoting. Grasp the connecting rod securely, or mount it in a vise, and try to rock the piston back and forth along the centerline of the wristpin. There should not be any excessive play evident between the piston and the pin. If there are C-clips retaining the pin in the piston then you have wrist pin bushings in

TCCS3210

Measure the piston's outer diameter, perpendicular to the wrist pin, with a micrometer

the rods. There should not be any excessive play between the wrist pin and the rod bushing. Normal clearance for the wrist pin is approx. 0.001–0.002 in. (0.025mm–0.051mm).

Use a micrometer and measure the diameter of the piston, perpendicular to the wrist pin, on the skirt. Compare the reading to its original cylinder measurement obtained earlier. The difference between the two readings is the piston-to-wall clearance. If the clearance is within specifications, the piston may be used as is. If the piston is out of specification, but the bore is not, you will need a new piston. If both are out of specification, you will need the cylinder rebored and oversize pistons installed. Generally if two or more pistons/bores are out of specification, it is best to rebore the entire block and purchase a complete set of oversize pistons.

CONNECTING ROD

You should have the connecting rod checked for straightness at a machine shop. If the connecting rod is bent, it will unevenly wear the bearing and piston, as well as place greater stress on these components. Any bent or twisted connecting rods must be replaced. If the rods are straight and the wrist pin clearance is within specifications, then only the bearing end of the rod need be checked. Place the connecting rod into a vice, with the bearing inserts in place, install the cap to the rod and tighten the fasteners to specifications. Use a telescoping gauge and carefully measure the inside diameter of the bearings. Compare this reading to the rods original crankshaft journal diameter measurement. The difference is the oil clearance. If the oil clearance is not within specifications, install new bearings in the rod and take another measurement. If the clearance is still out of specifications, and the crankshaft is not, the rod will need to be reconditioned by a machine shop.

➡You can also use Plastigage® to check the bearing clearances. The assembling section has complete instructions on its use.

Camshaft

Inspect the camshaft and lifters/followers as described earlier in this section.

Bearings

All of the engine bearings should be visually inspected for wear and/or damage. The bearing should look evenly worn all around with no deep scores or pits. If the bearing is severely worn, scored, pitted or heat blued, then the bearing, and the components that use it, should be brought to a machine shop for inspection. Full-circle bearings (used on most camshafts, auxiliary shafts, balance shafts, etc.) require specialized tools for removal and installation, and should be brought to a machine shop for service.

Oil Pump

➡The oil pump is responsible for providing constant lubrication to the whole engine and so it is recommended that a new oil pump be installed when rebuilding the engine.

Completely disassemble the oil pump and thoroughly clean all of the components. Inspect the oil pump gears and housing for wear and/or damage. Insure that the pressure relief valve operates properly and there is no binding or sticking due to varnish or debris. If all of the parts are in proper working condition, lubricate the gears and relief valve, and assemble the pump.

REFINISHING

Almost all engine block refinishing must be performed by a machine shop. If the cylinders are not to be rebored, then the cylinder glaze can be removed with a ball hone. When removing cylinder glaze with a ball hone, use a light or penetrating type oil to lubricate the hone. Do not allow the hone to run dry as this may cause excessive scoring of the cylinder bores and wear on the hone. If new pistons are required, they will need to be installed to the connecting rods. This should be performed by a machine shop as the pistons must be installed in the correct relationship to the rod or engine damage can occur.

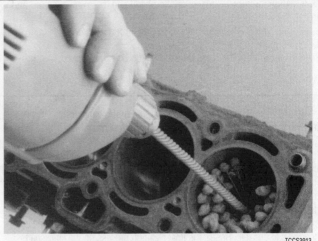

TCCS3913

Use a ball type cylinder hone to remove any glaze and provide a new surface for seating the piston rings

Pistons and Connecting Rods

Only pistons with the wrist pin retained by C-clips are serviceable by the home-mechanic. Press fit pistons require special presses and/or heaters to remove/install the connecting rod and should only be performed by a machine shop.

All pistons will have a mark indicating the direction to the front of the engine and the must be installed into the engine in that manner. Usually it is a notch or arrow on the top of the piston, or it may be the letter F cast or stamped into the piston.

C-CLIP TYPE PISTONS

1. Note the location of the forward mark on the piston and mark the connecting rod in relation.
2. Remove the C-clips from the piston and withdraw the wrist pin.

➡Varnish build-up or C-clip groove burrs may increase the difficulty of removing the wrist pin. If necessary, use a punch or drift to carefully tap the wrist pin out.

3. Insure that the wrist pin bushing in the connecting rod is usable, and lubricate it with assembly lube.
4. Remove the wrist pin from the new piston and lubricate the pin bores on the piston.

TCCS3814

Most pistons are marked to indicate positioning in the engine (usually a mark means the side facing the front)

5. Align the forward marks on the piston and the connecting rod and install the wrist pin.

6. The new C-clips will have a flat and a rounded side to them. Install both C-clips with the flat side facing out.

7. Repeat all of the steps for each piston being replaced.

ASSEMBLY

Before you begin assembling the engine, first give yourself a clean, dirt free work area. Next, clean every engine component again. The key to a good assembly is cleanliness.

Mount the engine block into the engine stand and wash it one last time using water and detergent (dishwashing detergent works well). While washing it, scrub the cylinder bores with a soft bristle brush and thoroughly clean all of the oil passages. Completely dry the engine and spray the entire assembly down with an anti-rust solution such as WD-40® or similar product. Take a clean lint-free rag and wipe up any excess anti-rust solution from the bores, bearing saddles, etc. Repeat the final cleaning process on the crankshaft. Replace any freeze or oil galley plugs which were removed during disassembly.

Crankshaft

1. Remove the main bearing inserts from the block and bearing caps.

2. If the crankshaft main bearing journals have been refinished to a definite undersize, install the correct undersize bearing. Be sure that the bearing inserts and bearing bores are clean. Foreign material under inserts will distort bearing and cause failure.

3. Place the upper main bearing inserts in bores with tang in slot.

➡ **The oil holes in the bearing inserts must be aligned with the oil holes in the cylinder block.**

4. Install the lower main bearing inserts in bearing caps.

5. Clean the mating surfaces of block and rear main bearing cap.

6. Carefully lower the crankshaft into place. Be careful not to damage bearing surfaces.

7. Check the clearance of each main bearing by using the following procedure:

a. Place a piece of Plastigage® or its equivalent, on bearing surface across full width of bearing cap and about ¼ in. off center.

b. Install cap and tighten bolts to specifications. Do not turn crankshaft while Plastigage® is in place.

c. Remove the cap. Using the supplied Plastigage® scale, check width of Plastigage® at widest point to get maximum clearance. Difference between readings is taper of journal.

d. If clearance exceeds specified limits, try a 0.001 in. or 0.002 in. undersize bearing in combination with the standard bearing. Bearing clearance must be within specified limits. If standard and 0.002 in. undersize bearing does not bring clearance within desired limits, refinish crankshaft journal, then install undersize bearings.

8. After the bearings have been fitted, apply a light coat of engine oil to the journals and bearings. Install the rear main bearing cap. Install all bearing caps except the thrust bearing cap. Be sure that main bearing caps are installed in original locations. Tighten the bearing cap bolts to specifications.

9. Install the thrust bearing cap with bolts finger-tight.

10. Pry the crankshaft forward against the thrust surface of upper half of bearing.

11. Hold the crankshaft forward and pry the thrust bearing cap to the rear. This aligns the thrust surfaces of both halves of the bearing.

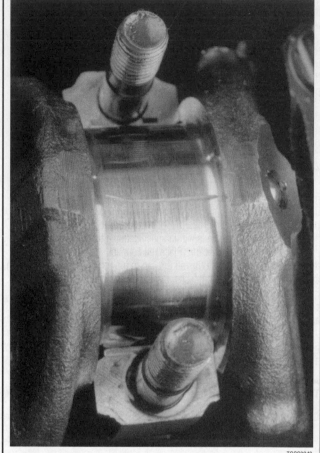

Apply a strip of gauging material to the bearing journal, then install and tighten the cap

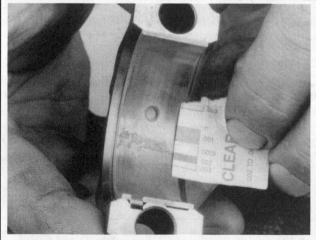

After the cap is removed again, use the scale supplied with the gauging material to check the clearance

TCCS3805

A dial gauge may be used to check crankshaft end-play

12. Retain the forward pressure on the crankshaft. Tighten the cap bolts to specifications.

13. Measure the crankshaft end-play as follows:

a. Mount a dial gauge to the engine block and position the tip of the gauge to read from the crankshaft end.

b. Carefully pry the crankshaft toward the rear of the engine and hold it there while you zero the gauge.

c. Carefully pry the crankshaft toward the front of the engine and read the gauge.

d. Confirm that the reading is within specifications. If not, install a new thrust bearing and repeat the procedure. If the reading is still out of specifications with a new bearing, have a machine shop inspect the thrust surfaces of the crankshaft, and if possible, repair it.

14. Rotate the crankshaft so as to position the first rod journal to the bottom of its stroke.

15. Install the rear main seal.

TCCS3806

Carefully pry the crankshaft back and forth while reading the dial gauge for end-play

Pistons and Connecting Rods

1. Before installing the piston/connecting rod assembly, oil the pistons, piston rings and the cylinder walls with light engine oil. Install connecting rod bolt protectors or rubber hose onto the connecting rod bolts/studs. Also perform the following:

a. Select the proper ring set for the size cylinder bore.

b. Position the ring in the bore in which it is going to be used.

c. Push the ring down into the bore area where normal ring wear is not encountered.

d. Use the head of the piston to position the ring in the bore so that the ring is square with the cylinder wall. Use caution to avoid damage to the ring or cylinder bore.

e. Measure the gap between the ends of the ring with a feeler gauge. Ring gap in a worn cylinder is normally greater than specification. If the ring gap is greater than the specified limits, try an oversize ring set.

TCCS3923

Checking the piston ring-to-ring groove side clearance using the ring and a feeler gauge

TCCS3917

The notch on the side of the bearing cap matches the tang on the bearing insert

TCCS3914

Install the piston and rod assembly into the block using a ring compressor and the handle of a hammer

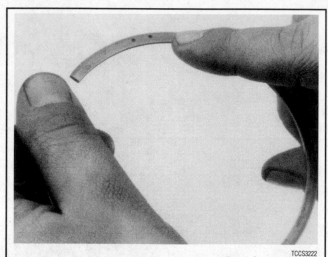

TCCS3222

Most rings are marked to show which side of the ring should face up when installed to the piston

f. Check the ring side clearance of the compression rings with a feeler gauge inserted between the ring and its lower land according to specification. The gauge should slide freely around the entire ring circumference without binding. Any wear that occurs will form a step at the inner portion of the lower land. If the lower lands have high steps, the piston should be replaced.

2. Unless new pistons are installed, be sure to install the pistons in the cylinders from which they were removed. The numbers on the connecting rod and bearing cap must be on the same side when installed in the cylinder bore. If a connecting rod is ever transposed from one engine or cylinder to another, new bearings should be fitted and the connecting rod should be numbered to correspond with the new cylinder number. The notch on the piston head goes toward the front of the engine.

3. Install all of the rod bearing inserts into the rods and caps.
4. Install the rings to the pistons. Install the oil control ring first, then the second compression ring and finally the top compression ring. Use a piston ring expander tool to aid in installation and to help reduce the chance of breakage.
5. Make sure the ring gaps are properly spaced around the circumference of the piston. Fit a piston ring compressor around the piston and slide the piston and connecting rod assembly down into the cylinder bore, pushing it in with the wooden hammer handle. Push the piston down until it is only slightly below the top of the cylinder bore. Guide the connecting rod onto the crankshaft bearing journal carefully, to avoid damaging the crankshaft.
6. Check the bearing clearance of all the rod bearings, fitting them to the crankshaft bearing journals. Follow the procedure in the crankshaft installation above.
7. After the bearings have been fitted, apply a light coating of assembly oil to the journals and bearings.
8. Turn the crankshaft until the appropriate bearing journal is at the bottom of its stroke, then push the piston assembly all the way down until the connecting rod bearing seats on the crankshaft journal. Be careful not to allow the bearing cap screws to strike the crankshaft bearing journals and damage them.
9. After the piston and connecting rod assemblies have been installed, check the connecting rod side clearance on each crankshaft journal.
10. Prime and install the oil pump and the oil pump intake tube.
11. Install the auxiliary/balance shaft(s)/assembly(ies).
12. Install the cylinder head(s) using new gaskets.
13. Install the timing sprockets/gears and the belt/chain assemblies.

Engine Covers and Components

Install the timing cover(s) and oil pan. Refer to your notes and drawings made prior to disassembly and install all of the components that were removed. Install the engine into the vehicle.

Engine Start-up and Break-in

STARTING THE ENGINE

Now that the engine is installed and every wire and hose is properly connected, go back and double check that all coolant and vacuum hoses are connected. Check that you oil drain plug is installed and properly tightened. If not already done, install a new oil filter onto the engine. Fill the crankcase with the proper amount and grade of engine oil. Fill the cooling system with a 50/50 mixture of coolant/water.

1. Connect the vehicle battery.
2. Start the engine. Keep your eye on your oil pressure indicator; if it does not indicate oil pressure within 10 seconds of starting, turn the vehicle off.

❄❄ WARNING

Damage to the engine can result if it is allowed to run with no oil pressure. Check the engine oil level to make sure that it is full. Check for any leaks and if found, repair the leaks before continuing. If there is still no indication of oil pressure, you may need to prime the system.

3. Confirm that there are no fluid leaks (oil or other).
4. Allow the engine to reach normal operating temperature (the upper radiator hose will be hot to the touch).
5. If necessary, set the ignition timing.
6. Install any remaining components such as the air cleaner (if removed for ignition timing) or body panels which were removed.

BREAKING IT IN

Make the first miles on the new engine, easy ones. Vary the speed but do not accelerate hard. Most importantly, do not lug the engine, and avoid sustained high speeds until at least 100 miles. Check the engine oil and coolant levels frequently. Expect the engine to use a little oil until the rings seat. Change the oil and filter at 500 miles, 1500 miles, then every 3000 miles past that.

KEEP IT MAINTAINED

Now that you have just gone through all of that hard work, keep yourself from doing it all over again by thoroughly maintaining it. Not that you may not have maintained it before, heck you could have had one to two hundred thousand miles on it before doing this. However, you may have bought the vehicle used, and the previous owner did not keep up on maintenance. Which is why you just went through all of that hard work. See?

TORQUE SPECIFICATIONS

Component		U.S.	Metric
4A-F Engine:			
Camshaft timing pulley		43 ft. lbs.	59 Nm
Center crossmember-to-body		45 ft. lbs.	61 Nm
Center crossmember-to-transaxle mounting bracket		45 ft. lbs.	61 Nm
Clutch cover-to-flywheel		14 ft. lbs.	19 Nm
Clutch line union		11 ft. lbs.	15 Nm
Clutch master cylinder set nut		9 ft. lbs.	13 Nm
Clutch slave cylinder set bolt		9 ft. lbs.	13 Nm
Cold start injector pipe-to-cold start injector		13 ft. lbs.	18 Nm
Connecting rod cap connecting rod		36 ft. lbs.	49 Nm
Crankshaft flywheel		58 ft. lbs.	78 Nm
Crankshaft pulley		87 ft. lbs.	118 Nm
Cylinder head bolt		44 ft. lbs.	60 Nm
Cylinder head camshaft bearing cap		9 ft. lbs.	13 Nm
Cylinder head crankshaft bearing cap		44 ft. lbs.	60 Nm
Cylinder head exhaust manifold		18 ft. lbs.	25 Nm
Cylinder head intake manifold		14 ft. lbs.	19 Nm
Cylinder head oil pan		43 inch lbs.	5 Nm
Cylinder head oil pump		16 ft. lbs.	21 Nm
Cylinder head spark plug		13 ft. lbs.	18 Nm
Cylinder head timing belt idler pulley		27 ft. lbs.	37 Nm
Exhaust pipe-to-converter		32 ft. lbs.	43 Nm
Exhaust pipe-to-manifold		46 ft. lbs.	62 Nm
Fuel inlet pipe delivery pipe		22 ft. lbs.	29 Nm
Oil pump strainer		82 inch lbs.	9 Nm
Pressure regulator delivery pipe		65 inch lbs.	7 Nm
Starter-to-manual transaxle		29 ft. lbs	39 Nm
Transaxle-to-engine	10mm bolt	34 ft. lbs.	46 Nm
Transaxle-to-engine	12mm bolt	47 ft. lbs.	64 Nm
4A-GE Engine:			
Camshaft timing pulley		43 ft. lbs.	59 Nm
Connecting rod connection rod cap	1st	29 ft . lbs.	39 Nm
Connecting rod connection rod cap	2nd	additional 90°	additional 90°
Crankshaft pulley		101 ft. lbs.	137 Nm
Crankshaft-to-flywheel		54 ft. lbs.	74 Nm
Cylinder block idler pulley		27 ft. lbs.	37 Nm
Cylinder block main bearing cap		44 ft. lbs.	60 Nm
Cylinder block-to-oil knozzle		18 ft. lbs.	25 Nm
Cylinder head camshaft bearing cap		9 ft. lbs.	13 Nm
Cylinder head-to-cylinder block	1st	22 ft. lbs.	29 Nm
Cylinder head-to-cylinder block	2nd	90° turns	90° turns
Cylinder head-to-cylinder block	3rd	90° turns	90° turns
Clutch master cylinder set nut		9 ft. lbs.	13 Nm
Cold start injector pipe-to-delivery pipe		13 ft. lbs.	18 Nm
Cylinder head-to-exhaust manifold		29 ft. lbs.	39 Nm

88273C20

TORQUE SPECIFICATIONS

Component		U.S.	Metric
4A-GE Engine:			
Cylinder head-to-intake manifold		20 ft. lbs.	27 Nm
Cylinder head union		22 ft. lbs.	29 Nm
EGR pipe-to-exhaust manifold		51 ft. lbs.	69 Nm
Engine mounting	automatic	38 ft. lbs.	52 Nm
Engine mounting center member		45 ft. lbs.	61 Nm
Engine mounting bracket-to-transaxle		57 ft. lbs.	77 Nm
Engine mounting LH to bracket	manual	35 ft. lbs.	48 Nm
Engine mounting LH to transaxle	manual	38 ft. lbs.	52 Nm
Engine mounting LH stay	manual	15 ft. lbs.	21 Nm
Engine mounting RH to bracket	manual	31 ft. lbs.	42 Nm
Engine mounting RH to engine	manual-nut	38 ft. lbs.	52 Nm
Engine mounting RH to engine	manual-bolt	47 ft. lbs.	64 Nm
Engine mounting	front	35 ft. lbs.	48 Nm
Engine mounting	center	38 ft. lbs.	52 Nm
Engine mounting	rear	42 ft. lbs.	57 Nm
Engine rear mounting bolt		64 ft. lbs.	87 Nm
Engine front mounting bolt		64 ft. lbs.	87 Nm
Exhaust front pipe-to-center pipe		32 ft. lbs.	43 Nm
Exhaust manifold stay-to-cylinder block		29 ft. lbs.	39 Nm
Exhaust manifold stay-to-exhaust manifold		29 ft. lbs.	39 Nm
Exhaust manifold-to-front pipe		46 ft. lbs.	62 Nm
Fuel inlet pipe-to-delivery pipe		22 ft. lbs.	29 Nm
Intake manifold stay-to-manifold		16 ft. lbs.	39 Nm
Transaxle-to-engine	10mm bolt	47 ft. lbs.	64 Nm
	12mm bolt	34 ft. lbs.	46 Nm
4A-FE and 7A-FE Engines:			
1989-92			
Clutch line union		11 ft. lbs.	15 Nm
Clutch master cylinder set nut		9 ft. lbs.	13 Nm
Clutch slave cylinder set bolt		9 ft. lbs.	13 Nm
Cold start injector pipe-to-cold start injector		13 ft. lbs.	18 Nm
Connecting rod cap		36 ft. lbs.	49 Nm
Crankshaft pulley		87 ft. lbs.	118 Nm
Crankshaft driveplate	automatic	47 ft. lbs.	64 Nm
Crankshaft flywheel	manual	58 ft. lbs.	78 Nm
Camshaft timing pulley		43 ft. lbs.	59 Nm
Cylinder block oil pump		16 ft. lbs.	21 Nm
Cylinder head bolt		44 ft. lbs.	60 Nm
Cylinder head camshaft bearing cap		9 ft. lbs.	13 Nm
Cylinder head crankshaft bearing cap		44 ft. lbs.	60 Nm
Cylinder head spark plugs		13 ft. lbs.	18 Nm
Cylinder head-to-exhaust manifold		18 ft. lbs.	25 Nm
Cylinder head-to-intake manifold		14 ft. lbs.	19 Nm
Exhaust manifold-to-front pipe		45 ft. lbs.	62 Nm
Engine mounting bracket-to-crossmember		35 ft. lbs.	48 Nm
Engine mounting	automatic	38 ft. lbs.	52 Nm

88273C21

TORQUE SPECIFICATIONS

Component		U.S.	Metric
4A-FE and 7A-FE Engines:			
1988-92			
Engine mounting bracket-to-transaxle		57 ft. lbs.	77 Nm
Engine mounting LH to bracket	manual	35 ft. lbs.	48 Nm
Engine mounting LH to transaxle	manual	38 ft. lbs.	52 Nm
Engine mounting LH to transaxle	manual	15 ft. lbs.	21 Nm
Engine mounting RH to bracket	manual	31 ft. lbs.	42 Nm
Engine mounting RH to engine	manual-nut	38 ft. lbs.	52 Nm
Engine mounting RH to engine	manual-bolt	47 ft. lbs.	64 Nm
Fuel inlet pipe-to-delivery pipe		22 ft. lbs.	29 Nm
Oil pump-to-strainer		82 inch lbs.	9 Nm
4A-FE and 7A-FE Engines:			
1993-97			
Alternator bracket-to-cylinder head		20 ft. lbs.	26 Nm
Camshaft timing pulley		43 ft. lbs.	59 Nm
Center member-to-body (A)		61 ft. lbs.	45 Nm
Center member-to-body (B)		64 ft. lbs.	47 Nm
Center member-to-body (C)		48 ft. lbs.	35 Nm
Center member-to-body nut		57 ft. lbs.	42 Nm
Connecting rod cap-to-connecting rod	4A-FE 1st	22 ft. lbs.	29 Nm
Connecting rod cap-to-connecting rod	4A-FE 2nd	Turn 90°	Turn 90°
Connecting rod cap-to-connecting rod	7A-FE 1st	18 ft. lbs.	25 Nm
Connecting rod cap-to-connecting rod	7A-FE 2nd	Turn 90°	Turn 90°
Crankshaft pulley		87 ft. lbs.	118 Nm
Cylinder block idler pulley		27 ft. lbs.	37 Nm
Cylinder head camshaft bearing cap		9 ft. lbs.	13 Nm
Cylinder head cover		52 inch lbs.	6 Nm
Cylinder head delivery pipe		11 ft. lbs.	15 Nm
Cylinder head distributor		14 ft. lbs.	20 Nm
Cylinder head-to block	1st pass	22 ft. lbs.	29 Nm
Cylinder head-to block	2nd pass	90° turn	90° turn
Cylinder head-to block	3rd pass	90° turn	90° turn
Drive plate	automatic	47 ft. lbs.	64 Nm
Engine mounting bracket-to-block		38 ft. lbs.	51 Nm
Engine mounting insulator RH body (A)		47 ft. lbs.	64 Nm
Engine mounting insulator RH body (C)		19 ft. lbs.	25 Nm
Engine mounting RH insulator bracket bolt		47 ft. lbs.	64 Nm
Engine mounting RH insulator bracket nut		38 ft. lbs.	52 Nm
Exhaust manifold stay-to-cylinder block		29 ft. lbs.	39 Nm
Exhaust manifold stay-to-manifold		29 ft. lbs.	39 Nm
Exhaust manifold-to-cylinder head		25 ft. lbs	34 Nm
Flywheel	manual	58 ft. lbs.	78 Nm
Front engine mounting bracket-to-transaxle		57 ft. lbs..	77 Nm
Front engine mounting insulator-to-bracket		87 ft. lbs.	64 Nm
Front exhaust pipe-to-catalyst		32 ft. lbs.	43 Nm
Front exhaust pipe-to-exhaust manifold		46 ft. lbs.	62 Nm
Intake manifold stay-to-bracket		29 ft. lbs.	39 Nm
Intake manifold stay-to-manifold		14 ft. lbs.	19 Nm
Intake manifold-to-cylinder head	4A-FE	14 ft. lbs.	19 Nm

TORQUE SPECIFICATIONS

Component		U.S.	Metric
4A-FE and 7A-FE Engines:			
1993-97			
Intake manifold-to-cylinder head	7A-FE EGR port	9 ft. lbs.	13 Nm
Intake manifold-to-cylinder head	7A-FE others	14 ft. lbs.	19 Nm
Knock sensor-o-block		27 ft. lbs.	37 Nm
Main bearing cap-to-cylinder block		44 ft. lbs.	60 Nm
Mounting bracket LH		38 ft. lbs.	52 Nm
Mounting bracket LH-to-mounting bracket		56 ft. lbs.	41 Nm
Mounting isolator LH-to-body		87 ft. lbs.	64 Nm
Mounting stay LH-to-insulator		21 ft. lbs.	15 Nm
Mounting stay LH-to-transaxle		21 ft. lbs.	15 Nm
Oil dipstick guide No. 2 water outlet		82 inch lbs.	9 Nm
Oil pan No. 1-to-block	7A-FE	12 ft. lbs.	16 Nm
Oil pan No. 1-to-oil pan No. 2	7A-FE	43 inch lbs.	5 Nm
Oil pan-to-block	4A-FE	43 inch lbs.	5 Nm
Oil pan-to-oil pump	4A-FE	43 inch lbs.	5 Nm
Oil pan-to-oil pump	7A-FE	69 inch lbs.	8 Nm
Rear engine mounting bracket-to-transaxle		57 ft. lbs.	77 Nm
Rear engine mounting insulator-to-bracket		87 ft. lbs.	64 Nm
Rear oil seal retainer-to-cylinder block		82 inch lbs.	9 Nm
Water inlet housing-to-cylinder head		14 ft. lbs.	20 Nm
Water inlet No. 2 cylinder head		11 ft. lbs.	15 Nm
Water outlet-to-cylinder head		11 ft lbs.	15 Nm
Water pump pulley		7 inch lbs.	9 Nm
Water pump-to-cylinder block		11 ft. lbs.	14 Nm

88273C23

USING A VACUUM GAUGE

White needle = steady needle   *Dark needle = drifting needle*

The vacuum gauge is one of the most useful and easy-to-use diagnostic tools. It is inexpensive, easy to hook up, and provides valuable information about the condition of your engine.

Indication: Normal engine in good condition

Gauge reading: Steady, from 17–22 in./Hg.

Indication: Sticking valve or ignition miss

Gauge reading: Needle fluctuates from 15–20 in./Hg. at idle

Indication: Late ignition or valve timing, low compression, stuck throttle valve, leaking carburetor or manifold gasket.

Gauge reading: Low (15–20 in./Hg.) but steady

Indication: Improper carburetor adjustment, or minor intake leak at carburetor or manifold

NOTE: Bad fuel injector O-rings may also cause this reading.

Gauge reading: Drifting needle

Indication: Weak valve springs, worn valve stem guides, or leaky cylinder head gasket (vibrating excessively at all speeds).

NOTE: A plugged catalytic converter may also cause this reading.

Gauge reading: Needle fluctuates as engine speed increases

Indication: Burnt valve or improper valve clearance. The needle will drop when the defective valve operates.

Gauge reading: Steady needle, but drops regularly

Indication: Choked muffler or obstruction in system. Speed up the engine. Choked muffler will exhibit a slow drop of vacuum to zero.

Gauge reading: Gradual drop in reading at idle

Indication: Worn valve guides

Gauge reading: Needle vibrates excessively at idle, but steadies as engine speed increases

TCCS3C01

Troubleshooting Engine Mechanical Problems

Problem	Cause	Solution
External oil leaks	• Cylinder head cover RTV sealant broken or improperly seated	• Replace sealant; inspect cylinder head cover sealant flange and cylinder head sealant surface for distortion and cracks
	• Oil filler cap leaking or missing	• Replace cap
	• Oil filter gasket broken or improperly seated	• Replace oil filter
	• Oil pan side gasket broken, improperly seated or opening in RTV sealant	• Replace gasket or repair opening in sealant; inspect oil pan gasket flange for distortion
	• Oil pan front oil seal broken or improperly seated	• Replace seal; inspect timing case cover and oil pan seal flange for distortion
	• Oil pan rear oil seal broken or improperly seated	• Replace seal; inspect oil pan rear oil seal flange; inspect rear main bearing cap for cracks, plugged oil return channels, or distortion in seal groove
	• Timing case cover oil seal broken or improperly seated	• Replace seal
	• Excess oil pressure because of restricted PCV valve	• Replace PCV valve
	• Oil pan drain plug loose or has stripped threads	• Repair as necessary and tighten
	• Rear oil gallery plug loose	• Use appropriate sealant on gallery plug and tighten
	• Rear camshaft plug loose or improperly seated	• Seat camshaft plug or replace and seal, as necessary
Excessive oil consumption	• Oil level too high	• Drain oil to specified level
	• Oil with wrong viscosity being used	• Replace with specified oil
	• PCV valve stuck closed	• Replace PCV valve
	• Valve stem oil deflectors (or seals) are damaged, missing, or incorrect type	• Replace valve stem oil deflectors
	• Valve stems or valve guides worn	• Measure stem-to-guide clearance and repair as necessary
	• Poorly fitted or missing valve cover baffles	• Replace valve cover
	• Piston rings broken or missing	• Replace broken or missing rings
	• Scuffed piston	• Replace piston
	• Incorrect piston ring gap	• Measure ring gap, repair as necessary
	• Piston rings sticking or excessively loose in grooves	• Measure ring side clearance, repair as necessary
	• Compression rings installed upside down	• Repair as necessary
	• Cylinder walls worn, scored, or glazed	• Repair as necessary

TCCS3C02

Troubleshooting Engine Mechanical Problems

Problem	Cause	Solution
Excessive oil consumption (cont.)	• Piston ring gaps not properly staggered	• Repair as necessary
	• Excessive main or connecting rod bearing clearance	• Measure bearing clearance, repair as necessary
No oil pressure	• Low oil level	• Add oil to correct level
	• Oil pressure gauge, warning lamp or sending unit inaccurate	• Replace oil pressure gauge or warning lamp
	• Oil pump malfunction	• Replace oil pump
	• Oil pressure relief valve sticking	• Remove and inspect oil pressure relief valve assembly
	• Oil passages on pressure side of pump obstructed	• Inspect oil passages for obstruction
	• Oil pickup screen or tube obstructed	• Inspect oil pickup for obstruction
	• Loose oil inlet tube	• Tighten or seal inlet tube
Low oil pressure	• Low oil level	• Add oil to correct level
	• Inaccurate gauge, warning lamp or sending unit	• Replace oil pressure gauge or warning lamp
	• Oil excessively thin because of dilution, poor quality, or improper grade	• Drain and refill crankcase with recommended oil
	• Excessive oil temperature	• Correct cause of overheating engine
	• Oil pressure relief spring weak or sticking	• Remove and inspect oil pressure relief valve assembly
	• Oil inlet tube and screen assembly has restriction or air leak	• Remove and inspect oil inlet tube and screen assembly. (Fill inlet tube with lacquer thinner to locate leaks.)
	• Excessive oil pump clearance	• Measure clearances
	• Excessive main, rod, or camshaft bearing clearance	• Measure bearing clearances, repair as necessary
High oil pressure	• Improper oil viscosity	• Drain and refill crankcase with correct viscosity oil
	• Oil pressure gauge or sending unit inaccurate	• Replace oil pressure gauge
	• Oil pressure relief valve sticking closed	• Remove and inspect oil pressure relief valve assembly
Main bearing noise	• Insufficient oil supply	• Inspect for low oil level and low oil pressure
	• Main bearing clearance excessive	• Measure main bearing clearance, repair as necessary
	• Bearing insert missing	• Replace missing insert
	• Crankshaft end-play excessive	• Measure end-play, repair as necessary
	• Improperly tightened main bearing cap bolts	• Tighten bolts with specified torque
	• Loose flywheel or drive plate	• Tighten flywheel or drive plate attaching bolts
	• Loose or damaged vibration damper	• Repair as necessary

TCCS3C03

Troubleshooting Engine Mechanical Problems

Problem	Cause	Solution
Connecting rod bearing noise	• Insufficient oil supply	• Inspect for low oil level and low oil pressure
	• Carbon build-up on piston	• Remove carbon from piston crown
	• Bearing clearance excessive or bearing missing	• Measure clearance, repair as necessary
	• Crankshaft connecting rod journal out-of-round	• Measure journal dimensions, repair or replace as necessary
	• Misaligned connecting rod or cap	• Repair as necessary
	• Connecting rod bolts tightened improperly	• Tighten bolts with specified torque
Piston noise	• Piston-to-cylinder wall clearance excessive (scuffed piston)	• Measure clearance and examine piston
	• Cylinder walls excessively tapered or out-of-round	• Measure cylinder wall dimensions, rebore cylinder
	• Piston ring broken	• Replace all rings on piston
	• Loose or seized piston pin	• Measure piston-to-pin clearance, repair as necessary
	• Connecting rods misaligned	• Measure rod alignment, straighten or replace
	• Piston ring side clearance excessively loose or tight	• Measure ring side clearance, repair as necessary
	• Carbon build-up on piston is excessive	• Remove carbon from piston
Valve actuating component noise	• Insufficient oil supply	• Check for: (a) Low oil level (b) Low oil pressure (c) Wrong hydraulic tappets (d) Restricted oil gallery (e) Excessive tappet to bore clearance
	• Rocker arms or pivots worn	• Replace worn rocker arms or pivots
	• Foreign objects or chips in hydraulic tappets	• Clean tappets
	• Excessive tappet leak-down	• Replace valve tappet
	• Tappet face worn	• Replace tappet; inspect corresponding cam lobe for wear
	• Broken or cocked valve springs	• Properly seat cocked springs; replace broken springs
	• Stem-to-guide clearance excessive	• Measure stem-to-guide clearance, repair as required
	• Valve bent	• Replace valve
	• Loose rocker arms	• Check and repair as necessary
	• Valve seat runout excessive	• Regrind valve seat/valves
	• Missing valve lock	• Install valve lock
	• Excessive engine oil	• Correct oil level

TCCS3C04

Troubleshooting Engine Performance

Problem	Cause	Solution
Hard starting (engine cranks normally)	• Faulty engine control system component	• Repair or replace as necessary
	• Faulty fuel pump	• Replace fuel pump
	• Faulty fuel system component	• Repair or replace as necessary
	• Faulty ignition coil	• Test and replace as necessary
	• Improper spark plug gap	• Adjust gap
	• Incorrect ignition timing	• Adjust timing
	• Incorrect valve timing	• Check valve timing; repair as necessary
Rough idle or stalling	• Incorrect curb or fast idle speed	• Adjust curb or fast idle speed (If possible)
	• Incorrect ignition timing	• Adjust timing to specification
	• Improper feedback system operation	• Refer to Chapter 4
	• Faulty EGR valve operation	• Test EGR system and replace as necessary
	• Faulty PCV valve air flow	• Test PCV valve and replace as necessary
	• Faulty TAC vacuum motor or valve	• Repair as necessary
	• Air leak into manifold vacuum	• Inspect manifold vacuum connections and repair as necessary
	• Faulty distributor rotor or cap	• Replace rotor or cap (Distributor systems only)
	• Improperly seated valves	• Test cylinder compression, repair as necessary
	• Incorrect ignition wiring	• Inspect wiring and correct as necessary
	• Faulty ignition coil	• Test coil and replace as necessary
	• Restricted air vent or idle passages	• Clean passages
	• Restricted air cleaner	• Clean or replace air cleaner filter element
Faulty low-speed operation	• Restricted idle air vents and passages	• Clean air vents and passages
	• Restricted air cleaner	• Clean or replace air cleaner filter element
	• Faulty spark plugs	• Clean or replace spark plugs
	• Dirty, corroded, or loose ignition secondary circuit wire connections	• Clean or tighten secondary circuit wire connections
	• Improper feedback system operation	• Refer to Chapter 4
	• Faulty ignition coil high voltage wire	• Replace ignition coil high voltage wire (Distributor systems only)
	• Faulty distributor cap	• Replace cap (Distributor systems only)
Faulty acceleration	• Incorrect ignition timing	• Adjust timing
	• Faulty fuel system component	• Repair or replace as necessary
	• Faulty spark plug(s)	• Clean or replace spark plug(s)
	• Improperly seated valves	• Test cylinder compression, repair as necessary
	• Faulty ignition coil	• Test coil and replace as necessary

TCCS3C05

Troubleshooting Engine Performance

Problem	Cause	Solution
Faulty acceleration (cont.)	• Improper feedback system operation	• Refer to Chapter 4
Faulty high speed operation	• Incorrect ignition timing	• Adjust timing (if possible)
	• Faulty advance mechanism	• Check advance mechanism and repair as necessary (Distributor systems only)
	• Low fuel pump volume	• Replace fuel pump
	• Wrong spark plug air gap or wrong plug	• Adjust air gap or install correct plug
	• Partially restricted exhaust manifold, exhaust pipe, catalytic converter, muffler, or tailpipe	• Eliminate restriction
	• Restricted vacuum passages	• Clean passages
	• Restricted air cleaner	• Cleaner or replace filter element as necessary
	• Faulty distributor rotor or cap	• Replace rotor or cap (Distributor systems only)
	• Faulty ignition coil	• Test coil and replace as necessary
	• Improperly seated valve(s)	• Test cylinder compression, repair as necessary
	• Faulty valve spring(s)	• Inspect and test valve spring tension, replace as necessary
	• Incorrect valve timing	• Check valve timing and repair as necessary
	• Intake manifold restricted	• Remove restriction or replace manifold
	• Worn distributor shaft	• Replace shaft (Distributor systems only)
	• Improper feedback system operation	• Refer to Chapter 4
Misfire at all speeds	• Faulty spark plug(s)	• Clean or relace spark plug(s)
	• Faulty spark plug wire(s)	• Replace as necessary
	• Faulty distributor cap or rotor	• Replace cap or rotor (Distributor systems only)
	• Faulty ignition coil	• Test coil and replace as necessary
	• Primary ignition circuit shorted or open intermittently	• Troubleshoot primary circuit and repair as necessary
	• Improperly seated valve(s)	• Test cylinder compression, repair as necessary
	• Faulty hydraulic tappet(s)	• Clean or replace tappet(s)
	• Improper feedback system operation	• Refer to Chapter 4
	• Faulty valve spring(s)	• Inspect and test valve spring tension, repair as necessary
	• Worn camshaft lobes	• Replace camshaft
	• Air leak into manifold	• Check manifold vacuum and repair as necessary
	• Fuel pump volume or pressure low	• Replace fuel pump
	• Blown cylinder head gasket	• Replace gasket
	• Intake or exhaust manifold passage(s) restricted	• Pass chain through passage(s) and repair as necessary
Power not up to normal	• Incorrect ignition timing	• Adjust timing
	• Faulty distributor rotor	• Replace rotor (Distributor systems only)

TCCS3C06

Troubleshooting Engine Performance

Problem	Cause	Solution
Power not up to normal (cont.)	• Incorrect spark plug gap	• Adjust gap
	• Faulty fuel pump	• Replace fuel pump
	• Faulty fuel pump	• Replace fuel pump
	• Incorrect valve timing	• Check valve timing and repair as necessary
	• Faulty ignition coil	• Test coil and replace as necessary
	• Faulty ignition wires	• Test wires and replace as necessary
	• Improperly seated valves	• Test cylinder compression and repair as necessary
	• Blown cylinder head gasket	• Replace gasket
	• Leaking piston rings	• Test compression and repair as necessary
	• Improper feedback system operation	• Refer to Chapter 4
Intake backfire	• Improper ignition timing	• Adjust timing
	• Defective EGR component	• Repair as necessary
	• Defective TAC vacuum motor or valve	• Repair as necessary
Exhaust backfire	• Air leak into manifold vacuum	• Check manifold vacuum and repair as necessary
	• Faulty air injection diverter valve	• Test diverter valve and replace as necessary
	• Exhaust leak	• Locate and eliminate leak
Ping or spark knock	• Incorrect ignition timing	• Adjust timing
	• Distributor advance malfunction	• Inspect advance mechanism and repair as necessary (Distributor systems only)
	• Excessive combustion chamber deposits	• Remove with combustion chamber cleaner
	• Air leak into manifold vacuum	• Check manifold vacuum and repair as necessary
	• Excessively high compression	• Test compression and repair as necessary
	• Fuel octane rating excessively low	• Try alternate fuel source
	• Sharp edges in combustion chamber	• Grind smooth
	• EGR valve not functioning properly	• Test EGR system and replace as necessary
Surging (at cruising to top speeds)	• Low fuel pump pressure or volume	• Replace fuel pump
	• Improper PCV valve air flow	• Test PCV valve and replace as necessary
	• Air leak into manifold vacuum	• Check manifold vacuum and repair as necessary
	• Incorrect spark advance	• Test and replace as necessary
	• Restricted fuel filter	• Replace fuel filter
	• Restricted air cleaner	• Clean or replace air cleaner filter element
	• EGR valve not functioning properly	• Test EGR system and replace as necessary
	• Improper feedback system operation	• Refer to Chapter 4

TCCS3C07

Troubleshooting the Serpentine Drive Belt

Problem	Cause	Solution
Tension sheeting fabric failure (woven fabric on outside circumference of belt has cracked or separated from body of belt)	• Grooved or backside idler pulley diameters are less than minimum recommended • Tension sheeting contacting (rubbing) stationary object • Excessive heat causing woven fabric to age • Tension sheeting splice has fractured	• Replace pulley(s) not conforming to specification • Correct rubbing condition • Replace belt • Replace belt
Noise (objectional squeal, squeak, or rumble is heard or felt while drive belt is in operation)	• Belt slippage • Bearing noise • Belt misalignment • Belt-to-pulley mismatch • Driven component inducing vibration • System resonant frequency inducing vibration	• Adjust belt • Locate and repair • Align belt/pulley(s) • Install correct belt • Locate defective driven component and repair • Vary belt tension within specifications. Replace belt.
Rib chunking (one or more ribs has separated from belt body)	• Foreign objects imbedded in pulley grooves • Installation damage • Drive loads in excess of design specifications • Insufficient internal belt adhesion	• Remove foreign objects from pulley grooves • Replace belt • Adjust belt tension • Replace belt
Rib or belt wear (belt ribs contact bottom of pulley grooves)	• Pulley(s) misaligned • Mismatch of belt and pulley groove widths • Abrasive environment • Rusted pulley(s) • Sharp or jagged pulley groove tips • Rubber deteriorated	• Align pulley(s) • Replace belt • Replace belt • Clean rust from pulley(s) • Replace pulley • Replace belt
Longitudinal belt cracking (cracks between two ribs)	• Belt has mistracked from pulley groove • Pulley groove tip has worn away rubber-to-tensile member	• Replace belt • Replace belt
Belt slips	• Belt slipping because of insufficient tension • Belt or pulley subjected to substance (belt dressing, oil, ethylene glycol) that has reduced friction • Driven component bearing failure • Belt glazed and hardened from heat and excessive slippage	• Adjust tension • Replace belt and clean pulleys • Replace faulty component bearing • Replace belt
"Groove jumping" (belt does not maintain correct position on pulley, or turns over and/or runs off pulleys)	• Insufficient belt tension • Pulley(s) not within design tolerance • Foreign object(s) in grooves	• Adjust belt tension • Replace pulley(s) • Remove foreign objects from grooves

TCCS3C09

Troubleshooting the Serpentine Drive Belt

Problem	Cause	Solution
"Groove jumping" (belt does not maintain correct position on pulley, or turns over and/or runs off pulleys)	• Excessive belt speed • Pulley misalignment • Belt-to-pulley profile mismatched • Belt cordline is distorted	• Avoid excessive engine acceleration • Align pulley(s) • Install correct belt • Replace belt
Belt broken (Note: identify and correct problem before replacement belt is installed)	• Excessive tension • Tensile members damaged during belt installation • Belt turnover • Severe pulley misalignment • Bracket, pulley, or bearing failure	• Replace belt and adjust tension to specification • Replace belt • Replace belt • Align pulley(s) • Replace defective component and belt
Cord edge failure (tensile member exposed at edges of belt or separated from belt body)	• Excessive tension • Drive pulley misalignment • Belt contacting stationary object • Pulley irregularities • Improper pulley construction • Insufficient adhesion between tensile member and rubber matrix	• Adjust belt tension • Align pulley • Correct as necessary • Replace pulley • Replace pulley • Replace belt and adjust tension to specifications
Sporadic rib cracking (multiple cracks in belt ribs at random intervals)	• Ribbed pulley(s) diameter less than minimum specification • Backside bend flat pulley(s) diameter less than minimum • Excessive heat condition causing rubber to harden • Excessive belt thickness • Belt overcured • Excessive tension	• Replace pulley(s) • Replace pulley(s) • Correct heat condition as necessary • Replace belt • Replace belt • Adjust belt tension

TCCS3C10

Troubleshooting the Cooling System

Problem	Cause	Solution
High temperature gauge indication—overheating	• Coolant level low • Improper fan operation • Radiator hose(s) collapsed • Radiator airflow blocked • Faulty pressure cap • Ignition timing incorrect • Air trapped in cooling system • Heavy traffic driving • Incorrect cooling system component(s) installed • Faulty thermostat • Water pump shaft broken or impeller loose • Radiator tubes clogged • Cooling system clogged • Casting flash in cooling passages • Brakes dragging • Excessive engine friction • Antifreeze concentration over 68% • Missing air seals • Faulty gauge or sending unit • Loss of coolant flow caused by leakage or foaming • Viscous fan drive failed	• Replenish coolant • Repair or replace as necessary • Replace hose(s) • Remove restriction (bug screen, fog lamps, etc.) • Replace pressure cap • Adjust ignition timing • Purge air • Operate at fast idle in neutral intermittently to cool engine • Install proper component(s) • Replace thermostat • Replace water pump • Flush radiator • Flush system • Repair or replace as necessary. Flash may be visible by removing cooling system components or removing core plugs. • Repair brakes • Repair engine • Lower antifreeze concentration percentage • Replace air seals • Repair or replace faulty component • Repair or replace leaking component, replace coolant • Replace unit
Low temperature indication—undercooling	• Thermostat stuck open • Faulty gauge or sending unit	• Replace thermostat • Repair or replace faulty component
Coolant loss—boilover	• Overfilled cooling system • Quick shutdown after hard (hot) run • Air in system resulting in occasional "burping" of coolant • Insufficient antifreeze allowing coolant boiling point to be too low • Antifreeze deteriorated because of age or contamination • Leaks due to loose hose clamps, loose nuts, bolts, drain plugs, faulty hoses, or defective radiator	• Reduce coolant level to proper specification • Allow engine to run at fast idle prior to shutdown • Purge system • Add antifreeze to raise boiling point • Replace coolant • Pressure test system to locate source of leak(s) then repair as necessary

TCCS3C11

Troubleshooting the Cooling System (cont.)

Problem	Cause	Solution
Coolant loss—boilover	• Faulty head gasket • Cracked head, manifold, or block • Faulty radiator cap	• Replace head gasket • Replace as necessary • Replace cap
Coolant entry into crankcase or cylinder(s)	• Faulty head gasket • Crack in head, manifold or block	• Replace head gasket • Replace as necessary
Coolant recovery system inoperative	• Coolant level low • Leak in system • Pressure cap not tight or seal missing, or leaking • Pressure cap defective • Overflow tube clogged or leaking • Recovery bottle vent restricted	• Replenish coolant to FULL mark • Pressure test to isolate leak and repair as necessary • Repair as necessary • Replace cap • Repair as necessary • Remove restriction
Noise	• Fan contacting shroud • Loose water pump impeller • Glazed fan belt • Loose fan belt • Rough surface on drive pulley • Water pump bearing worn • Belt alignment	• Reposition shroud and inspect engine mounts (on electric fans inspect assembly) • Replace pump • Apply silicone or replace belt • Adjust fan belt tension • Replace pulley • Remove belt to isolate. Replace pump. • Check pulley alignment. Repair as necessary.
No coolant flow through heater core	• Restricted return inlet in water pump • Heater hose collapsed or restricted • Restricted heater core • Restricted outlet in thermostat housing • Intake manifold bypass hole in cylinder head restricted • Faulty heater control valve • Intake manifold coolant passage restricted	• Remove restriction • Remove restriction or replace hose • Remove restriction or replace core • Remove flash or restriction • Remove restriction • Replace valve • Remove restriction or replace intake manifold

NOTE: *Immediately after shutdown, the engine enters a condition known as heat soak. This is caused by the cooling system being inoperative while engine temperature is still high. If coolant temperature rises above boiling point, expansion and pressure may push some coolant out of the radiator overflow tube. If this does not occur frequently it is considered normal.*

TCCS3C12

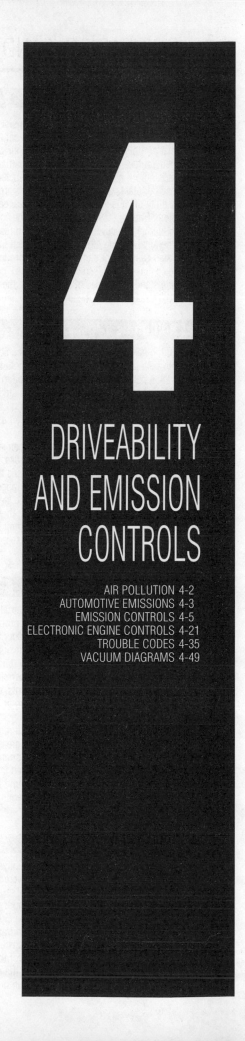

4

DRIVEABILITY AND EMISSION CONTROLS

AIR POLLUTION

The earth's atmosphere, at or near sea level, consists approximately of 78 percent nitrogen, 21 percent oxygen and 1 percent other gases. If it were possible to remain in this state, 100 percent clean air would result. However, many varied sources allow other gases and particulates to mix with the clean air, causing our atmosphere to become unclean or polluted.

Some of these pollutants are visible while others are invisible, with each having the capability of causing distress to the eyes, ears, throat, skin and respiratory system. Should these pollutants become concentrated in a specific area and under certain conditions, death could result due to the displacement or chemical change of the oxygen content in the air. These pollutants can also cause great damage to the environment and to the many man made objects that are exposed to the elements.

To better understand the causes of air pollution, the pollutants can be categorized into 3 separate types, natural, industrial and automotive.

Natural Pollutants

Natural pollution has been present on earth since before man appeared and continues to be a factor when discussing air pollution, although it causes only a small percentage of the overall pollution problem. It is the direct result of decaying organic matter, wind born smoke and particulates from such natural events as plain and forest fires (ignited by heat or lightning), volcanic ash, sand and dust which can spread over a large area of the countryside.

Such a phenomenon of natural pollution has been seen in the form of volcanic eruptions, with the resulting plume of smoke, steam and volcanic ash blotting out the sun's rays as it spreads and rises higher into the atmosphere. As it travels into the atmosphere the upper air currents catch and carry the smoke and ash, while condensing the steam back into water vapor. As the water vapor, smoke and ash travel on their journey, the smoke dissipates into the atmosphere while the ash and moisture settle back to earth in a trail hundreds of miles long. In some cases, lives are lost and millions of dollars of property damage result.

Industrial Pollutants

Industrial pollution is caused primarily by industrial processes, the burning of coal, oil and natural gas, which in turn produce smoke and fumes. Because the burning fuels contain large amounts of sulfur, the principal ingredients of smoke and fumes are sulfur dioxide and particulate matter. This type of pollutant occurs most severely during still, damp and cool weather, such as at night. Even in its less severe form, this pollutant is not confined to just cities. Because of air movements, the pollutants move for miles over the surrounding countryside, leaving in its path a barren and unhealthy environment for all living things.

Working with Federal, State and Local mandated regulations and by carefully monitoring emissions, big business has greatly reduced the amount of pollutant introduced from its industrial sources, striving to obtain an acceptable level. Because of the mandated industrial emission clean up, many land areas and streams in and around the cities that were formerly barren of vegetation and life, have now begun to move back in the direction of nature's intended balance.

Automotive Pollutants

The third major source of air pollution is automotive emissions. The emissions from the internal combustion engines were not an appreciable problem years ago because of the small number of registered vehicles and the nation's small highway system. However, during the early 1950's, the trend of the American people was to move from the cities to the surrounding suburbs. This caused an immediate problem in transportation because the majority of suburbs were not afforded mass transit conveniences. This lack of transportation created an attractive market for the automobile manufacturers, which resulted in a dramatic increase in the number of vehicles produced and sold, along with a marked increase in highway construction

between cities and the suburbs. Multi-vehicle families emerged with a growing emphasis placed on an individual vehicle per family member. As the increase in vehicle ownership and usage occurred, so did pollutant levels in and around the cities, as suburbanites drove daily to their businesses and employment, returning at the end of the day to their homes in the suburbs.

It was noted that a smoke and fog type haze was being formed and at times, remained in suspension over the cities, taking time to dissipate. At first this "smog," derived from the words "smoke" and "fog," was thought to result from industrial pollution but it was determined that automobile emissions shared the blame. It was discovered that when normal automobile emissions were exposed to sunlight for a period of time, complex chemical reactions would take place.

It is now known that smog is a photo chemical layer which develops when certain oxides of nitrogen (NOx) and unburned hydrocarbons (HC) from automobile emissions are exposed to sunlight. Pollution was more severe when smog would become stagnant over an area in which a warm layer of air settled over the top of the cooler air mass, trapping and holding the cooler mass at ground level. The trapped cooler air would keep the emissions from being dispersed and diluted through normal air flows. This type of air stagnation was given the name "Temperature Inversion."

TEMPERATURE INVERSION

In normal weather situations, surface air is warmed by heat radiating from the earth's surface and the sun's rays. This causes it to rise upward, into the atmosphere. Upon rising it will cool through a convection type heat exchange with the cooler upper air. As warm air rises, the surface pollutants are carried upward and dissipated into the atmosphere.

When a temperature inversion occurs, we find the higher air is no longer cooler, but is warmer than the surface air, causing the cooler surface air to become trapped. This warm air blanket can extend from above ground level to a few hundred or even a few thousand feet into the air. As the surface air is trapped, so are the pollutants, causing a severe smog condition. Should this stagnant air mass extend to a few thousand feet high, enough air movement with the inversion takes place to allow the smog layer to rise above ground level but the pollutants still cannot dissipate. This inversion can remain for days over an area, with the smog level only rising or lowering from ground level to a few hundred feet high. Meanwhile, the pollutant levels increase, causing eye irritation, respiratory problems, reduced visibility, plant damage and in some cases, even disease.

This inversion phenomenon was first noted in the Los Angeles, California area. The city lies in terrain resembling a basin and with certain weather conditions, a cold air mass is held in the basin while a warmer air mass covers it like a lid.

Because this type of condition was first documented as prevalent in the Los Angeles area, this type of trapped pollution was named Los Angeles Smog, although it occurs in other areas where a large concentration of automobiles are used and the air remains stagnant for any length of time.

HEAT TRANSFER

Consider the internal combustion engine as a machine in which raw materials must be placed so a finished product comes out. As in any machine operation, a certain amount of wasted material is formed. When we relate this to the internal combustion engine, we find that through the input of air and fuel, we obtain power during the combustion process to drive the vehicle. The by-product or waste of this power is, in part, heat and exhaust gases with which we must dispose.

The heat from the combustion process can rise to over 4000°F (2204°C). The dissipation of this heat is controlled by a ram air effect, the use of cooling fans to cause air flow and a liquid coolant solution surrounding the combustion area to transfer the heat of combustion through the cylinder walls and into the coolant. The coolant is then directed to a thin-finned, multi-tubed radiator, from which the excess heat is transferred to the atmosphere by 1 of the 3 heat transfer methods, conduction, convection or radiation.

The cooling of the combustion area is an important part in the control of exhaust emissions. To understand the behavior of the combustion and transfer of its heat, consider the air/fuel charge. It is ignited and the flame front burns progressively across the combustion chamber until the burning charge reaches the cylinder walls. Some of the fuel in contact with the walls is not hot enough to burn, thereby snuffing out or quenching the combustion process. This leaves unburned fuel in the combustion chamber. This

unburned fuel is then forced out of the cylinder and into the exhaust system, along with the exhaust gases.

Many attempts have been made to minimize the amount of unburned fuel in the combustion chambers due to quenching, by increasing the coolant temperature and lessening the contact area of the coolant around the combustion area. However, design limitations within the combustion chambers prevent the complete burning of the air/fuel charge, so a certain amount of the unburned fuel is still expelled into the exhaust system, regardless of modifications to the engine.

AUTOMOTIVE EMISSIONS

Before emission controls were mandated on internal combustion engines, other sources of engine pollutants were discovered along with the exhaust emissions. It was determined that engine combustion exhaust produced approximately 60 percent of the total emission pollutants, fuel evaporation from the fuel tank and carburetor vents produced 20 percent, with the final 20 percent being produced through the crankcase as a by-product of the combustion process.

Exhaust Gases

The exhaust gases emitted into the atmosphere are a combination of burned and unburned fuel. To understand the exhaust emission and its composition, we must review some basic chemistry.

When the air/fuel mixture is introduced into the engine, we are mixing air, composed of nitrogen (78 percent), oxygen (21 percent) and other gases (1 percent) with the fuel, which is 100 percent hydrocarbons (HC), in a semi-controlled ratio. As the combustion process is accomplished, power is produced to move the vehicle while the heat of combustion is transferred to the cooling system. The exhaust gases are then composed of nitrogen, a diatomic gas (N_2), the same as was introduced in the engine, carbon dioxide (CO_2), the same gas that is used in beverage carbonation, and water vapor (H_2O). The nitrogen (N_2), for the most part, passes through the engine unchanged, while the oxygen (O_2) reacts (burns) with the hydrocarbons (HC) and produces the carbon dioxide (CO_2) and the water vapors (H_2O). If this chemical process would be the only process to take place, the exhaust emissions would be harmless. However, during the combustion process, other compounds are formed which are considered dangerous. These pollutants are hydrocarbons (HC), carbon monoxide (CO), oxides of nitrogen (NOx) oxides of sulfur (SOx) and engine particulates.

HYDROCARBONS

Hydrocarbons (HC) are essentially fuel which was not burned during the combustion process or which has escaped into the atmosphere through fuel evaporation. The main sources of incomplete combustion are rich air/fuel mixtures, low engine temperatures and improper spark timing. The main sources of hydrocarbon emission through fuel evaporation on most vehicles used to be the vehicle's fuel tank and carburetor float bowl.

To reduce combustion hydrocarbon emission, engine modifications were made to minimize dead space and surface area in the combustion chamber. In addition, the air/fuel mixture was made more lean through the improved control which feedback carburetion and fuel injection offers and by the addition of external controls to aid in further combustion of the hydrocarbons outside the engine. Two such methods were the addition of air injection systems, to inject fresh air into the exhaust manifolds and the installation of catalytic converters, units that are able to burn traces of hydrocarbons without affecting the internal combustion process or fuel economy.

To control hydrocarbon emissions through fuel evaporation, modifications were made to the fuel tank to allow storage of the fuel vapors during periods of engine shut-down. Modifications were also made to the air intake system so that at specific times during engine operation, these vapors may be purged and burned by blending them with the air/fuel mixture.

CARBON MONOXIDE

Carbon monoxide is formed when not enough oxygen is present during the combustion process to convert carbon (C) to carbon dioxide (CO_2). An increase in the carbon monoxide (CO) emission is normally accompanied by an increase in the hydrocarbon (HC) emission because of the lack of oxygen to completely burn all of the fuel mixture.

Carbon monoxide (CO) also increases the rate at which the photo chemical smog is formed by speeding up the conversion of nitric oxide (NO) to nitrogen dioxide (NO_2). To accomplish this, carbon monoxide (CO) combines with oxygen (O_2) and nitric oxide (NO) to produce carbon dioxide (CO_2) and nitrogen dioxide (NO_2). ($CO + O_2 + NO = CO_2 + NO_2$).

The dangers of carbon monoxide, which is an odorless and colorless toxic gas are many. When carbon monoxide is inhaled into the lungs and passed into the blood stream, oxygen is replaced by the carbon monoxide in the red blood cells, causing a reduction in the amount of oxygen supplied to the many parts of the body. This lack of oxygen causes headaches, lack of coordination, reduced mental alertness and, should the carbon monoxide concentration be high enough, death could result.

NITROGEN

Normally, nitrogen is an inert gas. When heated to approximately 2500°F (1371°C) through the combustion process, this gas becomes active and causes an increase in the nitric oxide (NO) emission.

Oxides of nitrogen (NOx) are composed of approximately 97–98 percent nitric oxide (NO). Nitric oxide is a colorless gas but when it is passed into the atmosphere, it combines with oxygen and forms nitrogen dioxide (NO_2). The nitrogen dioxide then combines with chemically active hydrocarbons (HC) and when in the presence of sunlight, causes the formation of photochemical smog.

Ozone

To further complicate matters, some of the nitrogen dioxide (NO_2) is broken apart by the sunlight to form nitric oxide and oxygen. ($NO_2 + sunlight = NO + O$). This single atom of oxygen then combines with diatomic (meaning 2 atoms) oxygen (O_2) to form ozone (O_3). Ozone is one of the smells associated with smog. It has a pungent and offensive odor, irritates the eyes and lung tissues, affects the growth of plant life and causes rapid deterioration of rubber products. Ozone can be formed by sunlight as well as electrical discharge into the air.

The most common discharge area on the automobile engine is the secondary ignition electrical system, especially when inferior quality spark plug cables are used. As the surge of high voltage is routed through the secondary cable, the circuit builds up an electrical field around the wire, which acts upon the oxygen in the surrounding air to form the ozone. The faint glow along the cable with the engine running that may be visible on a dark night, is called the "corona discharge." It is the result of the electrical field passing from a high along the cable, to a low in the surrounding air, which forms the ozone gas. The combination of corona and ozone has been a major cause of cable deterioration. Recently, different and better quality insulating materials have lengthened the life of the electrical cables.

Although ozone at ground level can be harmful, ozone is beneficial to the earth's inhabitants. By having a concentrated ozone layer called the "ozonosphere," between 10 and 20 miles (16–32 km) up in the atmosphere, much of the ultra violet radiation from the sun's rays are absorbed and screened. If this ozone layer were not present, much of the earth's surface would be burned, dried and unfit for human life.

OXIDES OF SULFUR

Oxides of sulfur (SOx) were initially ignored in the exhaust system emissions, since the sulfur content of gasoline as a fuel is less than $\frac{1}{10}$ of 1 percent. Because of this small amount, it was felt that it contributed very little to the overall pollution problem. However, because of the difficulty in solving the sulfur emissions in industrial pollutions and the introduction of catalytic converter to the automobile exhaust systems, a change was mandated. The automobile exhaust system, when equipped with a catalytic converter, changes the sulfur dioxide (SO_2) into sulfur trioxide (SO_3).

When this combines with water vapors (H_2O), a sulfuric acid mist (H_2SO_4) is formed and is a very difficult pollutant to handle since it is extremely corrosive. This sulfuric acid mist that is formed, is the same mist that rises from the vents of an automobile battery when an active chemical reaction takes place within the battery cells.

When a large concentration of vehicles equipped with catalytic converters are operating in an area, this acid mist may rise and be distributed over a large ground area causing land, plant, crop, paint and building damage.

PARTICULATE MATTER

A certain amount of particulate matter is present in the burning of any fuel, with carbon constituting the largest percentage of the particulates. In gasoline, the remaining particulates are the burned remains of the various other compounds used in its manufacture. When a gasoline engine is in good internal condition, the particulate emissions are low but as the engine wears internally, the particulate emissions increase. By visually inspecting the tail pipe emissions, a determination can be made as to where an engine defect may exist. An engine with light gray or blue smoke emitting from the tail pipe normally indicates an increase in the oil consumption through burning due to internal engine wear. Black smoke would indicate a defective fuel delivery system, causing the engine to operate in a rich mode. Regardless of the color of the smoke, the internal part of the engine or the fuel delivery system should be repaired to prevent excess particulate emissions.

Diesel and turbine engines emit a darkened plume of smoke from the exhaust system because of the type of fuel used. Emission control regulations are mandated for this type of emission and more stringent measures are being used to prevent excess emission of the particulate matter. Electronic components are being introduced to control the injection of the fuel at precisely the proper time of piston travel, to achieve the optimum in fuel ignition and fuel usage. Other particulate after-burning components are being tested to achieve a cleaner emission.

Good grades of engine lubricating oils should be used, which meet the manufacturers specification. Cut-rate oils can contribute to the particulate emission problem because of their low flash or ignition temperature point. Such oils burn prematurely during the combustion process causing emission of particulate matter.

The cooling system is an important factor in the reduction of particulate matter. The optimum combustion will occur, with the cooling system operating at a temperature specified by the manufacturer. The cooling system must be maintained in the same manner as the engine oiling system, as each system is required to perform properly in order for the engine to operate efficiently for a long time.

Crankcase Emissions

Crankcase emissions are made up of water, acids, unburned fuel, oil fumes and particulates. These emissions are classified as hydrocarbons (HC) and are formed by the small amount of unburned, compressed air/fuel mixture entering the crankcase from the combustion area (between the cylinder walls and piston rings) during the compression and power strokes. The head of the compression and combustion help to form the remaining crankcase emissions.

Since the first engines, crankcase emissions were allowed into the atmosphere through a road draft tube, mounted on the lower side of the engine block. Fresh air came in through an open oil filler cap or breather. The air passed through the crankcase mixing with blow-by gases. The motion of the vehicle and the air blowing past the open end of the road draft tube caused a low pressure area (vacuum) at the end of the tube. Crankcase emissions were simply drawn out of the road draft tube into the air.

To control the crankcase emission, the road draft tube was deleted. A hose and/or tubing was routed from the crankcase to the intake manifold so the blow-by emission could be burned with the air/fuel mixture. However, it was found that intake manifold vacuum, used to draw the crankcase emissions into the manifold, would vary in strength at the wrong time and not allow the proper emission flow. A regulating valve was needed to control the flow of air through the crankcase.

Testing, showed the removal of the blow-by gases from the crankcase as quickly as possible, was most important to the longevity of the engine. Should large accumulations of blow-by gases remain and condense, dilution of the engine oil would occur to form water, soots, resins, acids and lead salts, resulting in the formation of sludge and varnishes. This condensation of the blow-by gases occurs more frequently on vehicles used in numerous starting and stopping conditions, excessive idling and when the engine is not allowed to attain normal operating temperature through short runs.

Evaporative Emissions

Gasoline fuel is a major source of pollution, before and after it is burned in the automobile engine. From the time the fuel is refined, stored, pumped and transported, again stored until it is pumped into the fuel tank of the vehicle, the gasoline gives off unburned hydrocarbons (HC) into the atmosphere. Through the redesign of storage areas and venting systems, the pollution factor was diminished, but not eliminated, from the refinery standpoint. However, the automobile still remained the primary source of vaporized, unburned hydrocarbon (HC) emissions.

Fuel pumped from an underground storage tank is cool but when exposed to a warmer ambient temperature, will expand. Before controls were mandated, an owner might fill the fuel tank with fuel from an underground storage tank and park the vehicle for some time in warm area, such as a parking lot. As the fuel would warm, it would expand and should no provisions or area be provided for the expansion, the fuel would spill out of the filler neck and onto the ground, causing hydrocarbon (HC) pollution and creating a severe fire hazard. To correct this condition, the vehicle manufacturers added overflow plumbing and/or gasoline tanks with built in expansion areas or domes.

However, this did not control the fuel vapor emission from the fuel tank. It was determined that most of the fuel evaporation occurred when the vehicle was stationary and the engine not operating. Most vehicles carry 5–25 gallons (19–95 liters) of gasoline. Should a large concentration of vehicles be parked in one area, such as a large parking lot, excessive fuel vapor emissions would take place, increasing as the temperature increases.

To prevent the vapor emission from escaping into the atmosphere, the fuel systems were designed to trap the vapors while the vehicle is stationary, by sealing the system from the atmosphere. A storage system is used to collect and hold the fuel vapors from the carburetor (if equipped) and the fuel tank when the engine is not operating. When the engine is started, the storage system is then purged of the fuel vapors, which are drawn into the engine and burned with the air/fuel mixture.

EMISSION CONTROLS

Due to varying state, federal, and provincial regulations, specific emission control equipment may vary by area of sale. The U.S. emission equipment is divided into two categories: California and 49 State (or Federal). In this section, the term "California" applies only to cars originally built to be sold in California. Some California emissions equipment is not shared with equipment installed on cars built to be sold in the other 49 states. Models built to be sold in Canada also have specific emissions equipment, although in many cases the 49 State and Canadian equipment is the same.

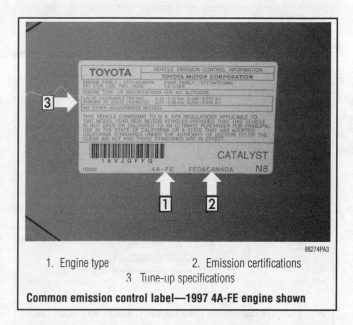

1. Engine type
2. Emission certifications
3. Tune-up specifications

Common emission control label—1997 4A-FE engine shown

Crankcase Ventilation System

OPERATION

▶ **See Figures 1 and 2**

A closed positive crankcase ventilation system is used on all Toyota models. This system cycles incompletely burned fuel which works its way

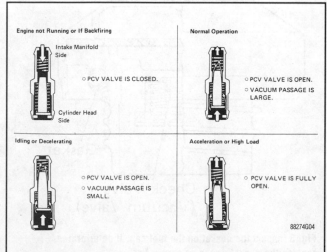

Fig. 1 The PCV valve opens and closes according to engine operating conditions

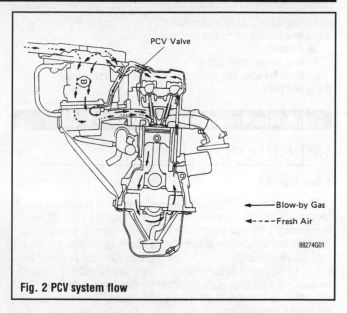

Fig. 2 PCV system flow

past the piston rings back into the intake manifold for reburning with the fuel/air mixture. The oil filler cap is sealed and the air is drawn from the top of the crankcase into the intake manifold through a valve with a variable orifice.

This valve (commonly known as the PCV valve) regulates the flow of air into the manifold according to the amount of manifold vacuum.

A plugged valve or hose may cause a rough idle, stalling or low idle speed, oil leaks in the engine and/or slugging and oil deposits within the engine and air cleaner. A leaking valve or hose could cause an erratic idle or stalling.

COMPONENT TESTING

Inspect the PCV system hoses and connections at each tune-up and replace any deteriorated hoses. Check the PCV valve at every tune-up and replace it at 30,000 mile (48,000 km) intervals.

The PCV valve is easily checked with the engine running at normal idle speed (warmed up).

1. Remove the PCV valve from the valve cover or intake manifold, but leave it connected to its hose.
2. Start the engine.
3. Place your thumb over the end of the valve to check for vacuum. If there is no vacuum, check for plugged hoses or ports. If these are open, the valve is faulty.
4. With the engine **OFF**, remove the valve completely. Shake it end-to-end, listening for the rattle of the needle inside the valve. If no rattle is heard, the needle is jammed (probably due to oil sludge) and the valve should be replaced.

✳✳ CAUTION

Don't blow directly into the valve; petroleum deposits within the valve can be harmful.

An engine without crankcase ventilation is quickly damaged. It is important to check the PCV at regular intervals. When replacing a PCV valve you must use the correct one for the engine. Many valves look alike on the outside, but have different mechanical values. Putting the incorrect valve on a vehicle can cause a great deal of driveability problems.

REMOVAL & INSTALLATION

1. Pull the PCV valve from the valve cover.
2. Remove the hose from the valve.

3. Check the valve for proper operation. While the valve is removed, the hoses should be checked for splits, kinks and blockages. Check the vacuum port (that the hoses connect to) for any clogging.

4. Inspect the rubber grommet the PCV valve fits into. If it is in any way deteriorated or oil soaked, replace it.

To install:

5. Insert a new valve into the hose.

6. Push the valve into the rubber grommet. Make sure the valve is firmly into place.

Evaporative Emission Control (EVAP) System

SYSTEM OPERATION

▶ **See Figure 3**

The Evaporative Emission Control (EVAP) system is designed to prevent fuel tank vapors from being emitted into the atmosphere. When the engine is not running, gasoline vapors from the tank are stored in a charcoal canister. The charcoal canister absorbs the gasoline vapors and stores them until certain engine conditions are met and the vapors can be purged and burned by the engine. In some vehicles, any liquid fuel entering the canister goes into a reservoir in the bottom of the canister to protect the integrity of the carbon element in the canister above. These systems employ the following components:

4A-F engine:
*   Fuel tank cap
*   Charcoal canister
*   Outer vent control valve
*   Vacuum Switching Valve (VSV)
*   Check valve
*   Tempreture switch

4A-GE engine:
*   Bimetal Vacuum Switching Valve (BVSV)
*   Check valve
*   Charcoal canister
*   Fuel tank cap

4A-FE and 7A-FE engines:
*   Charcoal canister
*   Bimetal vacuum switching valve (BVSV)—1988–92 models
*   Fuel tank cap
*   Thermal Vacuum Valve (TVV)—1993–97 models

COMPONENT TESTING

▶ **See Figure 4**

Before embarking on component removal or extensive diagnosis, perform a complete visual check of the system. Every vacuum line and vapor line (including the lines running to the tank) should be inspected for cracking, loose clamps, kinks and obstructions. Additionally, check the tank for any signs of deformation or crushing. Each vacuum port on the engine or manifold should be checked for restriction by dirt or sludge.

The evaporative control system is generally not prone to component failure in normal circumstances; most problems can be tracked to the causes listed above.

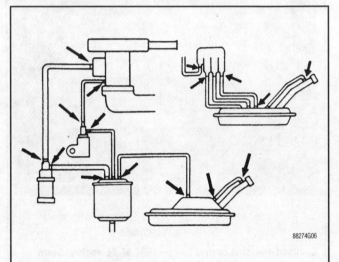

Fig. 4 Always inspect the lines for kinks, cracks and loose connections

Fuel Filler Cap

▶ **See Figure 5**

Check that the filler cap seals effectively. Replace the filler cap if the seal is defective.

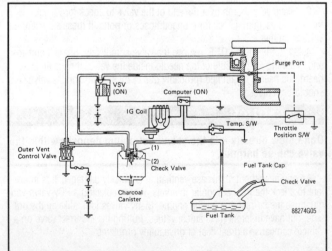

Fig. 3 Evaporative Emission Control (EVAP) system components-4A-F engine shown, others similar

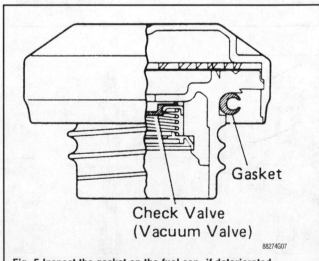

Fig. 5 Inspect the gasket on the fuel cap, if deteriorated, replace the gasket or cap as necessary

Charcoal Canister and Check Valves

▶ See Figures 6 and 7

1. Remove the charcoal canister from the vehicle.
2. Visually check the charcoal canister for cracks or damage.
3. Check for a clogged filter and stuck check valve. Using low pressure compressed air (0.68 psi. or 4 kPa), blow into the tank pipe and check that the air flows without resistance from the other pipes. If this does not test positive replace the canister.
4. Clean the filter in the canister by blowing no more than 43 psi (294 kPa) of compressed air into the pipe to the outer vent control valve while holding the other upper canister pipes closed.

➡ **Do not attempt to wash the charcoal canister. Also be sure that no activated carbon comes out of the canister during the cleaning process.**

5. Replace or reinstall the canister as needed.

Outer Vent Control Valve

▶ See Figures 8 and 9

1. Disconnect the hoses from the valve.
2. Check that the valve opens when the ignition switch is OFF.
3. Check that the valve is closed when the ignition switch is ON.
4. Reattach the hoses to the proper locations. If the valve does not respond correctly to this test, replace the valve.

Vacuum Switching Valve (VSV)

▶ See Figure 10

1. Remove the VSV from the engine. Connect the VSV terminals to the battery terminals.
2. Blow into the pipe of the valve, check that the VSV is open.
3. Disconnect the positive terminal of the battery.
4. Blow into the pipe again and check that the valve is closed. If the testing is not found to be to standards, replace the valve.

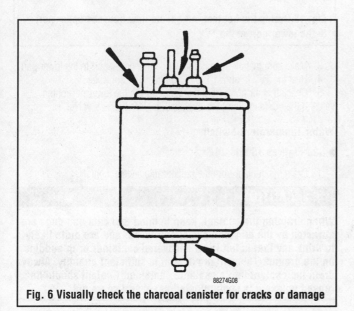

Fig. 6 Visually check the charcoal canister for cracks or damage

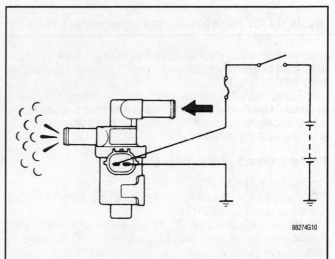

Fig. 8 Check that the outer vent control opens when the ignition is OFF

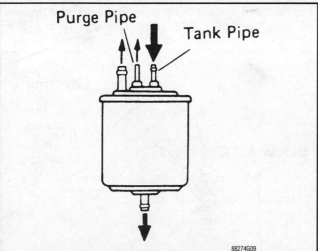

Fig. 7 To check for a clogged filter or check valve, blow compressed air into the pipes as shown

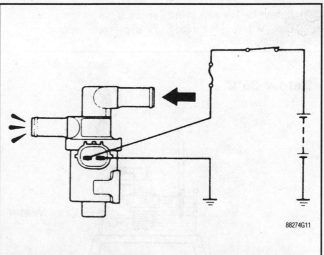

Fig. 9 Check that the outer vent control closes when the ignition is ON

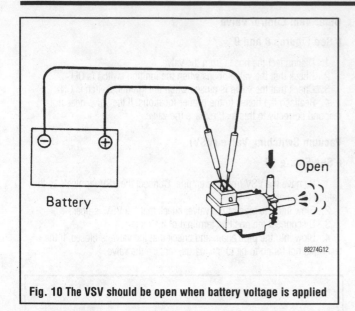

Fig. 10 The VSV should be open when battery voltage is applied

5. To test for a short in the valve; attach an ohmmeter, and check for continuity at the positive terminal and the body of the valve. If continuity is found, the valve is faulty.

6. Testing the VSV for and open circuit. Using an ohmmeter, measure the resistance between the positive terminal and the other terminals. Resistance should be 38–44 ohms at 68° F (20° C). If the resistance is not within specifications, replace the VSV.

Bimetal Vacuum Switching Valve (BVSV)

1. Remove the BVSV.

2. Cool the BVSV to below 104° F (40° C) with cool water. Blow air into pipe and check that the BVSV is closed.

3. Heat the BVSV to above 129° F (54° C) with hot water. Blow air into pipe and check that the BVSV is open. If a problem is found, replace the valve.

4. Apply liquid sealer to the threads of the BVSV and reinstall.

Thermal Vacuum Valve (TVV)

▶ See Figures 11 and 12

1. Remove the TVV valve from the engine.
2. Cool the valve to below 95° F (35° C) with cool water.

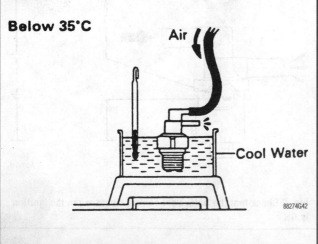

Fig. 11 During the cold test, air should not flow from the upper port to the lower port of the TVV

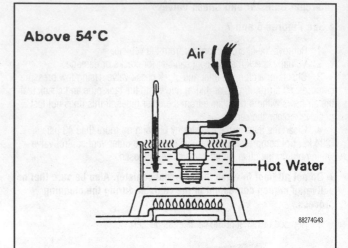

Fig. 12 During the hot test, air should flow from the upper port to the lower port of the TVV

3. Make sure that air does not flow from the upper port to the lower port.
4. Heat the TVV to above 129° F (54° C) with hot water.
5. Check that air flows from the upper port to the lower port of the valve. If the operation is not as specified, replace the TVV valve.

Water Temperature Switch

▶ See Figures 13 and 14

1. Drain the coolant from the radiator into a clean container.

❊❊ CAUTION

When draining the coolant, keep in mind that cats and dogs are attracted by the ethylene glycol antifreeze, and are quite likely to drink any that is left in an uncovered container or in puddles on the ground. This will prove fatal in sufficient quantity. Always drain the coolant into a sealable container. Coolant should be reused unless it is contaminated or several years old.

2. Remove the thermo switch.
3. Cool the switch off until the temperature is below 109°F (43°C). Check that there is continuity through the switch by the use of an ohmmeter.
4. Using hot water, bring the temperature of the switch to above 131°F

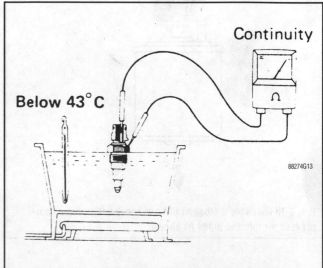

Fig. 13 Cool the temperature switch and check for continuity

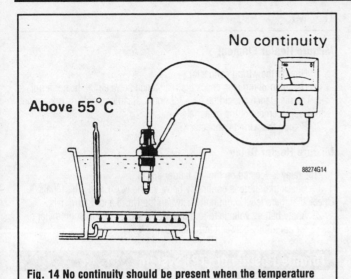

Fig. 14 No continuity should be present when the temperature switch is heated

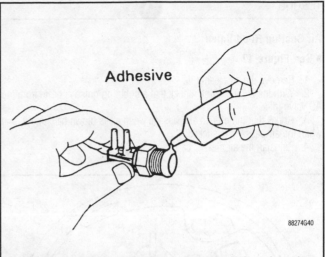

Fig. 15 Apply adhesive to the first few threads of the valve prior to installation

(55°C). Check that there is no continuity when the switch is above this temperature.

5. Apply sealer to the threads of the switch and reinstall it.
6. Refill the radiator with coolant.

REMOVAL & INSTALLATION

➡**When replacing any EVAP system hoses, always use hoses that are fuel-resistant or are marked EVAP. Use of hose which is not fuel-resistant will lead to premature hose failure.**

Charcoal Canister

1. Label and disconnect the lines running to the canister. Remove the charcoal canister from the vehicle.

➡**Do not attempt to wash the charcoal canister. Also be sure that no activated carbon comes out of the canister during the cleaning process.**

2. Attach the charcoal canister to its mounting bracket and secure. Connect the vacuum hoses in their proper locations.

Bimetal Vacuum Switching Valve (BVSV)

1. Drain the engine coolant from the radiator into a suitable container.
2. Unscrew the BVSV from the engine.
To install:
3. Apply liquid sealer to the threads of the BVSV. carefully thread the valve into the engine.
4. Fill the radiator with coolant. Start the engine, check and top off the fluid level.

Thermal Vacuum Valve (TVV)

▶ **See Figure 15**

1. Drain the coolant the from the radiator.
2. Disconnect the vacuum hoses from the charcoal canister (1) and throttle body (2).
3. Remove the TVV valve from the engine.
To install:
4. Apply adhesive to 2 or 3 of the threads of the TVV, then tighten the valve to 22 ft. lbs. (29 Nm).
5. Reattach the vacuum hoses.
6. Refill the engine with coolant. Start the engine, check and top off fluid level.

Outer Vent Control Valve

1. Disconnect and label the hoses from the valve.
2. Remove the valve from its mounting bracket.
3. Place a new valve into position on the bracket. Attach the hoses.

Air Suction (AS) System

➡**This system is only used on the 4A-F engines.**

OPERATION

▶ **See Figure 16**

The air suction (AS) system brings fresh, filtered air into the exhaust ports to reduce HC and CO emissions. On some applications, it also supplies the air necessary for the oxidizing reaction in the catalytic converter. The air suction system is different for the Federal models vs. the California models. Federal models are only equipped with an air reed, whereas the California models are equipped with a shut-off valve and air reed.

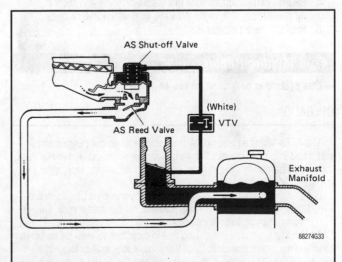

Fig. 16 Air Suction (AS) system airflow—California shown, others similar

TESTING

Air Suction Reed Valve

▶ See Figure 17

1. Remove the air cleaner lid.
2. With the engine idling, check that a bubbling noise is heard from the AS valve inlet.
3. Check that there is no air passage when air is blown hard into it, and when the air passage is sucked.
4. Reinstall the air cleaner cap.

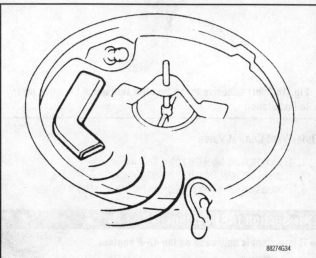

Fig. 17 Listen for a bubbling noise from the air suction reed valve inlet during idle

Air Suction Shut-Off Valve

➡This valve is only found on California models.

1. Disconnect the vacuum hose from the shut-off valve and plug the hose end.
2. Remove the air cleaner lid.
3. Start the engine.
4. Reconnect the vacuum hose to the shut-off valve and check that a bubbling noise is heard from the AS valve inlet within 2–6 seconds.
5. Resinatll the air cleaner lid.

Cold Mixture Heater

➡This system is only used on the 4A-F engines.

OPERATION

The Cold-Mixture Heater (CMH) system reduces cold engine emissions and improves driveability during engine warm-up. The intake manifold is heated during cold engine warm-up to accelerate vaporization of the fuel.

If the engine is running and the coolant temperature is below a predetermined limit, the computer energizes the cold mixture heater relay. This in turn allows battery voltage to be applied to the cold mixture heater. The CMH is a Multi-element heater ring that is mounted between the carburetor base and the intake manifold. Once the coolant temperature exceeds a certain limit, the CMH relay is de-energized and the heater elements turn off.

TESTING

Mixture Heater Element

1. Unplug the wiring connector.
2. Using an ohmmeter, check the resistance between the heater terminals. The resistance should be 0.5–2.2 ohms. Readings outside this range require replacement of the heater element.
3. Replug the wiring connector.

Mixture Heater Relay

This relay is located on the left fender apron.
1. Check that there is continuity between the No. 1 and 2 terminals. Check that there is NO continuity between the No. 3 and 4 terminals.
2. Apply battery voltage to terminal No. 1 and 2. Use the ohmmeter to check for continuity between terminals 3 and 4.

Throttle Positioner (TP) System

➡This system is only used on 4A-F engines.

OPERATION

▶ See Figure 18

To reduce HC and CO emissions, the Throttle Positioner (TP) opens the throttle valve to slightly more than the idle position when decelerating. This keeps the air/fuel ratio from becoming excessively rich when the throttle valve is quickly closed. In addition, the TP is used to increase idle rpm when power steering fluid pressure exceeds a calibrated value and/or when a large electrical load is placed on the electrical system (headlights, rear defogger etc).

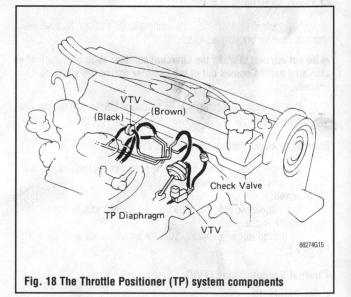

Fig. 18 The Throttle Positioner (TP) system components

TESTING

Vacuum Transmitting Valve (VTV)

▶ See Figure 19

1. Check that air flows without resistance from **B** to **A**.
2. Check that air flows with difficulty from **A** to **B**.
3. If a problem is found, replace the vacuum delay valve.

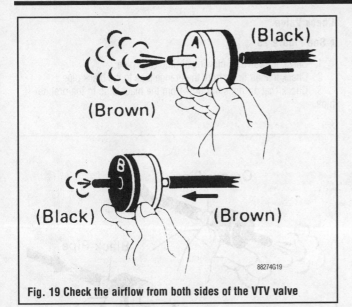

Fig. 19 Check the airflow from both sides of the VTV valve

➡When replacing the vacuum transmitting valve, side A should face the throttle positioner.

Vacuum Switching Valve (VSV)

◆ See Figures 20, 21 and 22

1. Warm the engine to operating temperature.
2. Check the idle speed and adjust if necessary.
3. Disconnect the hose from the TVSV **M** port and plug the port.
4. Check the throttle positioner setting speed and operation of the VTV. Disconnect the vacuum hose from the TP diaphragm and plug the hose end.
5. Check that the TP is set to 900 rpm. If it is not at the specified speed, adjust with the TP adjusting screw. Make the adjustment with the cooling fan OFF.
6. Reconnect the vacuum hose to the TP diaphragm and check that the engine returns to idle speed within 2–6 seconds. Reconnect the vacuum hose to the diaphragm.
7. Reconnect the hose to the TVSV **M** port. If no problem is found with this inspection, the system is OK; otherwise inspect each part.

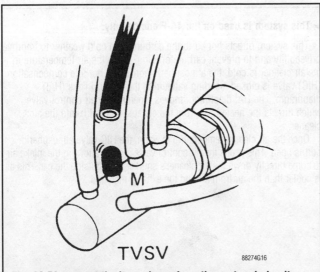

Fig. 20 Disconnect the hose shown from the port and plug it

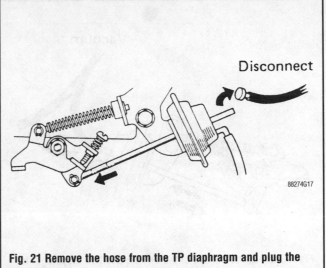

Fig. 21 Remove the hose from the TP diaphragm and plug the hose end

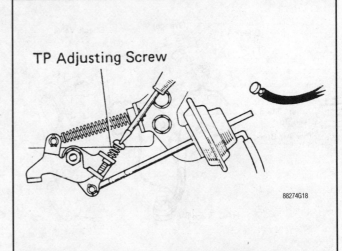

Fig. 22 Turn the screw to adjust the TP setting speed if necessary

Throttle Positioner Diaphragm

◆ See Figure 23

Check that the linkage moves in accordance with applied vacuum.

High Altitude Compensation (HAC)

OPERATION

◆ See Figure 24

➡This system is used on the 4A-FE engines only.

As altitude increases, air density decreases. This causes the air/fuel mixture to become richer (the same amount of fuel is mixing with less air). The high altitude compensation (HAC) system insures a proper air/fuel mixture by supplying additional air to the primary low and high speed circuits of the carburetor and advancing the ignition timing to improve driveability at altitudes above 3,930 feet (1,200 m). At altitudes below 2,570 feet (783 m), normal operation is resumed.

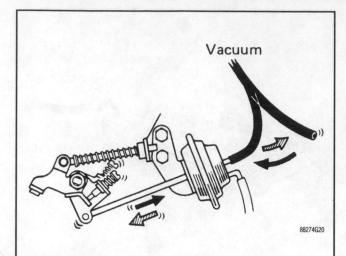

Fig. 23 Check the linkage of the throttle position diaphragm for smooth movement

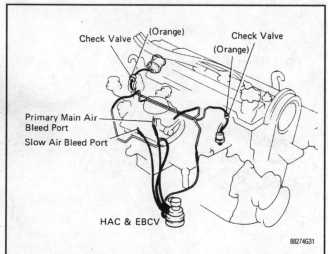

Fig. 24 Components of the High Altitude Compensation (HAC) system

TESTING

HAC Valve

1. Visually check and clean the air filter in the HAC valve.
2. Check the HAC valve as follows:
   a. Above 3,930 ft. (1,200 m), blow into any one of the two ports on top of the HAC valve with the engine idling and check that the HAC valve is open (air flows through the bottom of the valve).
   b. Below 2,570 ft. (783 m), blow into any one of the two ports on top of the HAC valve with the engine idling and check that the HAC valve is closed (no air flow through the bottom of the valve).

Check Valve

♦ **See Figure 25**

1. Check the valve by blowing air into each pipe:
2. Check that air flows from the orange pipe to the black pipe.
3. Check that air does not flow from the black pipe to the orange pipe.

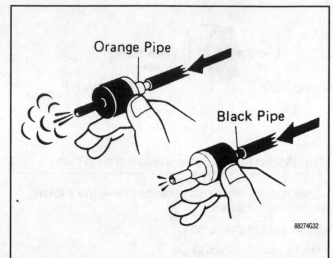

Fig. 25 Air should flow from the orange pipe to the black pipe, but not from the black pipe to the orange pipe

Distributor Vacuum Advance

1. Remove the distributor cap and rotor.
2. Plug one port of the sub-diaphragm. Using a hand-held vacuum pump, apply vacuum to the diaphragm, checking that the vacuum advance moves when the vacuum is applied.
3. Reinstall the rotor and distributor cap.

Hot Air Intake (HAI) System

OPERATION

➡**This system is used on the 4A-F engine only.**

This system directs hot air to the carburetor in cold weather to improve driveability and to prevent carburetor icing. When the air temperature in the air cleaner is cold, the atmospheric port in the hot idle compensation (HIC) valve is closed, sending vacuum to the hot air intake (HAI) diaphragm. The HAI diaphragm moves, opening the air control valve which directs the heated air (from the exhaust manifold) into the air cleaner.

Once the air cleaner temperature is warm, the HIC valve atmospheric port is open. This keeps the air control valve closed, allowing the intake air to come directly down the air cleaner's snorkel from outside the car. This air is cooler than the air from around the exhaust manifold.

TESTING

▶ **See Figures 26 and 27**

1. Remove the air cleaner cover and cool the HIC valve by blowing compressed air on it.
2. Check that the air control valve closes the cool air passage.
3. Reinstall the air cleaner cover and warm up the engine.
4. Check that the air control valve opens the cool air passage at idle.
5. Visually check the hoses and connections for cracks, leaks or damage.

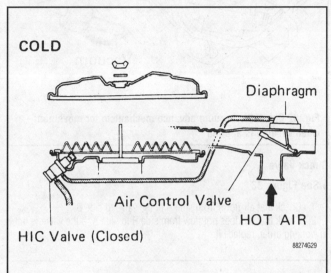

Fig. 26 On a cold engine, the HIC valve should stayed closed

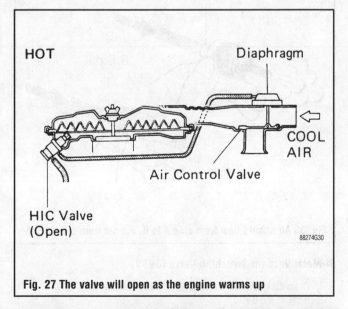

Fig. 27 The valve will open as the engine warms up

Hot Idle Compensation (HIC) System

OPERATION

▶ **See Figure 28**

➡**This system is used on the 4A-F engines only.**

The Hot Idle Compensation (HIC) system allows additional air to enter the intake manifold, maintaining a proper air/fuel mixture during

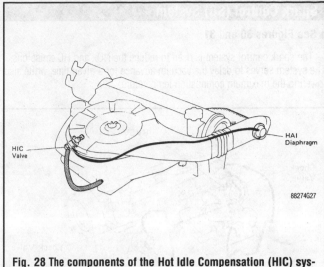

Fig. 28 The components of the Hot Idle Compensation (HIC) system are located on the air cleaner

idle at high temperatures. It also controls the vacuum supplied to the HAI valve, allowing heated air to enter the air cleaner during cold operation.

TESTING

▶ **See Figure 29**

1. Check that air flows from the HAI diaphragm side to the carburetor side while closing the atmospheric port.
2. Check that air does not flow from the carburetor side to the HAI diaphragm side with the atmospheric port open.
3. Check that air does NOT flow from the HAI diaphragm side to the atmosphere port while closing the carburetor side below this temperature 72°F (22°C). Using a hotwater bath, heat the HIC valve to above 84°F (29°C).

➡**Do not allow water to get inside the valve.**

4. Check that air flows from the HAI diaphragm side to the atmospheric port while closing the carburetor side.

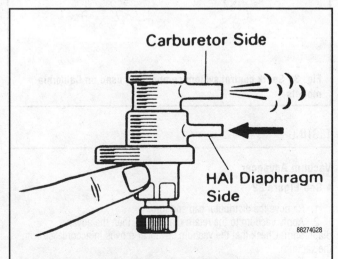

Fig. 29 Test for air flowing from the HAI diaphragm side to the carburetor side with the port of the valve closed

Spark Control (SC) System

♦ **See Figures 30 and 31**

The spark control system is used to reduce the NOx and HC emissions. The system serves to delay the vacuum advance for a given time, while also lowering the maximum combustion temperature.

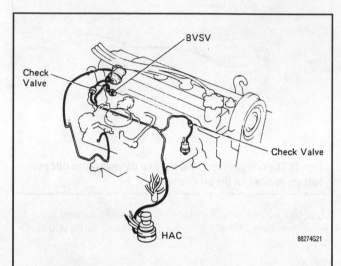

Fig. 30 Spark Control (SC) system components—except California models

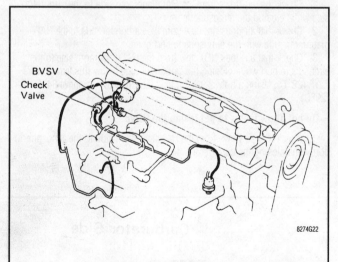

Fig. 31 Spark control system components used on California models

TESTING

Vacuum Advancer

♦ **See Figure 32**

1. Remove the distributor cap and rotor.
2. Apply vacuum to the retard diaphragm, then the advance diaphragm. Check that the vacuum advancer moves in accordance with the vacuum.
3. If a problem is found, replace the vacuum advancer. Install the cap and rotor.

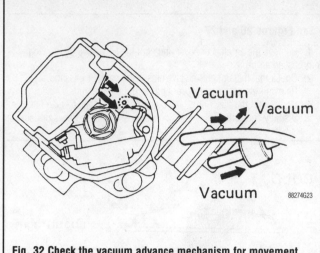

Fig. 32 Check the vacuum advance mechanism for movement when vacuum is applied

Check Valve

♦ **See Figure 33**

1. Check that air flows from side A of the valve to side B.
2. Check that air does not flow from side B to side A. If the valve is not in working order, replace it.

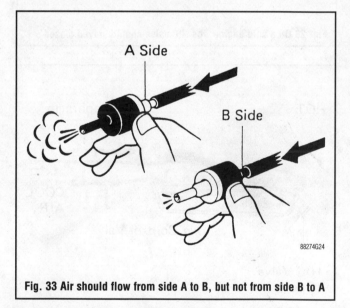

Fig. 33 Air should flow from side A to B, but not from side B to A

Bi-Metal Vacuum Switching Valve (BVSV)

1. Drain the coolant from the radiator into a suitable container.
2. Remove the BVSV.
3. Cool the BVSV in water below 104°F (40° C).
4. Blow air into a pipe and check that the BVSV is closed.
5. Heat the valve in water above 129° F (54° C).
6. Blow air into the pipe and check that the valve is open.
7. Apply liquid sealer to the first few threads of the valve and reinstall it in the engine.
8. Fill the radiator with coolant and water mixture. Start the engine and check for leaks.
9. If a problem is found with the testing of the BVSV, replace the valve.

Dash Pot (DP) System

SYSTEM OPERATION

▶ **See Figure 34**

The operation of this system reduces the HC and CO emissions. When decelerating, the dash pot opens the throttle valve slightly more than at idle. This causes the air-fuel mixture to burn completely.

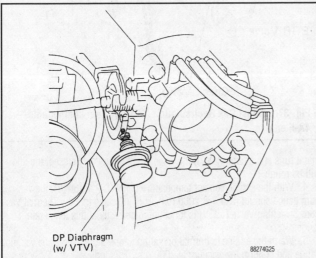

Fig. 34 The dash pot actuates the throttle lever—4A-GE engine shown

ADJUSTMENT

4A-GE Engine

▶ **See Figure 35**

1. Warm up and stop engine.
2. Check idle speed.
3. Disconnect the throttle cables from the throttle cam.
4. Remove the VTV cap, filter and separator from the dash pot.
5. Adjust DP setting speed as follows:

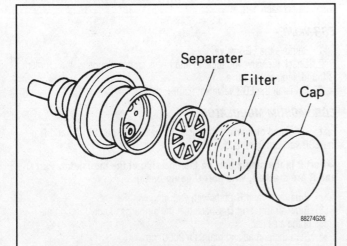

Fig. 35 Exploded view of the Vacuum Thermal Valve (VTV) assembly

a. Race the engine at 2500 rpm for a few seconds. Plug the VTV hole with your finger in the dash pot assembly.
b. Release the throttle valve.
c. Check the DP setting speed. The DP setting speed is 1800 rpm with cooling fan OFF.
d. Adjust the DP setting speed by turning the DP adjusting screw.
6. Reinstall the DP separator, filter and VTV cap.
7. Connect the throttle cables to the throttle cam.
8. Check system operation by racing the engine at 2500 rpm for a few seconds, release the throttle valve and check that the engine returns to idle speed in a few seconds.

4A-FE Engine

➡ **The 1993–97 4A-FE engines do not use this system.**

1. Warm up and stop engine.
2. Check idle speed and adjust, if necessary.
3. Remove the cap, filter and separator from the dash pot.
4. Adjust DP setting speed as follows:
   a. Connect terminals TE_1 and E_1 in the check connector.
   b. On 2WD California and 4WD, disconnect the EGR VSV connector.
   c. Race the engine at 3000 rpm (2WD) or 3500 rpm (4WD) for a few seconds. Plug the VTV hole with your finger in the dash pot assembly.
   d. Release the throttle valve.
   e. Check the DP setting speed. The DP setting speed should be 1500 rpm on 2WD, 1800 rpm on 4WD with M/T or 2200 rpm on 4WD with A/T, with cooling fan OFF.
   f. Adjust the DP setting speed by turning the DP adjusting screw.
   g. Connect the EGR VSV connector if so equipped. Remove the SST or jumper from the check connector.
5. Reinstall the DP separator, filter and cap.
6. Check system operation by racing the engine at 3000 rpm (2WD) or 3500 rpm (4WD) for a few seconds, release the throttle valve and check that the engine returns to idle speed in a few seconds.

REMOVAL & INSTALLATION

1. To remove the dash pot assembly, unplug the vacuum hose then remove the dash pot mounting screws.
2. Remove the assembly from the throttle body.
3. Installation is the reverse of removal. Replace the dash pot assembly and adjust if necessary.

Auxiliary Acceleration Pump (AAP) System

OPERATION

▶ **See Figure 36**

To reduce emissions, carburetor air/fuel mixtures are calibrated to be as lean as possible. Although a lean mixture will burn readily at hotter temperatures, it is reluctant to ignite when cold because fuel vaporizes less readily when cold. Thus, increasing the amount of fuel in a cold air/fuel mixture increases the amount of vaporized fuel available.

The problem of a poor air/vaporized fuel mixture in a cold engine is accentuated when accelerating. Although the carburetor is equipped with an acceleration pump for the normal demands of an accelerating engine, its capacity is insufficient for a cold engine. The Auxiliary Acceleration Pump (AAP) is designed to send additional fuel into the acceleration nozzle in the carburetor independent of the regular acceleration pump.

The AAP itself is an integral part of the carburetor. It consists of two check valves controlled by springs and a diaphragm controlled by both a spring and engine vacuum. At constant speeds, intake manifold vacuum draws the AAP diaphragm back, enlarging the chamber and allowing gaso-

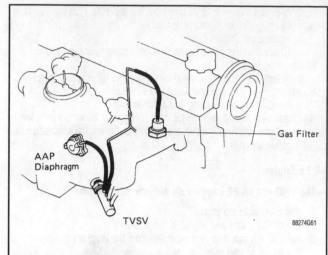

Fig. 36 Auxiliary Acceleration Pump (AAP) system components—4A-GE engine shown, others similar

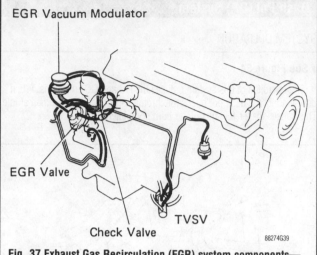

Fig. 37 Exhaust Gas Recirculation (EGR) system components—4A-F engine

line to enter. When the engine is accelerated, intake manifold vacuum drops, allowing the AAP diaphragm to be pushed back by the spring. The resultant reduction in chamber volume forces the gasoline out through the other check valve, into the acceleration nozzle.

AAP operation is governed by the same switching valve used in the choke breaker system. At cold coolant temperatures, the valve allows intake manifold vacuum to reach the AAP diaphragm. At approximately 131°F (55°C), it closes off the passage to vacuum, thus shutting off the AAP function on a fully warmed engine.

INSPECTION

The vacuum hose should be checked for leaks, kinks, or improper connection.

1. With the engine cold and idling, remove the air cleaner cap and look into the carburetor.
2. Pinch the AAP hose shut and stop the engine.
3. Release the hose; check that a spurt of gas is seen from the acceleration nozzle at the instant the vacuum hose is released.
4. Fully warm the engine to normal temperature and repeat the test.
5. No gasoline should spurt from the acceleration nozzle.
6. Reinstall the air cleaner.

Exhaust Gas Recirculation (EGR) System

SYSTEM OPERATION

The EGR system reduces oxides of nitrogen. This is accomplished by recirculating some of the exhaust gases through the EGR valve to the intake manifold, lowering peak combustion temperatures.

INSPECTION & TESTING

4A-F Engine

SYSTEM CHECK

♦ See Figure 37

1. Check and clean the filter in the EGR vacuum modulator. Use compressed air (if possible) to blow the dirt out of the filters and check the filters for contamination or damage.
2. Using a tee (3-way connector), connect a vacuum gauge to the hose between the EGR valve and the vacuum modulator.
3. Check the seating of the EGR valve by starting the engine and seeing

that it runs at a smooth idle. If the valve is not completely closed, the idle will be rough.

4. With the engine coolant temperature below 122°F (50°C), the vacuum gauge should read 0 at 2000 rpm. This indicates that the Thermal Vacuum Switching Valve (TVSV) is functioning correctly at this temperature range.
5. Warm the engine to normal operating temperature. Check the vacuum gauge and confirm low vacuum at 2000 rpm. This indicates the TVSV and the EGR vacuum modulator are working correctly in this temperature range.
6. Disconnect the vacuum hose from the **R** port on the EGR vacuum modulator and, using another piece of hose, connect the **R** port directly to the intake manifold. Check that the vacuum gauge indicates high vacuum at 2000 rpm.

➥**Port R is the lower of the two ports. As a large amount of exhaust gas enters, the engine will misfire slightly at this time.**

7. Disconnect the vacuum gauge and reconnect the vacuum hoses to their proper locations.
8. Check the EGR valve by applying vacuum directly to the valve with the engine at idle. (This may be accomplished either by bridging vacuum directly from the intake manifold or by using a hand-held vacuum pump.) The engine should falter and die as the full load of recirculated gasses enters the engine.
9. If no problem is found with this inspection, the system is OK; otherwise inspect each part.

EGR VALVE

1. Remove the EGR valve.
2. Check the valve for sticking and heavy carbon deposits. If a problem is found, replace the valve.
3. Reinstall the EGR valve with a new gasket.

EGR VACUUM MODULATOR

1. Label and disconnect the vacuum hoses from ports **P, Q,** and **R** of the EGR vacuum modulator.

➥**Port P is the single port on the one side of the modulator. Port Q and R are stacked, with port Q being on top.**

2. Plug the **P** and **R** ports with your fingers.
3. Blow air into port **Q**. Check that the air passes freely through the sides of the air filter.
4. Start the engine and maintain 2000 rpm.
5. Repeat the test above. Check that there is a strong resistance to air flow.
6. Reconnect the vacuum hoses to the proper locations.

THERMAL VACUUM SWITCHING VALVE (TVSV)

▶ **See Figure 38**

1. Drain the coolant from the radiator into a suitable container.
2. Remove the TVSV from the engine.
3. Plac the TVSV into cool water below 45° F (7°C).
4. See if air flows from pipe **J** to pipes **M** and **L**, and flows from pipe **K** to pipe **N**.
5. Place the TVSV into hot water at 63–122° F (17–50° C).
6. See if air flows from pipe **K** to pipes **N** and **L**, and flows from pipe **J** to pipe **M**.
7. Heat the TVSV to above 154° F (68° C).
8. See if air flows from pipe **K** to pipes **M** and **L**, and does not flow from pipe **J** to the other pipes.
9. Apply liquid sealer to the first few threads of the TVSV and reinstall it in the engine.
10. Fill the radiator with the correct coolant water mixture. Start the vehicle and check for leaks, top off if necessary.

➡**If a problem was found during testing, replace the TVSV.**

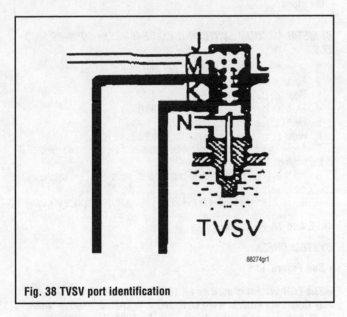

Fig. 38 TVSV port identification

4A-GE Engine

SYSTEM CHECK-1988-89 MODELS

▶ **See Figure 39**

1. Check and clean the filter in the EGR vacuum modulator. Use compressed air (if possible) to blow the dirt out of the filters and check the filters for contamination or damage.
2. Using a tee (3-way connector), connect a vacuum gauge to the hose between the EGR valve and the vacuum modulator.
3. Check the seating of the EGR valve by starting the engine and seeing that it runs at a smooth idle. If the valve is not completely closed, the idle will be rough.
4. With the engine coolant temperature below 95°F (35°C), the vacuum gauge should read 0 at 3500 rpm. This indicates that the Bimetal Vacuum Switching Valve (BVSV) is functioning correctly at this temperature range.
5. Warm the engine to normal operating temperature. Check the vacuum gauge and confirm low vacuum at 3500 rpm. Check that the vacuum gauge is at 5000 rpm at zero. This indicates the BVSV, VSV and the EGR vacuum modulator are working correctly in this temperature range.
6. Disconnect the vacuum hose from the **R** port on the EGR vacuum modulator and, using another piece of hose, connect the **R** port directly to

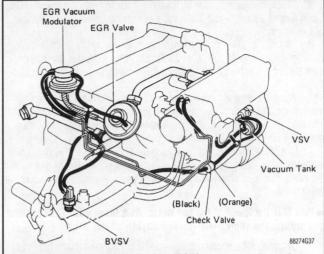

Fig. 39 Exhaust Gas Recirculation (EGR) system components— 1988–89 4A-GE engines

the intake manifold. Check that the vacuum gauge indicates high vacuum at 3500 rpm.

➡**Port R is the lower of the two ports. As a large amount of exhaust gas enters, the engine will misfire slightly at this time.**

7. Disconnect the vacuum gauge and reconnect the vacuum hoses to their proper locations.
8. Check the EGR valve by applying vacuum directly to the valve with the engine at idle. (This may be accomplished either by bridging vacuum directly from the intake manifold or by using a hand-held vacuum pump.) The engine should falter and die as the full load of recirculated gasses enters the engine.
9. If no problem is found with this inspection, the system is OK; otherwise inspect each part.

SYSTEM CHECK—1990–91 MODELS

▶ **See Figure 40**

1. Check and clean the filter in the EGR vacuum modulator. Use compressed air (if possible) to blow the dirt out of the filters and check the filters for contamination or damage.
2. Using a tee (3-way connector), connect a vacuum gauge to the hose between the EGR valve and the vacuum modulator.

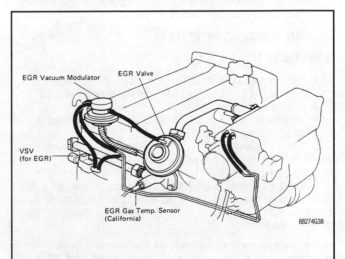

Fig. 40 Exhaust Gas Recirculation (EGR) system components— 1990–91 4A-GE engines

3. Check the seating of the EGR valve by starting the engine and seeing that it runs at a smooth idle. If the valve is not completely closed, the idle will be rough.

4. With the engine coolant temperature below 129°F (54°C), the vacuum gauge should read 0 at 2500 rpm. This indicates that the Vacuum Switching Valve (VSV) is functioning correctly at this temperature range.

5. Warm the engine to normal operating temperature. Check the vacuum gauge and confirm low vacuum at 3500 rpm. This indicates the VSV and the EGR vacuum modulator are working correctly in this temperature range.

6. Disconnect the vacuum hose from the **R** port on the EGR vacuum modulator and, using another piece of hose, connect the **R** port directly to the intake manifold. Check that the vacuum gauge indicates high vacuum at 2500 rpm.

➥Port R is the lower of the two ports. As a large amount of exhaust gas enters, the engine will misfire slightly at this time.

7. Disconnect the vacuum gauge and reconnect the vacuum hoses to their proper locations.

8. Check the EGR valve by applying vacuum directly to the valve with the engine at idle. (This may be accomplished either by bridging vacuum directly from the intake manifold or by using a hand-held vacuum pump.) The engine should falter and die as the full load of recirculated gasses enters the engine.

9. If no problem is found with this inspection, the system is OK; otherwise inspect each part.

EGR VALVE

1. Remove the EGR valve.
2. Check the valve for sticking and heavy carbon deposits. If a problem is found, replace the valve.
3. Reinstall the EGR valve with a new gasket.

EGR VACUUM MODULATOR

1. Label and disconnect the vacuum hoses from ports **P, Q**, and **R** of the EGR vacuum modulator.
2. Plug the **P** and **R** ports with your fingers.
3. Blow air into port **Q**. Check that the air passes freely through the sides of the air filter.

➥Port P is the single port on the one side of the modulator. Port Q and R are stacked, with port Q being on top.

4. Start the engine and maintain 3500 rpm on 1988–89 models; and 2500 rpm on 1990–91 models.
5. Repeat the test above. Check that there is a strong resistance to air flow.
6. Reconnect the vacuum hoses to the proper locations.

VACUUM SWITCHING VALVE (VSV)

◆ See Figure 41

1. Connect the vacuum switching valve terminals to the battery.
2. Blow air into pipe **E** and check that the air comes out of pipe **F**.
3. Disconnect the battery terminals.
4. Blow air into pipe **E** and check that air comes out of air filter. If a problem is found, replace the VSV.
5. Check for a short circuit within the valve. Using an ohmmeter, check that there is no continuity between the terminal and the VSV body. If there is continuity, replace the VSV.
6. Check for an open circuit. Using an ohmmeter, measure the resistance (ohms) between the two terminals of the valve. The resistance should be 33–39 ohms at 68°F (20°C). If the resistance is not within specifications, replace the VSV.

➥The resistance will vary slightly with temperature. It will decrease in cooler temperatures and increase with heat. Slight variations due to temperature range are not necessarily a sign of a failed valve.

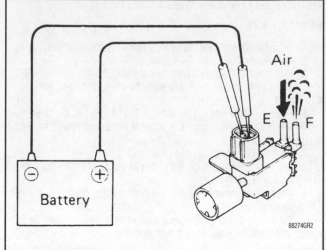

Fig. 41 With battery voltage applied, air should pass through the pipes

BI-METAL VACUUM SWITCHING VALVE (BVSV)—1988–89 MODELS

1. Drain the coolant from the radiator into a suitable container.
2. Remove the BVSV.
3. Cool the BVSV in water below 95°F (35° C).
4. Blow air into a pipe and check that the BVSV is closed.
5. Heat the valve in water above 129° F (54° C).
6. Blow air into the pipe and check that the valve is open.
7. Apply liquid sealer to the first few threads of the valve and reinstall it in the engine.
8. Fill the radiator with coolant and water mixture. Start the engine and check for leaks.
9. If a problem is found with the testing of the BVSV, replace the valve.

4AFE And 7A-FE Engines

SYSTEM CHECK

◆ See Figure 42

➥The EGR system is used on all 1988–92 models. From 1993–94 only California models were equipped with EGR. In 1995 only the 7A-FE engine was equipped with EGR. On 1996–97 models, both the 4A-FE and 7A-FE engines had EGR.

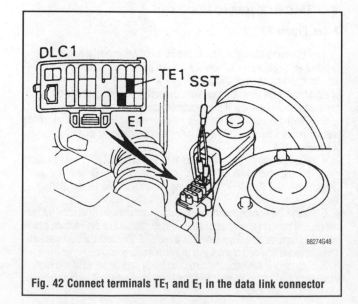

Fig. 42 Connect terminals TE₁ and E₁ in the data link connector

1. Check and clean the filter in the EGR vacuum modulator. Use compressed air (if possible) to blow the dirt out of the filters and check the filters for contamination or damage.

2. Using a tee (3-way connector), connect a vacuum gauge to the hose between the EGR valve and the vacuum modulator.

3. Check the seating of the EGR valve by starting the engine and seeing that it runs at a smooth idle. If the valve is not completely closed, the idle will be rough.

4. With the engine coolant temperature below 117°F (47°C), the vacuum gauge should read 0 at 2500 rpm.

➡ **The check connector is located near the air cleaner.**

5. On 1988–94 models perform the following:
   a. Connect terminals TE_1 and E_1 in the check connector.
   b. Inspect VSV and EGR vacuum modulator operation with hot engine. With the engine coolant temperature above 127°F (53°C), check the vacuum gauge and confirm low vacuum at 2500 rpm. This indicates the VSV and the EGR vacuum modulator are working correctly in this temperature range.

6. On 1995–97 models perform the following:
   a. Warm the engine up above 127°F (53°C). check that the vacuum gauge indicates low vacuum at 2500 rpm.
   b. Disconnect the hose from port **R** of the EGR vacuum modulator and connect port **R** directly to the intake manifold with another hose. Check the vacuum and make sure the reading is high at 2500 rpm.

➡ **Port R is the lower of the two ports. As a large amount of exhaust gas enters, the engine will misfire slightly at this time.**

7. Disconnect the vacuum gauge, SST or jumper wire and reconnect the vacuum hoses to their proper locations.

8. Check the EGR valve by applying vacuum directly to the valve with the engine at idle. (This may be accomplished either by bridging vacuum directly from the intake manifold or by using a hand-held vacuum pump.) The engine should falter and die as the full load of recirculated gasses enters the engine.

9. Remove the jumper from the check connector.

10. If no problem is found with this inspection, the system is OK; otherwise inspect each part.

EGR VALVE

1. Remove the EGR valve.
2. Check the valve for sticking and heavy carbon deposits. If a problem is found, replace the valve.
3. Reinstall the EGR valve with a new gasket.

EGR VACUUM MODULATOR

▸ See Figures 43 and 44

1. Label and disconnect the vacuum hoses from ports **P**, **Q**, and **R** of the EGR vacuum modulator.
2. Plug the **P** and **R** ports with your fingers.
3. Blow air into port **Q**. Check that the air passes freely through the sides of the air filter.
4. Start the engine and maintain 2500 rpm.
5. Repeat the test above. Check that there is a strong resistance to air flow.
6. Reconnect the vacuum hoses to the proper locations.

VACUUM SWITCHING VALVE (VSV)

▸ See Figures 45 and 46

1. Check that air flows from port **E** to the filter.
2. Connect the vacuum switching valve terminals to the battery.
3. Check that air flows from port **E** to port **F**.
4. If the VSV fails this test replace it. Any doubts perform the following test.
5. Remove the VSV.

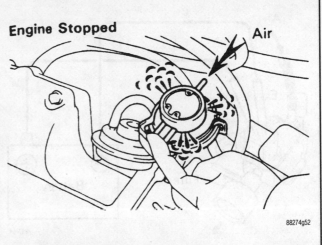

Fig. 43 Blow air into port Q and check that the air passes freely through filter of the vacuum modulator

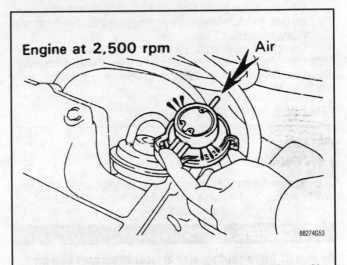

Fig. 44 Repeat the test with the engine running at 2500 rpm. Air should not pass through the filter

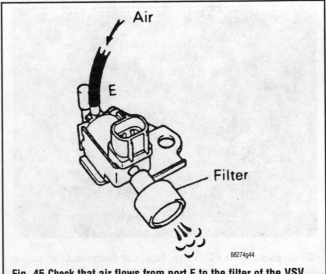

Fig. 45 Check that air flows from port E to the filter of the VSV

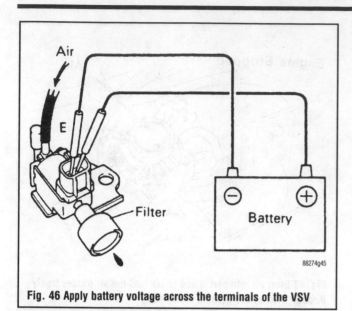

Fig. 46 Apply battery voltage across the terminals of the VSV

6. Check for a short circuit within the valve. Using an ohmmeter, check that there is no continuity between the terminals and the VSV body. If there is continuity, replace the VSV.

7. Check for an open circuit. Using an ohmmeter, measure the resistance (ohms) between the two terminals of the valve. The resistance (cold) should be 37–44 ohms. If the resistance is not within specifications, replace the VSV.

REMOVAL & INSTALLATION

EGR Valve

▶ See Figure 47

On some models the EGR valve can be unbolted, hoses labeled and removed from the vehicle. On other models the following procedure will be required.

1. Disconnect the negative battery cable.

✳✳ CAUTION

On models with an airbag, wait at least 90 seconds from the time that the ignition switch is turned to the LOCK position and the battery is disconnected before performing any further work. Refer to Section 7 for all air bag warnings.

When removing the EGR valve, label and disconnect the vacuum hoses

Remove the EGR retaining nuts . . .

. . . then lift the valve off the intake manifold

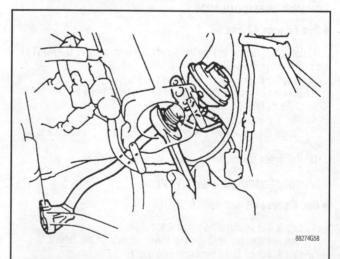

Fig. 47 On some engines, you must loosen the union from the EGR valve pipe

2. Remove the air cleaner hose and lid. Disconnect the IAT sensor wiring.
3. Disconnect the accelerator cable bracket from the throttle body.
4. Remove the throttle body from the air intake chamber.
5. Unbolt and remove the engine hanger, air intake chamber stay and EGR vacuum modulator. Discard the vacuum modulator gasket.
6. Loosen the union nut of the EGR valve. Disconnect and label the hoses attached to the valve.
7. Disconnect the EGR gas temperature sensor wiring.
8. Remove the nuts, EGR valve and pipe. Discard the gaskets.
To install:
9. Place a new gasket on the cylinder head facing the protrusion downward. Install another gasket on the EGR valve and pipe and secure with the mounting nuts. Tighten them to 9 ft. lbs. (13 Nm).

10. Connect the EGR gas temperature sensor wiring.
11. Attach the vacuum hoses to the valve in their proper locations.
12. Tighten the union nut on the EGR valve to 43 ft. lbs. (59 Nm).
13. Install the air intake chamber stay, vacuum modulator and engine hanger. Place a new gasket into position facing the protrusion downward. Tighten the assembly down with the bolt and nut to 21 ft. lbs. (28 Nm). Attach the hoses.
14. Install the throttle body with a new gasket. Tighten the bolts and nuts to 16 ft. lbs. (22 Nm). Attach all wiring and hoses removed.
15. Connect the accelerator cable bracket to the throttle body, tightening the bolts to 8 ft. lbs. (11 Nm).
16. Install the air cleaner and hose. Attach the IAT sensor connection.
17. Attach the negative battery cable.

ELECTRONIC ENGINE CONTROLS

Computerized Engine Systems

OPERATION

Engines equipped with a feedback carburetor use a simple system designed to keep the air/fuel ratio at an optimum of 14.7:1; excluding warm-up and acceleration. The carburetor is designed to run richer than it normally should. This sets up a rich limit of system operation. When a leaner operation is desired, the computer (ECM) energizes the electronic air bleed control valve (EBCV) to introduce additional air into the carburetor's main metering system and into the carburetor's primary bore. Once the air/fuel ratio is detected as being too lean by the oxygen sensor, the ECM will de-energize the EBCV and close both bleed ports. By shutting off the air, the mixture begins moving back towards the rich limit. The system is operating in the "closed loop" mode, during which it will adjust itself and react to these adjustments. On these engines, the ECM receives information from the oxygen sensor, vacuum switches and the distributor.

The Electronic Fuel Injection (EFI) system precisely controls fuel injection to match engine requirements. This in turn reduces emissions and increases driveability. The ECM receives input from various sensors to determine engine operating conditions. These sensors provide the input to the control unit which determines the amount of fuel to be injected as well as other variables such as idle speed. These inputs and their corresponding sensors include:
- Intake manifold absolute pressure—MAP or Vacuum Sensor
- Intake air temperature—Intake Air Temperature Sensor
- Coolant temperature—Water Temperature Sensor
- Engine speed—Pulse signal from the distributor
- Throttle valve opening—Throttle Position Sensor
- Exhaust oxygen content—Oxygen Sensor

Electronic Control Module (ECM)

OPERATION

The ECM receives signals from various sensors on the engine. It will then process this information and calculate the correct air/fuel mixture under all operating conditions. The ECM is a very fragile and expensive component. Always follow the precautions when servicing the electronic control system.

PRECAUTIONS

- Do not permit parts to receive a severe impact during removal or installation. Always handle all fuel injection parts with care, especially the ECM. DO NOT open the ECM cover!
- Before removing the fuel injected wiring connectors, terminals, ect., first disconnect the power by either disconnecting the negative battery cable or turning the ignition switch **OFF**.

- Do not be careless during troubleshooting as there are numerous amounts of transistor circuits; even a slight terminal contact can induce troubles.
- When inspecting during rainy days, take extra caution not to allow entry of water in or on the unit. When washing the engine compartment, prevent water from getting on the fuel injection parts and wiring connectors.

REMOVAL & INSTALLATION

▶ See Figure 48

1. Disconnect the negative battery cable.

❈❈ CAUTION

On models with an airbag, wait at least 90 seconds from the time that the ignition switch is turned to the LOCK position and the battery is disconnected before performing any further work. Refer to Section 7 for all air bag warnings.

2. Remove any necessary trim panel to gain access to the ECM floor mat bracket bolts.
3. Remove the ECM floor mat bracket bolts.
4. Locate the ECM and release the lock, then pull out the connector. Pull on the connectors only!
5. Unbolt the ECM from its mounting area.
To install:
6. Install the ECM floor mat bracket bolts.
7. Fully insert the connector, then check that it is locked.

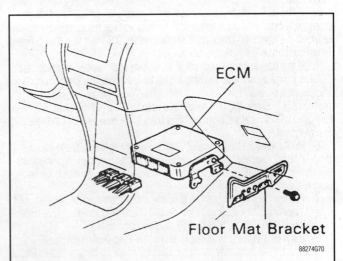

Fig. 48 Remove the floor mat bracket attached to the side of the ECM

8. Install any necessary trim panel. Reconnect the negative battery cable.

9. Start engine and check for proper operation.

Oxygen Sensor

OPERATION

The exhaust oxygen sensor or O2S, is mounted in the exhaust stream where it monitors oxygen content in the exhaust gas. The oxygen content in the exhaust is a measure of the air/fuel mixture going into the engine. The oxygen in the exhaust reacts with the oxygen sensor to produce a voltage which is read by the ECM.

There are two types of oxygen sensors used in these vehicles. They are the single wire oxygen sensor (02S) and the heated oxygen sensor (H02S). The oxygen sensor is a spark plug shaped device that is screwed into the exhaust manifold. It monitors the oxygen content of the exhaust gases and sends a voltage signal to the Electronic Control Module (ECM). The ECM monitors this voltage and, depending on the value of the received signal, issues a command to the mixture control solenoid on the carburetor to adjust for rich or lean conditions.

The heated oxygen sensor has a heating element incorporated into the sensor to aid in the warm up to the proper operating temperature and to maintain that temperature.

The proper operation of the oxygen sensor depends upon four basic conditions:

• Good electrical connections. Since the sensor generates low currents, good clean electrical connections at the sensor are a must.

• Outside air supply. Air must circulate to the internal portion of the sensor. When servicing the sensor, do not restrict the air passages.

• Proper operating temperatures. The ECM will not recognize the sensor's signals until the sensor reaches approximately 600°F (316°C).

• Non-leaded fuel. The use of leaded gasoline will damage the sensor very quickly.

TESTING

Single Wire Sensor

1. Start the engine and bring it to normal operating temperature, then run the engine above 1200 rpm for two minutes.

2. Backprobe with a high impedance averaging voltmeter (set to the DC voltage scale) between the oxygen sensor (02S) and battery ground.

3. Verify that the 02S voltage fluctuates rapidly between 0.40–0.60 volts.

4. If the 02S voltage is stabilized at the middle of the specified range (approximately 0.45–0.55 volts) or if the 02S voltage fluctuates very slowly between the specified range (02S signal crosses 0.5 volts less than 5 times in ten seconds), the 02S may be faulty.

5. If the 02S voltage stabilizes at either end of the specified range, the ECM is probably not able to compensate for a mechanical problem such as a vacuum leak or a faulty pressure regulator. These types of mechanical problems will cause the 02S to sense a constant lean or constant rich mixture. The mechanical problem will first have to be repaired and then the 02S test repeated.

6. Pull a vacuum hose located after the throttle plate. Voltage should drop to approximately 0.12 volts (while still fluctuating rapidly). This tests the ability of the 02S to detect a lean mixture condition. Reattach the vacuum hose.

7. Richen the mixture using a propane enrichment tool. Voltage should rise to approximately 0.90 volts (while still fluctuating rapidly). This tests the ability of the 02S to detect a rich mixture condition.

8. If the 02S voltage is above or below the specified range, the 02S and/or the 02S wiring may be faulty. Check the wiring for any breaks, repair as necessary and repeat the test.

Heated Oxygen Sensor

1. Start the engine and bring it to normal operating temperature, then run the engine above 1200 rpm for two minutes.

2. Turn the ignition **OFF** disengage the H02S harness connector.

3. Connect a test light between harness terminals A and B. With the ignition switch **ON** and the engine off, verify that the test light is lit. If the test light is not lit, either the supply voltage to the H02S heater or the ground circuit of the H02S heater is faulty. Check the H02S wiring and the fuse.

4. Next, connect a high impedance ohmmeter between the H02S terminals of the heating element and verify that the resistance is 11.0–16.0 ohms.

5. If the H02S heater resistance is not as specified, the H02S may be faulty.

6. Start the engine and bring it to normal operating temperature, then run the engine above 1200 rpm for two minutes.

7. Backprobe with a high impedance averaging voltmeter (set to the DC voltage scale) between the oxygen sensor (02S) signal wire and battery ground.

8. Verify that the 02S voltage fluctuates rapidly between 0.40–0.60 volts.

9. If the 02S voltage is stabilized at the middle of the specified range (approximately 0.45–0.55 volts) or if the 02S voltage fluctuates very slowly between the specified range (02S signal crosses 0.5 volts less than 5 times in ten seconds), the 02S may be faulty.

10. If the 02S voltage stabilizes at either end of the specified range, the ECM is probably not able to compensate for a mechanical problem such as a vacuum leak or a faulty fuel pressure regulator. These types of mechanical problems will cause the 02S to sense a constant lean or constant rich mixture. The mechanical problem will first have to be repaired and then the 02S test repeated.

11. Pull a vacuum hose located after the throttle plate. Voltage should drop to approximately 0.12 volts (while still fluctuating rapidly). This tests the ability of the 02S to detect a lean mixture condition. Reattach the vacuum hose.

12. Richen the mixture using a propane enrichment tool. Voltage should rise to approximately 0.90 volts (while still fluctuating rapidly). This tests the ability of the 02S to detect a rich mixture condition.

13. If the 02S voltage is above or below the specified range, the 02S and/or the 02S wiring may be faulty. Check the wiring for any breaks, repair as necessary and repeat the test.

REMOVAL & INSTALLATION

The oxygen sensor can be located in several places. Either in the exhaust manifold, front pipe or catalytic converter.

✳✳ WARNING

Care should be used during the removal of the oxygen sensor. Both the sensor and its wire can be easily damaged.

1. The best condition in which to remove the sensor is when the engine is moderately warm. This is generally achieved after two to five minutes (depending on outside temperature) of running after a cold start. The exhaust manifold has developed enough heat to expand and make the removal easier but is not so hot that it has become untouchable. Wearing heat resistant gloves is highly recommended during this repair.

2. With the ignition **OFF**, unplug the connector for the sensor.

3. Remove the two sensor attaching bolts.

4. Remove the oxygen sensor from its mounting place and discard the gasket.

To install:

5. During and after the removal, use great care to protect the tip of the sensor if it is to be reused. Do not allow it to come in contact with fluids or dirt. Do not attempt to clean it or wash it.

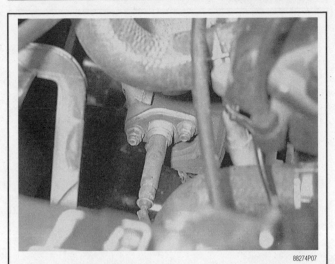

The oxygen sensor is secured to the exhaust manifold or exhaust pipe by two bolts

88274P07

. . . then separate the wiring

88274P10

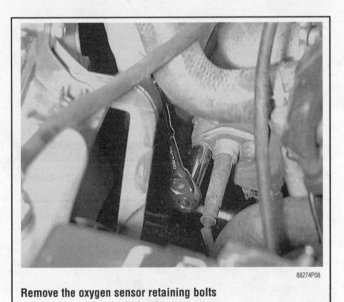

Remove the oxygen sensor retaining bolts

88274P08

Don't forget to discard the old gasket

88274P11

6. Apply a coat of anti-seize compound to the bolt threads but DO NOT allow any to get on the tip of the sensor.
7. Install and secure the sensor. Remember to install a new gasket.
8. Reconnect the electrical wiring and insure a clean, tight connection.

Electronic Air Bleed Control Valve (EBCV)

TESTING

♦ See Figures 49 and 50

➡Used on 4A-F engines.

1. Check for a short circuit. Using an ohmmeter, check that there is no continuity between the positive (+) terminal and the EBCV body. If there is continuity, replace the EBCV.
2. Check for an open circuit. Using an ohmmeter, measure the resistance between the two terminals. The resistance should be between 11–13 ohms at 68°F (20°C). If the resistance is not within specification, replace the EBCV. Remember that the resistance will vary slightly with temperature. Resistance (ohms) will decrease as the temperature drops.

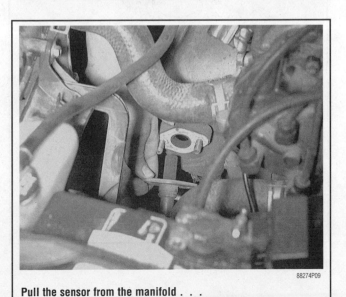

Pull the sensor from the manifold . . .

88274P09

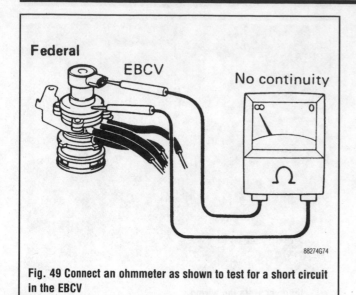

Fig. 49 Connect an ohmmeter as shown to test for a short circuit in the EBCV

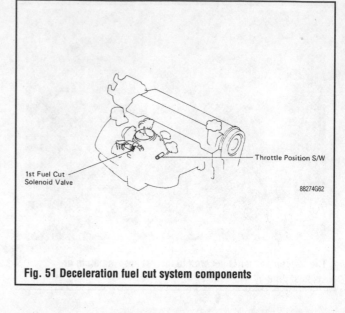

Fig. 51 Deceleration fuel cut system components

TESTING

◗ See Figures 52 and 53

1. Connect a tachometer to the engine.
2. Start the engine and check that it runs normally.
3. Disconnect the throttle position switch terminal.
4. Gradually increase the engine speed to 2300 rpm. Check that the engine slightly fluctuates.

✳✳ WARNING

Perform this procedure quickly to avoid overheating the catalytic converter.

5. Reconnect the throttle position switch terminal. Again gradually increase the engine speed to 2300 rpm. and check that the engine operation is normal.

Fig. 50 Measure the resistance between the terminals of the EBCV

REMOVAL & INSTALLATION

Replacing the EBCV simply requires labeling and unplugging the vacuum and/or electrical connections, then unbolting the valve. Inspect the vacuum hose over its entire length for any signs of cracking or splitting. The slightest leak can cause improper operation.

Deceleration Fuel Cut System

OPERATION

◗ See Figure 51

➡This system only applies to the 4A-F engine.

This system cuts off part of the fuel in the slow circuit of the carburetor to prevent overheating and afterburning of the exhaust system.

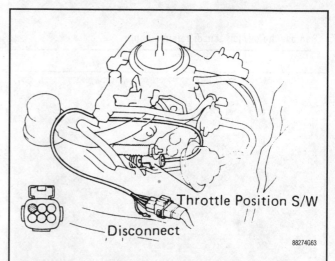

Fig. 52 Disconnect the throttle position switch wire from the harness

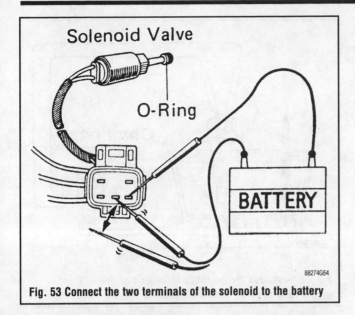

Fig. 53 Connect the two terminals of the solenoid to the battery

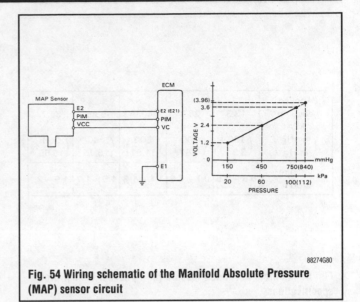

Fig. 54 Wiring schematic of the Manifold Absolute Pressure (MAP) sensor circuit

6. With the engine at idle unplug the solenoid valve. Connect two terminals and the battery terminals as shown.

7. Check for a click in the solenoid valve when the battery is connected and disconnected.

8. Check the O-ring for damages.

9. Reinstall the valves and reattach the wiring.

REMOVAL & INSTALLATION

Fuel Cut Solenoid Valve

➡This solenoid valve is only applicable to the 4A-F carbureted engines.

1. Disconnect the solenoid valve wiring.

2. Carefully unscrew the valve from the carburetor. Discard the old O-ring.

3. Place a new O-ring on the end of the valve and securely tighten the unit into the carburetor.

Manifold Absolute Pressure (MAP) Sensor

OPERATION

This sensor advises the ECM of pressure changes in the intake manifold. It consists of a semi-conductor pressure converting element which converts a pressure change into an electrical signal. The ECM sends a reference signal to the MAP sensor; the change in air pressure changes the resistance within the sensor. The ECM reads the change from its reference voltage and signals its systems to react accordingly.

TESTING

◆ See Figures 54, 55, 56 and 57

➡Use only a 10 megaohm digital multi-meter when testing. The use of any other type of equipment may damage the ECM and other components.

1. Unplug the vacuum sensor connector.

2. Turn the ignition switch ON.

3. Using a voltmeter, measure the voltage between terminals VCC and E2 of the vacuum sensor connector. It should be between 4–6 volts.

4. Turn the ignition switch OFF.

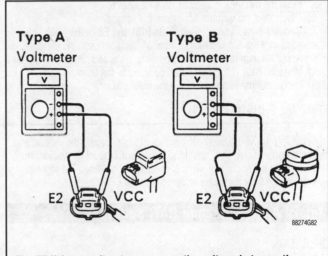

Fig. 55 Using a voltmeter, measure the voltage between the MAP connector terminals

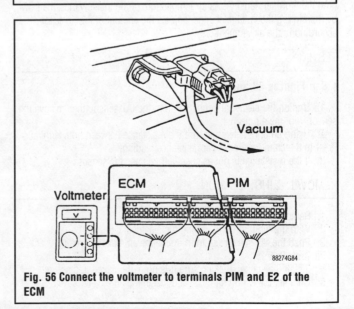

Fig. 56 Connect the voltmeter to terminals PIM and E2 of the ECM

Applied Vacuum kPa $\left(\begin{smallmatrix}mmHg\\in.Hg\end{smallmatrix}\right)$	13.3 $\left(\begin{smallmatrix}100\\3.94\end{smallmatrix}\right)$	26.7 $\left(\begin{smallmatrix}200\\7.87\end{smallmatrix}\right)$	40.0 $\left(\begin{smallmatrix}300\\11.81\end{smallmatrix}\right)$	53.5 $\left(\begin{smallmatrix}400\\15.75\end{smallmatrix}\right)$	66.7 $\left(\begin{smallmatrix}500\\19.69\end{smallmatrix}\right)$
Voltage drop V	0.3 – 0.5	0.7 – 0.9	1.1 – 1.3	1.5 – 1.7	1.9 – 2.1

88274G83

Fig. 57 Manifold Absolute Pressure (MAP) sensor voltage drop specifications[8]

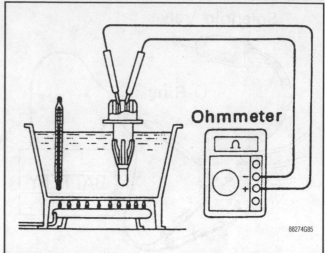

Fig. 58 Submerge the sensor tip in water and check for the proper resistance between the terminals

5. Push the electrical connector back into place.
6. Disconnect the vacuum hose from the sensor.
7. Connect the voltmeter to terminals **PIM** and **E2** of the ECM. Measure and record the output voltage under ambient atmospheric pressure.
8. Apply vacuum to the sensor according to the segments show on the chart. Measure each voltage drop and compare to the chart.
9. Reconnect the vacuum hose to the MAP sensor.

REMOVAL & INSTALLATION

Replacing the MAP sensor simply requires unplugging the vacuum and electrical connections, then unbolting the sensor. Inspect the vacuum hose over its entire length for any signs of cracking or splitting. The slightest leak can cause false messages to be send to the ECM.

Intake Air Temperature (IAT) Sensor

OPERATION

The IAT sensor advises the ECM of changes in intake air temperature (and therefore air density). As air temperature of the intake varies, the ECM, by monitoring the voltage change, adjusts the amount of fuel injection according to the air temperature.

TESTING

▶ **See Figures 58 and 59**

1. Unplug the electrical connector from the IAT sensor, then remove the sensor from the air cleaner.
2. Using an ohmmeter, measure the resistance between both terminals. Refer to the chart for the proper resistance reading.
3. If the resistance is not as specified, replace the sensor.

REMOVAL & INSTALLATION

1. Remove the air cleaner cover.
2. With the ignition **OFF**, unplug the electrical connector.
3. Push the IAT sensor out from inside the air cleaner housing.
To install:
4. Install the sensor, making sure it is properly placed and secure.
5. Connect the wiring harness, and install the air cleaner cover.

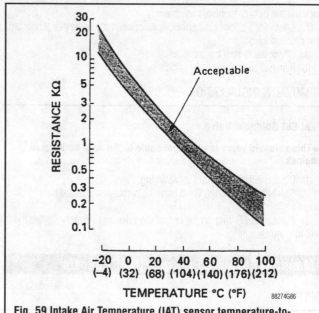

Fig. 59 Intake Air Temperature (IAT) sensor temperature-to-resistance graph

Water Temperature Sensor

OPERATION

The water temperature sensor's function is to advise the ECM of changes in engine temperature by monitoring the changes in coolant temperature. The sensor must be handled carefully during removal. It can be damaged (thereby affecting engine performance) by impact.

TESTING

▶ **See Figures 60 and 61**

1. Unplug the electrical connector from the sensor.
2. Using an ohmmeter, measure the resistance between both terminals. Refer to the chart for the proper resistance reading.
3. If the resistance is not as specified, replace the sensor.

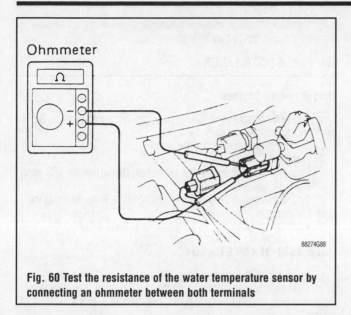

Fig. 60 Test the resistance of the water temperature sensor by connecting an ohmmeter between both terminals

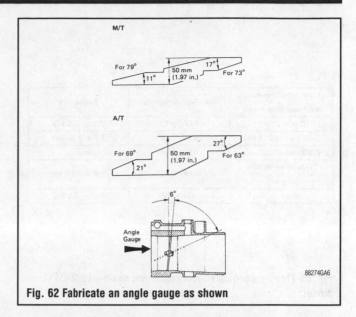

Fig. 62 Fabricate an angle gauge as shown

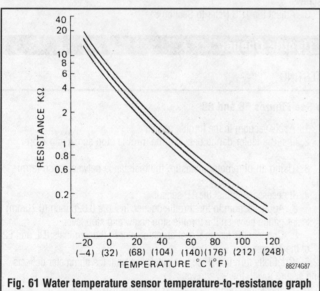

Fig. 61 Water temperature sensor temperature-to-resistance graph

REMOVAL & INSTALLATION

➡ **Perform this procedure only on a cold engine.**

1. Drain the cooling system as necessary.
2. With the ignition **OFF**, unplug the electrical connector to the sensor.
3. Using the proper sized wrench, carefully unscrew the sensor from the engine.

To install:

4. Coat the threads of the sensor with a sealant. Install the sensor and tighten it to 18 ft. lbs. (24 Nm).
5. Plug the electrical connector into the sensor.
6. Refill the coolant to the proper level. Road test the vehicle for proper operation.

Throttle Position (TP) Sensor

TESTING

▶ **See Figures 62 thru 67**

1. Unplug the TP sensor connector.
2. Insert a thickness gauge between the throttle stop screw and the stop lever.

Throttle valve opening angle		Continuity		
M/T	A/T	IDL—E2	PSW—E2	IDL—PSW
73° from vertical	63° from vertical	No continuity	No continuity	No continuity
79° from vertical	69° from vertical	No continuity	Continuity	No continuity
Less than 7.5° from vertical		Continuity	No continuity	No continuity

Fig. 63 Check that the throttle position sensor performs as indicated—4A-FE engines

Clearance between lever and stop screw	Between terminals	Resistance
0 mm (0 in.)	VTA — E2	0.2 — 0.8 kΩ
0.35 mm (0.0138 in.)	IDL — E2	Less than 2.3 kΩ
0.59 mm (0.0232 in.)	IDL — E2	Infinity
Throttle valve fully open	VTA — E2	3.3 — 10 kΩ
—	VC — E2	3 — 7 kΩ

Fig. 64 Check for resistance between the terminals indicated—4A-GE engines

Clearance between lever and stop screw	Between terminals	Resistance
0 mm (0 in.)	VTA — E2	0.2 — 6.0 kΩ
0.40 mm (0.016 in.)	IDL — E2	2.3 kΩ or less
0.90 mm (0.035 in.)	IDL — E2	Infinity
Throttle valve fully open	VTA — E2	3.3 — 10.0 kΩ
—	VC — E2	4.0 — 8.5 kΩ

88274GA8

Fig. 65 Throttle position sensor resistance chart—1992–94 models

Clearance between lever and stop screw	Between terminals	Resistance
0 mm (0 in.)	VTA — E2	0.2 — 5.7 kΩ
0.40 mm (0.016 in.)	IDL — E2	2.3 kΩ or less
0.90 mm (0.035 in.)	IDL — E2	Infinity
Throttle valve fully open	VTA — E2	2.0 — 10.2 kΩ
—	VC — E2	2.5 — 5.9 kΩ

88274GB2

Fig. 66 The throttle position sensor should perform as indicated—1995–97 models

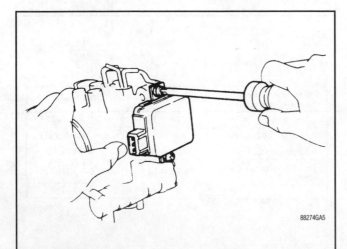

Fig. 67 If necessary, loosen the screws and adjust the throttle position sensor

3. Using an ohmmeter, measure the resistance between each terminal. Compare the readings to the chart.

REMOVAL & INSTALLATION

1988–91 4A-FE Engines

1. Secure the throttle valve opening at approximately 45 degrees. Be careful not to damage any components.
2. Remove the two screws and the sensor.
   To install:
3. Place the TPS over the throttle valve shaft. Do not turn the TPS when it is being installed.
4. Temporarily install the two screws. Remove the device securing the throttle valve angle.
5. Adjust the throttle position sensor (refer to Section 5).

Except 1988–91 4A-FE Engines

1. Remove the two screws and the TPS.
2. To install, place the sensor on the throttle body. Turn the sensor clockwise until the ohmmeter defects, then secure with the two screws.
3. Adjust the TPS (refer to Section 5).

Throttle Opener

TESTING

♦ **See Figures 68 and 69**

1. Apply vacuum to the throttle opener.
2. Insert a feeler gauge between the throttle stop screw and stop lever.
3. Using an ohmmeter, measure the resistance between each terminal.
4. If necessary, adjust the TP sensor.
   a. Apply vacuum to the throttle opener. Insert a 0.028 inch (0.70mm) feeler gauge between the throttle stop screw and stop lever.
   b. Connect the test probe of an ohmmeter to the terminals IDL and E2 of the TP sensor.
5. Gradually turn the TP sensor clockwise until the ohmmeter deflects, and secure it with the set screws.
6. Recheck the continuity between terminals IDL and E2.

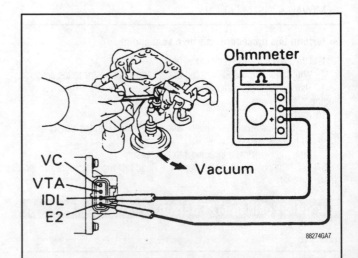

Fig. 68 Check for resistance between these two terminals of the throttle position sensor

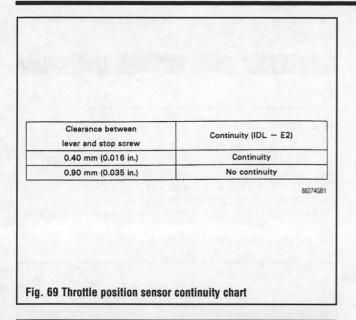

Clearance between lever and stop screw	Continuity (IDL — E2)
0.40 mm (0.016 in.)	Continuity
0.90 mm (0.035 in.)	No continuity

88274GB1

Fig. 69 Throttle position sensor continuity chart

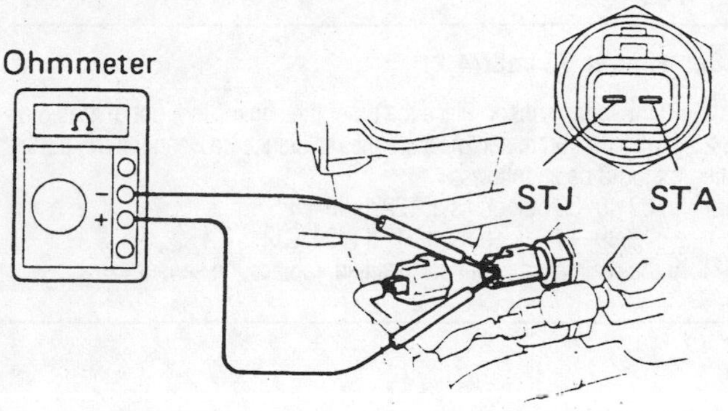

Cold Start Injector Time Switch

OPERATION

The start injector time switch controls the length of time the injector will stay on depending on engine temperature.

TESTING

▶ **See Figures 70, 71 and 72**

1. Using an ohmmeter, measure the resistance between each of the terminals. They should be as follows:
   a. Terminals **STA** and **STJ**—20–40 ohms below 86°F (30°C) or 40–60 ohms when above 104°F (40°C)
   b. Terminal **STA** and ground—20–80 ohms.
2. If the resistance is not as specified, replace the switch.

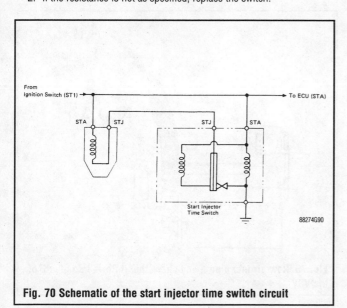

Fig. 70 Schematic of the start injector time switch circuit

Ohmmeter

Fig. 71 Measure the resistance between the terminals of the time switch

Between terminals	Resistance (Ω)	Coolant temp.
STA – STJ	20 – 40	Below 30°C (86°F)
	40 – 60	Above 40°C (104°F)
STA – Ground	20 – 80	—

88274G92

Fig. 72 The time switch should exhibit the values shown

REMOVAL & INSTALLATION

➡**Perform this procedure only on a cold engine.**

1. Drain the cooling system as necessary.
2. With the ignition **OFF**, unplug the electrical connector to the switch.
3. Using the proper sized wrench, carefully unscrew the switch from the engine.

To install:

4. Coat the threads of the switch with a sealant and install it.
5. Plug the electrical connector into the switch.
6. Refill the coolant to the proper level. Road test the vehicle for proper operation.

EGR Gas Temperature Sensor

TESTING

▶ **See Figures 73 and 74**

1. Remove the sensor. Place the tip of the sensor in a pot of heated oil.
2. Using an ohmmeter, measure the resistance between the two terminals. It should be as follows:
   a. 69.40–88.50k ohms at 122°F(50°C)
   b. 11.89–14.37k ohms at 212°F(100°C)
3. If the resistance is not as specified, replace the sensor.

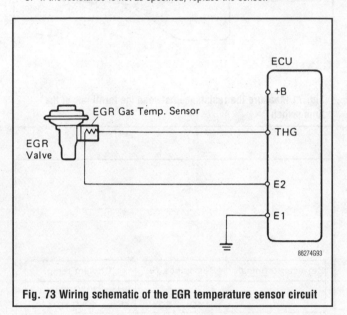

Fig. 73 Wiring schematic of the EGR temperature sensor circuit

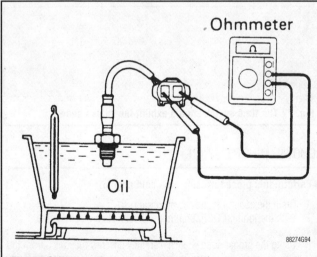

Fig. 74 Submerge the sensor tip in oil and measure the resistance of the sensor

REMOVAL & INSTALLATION

1. With the ignition **OFF**, unplug the electrical connector to the sensor.
2. Using the proper sized wrench, carefully unscrew the sensor from the engine.
   To install:
3. Install the sensor.
4. Plug the electrical connector into the sensor.

5. Refill the coolant to the proper level. Road test the vehicle for proper operation.

Idle-Up System

TESTING

▶ **See Figures 75 and 76**

1. Make sure all accessories are off.
2. Test the VSV using a voltmeter, check the meter indicates battery voltage during cranking and fir ten seconds after starting.
3. If it is not as specified, replace the VSV.
4. Check that air does not blow from pipe E to F.
5. Apply battery voltage across the terminals. Check that air flows from pipe E to F.
6. If operation is not as specified, replace the VSV.

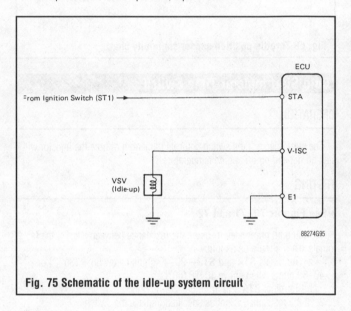

Fig. 75 Schematic of the idle-up system circuit

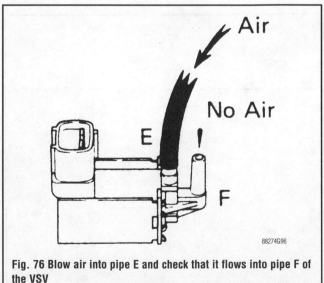

Fig. 76 Blow air into pipe E and check that it flows into pipe F of the VSV

REMOVAL & INSTALLATION

Replacing the various vacuum switches simply requires unplugging the vacuum and/or electrical connections, then unbolting the switch.

Inspect the vacuum hose over its entire length for any signs of cracking or splitting. The slightest leak can cause improper operation.

Knock Sensor

TESTING

1. Disconnect the wiring from the knock sensor.
2. Using tool 09816–30010 or an equivalent socket, remove the knock sensor from the vehicle.
3. Using an ohmmeter, check that there is no continuity between the terminal and the body.
4. If there is continuity, replace the sensor.
5. Install the knock sensor with the special tool, tighten securely to 33 ft. lbs. (44 Nm).
6. Connect the sensor wiring.

REMOVAL & INSTALLATION

▶ **See Figure 77**

1. Disconnect the wiring from the knock sensor.
2. Using tool, 09816–30010 or an equivalent socket, remove the knock sensor from the vehicle.
3. Inspect the vacuum hose over its entire length for any signs of cracking or splitting. The slightest leak can cause improper operation.

To install:
4. Install the knock sensor with the special tool, tighten securely to 33 ft. lbs. (44 Nm).
5. Connect the sensor wiring.

Inspect the vacuum hose over its entire length for any signs of cracking or splitting. The slightest leak can cause improper operation.

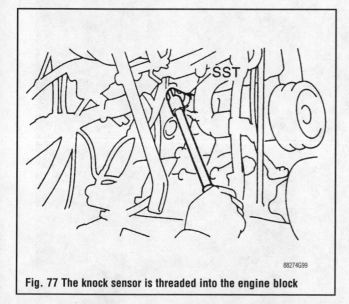

Fig. 77 The knock sensor is threaded into the engine block

Idle Air Control (IAC) Valve

TESTING

▶ **See Figure 78**

1. Remove the throttle body as described in Section 5.
2. Remove the IAC valve.

3. Connect the positive lead from the battery to terminal B+ and the negative lead to terminal RSC. Check that the valve is closed.
4. Connect the positive lead from the battery to terminal B+ and the negative lead to terminal RSO, then check that the valve is open.
5. If the valve is not properly functioning during testing, then replace the valve.

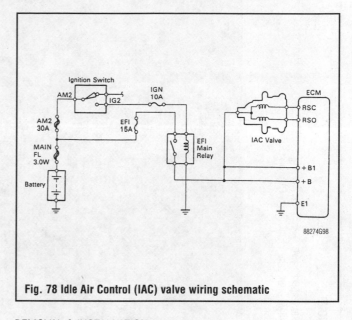

Fig. 78 Idle Air Control (IAC) valve wiring schematic

REMOVAL & INSTALLATION

▶ **See Figure 79**

1. Remove the throttle body as described in Section 5.
2. Remove the 4 screws retaining the IAC valve and pull the unit from the engine. Discard the old gasket.
To install:
3. Place a new gasket into position on the throttle body.
4. Position the IAC valve and secure the retaining screws.
5. Install the throttle body as described in Section 5.

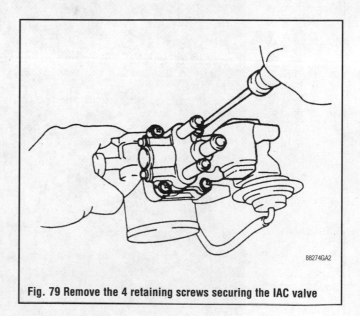

Fig. 79 Remove the 4 retaining screws securing the IAC valve

COMPONENT LOCATIONS

EMISSION COMPONENT LOCATIONS

1. Exhaust Gas Recirculation (EGR) valve
2. Exhaust Gas Recirculation (EGR) vacuum modulator
3. Electronic Bleed Control Valve (EBCV)
4. Vacuum check valve
5. Positive Crankcase Ventilation (PCV) valve
6. O_2 sensor

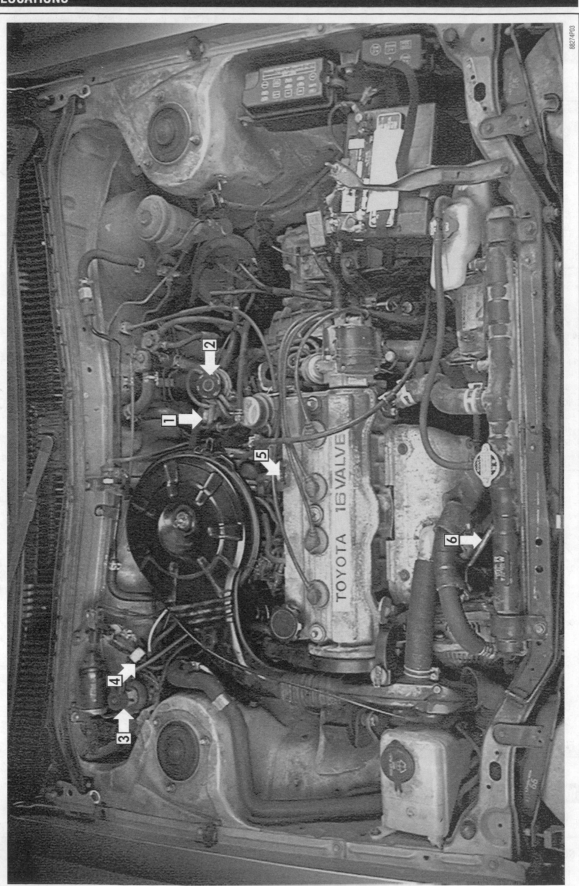

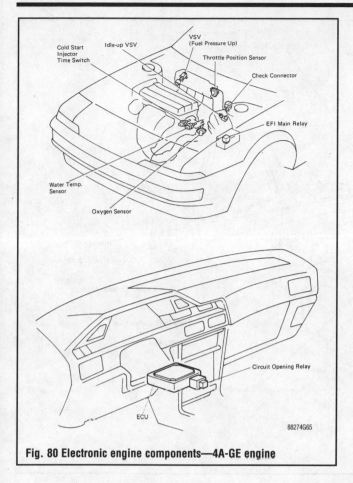

Fig. 80 Electronic engine components—4A-GE engine

88274G65

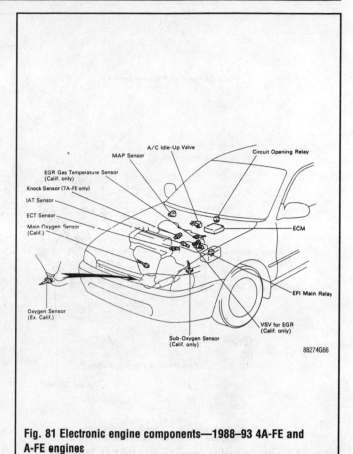

Fig. 81 Electronic engine components—1988–93 4A-FE and A-FE engines

88274G66

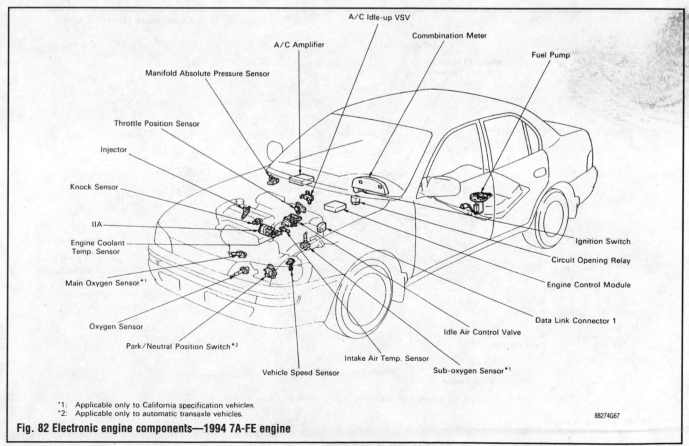

*1: Applicable only to California specification vehicles
*2: Applicable only to automatic transaxle vehicles.

88274G67

Fig. 82 Electronic engine components—1994 7A-FE engine

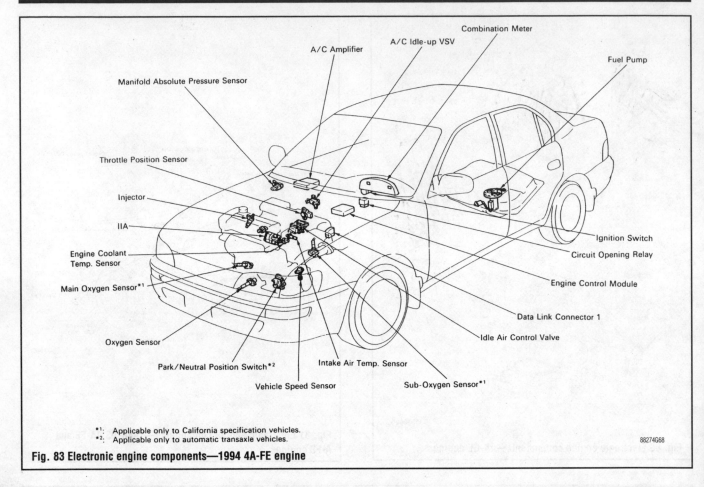

Fig. 83 Electronic engine components—1994 4A-FE engine

*1: Applicable only to California specification vehicles.
*2: Applicable only to automatic transaxle vehicles.

88274G68

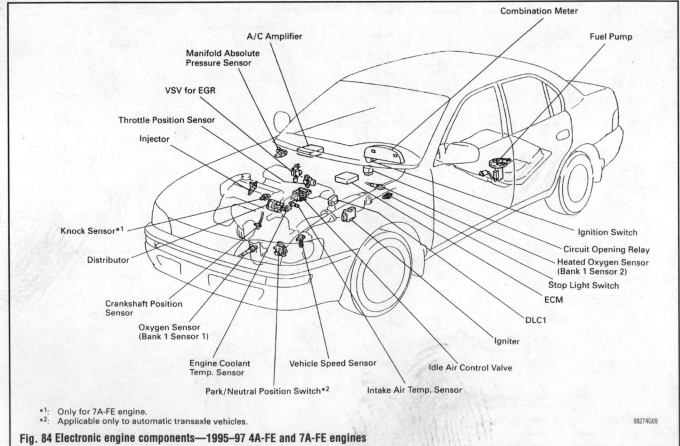

*1: Only for 7A-FE engine.
*2: Applicable only to automatic transaxle vehicles.

88274G69

Fig. 84 Electronic engine components—1995–97 4A-FE and 7A-FE engines

TROUBLE CODES

General Information

The ECM contains a built-in, self-diagnosis system which detects troubles within the engine signal network. Once a malfunction is detected, the Malfunction Indicator Lamp (MIL), located on the instrument panel, will light.

By analyzing various signals, the ECM detects system malfunctions related to the operating sensors. The ECM stores the failure code associated with the detected failure until the diagnosis system is cleared.

The MIL on the instrument panel informs the driver that a malfunction has been detected. The light will go out automatically once the malfunction has been cleared.

DATA LINK CONNECTOR (DLC)

◆ **See Figures 85 and 86**

The DLC1 is located in the engine compartment. The DLC3 is located in the interior of the vehicle, under the driver's side dash.

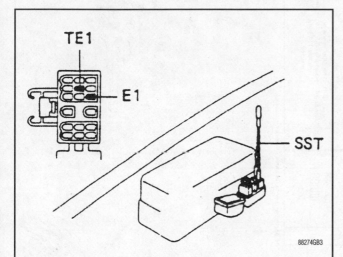

Fig. 85 The DLC1 is located in the engine compartment, on the side of the fuse block

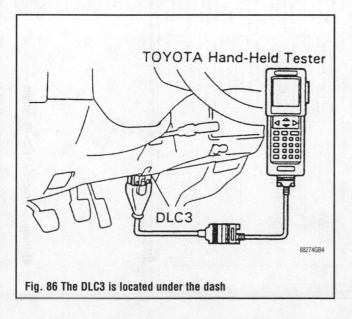

Fig. 86 The DLC3 is located under the dash

Reading Codes

1989–95 MODELS

1. Make sure the battery voltage is at least 11 volts.
2. Make sure the throttle valve is fully closed.
3. Place the gear shift lever in Neutral. Turn all accessories off.
4. The engine should be at normal operating temperature.
5. Using a jumper wire, connect terminals TE1 and E1 of the Data Link Connector 1 (DLC1).
6. Turn the ignition switch **ON**, but do not start the engine. Read the diagnostic code by the counting the number of flashes of the malfunction indicator lamp.
7. Codes will flash in numerical order. If no faults are stored, the lamp flashes continuously every ½ second. This is sometimes called the Normal or System Clear signal.
8. After the diagnosis check, turn the ignition **OFF** and remove the jumper wire.
9. Compare the codes found to the applicable diagnostic code chart. If necessary, refer to the individual component tests in this section. If the component tests are OK, test the wire harness and connectors for shorts, opens and poor connections.

1996–97 MODELS

➡ **These models require the use of the Toyota's hand held scan tool or an equivalent OBD II compliant scan tool.**

1. Prepare the scan tool according to the manufacturers instructions.
2. Connect the OBD II scan tool, to the DLC3 under the instrument panel.

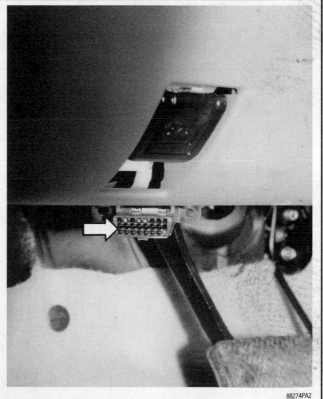

The DLC3 on the 1996–97 models is located on the drivers side under the dash

➡When the diagnosis system is switched from the normal mode to the check mode, it erases all Diagnostic Trouble Codes (DTC) and freeze frame data recorded. Before switching modes, always check the DTC and freeze frame data and write them down.

3. Turn the ignition switch to the **ON** and switch the OBD II scan tool switch on.

4. Use the OBD II scan tool to check the DTC and freeze frame data. Write them down.

5. Compare the codes found to the applicable diagnostic code chart. If necessary, refer to the individual component tests in this section. If the component tests are OK, test the wire harness and connectors for shorts, opens and poor connections.

Clearing Trouble Codes

After repair of the circuit, the diagnostic code(s) must be removed from the ECM memory. With the ignition turned **OFF**, remove the 15 amp EFI fuse for 30 seconds or more. Once the time period has been observed, reinstall the fuse and check for normal code output.

If the diagnostic code is not erased, it will be retained by the ECM and appear along with a new code in event of future trouble.

Cancellation of the trouble code can also be accomplished by disconnecting the negative battery cable. However, disconnecting the battery cable will erase the other memory systems including the clock and radio settings. If this method is used, always reset these components once the trouble code has been erased.

DIAGNOSTIC CODES

Code No.	Number of blinks "CHECK ENGINE"	System	Diagnosis	Trouble area
–		Normal	This appears when none of the other codes are identified.	–
12		RPM Signal	• No "NE" signal to ECU within 2 seconds after the engine is cranked. • No "G" signal to ECU 2 times in succession when engine speed is between 500 rpm and 4000 rpm.	• Distributor circuit • Distributor • Starter signal circuit • ECU
13		RPM Signal	No "NE" signal to ECU when the engine speed is above 1500 rpm	• Distributor circuit • Distributor • ECU
14		Ignition Signal	No "IGF" signal to ECU 4 times in succession.	• Igniter circuit • Igniter • ECU
21		Oxygen Sensor Signal/Main Oxygen Sensor Signal	During air-fuel ratio feedback correction, voltage output from the oxygen sensor does not exceed a set value on the lean side and the rich side continuously for a certain period (OX1).	• Oxygen sensor circuit • Oxygen sensor • ECU
22		Oxygen Sensor Heater Circuit	Open or short circuit in oxygen sensor heater signal (HT).	• Oxygen sensor heater circuit • Oxygen sensor • ECU
22		Water Temp. Sensor Signal	Open or short circuit in water temp. sensor signal (THW).	• Water temp. sensor circuit • Water temp. sensor • ECU
24		Intake Air Temp. Sensor Signal	Open or short circuit in intake air temp. sensor signal (THA).	• Intake air temp. sensor circuit • Intake air temp. sensor • ECU
*1 25		Air-Fuel Ratio Lean Malfunction	(1) When air-fuel ratio feedback correction value or adaptive control value continues at the upper (lean) or lower (rich) limit for a certain period of time or adaptive control value is not renewed for a certain period of time.	• Injector circuit • Injector • Fuel line pressure • Oxygen sensor • Air flow meter • Water temp. sensor • ECU
*1 26		Air-Fuel Ratio Rich Malfunction	(2) When marked variation is detected in engine revolutions for each cylinder during idle switch on and feedback condition. (3) Open or short circuit in oxygen sensor signal (OXI).	• Injector circuit • Injector • Fuel line pressure • Cold start injector circuit • Cold start injector • Oxygen sensor • Air flow meter • Water temp. sensor • ECU

DIAGNOSTIC CODES (Cont'd)

Code No.	Number of blinks "CHECK ENGINE"	System	Diagnosis	Trouble area
*2 27		Sub-Oxygen Sensor Signal	Open or short circuit in sub-oxygen sensor signal (OX2).	• Sub-oxygen sensor circuit • Sub-oxygen sensor • ECU
31		Air Flow Meter Signal	Short circuit between VC and VB, VC and E2, or VS and VC.	• Air flow meter circuit • Air flow meter • ECU
41		Throttle Position Sensor Signal	Open or short circuit in throttle position sensor signal (VTA).	• Throttle position sensor circuit • Throttle position sensor • ECU
42		Vehicle Speed Sensor Signal	No "SPD" signal for 8 seconds when engine speed is between 2,500 rpm and 4,500 rpm	• Vehicle speed sensor circuit • Vehicle speed sensor • ECU
43		Starter Signal	No "STA" signal to ECU until engine speed reaches 800 rpm with vehicle not moving.	• Starter signal circuit • Ignition switch, main relay circuit • ECU
52		Knock Sensor Signal	Open or short circuit in knock sensor signal (KNK).	• Knock sensor circuit • Knock sensor • ECU
53		Knock Control Signal in ECU	Knock control in ECU faulty.	• ECU
*2 71		EGR System Malfunction	• EGR gas temp. below predetermined level during EGR operation (THG). • Open circuit in EGR gas temp. sensor signal (THG).	• EGR system (EGR valve, EGR hose etc.) • EGR gas temp. sensor circuit • EGR gas temp. sensor • VSV for EGR • VSV for EGR circuit • ECU
51		Switch Condition Signal	No "IDL" signal or "A/C" signal to ECU, with the check terminals TE1 and E1 connected.	• A/C switch circuit • A/C switch • A/C amplifire • Throttle position sensor circuit • Throttle position sensor • ECU

*2 Applicable only to California specification vehicles.

*1 No. (1) and (2) in the diagnostic contents of codes No. 25 and 26 apply to California specification vehicles only, while (3) applies to all models.

Fig. 87 Diagnostic codes—1988–90 models

88274GB5

88274G86

DIAGNOSTIC CODES

Code No.	System	Number of blinks "CHECK ENGINE" Warning Light	*1 "CHECK ENGINE" Warning Light	Diagnosis	Trouble Area	*2 Memory
1	Normal	(blink pattern)	—	Output when no other code is recorded.	—	—
12	RPM Signal	(blink pattern)	ON	No G or NE signal is input to the ECU for 2 secs. or more after STA turns ON.	• Open or short in NE, G circuit • Distributor • Open or short in STA circuit • ECU	○
13	RPM Signal	(blink pattern)	ON	NE signal is not input to ECU for 300 msec. or more when engine speed is 1500 rpm or more.	• Open or short in NE circuit • Distributor • ECU	○
14	Ignition Signal	(blink pattern)	ON	IGF signal from igniter is not input to ECU for 4 consecutive ignition.	• Open or short in IGF or IGT circuit from igniter to ECU • Igniter • ECU	○
21	Main Oxygen Sensor Signal	(blink pattern)	ON	(1) Open or short in heater circuit of main oxygen sensor for 500 msec. or more. (HT) (2) At normal driving speed (below 60 mph and engine speed is above 1900 rpm), amplitude of main oxygen sensor signal (OX1) is reduced to between 0.35—0.70 V continuously for 60 secs. or more. *6 (2 trip detection logic) (2)	• Open or short in heater circuit of main oxygen sensor • Main oxygen sensor heater • ECU • Open or short in main oxygen sensor circuit • Main oxygen sensor • ECU	○
22	Water Temp. Sensor Signal	(blink pattern)	ON	Open or short in water temp. sensor circuit for 500 msec. or more. (THW)	• Open or short in water temp. sensor circuit. • Water temp. sensor • ECU	○
24	Intake Air Temp. Sensor Signal	(blink pattern)	*3 ON	Open or short in intake air temp. sensor circuit for 500 msec. or more. (THA)	• Open or short in intake air temp. circuit. • Intake air temp. sensor • ECU	○
25	Air-Fuel Ratio Lean Malfunction	(blink pattern)	ON	(1) Oxygen sensor output is less than 0.45 V when warmed up, when idle switch is off, air-fuel ratio feedback compensation values are deviating. when main oxygen sensor is not warmed 120 sec. (racing at 2000 rpm). (only for code 25) *4 (2) When air-fuel ratio feedback correction value or adaptive control value continues at the upper (lean) or lower (rich) limit for a certain period of time or limit for a certain period of time and adaptive control value is not renewed for a certain period of time. *4	• Oxygen sensor • Ignition system • Water temp. sensor • Air flow meter • ECU	○
26	Air-Fuel Ratio Rich Malfunction	(blink pattern)	ON	(3) When marked variation is detected in engine revolutions for each cylinder during idle switch on and feedback condition. Furthermore, when idle switch is off, air-fuel ratio feedback compensation values are deviating. *6 (2 trip detection logic) (1)-(3)	• Engine ground bolt loose • Open in E1 circuit • Short in injector circuit • Fuel line pressure (injector leakage, etc.) • Open or short in cold start injector circuit • Cold start injector • Open or short in oxygen sensor circuit • Oxygen sensor • Water temp. sensor • Air flow meter • Compression pressure • ECU	○

DIAGNOSTIC CODES (Cont'd)

Code No.	System	Number of blinks "CHECK ENGINE" Warning Light	*1 "CHECK ENGINE" Warning Light	Diagnosis	Trouble Area	*2 Memory
*5 27	Sub-Oxygen Sensor Signal	(blink pattern)	ON	When sub-oxygen sensor is warmed up and full acceleration continues for 2 seconds, output of main oxygen sensor is 0.45 V or more (rich) and output of sub-oxygen sensor is 0.45 V or less (lean). (OX2) *6 (2 trip detection logic)	• Short or open in sub-oxygen sensor circuit. • Sub-oxygen sensor • ECU	○
31	Air Flow Meter Signal	(blink pattern)	ON	Open or short detected continuously for 500 msec. or more in air flow meter circuit. • Open – VC or E2 • Short – VC – E2 or VS – VC	• Open or short in air flow meter circuit • Air flow meter • ECU	○
41	Throttle Position Sensor Signal	(blink pattern)	*3 ON	Open or short detected in throttle position sensor signal (VTA) for 500 msec. or more.	• Open or short in throttle position sensor circuit • Throttle position sensor • ECU	○
42	Vehicle Speed Sensor Signal	(blink pattern)	OFF	SPD signal is not input to the ECU for at least 8 seconds during high load driving when engine speed between 2500 rpm and 5500 rpm.	• Open or short in vehicle speed sensor circuit • Vehicle speed sensor • ECU	○
43	Starter Signal	(blink pattern)	OFF	Starter signal (STA) is not input to ECU even once until engine reaches 800 rpm or more when cranking.	• Open or short in starter signal circuit. • Open or short in IG SW circuit. • ECU	○
52	Knock Sensor Signal	(blink pattern)	ON	With engine speed between 1950 rpm – 6450 rpm, signal from knock sensor is not input to ECU for revolution. (KNK)	• Open or short knock sensor circuit. • Knock sensor • ECU	○
53	Knock Control Signal	(blink pattern)	ON	Engine control computer (for knock control) malfunction is detected.	• ECU	✕
*5 71	EGR System Malfunction	(blink pattern)	ON	EGR gas temp. sensor signal (THG) is below total temp. of intake air temp. plus 55°C (99°F) after driving for 42D seconds in EGR operation range. *6 (2 trip detection logic)	• Open in EGR gas temp. sensor circuit • Open in VSV circuit for EGR • EGR vacuum hose disconnected, valve stuck • ECU • Clogged EGR gas passage	○
51	Switch Condition Signal	(blink pattern)	OFF	Displayed when A/C is ON or IDL contact OFF, with the check terminals E1 and TE1 connected.	• A/C switch circuit • Throttle position sensor IDL circuit • Neutral start switch circuit • Accelerator pedal, cable • ECU	✕

REMARKS

*1: "ON" displayed in the diagnosis mode column indicates that the "CHECK ENGINE" Warning Light is lighted up when a malfunction is detected. "OFF" indicates that the "CHECK ENGINE" Warning Light does not light up during malfunction diagnosis, even if a malfunction is detected.

*2: "○" in the memory column indicates that a diagnostic code is recorded in the ECU memory when a malfunction occurs. "✕" indicates that a diagnostic code is not recorded in the ECU memory even if a malfunction occurs. Accordingly, output of diagnostic results is performed with the IG SW ON.

*3: The "CHECK ENGINE" Warning Light comes on if malfunction occurs only for California specifications.

*4: No. (2) and (3) in the diagnostic contents of codes No.25 and 26 apply to California specification vehicles only. while (1) applies to all models.

*5: Codes 27 and 71 are used only for California specifications.

*6: "2 trip detection logic"

Fig. 88 Diagnostic codes—1991–92 models

DIAGNOSTIC TROUBLE CODE CHART

Parameters listed in the chart may not be exactly same as your reading due to type of the instruments or other factors.

If a malfunction code is displayed during the diagnostic trouble code check in test mode, check the circuit for that code listed in the table below

DTC No.	Number of MIL Blinks	Circuit	Diagnostic Trouble Code Detecting Condition	Trouble Area	Malfunction Indicator Lamp[1] Normal Mode	Malfunction Indicator Lamp[1] Test Mode	Memory[2]
–	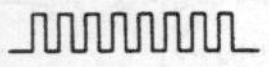 ⎍⎍⎍⎍⎍⎍⎍	Normal	No code is recorded.	–	–	–	–
12	 ⎍⎍	G, NE signal	No NE signal to ECM within 2 sec. after cranking. No G signal to ECM for 3 sec. or more with engine speed between 600 rpm and 4,000 rpm.	• Open or short in NE, G circuit • IIA • Open or short in STA circuit • ECM	ON	N.A.	○
13	⎍⎍⎍	G, NE signal	No NE signal to ECM for 0.3 sec. or more at 1,500 rpm or more. No G signal to ECM while NE signal is input 4 times to ECM when engine speed is between 500 rpm and 4,000 rpm.	• Open or short in NE circuit • IIA • ECM • Open or short in NE circuit • IIA • ECM	ON N.A.	N.A. ON	○
14	 ⎍⎍⎍⎍	Ignition Signal	No IGF signal to ECM for 4 consecutive IGT signal.	• Open or short in IGF or IGT circuit from IIA to ECM • IIA • ECM	ON	N.A.	○
21	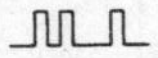 ⎍⎍	Main Oxygen Sensor Signal	Main oxygen sensor signal voltage is reduced to between 0.35 V and 0.70 V for 60 sec. under conditions (a) ~ (d). (2 trip detection logic)[5] (a) Engine coolant temp.: 80°C (176°F) or more. (b) Engine speed: 1,500 rpm or more. (c) Load driving (Ex. A/T in 3rd speed (5th for M/T), A/C ON, Flat road, 50 mph (80 km/h)). (d) Main oxygen sensor signal voltage: Alternating above and below 0.45 V.	• Main oxygen sensor circuit • Main oxygen sensor	ON	ON	○
22	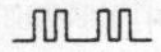 ⎍⎍	Engine Coolant Temp. Sensor Signal	Open or short in Engine Coolant temp. sensor circuit for 0.5 sec. or more.	• Open or short in engine coolant temp. sensor circuit • Engine coolant temp. sensor • ECM	ON	ON	○

Fig. 89 Diagnostic codes—1993–95 4A-FE engine

88274GB7

DTC No.	Number of MIL Blinks	Circuit	Diagnostic Trouble Code Detecting Condition	Trouble Area	Malfunction Indicator Lamp[1] Normal Mode	Malfunction Indicator Lamp[1] Test Mode	Memory[2]
24	⎍⎍⎍⎍⎍	Intake Air Temp. Sensor Signal	Open or short in intake air temp. sensor circuit for 0.5 sec. or more.	• Open or short in intake air temp. sensor circuit • Intake air temp. sensor • ECM	OFF ON[3]	ON	O
25	⎍⎍_⎍⎍⎍⎍	Air-Fuel Ratio Lean Malfunction	(1) Main oxygen sensor voltage is 0.45 V or less (lean) for 90 sec. under conditions (a) ~ (c). (2 trip detection logic)[5] (a) Engine coolant temp.: 50°C (122°F) or more. (b) Engine speed: 1,500 rpm or more. (c) Vehicle speed: Below 62 mph (100 km/h). (2)[3] Engine speed varies by more than 15 rpm over the preceding crank angle period during a period of 30 sec. or more under conditions (a) and (b). (2 trip detection logic)[5] (a) Engine speed: Idling (b) Engine coolant temp.: 80°C (176°F) or more.	• Open or short in main oxygen sensor circuit • Main oxygen sensor • Ignition system • ECM • Open or short in injector circuit • Fuel line pressure (injector leak, blockage) • Mechanical system malfunction (skipping teeth of timing belt) • Ignition system • Compression pressure (foreign object caught in valve) • Air leakage • ECM	ON	ON	O
26[3]	⎍⎍_⎍⎍⎍⎍⎍	Air-Fuel Ratio Rich Malfunction	Engine speed varies by more than 15 rpm over the preceding crank angle period of 30 sec. or more under conditions (a) and (b). (2 trip detection logic)[5] (a) Engine speed: Idling (b) Engine coolant temp.: 80°C (176°F) or more.	• Open or short in injector circuit • Fuel line pressure (injector leak, blockage) • Mechanical system malfunction (skipping teeth of timing belt) • Ignition system • Compression pressure (foreign object caught in valve) • Air leakage • ECM	ON	ON	O
27[3]	⎍⎍_⎍⎍⎍⎍⎍⎍	Sub - Oxygen Sensor Signal	Main oxygen sensor signal is 0.45 V or more and sub-oxygen sensor signal is 0.45 V or less under conditions (a) ~ (c). (2 trip detection logic)[5] (a) Engine coolant temp.: 80°C (176°F) or more. (b) Engine speed: 1,500 rpm or more. (c) Accel. pedal: Fully depressed for 2 sec. or more.	• Open or short in sub-oxygen sensor circuit • Sub-oxygen sensor • ECM	ON	ON	O

Fig. 90 Diagnostic codes—1993–95 4A-FE engine (continued)

88274GB8

DTC No.	Number of MIL Blinks	Circuit	Diagnostic Trouble Code Detecting Condition	Trouble Area	Malfunction Indicator Lamp*1 Normal Mode	Malfunction Indicator Lamp*1 Test Mode	Memory*2
31	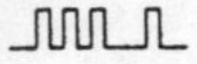 (blinks)	Manifold Absolute Pressure Sensor Signal	Open or short in manifold absolute pressure sensor circuit for 0.5 sec. or more.	• Open or short in Manifold absolute pressure sensor circuit • Manifold absolute pressure sensor • ECM	ON	ON	○
41	 (blinks)	Throttle Position Sensor Signal	Open or short in throttle position sensor circuit for 0.5 sec. or more.	• Open or short in throttle position sensor circuit • Throttle position sensor • ECM	OFF / ON*3	ON	○
42	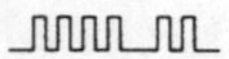 (blinks)	Vehicle speed Sensor Signal (for A/T)	All conditions below are detected continuously for 8 sec. or more. (a) Vehicle speed signal: 0 km/h (mph). (b) Engine speed: 3,000 rpm or more. (c) Park/Neutral position switch (NSW): OFF	• Open or short in vehicle speed sensor circuit • Vehicle speed sensor • Combination meter • ECM	ON	OFF	○
		Vehicle Speed Sensor Signal (for M/T)	All conditions below are detected continuously for 8 sec. or more. (a) Vehicle speed signal: 0 km/h (mph). (b) Engine speed: Between 3,000 rpm and 5,000 rpm. (c) Engine coolant temp.: 80°C (176°F) or more. (d) Load driving.				
43	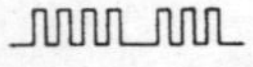 (blinks)	Starter Signal	No starter signal to ECM.	• Open or short in starter signal circuit • Open or short in ignition switch or starter relay circuit • ECM	N.A.	OFF	X

88274GB9

Fig. 91 Diagnostic codes—1993–95 4A-FE engine (continued)

88274GC1

DTC No.	Number of MIL Blinks	Circuit	Diagnostic Trouble Code Detecting Condition	Trouble Area	Malfunction Indicator Lamp*4		Memory*2
					Normal Mode	Test Mode	
71*3	⎍⎍⎍⎍⎍⎍⎍⎍_	EGR System Malfunction	EGR gas temp. is 70°C (158°F) or below for 50 sec. under conditions (a) and (b). (2 trip detection logic)*5 (a) Engine coolant temp.: 60°C (140°F) or more. (b) EGR operation possible (Ex. A/T in 3rd speed (5th for M/T, 55 ~ 60 mph (88 ~ 96 km/h). Flat road).	• Open in EGR gas temp. sensor circuit • Open or short in VSV circuit for EGR • EGR hose disconnected, valve stuck • Clogged EGR gas passage • ECM	ON	ON	O
51	⎍⎍⎍⎍⎍_⎍	Switch Condition Signal	(1) 3 sec. or more after engine starts, idle switch OFF (IDL). (2)*4 Park/Neutral position switch OFF (NSW). (Shift position in "R", "D", "2", or "1" ranges). (3) A/C switch ON.	• Throttle position sensor IDL circuit • Accelerator pedal and cable • Park/Neutral position switch circuit • A/C switch circuit • ECM	N.A.	OFF	X

*1: "ON" displayed in the diagnosis mode column indicates that the malfunction indicator lamp is lighted up when a malfunction is detected. "OFF" indicates that the "CHECK" does not light up during malfunction diagnosis, even if a malfunction is detected. "N.A." indicates that the item is not included in malfunction diagnosis.

*2: "C" in the memory column indicates that a diagnostic trouble code is recorded in the ECM memory when a malfunction occurs. "X" indicates that a diagnostic trouble code is not recorded in the ECM memory even if a malfunction occurs. Accordingly, output of diagnostic results in normal or test mode is performed with the IG switch ON.

*3: Only for California specification vehicles.

*4: Only for automatic transaxle vehicles.

*5: This indicates items for which "2 trip detection logic" is used. With this logic, when a logic malfunction is first detected, the malfunction is temporarily stored in the ECM memory. If the same case is detected again during the second drive test, this second detection causes the malfunction indicator lamp to light up.
The 2 trip repeats the same mode a 2nd time. (However, the IG switch must be turned OFF between the 1st trip and 2nd trip).
In the Test Mode, the malfunction indicator lamp lights up the 1st trip a malfunction is detected.

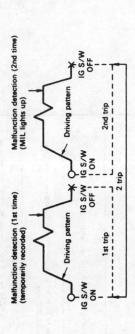

Fig. 92 Diagnostic codes—1993–95 4A-FE engine (continued)

DIAGNOSTIC TROUBLE CODE CHART

Parameters listed in the chart may not be exactly same as your reading due to type of the instruments or other factors.

DTC No.	Number of MIL Blinks	Circuit	Diagnostic Trouble Code Detecting Condition
—	(blink pattern)	Normal	No code is recorded.
12	(blink pattern)	G, NE Signal	No NE signal to ECM within 2 sec. after cranking. No G signal to ECM for 3 sec. or more with engine speed between 600 rpm and 4,000 rpm.
13	(blink pattern)	G, NE Signal	No NE signal to ECM for 0.3 sec. or more at 1,500 rpm or more. No G signal to ECM while NE signal is input 4 times to ECM when engine speed is between 500 rpm and 4,000 rpm.
14	(blink pattern)	Ignition Signal	No IGF signal to ECM for 4 consecutive IGT signal.
16[*4]	(blink pattern)	A/T Control Signal	Fault in communications between the engine CPU and A/T CPU in the ECM.
21	(blink pattern)	Main Oxygen Sensor Signal	Main oxygen sensor signal voltage is reduced to between 0.35 V and 0.70 V for 60 sec. under conditions (a) ~ (d). (2 trip detection logic)[*5] (a) Engine coolant temp.: 80°C (176°F) or more. (b) Engine speed: 1,500 rpm or more. (c) Load driving (Ex. A/T in 4th speed (5th for M/T), Flat road, 50 mph (80 km/h)). (d) Main oxygen sensor signal voltage: Alternating above and below 0.45V.

88274GC3

Fig. 93 Diagnostic codes—1993–95 7A-FE engine

If a malfunction code is displayed during the diagnostic trouble code check in test mode, check the circuit for that code listed in the table below

Trouble Area	Malfunction Indicator Lamp[1] Normal Mode	Malfunction Indicator Lamp[1] Test Mode	Memory[2]	DTC No.	Number of MIL Blinks	Circuit	Diagnostic Trouble Code Detecting Condition
• Open or short in NE, G circuit • IIA • Open or short in STA circuit • ECM	—	—	—				
• Open or short in NE circuit • IIA • ECM	ON	N.A.	○	22		Engine Coolant Temp. Sensor Circuit	Open or short in engine coolant temp. sensor circuit for 0.5 sec. or more.
• Open or short in NE circuit • IIA • ECM	ON	N.A.	○	24		Intake Air Temp. Sensor Signal	Open or short in intake air temp. sensor circuit for 0.5 sec. or more.
• Open or short in IGF or IGT circuit from IIA to ECM • IIA • ECM	N.A.	ON	○	25		Air-Fuel Ratio Lean Malfunction	(1) Main oxygen sensor voltage is 0.45 V or less (lean) for 90 sec. under conditions (a) ~ (c). (2 trip detection logic)*5 (a) Engine coolant temp.: 50°C (122°F) or more. (b) Engine speed: 1,500 rpm or more. (c) Vehicle speed: Below 100 km/h (62 mph). (2)*3 Engine speed varies by more than 15 rpm over the preceding crank angle period during a period of 30 sec. or more under conditions (a) and (b). (2 trip detection logic)*5 (a) Engine speed: Idling (b) Engine coolant temp.: 80°C (176°F) or more.
• ECM	ON	N.A.	×				
• Main oxygen sensor circuit • Main oxygen sensor	ON	ON	○	26*3		Air-Fuel Ratio Rich Malfunction	Engine speed varies by more than 15 rpm over the preceding crank angle period during a period of 30 sec. or more under conditions (a) and (b). (2 trip detection logic)*5 (a) Engine speed: Idling (b) Engine coolant temp.: 80°C (176°F) or more.

88274GC4

Fig. 94 Diagnostic codes—1993–95 7A-FE engine (continued)

88274GC5

DTC No.	Number of MIL Blinks	Circuit	Diagnostic Trouble Code Detecting Condition
27*3	(blink pattern)	Sub-Oxygen Sensor Signal	Main oxygen sensor signal is 0.45 V or more and sub-oxygen sensor signal is 0.45 V or less under conditions (a) ~ (c). (2 trip detection logic)*5 (a) Engine coolant temp.: 80°C (176°F) or more (b) Engine speed: 1,500 rpm or more (c) Accel. pedal: Fully depressed for 2 sec. or more.
31	(blink pattern)	Manifold Absolute Pressure Sensor Signal	Open or short in manifold absolute pressure sensor circuit for 0.5 sec. or more.
41	(blink pattern)	Throttle Position Sensor Signal	Open or short in throttle position sensor circuit for 0.5 sec. or more.
42	(blink pattern)	Vehicle Speed Sensor Signal (for A/T)	All conditions below are detected continuously for 8 sec. or more. (a) Vehicle speed signal: 0 km/h (mph). (b) Engine speed: 3,000 rpm or more. (c) Park/Neutral position switch: OFF
42	(blink pattern)	Vehicle Speed Sensor Signal (for M/T)	All conditions below are detected continuously for 8 sec. or more. (a) Vehicle speed signal: 0 km/h (mph). (b) Engine speed: Between 3,000 rpm and 5,000 rpm. (c) Engine coolant temp.: 80°C (176°F) or more. (d) Load driving
43	(blink pattern)	Starter Signal	No starter signal to ECM.

Trouble Area	Malfunction Indicator Lamp*1 Normal Mode	Malfunction Indicator Lamp*1 Test Mode	Memory*2
• Open or short in engine coolant temp. sensor circuit. • Engine coolant temp. sensor • ECM	ON	ON	○
• Open or short in intake air temp. sensor circuit. • Intake air temp. sensor • ECM	OFF / ON*3	ON	○
• Open or short in main oxygen sensor circuit. • Main oxygen sensor • Ignition system • ECM		ON	○
• Open or short in injector circuit. • Fuel line pressure (injector leak, blockage) • Mechanical system malfunction (skipping teeth of timing belt) • Ignition system • Compression pressure (foreign object caught in valve) • Air leakage • ECM	ON	ON	
• Open or short in injector circuit. • Fuel line pressure (injector leak, blockage) • Mechanical system malfunction (skipping teeth of timing belt) • Ignition system • Compression pressure (foreign object caught in valve) • Air leakage • ECM	ON	ON	○

Fig. 95 Diagnostic codes—1993-95 7A-FE engine (continued)

Trouble Area	Malfunction Indicator Lamp*1		Memory*2
	Normal Mode	Test Mode	
• Open or short in sub-oxygen sensor circuit • Sub-oxygen sensor • ECM	ON	ON	○
• Open or short in manifold absolute pressure sensor circuit. • Manifold absolute pressure sensor • ECM	ON	ON	○
• Open or short in throttle position sensor circuit. • Throttle position sensor • ECM	OFF ON*3	ON	○
• Open or short in vehicle speed sensor circuit. • Vehicle speed sensor • Combination meter • ECM	ON	OFF	○
• Open or short in starter signal circuit • Open or short in ignition switch or starter relay circuit. • ECM	N.A.	OFF	X

DTC No.	Number of MIL Blinks	Circuit	Diagnostic Trouble Code Detecting Condition
52	BE3935	Knock Sensor Signal	Open or short in knock sensor circuit with engine speed between 1,200 rpm and 6,000 rpm.
71*3	BE3937	EGR System Malfunction	EGR gas temp. is 70°C (158°F) or below for 50 sec. under conditions (a) and (b). (2 trip detection logic)*5 (a) Engine coolant temp.: 60°C (140°F) or more. (b) EGR operation possible (Ex. A/T in 3rd speed (5th for M/T), 55 ~ 60 mph (88 ~ 96 km/h), Flat road).
51	BE3935	Switch Condition Signal	(1) 3 sec. or more after engine starts, idle switch OFF (IDL). (2)*4 Park/neutral position switch OFF (Shift position in "R", "D", "2", or "1" ranges). (3) A/C switch ON.

*1: "ON" displayed in the diagnosis mode column indicates that the Malfunction Indicator Lamp is lighted up when a malfunction is detected. "OFF" indicates that the "CHECK" does not light up during malfunction diagnosis, even if a malfunction is detected. "N.A." indicates that the item is not included in malfunction diagnosis.

*2: "○" in the memory column indicates that a diagnostic trouble code is recorded in the ECM memory when a malfunction occurs. "X" indicates that a diagnostic trouble code is not recorded in the ECM memory even if a malfunction occurs. Accordingly, output of diagnostic results in normal or test mode is performed with the IG switch ON.

*3: Only for California specification vehicles.

*4: Only vehicles with A/T.

88274GC6

Fig. 96 Diagnostic codes continued—1993–95 7A-FE engine

HINT: Parameters listed in the chart may not be exactly the same as your reading due to the type of instrument or other factors.

If a malfunction code is displayed during the DTC check in check mode, check the circuit for that code listed in the table below, for details of each code, turn to the page referred to under the "See Page" for the respective "DTC No." in the DTC chart.

DTC No.	Detection Item	Trouble Area	MIL*	Memory
P0105	Manifold Absolute Pressure/Barometric Pressure Circuit Malfunction	• Open or short in manifold absolute pressure sensor circuit • Manifold absolute pressure sensor • ECM	○	○
P0106	Manifold Absolute Pressure/Barometric Pressure Circuit Range/Performance Problem	• Manifold absolute pressure sensor	○	○
P0110	Intake Air Temp. Circuit Malfunction	• Open or short in intake air temp. sensor circuit • Intake air temp. sensor • ECM	○	○
P0115	Engine Coolant Temp. Circuit Malfunction	• Open or short in engine coolant temp. sensor circuit • Engine coolant temp. sensor • ECM	○	○
P0116	Engine Coolant Temp. Circuit Range/Performance Problem	• Engine coolant temp. sensor • Cooling system	○	○
P0120	Throttle/Pedal Position Sensor/Switch "A" Circuit Malfunction	• Open or short in throttle position sensor circuit • Throttle position sensor • ECM	○	○
P0121	Throttle/Pedal Position Sensor/Switch "A" Circuit Range/Performance Problem	• Throttle position sensor	○	○
P0125	Insufficient Coolant Temp. for Closed Loop Fuel Control	• Open or short in oxygen sensor (bank 1 senser 1) circuit • Oxygen sensor (bank 1 sensor 1)	○	○
P0130	Oxygen Sensor Circuit Malfunction (Bank 1 Sensor 1)	• Oxygen sensor • Fuel trim malfunction	○	○
P0133	Oxygen Sensor Circuit Slow Response (Bank 1 Sensor 1)	• Oxygen sensor	○	○

*: ○...... MIL lights up

Fig. 98 Diagnostic codes—1996–97 models

Trouble Area	Malfunction Indicator Lamp*1		Memory*2
	Normal Mode	Test Mode	
• Open or short in knock sensor circuit • Knock sensor (looseness). • ECM	ON	N.A.	○
• Open in EGR gas temp. sensor circuit. • Open or short in VSV circuit for EGR. • EGR hose disconnected, valve stuck • Clogged EGR gas passage • ECM	ON	ON	○
• Throttle position sensor IDL circuit. • Accelerator pedal and cable • Park/neutral position switch circuit • A/C switch circuit • ECM	N.A.	OFF	×

*5: This indicates items for which "2 trip detection logic" is used. With this logic, when a logic malfunction is first detected, the malfunction is temporarily stored in the ECM memory. If the same case is detected again during the second drive test, this second detection causes the Malfunction Indicator Lamp to light up.
The 2 trip repeats the same mode a 2nd time. (However, the IG switch must be turned OFF between the 1st trip and 2nd trip).
In the Test Mode, the Malfunction Indicator Lamp lights up the 1st trip a malfunction is detected.

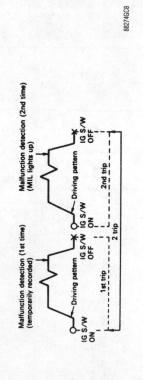

Fig. 97 Diagnostic codes—1993–95 7A-FE engine (continued)

DTC No.	Detection Item	Trouble Area	MIL*	Memory
P0336	Crankshaft Position Sensor "A" circuit Range/Performance	• Distributor • ECM	○	○
P0340	Camshaft Position Sensor Circuit Malfunction	• Open or short in camshaft position sensor circuit • Camshaft position sensor • Starter • ECM	○	○
P0401	Exhaust Gas Recirculation Flow Insufficient Detected	• EGR valve stuck closed • Open or short in VSV circuit for EGR • Vacuum or EGR hose disconnected • Manifold absolute pressure sensor • EGR VSV open or close malfunction • ECM	○	○
P0402	Exhaust Gas Recirculation Flow Excessive Detected	• EGR valve stuck open • Vacuum or EGR hose in connected to wrong post • Manifold absolute pressure sensor • ECM	○	○
P0420	Catalyst System Efficiency Below Threshold	• Three-way catalytic converter • Oxygen sensor	○	○
P0500	Vehicle Speed Sensor Malfunction	• Open or short in vehicle speed sensor circuit • Vehicle speed sensor • Combination meter • ECM	○	○
P0505	Idle Control System Malfunction	• IAC valve is stuck or closed • Open or short in IAC valve circuit • Open or short AC1 signal circuit • Air intake (hose loose)	○	○

*: ○ ...... MIL lights up

88274G03

Fig. 100 Diagnostic codes—1996–97 models (continued)

DTC No.	Detection Item	Trouble Area	MIL*1	Memory
P0136	Heated Oxygen Sensor Circuit Malfunction (Bank 1 Sensor 2)	• Heated oxygen sensor	○	○
P0141	Heated oxygen Sensor Heater Circuit Malfunction (Bank 1 Sensor 2)	• Open or short in heater circuit of heated oxygen sensor • Heated oxygen sensor heater • ECM	○	○
P0171	System too Lean (Fuel Trim)	• Air intake (hose loose) • Fuel line pressure • Injector blockage • Oxygen sensor (bank 1 sensor 1) malfunction • Manifold absolute pressure sensor • Engine coolant temp. sensor	○	○
P0172	System too Rich (Fuel Trim)	• Fuel line pressure • Injector leak blockage • Oxygen sensor (bank 1 sensor 1) malfunction • Manifold absolute pressure sensor • Engine coolant temp. sensor	○	○
P0300	Random/Multiple Cylinder Misfire Detected	• Ignition system • Injector • Fuel line pressure • EGR	○	○
P0301 P0302 P0303 P0304	Misfire Detected – Cylinder 1 – Cylinder 2 – Cylinder 3 – Cylinder 4	• Compression pressure • Valve clearance not to specification • Valve timing • Manifold absolute pressure sensor • Engine coolant temp. sensor	○	○
P0325*2	Knock Sensor 1 Circuit Malfunction	• Open or short in knock sensor 1 circuit • Knock sensor 1 (looseness) • ECM	○	○
P0335	Crankshaft Position Sensor "A" Circuit Malfunction	• Open or short in crankshaft position sensor circuit • Crankshaft position sensor • Starter • ECM	○	○

*1: ○ ...... MIL lights up
*2: Only for 7A-FE engine.

88274G02

Fig. 99 Diagnostic codes—1996–97 models (continued)

DTC No.	Detection Item	Trouble Area	SRS Warning Light
(Normal)	• System normal	—	OFF
	• Source voltage drop	• Battery • Airbag sensor assembly	ON
11	• Short in squib circuit (to ground)	• Steering wheel pad (D squib) • Front passenger airbag assembly (P squib) • Spiral cable • Airbag sensor assembly • Wire harness	ON
12	• Short in squib circuit (to B+)	• Steering wheel pad (D squib) • Front passenger airbag assembly (P squib) • Spiral cable • Airbag sensor assembly • Wire harness	ON
13	• Short in D squib circuit	• Steering wheel pad (D squib) • Spiral cable • Airbag sensor assembly • Wire harness	ON
14	• Open in D squib circuit	• Steering wheel pad (D squib) • Spiral cable • Airbag sensor assembly • Wire harness	ON
31	• Airbag sensor assembly malfunction	• Airbag sensor assembly	ON
53	• Short in P squib circuit	• Front passenger airbag assembly (P squib) • Airbag sensor assembly • Wire harness	ON
54	• Open in P squib circuit	• Front passenger airbag assembly (P squib) • Airbag sensor assembly • Wire harness	ON

HINT:
• When the SRS warning light remains lit up and the DTC is the normal code, this means a source voltage drop.
  This malfunction is not stored in memory by the airbag sensor assembly and if the power source voltage returns to normal, after approx. 10 seconds the SRS warning light will automatically go out.
• When 2 or more codes are indicated, the codes will be displayed in numeral order starting from the lowest numbered code.
• If a code not listed on the chart is displayed, the airbag sensor assembly is faulty.

Fig. 102 Diagnostic codes (SRS system)—1996–97 models

DTC No.	Detection Item	Trouble Area	MIL *1	Memory
P1300	Igniter Circuit Malfunction	• Open or short in IGF or IGT circuit from igniter to ECM • Igniter • ECM	○	○
P1335	Crankshaft Position Sensor Circuit Malfunction (during engine running)	• Open or short in crankshaft position sensor circuit • Crankshaft position sensor • ECM	—	○
P1520 *2	Stop Light Switch Signal Malfunction	• Short in stop light switch signal circuit • Stop light switch • ECM	○	○
P1600	ECM BATT Malfunction	• Open in back up power source circuit • ECM	○	○
P1780	Park/Neutral Position Switch Malfunction	• Short in park/neutral position switch circuit • Park/neutral position switch • ECM	○	○

*1: — ..... MIL does not light up
    ○ ..... MIL lights up
*2: Only for 7A-FE engine with A/T vehicles.

Fig. 101 Diagnostic codes—1996–97 models (continued)

VACUUM DIAGRAMS

Following are vacuum diagrams for most of the engine and emissions package combinations covered by this manual. Because vacuum circuits will vary based on various engine and vehicle options, always refer first to the vehicle emission control information label, if present. Should the label be missing, or should vehicle be equipped with a different engine from the vehicle's original equipment, refer to the diagrams below for the same or similar conguration.

If you wish to obtain a replacement emissions label, most manufacturers make the labels available for purchase. The labels can usually be ordered from a local dealer.

View of a common vacuum hose routing label—4A-F engine shown

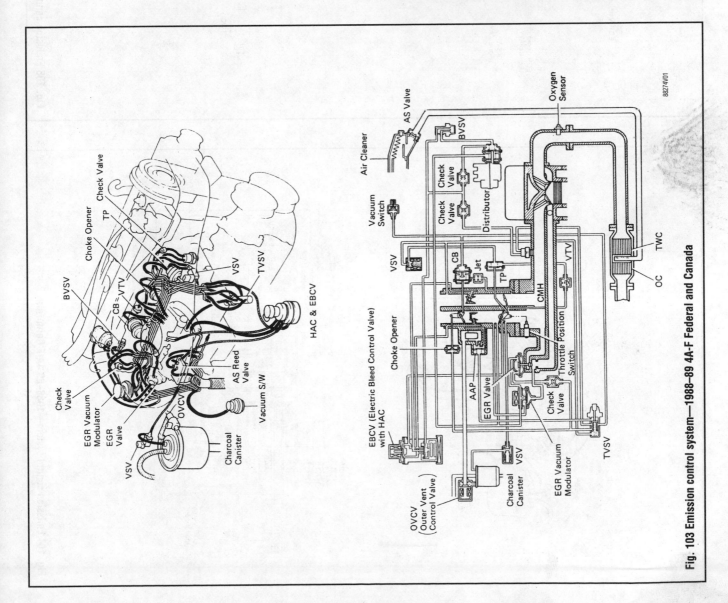

Fig. 103 Emission control system—1988–89 4A-F Federal and Canada

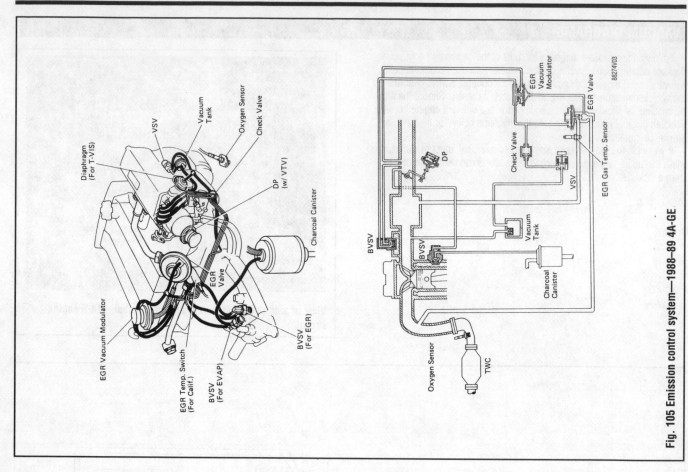

Fig. 105 Emission control system—1988-89 4A-GE

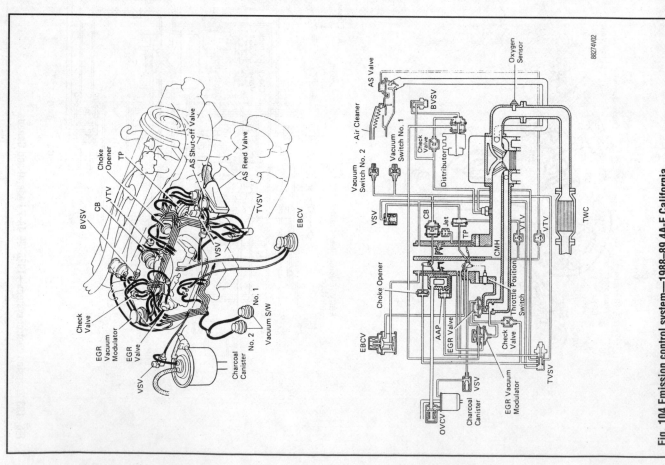

Fig. 104 Emission control system—1988-89 4A-F California

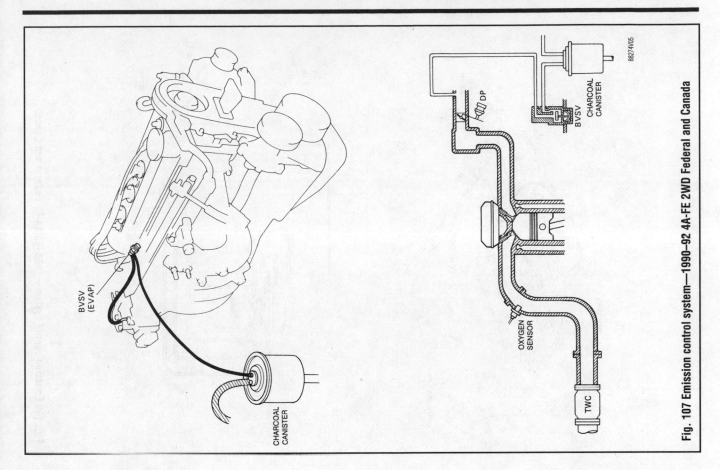

Fig. 107 Emission control system—1990–92 4A-FE 2WD Federal and Canada

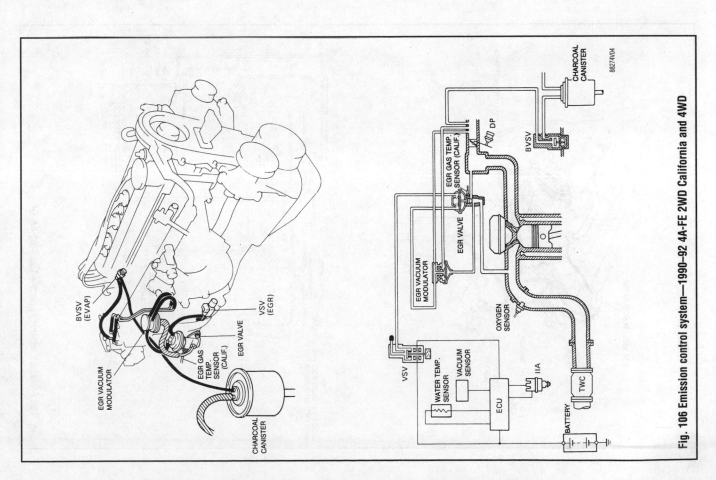

Fig. 106 Emission control system—1990–92 4A-FE 2WD California and 4WD

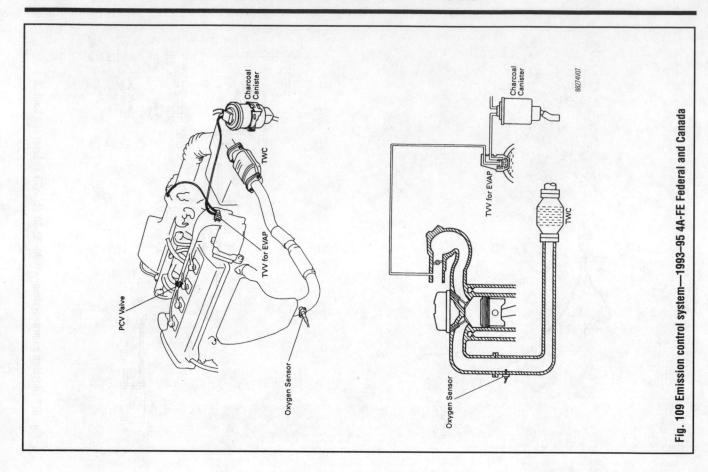

Fig. 109 Emission control system—1993–95 4A-FE Federal and Canada

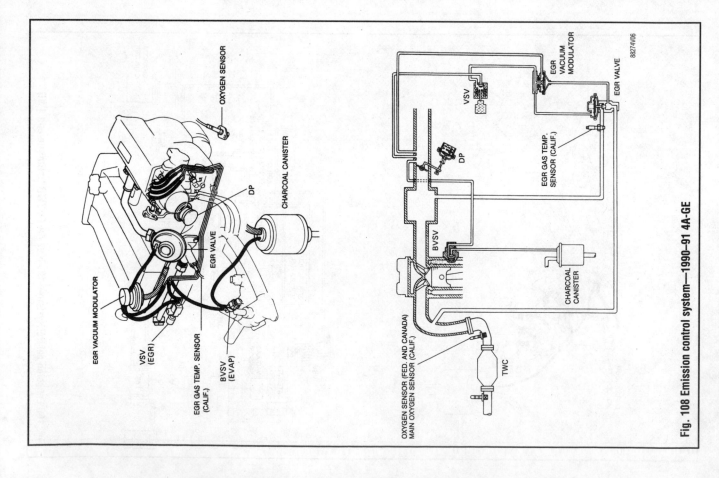

Fig. 108 Emission control system—1990–91 4A-GE

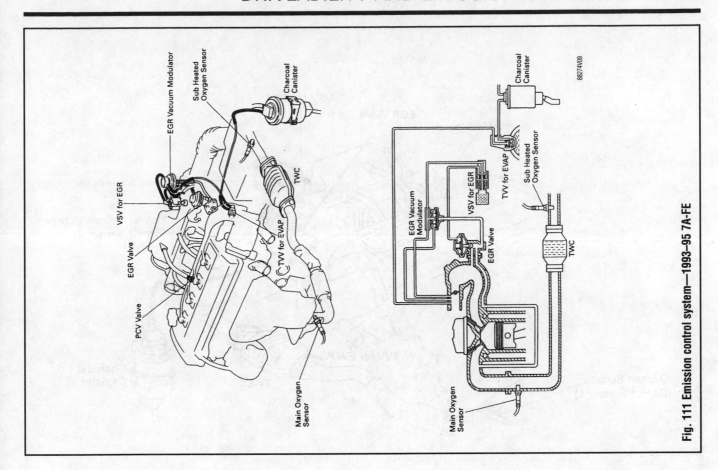

Fig. 111 Emission control system—1993–95 7A-FE

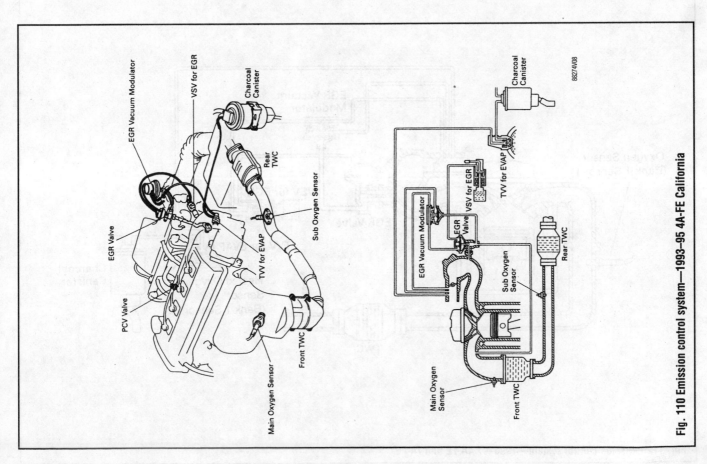

Fig. 110 Emission control system—1993–95 4A-FE California

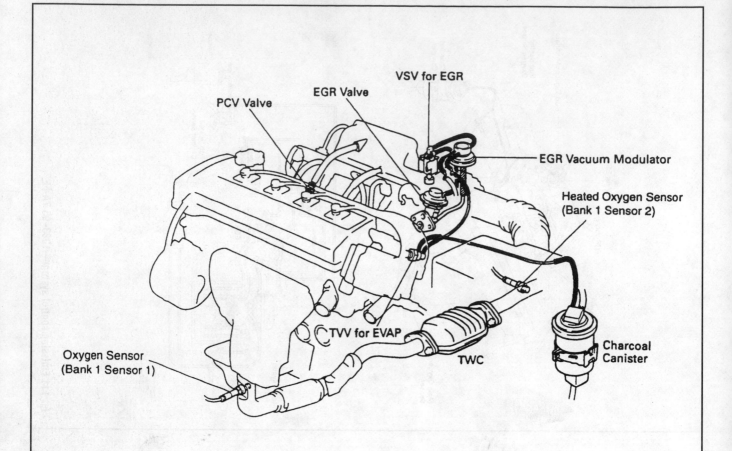

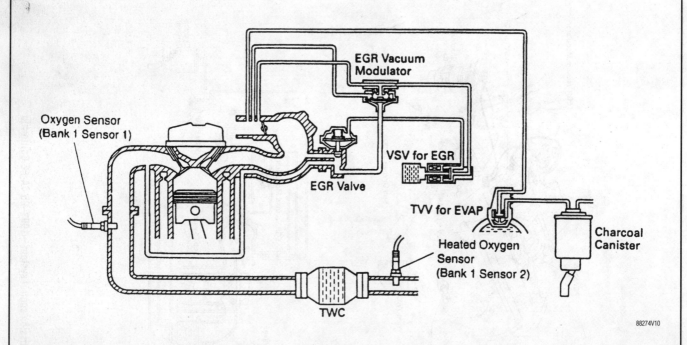

Fig. 112 Emission control system—1996–97 4A-FE and 7A-FE

88274V10

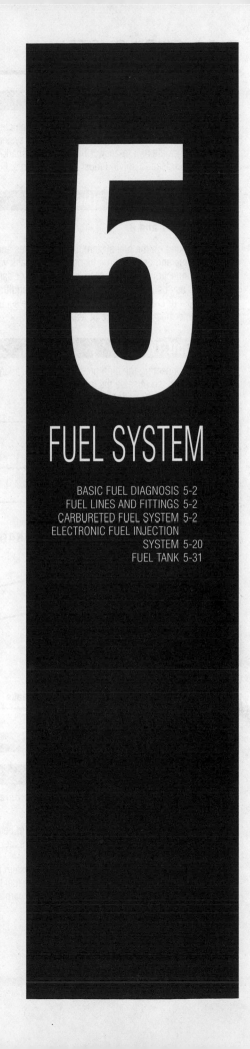

5

FUEL SYSTEM

BASIC FUEL DIAGNOSIS

When there is a problem starting or driving a vehicle, two of the most important checks involve the ignition and the fuel systems. The questions most mechanics attempt to answer first, "is there spark?" and "is there fuel?" will often lead to solving most basic problems. For ignition system diagnosis and testing, please refer to the information on engine electrical components and ignition systems found earlier in this manual. If the ignition system checks out (there is spark), then you must determine if the fuel system is operating properly (is there fuel?).

FUEL LINES AND FITTINGS

▶ **See Figures 1 and 2**

When working on the fuel system, insect the lines and connections for cracks, leakage and deformation. Inspect the fuel tank vapor vent system hose and connections for looseness, sharp bends or damage. Check the fuel tank for any deformation due to bad driving conditions. Inspect the bands for rust or cracks. The tank bands should be secure and not loose. Check the filler neck for damage or leakage.

Union Bolt Type

When disconnecting the high pressure fuel line, a large amount of gasoline will spill out, so observe the following.
• Place a container under the connection.

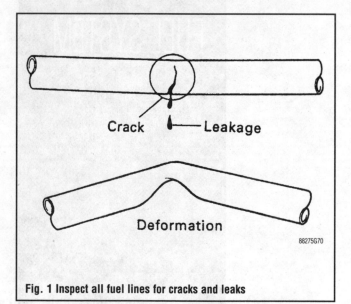

Fig. 1 Inspect all fuel lines for cracks and leaks

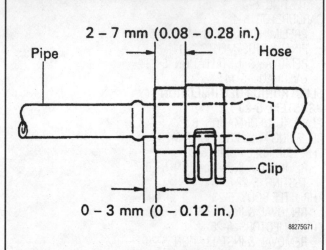

Fig. 2 When placing a hose clamp, install in the position illustrated for a secure hold

• Slowly loosen the connection. Have a rag handy to clean up any split fuel.
• Separate the connection.
• Plug the connection with a rubber plug.
• When connecting the union bolt on the high pressure line, always use a new gasket.
• Always tighten the union bolt by hand. Tighten the bolt to 22 ft. lbs. (29 Nm).

Flare Nut Type

Apply a light coat of engine oil to the flare and tighten the flare nut by hand. Using a torque wrench, tighten the flare nut to 22 ft. lbs. (30 Nm).

CARBURETED FUEL SYSTEM

General Information

➡**Only the 4A-F engine is equipped with a carburetor. All other engines are fuel injected.**

An automotive fuel system consists of everything between the fuel tank and the carburetor. This includes the tank itself, the fuel lines, one fuel filter, a mechanical fuel pump, and the carburetor.

With the exception of the carburetor, the fuel system is quite simple in operation. Fuel is drawn from the tank through the fuel line by the fuel pump, which forces it through the fuel filter to the carburetor, where it is distributed to the cylinders.

Mechanical Fuel Pump

REMOVAL & INSTALLATION

▶ **See Figure 3**

1. Disconnect the negative battery cable.
2. With the engine cold and the key removed from the ignition, label, disconnect and plug the fuel lines from the pump.
3. Unscrew the two fuel pump retaining bolts. Remove the fuel pump, gaskets and insulator.

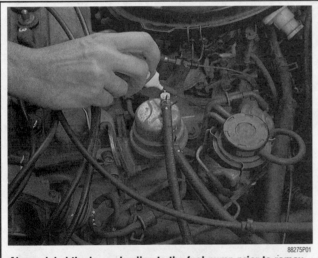

Fig. 3 Cutaway view of the mechanical fuel pump

Remove the hoses connected to the pump. Make sure a rag is handy for spilt fuel

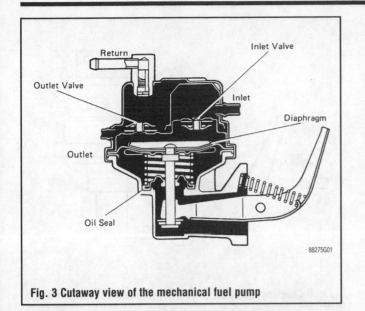

Always label the hoses leading to the fuel pump prior to removing them

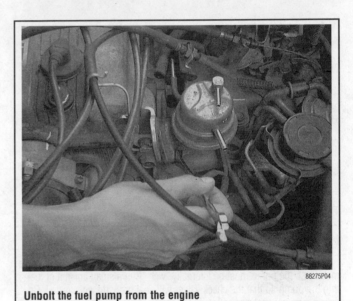

Unbolt the fuel pump from the engine

Slide the hose clamps far enough to pull the hoses off the pump

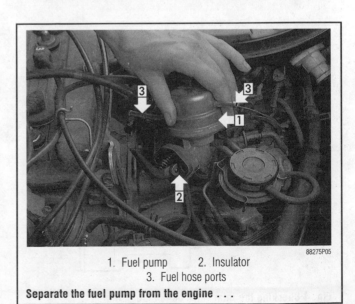

1. Fuel pump   2. Insulator
3. Fuel hose ports

Separate the fuel pump from the engine . . .

. . . then pull the insulator and gaskets from the pump and mating surfaces

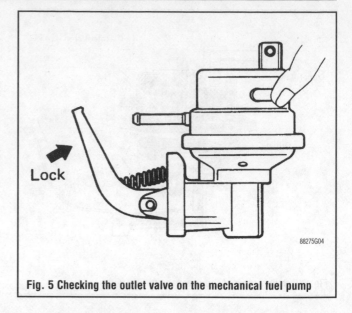

Fig. 5 Checking the outlet valve on the mechanical fuel pump

4. Inspect the insulator for any cracks or damage. Replace if necessary.

5. Cover the mating surface of the cylinder head where the fuel pump sits to prevent dirt entering.

To install:

6. Place new gaskets on either side of the insulator. Insert the pump arm through the hole of the insulator/gaskets and mount on the engine. Tighten the two mounting screws to 13 ft. lbs. (18 Nm).

➡**Always use new gaskets when installing the fuel pump.**

7. Reconnect the fuel lines.
8. Connect the negative battery cable.
9. Start the engine and check for any leaks.

TESTING

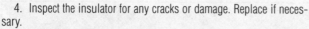 **See Figures 4, 5, 6 and 7**

Before performing and checks on the fuel pump, two conditions must be met. First, the pump must be internally "wet". Run a small amount of fuel into the pump so that the check valves will seal properly when tested. Dry valves may not seal and will yield false test results.

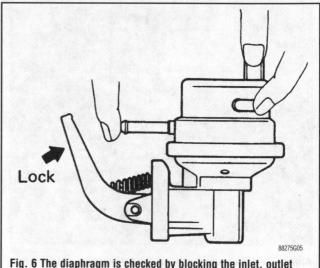

Fig. 6 The diaphragm is checked by blocking the inlet, outlet and return pipes

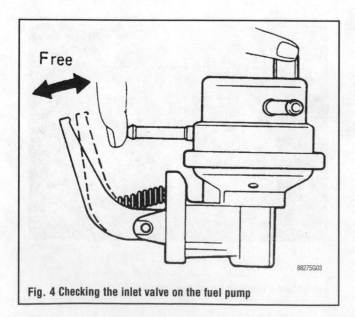

Fig. 4 Checking the inlet valve on the fuel pump

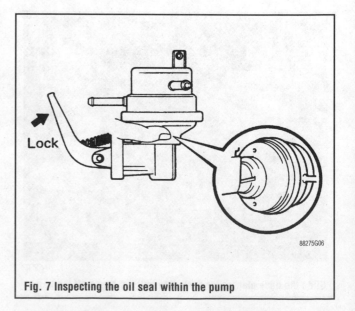

Fig. 7 Inspecting the oil seal within the pump

Hold the pump with out blocking either pipe and operate the pump lever, noting the amount of force needed to move it. This is the reference point for all tests. Do not apply more than this amount of force to the lever during the testing. Excessive force can damage an otherwise useable pump.

1. Block off the outlet and return pipes with your fingers. Operate the lever. There should be an increase in arm play and it should move freely.

2. Block the inlet port with your finger and operate the lever. The arm should lock when the normal amount of force is applied.

3. The diaphragm is checked by blocking the inlet, outlet and return pipes. When normal force is applied to the lever, the lever should lock and not move. Any lever motion indicates a ruptured diaphragm. This is a common cause of poor fuel mileage and poor acceleration since the correct amount of fuel is not being delivered to the carburetor.

➡**The fuel pump must pass all three of these tests to be considered usable. If the pump fails one or more of these tests, it must be replaced.**

4. Check the oil seal within the pump. Block off the vent hole in the lower part of the pump housing. The lever arm should lock when normal force is applied.

Carburetor

◆ **See Figures 8 and 9**

The carburetor is the most complex part of the fuel system. Carburetors vary greatly in construction, but they all operate basically the same way; their job is to supply the correct mixture of fuel and air to the engine in response to varying conditions.

Despite their complexity in operation, carburetors function because of a simple physical principle; the venturi principle. Air is drawn into the engine by the pumping action of the pistons. As the air enters the top of the carburetor, it passes through a venturi, which is nothing more than a restriction in the throttle bore. The air speeds up as it passes through the venturi, causing a slight drop in pressure. This pressure drop pulls fuel from the float bowl through a nozzle into the throttle bore, where it mixes with the air and forms a fine mist, which is distributed to the cylinders through the intake manifold.

There are multiple systems (air/fuel circuits) in a carburetor that make it work:

- Float
- Main Metering

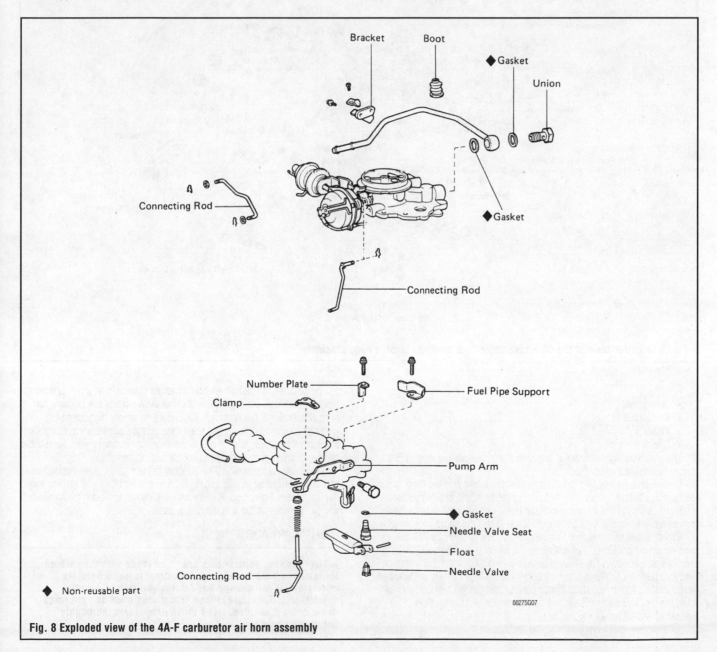

Fig. 8 Exploded view of the 4A-F carburetor air horn assembly

◆ Non-reusable part

00275G07

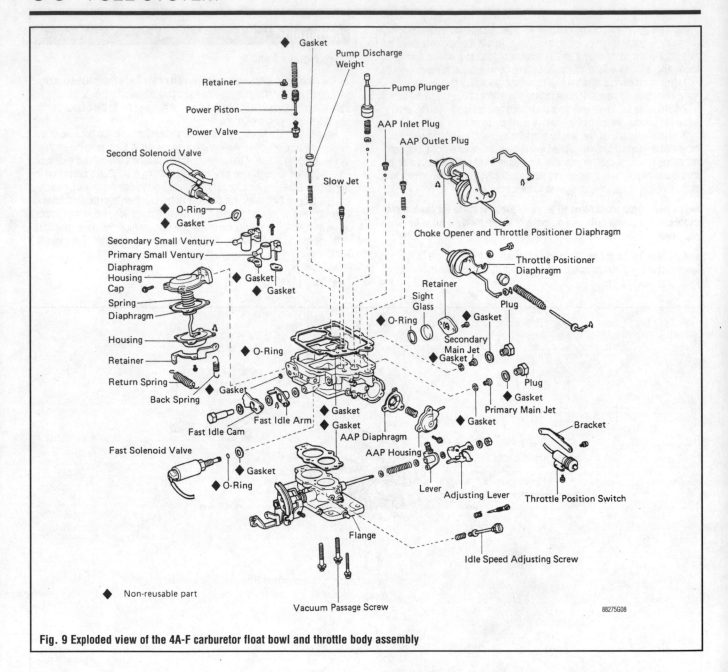

Fig. 9 Exploded view of the 4A-F carburetor float bowl and throttle body assembly

- Idle
- Low-Speed
- Accelerator Pump
- Power
- Choke system

The way these systems are arranged in the carburetor determines the carburetor's size and shape.

Carburetors all function in the same fashion; larger engines have larger carburetors to move more air and fuel, but the principle is still the same. Older units don't have as many external linkages and controls to manage emissions and driveability, but the principle is still the same.

It's important to remember that carburetors seldom give trouble during normal operation. Other than changing the fuel and air filters and making sure the idle speed is OK at every tune-up, there's not much maintenance you can perform on the average carburetor. Quality of fuel and presence of water in the system will affect the carburetor; dirt particles in the fuel can clog the jets and water causes rust and corrosion. If the vehicle is to be parked or stored for a long period of time, drain the carburetor to prevent the evaporating fuel from gumming up the system.

The carburetors used on 4A-F engines are conventional 2 bbl, downdraft types similar to domestic carburetors. The main circuits are: primary, for normal operational requirements; secondary, to supply high speed/high load fuel needs; float, to supply fuel to the primary and secondary circuits; accelerator, to supply fuel for quick and safe acceleration; choke, for reliable starting in cold weather; power valve, for fuel economy.

It is important to know that carburetors seldom give trouble during normal operation. Other than changing the fuel and air filters and making sure the idle speeds are correct at every tune-up, there's not much maintenance you can perform on the average carburetor.

PRELIMINARY ADJUSTMENTS

➡**The following adjustments are to be made with the carburetor removed from the engine. Adjustments on carburetors interrelate; if you change one setting you may affect other adjustments. Therefore, these procedures must be performed in the order presented. Read these procedures thoroughly before continuing.**

Float

▶ See Figures 10 thru 15

It will be necessary to remove the air horn from the carburetor to gain access to the float. Follow the procedures outlined in the carburetor overhaul.

1. Remove the float, needle valve, spring and plunger.
2. Remove the pin clip from the needle valve.
3. Install the needle valve, spring, and plunger onto the seat.
4. Install the float and pivot pin.
5. Allow the float to hang down on its own weight. Check the clearance between the float tip and the air horn without the gasket on the air horn. Float level should be 0.283 inch (7.2mm).
6. Adjust if necessary, by bending the portion of the float lip marked (A) in the illustration.
7. Lift up the float and check the clearance between the needle valve plunger and the float lip. Clearance should be 0.0657–0.0783 inch (1.67–1.99mm).
8. If not within specification, adjust by bending the portion of the float lip marked (B) in the illustration.
9. After adjusting the float level, remove the float, plunger, spring and needle valve.

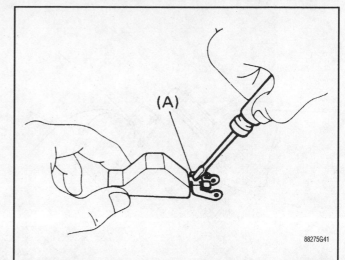

Fig. 12 Bend the portion of the float lip marked (A) to adjust the float

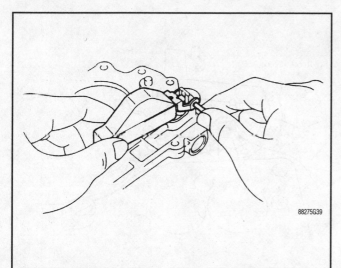

Fig. 10 Installing the float and pivot pin to the side of the carburetor

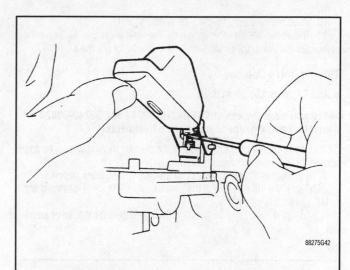

Fig. 13 Lift up the float and check the clearance between the needle valve plunger and the float lip

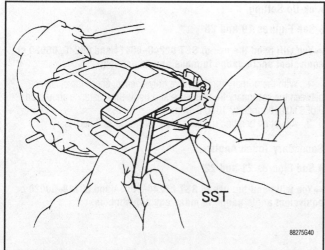

Fig. 11 With the float hanging, check the clearance between the float tip and air horn

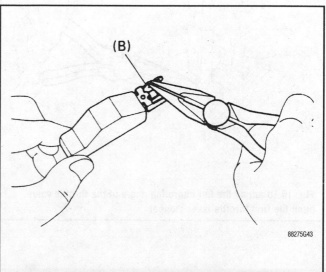

Fig. 14 Adjust the float lip by bending the portion marked (B)

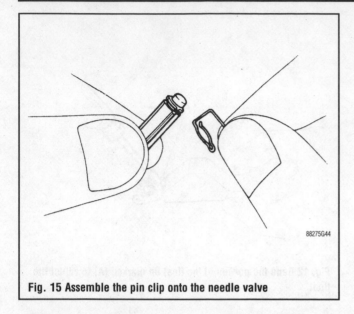

Fig. 15 Assemble the pin clip onto the needle valve

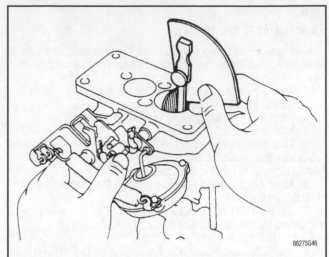

Fig. 17 Check the full opening of the secondary throttle valve from horizontal plane

10. Assemble the pin clip onto the needle valve.

11. Install the needle valve assembly, float and pivot pin. Assemble the carburetor following the procedures in the carburetor overhaul.

Throttle Valve Opening

▶ See Figures 16, 17 and 18

➡You will need the use of SST 09240–00014 and 09240–00020 or equivalent angle gauge to make any adjustments.

1. Check the full operating angle of the primary throttle valve. The angle should be 90° from horizontal plane.

2. If adjustment is necessary, bend the first throttle lever stopper.

3. Check the full opening of the secondary throttle valve. Standard and is 80° from horizontal plane.

4. Adjust if necessary by bending the secondary throttle lever stopper.

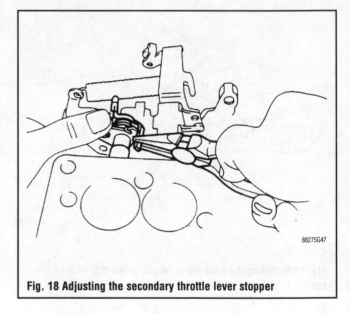

Fig. 18 Adjusting the secondary throttle lever stopper

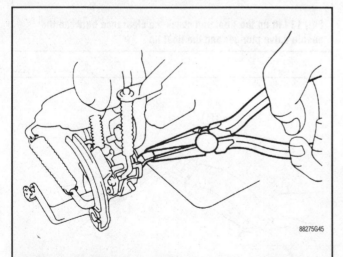

Fig. 16 To adjust the full operating angle of the throttle valve, bend the first throttle lever stopper

Kick-Up Setting

▶ See Figures 19 and 20

➡You will need the use of SST 09240–00014 and 09240–00020 or equivalent angle gauge to make any adjustments.

1. With the primary throttle valve fully opened, check the clearance between the secondary throttle valve and body. the clearance should be 0.0063 0.0106 inch (0.16–0.27mm).

2. Adjust by bending the secondary throttle lever if necessary.

Secondary Touch Angle

▶ See Figures 21 and 22

➡You will need the use of SST 09240–00014 and 09240–00020 or equivalent angle gauge to make any adjustments.

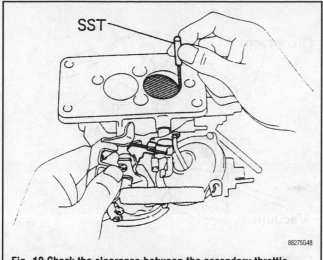

Fig. 19 Check the clearance between the secondary throttle valve and body for the kick-up setting

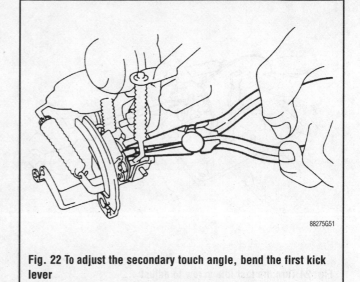

Fig. 22 To adjust the secondary touch angle, bend the first kick lever

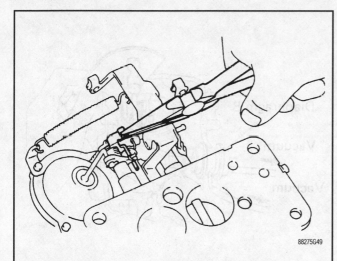

Fig. 20 Adjust the kick-up setting by bending the secondary throttle lever

1. Check the primary throttle valve opening angle when the first kick lever touches the second kick lever.
2. Standard angle should be 45° from horizontal plane.
3. Adjustment is done by bending the first kick lever.

Fast Idle Setting

▶ See Figures 23 and 24

➡You will need the use of SST 09240–00014 and 09240–00020 or equivalent angle gauge to make any adjustments.

1. Set the throttle shaft lever to the first step of the fast idle cam as shown in the illustration.
2. With the choke valve fully closed, check the primary throttle valve angle.
3. Adjustment is done by turning the fast idle adjusting screw. Standard angle is 21° from horizontal plane.

Choke Unloader

➡You will need the use of SST 09240–00014 and 09240–00020 or equivalent angle gauge to make any adjustments.

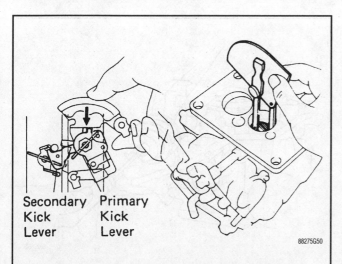

Secondary Kick Lever   Primary Kick Lever

Fig. 21 You will need the use of an angle gauge to make any adjustments for the secondary touch angle

Fig. 23 Set the throttle shaft lever to the first step of the fast idle cam

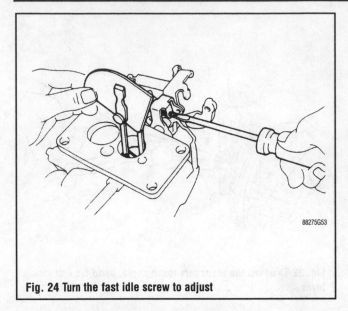

Fig. 24 Turn the fast idle screw to adjust

1. With the primary throttle valve fully opened, check the valve angel. Standard angle is 41° from horizontal plane.
2. If adjustment is necessary, bend the fast idle lever.

Choke Opener

1. Set the fast idle cam.
2. While holding the throttle slightly open, push the choke valve closed, and hold it closed as you release the throttle valve.
3. Apply vacuum to the choke opener diaphragm.
4. Check the choke valve angle, standard angle is 74° from horizontal plane.
5. Adjust if necessary by bending the relief lever.

Choke Breaker

▶ **See Figures 25, 26, 27 and 28**

1. Set the fast idle cam. While holding the throttle slightly open, push the choke valve closed, and hold it closed as you release the throttle valve.
2. Fully close the choke valve and check the choke opening angle.
3. Apply vacuum to the choke breaker diaphragm (A).
4. Check the choke valve angle. The standard angle is 38° from horizontal plane.

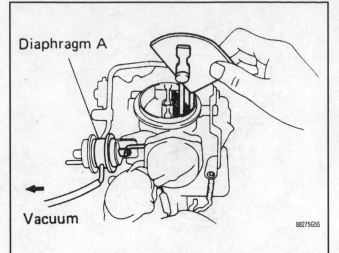

Fig. 26 Apply vacuum to the diaphragm and check the choke valve angle

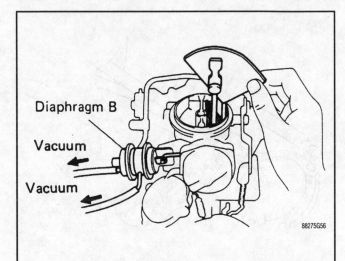

Fig. 27 Apply vacuum to the choke breaker diaphragms (A) and (B)

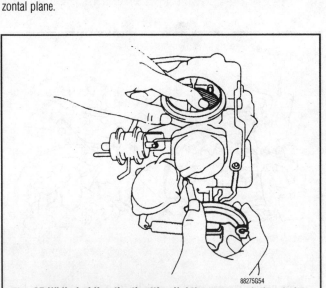

Fig. 25 While holding the throttle slightly open, push the choke valve closed, and hold it closed as you release the throttle valve

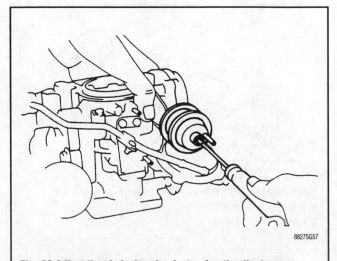

Fig. 28 Adjust the choke breaker by turning the diaphragm screw

5. Adjust the angler by bending the relief lever.
6. Apply vacuum to the choke breaker diaphragms (A) and (B).
7. Check the choke valve angle, standard angle is 58° from horizontal plane.
8. Adjust by turning the diaphragm adjusting screw.

Pump Stroke

▶ **See Figure 29**

1. With the choke valve fully opened, check the length of the stroke.
2. Standard stroke is 0.157 inch (4.0mm).
3. Adjust the pump stroke by bending the connecting link (A).

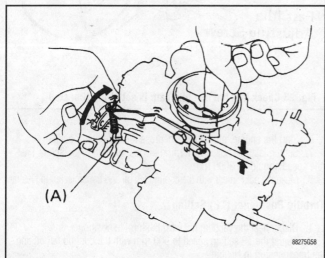

Fig. 29 Test the pump stroke with the choke valve fully opened, check the length of the stroke

Throttle Position Switch

1. Connect ohmmeter probes to the harness and switch body.
2. With the throttle valve fully opened, check that there is continuity.
3. Slowly return the throttle valve from fully open. At the point where there is no continuity, measure the throttle valve angle. Standard angle is 9° from horizontal plane.
4. If not, adjust the throttle position switch using the adjusting screw.
5. Check for smooth operation of each component.

FINAL ADJUSTMENTS

▶ **See Figures 30 and 31**

To perform the final carburetor adjustments, the following conditions must be met:
• All accessories must be off
• The ignition timing set correctly
• The transmission is in the Neutral range
• Warm the engine to operating temperature
• The float level should be even with the correct level in the sight glass.
• Check that the choke valve opens fully.
• Connect a tachometer. Remove the rubber cap and attach the tachometer to the positive terminal of the service connector at the IIA distributor.

⁕⁕ WARNING

Some tachometers are not compatible with this ignition system, it is recommended to confirm the capability of your unit prior to use.

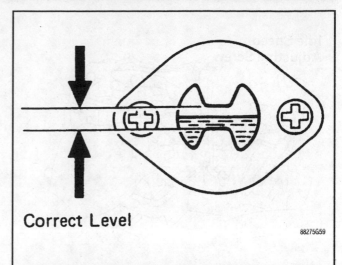

Fig. 30 The float level should be even with the correct level in the sight glass

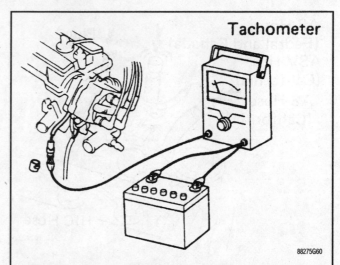

Fig. 31 Connect the tachometer to the positive terminal of the service connector at IIA distributor

Idle Speed

▶ **See Figure 32**

Adjust the idle speed by turning the idle speed adjusting screw. It should be 650 rpm on M/T and 750 rpm on A/T. Leave the tachometer attached for further adjustments.

Fast Idle

▶ **See Figures 33, 34 and 35**

1. Stop the engine and remove the air cleaner.
2. Plug the Air Switching (AS) hose on Federal and Canadian models, to prevent leakage of the exhaust gas. Or plug the Air Switching Valve (ASV) for California models. Plug the HIC hose to prevent rough idling.
3. Disconnect the hose from the TVSV (M) port and plug the (M) port.
4. This will shut off the choke opener and EGR systems.
5. Set the fast idle cam. While holding the throttle valve slightly open, pull up the fast idle cam and hold it closed as you release the throttle valve.

➡Check the fast idle cam is set at the first step.

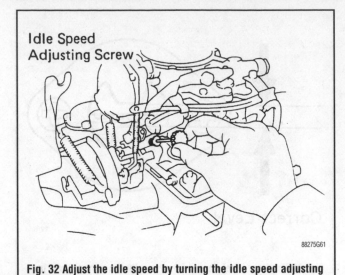

Fig. 32 Adjust the idle speed by turning the idle speed adjusting screw

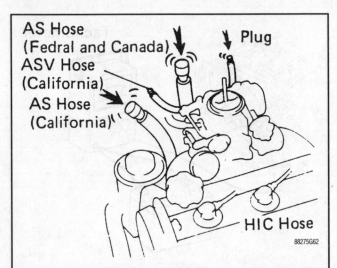

Fig. 33 Make sure to plug these hoses prior to adjusting the fast idle

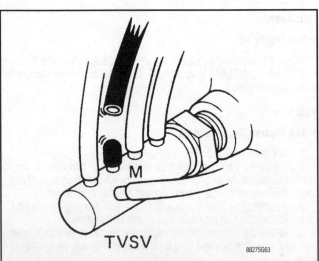

Fig. 34 Disconnect the hose from the TVSV (M) port and plug the port

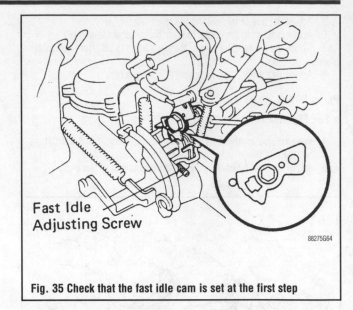

Fig. 35 Check that the fast idle cam is set at the first step

6. Start the engine, but do **NOT** depress the accelerator pedal.

7. Set the fast idle speed by turning the fast idle adjusting screw. Fast idle speed should be 3000 rpm.

8. Make the adjustment with the cooling fan off and transmission in Neutral.

Throttle Positioner (TP) Setting

1. Disconnect the vacuum hose fro the throttle positioner.

2. Adjust the TP setting speed to 900 rpm with the cooling fan off and the transmission in Neutral.

3. Reconnect the vacuum hose to the throttle positioner.

Throttle Position (TP) Switch

1. Disconnect the throttle position switch terminal.

2. Using an ohmmeter, place one terminal to throttle switch connector and the other to the carburetor body.

3. Slowly raise the engine rpms.

4. Adjust the throttle position switch setting speed when the ohmmeter shows continuity. The setting speed should be 1800 rpms.

5. Reconnect the vacuum hose to the TVSV (M) port.

Idle Mixture Screw

♦ See Figures 36 and 37

As stated in Section 2, the Mixture Adjusting Screw (MAS) should be the very last item you try to adjust during tune-up or troubleshooting. The MAS is concealed behind a plug; the plug cannot be removed with the carburetor on the car. If adjustment is to be done, great care must be taken during removal of the plug; clearances are very tight and damage to the carburetor can occur.

1. Tag and disconnect all hoses and linkages attached to the carburetor.

2. Remove the carburetor.

3. Plug each carburetor vacuum port to prevent entry of metal particles.

4. Mark the center of the MAS plug with a punch. Drill a 0.256 in. (6.5mm) hole in the center of the plug.

✳✳ WARNING

The head of the screw is only 0.04 in. (1mm) below the plug—drill carefully and slowly to avoid damage.

5. The plug may come out with the drill at this time. If not, use a small screwdriver to reach through the hole and gently turn the adjusting screw all the way in. Do NOT overtighten the screw; just tighten it until it touches bottom.

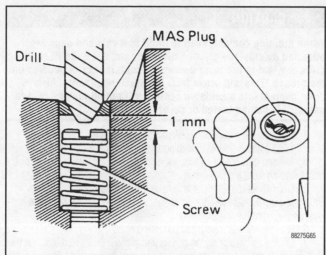

Fig. 36 The head of the screw is only 0.04 in. (1mm) below the plug. Drill carefully and slowly to avoid damage

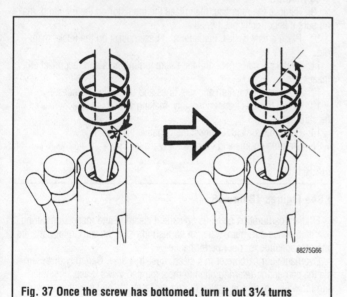

Fig. 37 Once the screw has bottomed, turn it out 3¼ turns

6. Use a 0.295 in. (7.5mm) drill to force the plug off.
7. Remove the adjusting screw. Inspect the tip for any damage; remove any steel particles. If the drill has damaged the top of the screw, it must be replaced.
8. Reinstall the adjusting screw. Turn it all the way in, just touching bottom.
9. Once the screw has bottomed, turn it out 3¼ turns.
10. Reinstall the carburetor and air cleaner.
11. Before adjusting idle speed and mixture, ALL the following conditions must be met:
   a. Air cleaner properly installed.
   b. Engine running at normal operating temperature.
   c. Choke fully opened.
   d. All accessories OFF.
   e. All vacuum lines connected.
   f. Ignition timing correctly set.
   g. Transmission in neutral.
   h. Fuel level should be approximately centered in float glass.
   i. For Calif. vehicles, EBCV off.
12. Connect a tachometer.
13. Start the engine.

14. Turn the MAS until the highest possible rpm is achieved.
15. Turn the idle speed adjusting screw until 700 rpm is achieved. The idle speed adjusting screw is located above and to the left (10 o'clock) of the mixture adjusting screw.
16. Repeat the last two steps several times. When the idle does not rise no matter how much the MAS is turned, proceed to the next Step.
17. Turn the MAS screw IN to set the idle to 650 rpm.
18. Turn the engine OFF. Remove the air cleaner.
19. Gently tap a new plug into place over the MAS plug. Check and adjust the fast idle speed to 650 rpm on M/T and 750 rpm on A/T transmissions.

➡The method used to set the idle mixture and speed is also known as the Lean Drop Method.

REMOVAL & INSTALLATION

◗ See Figures 38, 39, 40, 41 and 42

1. Disconnect the negative battery cable.
2. Loosen the radiator drain plug and drain the coolant into a suitable container.

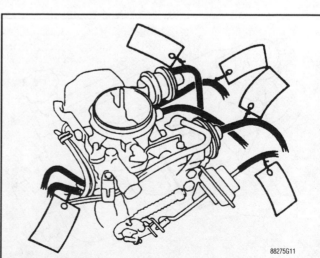

Fig. 38 Remove the air cleaner to access the carburetor

Fig. 39 Tag and disconnect all fuel, vacuum, coolant and electrical lines or hoses

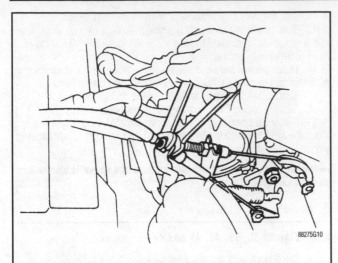

Fig. 40 Disconnect the accelerator and throttle linkages from the carburetor

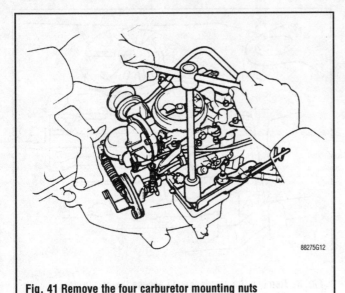

Fig. 41 Remove the four carburetor mounting nuts

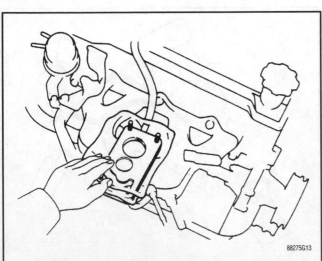

Fig. 42 Discard the base gasket and remove the insulator; do not discard the insulator

✳✳✳ **CAUTION**

When draining coolant, keep in mind that cats and dogs are attracted by ethylene glycol antifreeze, and are quite likely to drink any that is left in an uncovered container or in puddles on the ground. This will prove fatal in sufficient quantity. Always drain coolant into a sealable container. Coolant may be reused unless it is contaminated or several years old.

3. Unscrew the mounting screws and remove the air filter housing. Disconnect all hoses and lines leading from the air cleaner.

4. Tag and disconnect all fuel, vacuum, coolant and electrical lines or hoses leading from the carburetor.

5. Disconnect the accelerator linkage from the carburetor. On cars equipped with an automatic transmission, disconnect the throttle cable linkage running from the transmission.

6. Remove the four carburetor mounting nuts.

7. Lift the carburetor off the engine and place it on a clean cloth on the workbench. If desired, the insulator (base gasket) may also be removed.

8. Cover the inlet area of the manifold with clean rags or a plastic bag. This will prevent the entry of dust, dirt and loose parts.

To install:

9. Remove the rags/bag, then place the insulator on the manifold, making sure it is correctly positioned.

10. Place a new gasket, insulator and base gasket on the intake manifold.

11. Install the carburetor, tighten the mounting nuts and reconnect all linkages.

12. Connect the vacuum and fuel lines and the wiring harness.

13. Install the air cleaner assembly, making sure it is correctly seated on the carburetor.

14. Refill the coolant. Connect the negative battery cable.

15. Start the engine and check for any leaks. Check the float level.

OVERHAUL

▶ **See Figures 43 thru 65**

Efficient carburetion depends on careful cleaning and inspection during overhaul, since dirt, gum, water, or varnish in or on the carburetor parts are often responsible for poor performance.

Overhaul your carburetor in a clean, dust-free area. Carefully disassemble the carburetor, referring often to the exploded views. Keep all similar and look-alike parts segregated during disassembly and cleaning to avoid accidental interchange during assembly.

Carburetor overhaul kits are recommended for each overhaul. These kits contain all gaskets and new parts to replace those that deteriorate most rapidly. Failure to replace all parts supplied with the kit (especially gaskets) can result in poor performance and a leaks.

➡ **The following procedure is organized so that only one group of components is worked on at a time. This will help eliminate confusion of parts or sub-assemblies on the bench. Always keep parts in order; take great care not to lose small parts or clips.**

1. To remove the air horn, unscrew the air cleaner setting bolt.

2. Remove the fuel pipe clamp, union, fuel pipe and gaskets.

3. Label and disconnect the vacuum hoses. Inspect them for replacement.

4. Remove the pump arm pivot screw and pump arm with connecting link.

5. Disconnect the choke link.

6. Disconnect the choke opener linkage.

7. Remove the eight retaining screws along with the number plate, fuel pipe support and choke and solenoid wire clamps.

8. Lift the air horn with gasket from the carburetor body. Throw away the old gasket.

9. Disconnect the solenoid valve wires from the harness.

10. Disconnect the throttle position switch wire from the harness.

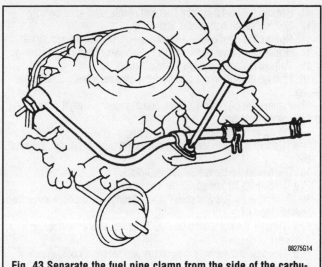

Fig. 43 Separate the fuel pipe clamp from the side of the carburetor

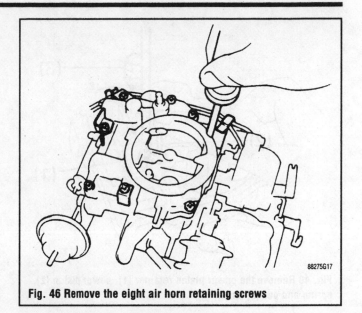

Fig. 46 Remove the eight air horn retaining screws

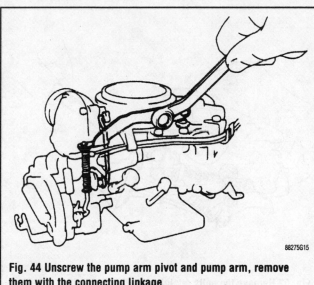

Fig. 44 Unscrew the pump arm pivot and pump arm, remove them with the connecting linkage

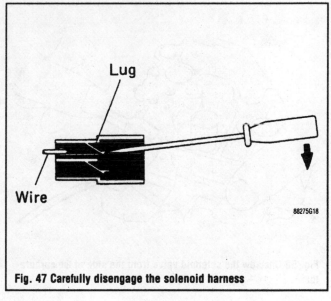

Fig. 47 Carefully disengage the solenoid harness

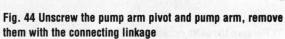

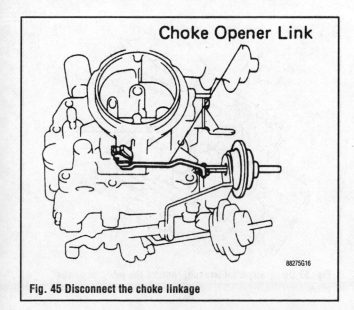

Fig. 45 Disconnect the choke linkage

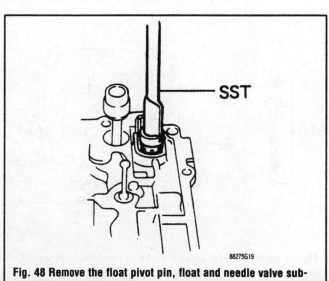

Fig. 48 Remove the float pivot pin, float and needle valve subassembly from the body

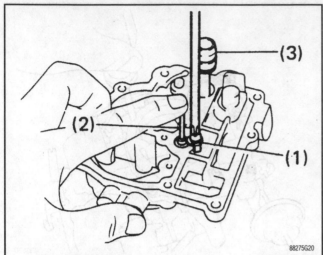

Fig. 49 Remove the power piston retainer (1), power piston (2), spring and pump plunger (3)

11. Remove the float pivot pin, float and needle valve subassembly.
12. Remove the air horn gasket and discard.
13. Remove the needle valve seat and gasket. Discard the old gasket.
14. Remove the power piston retainer (1), power piston (2) and spring.
15. Pull out the pump plunger (3) and remove the boot.
16. Remove the solenoid valves from the carburetor body. Discard the O-ring.
17. Remove the (a) stopper gasket, pump discharge weight, long spring and discharge large ball.
    a. Remove the (b) pump damping spring.
    b. Using a pair of tweezers, remove the (c) plunger retainer and small ball.
18. Disconnect the throttle positioner linkage.
    a. Unbolt the throttle positioner and remove.
19. To remove the jets and power valve, disengage the power valve, then remove the slow jet.
    a. Remove the nut, spring washer, TP levers, washer and spring in that order.
    b. Unscrew and separate the primary and secondary passage plugs from the body.
    c. Remove the primary and secondary main jets with gaskets. Discard the old gaskets.

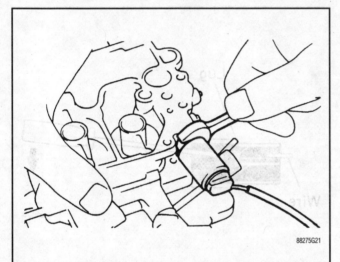

Fig. 50 Unscrew the solenoid valve from the side of the carburetor

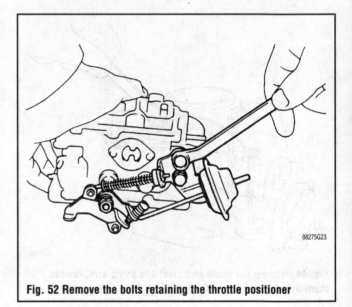

Fig. 52 Remove the bolts retaining the throttle positioner

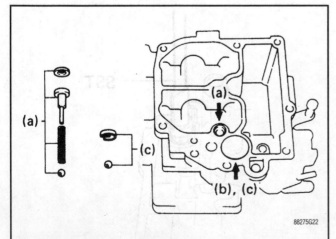

Fig. 51 Remove the (a) stopper gasket, pump discharge weight, long spring, discharge large ball, (b) pump damping spring, (c) plunger retainer and small ball

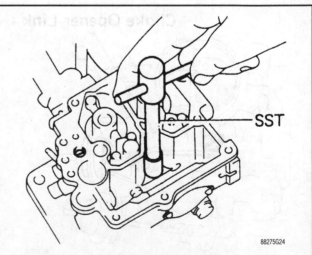

Fig. 53 Using a special wrench, remove the jets and power valve

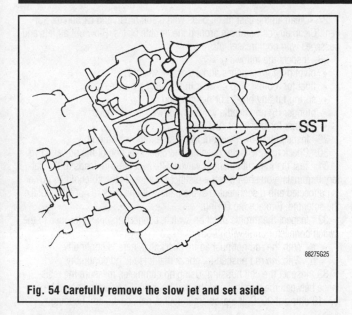

Fig. 54 Carefully remove the slow jet and set aside

20. Unscrew the AAP housing and remove the spring and diaphragm.
   a. Remove the AAP inlet plug and small ball.
   b. Remove the AAP outlet plug, short spring and small ball. Be careful with these small components. Do not loose or mix them up.
21. Remove the primary and secondary small venturies and gaskets. Discard the gaskets.
22. Unscrew and remove the sight glass retainer, glass and O-ring. Discard the O-ring.
23. On the fast idle cam, remove the throttle return spring and throttle back spring.
   a. Remove the bolt, washer, fast idle cam, washer, arm and washer in that order for the fast idle cam subassembly.
24. To remove the secondary throttle valve diaphragm, disconnect the linkage.
   a. Next, remove the two screws, diaphragm assembly and gasket.
   b. Remove the four screws, and disassemble the cap, spring, throttle valve diaphragm, housing and retainer.
25. Remove the screws retaining the throttle position switch with bracket.
26. To separate the body and flange, remove the screws and vacuum passage screw.
   a. Separate the body and flange. Remove the washer from the throttle valve shaft.
   b. Remove the idle mixture and idle speed adjusting screws.

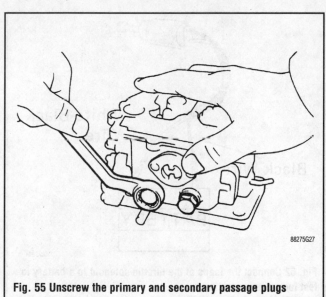

Fig. 55 Unscrew the primary and secondary passage plugs

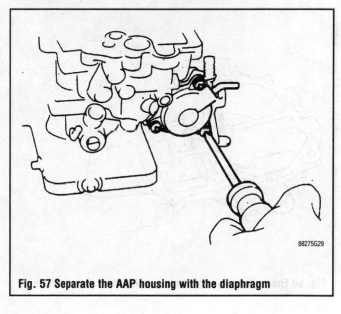

Fig. 57 Separate the AAP housing with the diaphragm

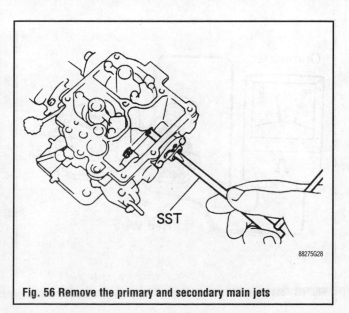

Fig. 56 Remove the primary and secondary main jets

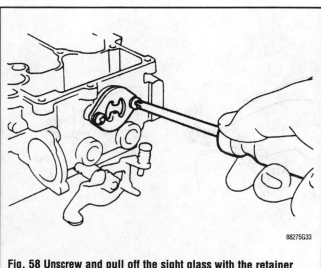

Fig. 58 Unscrew and pull off the sight glass with the retainer and O-ring

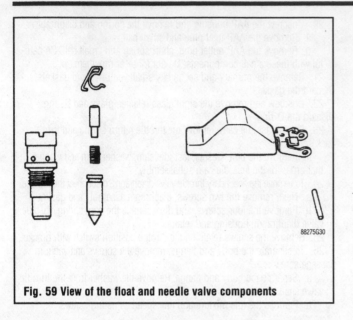

Fig. 59 View of the float and needle valve components

27. Clean all the cast metal parts with a soft brush and carburetor solvent. Clean any carbon from around the throttle plates. Blow out all jets and passages with compressed air.

28. Inspect the following:
- pivot pin for scratches and excessive wear (1)
- float for a broken lip or wear in the pivot pin holes (2)
- spring for any breaks or deformation (3)
- plunger (5) and needle valve (4) for wear or damages
- strainer for breaks or rust (6)

29. Inspect the power piston. Make sure it moves smoothly.

30. Check for any faulty opening and closing action of the power valve.

31. Test the fuel cut solenoid valves. Connect the wire leads to the battery terminals; you should feel a distinct click inside the solenoid as power is connected and disconnected at the battery. If this click is not felt, replace the solenoid. Replace the O-ring.

32. Inspect the throttle position switch, connect ohmmeter probes to the switch connector and switch body.
  a. With the rod not pushed in, check that there is continuity.
  b. With the rod pushed in, check that there is no continuity.

33. Inspect the coil housing. Using an ohmmeter, measure the resistance between the terminal and the coil housing. Resistance should be 17–19 ohms at 20°C. If a problem is found, replace the coil housing.

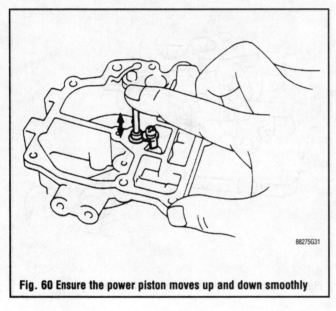

Fig. 60 Ensure the power piston moves up and down smoothly

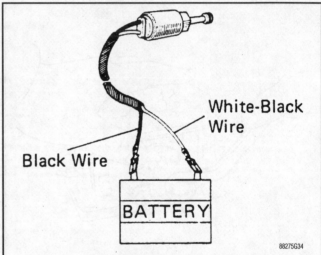

Fig. 62 Connect the leads of the throttle solenoid to a battery to test for proper operation

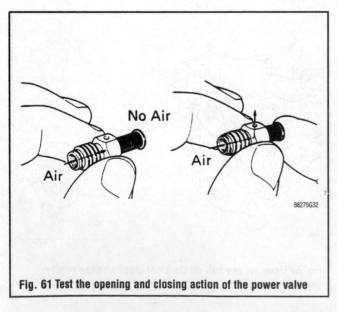

Fig. 61 Test the opening and closing action of the power valve

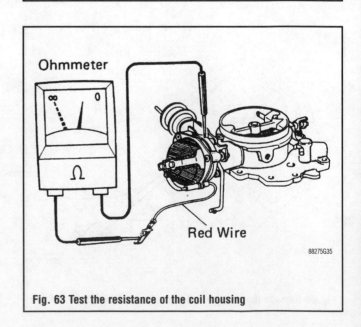

Fig. 63 Test the resistance of the coil housing

To assemble:

➡**Place new gaskets and O-rings throughout the carburetor assembly.**

34. Place a new gasket in position on the flange; install the body and tighten the 3 screws.

35. Assmeble the carburetor body and flange.
   a. Install the idle speed adjusting and idle mixture screws.
   b. Install the washer to the throttle valve shaft.
   c. Place a new gasket and body onto flange.
   d. Install a vacuum passage screw as shown in the illustration. Install the three screws.

36. Install the throttle position switch and bracket with the two screws.

37. To install the secondary throttle valve diaphragm, assemble the housing (1), diaphragm (2), spring (3) and cap (4). Install the four screws with the retainer.
   a. Place a new gasket into position.
   b. Install the diaphragm assembly with two screws.
   c. Connect the linkage from secondary throttle lever.
   d. Install the throttle back and return springs.

38. To install the fast idle cam, place the washer, fast idle cam, washer, cam with washer and bolt in place.

39. Install a new O-ring, sight glass and sight glass retainer.

40. Place the primary and secondary small venturies over the new gaskets.

41. When attaching the AAP, install the small ball, AAP outlet plug and short spring. Next install the other small ball and AAP inlet plug.
   a. Secure the diaphragm, spring and AAP housing with the three retaining screws.

42. Install the jets and power valve with new gaskets. Secure the primary and secondary passage plugs. Make sure to install new gaskets.
   a. Install the spring, washer, throttle levers with the spring washer and nuts. Install the slow jet and power valve.

43. Install the throttle positioner with the two bolts. connect the throttle positioner linkage.

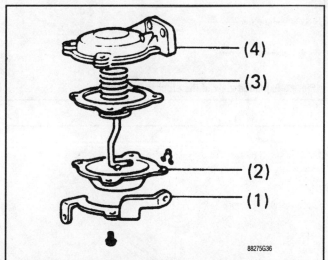

Fig. 64 Place the secondary throttle valve components in this order during assembly

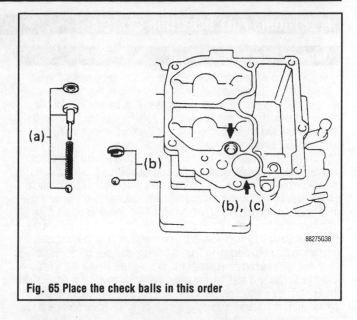

Fig. 65 Place the check balls in this order

44. Install the solenoid valves with a new gasket into the carburetor gasket.

45. Install the check balls for the acceleration as follows. Install all discharge large ball, long spring, pump discharge weight and stopper gasket.
   a. Using tweezers, insert the plunger small ball and retainer.
   b. Install the pump damping spring.

46. On the air horn, install the valve seat over the gasket into the fuel inlet.

47. Measure and adjust the float level by following the procedures outlined earlier in this section.

48. Install the power piston spring and piston into its bore and install the retainer.

49. Install the acceleration pump plunger and its boot.

50. Place a new gasket onto the air horn.

51. Install the needle valve assembly, the float and the pivot pin. Insert the float lip between the plunger and the clip when installing the float.

52. Install the solenoid valves with new gaskets and O-rings into the body of the carburetor.

53. Assemble the air horn and body. Install the eight screws, paying particular attention to the various brackets, wire clamps and steel number plate. Tighten the screws evenly, in steps, using a criss-cross pattern.

54. Install the accelerator pump arm. Install the pump arm to the air horn with the pump plunger hole and lever aligned.

55. Connect the choke link and the pump connecting link.

56. Install the fuel pipe and union.

57. With the carburetor still on the bench, move the various linkages by hand, checking for smooth operation. Follow the adjustment procedures outlined earlier.

58. Reinstall the carburetor on the intake manifold, following the procedure outlined earlier.

59. Start the engine and allow it to warm up normally. During this time, pay careful attention to the high idle speed, the operation of the choke and its controls and the idle quality. If you worked carefully and accurately, and performed the bench set-up properly, the carburetor should need very little adjustment after reinstallation.

ELECTRONIC FUEL INJECTION SYSTEM

General Information

Fuel injected engines are equipped with the Toyota Computer Control System (TCCS). This integrated control system allows the Engine Control Module (ECM) to control other systems as well as the fuel injection. On earlier systems, the fuel management was performed by the EFI computer; in the current system, the control unit also oversees ignition timing and advance, EGR function, idle speed control (ISC system), Electronically Controlled Transmission (ECT) function as well as on-board diagnostics and back-up or fail-safe functions. The control unit is a sophisticated micro-computer, receiving input signals from many sources and locations on the vehicle. It is capable of rapid calculation of many variables and controls several output circuits simultaneously. This system is broken down into 3 major sub-systems: the Fuel System, Air Induction System and the Electronic Control System. Keeping these divisions in mind will shorten troubleshooting and diagnostic time. An electric fuel pump supplies sufficient fuel, under a constant pressure, to the injectors. These injectors allow a metered quantity of fuel into the intake manifold according to signals from the ECM. The air induction system provides sufficient air for the engine operation. This system includes the throttle body, air intake device and idle control system components.

Relieving Fuel Pressure

1. Disconnect the negative battery cable.
2. Unbolt the retaining screws and remove the protective shield for the fuel filter (if so equipped).
3. Place a large pan under the delivery pipe (large connection) to catch the dripping fuel and SLOWLY loosen the union bolt to bleed off the fuel pressure.

Electric Fuel Pump

REMOVAL & INSTALLATION

The electric fuel pump is contained within the fuel tank. On 1988–92 models, it is necessary to remove the fuel tank from the vehicle in order to reach the pump. On 1993–97 models, the fuel pump can be accessed by removing the rear seat cushion and service hole cover.

1988–92 Models

♦ **See Figures 66, 67, 68 and 69**

➡Before disconnecting fuel system lines, clean the fittings with a spray-type engine cleaner. Follow the instructions on the cleaner. Do not soak fuel system parts in liquid cleaning solvent.

❊❊ CAUTION

The fuel injection system is under pressure. Release pressure slowly and contain spillage. Observe "no smoking/no open flame" precautions. Have a Class B-C (dry powder) fire extinguisher within arm's reach at all times.

1. Disconnect the negative battery cable and relieve the fuel pressure. Remove the filler cap.
2. Remove the fuel tank from the vehicle.
3. Remove the fuel pump bracket attaching screws, then remove the fuel pump/bracket assembly from the tank.
4. Pull the lower side of the fuel pump from the bracket.
5. Remove the nuts attaching the wires to the fuel pump.
6. Disconnect the hose from the pump.
7. Separate the filter from the pump. Use a small screwdriver to remove the attaching clip.

8. While the tank is out and disassembled, inspect it for any signs of rust, leakage or metal damage. If any problem is found, replace the tank.
9. Inspect all of the lines, hoses and fittings for any sign of corrosion, wear or damage to the surfaces. Check the pump outlet hose and the filter for restrictions.
10. When reassembling, ALWAYS replace the sealing gaskets with new ones. Also replace any rubber parts showing any sign of deterioration.

To install:
11. Install the pump filter using a new clip. Install the rubber cushion under the filter.
12. Connect the outlet hose to the pump, then attach the pump to the bracket.
13. Connect the wires to the fuel pump with the nuts.
14. Install the fuel pump and bracket assembly onto the tank. Use new gaskets.
15. Install the fuel tank.
16. Start the engine and check carefully for any sign of leakage around the tank and lines. Road test the vehicle for proper operation.

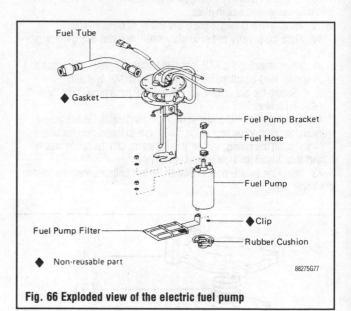

Fig. 66 Exploded view of the electric fuel pump

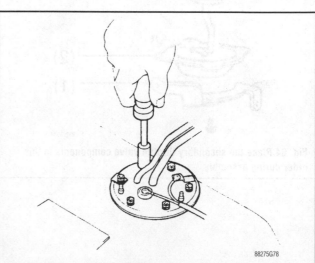

Fig. 67 Remove the bolts retaining the pump bracket to the fuel tank

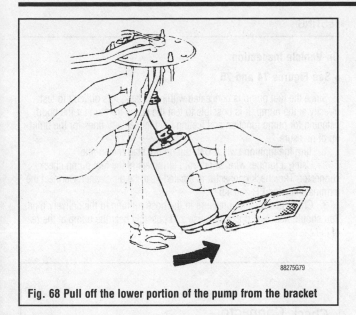

Fig. 68 Pull off the lower portion of the pump from the bracket

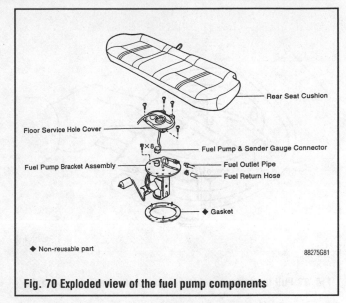

Fig. 70 Exploded view of the fuel pump components

◆ Non-reusable part

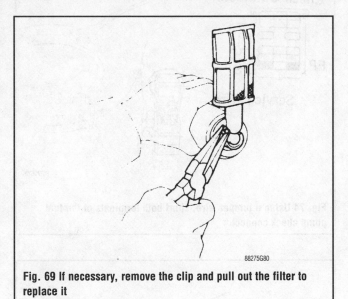

Fig. 69 If necessary, remove the clip and pull out the filter to replace it

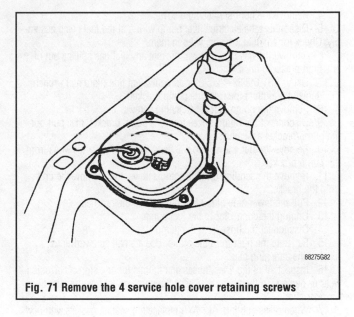

Fig. 71 Remove the 4 service hole cover retaining screws

1993–97 Models

▶ See Figures 70, 71, 72 and 73

※※ CAUTION

The fuel injection system is under pressure. Release pressure slowly and contain spillage. Observe no smoking/no open flame precautions. Have a Class B-C (dry powder) fire extinguisher within arm's reach at all times.

1. Disconnect the negative battery cable.

※※ CAUTION

On models with an airbag, wait at least 90 seconds from the time that the ignition switch is turned to the LOCK position and the battery is disconnected before performing any further work. Refer to Section 7 for all air bag warnings.

2. Relieve the fuel pressure.
3. Remove the rear seat cushion.

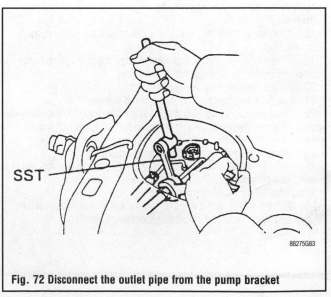

Fig. 72 Disconnect the outlet pipe from the pump bracket

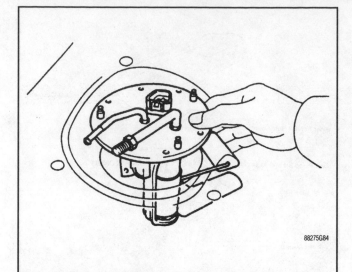

Fig. 73 Pull the pump bracket with pump attached from the tank

4. Remove the floor service hole cover.

5. Disconnect the electrical fuel pump wiring at the fuel pump assembly. Check for any fuel leakage while in there.

6. Remove the gas cap, this will prevent any fuel gas spilling out of any high pressure lines.

7. Using SST 09631–22020 or an equivalent line (flare nut) wrench, disconnect the outlet pipe from the pump bracket.

8. Remove the pump bracket attaching screws.

9. Disconnect the return hoses from the pump bracket, then pull out the pump/bracket assembly.

10. Remove the nut and spring washer, then disconnect the wires from the pump bracket.

11. Remove the sending unit attaching screws, then remove the unit from the bracket.

12. Pull the lower side of the fuel pump from the bracket.

13. Unplug the connector to the fuel pump.

14. Disconnect the hose from the pump.

15. Separate the filter from the pump. Use a small screwdriver to remove the attaching clip.

16. Inspect all of the lines, hoses and fittings for any sign of corrosion, wear or damage to the surfaces. Check the pump outlet hose and the filter for restrictions.

17. When reassembling, ALWAYS replace the sealing gaskets with new ones. Also replace any rubber parts showing any sign of deterioration.

To install:

18. Install the pump filter using a new clip. Install the rubber cushion under the filter.

19. Connect the outlet hose to the pump, then attach the pump to the bracket and tighten to 22–25 ft. lbs. (29–34 Nm).

20. Engage the connector to the fuel pump.

21. Install the fuel sending unit to the pump bracket.

22. Install the fuel pump and bracket assembly onto the tank. Use new gaskets. Tighten the pump bracket retaining screws to 34 inch lbs. (4 Nm).

23. Connect the return hoses to the pump bracket.

24. Install the service hole cover, then the engage the fuel pump and sending unit connector.

25. Install the rear seat cushion.

26. Start the engine and check carefully for any sign of leakage around the tank and lines. Road test the vehicle for proper operation.

TESTING

On-Vehicle Inspection

♦ **See Figures 74 and 75**

Since the fuel pump is concealed within the tank, it is difficult to test directly at the pump. It is possible to test the pump from under the hood, listening for pump function and feeling the fuel delivery lines for the build-up of pressure.

1. Turn the ignition switch **ON**, but do not start the engine.

2. Using a jumper wire, short both terminals of the fuel pump check connector. The check connector is located near the air cleaner. Connect the terminals labeled **FP** and **+B**.

3. Check that there is pressure in the hose running to the delivery pipe. You should hear fuel pressure noise and possibly hear the pump at the rear of the car.

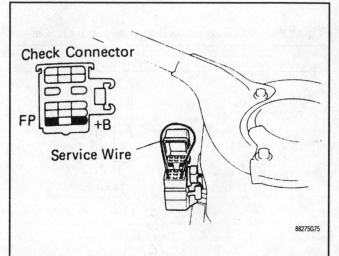

Fig. 74 Using a jumper wire, short both terminals of the fuel pump check connector

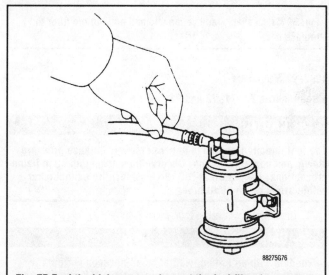

Fig. 75 Feel the high pressure hose at the fuel filter for pressure

4. If the fuel pump failed to function, it may indicate a faulty pump, but before removing the fuel pump, check the following items within the pump system:

   a. All fusible links
   b. All fuses (EFI—15amp and IGN—10.0amp)
   c. H- fuse (AM2 30A)
   d. EFI main relay
   e. Fuel pump
   f. Circuit opening relay
   g. All wiring connections and grounds.
5. Turn the ignition to **OFF**.
6. Remove the jumper wire.

Fuel Pressure

▶ See Figure 76

1. Check that the battery voltage is approximately 12 volts.
2. Disconnect the negative battery cable.

✳✳ CAUTION

On models with an airbag, wait at least 90 seconds from the time that the ignition switch is turned to the LOCK position and the battery is disconnected before performing any further work. Refer to Section 7 for all air bag warnings.

3. Relieve the fuel system pressure.
4. Disconnect the hose from the fuel filter outlet.
5. Connect the hose and a fuel pressure gauge to the fuel filter outlet with three new gaskets and the union bolt.
6. Wipe any spilled gasoline.
7. Connect the negative battery cable.
8. Using a jumper wire, short terminals FP and +B of the check connector.
9. Turn the ignition switch **ON**, but do not start the car.
10. The fuel pressure should read 38–44 psi (265–304 kPa).
11. If the pressure is too high, the pressure regulator is probably defective. If it is too low, check for the following:
   a. Fuel hoses and connections for leaks or restrictions.
   b. Defective fuel pump.
   c. Clogged fuel filter.
   d. Defective pressure regulator.
12. After checking the fuel pressure, turn the ignition **OFF** and remove the jumper wire from the check connector.
13. Disconnect the negative battery cable.

14. Relieve the fuel system pressure and remove the pressure gauge.
15. Connect the hose to the fuel filter outlet using new gaskets.
16. Wipe any fuel spillage.
17. Connect the negative battery cable, then start the engine and check for leaks.

Throttle Body

REMOVAL & INSTALLATION

4A-GE Engine

▶ See Figures 77, 78 and 79

1. Disconnect the negative battery cable.
2. Either drain the coolant from the throttle body by disconnecting a coolant hose or open the engine draincock.
3. Disconnect the throttle return spring.
4. Disconnect the throttle cable.
5. Label and disconnect the vacuum hose.
6. Carefully remove the throttle position sensor wiring connector.

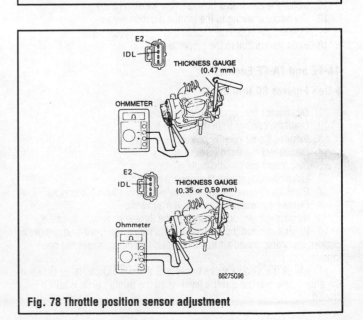

Fig. 77 Remove the throttle body bolts and nuts to separate the unit from the engine

Fig. 76 Fuel pressure can be checked using an inexpensive pressure/vacuum gauge

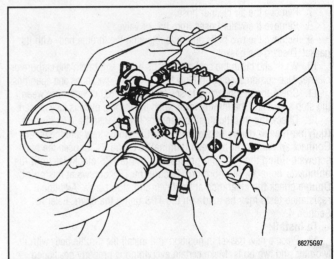

Fig. 78 Throttle position sensor adjustment

Clearance between lever and stop screw	Between terminals	Resistance
0 mm (0 in.)	VTA – E_2	0.2 – 0.8 kΩ
0.35 mm (0.0138 in.)	IDL – E_2	Less than 2.3 kΩ
0.59 mm (0.0232 in.)	IDL – E_2	Infinity
Throttle valve fully opened position	VTA – E_2	3.3 – 10 kΩ
–	Vcc – E_2	3 – 7 kΩ

88275G96

Fig. 79 Throttle position sensor adjustment specifications

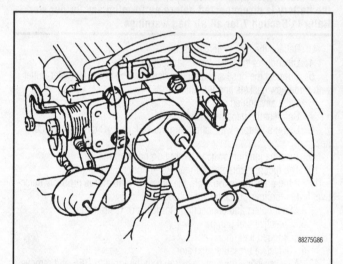

The throttle body is attached to the air intake chamber

88275PA2

7. Remove the air cleaner hose.

8. Remove the water hoses from the air valve.

9. Remove the two bolts and nuts retaining the throttle body with its gasket. Discard the gasket.

10. Wash and clean the cast metal parts with a soft brush and carburetor cleaner. Use compressed air to blow through all the passages and openings.

11. Check the throttle valve to see that there is NO clearance between the stop screw and the throttle lever when the throttle plate is fully closed.

12. Check the throttle position sensor (TPS). Insert a 0.0185 inch (0.47mm) feeler gauge between the throttle stop screw and the lever. Connect an ohmmeter between terminal **IDL** and **E₂**. Loosen the two screws holding the TPS and gradually turn the TPS clockwise until the ohmmeter deflects, but no more. Secure the TPS screws at this point. Double check the clearance at the lever and stop screw. Additional resistance tests may be made on the TPS using the chart. Refer to Section 4.

To install:

13. Place a new gasket in position and install the throttle body with its two nuts and two bolts. Make certain everything is properly positioned before securing the unit. Tighten the bolts to 16 ft. lbs. (22 Nm).

14. Connect the water hoses to the air valve.

15. Install the air cleaner hose and the vacuum hoses.

16. Connect the wiring to the throttle position sensor.

17. Connect the accelerator cable and its return spring.

18. Refill the coolant to the proper level.

4A-FE and 7A-FE Engines

♦ See Figures 80 thru 86

1. Disconnect the negative battery cable.

2. Drain the coolant from the throttle body.

3. Remove the air cleaner hose.

4. Disconnect the throttle return spring.

5. Disconnect the throttle cable.

6. Label and disconnect the vacuum hoses.

7. Carefully remove the throttle position sensor wiring connector.

8. Remove the water hoses from the air valve.

9. Remove the two bolts, nuts and the throttle body with its gasket.

10. Wash and clean the cast metal parts with a soft brush and carburetor cleaner. Use compressed air to blow through all the passages and openings.

11. Check the throttle valve to see that there is NO clearance between the stop screw and the throttle lever when the throttle plate is fully closed.

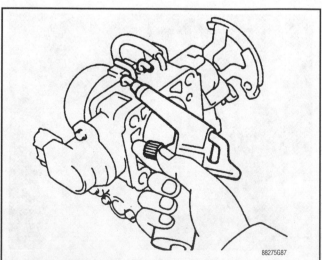

Fig. 80 Remove the 2 bolts and nuts to detach the throttle body from the air intake chamber

88275G86

Fig. 81 Use compressed air to clean all passages and openings in the throttle body

88275G87

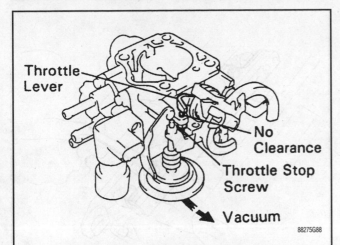

Fig. 82 Check the throttle valve to see that there is NO clearance between the stop screw and the throttle lever when the throttle plate is fully closed

➡On 1993–97 4A-FE and 7A-FE models equipped with a throttle opener, apply vacuum to the opener before inserting the feeler gauge between the throttle stop screw and the lever.

12. Check the throttle position sensor (TPS). Insert a 0.028 inch (0.70mm) feeler gauge between the throttle stop screw and the lever. Connect an ohmmeter between terminal IDL and E₂. Loosen the two screws holding the TPS and gradually turn the TPS clockwise until the ohmmeter deflects, but no more. Secure the TPS screws at this point. Double check the clearance at the lever and stop screw.

To install:

13. Place a new gasket in position and install the throttle body with its two nuts and two bolts. On the 1993–97 4A-FE and 7A-FE engines install the throttle body (with new gasket facing the protrusion downward) with the 2 bolts and nuts, tighten in the correct sequence. Make certain everything is properly positioned before securing the unit. Tighten the bolts to 16 ft. lbs. (21 Nm).

14. Attach all wiring to each labeled component.
15. Connect the all water and vacuum hoses.
16. Install the air cleaner hose.
17. Connect the wiring to the throttle position sensor.
18. Connect the accelerator cable and its return spring.
19. Refill the coolant to the proper level.

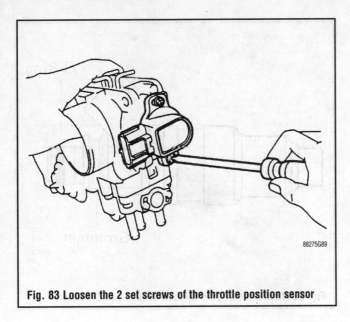

Fig. 83 Loosen the 2 set screws of the throttle position sensor

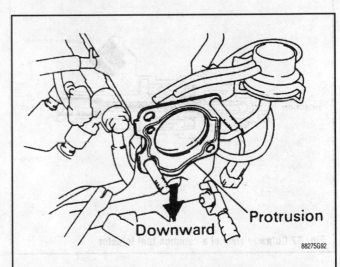

Fig. 85 Place the new gasket on the air intake chamber with the protrusion facing downward

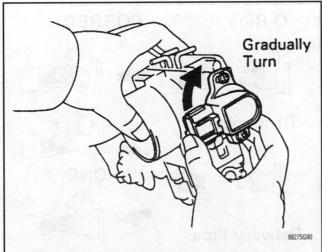

Fig. 84 Gradually turn the TPS clockwise until the ohmmeter deflects

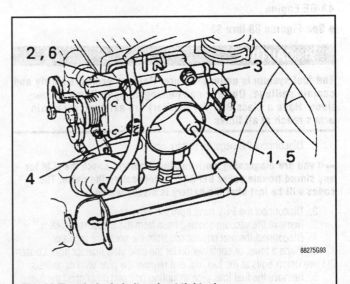

Fig. 86 Throttle body bolt and nut tightening sequence

Fuel Injectors

♦ **See Figure 87**

The injectors deliver a measured quantity of fuel into the intake manifold according to signals from the ECM. As driving conditions change, the computer signals each injector to stay open a longer or shorter period of time, thus controlling the amount of fuel introduced into the engine. An injector, being an electric component, is either on or off (open or closed); there is no variable control for an injector other than duration.

Cleanliness equals success when working on a fuel injected system. Every component must be treated with the greatest care and be protected from dust, grime and impact damage. The miniaturized and solid state circuitry is easily damaged by a jolt. Additionally, care must be used in dealing with electrical connectors. Look for and release any locking mechanisms on the connector before separating the connectors. When reattaching, make sure each pin is properly lined up and seated before pushing the connector closed.

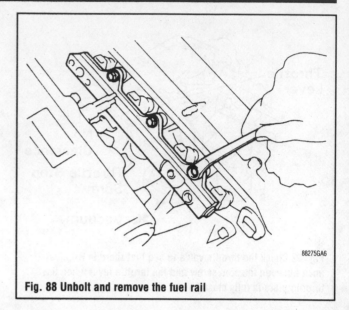

Fig. 88 Unbolt and remove the fuel rail

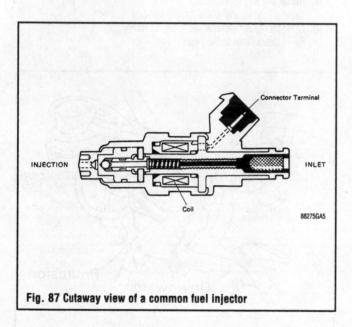

Fig. 87 Cutaway view of a common fuel injector

REMOVAL & INSTALLATION

4A-GE Engine

♦ **See Figures 88 thru 93**

> ❊❊❊ **CAUTION**

The fuel system is under pressure. Release pressure slowly and contain spillage. Observe no smoking/no open flame precautions. Have a Class B-C (dry powder) fire extinguisher within arm's reach at all times.

1. Disconnect the negative battery cable.

➡**If you are diagnosing a driveability problem, check the ECM for any stored trouble codes BEFORE disconnecting the cable. The codes will be lost after the battery is disconnected.**

2. Disconnect the PCV hose from the valve cover.
3. Remove the vacuum sensing hose from the pressure regulator.
4. Disconnect the fuel return hose from the pressure regulator.
5. Place a towel or container under the cold start injector pipe. Loosen the two union bolts at the fuel line and remove the pipe with its gaskets.
6. Remove the fuel inlet pipe mounting bolt and disconnect the fuel inlet hose by removing the fuel union bolt, the two gaskets and the hose.

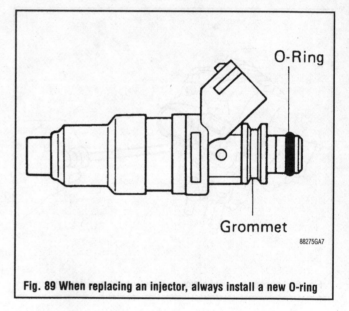

Fig. 89 When replacing an injector, always install a new O-ring

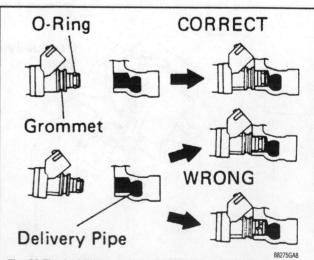

Fig. 90 The fuel injectors must be installed properly into the fuel rail

7. Disconnect the injector electrical wiring.

8. At the fuel delivery pipe (rail), remove the three bolts. Lift the delivery pipe and the injectors free of the engine. DON'T drop the injectors.

9. Remove the four insulators and three collars from the cylinder head.

10. Pull the injectors free of the delivery pipe.

To install:

11. Before installing the injectors back into the fuel rail, install a NEW O-ring on each injector.

12. Coat each O-ring with a light coat of gasoline (NEVER use oil of any sort) and install the injectors into the delivery pipe. Make certain each injector can be smoothly rotated. If they do not rotate smoothly, the O-ring is not in its correct position.

13. Install the insulators into each injector hole. Place the three spacers on the delivery pipe mounting holes in the cylinder head.

14. Place the delivery pipe and injectors on the cylinder head and again check that the injectors rotate smoothly. Install the three bolts and tighten them to 13 ft. lbs. (17 Nm).

15. Connect the electrical connectors to each injector.

16. Install two new gaskets and attach the inlet pipe and fuel union bolt. Tighten the bolt to 22 ft. lbs. (30 Nm). Install the mounting bolt.

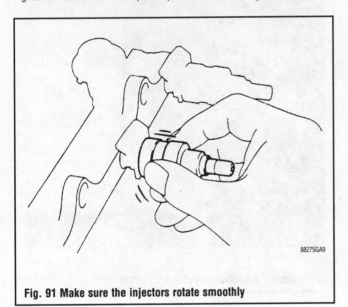

Fig. 91 Make sure the injectors rotate smoothly

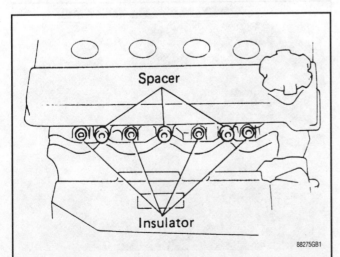

Fig. 92 Make sure the insulators and spacers are correctly positioned on the cylinder head

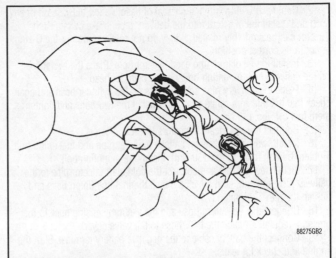

Fig. 93 Once the injectors are installed, again make sure they rotate smoothly

17. Install new gaskets and connect the cold start injector pipe to the delivery pipe and cold start injector. Install the fuel line union bolts and tighten them to 13 ft. lbs. (17 Nm).

18. Connect the fuel return hose and the vacuum sensing hose to the pressure regulator. Attach the PCV hose to the valve cover.

19. Connect the battery cable to the negative battery terminal. Start the engine and check for leaks.

✷✷ CAUTION

If there is a leak at any fitting, the line will be under pressure and the fuel may spray in a fine mist. This mist is extremely explosive. Shut the engine off immediately if any leakage is detected. Use rags to wrap the leaking fitting until the pressure diminishes and wipe up any fuel from the engine area.

4A-FE Engine

1990–92 MODELS

✷✷ CAUTION

The fuel system is under pressure. Release pressure slowly and contain spillage. Observe no smoking/no open flame precautions. Have a Class B-C (dry powder) fire extinguisher within arm's reach at all times.

1. Disconnect the negative battery cable.

2. Disconnect the PCV hose from the valve cover.

3. Remove the vacuum sensing hose from the pressure regulator.

4. Disconnect the fuel return hose from the pressure regulator.

5. Place a towel or container under the cold start injector pipe. Loosen the two union bolts at the fuel line and remove the pipe with its gasket.

6. Remove the fuel inlet pipe mounting bolt and disconnect the fuel inlet hose by removing the fuel union bolt, the two gaskets and the hose.

7. Disconnect the injector electrical connection.

8. At the fuel delivery pipe (rail), remove the two bolts. Lift the delivery pipe and the injectors free of the engine. DON'T drop the injector.

9. Remove the 4 insulators and 2 collars from the cylinder head.

10. Pull the injectors free of the delivery pipe.

To Install:

11. Before installing the injectors back into the fuel rail, install a NEW O-ring on each injector.

12. Coat each O-ring with a light coat of gasoline (NEVER use oil of any sort) and install the injectors into the delivery pipe. Make certain each injector can be smoothly rotated. If they do not rotate smoothly, the O-ring is not in its correct position.

13. Install the insulators into each injector hole. Place the two spacers on the delivery pipe mounting holes in the cylinder head.

14. Place the delivery pipe and injectors on the cylinder head and again check that the injectors rotate smoothly. Install the two bolts and tighten them to 11 ft. lbs. (15 Nm)

15. Connect the electrical connectors to each injector.

16. Install two new gaskets and attach the inlet pipe and fuel union bolt. Tighten the bolt to 22 ft. lbs. (30 Nm). Install the mounting bolt.

17. Install new gaskets and connect the cold start injector pipe to the delivery pipe and cold start injector. Install the fuel line union bolts and tighten them to 13 ft. lbs. (17 Nm).

18. Connect the fuel return hose and the vacuum sensing hose to the pressure regulator. Attach the PCV hose to the valve cover.

19. Connect the battery cable to the negative battery terminal. Start the engine and check for leaks.

⚙ CAUTION

If there is a leak at any fitting, the line will be under pressure and the fuel may spray in a fine mist. This mist is extremely explosive. Shut the engine OFF immediately if any leakage is detected. Use rags to wrap the leaking fitting until the pressure diminishes and wipe up any fuel from the engine area.

4A-FE and 7A-FE Engines

1993–97 MODELS

⚙ CAUTION

The fuel system is under pressure. Release pressure slowly and contain spillage. Observe no smoking/no open flame precautions. Have a Class B-C (dry powder) fire extinguisher within arm's reach at all times.

1. Disconnect the negative battery cable.

⚙ CAUTION

On models with an airbag, wait at least 90 seconds from the time that the ignition switch is turned to the LOCK position and the battery is disconnected before performing any further work. Refer to Section 7 for all air bag warnings.

2. Relieve the fuel pressure.
3. Remove the air cleaner hose and cap.
4. Disconnect the accelerator cable bracket from the throttle body.
5. Disconnect the throttle body from the air intake chamber. Using a 6mm hexagon wrench, remove the 3 bolts and 2 nuts, then disconnect the throttle body and chamber cover assembly from the intake manifold. Remove and discard the gasket.
6. Remove the engine hanger and air intake chamber stay and EGR vacuum modulator if so equipped.
7. Remove the EGR valve and pipe if so equipped.
8. Remove all necessary hoses/electrical connections.
9. Separate the injector electrical wiring.
10. Detach the fuel inlet hose from the delivery pipe.
11. Disconnect the fuel return hose from the fuel pressure regulator.
12. At the fuel delivery pipe (rail), remove the two bolts. Lift the delivery pipe and the injectors free of the engine. DON'T drop the injectors.
13. Remove the 4 insulators and 2 collars from the intake manifold. Pull the injectors free of the delivery pipe.
14. Remove the O-rings and grommet from each of the injectors and discard.

To install:

15. Before installing the injectors back into the fuel rail, install a NEW O-ring on each injector.

16. Coat each O-ring with a light coat of gasoline (NEVER use oil of any sort) and install the injectors with a turning motion into the delivery pipe. Make certain each injector can be smoothly rotated. If they do not rotate smoothly, the O-ring is not in its correct position.

| 1. Injectors | 2. Injector wiring |

Fuel injectors are attached to the side of the fuel rail

Label and disconnect the wiring to each injector

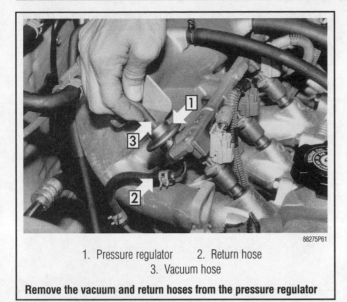

1. Pressure regulator   2. Return hose
3. Vacuum hose

88275P61

Remove the vacuum and return hoses from the pressure regulator

17. Install the insulators into each injector hole. Place the two spacers on the delivery pipe mounting holes in the intake manifold.

18. Place the delivery pipe and injectors on the intake manifold and again check that the injectors rotate smoothly. Position the injector connector upward. Install the two bolts and tighten them to 11 ft. lbs. (15 Nm).

➡**The No. 1 and No. 3 injector connections are gray and the No. 2 and No. 4 injector connections are dark gray.**

19. Connect the electrical wiring to each injector.

20. Install two new gaskets and attach the inlet pipe and fuel union bolt. Tighten the bolt to 22 ft. lbs. (30 Nm). Install the mounting bolt.

21. Install the air intake chamber cover with a NEW gasket. Tighten the retaining bolts in steps to 14 ft. lbs. (19 Nm).

22. Install all necessary hoses and electrical connections.

23. Install the EGR valve and pipe if so equipped.

24. Install the engine hanger and air intake chamber stay and EGR vacuum modulator if so equipped.

25. Install a new gasket on the air intake chamber stay, facing the protrusion downward. Install the throttle body and tighten the bolts evenly (in a X-pattern) to 16 ft. lbs. (21 Nm).

26. Connect the accelerator cable bracket to the throttle body.

27. Install the air cleaner hose and cap.

28. Connect the battery cable to the negative battery terminal. Start the engine and check for leaks.

❊❊ CAUTION

If there is a leak at any fitting, the line will be under pressure and the fuel may spray in a fine mist. This mist is extremely explosive. Shut the engine OFF immediately if any leakage is detected. Use rags to wrap the leaking fitting until the pressure diminishes and wipe up any fuel from the engine area.

TESTING

♦ **See Figure 94**

The simplest way to test the injectors is simply to listen to them with the engine running. Use either a stethoscope-type tool or the blade of a long screw driver to touch each injector while the engine is idling. You should hear a distinct clicking as each injector opens and closes.

Additionally, the resistance of the injector can be easily checked. Disconnect the negative battery cable and remove the electrical connector from the injector to be tested. Use an ohmmeter to check the resistance

TCCS5P03

Fig. 94 Fuel injector testers can be purchased or sometimes rented

across the terminals of the injector. Correct ohmmage is approximately 13.8 ohms at 68°F (20°C); slight variations are acceptable due to temperature conditions.

Never attempt to check a removed injector by hooking it directly to the battery. The injector runs on a much smaller voltage and the 12 volts from the battery will destroy it internally.

Cold Start Injector

REMOVAL & INSTALLATION

4A-GE and 4A-FE Engines

♦ **See Figure 95**

Only the 1988–92 4A-GE and 4A-FE engines are equipped with a cold start injector.

❊❊ CAUTION

The fuel system is under pressure. Release pressure slowly and contain spillage. Observe no smoking/no open flame precautions. Have a Class B-C (dry powder) fire extinguisher within arm's reach at all times.

1. Disconnect the negative battery cable.

2. Remove the wiring connector at the cold start injector.

3. Wrap the fuel pipe connection in a rag or towel. Remove the two union bolts and the cold start injector pipe with its gaskets. Slowly loosen the union bolt.

4. Remove the two retaining bolts and remove the cold start injector with its gasket.

5. When reinstalling, always use a new gasket for the injector. Install it with the injector, then tighten the two mounting bolts to 7 ft. lbs. (82 inch lbs.).

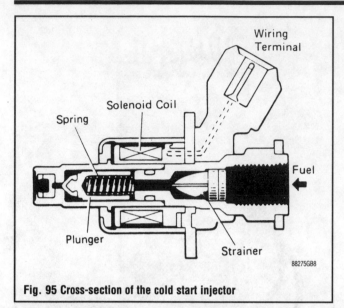

Fig. 95 Cross-section of the cold start injector

6. Again using new gaskets, connect the cold start injector pipe to the delivery pipe (fuel rail) and to the cold start injector. Tighten the bolts to 13 ft. lbs. (17 Nm).

7. Install the wiring to the cold start injector.

8. Connect the negative battery cable. Start the engine and check for leaks.

TESTING

▶ **See Figure 96**

1. Switch the ignition **OFF**.

2. Disconnect the electrical connector from the cold start injector

3. Use an ohmmeter to check the resistance of the injector. Correct resistance is 2–4 ohms. at 68°F (20°C) on the 4A-FE engine and 3–5 ohms. at 68°F (20°C) on the 4A-GE engine. The resistance specification may vary slightly with the temperature of the injector. Use common sense and good judgment when testing.

4. If the resistance is not within specifications, it must be replaced.

5. Reconnect the electrical wiring to the cold start injector.

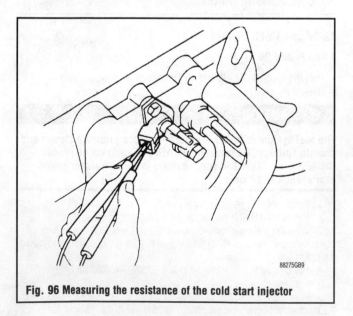

Fig. 96 Measuring the resistance of the cold start injector

REMOVAL & INSTALLATION

4A-GE Engine

▶ **See Figures 97 and 98**

1. Disconnect the negative battery cable. Relieve the fuel pressure. Remove the vacuum sensing hose from the fuel pressure regulator.

2. Remove the fuel hose from the regulator.

3. Remove the two retaining bolts and pull the regulator out of the fuel rail.

To install:

4. When reinstalling (replace O-ring) the two retaining bolts are tightened to 5 ft. lbs. (65 inch lbs.) Connect the two hoses (fuel and vacuum).

5. Start the engine and check carefully for leaks.

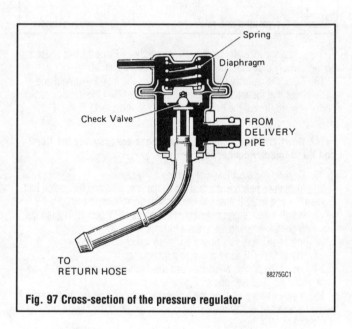

Fig. 97 Cross-section of the pressure regulator

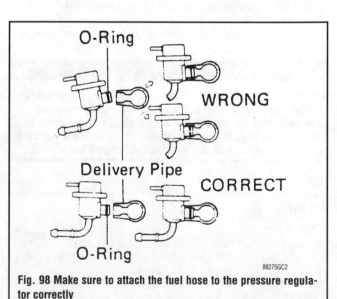

Fig. 98 Make sure to attach the fuel hose to the pressure regulator correctly

4A-FE and 7A-FE Engines

1. Disconnect the negative battery cable.
2. Relieve fuel system pressure.

✳✳ CAUTION

The fuel system is under pressure. Release pressure slowly and contain spillage. Observe "no smoking/no open flame" precautions. Have a Class B-C (dry powder) fire extinguisher within arm's reach at all times.

3. Unplug the vacuum sensing hose from the fuel pressure regulator.

FUEL TANK

Tank Assembly

REMOVAL & INSTALLATION

▶ See Figures 99 and 100

➡Before removing fuel system parts, clean them with a spray-type engine cleaner. Follow the instructions on the cleaner. Do not soak fuel system parts in liquid cleaning solvent. Refer to illustration of fuel tank and fuel pump assembly before starting this service repair.

✳✳ CAUTION

The fuel injection system is under pressure. Release pressure slowly and contain spillage. Observe no smoking/no open flame precautions. Have a Class B-C (dry powder) fire extinguisher within arm's reach at all times.

1. Disconnect the negative battery cable. Relieve the fuel pressure. Remove the filler cap. Using a siphon or pump, drain the fuel from the tank and store it in a proper metal container with a tight cap. If equipped with a drain plug drain the fuel tank by removing the drain plug.
2. Remove the fuel tank pipe protector.
3. On the 1993–97 models, remove the rear seat cushion to gain access to the electrical wiring.
4. On all models, disconnect the fuel pump and sending unit wiring at the connector.
5. Raise the vehicle and safely support it on jackstands.
6. Loosen the clamp and remove the filler neck assembly and overflow pipe assembly from the tank.
7. Remove the supply hose from the tank. Wrap a rag around the fitting to collect escaping fuel. Disconnect the breather hose or vent tube from the tank, again using a rag to control spillage.
8. Cover or plug the end of each disconnected line to keep dirt out and fuel in.
9. Support the fuel tank with a floor jack or transmission jack. Use a broad piece of wood to distribute the load. Be careful not to deform the bottom of the tank.
10. Remove the fuel tank support strap bolts.
11. Swing the straps away from the tank and lower the jack. Balance the tank with your other hand or have a helper assist you. The tank is bulky and may have some fuel left in it. If its balance changes suddenly, the tank may fall.
12. Remove the fuel filler pipe extension, the vent pipe assembly, fuel

4. Disconnect the fuel pipe from the regulator.
5. Remove the two retaining bolts and pull the regulator out of the fuel rail.
To install:
6. Apply a light coat of gasoline to a new O-ring, then install it on the regulator.
7. Rotate the regulator to the left and right while installing it in the fuel rail. Make certain it can be smoothly rotated. If it does not rotate smoothly, the O-ring is not seated correctly and should be replaced.
8. Install the two retaining bolts. Tighten them to 82 inch lbs. (9 Nm).
9. Connect the fuel and vacuum hoses.
10. Start the engine and check carefully for leaks.

pump and or the sending unit assembly. Keep these items in a clean, protected area away from the car.

➡On the 1988–92 models, the fuel pump and fuel sender gauge are two different assemblies. On the 1993–97 models, the fuel pump and fuel sender gauge are one unit.

13. While the tank is out and disassembled, inspect it for any signs of rust, leakage or metal damage. If any problem is found, replace the fuel tank. Clean the inside of the tank with water and a light detergent and rinse the tank thoroughly several times.
14. Inspect all of the lines, hoses and fittings for any sign of corrosion, wear or damage to the surfaces. Check the pump outlet hose and the filter for restrictions.
15. When reassembling, ALWAYS replace the sealing gaskets with new ones. Also replace any rubber parts showing any sign of deterioration.
16. Connect the vent pipe assembly and the filler pipe extension to the fuel tank. Always use new hose clamps as necessary.
17. Install the fuel pump and bracket assembly into the tank with a NEW gasket and tighten retaining bolts to 30 inch lbs. (40 Nm).
18. Install the fuel sending unit assembly into the tank with a NEW gasket and tighten retaining bolts to 30 inch lbs. (40 Nm).

➡Tighten the vent or breather tube screw to 17 inch lbs. (23 Nm) and all other attaching screws to 30 inch lbs. (40 Nm).

19. Place the fuel tank on the jack and elevate it into place within the car. Attach the straps and install the strap bolts, tightening them to EVENLY 29 ft. lbs. (39 Nm).

➡Make sure that fuel tank cushions are installed in the correct location before installing the fuel tank to the vehicle. The fuel tank cushions prevent vibration and noise during vehicle operation.

20. Connect the breather hose or vent to the tank pipe, the return hose to the tank pipe and the supply hose to its tank pipe. tighten the supply hose fitting to 21 ft. lbs. (28 Nm).
21. Connect the filler neck and overflow pipe to the vehicle. Make sure the clamps are properly seated and secure.
22. Lower the vehicle to the ground.
23. Connect the pump and sending unit electrical connectors to the harness.
24. Install the rear seat cushion.
25. Using a funnel, pour the fuel that was drained from its container into the fuel filler.
26. Install the fuel filler cap.
27. Start the engine and check carefully for any sign of leakage around the tank and lines.

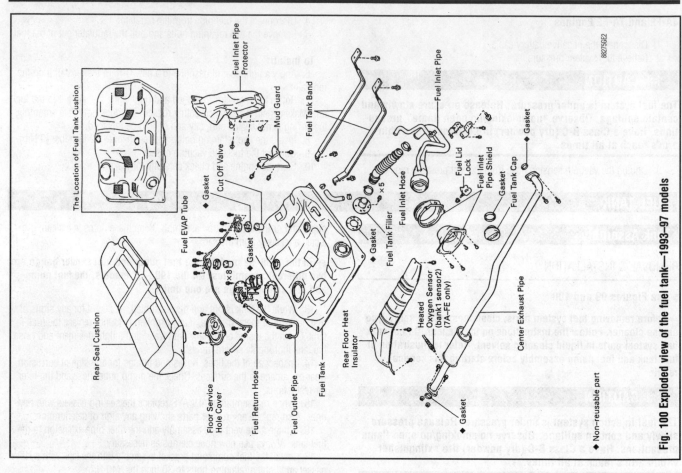

Fig. 100 Exploded view of the fuel tank—1993–97 models

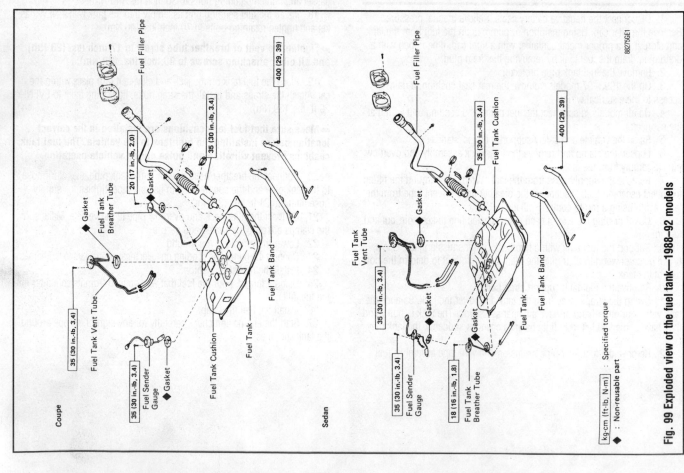

Fig. 99 Exploded view of the fuel tank—1988–92 models

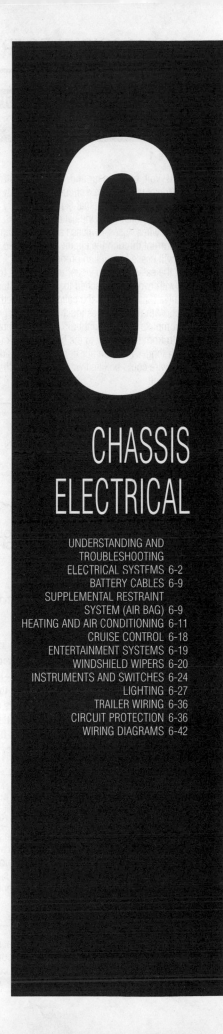

6

CHASSIS ELECTRICAL

UNDERSTANDING AND TROUBLESHOOTING ELECTRICAL SYSTEMS

Basic Electrical Theory

♦ See Figure 1

For any 12 volt, negative ground, electrical system to operate, the electricity must travel in a complete circuit. This simply means that current (power) from the positive terminal (+) of the battery must eventually return to the negative terminal (-) of the battery. Along the way, this current will travel through wires, fuses, switches and components. If, for any reason, the flow of current through the circuit is interrupted, the component fed by that circuit will cease to function properly.

Perhaps the easiest way to visualize a circuit is to think of connecting a light bulb (with two wires attached to it) to the battery—one wire attached to the negative (-) terminal of the battery and the other wire to the positive (+) terminal. With the two wires touching the battery terminals, the circuit would be complete and the light bulb would illuminate. Electricity would follow a path from the battery to the bulb and back to the battery. It's easy to see that with longer wires on our light bulb, it could be mounted anywhere. Further, one wire could be fitted with a switch so that the light could be turned on and off.

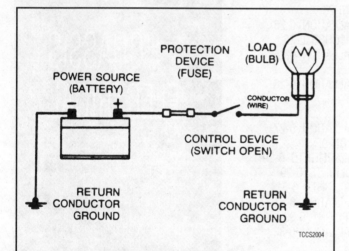

Fig. 1 This example illustrates a simple circuit. When the switch is closed, power from the positive (+) battery terminal flows through the fuse and the switch, and then to the light bulb. The light illuminates and the circuit is completed through the ground wire back to the negative (-) battery terminal. In reality, the two ground points shown in the illustration are attached to the metal chassis of the vehicle, which completes the circuit back to the battery.

The normal automotive circuit differs from this simple example in two ways. First, instead of having a return wire from the bulb to the battery, the current travels through the chassis of the vehicle. Since the negative (-) battery cable is attached to the chassis and the chassis is made of electrically conductive metal, the chassis of the vehicle can serve as a ground wire to complete the circuit. Secondly, most automotive circuits contain multiple components which receive power from a single circuit. This lessens the amount of wire needed to power components on the vehicle.

THE WATER ANALOGY

Electricity is the flow of electrons—hypothetical particles thought to constitute the basic "stuff" of electricity. Many people have been taught electrical theory using an analogy with water. In a comparison with water flowing through a pipe, the electrons would be the water.

The flow of electricity can be measured much like the flow of water through a pipe. The unit of measurement used is amperes, frequently abbreviated as amps (a). When connected to a circuit, an ammeter will measure the actual amount of current flowing through the circuit. When relatively few electrons flow through a circuit, the amperage is low. When many electrons flow, the amperage is high.

Just as water pressure is measured in units such as pounds per square inch (psi), electrical pressure is measured in units called volts (v). When a voltmeter is connected to a circuit, it is measuring the electrical pressure. The higher the voltage, the more current will flow through the circuit. The lower the voltage, the less current will flow.

While increasing the voltage in a circuit will increase the flow of current, the actual flow depends not only on voltage, but also on the resistance of the circuit. Resistance is the amount of force necessary to push the current through the circuit. The standard unit for measuring resistance is an ohm (W or omega). Resistance in a circuit varies depending on the amount and type of components used in the circuit. The main factors which determine resistance are:

• Material—some materials have more resistance than others. Those with high resistance are said to be insulators. Rubber is one of the best insulators available, as it allows little current to pass. Low resistance materials are said to be conductors. Copper wire is among the best conductors. Most vehicle wiring is made of copper.

• Size—the larger the wire size being used, the less resistance the wire will have. This is why components which use large amounts of electricity usually have large wires supplying current to them.

• Length—for a given thickness of wire, the longer the wire, the greater the resistance. The shorter the wire, the less the resistance. When determining the proper wire for a circuit, both size and length must be considered to design a circuit that can handle the current needs of the component.

• Temperature—with many materials, the higher the temperature, the greater the resistance. This principle is used in many of the sensors on the engine.

OHM'S LAW

The preceding definitions may lead the reader into believing that there is no relationship between current, voltage and resistance. Nothing can be further from the truth. The relationship between current, voltage and resistance can be summed up by a statement known as Ohm's law.

Voltage (E) is equal to amperage (I) times resistance (R): $E = I \times R$
Other forms of the formula are $R = E/I$ and $I = E/R$

In each of these formulas, E is the voltage in volts, I is the current in amps and R is the resistance in ohms. The basic point to remember is that as the resistance of a circuit goes up, the amount of current that flows in the circuit will go down, if voltage remains the same.

Electrical Components

POWER SOURCE

The power source for 12 volt automotive electrical systems is the battery. In most modern vehicles, the battery is a lead/acid electrochemical device consisting of six 2 volt subsections (cells) connected in series, so that the unit is capable of producing approximately 12 volts of electrical pressure. Each subsection consists of a series of positive and negative plates held a short distance apart in a solution of sulfuric acid and water.

The two types of plates are of dissimilar metals. This sets up a chemical reaction, and it is this reaction which produces current flow from the battery when its positive and negative terminals are connected to an electrical load. The power removed from the battery is replaced by the alternator, which forces electrons back through the battery, reversing the normal flow, and restoring the battery to its original chemical state.

GROUND

Two types of grounds are used in automotive electric circuits. Direct ground components are grounded through their mounting points. All other components use some sort of ground wire which is attached to the body or chassis of the vehicle. The electrical current runs through the chassis of the vehicle and returns to the battery through the ground (-) cable; if you look, you'll see that the battery ground cable connects between the battery and the body or chassis of the vehicle.

➡ It should be noted that a good percentage of electrical problems can be traced to bad grounds.

PROTECTIVE DEVICES

It is possible for large surges of current to pass through the electrical system of your vehicle. If this surge of current were to reach the load in the circuit, it could burn it out or severely damage it. To prevent this, fuses, circuit breakers and/or fusible links are connected into the supply wires of the electrical system. These items are nothing more than a built-in weak spot in the system. When an abnormal amount of current flows through the system, these protective devices work as follows to protect the circuit:
  • Fuse—when an excessive electrical current passes through a fuse, the fuse "blows" (the conductor melts) and opens the circuit, preventing the passage of current.
  • Circuit Breaker—a circuit breaker is basically a self-repairing fuse. It will open the circuit in the same fashion as a fuse, but when the surge subsides, the circuit breaker can be reset and does not need replacement.

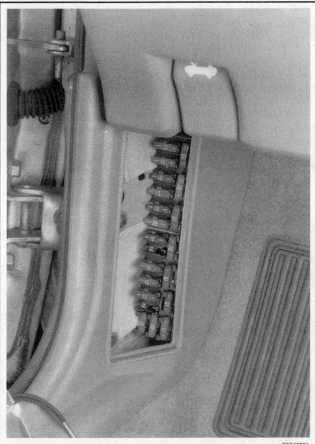

Most vehicles use one or more fuse panels. This one is located in the driver's side kick panel

TCCA6P01

  • Fusible Link—a fusible link (fuse link or main link) is a short length of special, Hypalon high temperature insulated wire that acts as a fuse. When an excessive electrical current passes through a fusible link, the thin gauge wire inside the link melts, creating an intentional open to protect the circuit. To repair the circuit, the link must be replaced. Some newer type fusible links are housed in plug-in modules, which are simply replaced like a fuse, while older type fusible links must be cut and spliced if they melt. Since this link is very early in the electrical path, it's the first place to look if nothing on the vehicle works, but the battery seems to be charged and is properly connected.

❋ CAUTION

Always replace fuses, circuit breakers and fusible links with identically rated components. Under no circumstances should a component of higher or lower amperage rating be substituted.

SWITCHES & RELAYS

▶ **See Figure 2**

Switches are used in electrical circuits to control the passage of current. The most common use is to open and close circuits between the battery and the various electric devices in the system. Switches are rated according to the amount of amperage they can handle. If a sufficient amperage rated switch is not used in a circuit, the switch could overload and cause damage.

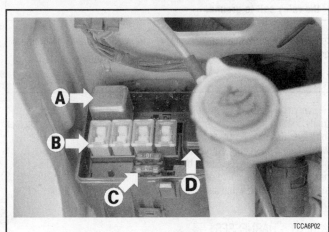

A. Relay   C. Fuse
B. Fusible link   d. Flasher

TCCA6P02

The underhood fuse and relay panel usually contains fuses, relays, flashers and fusible links

Some electrical components which require a large amount of current to operate use a special switch called a relay. Since these circuits carry a large amount of current, the thickness of the wire in the circuit is also greater. If this large wire were connected from the load to the control switch on the dashboard, the switch would have to carry the high amperage load and the dash would be twice as large to accommodate the increased size of the wiring harness. To prevent these problems, a relay is used.

Relays are composed of a coil and a switch. These two components are linked together so that when one operates, the other operates at the same time. The large wires in the circuit are connected from the battery to one side of the relay switch and from the opposite side of the relay switch to the load. Most relays are normally open, preventing current from passing through the circuit. Additional, smaller wires are connected from the relay coil to the control switch for the circuit and from the opposite side of the relay coil to ground. When the control switch is turned on, it grounds the smaller wire to the relay coil, causing the coil to operate. The coil pulls the relay switch closed, sending power to the component without routing it through the inside of the vehicle. Some common circuits which may use

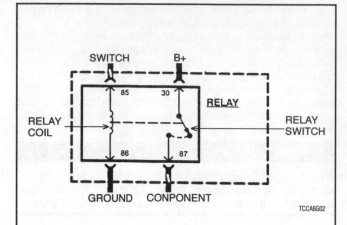

Fig. 2 Relays are composed of a coil and a switch. These two components are linked together so that when one operates, the other operates at the same time. The large wires in the circuit are connected from the battery to one side of the relay switch (B+) and from the opposite side of the relay switch to the load (component). Smaller wires are connected from the relay coil to the control switch for the circuit and from the opposite side of the relay coil to ground.

relays are the horn, headlights, starter, electric fuel pump and rear window defogger systems.

LOAD

Every complete circuit must include a "load" (something to use the electricity coming from the source). Without this load, the battery would attempt to deliver its entire power supply from one pole to another. The electricity would take a short cut to ground and cause a great amount of damage to other components in the circuit by developing a tremendous amount of heat. This condition could develop sufficient heat to melt the insulation on all the surrounding wires and reduce a multiple wire cable to a lump of plastic and copper.

WIRING & HARNESSES

The average automobile contains about ½ mile of wiring, with hundreds of individual connections. To protect the many wires from damage and to keep them from becoming a confusing tangle, they are organized into bundles, enclosed in plastic or taped together and called wiring harnesses. Different harnesses serve different parts of the vehicle. Individual wires are color coded to help trace them through a harness where sections are hidden from view.

Automotive wiring or circuit conductors can be either single strand wire, multi-strand wire or printed circuitry. Single strand wire has a solid metal core and is usually used inside such components as alternators, motors, relays and other devices. Multi-strand wire has a core made of many small strands of wire twisted together into a single conductor. Most of the wiring in an automotive electrical system is made up of multi-strand wire, either as a single conductor or grouped together in a harness. All wiring is color coded on the insulator, either as a solid color or as a colored wire with an identification stripe. A printed circuit is a thin film of copper or other conductor that is printed on an insulator backing. Occasionally, a printed circuit is sandwiched between two sheets of plastic for more protection and flexibility. A complete printed circuit, consisting of conductors, insulating material and connectors for lamps or other components is called a printed circuit board. Printed circuitry is used in place of individual wires or harnesses in places where space is limited, such as behind instrument panels.

Since automotive electrical systems are very sensitive to changes in resistance, the selection of properly sized wires is critical when systems are repaired. A loose or corroded connection or a replacement wire that is too small for the circuit will add extra resistance and an additional voltage drop to the circuit.

The wire gauge number is an expression of the cross-section area of the conductor. The most common system for expressing wire size is the American Wire Gauge (AWG) system. As gauge number increases, area decreases and the wire becomes smaller. An 18 gauge wire is smaller than a 4 gauge wire. A wire with a higher gauge number will carry less current than a wire with a lower gauge number. Gauge wire size refers to the size of the strands of the conductor, not the size of the complete wire. It is possible, therefore, to have two wires of the same gauge with different diameters because one may have thicker insulation than the other.

12 volt automotive electrical systems generally use 10, 12, 14, 16 and 18 gauge wire. Main power distribution circuits and larger accessories usually use 10 and 12 gauge wire. Battery cables are usually 4 or 6 gauge, although 1 and 2 gauge wires are occasionally used.

It is essential to understand how a circuit works before trying to figure out why it doesn't. An electrical schematic shows the electrical current paths when a circuit is operating properly. Schematics break the entire electrical system down into individual circuits. In a schematic, no attempt is made to represent wiring and components as they physically appear on the vehicle; switches and other components are shown as simply as possible. Face views of harness connectors show the cavity or terminal locations in all multi-pin connectors to help locate test points.

CONNECTORS

Three types of connectors are commonly used in automotive applications-weatherproof, molded and hard shell.

• Weatherproof—these connectors are most commonly used in the engine compartment or where the connector is exposed to the elements. Terminals are protected against moisture and dirt by sealing rings which provide a weathertight seal. All repairs require the use of a special terminal and the tool required to service it. Unlike standard blade type terminals, these weatherproof terminals cannot be straightened once they are bent. Make certain that the connectors are properly seated and all of the sealing rings are in place when connecting leads.

• Molded—these connectors require complete replacement of the connector if found to be defective. This means splicing a new connector assembly into the harness. All splices should be soldered to insure proper contact. Use care when probing the connections or replacing terminals in them, as it is possible to create a short circuit between opposite terminals. If this happens to the wrong terminal pair, it is possible to damage certain

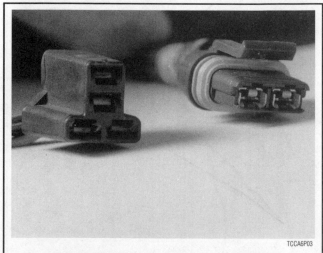

Hard shell (left) and weatherproof (right) connectors have replaceable terminals

Weatherproof connectors are most commonly used in the engine compartment or where the connector is exposed to the elements

components. Always use jumper wires between connectors for circuit checking and NEVER probe through weatherproof seals.

• Hard Shell—unlike molded connectors, the terminal contacts in hard-shell connectors can be replaced. Replacement usually involves the use of a special terminal removal tool that depresses the locking tangs (barbs) on the connector terminal and allows the connector to be removed from the rear of the shell. The connector shell should be replaced if it shows any evidence of burning, melting, cracks, or breaks. Replace individual terminals that are burnt, corroded, distorted or loose.

Test Equipment

Pinpointing the exact cause of trouble in an electrical circuit is most times accomplished by the use of special test equipment. The following describes different types of commonly used test equipment and briefly explains how to use them in diagnosis. In addition to the information covered below, the tool manufacturer's instructions booklet (provided with the tester) should be read and clearly understood before attempting any test procedures.

JUMPER WIRES

✳✳ CAUTION

Never use jumper wires made from a thinner gauge wire than the circuit being tested. If the jumper wire is of too small a gauge, it may overheat and possibly melt. Never use jumpers to bypass high resistance loads in a circuit. Bypassing resistance's, in effect, creates a short circuit. This may, in turn, cause damage and fire. Jumper wires should only be used to bypass lengths of wire.

Jumper wires are simple, yet extremely valuable, pieces of test equipment. They are basically test wires which are used to bypass sections of a circuit. Although jumper wires can be purchased, they are usually fabricated from lengths of standard automotive wire and whatever type of connector (alligator clip, spade connector or pin connector) that is required for the particular application being tested. In cramped, hard-to-reach areas, it is advisable to have insulated boots over the jumper wire terminals in order to prevent accidental grounding. It is also advisable to include a standard automotive fuse in any jumper wire. This is commonly referred to as a "fused jumper". By inserting an in-line fuse holder between a set of test

leads, a fused jumper wire can be used for bypassing open circuits. Use a 5 amp fuse to provide protection against voltage spikes.

Jumper wires are used primarily to locate open electrical circuits, on either the ground (-) side of the circuit or on the power (+) side. If an electrical component fails to operate, connect the jumper wire between the component and a good ground. If the component operates only with the jumper installed, the ground circuit is open. If the ground circuit is good, but the component does not operate, the circuit between the power feed and component may be open. By moving the jumper wire successively back from the component toward the power source, you can isolate the area of the circuit where the open is located. When the component stops functioning, or the power is cut off, the open is in the segment of wire between the jumper and the point previously tested.

You can sometimes connect the jumper wire directly from the battery to the "hot" terminal of the component, but first make sure the component uses 12 volts in operation. Some electrical components, such as fuel injectors, are designed to operate on about 4 volts, and running 12 volts directly to these components will cause damage.

TEST LIGHTS

The test light is used to check circuits and components while electrical current is flowing through them. It is used for voltage and ground tests. To use a 12 volt test light, connect the ground clip to a good ground and probe wherever necessary with the pick. The test light will illuminate when voltage is detected. This does not necessarily mean that 12 volts (or any particular amount of voltage) is present; it only means that some voltage is present. It is advisable before using the test light to touch its ground clip and probe across the battery posts or terminals to make sure the light is operating properly.

✳✳ WARNING

Do not use a test light to probe electronic ignition spark plug or coil wires. Never use a pick-type test light to probe wiring on computer controlled systems unless specifically instructed to do so. Any wire insulation that is pierced by the test light probe should be taped and sealed with silicone after testing.

Like the jumper wire, the 12 volt test light is used to isolate opens in circuits. But, whereas the jumper wire is used to bypass the open to operate

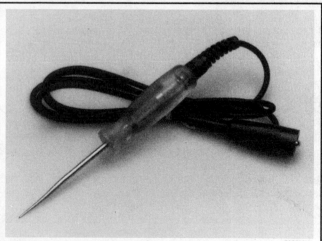

A 12 volt test light is used to detect the presence of voltage in a circuit

the load, the 12 volt test light is used to locate the presence of voltage in a circuit. If the test light illuminates, there is power up to that point in the circuit; if the test light does not illuminate, there is an open circuit (no power). Move the test light in successive steps back toward the power source until the light in the handle illuminates. The open is between the probe and a point which was previously probed.

The self-powered test light is similar in design to the 12 volt test light, but contains a 1.5 volt penlight battery in the handle. It is most often used in place of a multimeter to check for open or short circuits when power is isolated from the circuit (continuity test).

The battery in a self-powered test light does not provide much current. A weak battery may not provide enough power to illuminate the test light even when a complete circuit is made (especially if there is high resistance in the circuit). Always make sure that the test battery is strong. To check the battery, briefly touch the ground clip to the probe; if the light glows brightly, the battery is strong enough for testing.

➡️**A self-powered test light should not be used on any computer controlled system or component. The small amount of electricity transmitted by the test light is enough to damage many electronic automotive components.**

MULTIMETERS

Multimeters are an extremely useful tool for troubleshooting electrical problems. They can be purchased in either analog or digital form and have a price range to suit any budget. A multimeter is a voltmeter, ammeter and ohmmeter (along with other features) combined into one instrument. It is often used when testing solid state circuits because of its high input impedance (usually 10 megaohms or more). A brief description of the multimeter main test functions follows:

• Voltmeter—the voltmeter is used to measure voltage at any point in a circuit, or to measure the voltage drop across any part of a circuit. Voltmeters usually have various scales and a selector switch to allow the reading of different voltage ranges. The voltmeter has a positive and a negative lead. To avoid damage to the meter, always connect the negative lead to the negative (-) side of the circuit (to ground or nearest the ground side of the circuit) and connect the positive lead to the positive (+) side of the circuit (to the power source or the nearest power source). Note that the negative voltmeter lead will always be black and that the positive voltmeter will always be some color other than black (usually red).

• Ohmmeter—the ohmmeter is designed to read resistance (measured in ohms) in a circuit or component. All ohmmeters will have a selector switch which permits the measurement of different ranges of resistance (usually the selector switch allows the multiplication of the meter reading by 10, 100, 1,000 and 10,000). Since the meters are powered by an internal battery, the ohmmeter can be used as a self-powered test light. When the ohmmeter is connected, current from the ohmmeter flows through the circuit or component being tested. Since the ohmmeter's internal resistance and voltage are known values, the amount of current flow through the meter depends on the resistance of the circuit or component being tested. The ohmmeter can also be used to perform a continuity test for suspected open circuits. In using the meter for making continuity checks, do not be concerned with the actual resistance readings. Zero resistance, or any ohm reading, indicates continuity in the circuit. Infinite resistance indicates an opening in the circuit. A high resistance reading where there should be none indicates a problem in the circuit. Checks for short circuits are made in the same manner as checks for open circuits, except that the circuit must be isolated from both power and normal ground. Infinite resistance indicates no continuity to ground, while zero resistance indicates a dead short to ground.

Never use an ohmmeter to check the resistance of a component or wire while there is voltage applied to the circuit.

• Ammeter—an ammeter measures the amount of current flowing through a circuit in units called amperes or amps. At normal operating voltage, most circuits have a characteristic amount of amperes, called "current draw" which can be measured using an ammeter. By referring to a specified current draw rating, then measuring the amperes and comparing the two values, one can determine what is happening within the circuit to aid in diagnosis. An open circuit, for example, will not allow any current to flow, so the ammeter reading will be zero. A damaged component or circuit will have an increased current draw, so the reading will be high. The ammeter is always connected in series with the circuit being tested. All of the current that normally flows through the circuit must also flow through the ammeter; if there is any other path for the current to follow, the ammeter reading will not be accurate. The ammeter itself has very little resistance to current flow and, therefore, will not affect the circuit, but it will measure current draw only when the circuit is closed and electricity is flowing. Excessive current draw can blow fuses and drain the battery, while a reduced current draw can cause motors to run slowly, lights to dim and other components to not operate properly.

Troubleshooting

When diagnosing a specific problem, organized troubleshooting is a must. The complexity of a modern automotive vehicle demands that you approach any problem in a logical, organized manner. There are certain troubleshooting techniques which are standard:

• Establish when the problem occurs. Does the problem appear only under certain conditions? Were there any noises, odors or other unusual symptoms?

• Isolate the problem area. To do this, make some simple tests and observations, then eliminate the systems that are working properly. Check for obvious problems, such as broken wires and loose or dirty connections. Always check the obvious before assuming something complicated is the cause.

• Test for problems systematically to determine the cause once the problem area is isolated. Are all the components functioning properly? Is there power going to electrical switches and motors. Performing careful, systematic checks will often turn up most causes on the first inspection, without wasting time checking components that have little or no relationship to the problem.

• Test all repairs after the work is done to make sure that the problem is fixed. Some causes can be traced to more than one component, so a careful verification of repair work is important in order to pick up additional malfunctions that may cause a problem to reappear or a different problem to arise. A blown fuse, for example, is a simple problem that may require more than another fuse to repair. If you don't look for a problem that caused a fuse to blow, a shorted wire (for example) may go undetected.

Experience has shown that most problems tend to be the result of a fairly simple and obvious cause, such as loose or corroded connectors, bad grounds or damaged wire insulation which causes a short. This makes careful visual inspection of components during testing essential to quick and accurate troubleshooting.

Testing

OPEN CIRCUITS

1. Isolate the circuit from power and ground.
2. Connect the self-powered test light or ohmmeter ground clip to a good ground and probe sections of the circuit sequentially.

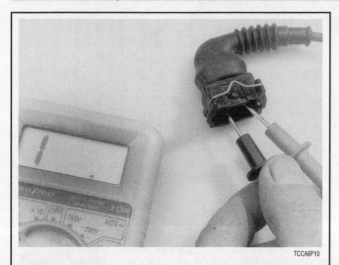

The infinite reading on this multimeter (1 .) indicates that the circuit is open

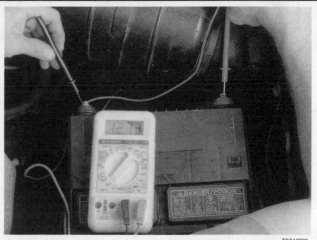

Using a multimeter to check battery voltage. This battery is fully charged

3. If the light is out or there is infinite resistance, the open is between the probe and the circuit ground.
4. If the light is on or the meter shows continuity, the open is between the probe and end of the circuit toward the power source.

SHORT CIRCUITS

➡**Never use a self-powered test light to perform checks for opens or shorts when power is applied to the electrical system under test. The 12 volt vehicle power will quickly burn out the light bulb in the test light.**

1. Isolate the circuit from power and ground.
2. Connect the self-powered test light or ohmmeter ground clip to a good ground and probe any easy-to-reach test point in the circuit.
3. If the light comes on or there is continuity, there is a short somewhere in the circuit.
4. To isolate the short, probe a test point at either end of the isolated circuit (the light should be on or the meter should indicate continuity).
5. Leave the test light probe engaged and sequentially open connectors or switches, remove parts, etc. until the light goes out or continuity is broken.
6. When the light goes out, the short is between the last two circuit components which were opened.

VOLTAGE

This test determines voltage available from the battery and should be the first step in any electrical troubleshooting procedure. Many electrical problems, especially on computer controlled systems, can be caused by a low state of charge in the battery. Excessive corrosion at the battery cable terminals can cause poor contact that will prevent proper charging and full battery current flow.
1. Set the voltmeter selector switch to the 20V position.
2. Connect the multimeter negative lead to the battery's negative (-) post or terminal and the positive lead to the battery's positive (+) post or terminal.
3. Turn the ignition switch **ON** to provide a load.
4. A well charged battery should register over 12 volts. If the meter reads below 11.5 volts, the battery power may be insufficient to operate the electrical system properly.

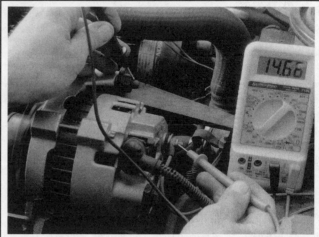

Testing voltage output between the alternator's BAT terminal and ground. This voltage reading is normal

VOLTAGE DROP

When current flows through a load, the voltage beyond the load drops. This voltage drop is due to the resistance created by the load and also by small resistance's created by corrosion at the connectors and damaged insulation on the wires. The maximum allowable voltage drop under load is critical, especially if there is more than one load in the circuit, since all voltage drops are cumulative.
1. Set the voltmeter selector switch to the 20 volt position.
2. Connect the multimeter negative lead to a good ground.
3. Operate the circuit and check the voltage prior to the first component (load).
4. There should be little or no voltage drop in the circuit prior to the first component. If a voltage drop exists, the wire or connectors in the circuit are suspect.
5. While operating the first component in the circuit, probe the ground side of the component with the positive meter lead and observe the voltage readings. A small voltage drop should be noticed. This voltage drop is caused by the resistance of the component.

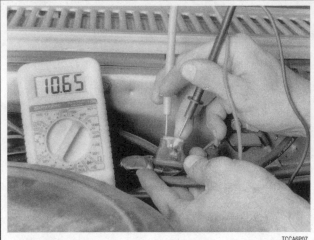

This voltage drop test revealed high resistance (low voltage) in the circuit

6. Repeat the test for each component (load) down the circuit.
7. If a large voltage drop is noticed, the preceding component, wire or connector is suspect.

RESISTANCE

1. Isolate the circuit from the vehicle's power source.
2. Ensure that the ignition key is **OFF** when disconnecting any components or the battery.
3. Where necessary, also isolate at least one side of the circuit to be checked, in order to avoid reading parallel resistance's. Parallel circuit

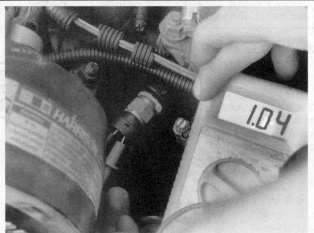

Checking the resistance of a coolant temperature sensor with an ohmmeter. Reading is 1.04 kilohms

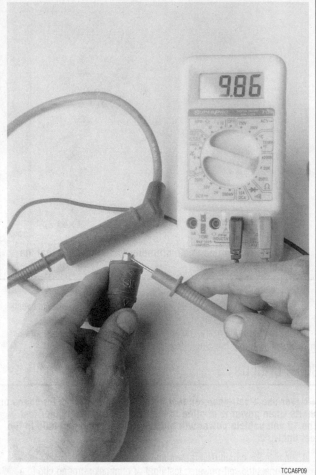

Spark plug wires can be checked for excessive resistance using an ohmmeter

resistance's will always give a lower reading than the actual resistance of either of the branches.
4. Connect the meter leads to both sides of the circuit (wire or component) and read the actual measured ohms on the meter scale. Make sure the selector switch is set to the proper ohm scale for the circuit being tested, to avoid misreading the ohmmeter test value.

Wire and Connector Repair

Almost anyone can replace damaged wires, as long as the proper tools and parts are available. Automotive wire and terminals are available to fit almost any need. Even the specialized weatherproof, molded and hard shell connectors are now available from aftermarket suppliers.

Be sure the ends of all the wires are fitted with the proper terminal hardware and connectors. Wrapping a wire around a stud is never a permanent solution and will only cause trouble later. Replace wires one at a time to avoid confusion. Always route wires exactly the same as the factory.

➡If connector repair is necessary, only attempt it if you have the proper tools. Weatherproof and hard shell connectors require special tools to release the pins inside the connector. Attempting to repair these connectors with conventional hand tools will damage them.

BATTERY CABLES

Disconnecting the Cables

When working on any electrical component on the vehicle, it is always a good idea to disconnect the negative (-) battery cable. This will prevent potential damage to many sensitive electrical components such as the Engine Control Module (ECM), radio, alternator, etc.

➡**Any time you disengage the battery cables, it is recommended that you disconnect the negative (-) battery cable first. This will prevent your accidentally grounding the positive (+) terminal to the body of the vehicle when disconnecting it, thereby preventing damage to the above mentioned components.**

Before you disconnect the cable(s), first turn the ignition to the **OFF** position. This will prevent a draw on the battery which could cause arcing (electricity trying to ground itself to the body of a vehicle, just like a spark plug jumping the gap) and, of course, damaging some components such as the alternator diodes.

When the battery cable(s) are reconnected (negative cable last), be sure to check that your lights, windshield wipers and other electrically operated safety components are all working correctly. If your vehicle contains an Electronically Tuned Radio (ETR), don't forget to also reset your radio stations. Ditto for the clock.

SUPPLEMENTAL RESTRAINT SYSTEM (AIR BAG)

General Information

▶ See Figure 3

The air bag system used on the 1993–97 Corollas is referred to as Supplemental Restraint System (SRS). The SRS provides additional protection for the driver, if a forward collision of sufficient force is encountered. The SRS assists the normal seatbelt restraining system by deploying an air bag, via the steering column.

The center air bag sensor is the heart of the SRS. It consists of safing sensors, ignition control and drive circuit, diagnosis circuit, etc. The center air bag receives signals from the air bag sensors and determines whether the air bag must be activated or not. The center air bag sensor is also used to diagnose system malfunctions.

The air bag warning light circuit is equipped with an electrical connection check mechanism which detects when the connector to the center air bag sensor assembly is not properly connected.

All connectors in the air bag system are colored yellow. These connectors use gold-plated terminals with twin-lock mechanism. This design assures positive locking; there-by, preventing the terminals from coming apart.

SYSTEM OPERATION

When the ignition switch is turn to the **ON** or **ACC** position, the air bag warning lamp will turned ON for approximately 6 seconds. If no malfunctions are detected in the system, after the 6 second period have elapse, the warning light will go **OFF**.

The safing sensors are designed to go ON at a lower deceleration rate than the front or center air bag sensor. When the vehicle is involved in a frontal collision, the shock is great enough to overcome the predetermine level of the front or center air bag sensor. When a safing sensor and a front air bag sensor and/or the center air bag sensor go ON simultaneously, it causes the squib of the air bag to ignite and the air bag is deployed automatically. The inflated bag breaks open the steering wheel pad.

After air bag deployment have occurred, the gas is discharged through the discharge holes provided behind the bag. The bag become deflated as a result.

The connector of the air bag contains a short spring plate, which provides an activation prevention mechanism. When the connector is disconnected, the short spring plate automatically connects the power source and grounding terminals of the inflator module (squib).

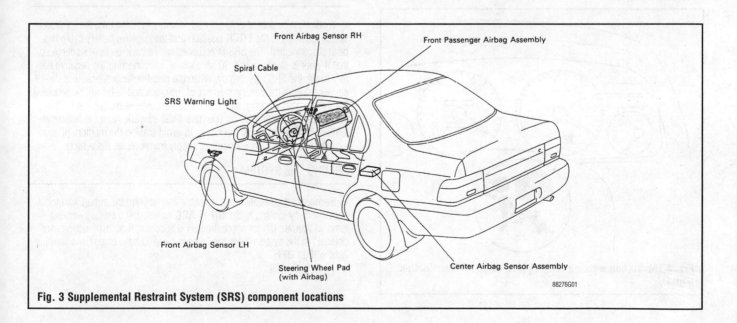

Fig. 3 Supplemental Restraint System (SRS) component locations

SYSTEM COMPONENTS

Front Air Bag Sensors

A front air bag sensor is mounted inside each of the front fenders. The sensor unit is basically a mechanical switch. When the sensor detects a deceleration force above a predetermined level in a collision, the contacts in the sensor close, sending a signal to the center air bag sensor assembly. The sensor cannot be disassembled.

Center Air Bag Sensor

The center air bag sensor is mounted on the floor inside the console box. The air bag sensor determines whether or not the air bag should be deployed and is also used to diagnose system malfunction.

Spiral Cable

The spiral cable, part of the combination switch, is used as an electrical joint from the vehicle body to the steering wheel. The spiral cable is referred to as a clock spring.

Drivers Air Bag

The drivers air bag, located in the steering wheel pad, contains a gas generant which will rapidly inflate the bag in a case of frontal collision.

Passengers Air Bag

The inflator and bag of the SRS are located in the front of the passengers air bag assembly and can not be disassembled. The air bag will inflate only when the sensor instructs it to do so.

SRS Warning Lamp

▶ See Figure 4

The air bag SRS warning lamp, located on the combination meter, is used to alert the driver of any malfunctions within the air bag system. In normal operating conditions when the ignition switch is turned to the **ON** or **ACC**, the light goes on for about 6 seconds and then goes off.

88276G05

Fig. 4 The air bag warning lamp is located on the combination meter

SRS Connectors

▶ See Figure 5

All connectors in the SRS are colored yellow to distinguish them from the other connectors. These connectors have special functions are specifically designed for the SRS. These connectors use durable gold-platted terminals.

SERVICE PRECAUTIONS

1. Work must be started after 90 seconds from the time the ignition switch is turned to the **LOCK** position and the negative battery cable has been disconnected. The SRS is equipped with a back-up power source so that if work is started within 90 seconds of disconnecting the negative battery cable, the SRS may deploy. When the negative terminal cable is disconnected from the battery, memory of the clock and radio will be canceled. Before you start working, make a note of the contents memorized by the audio memory system. When you have finished working, reset the audio systems and adjust the clock. Never use a back-up power supply from outside the vehicle.

2. In the event that of a minor frontal collision where the air bag does not deploy, the steering wheel pad, front air bag sensors and center air bag sensor assembly should be inspected.

3. Before repairs, remove the air bag sensors if shocks are likely to be applied to the sensors during repairs.

4. Never disassemble and repair the steering wheel pad, front air bag sensors or center air bag sensors.

5. Do not expose the steering wheel pad, front air bag sensors or center air bag sensor assembly directly to flames or hot air.

6. If the steering wheel pad, front air bag sensors or center air bag sensor assembly have been dropped, or there are cracks, dents or other defects in the case, bracket or connectors, have them replaced with new ones.

7. Information labels are attached to the periphery of the SRS components. Follow the instructions of the notices.

8. After arming the system, check for proper operation of the SRS warning light.

9. If the wiring harness in the SRS system is damaged, have the entire harness assembly replaced.

DISARMING THE SYSTEM

Work must be started only after 90 seconds from the time the ignition switch is turned to the **LOCK** position and the negative battery cable has been disconnected. The SRS is equipped with a back-up power source so that if work is started within 90 seconds of disconnecting the negative battery cable, the SRS may deploy. When the negative terminal cable is disconnected from the battery, memory of the clock and radio will be canceled. Before you start working, make a note of the contents memorized by the audio memory system. When you have finished work, reset the audio systems as before and adjust the clock. To avoid erasing the memory of each system, never use a back-up power supply from outside the vehicle.

ARMING THE SYSTEM

Reconnect the negative battery cable and perform the airbag warning light check by turning to the **ON** or **ACC** position, the air bag warning lamp will turned ON for approximately 6 seconds. If no malfunctions are detected in the system, after the 6 second period have elapse, the warning light will go **OFF**.

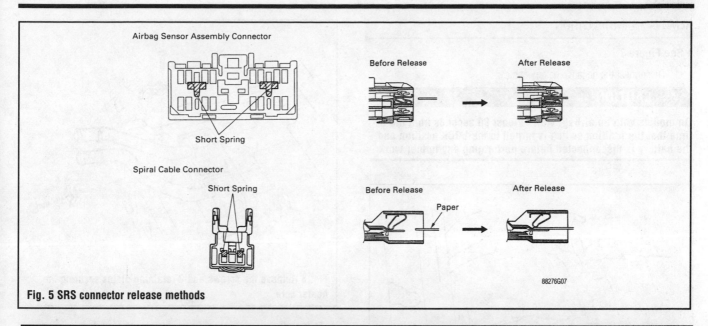

Fig. 5 SRS connector release methods

88276G07

HEATING AND AIR CONDITIONING

♦ See Figure 6

Blower Motor

The blower motor is located under the dashboard on the far right side of the car. The blower motor turns the fan, which circulates the heated, cooled or fresh air within the car. Aside from common electrical problems, the blower motor may need to be removed to clean out leaves or debris which have been sucked into the casing.

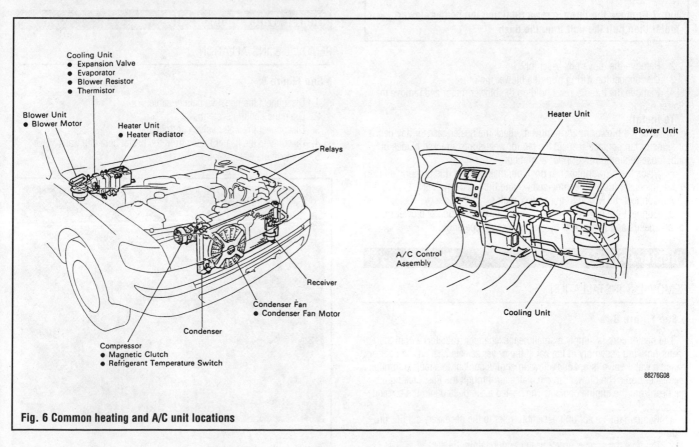

Fig. 6 Common heating and A/C unit locations

88276G08

REMOVAL & INSTALLATION

▶ See Figure 7

1. Disconnect the negative battery cable.

❊❊ CAUTION

On models with an airbag, wait at least 90 seconds from the time that the ignition switch is turned to the LOCK position and the battery is disconnected before performing any further work.

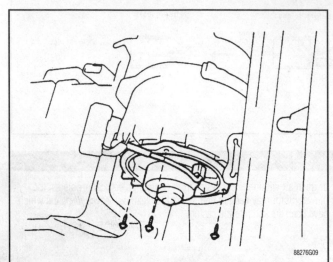

Fig. 7 Remove the three screws retaining the heater blower motor then pull the unit from the dash

2. Remove the glove box assembly.
3. Disconnect the wiring from the blower motor.
4. Remove the three screws holding the blower motor and remove the blower motor.
To install:
5. With the blower motor removed, check the heater case for any debris or signs of fan contact. Inspect the fan for wear spots, cracked blades or hub, loose retaining nut or poor alignment.
6. Place the blower motor in position, making sure it is properly aligned within the case. Install the three screws and tighten them EVENLY.
7. Connect the wiring to the blower motor.
8. Connect the negative battery cable. Check operation of blower motor for all speeds and heater A/C system for proper operation.

Heater Core

REMOVAL & INSTALLATION

▶ See Figure 8

The heater core is simply a small heat exchanger (radiator) within the heater housing assembly in the car. If the driver selects heat on the control panel, a water valve is opened allowing engine coolant to circulate through the heater core. The blower fan circulates air through the fins, picking up the heat from the engine coolant. The heated air is ducted into the car and the cool.
1. Remove the heater unit assembly-refer to the necessary service procedure.
2. Remove the screws and 2 heater core retaining plates.
3. Remove the heater core from the heater unit.

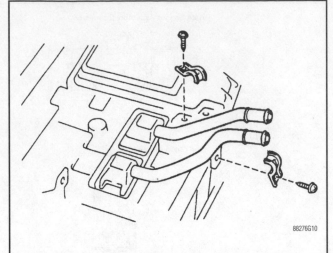

Fig. 8 Remove the screws and 2 retaining plates securing the heater core

To install:
4. Inspect the fins for blockage prior to installation if the old unit is being installed. Clean them with compressed air.
5. Insert the heater core into the unit. Secure with the screws and plates.
6. Install the heater unit.
7. Push the water hoses onto the heater core pipes as far as the ridge on the pipes. Refill the cooling system. Connect the negative battery cable. Check operation of heater and A/C system.

Heater Water Control Valve

REMOVAL & INSTALLATION

▶ See Figure 9

1. Disconnect the negative battery cable.
2. Drain the cooling system.
3. Disconnect the water valve control cable.
4. Disconnect the heater hoses from the heater core and water valve.
5. Remove the water valve.

Pull the tab retaining the heater valve cable to release it

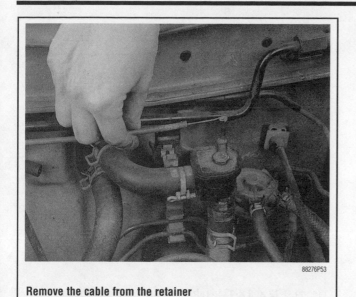

Remove the cable from the retainer

. . . then carefully pull the hose off the port on the firewall . . .

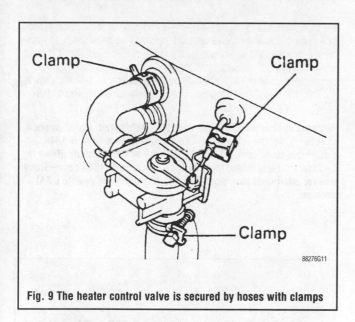

Clamp

Clamp

Clamp

Fig. 9 The heater control valve is secured by hoses with clamps

. . . and from the bottom of the valve

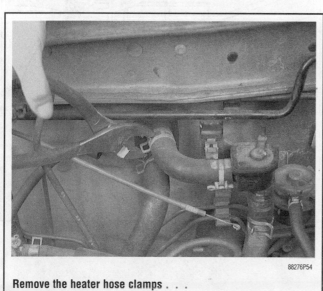

Remove the heater hose clamps . . .

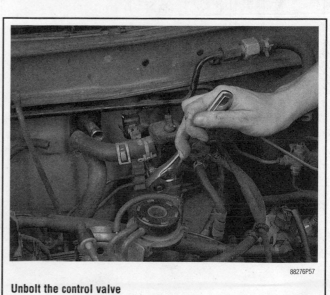

Unbolt the control valve

Pull the control valve away from the firewall

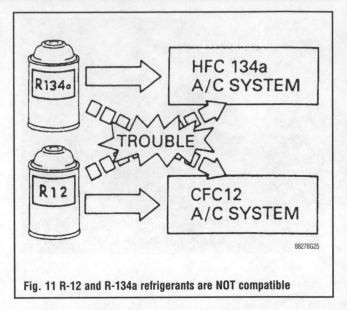

Fig. 11 R-12 and R-134a refrigerants are NOT compatible

To install:

6. Position the water control valve and secure with the retaining bolt.

7. Push the water hose onto the heater core pipe as far as the ridge on the pipe. Refill the cooling system.

8. Adjust control cable if necessary.

9. Connect the negative battery cable. Check operation of the system.

Air Conditioning Components

REMOVAL & INSTALLATION

 See Figures 10, 11, 12 and 13

Repair or service of air conditioning components is not covered by this manual, because of the risk of personal injury or death, and because of the legal ramifications of servicing these components without the proper EPA certification and experience. Cost, personal injury or death, environmental damage, and legal considerations (such as the fact that it is a federal crime to vent refrigerant into the atmosphere), dictate that the A/C components on your vehicle should be serviced only by a Motor Vehicle Air Conditioning (MVAC) trained, and EPA certified automotive technician.

➡**If your vehicle's A/C system uses R-12 refrigerant and is in need of recharging, the A/C system can be converted over to R-134a refrigerant (less environmentally harmful and expensive). Refer to Section 1 for additional information on R-12 to R-134a conversions, and for additional considerations dealing with your vehicle's A/C system.**

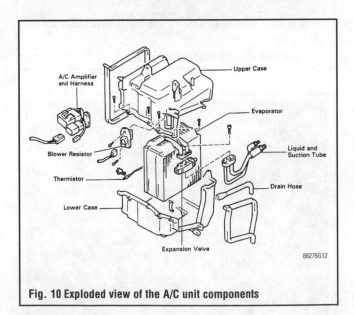

Fig. 10 Exploded view of the A/C unit components

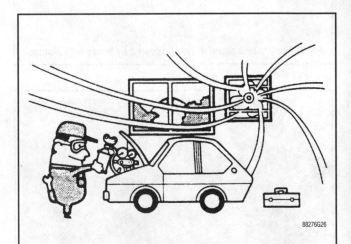

Fig. 12 A Motor Vehicle Air Conditioning (MVAC) trained, and EPA certified automotive technician are the only people that should service the A/C system

Fig. 13 Refrigerants can cause serious injury and even death if not handled correctly

Control Cables

REMOVAL & INSTALLATION

▶ **See Figure 14**

1. Remove the control panel.
2. Disengage the adjusting clip at the heater/cooling unit end of the cable.
3. Disengage the end of the control cable from the control lever.
4. Remove the cable from the vehicle.

To install:
5. Attach the cable to the end of the lever on the A/C or heater box.
6. Route the cable through the dash to the control lever and secure to the back of the unit.
7. Adjust the cable.
8. Install the control panel.

ADJUSTMENT

Air Inlet Door

▶ **See Figure 15**

1. Disengage the control cable from the lever at the heater/cooling unit end of the cable.
2. Set both the air inlet door and the control panel to the RECIRC position. Then, slide the control cable through the adjusting clip until the eyelet on the cable end can be engaged to the lever. Make sure the cable is secured in the clamps.
3. Move the control levers left and right and check for stiffness or binding through the full range of the levers. Test control cable operation.

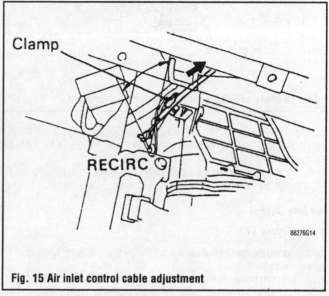

Fig. 15 Air inlet control cable adjustment

Mode Selector Door

▶ **See Figure 16**

1. Disengage the control cable from the lever at the heater/cooling unit end of the cable.
2. Set both the mode selector door and the control panel to the DEF

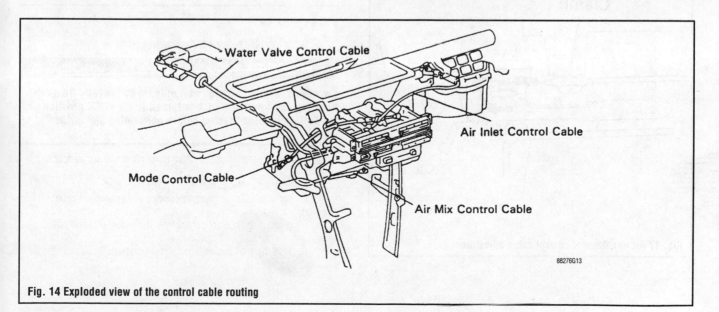

Fig. 14 Exploded view of the control cable routing

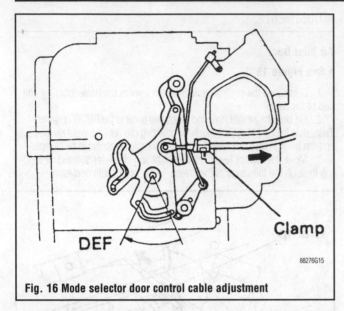

Fig. 16 Mode selector door control cable adjustment

position. Then, slide the control cable through the adjusting clip until the eyelet on the cable end can be engaged to the lever. Make sure the cable is secured in the clamps.

3. Move the control levers left and right and check for stiffness or binding through the full range of the levers. Test control cable operation.

Air Mix Door

♦ See Figure 17

1. Disengage the control cable from the lever at the heater/cooling unit end of the cable.

2. Set both the air mix door and the control panel to the COOL position. Then, slide the control cable through the adjusting clip until the eyelet on the cable end can be engaged to the lever. Make sure the cable is secured in the clamps.

3. Move the control levers left and right and check for stiffness or

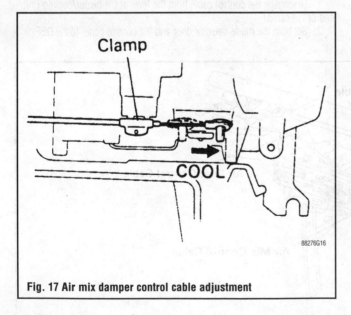

Fig. 17 Air mix damper control cable adjustment

binding through the full range of the levers. Test control cable operation.

Water Control Valve

♦ See Figure 18

1. Disengage the adjusting clip.

2. Place the water valve lever on the COOL position while pushing the outer cable in the COOL direction. Clamp the outer cable to the water valve bracket with the adjusting clip.

3. Move the control levers left and right and check for stiffness or binding through the full range of the levers. Test control cable operation.

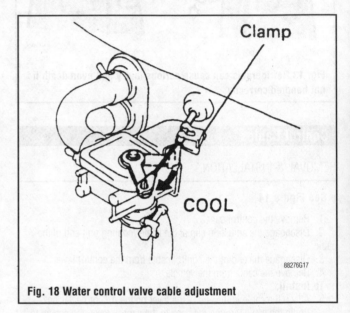

Fig. 18 Water control valve cable adjustment

Control Panel

REMOVAL & INSTALLATION

♦ See Figure 19

1. Disconnect the negative battery cable.

❄ CAUTION

On models with an airbag, wait at least 90 seconds from the time that the ignition switch is turned to the LOCK position and the battery is disconnected before performing any further work.

2. Remove the center cluster finish lower panel and stereo opening cover.

3. Remove the center cluster finish panel and radio.

4. On some models the glove box components may need to be removed.

5. Disconnect the control cables from the heater unit and water valve.

6. Remove the 4 screws and the control assembly. Disconnect the air

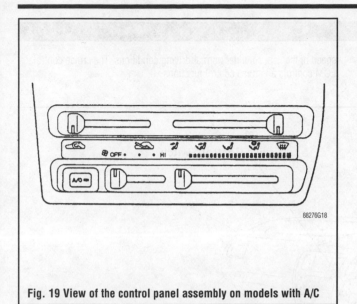

Fig. 19 View of the control panel assembly on models with A/C

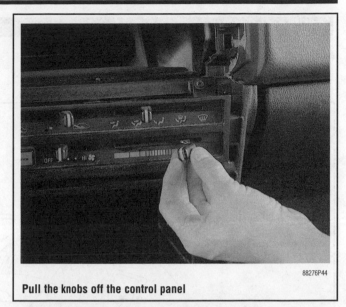

Pull the knobs off the control panel

Unscrew the center console . . .

Remove the screws retaining the control panel to the dash

. . . and remove it from the dash

inlet control cable from the control assembly. Disengage the blower switch connector. Remove the control assembly.

To install:

7. Attach the cables and wiring to the control assembly.

8. Position the control assembly into the dash and secure with the mounting screws.

9. Attach the control cables to the heater unit and water control valve. Adjust control cables as necessary.

10. If removed, install the glove box assembly.

11. Install the radio and center cluster finish panel.

12. Install and secure the center cluster finish lower panel and stereo opening cover.

13. Connect the negative battery cable. Check operation of the system.

CRUISE CONTROL

♦ **See Figure 20**

The cruise control, which is a speed control system, maintains a desired speed of the vehicle under normal driving conditions. The cruise control ECM controls all cruise control functions.

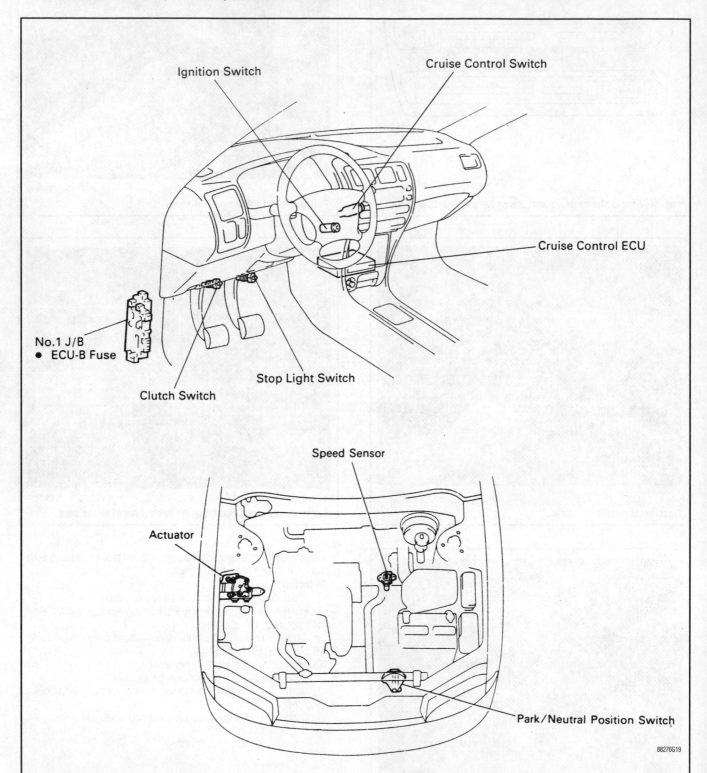

Fig. 20 View of the cruise control component locations

CRUISE CONTROL TROUBLESHOOTING

Problem	Possible Cause
Will not hold proper speed	Incorrect cable adjustment Binding throttle linkage Leaking vacuum servo diaphragm Leaking vacuum tank Faulty vacuum or vent valve Faulty stepper motor Faulty transducer Faulty speed sensor Faulty cruise control module
Cruise intermittently cuts out	Clutch or brake switch adjustment too tight Short or open in the cruise control circuit Faulty transducer Faulty cruise control module
Vehicle surges	Kinked speedometer cable or casing Binding throttle linkage Faulty speed sensor Faulty cruise control module
Cruise control inoperative	Blown fuse Short or open in the cruise control circuit Faulty brake or clutch switch Leaking vacuum circuit Faulty cruise control switch Faulty stepper motor Faulty transducer Faulty speed sensor Faulty cruise control module

Note: Use this chart as a guide. Not all systems will use the components listed.   TCCA6C01

ENTERTAINMENT SYSTEMS

Radio/Tape Player

REMOVAL & INSTALLATION

1. Disconnect the negative battery cable.

❊❊ CAUTION

On models with an airbag, wait at least 90 seconds from the time that the ignition switch is turned to the LOCK position and the battery is disconnected before performing any further work.

2. Remove the attaching screws from the trim panel.
3. Remove the trim panel, being careful of the concealed spring clips behind the panel.
4. Disconnect the wiring from the switches if so equipped mounted in the trim panel.
5. Remove the mounting screws from the radio.
6. Remove the radio from the dash until the wiring connectors are exposed.
7. Disconnect the electrical connectors and the antenna cable from the body of the radio and remove the radio from the car.

Remove the trim panel surrounding the stereo

88276P31

Remove the four radio retaining screws and pull the unit from the dash

To install:

8. Reconnect all the wiring and antenna cable first, then place the radio in position within the dash.

9. Install the attaching screws.
10. Reconnect the wiring harnesses to the switches if so equipped in the trim panel and make sure the switches if so equipped are secure in the panel.
11. Install the trim panel (make sure all the spring clips engage) and install the screws.
Connect the negative battery cable.
12. Check radio system for proper operation.

Speakers

REMOVAL & INSTALLATION

▶ **See Figure 21**

1. Remove the speaker cover on the door or back dash.
2. Remove the attaching screws for the speaker. Note location of speaker wires and .
3. Pull the speaker from its mounting surface.
To install:
4. Attach the speaker wiring to the back of the unit.
5. Position the speaker into its mounting surface and secure with the screws.
6. Secure the speaker cover. Check radio system for proper operation.

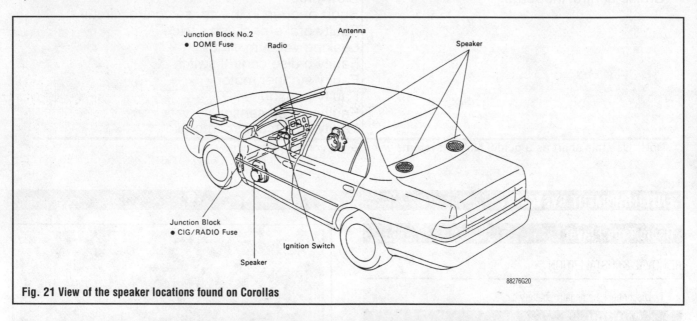

Fig. 21 View of the speaker locations found on Corollas

WINDSHIELD WIPERS

Wiper Blade and Arm

REMOVAL & INSTALLATION

1. To remove the wiper blades, lift up on the spring release tab on the wiper blade-to-wiper arm connector.
2. Pull the blade assembly off the wiper arm.
3. Press the old wiper blade insert down, away from the blade assembly, to free it from the retaining clips on the blade ends. Slide the insert out of the blade. Slide the new insert into the blade assembly and bend the insert upward slightly to engage the retaining clips.

➡**Prior to wiper arm removal, it is wise to mark the windshield-to-blade placement with crayon for installation. This will help with blade height.**

4. To replace a wiper arm, unscrew the acorn nut (a cap covers this retaining nut at the bottom of the wiper arm) which secures it to the pivot and carefully pull the arm upward and off the pivot. Install the arm by placing it on the pivot and tightening the nut to approximately 15 ft. lbs. (20 Nm). Remember that the arm MUST BE reinstalled in its EXACT previous position or it will not cover the correct area during use.

➡**If one wiper arm does not move when turned on or only moves a little bit, check the retaining nut at the bottom of the arm. The extra effort of moving wet snow or leaves off the glass can cause the nut to come loose—will turn without moving the arm.**

To remove the wiper blade, lift up on the spring release tab, then remove the blade

Remove the retaining nut . . .

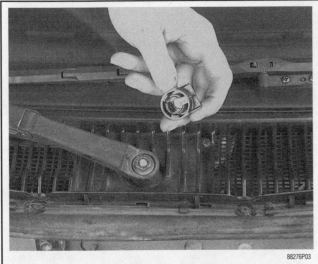

To remove the wiper arm, first remove the cap

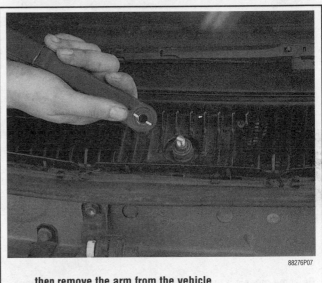

. . . then remove the arm from the vehicle

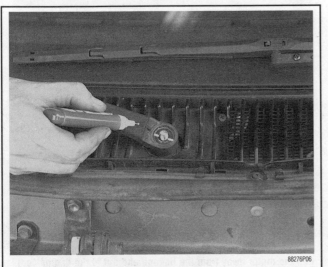

Place matchmarks on the shaft and arm

Windshield Wiper Motor

REMOVAL & INSTALLATION

Front

▶ **See Figure 22**

1. Disconnect the negative battery terminal.
2. Remove the wiper arms from the cowl panel.
3. On some models it may be necessary to remove the cowl panel.
4. Disconnect the electrical harness from the wiper motor.
5. Remove the wiper motor mounting bolts. Attach the claw of the wiper linkage to the cowl panel.
6. Separate the wiper motor from the linkage.
7. Installation is the reverse of removal. Check wiper system for proper operation.

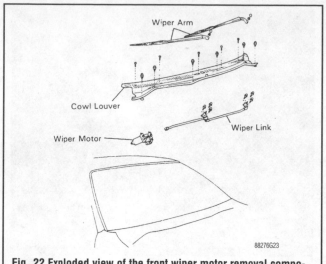

Fig. 22 Exploded view of the front wiper motor removal components

Loosen and remove the motor retaining bolts

On some models it may be necessary to remove the cowl panel

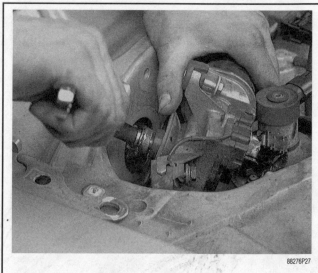

Remove the nut retaining the motor to the linkage

Disconnect the electrical harness from the wiper motor

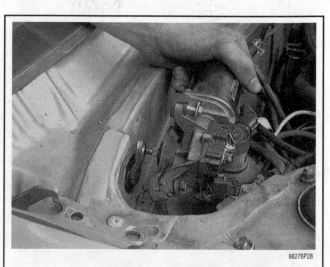

Pull the motor away from the linkage and out of the engine compartment

Rear

▶ **See Figure 23**

1. Remove the wiper arm from the pivot and remove the spacer and washer on the pivot.
2. Remove the cover (trim) panel on the inside of the hatch lock.
3. Remove the plastic cover on the wiper motor, then disconnect the wiring from the motor.
4. Remove the mounting nuts and bolts and remove the wiper motor.

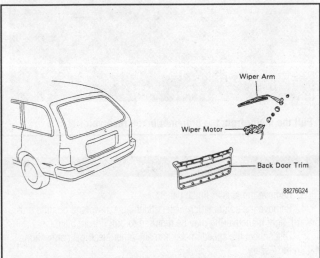

Fig. 23 The inner door trim must be removed to access the wiper motor on the wagon models

To install:

5. Position the motor and secure it in the hatch lid.
6. Connect the wiring harness and install the plastic cover.
7. Install the inner trim panel on the hatch lid.
8. Install the wiper arm with its washer and spacer, making sure the arm is correctly positioned before tightening the nut.

Windshield Washer Motor

REMOVAL & INSTALLATION

The windshield washer reservoir motor (pump) is located in the washer reservoir. The same pump is used for the front and rear washers.

1. Disconnect the negative battery cable.
2. Remove the washer reservoir/motor assembly from the vehicle.
3. Separate the washer fluid motor wiring from the harness.
4. Pull the motor from the rubber grommet retaining it to the washer reservoir.

To install:

5. Inspect the rubber grommet for deterioration and replace if necessary.
6. Apply petroleum jelly to the motor before inserting it into the grommet.
7. Attach the harness to the pump.
8. Secure the washer reservoir into the engine compartment.
9. Connect the negative battery cable and test the washer pump for operation.

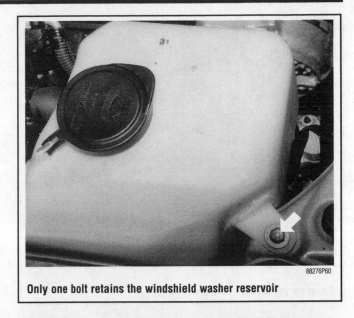

Only one bolt retains the windshield washer reservoir

Unbolt the washer reservoir . . .

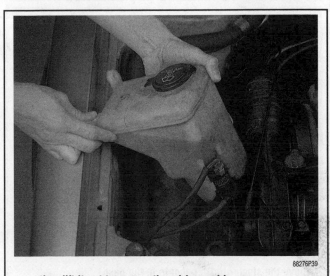

. . . then lift it out to access the wiring and hoses

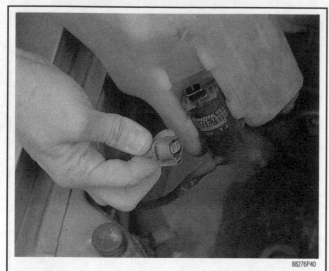
Separate the wiring at the pump motor

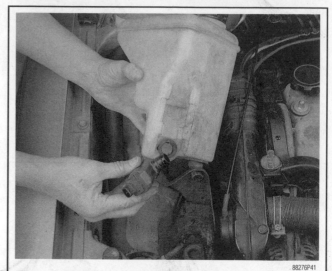
Pull the motor from the grommet in the reservoir

INSTRUMENTS AND SWITCHES

Instrument Cluster (Combination Meter)

REMOVAL & INSTALLATION

✳✳✳ CAUTION

To avoid personal injury and accidental deployment of the air bag, work must be started after about 90 seconds or longer from the time the ignition switch is turned to the LOCK position and the battery cable is disconnected from the battery.

1. Disconnect the negative battery cable.
2. Remove the steering column covers. Removing the steering wheel is not required, but may make the job easier. If the steering wheel is to be removed refer to Section 8.

➡**Be careful not to damage the collapsible steering column mechanism.**

3. Remove the cluster finish panel.
4. Remove the combination meter attaching screws and pull the unit forward. light maneuvering may be required to pull it from the dash.
5. Disconnect the speedometer and any other electrical connections that are necessary.
6. Remove the instruments from the combination meter as required.
7. Any blown combination meter bulbs can be replaced once the unit is removed. Simply twist the socket and pull.

To install:

8. Attach the components removed from the combination meter. Connect the harness to the back of the assembly and secure into the dash.
9. Attach the cluster finish panel securely.
10. Install and tighten the steering wheel column covers. Install the steering wheel if removed as per Section 8.
11. Attach the negative battery cable. Check meter operation.
12. Reset the radio, clock and any other electrical components from the battery cable being disconnected.

Remove the cluster finish panel from the dash

Unscrew the combination meter . . .

. . . then maneuver the meter out from behind the steering wheel

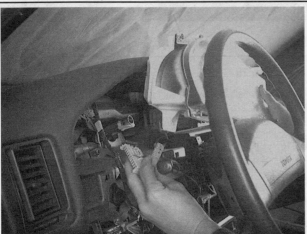

Disconnect all electrical harness from behind the meter assembly

Bulbs from behind the meter can be replaced if necessary

Gauges

REMOVAL & INSTALLATION

Disconnect the negative battery cable.
1. Remove the combination meter from the vehicle and disassemble the meter.
2. Remove the retaining screws and pull the gauge from the meter lens.

To install:
3. Attach the gauge to the combination meter. Connect the wiring harness to the assembly.
4. Insert the combination meter into the dash.
5. Connect the negative battery cable.
6. Check for proper operation.

Windshield Wiper/Washer Switch

REMOVAL & INSTALLATION

The windshield wiper/washer switch is part of the Combination Switch Assembly. Refer to Turn Signal/Combination Switch services procedures in Section 8 for additional information.

Rear Window Wiper/Washer Switch

REMOVAL & INSTALLATION

▶ See Figure 24

1. Disconnect the negative battery cable.
2. From under the dash, disconnect wiring from the switch assembly.
3. Pull the switch from the panel.

To install:
4. Insert the switch into the dash.
5. Connect the wiring to the back of the switch.
6. Connect the negative battery cable.
7. Check system for proper operation.

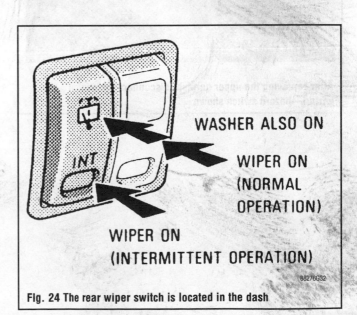

WASHER ALSO ON

WIPER ON (NORMAL OPERATION)

WIPER ON (INTERMITTENT OPERATION)

Fig. 24 The rear wiper switch is located in the dash

Headlight Switch

REMOVAL & INSTALLATION

The headlight switch is part of the Combination Switch Assembly. Refer to Turn Signal/Combination Switch services procedures in Section 8 for additional information.

Dash-Mounted Switches

REMOVAL & INSTALLATION

❊❊❊ CAUTION

On models equipped with a Supplemental Restraint System (SRS) or "air bag," work must NOT be started until at least 90 seconds have passed from the time that both the ignition switch is turned to the LOCK position and the negative cable is disconnected from the battery.

Most dash-mounted switches can be removed using the same basic procedure. Remove the trim panel which the switch is secured to. Trim panels are usually secured by a series of screws and/or clips. Make sure you remove all attaching screws before attempting to pull on the panel. Do not use excessive force as trim panels are easily damaged. Once the trim panel has been removed, unplug the switch connector, then remove its retaining screws or pry it from the mounting clip. Always disconnect the negative battery cable first.

88276P29

After removing the upper garnish, disconnect the switch wiring—hazard switch shown

88276P30

Remove the hazard switch retaining screws, then pull the unit from the trim

Clock

REMOVAL & INSTALLATION

▶ See Figure 25

On some models the clock is built into the radio assembly and cannot be removed separately. On all other models proceed with the following.
1. Disconnect the negative battery cable.
2. Using a small prytool, pry the clock loose from the dash panel. The clock is usually held in the dash panel by 2 small retaining clips.
3. Disconnect the electrical wiring from the rear of the clock and remove the clock.
4. Installation is the reverse of the removal procedure. Check the clock functions for proper operation. Reset the clock.

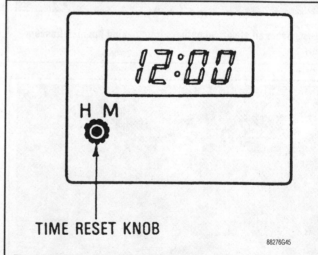

88276G45

Fig. 25 The digital clock is activated when the ignition key is in the ON or ACC position

LIGHTING

Headlights

REMOVAL & INSTALLATION

▶ **See Figure 26**

Sealed Beam Type

➡️If vehicle is equipped with retractable headlights raise the headlights and turn the lights off with the headlights raised. Then pull out the "RTR 30 AMP" fuse. Unless power is disconnected, headlights could suddenly retract causing injury.

1. Open the hood.
2. On some models it may be necessary to remove the air cleaner duct.
3. Remove the headlight bezel (trim).
4. The sealed beam is held in place by a retainer and either 2 or 4 small screws. Identify these screws before applying any tools.

➡️**DO NOT confuse the small retaining screws with the larger aiming screws! There will be two aiming screws or adjusters for each lamp. (One adjuster controls the up/down motion and the other controls the left/right motion.) Identify the adjusters and avoid them during removal. If they are not disturbed, the new headlamp will be in identical aim to the old one.**

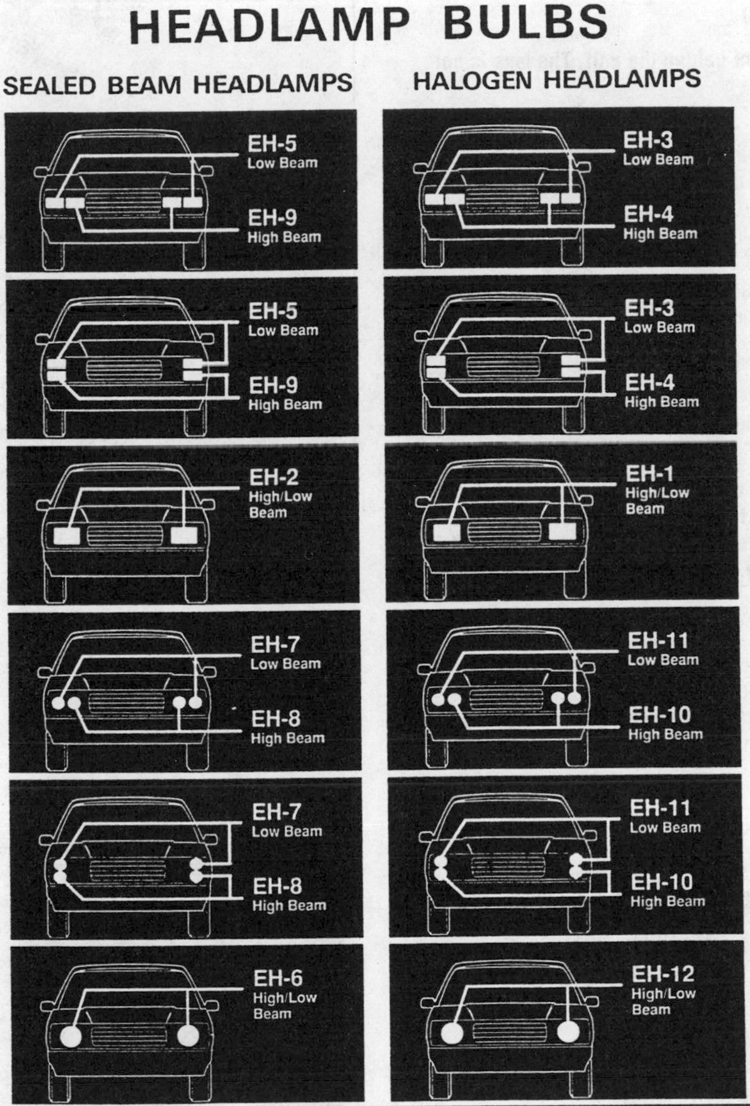

HEADLAMP BULBS

Bulb/Headlamp Number	Customer I.D.#	Bulb/Headlamp Number	Customer I.D.#	Bulb/Headlamp Number	Customer I.D.#
89	EB-6	13050	EB-10	H4651	EH-4
158	EB-8	4000	EH-7	H4656	EH-3
194	EB-7	4001/5001	EH-8	H5001	EH-10
1034	EB-4	4651	EH-9	H5006	EH-11
1073	EB-5	4652	EH-5	H6024	EH-12
1156	EB-3	6014	EH-6	H6054	EH-1
1157	EB-2	6052	EH-2	H6545	EH-13
12100	EB-9			H9004	EB-1

88276G43

Fig. 26 Headlight identification

5. Using a small screwdriver (preferably magnetic) and a pair of taper-nose pliers if necessary, remove the small screws in the headlamp retainer. DON'T drop the screws.

6. Remove the retainer and the headlamp may be gently pulled free from its mounts. Detach the connector (if the connector is tight wiggle it) from the back of the sealed beam unit and remove the unit from the car.

7. Place the new headlamp in position (single protrusion on the glass face upward) and connect the wiring harness. Remember to install the rubber boot on the back of the new lamp—its a water seal. Make sure the headlight is right-side up.

8. Turn on the headlights and check the new lamp for proper function, checking both high and low beams before final assembly.

9. Install the retainer and the small screws that hold it.

10. Reinstall the headlight bezel.

Fixed Lens Type

♦ See Figures 27, 28, 29 and 30

➡This type of light is replace from behind the unit. The lens is not removed or loosened.

1. Open and support the hood.

2. Remove the air cleaner duct on the left side if necessary. The duct is retained with a clip that may break, be careful during removal and installation.

3. Remove the wiring connector from the back the lamp. Be careful to release the locking tab completely before removal. If the connector is tight, wiggle it to remove.

4. Grasp the base of the bulb holder and collar, twist it counterclockwise (as viewed from the engine compartment) and carefully remove the bulb holder and bulb from the housing.

5. Using gloves or a rag, hold the bulb and release the clip on the holder. Remove the bulb.

6. Install the new bulb in the holder and make sure the clip engages firmly.

➡Hold the new bulb with a clean cloth or a piece of paper. DO NOT touch or grasp the bulb with your fingers. The oils from your skin will produce a hot spot on the glass envelope, shortening bulb life. If the bulb is touched accidentally, clean it with alcohol and a clean rag before installation.

7. Install the holder and bulb into the housing. Note that the holder has guides which must align with the housing. When the holder is correctly seated, turn the collar clockwise to lock the holder in place.

8. Connect the wiring harness. Turn on the headlights and check the function of the new bulb on both high and low beam.

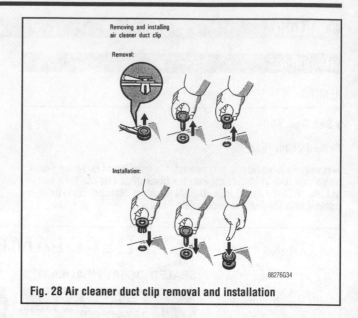

Fig. 28 Air cleaner duct clip removal and installation

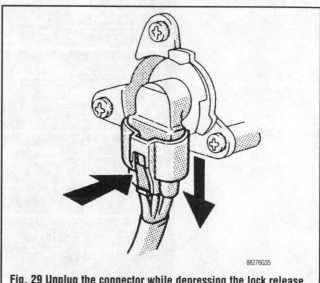

Fig. 29 Unplug the connector while depressing the lock release

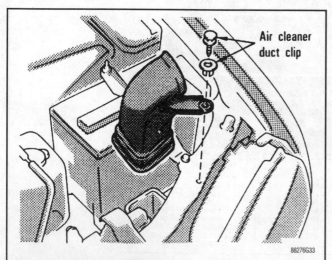

Fig. 27 Some models require the air cleaner duct to be removed to access the headlamp bulb

Inspect the connector for corrosion

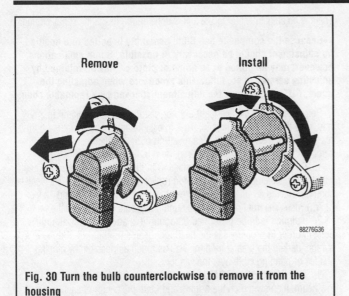

Fig. 30 Turn the bulb counterclockwise to remove it from the housing

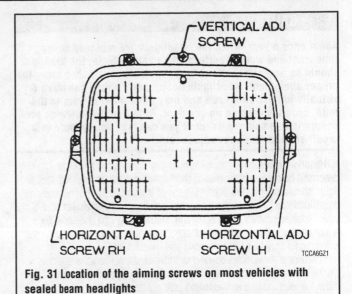

Fig. 31 Location of the aiming screws on most vehicles with sealed beam headlights

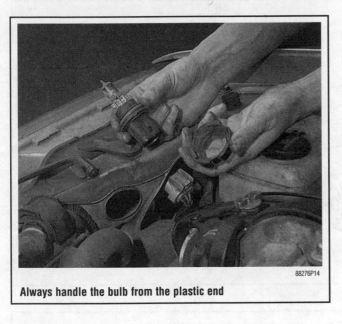

Always handle the bulb from the plastic end

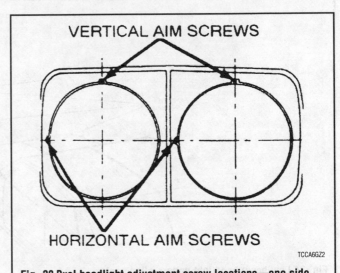

Fig. 32 Dual headlight adjustment screw locations—one side shown here (other side should be mirror image)

MANUAL OPERATION OF RETRACTABLE HEADLIGHTS

The retractable headlights can be manually operated if their electrical mechanism fails. To raise or lower the lights, Turn the ignition and headlight switches OFF and pull out the "RTR MTR 30A" fuse. Unless the power is disconnected, there is a danger of the headlights suddenly retracting. Remove the rubber cover from the manual operation knob (under the hood next to the headlight unit) and turn the knob clockwise. Manual operation should only be used if the system has failed; be sure to check the electrical operation of the lights as soon as possible. When the headlights are retracted, they should match the silhouette of the vehicle body.

AIMING THE HEADLIGHTS

♦ See Figures 31, 32, 33, 34 and 35

The headlights must be properly aimed to provide the best, safest road illumination. The lights should be checked for proper aim and adjusted as necessary. Certain state and local authorities have requirements for headlight aiming; these should be checked before adjustment is made.

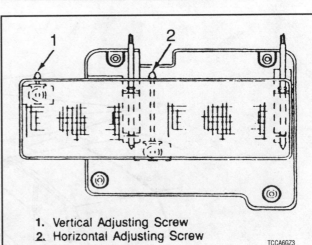

1. Vertical Adjusting Screw
2. Horizontal Adjusting Screw

Fig. 33 Example of headlight adjustment screw location for composite headlamps

☼ CAUTION

About once a year, when the headlights are replaced or any time front end work is performed on your vehicle, the headlight should be accurately aimed by a reputable repair shop using the proper equipment. Headlights not properly aimed can make it virtually impossible to see and may blind other drivers on the road, possibly causing an accident. Note that the following procedure is a temporary fix, until you can take your vehicle to a repair shop for a proper adjustment.

Headlight adjustment may be temporarily made using a wall, as described below, or on the rear of another vehicle. When adjusted, the lights should not glare in oncoming car or truck windshields, nor should they illuminate the passenger compartment of vehicles driving in front of you. These adjustments are rough and should always be fine-tuned by a repair shop which is equipped with headlight aiming tools. Improper adjustments may be both dangerous and illegal.

For most of the vehicles covered by this manual, horizontal and vertical aiming of each sealed beam unit is provided by two adjusting screws which move the retaining ring and adjusting plate against the tension of a coil spring.

There is no adjustment for focus; this is done during headlight manufacturing.

➡**Because the composite headlight assembly is bolted into position, no adjustment should be necessary or possible. Some applications, however, may be bolted to an adjuster plate or may be retained by adjusting screws. If so, follow this procedure when adjusting the lights, BUT always have the adjustment checked by a reputable shop.**

Before removing the headlight bulb or disturbing the headlamp in any way, note the current settings in order to ease headlight adjustment upon reassembly. If the high or low beam setting of the old lamp still works, this can be done using the wall of a garage or a building:

1. Park the vehicle on a level surface, with the fuel tank about ½ full and with the vehicle empty of all extra cargo (unless normally carried). The vehicle should be facing a wall which is no less than 6 feet (1.8m) high and 12 feet (3.7m) wide. The front of the vehicle should be about 25 feet from the wall.

2. If aiming is to be performed outdoors, it is advisable to wait until dusk in order to properly see the headlight beams on the wall. If done in a garage, darken the area around the wall as much as possible by closing shades or hanging cloth over the windows.

3. Turn the headlights **ON** and mark the wall at the center of each light's low beam, then switch on the brights and mark the center of each light's

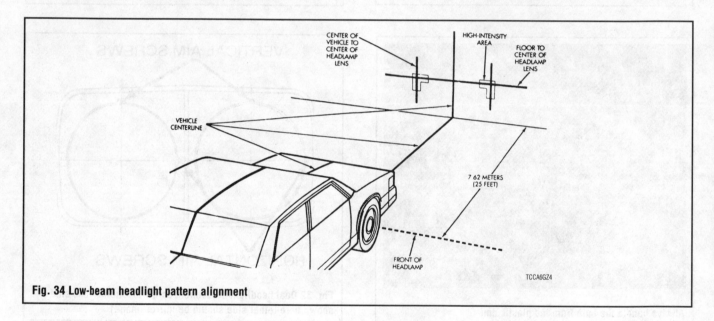

Fig. 34 Low-beam headlight pattern alignment

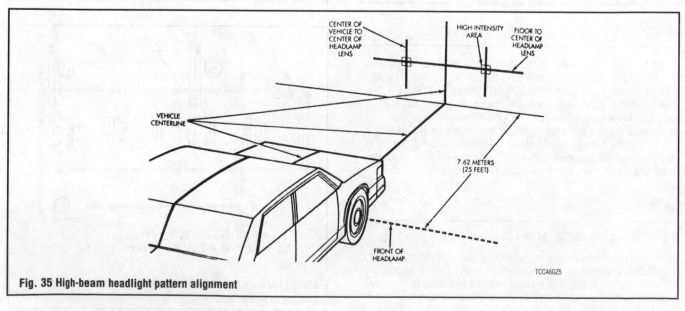

Fig. 35 High-beam headlight pattern alignment

high beam. A short length of masking tape which is visible from the front of the vehicle may be used. Although marking all four positions is advisable, marking one position from each light should be sufficient.

4. If neither beam on one side is working, and if another like-sized vehicle is available, park the second one in the exact spot where the vehicle was and mark the beams using the same-side light. Then switch the vehicles so the one to be aimed is back in the original spot. It must be parked no closer to or farther away from the wall than the second vehicle.

5. Perform any necessary repairs, but make sure the vehicle is not moved, or is returned to the exact spot from which the lights were marked. Turn the headlights **ON** and adjust the beams to match the marks on the wall.

6. Have the headlight adjustment checked as soon as possible by a reputable repair shop.

Signal and Marker Lights

REMOVAL & INSTALLATION

Front Turn Signals

◆ See Figure 36

➡ **This can be done with the car on the ground. Access is improved if the car is safely supported on jackstands.**

1. From behind the bumper, disconnect the electrical wiring.
2. Remove the two nuts from the housing.
3. Remove the turn signal lamp housing.

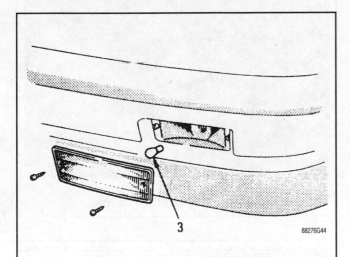

Fig. 36 If just removing the lens, loosen the two screws and pull it out from the front

➡ **If only the bulb is to be changed, the lens may be removed from the front. This requires the removal of two screws.**

To install:

4. Attach the lamp assembly into the front of the bumper.
5. Reassemble the housing in reverse order of disassembly procedure.

Side Marker Lights (Parking Lights)

FRONT

1. Remove the retaining screws. On some models, the screws are visible at the rear corner of the lens. On other models, the screw is under the hood.
2. Gently remove the lighting assembly from the body of the car.
3. Disconnect the bulb and socket(s) from the housing.
4. Reassemble in reverse order of removal procedure.

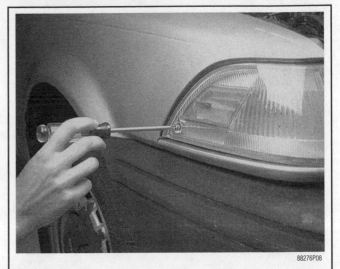

Loosen and remove the outer clearance lamp retaining screws

A hidden screw may be under the hood retaining the lamp

Pull the lamp assembly out from the body . . .

. . . then carefully disconnect the socket from the lamp housing

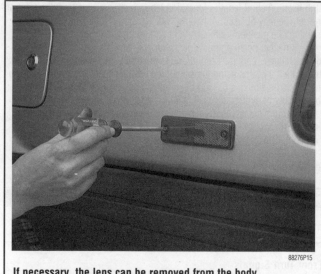

If necessary, the lens can be removed from the body

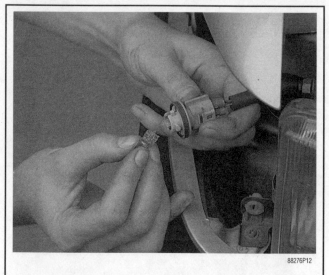

Pull the bulb from the socket. Inspect and replace if necessary

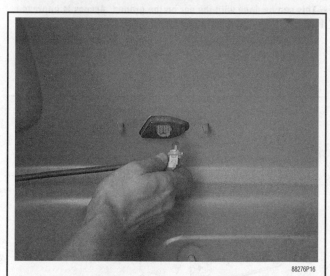

Pull the socket assembly out from behind the lens . . .

REAR

1. Some models incorporates the sidelights into the taillight assemblies. Remove the two screws in the sidemarker lens.
2. Remove the lighting assembly from the bodywork.
3. Disconnect the bulb and socket from the lighting assembly.
4. Reassemble in reverse order of the removal procedure.

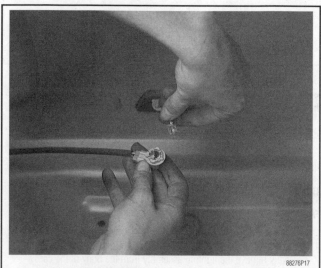

. . . and replace the light bulb

Rear Turn Signal, Brake and Parking Lights

▶ **See Figure 37**

1. Raise the trunk lid and remove or fold back the trunk carpeting.
2. Disconnect the wiring from the bulb holder(s).
3. If a bulb is to be changed, remove the bulb holder from the housing by pressing the tab and lifting out the holder assembly. Replace the bulb and reinsert the housing.
4. Remove the nuts holding the taillight assembly in place. Some may be difficult to reach.
5. Remove the lens assembly from the outside of the car.
6. When reinstalling the lens assembly, pay close attention to the placement of the gasket. It must be correctly positioned and evenly positioned to prevent water from entering the lens or trunk area. Double check the holes through which the threaded studs pass; caulk them with sealer if needed.
7. Install the retaining nuts and tighten them evenly. Do not overtighten them or the lens may crack.

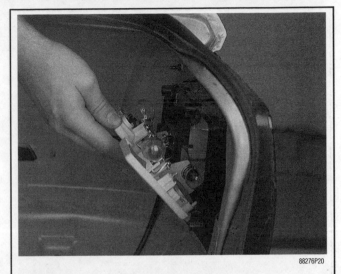

Pull the bulb socket housing down and out to remove

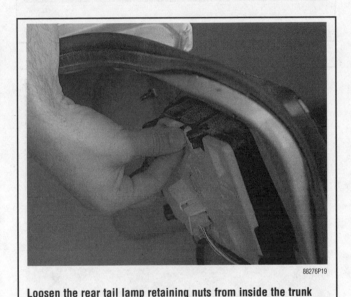

Loosen the rear tail lamp retaining nuts from inside the trunk

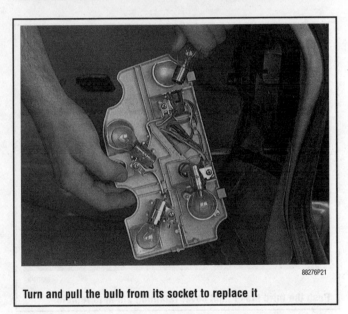

Turn and pull the bulb from its socket to replace it

8. Install the electrical connectors. Operate the lights while you check the function at the rear of the car. Replace the trunk carpet.

High Mounted Stoplight

REMOVAL & INSTALLATION

▶ **See Figure 38**

1. Remove the high mounted stoplight cover by pressing the center portion of the clip in while removing it.
2. Remove the bulb from the high mounted stoplight holder.
To install:
3. Insert a new bulb into the lamp socket.
4. Before installing the retaining clips, position the center of the clip correctly.
5. Attach the lens cover.

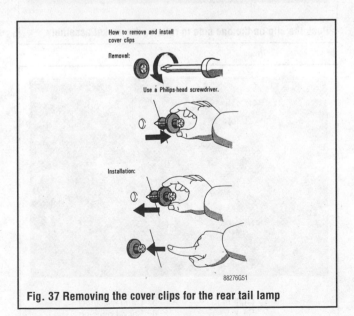

Fig. 37 Removing the cover clips for the rear tail lamp

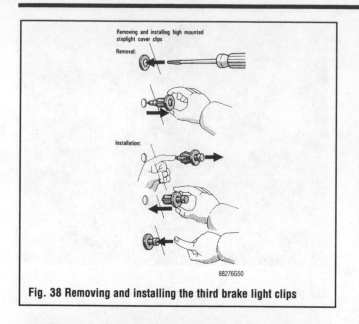

Fig. 38 Removing and installing the third brake light clips

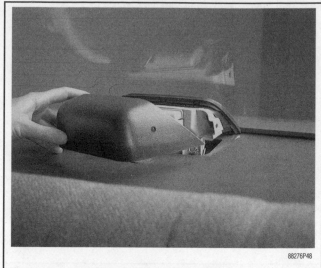

Pull the trim cover off the brake lamp assembly

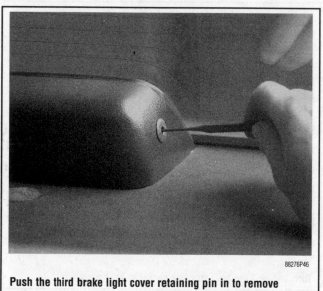

Push the third brake light cover retaining pin in to remove

Push the clip on the one side to release the socket assembly

Be careful when removing the clip, they break easily

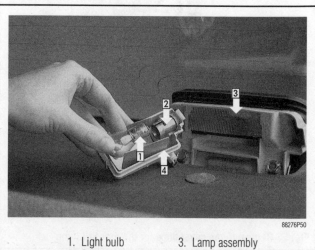

1. Light bulb   3. Lamp assembly
2. Socket   4. Socket housing

Remove the bulb and replace it if necessary

Dome Light

REMOVAL & INSTALLATION

1. Using a small prytool, carefully remove the cover lens from the lamp assembly.

2. Remove the bulb from its retaining clip contacts. If the bulb has tapered ends, gently depress the spring clip/metal contact and disengage the light bulb, then pull it free of the two metal contacts.

To install:

3. Before installing the light bulb into the metal contacts, ensure that all electrical conducting surfaces are free of corrosion or dirt.

4. Position the bulb between the two metal contacts. If the contacts have small holes, be sure that the tapered ends of the bulb are situated in them.

5. To ensure that the replacement bulb functions properly, activate the applicable switch to illuminate the bulb which was just replaced. If the replacement light bulb does not illuminate, either it is faulty or there is a problem in the bulb circuit or switch. Correct as necessary.

6. Install the cover lens until its retaining tabs are properly engaged.

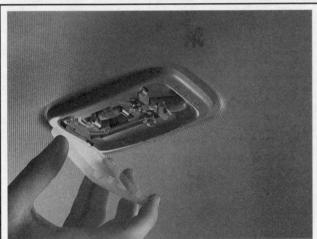

Remove the lens from the dome lamp by carefully pulling down on it

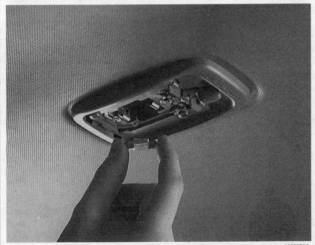

Pull the bulb from its retaining clasp in the lamp body

No.	Light Bulbs	Bulb No.	W
1	Parking lights**	194	3.8
2	Front side marker lights**	194	3.8
3	Front turn signal lights	1156	27
4	Daytime running lights	1156	27
5	Rear side marker lights**	194	3.8
6	Rear turn signal lights	1156	27
7	Stop and tail lights	1157	27/8
8	High mounted stop-light	1156	27
9	Back-up lights	1156	27
10	License plate lights Sedan	89	7.5
	All-Trac/4WD Wagon**	–	5
	Wagon	–	5
11	Trunk room light**	194	3.8
12	Luggage compartment light*	–	5
13	Interior light	–	10
14	Personal light	1853	10

Fig. 39 Light bulb applications—1988–92 models

Light bulbs	Bulb No.	W	Type
Headlights (inner bulb)	9005	65	A
Headlights (outer bulb)	9006	55	B
Parking and front side marker lights	194	3.8	D
Front turn signal lights	1156	27	C
Rear turn signal lights	1156	27	C
Stop and tail lights	1157	27/8	C
Rear side marker, stop and tail lights	1157	27/8	C
Buck up lights	1156	27	C
High mounted stop light	–	18	D
License plate lights	–	5	D
Interior light	–	8	E
Personal light	–	10	C
Luggage compartment light	–	5	E
Trunk light	194	3.8	D

A: HB3 halogen bulbs
B: HB4 halogen bulbs
C: Single end bulbs
D: Wedge base bulbs
E: Double end bulbs

Fig. 40 Light bulb applications—1993–97 models

TRAILER WIRING

Wiring the vehicle for towing is fairly easy. There are a number of good wiring kits available and these should be used, rather than trying to design your own.

All trailers will need brake lights and turn signals as well as tail lights and side marker lights. Most areas require extra marker lights for overwide trailers. Also, most areas have recently required back-up lights for trailers, and most trailer manufacturers have been building trailers with back-up lights for several years.

Additionally, some Class I, most Class II and just about all Class III trailers will have electric brakes. Add to this number an accessories wire, to operate trailer internal equipment or to charge the trailer's battery, and you can have as many as seven wires in the harness.

Determine the equipment on your trailer and buy the wiring kit necessary. The kit will contain all the wires needed, plus a plug adapter set which includes the female plug, mounted on the bumper or hitch, and the male plug, wired into, or plugged into the trailer harness.

When installing the kit, follow the manufacturer's instructions. The color coding of the wires is usually standard throughout the industry. One point to note: some domestic vehicles, and most imported vehicles, have separate turn signals. On most domestic vehicles, the brake lights and rear turn signals operate with the same bulb. For those vehicles with separate turn signals, you can purchase an isolation unit so that the brake lights won't blink whenever the turn signals are operated, or, you can go to your local electronics supply house and buy four diodes to wire in series with the brake and turn signal bulbs. Diodes will isolate the brake and turn signals. The choice is yours. The isolation units are simple and quick to install, but far more expensive than the diodes. The diodes, however, require more work to install properly, since they require the cutting of each bulb's wire and soldering in place of the diode.

One, final point, the best kits are those with a spring loaded cover on the vehicle mounted socket. This cover prevents dirt and moisture from corroding the terminals. Never let the vehicle socket hang loosely; always mount it securely to the bumper or hitch.

CIRCUIT PROTECTION

Fuses and Fusible Links

REPLACEMENT

▶ **See Figures 41 and 42**

➡**Vehicle fuses, fusible links and or relays are found in relay or junction blocks. Refer to the illustrations for location of relay and or junction block locations. The covers for the relay or junction blocks identify each fuse, fusible link or relay.**

All models have fuses, fusible links and relays found in various locations. One junction block (No. 1) is located within the cabin of the car, just under the extreme left side of the dashboard. This fuse block generally contains the fuses for body and cabin electrical circuits such as the wipers, rear defogger, ignition, cigarette lighter, etc. In addition, various relays and circuit breakers for other equipment are also mounted on or around this fuse block.

The second junction block (No. 2) is found under the hood on the forward part of the left wheelhouse (driver's side). The fuses, fusible links and relays in this junction block generally control the engine and major electrical systems on the car, such as headlights (separate fuses

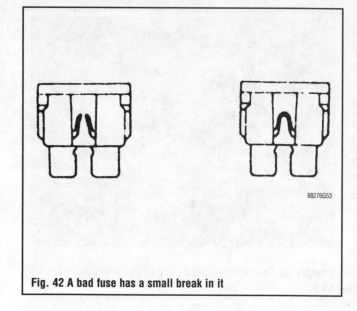

Fig. 42 A bad fuse has a small break in it

for left and right), air conditioning, horns, fuel injection, ECM, and fans.

All models have an additional small panel (relay/junction block No. 4) at the right kick panel area containing a fuse (air conditioner or heater) and a relay and circuit breaker for the heater system.

All models have a relay block (No. 5) near junction block (No. 2) which is found under the hood. On 1993–97 Canada vehicles, the relay block No. 6 is located in the front right engine compartment (passenger's side). These relay blocks contain various fuses, fusible links and relays for the vehicle. The covers for the relay or junction blocks identify each fuse, fusible link or relay for your vehicle

Each fuse and fusible link location is labeled on the fuseblock cover identifying its primary circuit, but designations such as "Engine", "CDS Fan" or "ECU-B" may not tell you what you need to know. A fuse and fusible link can control more than one circuit, so check related fuses. The sharing of fuses is necessary to conserve space and wiring.

The individual fuses are of the plastic or "slip-fuse" type. They connect into the fusebox with two small blades, similar to a household wall plug. Removing the fuse with the fingers can be difficult; there isn't a lot to grab onto. For this reason, the fuseblock contains a small plastic fuse remover which can be clipped over the back of the fuse and used as a handle to pull it free.

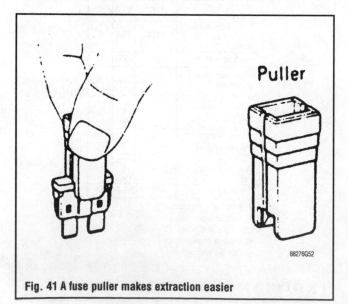

Fig. 41 A fuse puller makes extraction easier

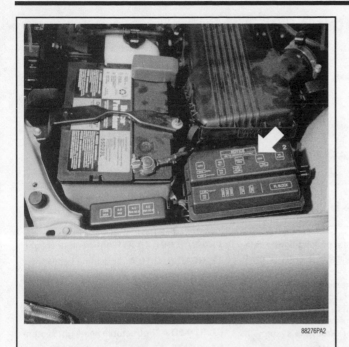

Look at the outside markings on the fuse block to determine the fuse location

Once the fuse is out, view the fusible element through the clear plastic of the fuse case. An intact fuse will show a continuous horseshoe-shaped wire within the plastic. This element simply connects one blade with the other; if it's intact, power can pass. If the fuse is blown, the link inside the fuse will show a break, possibly accompanied by a small black mark. This shows that the link broke when the electrical current exceeded the wires ability to carry it.

It is possible for the link to become weakened (from age or vibration) without breaking. In this case, the fuse will look good but fail to pass the proper amount of current, causing some electrical item to not work.

Once removed, any fuse may be checked for continuity with an ohmmeter. A reliable general rule is to always replace a suspect fuse with a new one. So doing eliminates one variable in the diagnostic path and may cure the problem outright. Remember, however, that a blown fuse is rarely the cause of a problem; the fuse is opening to protect the circuit from some other malfunction either in the wiring or the component itself. Always replace a fuse or

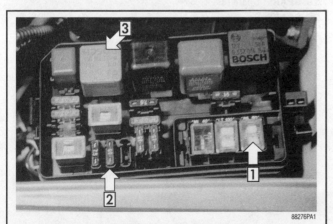

1. Fusible links   3. Relay
2. Fuse

Fuses, relays and fusible links can be found in the underhood fusebox

other electrical component with one of equal amperage rating; NEVER increase the ampere rating of the circuit. The number on the back of the fuse body (5, 7.5, 10, 15 ,etc.) indicates the rated amperage of the fuse.

Circuit Breakers

REPLACEMENT

◗ **See Figure 43**

The circuit breakers found on the junction and relay blocks mount to the blocks with blades similar to the fuses. Before removing a breaker, always disconnect the negative battery cable to prevent potentially damaging electrical "spikes" within the system. Simply remove the breaker by pulling straight out from the block. Do not twist the circuit breaker, because damage may occur to the connectors inside the housing.

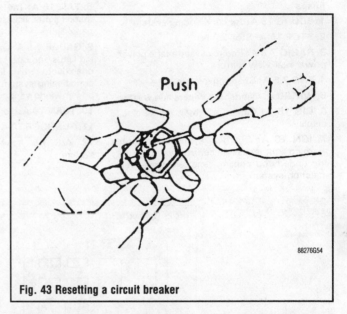

Fig. 43 Resetting a circuit breaker

➡**Some circuit breakers do not reset automatically. Once tripped, they must be reset by hand. Use a small screwdriver or similar tool; insert it in the hole in the back of the breaker and push gently. Once the breaker is reset, either check it for continuity with an ohmmeter or reinstall it and check the circuit for function.**

Reinstall the circuit breaker by pressing it straight in to its mount. Make certain the blades line up correctly and that the circuit breaker is fully seated. Reconnect the negative battery cable and check the circuit for function.

Turn Signal and Hazard Flasher

The combination turn signal and hazard flasher unit is located under the dash on the left side near junction block (No. 1). The flasher unit is not the classic round "can" found on many domestic cars; instead, it is a small box-shaped unit easily mistaken for another relay. Depending on the year of your vehicle, the flasher may be plugged directly into the junction block (No.1) or it may be plugged into its own connector and mounted near junction block (No. 1). The flasher unit emits the familiar ticking sound when the signals are in use and may be identified by touching the case and feeling the "click" as the system functions.

The flasher unit simply unplugs from its connector and a replacement may be installed. Assuming that all the bulbs on the exterior of the car are working properly, the correct rate of flash for the turn signals or hazard lights is 60–75 flashes per minute. Very rapid flashing on one side only or no flashing on one side generally indicates a failed bulb rather than a failed flasher.

1988–90 Corolla

Fuses and circuit breakers

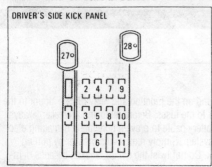

DRIVER'S SIDE KICK PANEL

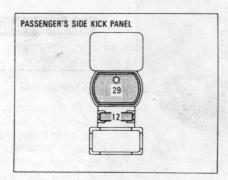

PASSENGER'S SIDE KICK PANEL

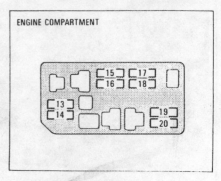

ENGINE COMPARTMENT

Fuses

1. ECU-IG 15 A: Air conditioning system

2. STOP 15 A: Stop lights

3. RADIO 7.5 A: Radio, cassette tape player, power rear view mirrors

4. ENG 7.5 A: Charging system

5. WIP 20 A: Windshield wipers and washer

6. CIG 15 A: Cigarette lighter, digital clock display

7. IGN 10 A: Charging system, discharge warning light, emission control system, electric underhood cooling fans, electronic fuel injection system

8. TAIL 15 A: Tail lights, parking lights, side marker lights, license plate lights, instrument panel lights

9. GAUGE 7.5 A: Gauges and meters, warning lights and buzzers (except discharge and open door warning lights), back-up lights, air conditioning system, rear window defogger, power windows, power door lock system

10. TURN 10 A: Turn signal lights

11. SUNROOF 30 A: Electric sun roof

12. A/C 7.5 A: Air conditioning cooling system

13. HEAD (RH) 10 A: Right-hand headlight

14. HEAD (LH) 10 A: Left-hand headlight

15. HAZ-HORN 15 A: Emergency flashers, horns

16. EFI 15 A: Electronic fuel injection system

17. RTR 30 A: Retractable headlight system

18. DOME 10 A: Interior light, personal light, trunk room light, clock, open door warning light

19. FAN-I/UP 7.5 A: Engine cooling fan control system

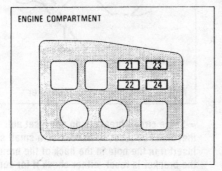

ENGINE COMPARTMENT

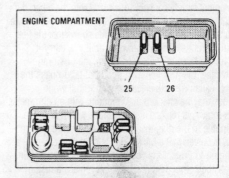

ENGINE COMPARTMENT

20. CHARGE 7.5 A: Charging system, discharge warning light, automatic choke

21. HEAD (LH-UPR) 10 A: Left-hand headlight (high beam)

22. HEAD (RH-UPR) 10 A: Right-hand headlight (high beam)

23. HEAD (LH-LWR) 10 A: Left-hand headlight (low beam)

24. HEAD (RH-LWR) 10 A: Right-hand headlight (low beam)

25. SPARE: Spare fuse (7.5 A)

26. SPARE: Spare fuse (15 A)

Circuit breakers

27. 30 A: Power windows, power door lock system

28. 30 A: Rear window defogger

29. 30 A: Air conditioning system

88276C03

1991–92 Corolla

Fuses and circuit breakers

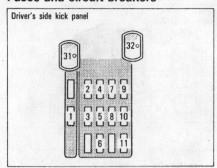

Driver's side kick panel

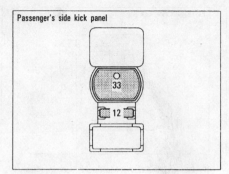

Passenger's side kick panel

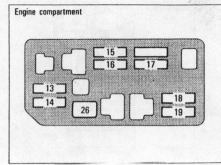

Engine compartment

Fuses (type A)

1. ECU-IG 15 A: Air conditioning system

2. STOP 15 A: High mounted stoplights

3. RADIO 7.5 A: Radio, cassette tape player, power rear view mirrors

4. ENG 7.5 A: Charging system

5. WIP 20 A: Windshield wipers and washer

6. CIG 15 A: Cigarette lighter, digital clock display

7. IGN 10 A: Charging system, discharge warning light, emission control system, electric underhood cooling fans, electronic fuel injection system

8. TAIL 15 A: Tail lights, parking lights, side marker lights, license plate lights, instrument panel lights

9. GAUGE 7.5 A: Gauges and meters, warning lights and buzzers (except discharge and open door warning lights), back-up lights, air conditioning system, rear window defogger, power windows, power door lock system

10. TURN 10 A: Turn signal lights

11. SUNROOF 30 A: Electric sun roof

12. A/C 7.5 A: Air conditioning cooling system

13. HEAD (RH) 10 A: Right-hand headlight

14. HEAD (LH) 10 A: Left-hand headlight

15. HAZ-HORN 15 A: Emergency flashers, horns

16. EFI 15 A: Electronic fuel injection system

17. DOME 10 A: Interior light, personal light, trunk room light, clock, open door warning light, daytime running light system

18. FAN-I/UP 7.5 A: Engine cooling fan control system

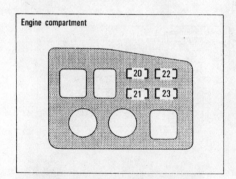

Engine compartment

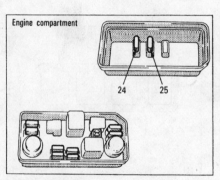

Engine compartment

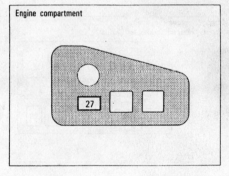

Engine compartment

19. CHARGE 7.5 A: Charging system, discharge warning light, automatic choke

20. HEAD (LH-UPR) 10 A: Left-hand headlight (high beam)

21. HEAD (RH-UPR) 10 A: Right-hand headlight (high beam)

22. HEAD (LH-LWR) 10 A: Left-hand headlight (low beam)

23. HEAD (RH-LWR) 10 A: Right-hand headlight (low beam)

24. SPARE: Spare fuse (7.5 A)

25. SPARE: Spare fuse (15 A)

Fuses (type B)

26. FAN 30 A: Radiator cooling fan

27. CDS FAN 30 A: Condenser cooling fan

28. ALT 100 A: Charging system

29. AM1 40 A: Starting system

30. AM2 30 A: Electronic fuel injection system

Circuit breakers

31. 30 A: Power windows, power door lock system

32. 30 A: Rear window defogger

33. 30 A: Air conditioning system

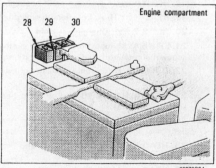

Engine compartment

88276C04

1993–95 Corolla

Fuses

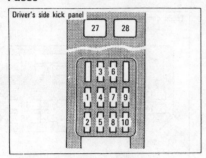

Driver's side kick panel

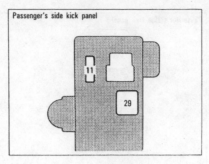

Passenger's side kick panel

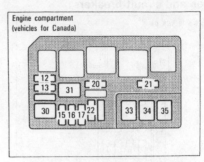

Engine compartment
(vehicles for Canada)

Fuses (type A)

1. CIG & RADIO 20 A: Cigarette lighter, digital clock display, air conditioning system, radio, cassette tape player, power rear view mirrors, automatic transmission shift lock system, theft deterrent system, SRS airbags

2. TAIL 15 A: Tail lights, parking lights, license plate lights, instrument panel lights, daytime running light system

3. IGN 10 A: Multiport fuel injection system/sequential multiport fuel injection system, electric cooling fans, discharge warining light, SRS airbags

4. ECU-B 10 A: Daytime running light system, cruise control system

5. DEF-I/UP 7.5 A: Multiport fuel injection system/sequential multiport fuel injection system

6. STOP 15 A: Stop lights, high mounted stoplight, cruise control system, automatic transmission shift lock system, anti-lock brake system

7. TURN 10 A: Turn signal lights, emergency flashers

8. ECU-IG 15 A: Starting system, anti-lock brake system, automatic transmission shift lock system

9. GAUGE 10 A: Gauges and meters, service reminder indicators (except discharge and open door warning lights), back-up light, air conditioning system, daytime running lights system

10. WIPER 20 A: Windshield wipers and washer, rear window wiper and washer

11. A/C 15 A: Air conditioning system

12. DOME 20 A: Interior light, luggage compartment light, trunk light, clock, open door warning light, radio, cassette tape player, anti-lock brake system

13. HAZ-HORN 20 A: Emergency flashers, horns

14. FAN-I/UP 7.5 A: Multiport fuel injection system/sequential multiport fuel injection system

15. SPARE 7.5 A: Spare fuse

16. SPARE 15 A: Spare fuse

17. SPARE 20 A: Spare fuse

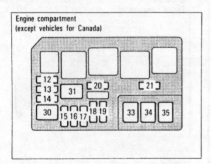

Engine compartment
(except vehicles for Canada)

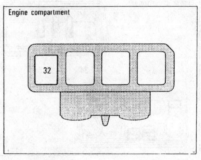

Engine compartment

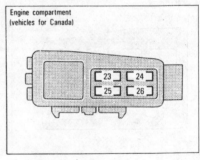

Engine compartment
(vehicles for Canada)

18. HEAD (RH) 15 A: Right-hand headlight

19. HEAD (LH) 15 A: Left-hand headlight

20. ALT-S 7.5 A: Charging system

21. EFI 15 A: Multiport fuel injection system/sequential multiport fuel injection system

22. D.R.L 7.5 A: Daytime running light system

23. HEAD (LH-UPR) 10 A: Left-hand headlight (high beam)

24. HEAD (LH-LWR) 10 A: Left-hand headlight (low beam)

25. HEAD (RH-UPR) 10 A: Right-hand headlight (high beam)

26. HEAD (RH-LWR) 10 A: Right-hand headlight (low beam)

Fuses (type B)

27. P/W 30 A: Power windows, power door lock system, electric sun roof

28. DEFOG 30 A: Rear window defogger

29. 40 A: Air conditioning system

30. AM 2 30 A: Starting system

31. FAN 30 A: Electric cooling fan

32. CDS 30 A: Electric cooling fan

Fuses (type C)

33. AM 1 40 A: Starting system, SRS airbags

34. ALT 100 A: Tail lights, "STOP", "ECU-B", "AM1" and "ABS" fuses

35. ABS 50 A: Anti-lock brake system

88276C05

1996–97 Corolla

Fuses

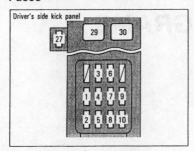

Driver's side kick panel

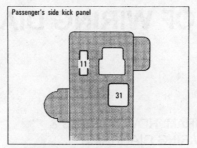

Passenger's side kick panel

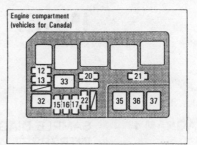

Engine compartment
(vehicles for Canada)

Fuses (type A)

1. **CIG & RADIO 20 A:** Cigarette lighter, digital clock display, air conditioning system, radio, cassette tape player, power rear view mirrors, automatic transmission shift lock system, theft deterrent system, SRS airbags

2. **TAIL 15 A:** Tail lights, parking lights, license plate lights, instrument panel lights, daytime running light system

3. **IGN 10 A:** Multiport fuel injection system/sequential multiport fuel injection system, discharge warning light, SRS airbags

4. **ECU–B 10 A:** Daytime running light system, cruise control system

5. **DEF–I/UP 7.5 A:** Multiport fuel injection system/sequential multiport fuel injection system

6. **STOP 15 A:** Stop lights, high mounted stoplight, cruise control system, automatic transmission shift lock system, anti–lock brake system

7. **TURN 7.5 A:** Turn signal lights

8. **ECU–IG 15 A:** Starting system, anti–lock brake system, automatic transmission shift lock system

9. **GAUGE 10 A:** Gauges and meters, service reminder indicators (except discharge and open door warning lights), back–up light, air conditioning system, daytime running light system, electronically controlled automatic transmission system

10. **WIP 20 A:** Windshield wipers and washer

11. **A/C 15 A:** Air conditioning system

12. **DOME 20 A:** Interior light, trunk light, clock, open door warning light, radio, cassette tape player, anti–lock brake system, theft deterrent system, electric sun roof

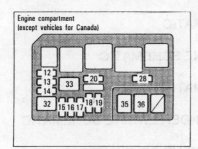

Engine compartment
(except vehicles for Canada)

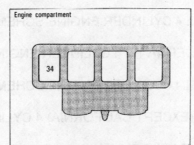

Engine compartment

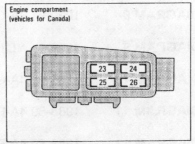

Engine compartment
(vehicles for Canada)

13. **HAZ–HONE 20 A:** Emergency flashers, hones

14. **FAN–I/UP 7.5 A:** Multiport fuel injection system/sequential multiport fuel injection system

15. **SPARE 7.5 A:** Spare fuse

16. **SPARE 15 A:** Spare fuse

17. **SPARE 20 A:** Spare fuse

18. **HEAD (RH) 15 A:** Right–hand headlight

19. **HEAD (LH) 15 A:** Left–hand headlight

20. **ALT–S 7.5 A:** Charging system

21. **EFI, F–HTR 15 A:** Multiport fuel injection system/sequential multiport fuel injection system, electronically controlled automatic transmission system

22. **DRL 7.5 A:** Daytime running light system

23. **HEAD (LH–UPR) 10 A:** Left–hand headlight (high beam)

24. **HEAD (LH–LWR) 10 A:** Left–hand headlight (low beam)

25. **HEAD (RH–UPR) 10 A:** Right–hand headlight (high beam)

26. **HEAD (RH–LWR) 10 A:** Right–hand headlight (low beam)

27. **OBD 7.5 A:** On–board diagnosis system

28. **EFI 15 A:** Multiport fuel injection system/sequential multiport fuel injection system, electronically controlled automatic transmission system

Fuses (type B)

29. **POWER 30 A:** Power windows, power door lock system, electric sun roof

30. **DEF 30 A:** Rear window defogger

31. **HEATER 40 A:** Air conditioning system

32. **AM2 30 A:** Starting system and "IGN" fuse

33. **FAN 30 A:** Electric cooling fan and "FAN–I/UP" fuse

34. **CDS 30 A:** Electric cooling fan

Fuses (type C)

35. **AM1 40 A:** "CIG & RADIO", "GAUGE", "TURN", "ECU–IG", "WIP", "DEF" and "OBD" fuses

36. **ALT 100A:** Tail lights, "DEF", "STOP", "ECU–B" and "AM 1" fuses

37. **ABS 50 A:** Anti–lock brake system

88276C06

INDEX OF WIRING DIAGRAMS

DIAGRAM 1	SAMPLE DIAGRAM: HOW TO READ & INTREPRET WIRING DIAGRAMS
DIAGRAM 2	WIRING DIAGRAM SYMBOLS
DIAGRAM 3	1996-97 4 CYLINDER ENGINE SCHEMATIC
DIAGRAM 4	1995 4 CYLINDER 7A-FE ENGINE SCHEMATIC
DIAGRAM 5	1995 4 CYLINDER 4A-FE ENGINE SCHEMATIC
DIAGRAM 6	1993-94 4 CYLINDER ENGINE SCHEMATIC
DIAGRAM 7	1992 4 CYLINDER & 1990-91 4A-FE 4 CYLINDER ENGINE SCHEMATIC
DIAGRAM 8	1990-91 4A-GE 4 CYLINDER ENGINE SCHEMATIC
DIAGRAM 9	1989 4 CYLINDER 4A-FE 4 CYLINDER ENGINE SCHEMATIC
DIAGRAM 10	1988-89 4A-GE 4 CYLINDER ENGINE SCHEMATIC
DIAGRAM 11	1988-89 4A-F (EXCEPT CALIFORNIA) 4 CYLINDER ENGINE SCHEMATIC
DIAGRAM 12	1988-89 4A-F (CALIFORNIA) 4 CYLINDER ENGINE SCHEMATIC
DIAGRAM 13	1993-97 STARTING, CHARGING, FUEL PUMP & POWER DOOR LOCKS
DIAGRAM 14	1993-97 BACKUP LIGHTS & HEADLIGHTS W & W/O DRL
DIAGRAM 15	1992 BACKUP LIGHTS & HEADLIGHTS CANADA & FEDERAL
DIAGRAM 16	1988-92 STARTING, CHARGING, FUEL PUMP & POWER DOOR LOCKS
DIAGRAM 17	1990-91 HEADLIGHTS (CANADA)
DIAGRAM 18	89-91 BACK-UP LIGHTS , 90-91 HEADLIGHTS (USA) & 88-89 HEADLIGHTS
DIAGRAM 19	1990-91 HEADLIGHTS (CANADA)

87276W01

Fig. 44 Index of wiring diagrams

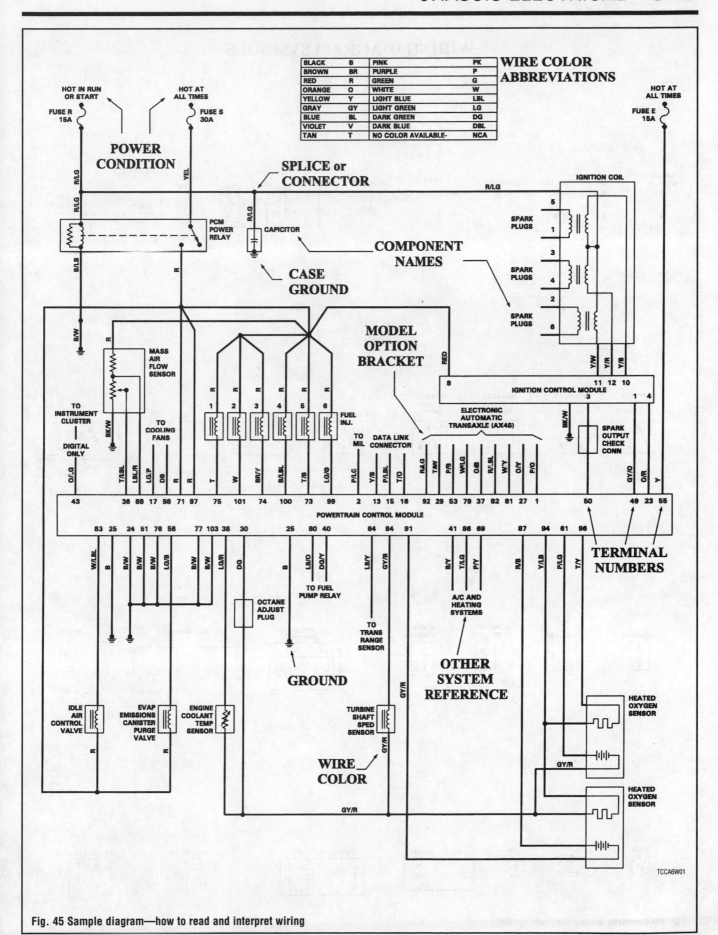

Fig. 45 Sample diagram—how to read and interpret wiring

WIRING DIAGRAM SYMBOLS

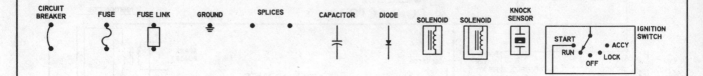

CIRCUIT BREAKER   FUSE   FUSE LINK   GROUND   SPLICES   CAPACITOR   DIODE   SOLENOID   SOLENOID   KNOCK SENSOR   IGNITION SWITCH (START, RUN, ACCY, OFF, LOCK)

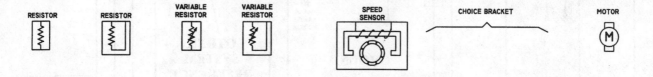

NORMALLY OPEN SWITCH   NORMALLY CLOSED SWITCH   NORMALLY OPEN SWITCH   NORMALLY CLOSED SWITCH   3 POSITION SWITCH   BATTERY   RELAY   RELAY

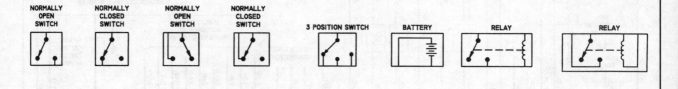

RESISTOR   RESISTOR   VARIABLE RESISTOR   VARIABLE RESISTOR   SPEED SENSOR   CHOICE BRACKET   MOTOR

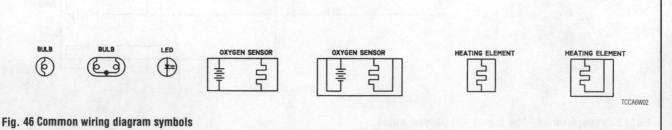

BULB   BULB   LED   OXYGEN SENSOR   OXYGEN SENSOR   HEATING ELEMENT   HEATING ELEMENT

TCCA6W02

Fig. 46 Common wiring diagram symbols

1996-97 4 CYLINDER ENGINE SCHEMATIC

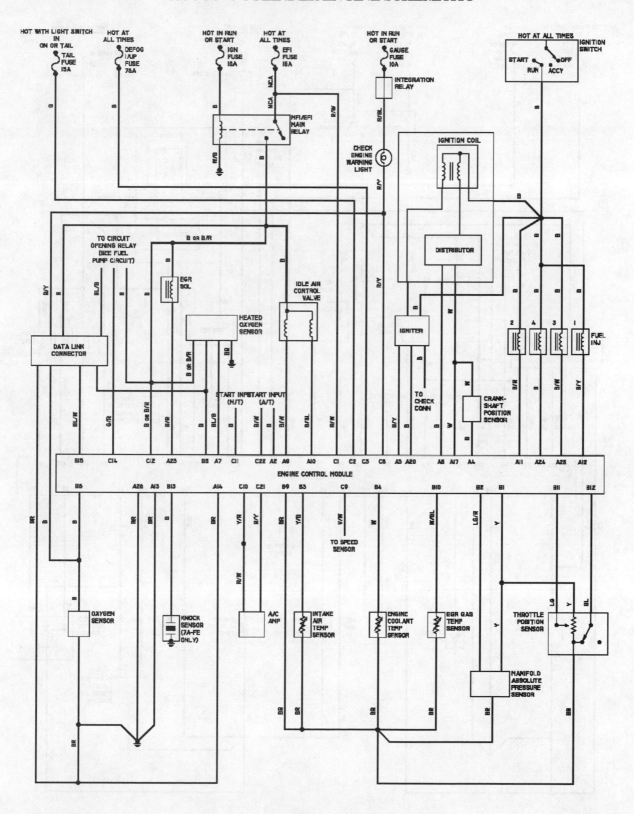

DIAGRAM 3

88276E11

1995 4 CYLINDER 7A-FE ENGINE SCHEMATIC

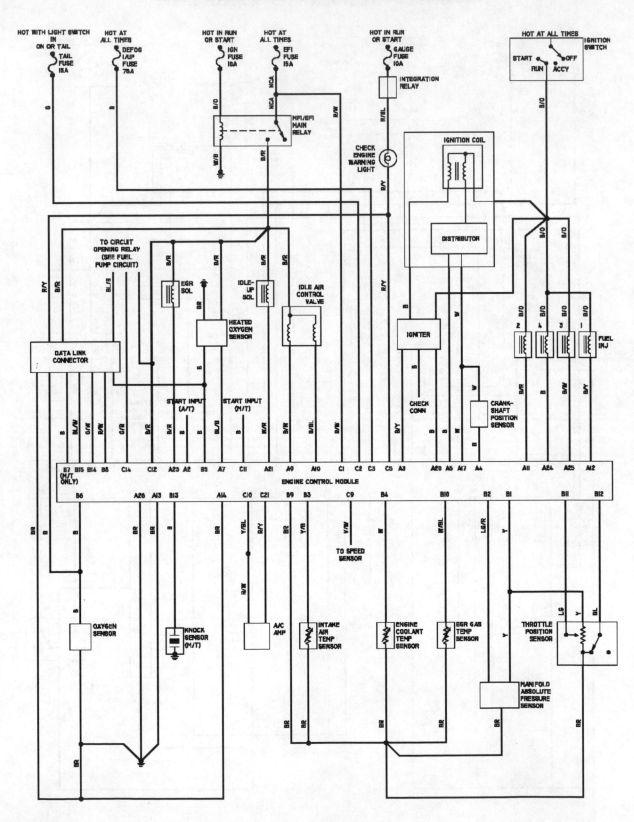

DIAGRAM 4

88276E10

1995 4 CYLINDER 4A-FE ENGINE SCHEMATIC

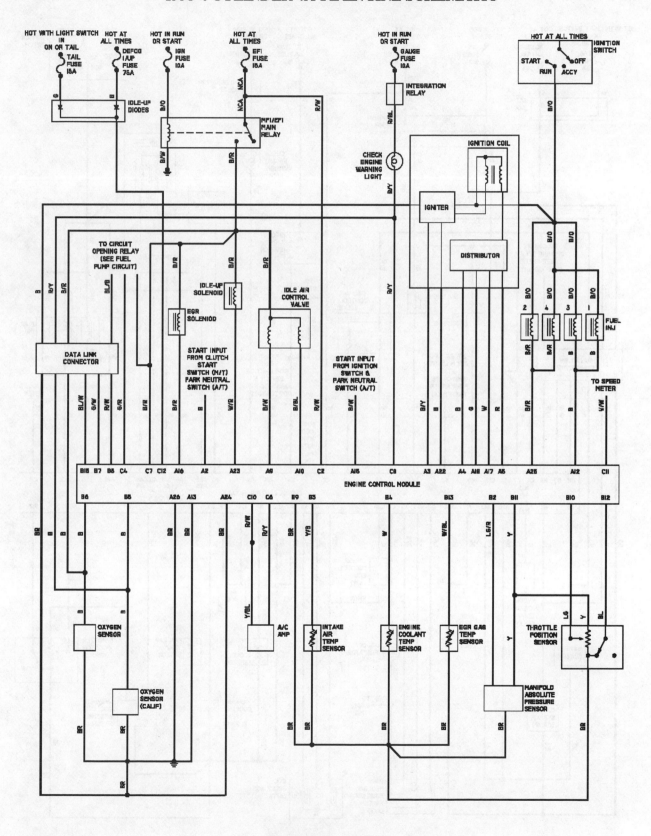

DIAGRAM 5

88276E09

1993-94 4 CYLINDER ENGINE SCHEMATIC

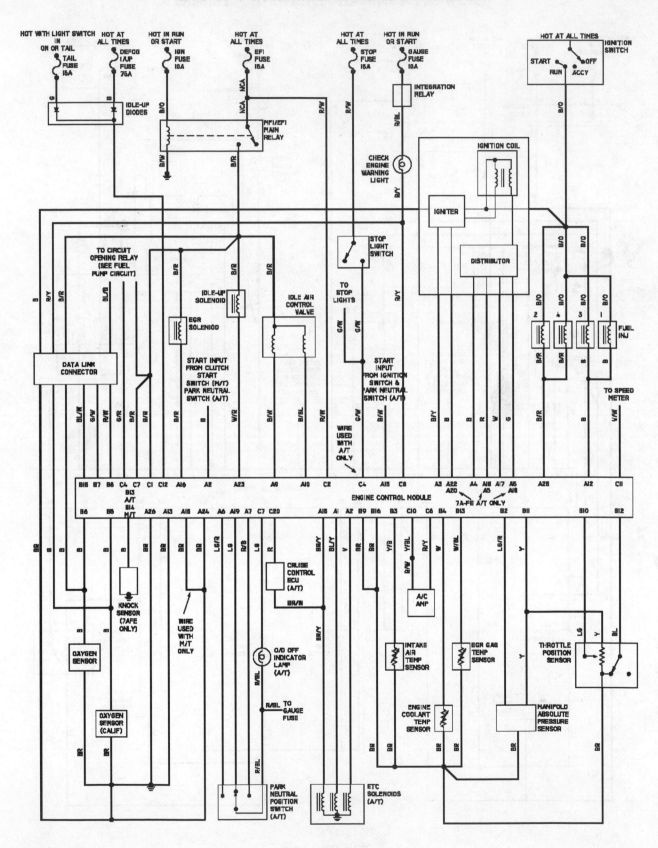

DIAGRAM 6

88276E01

1992 4 CYLINDER & 1990-91 4A-FE 4 CYLINDER ENGINE SCHEMATIC

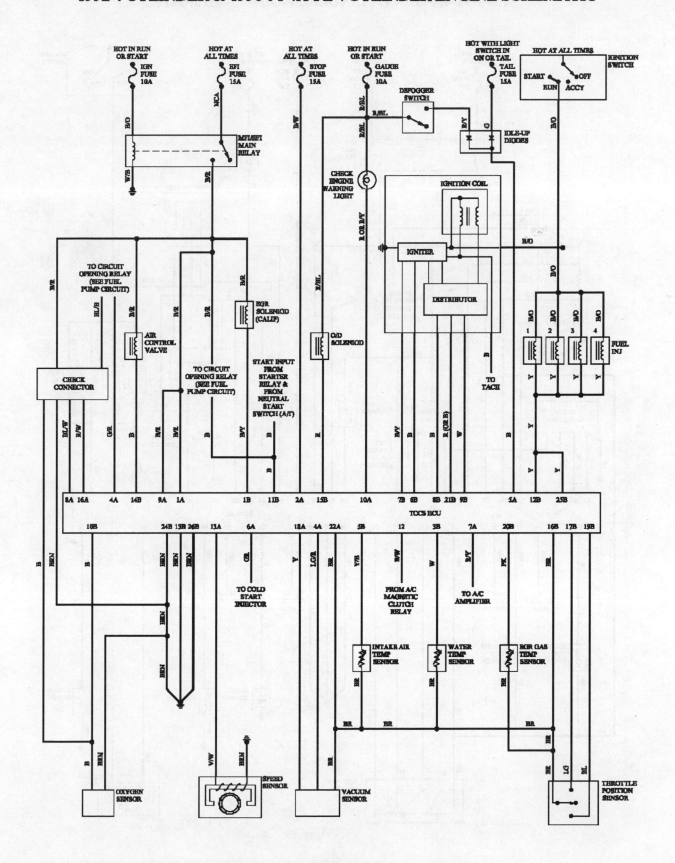

DIAGRAM 7

88276E03

1990-91 4A-GE 4 CYLINDER ENGINE SCHEMATIC

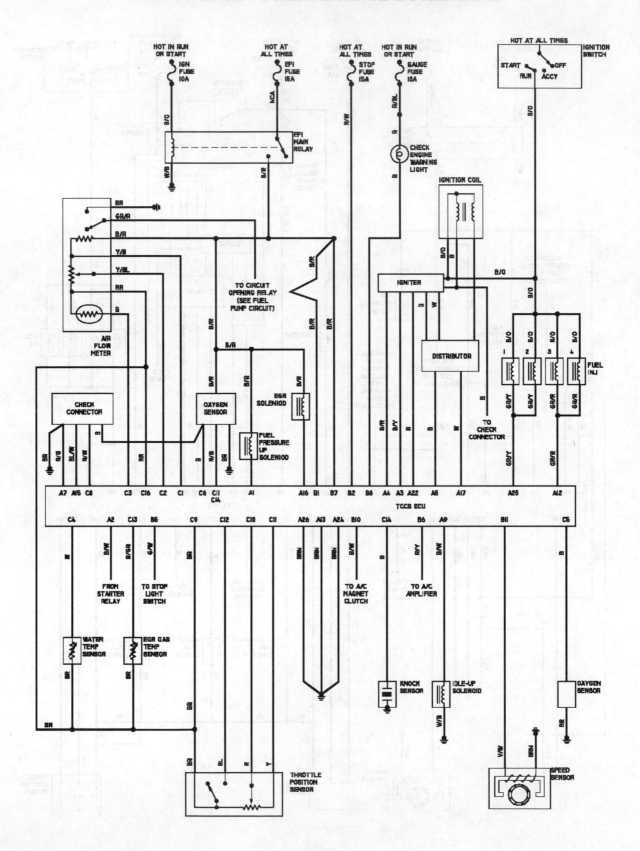

DIAGRAM 8

88276E04

1989 4 CYLINDER 4A-FE 4 CYLINDER ENGINE SCHEMATIC

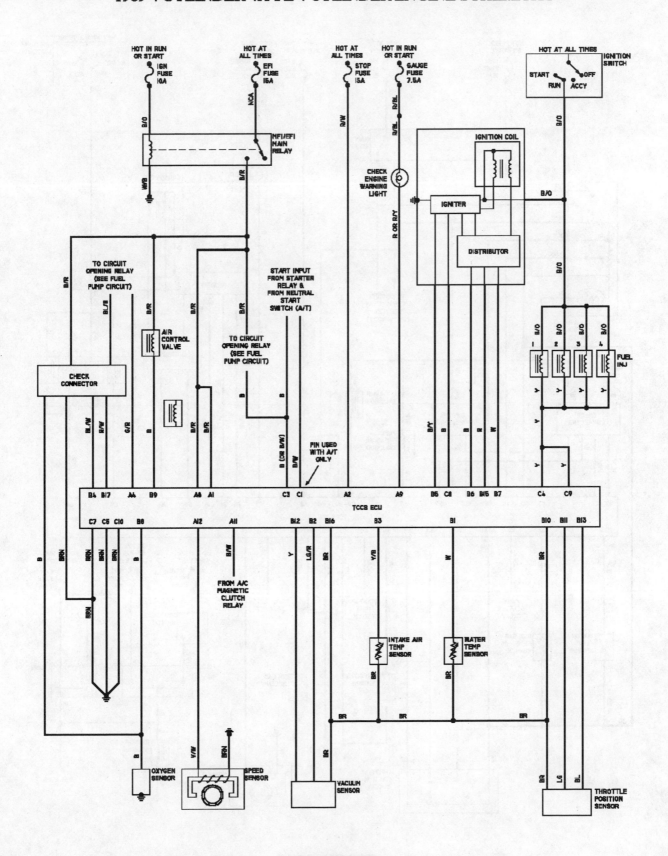

DIAGRAM 9

88276E05

1988-89 4A-GE 4 CYLINDER ENGINE SCHEMATIC

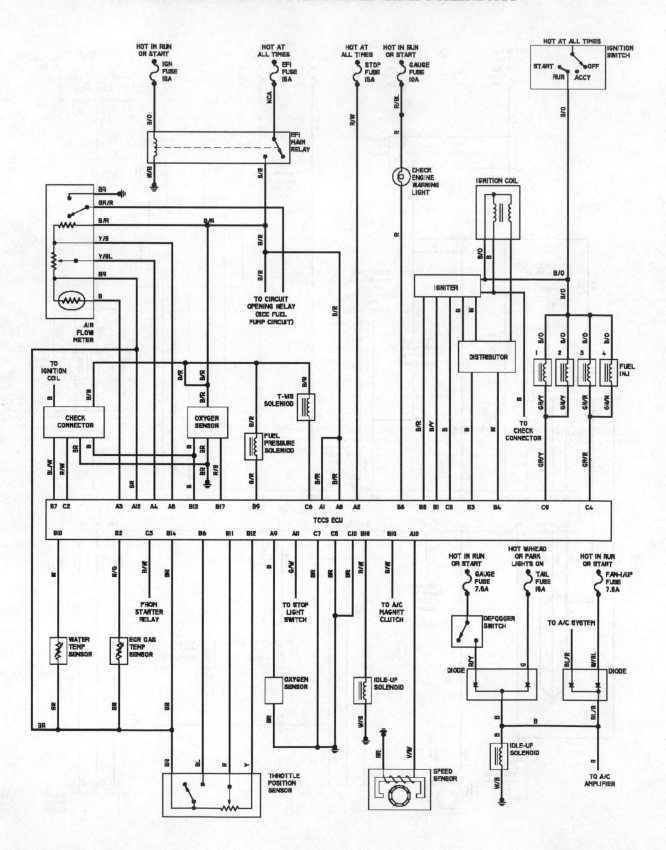

DIAGRAM 10

88276E06

1988-89 4A-F (EXCEPT CALIFORNIA) 4 CYLINDER ENGINE SCHEMATIC

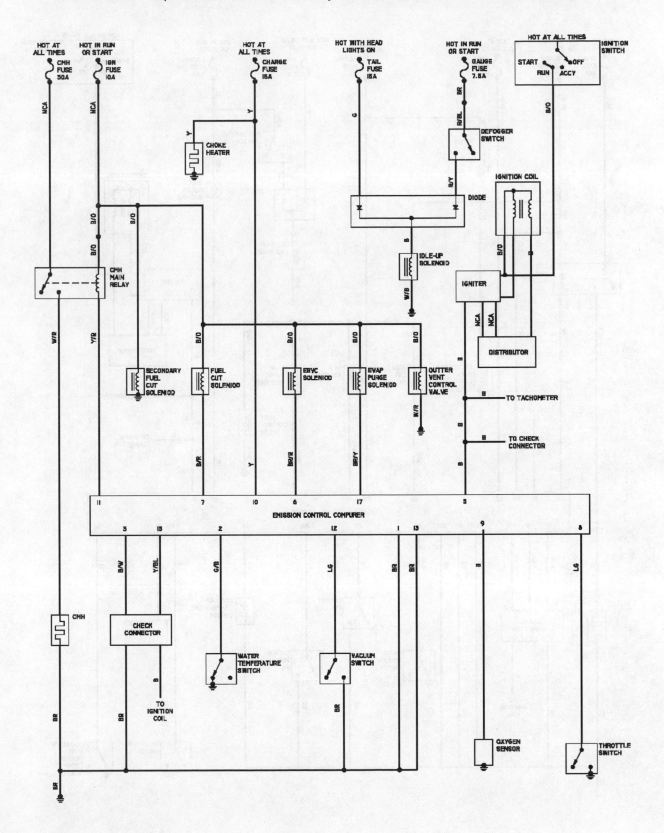

DIAGRAM 11

88276E08

1988-89 4A-F (CALIFORNIA) 4 CYLINDER ENGINE SCHEMATIC

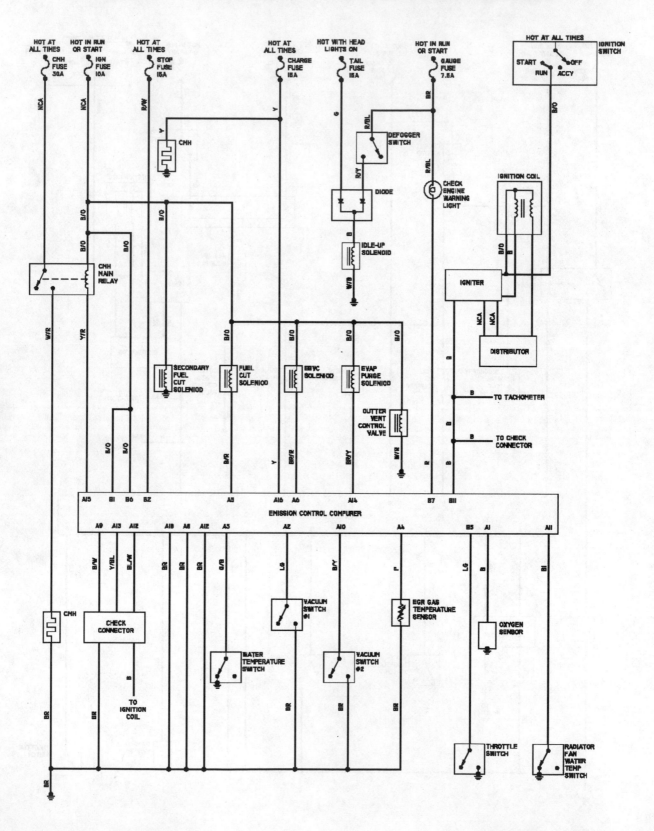

DIAGRAM 12

88276F07

1993-97 CHASSIS SCHEMATICS

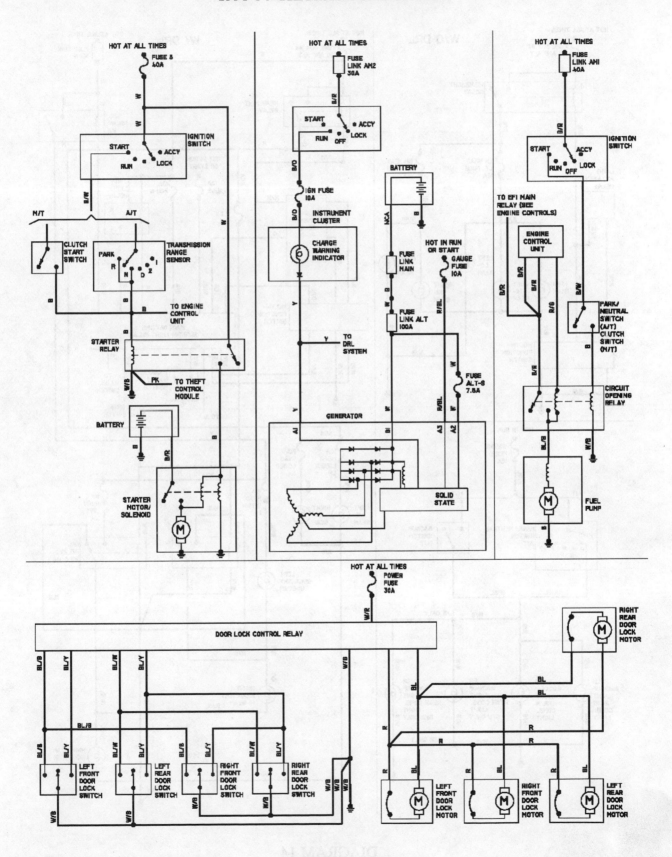

DIAGRAM 13

88276B01

1993-97 CHASSIS SCHEMATIC

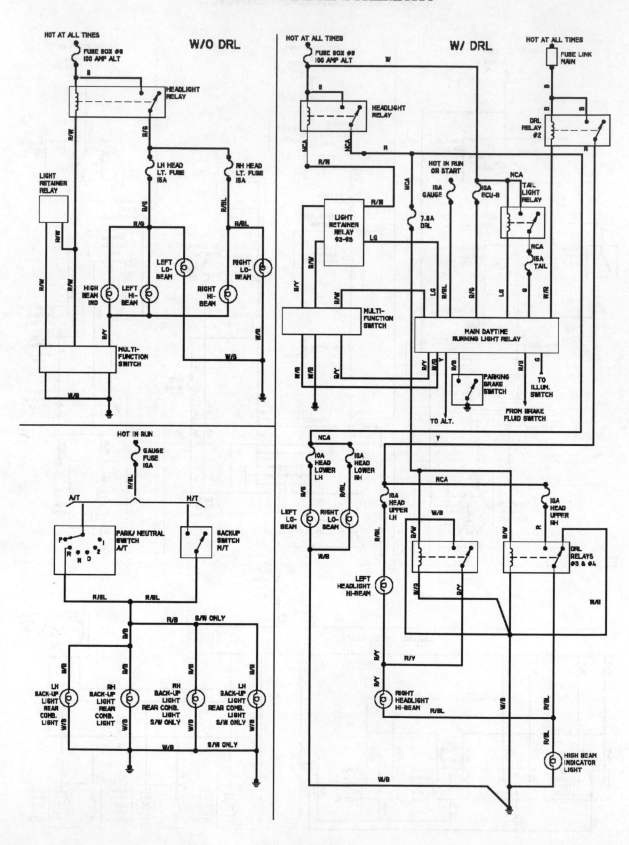

DIAGRAM 14

88276B05

1992 CHASSIS SCHEMATIC

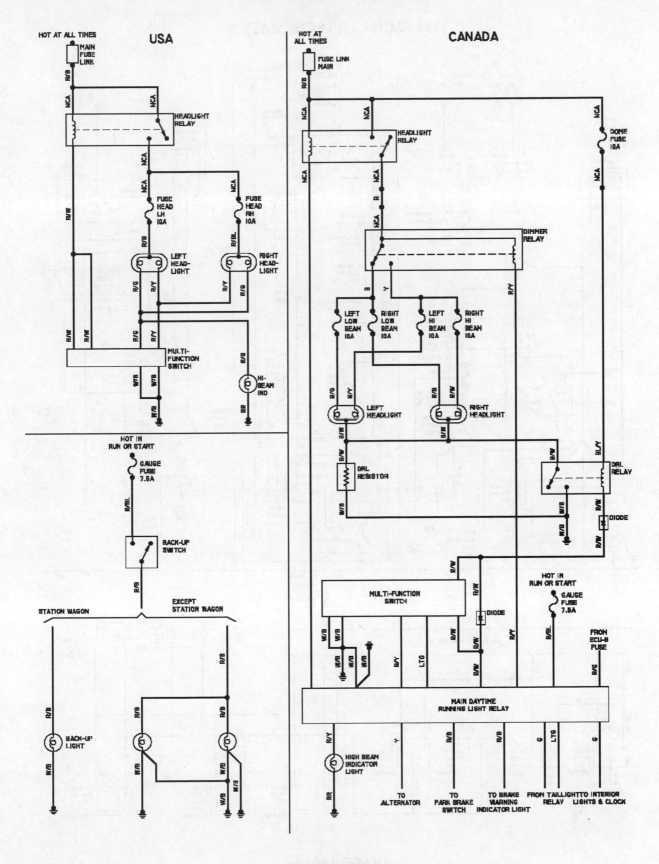

DIAGRAM 15

88276B06

1988-92 CHASSIS SCHEMATICS

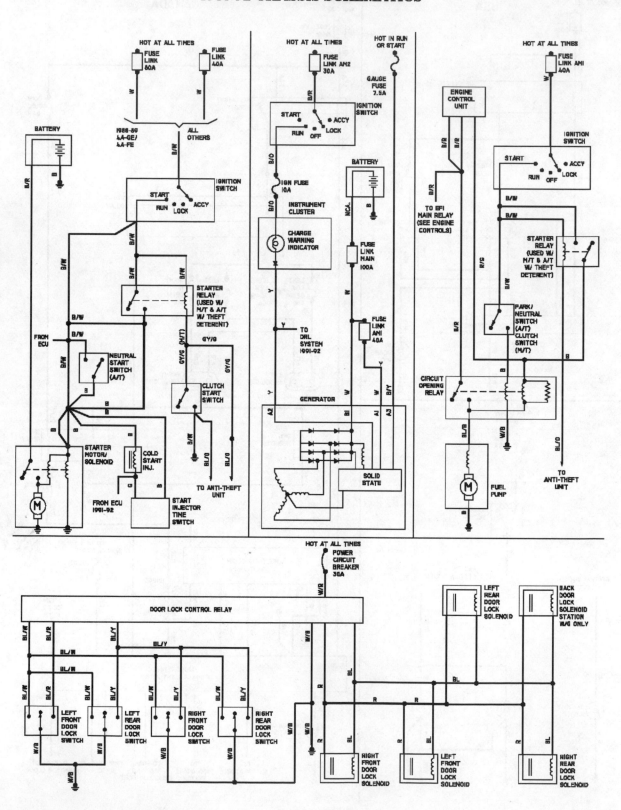

DIAGRAM 16

88276B02

1990-91 CHASSIS SCHEMATICS

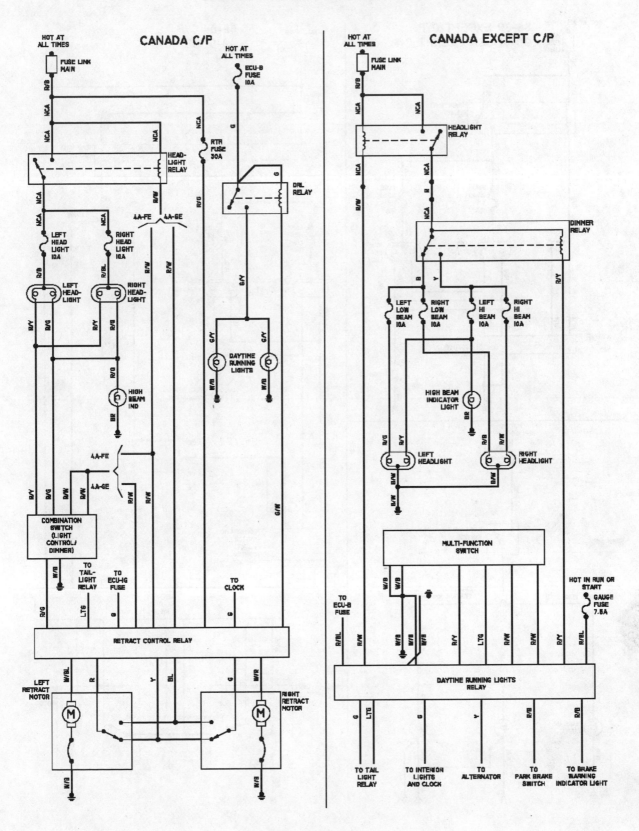

DIAGRAM 17

88276B08

1989-91 CHASSIS SCHEMATIC

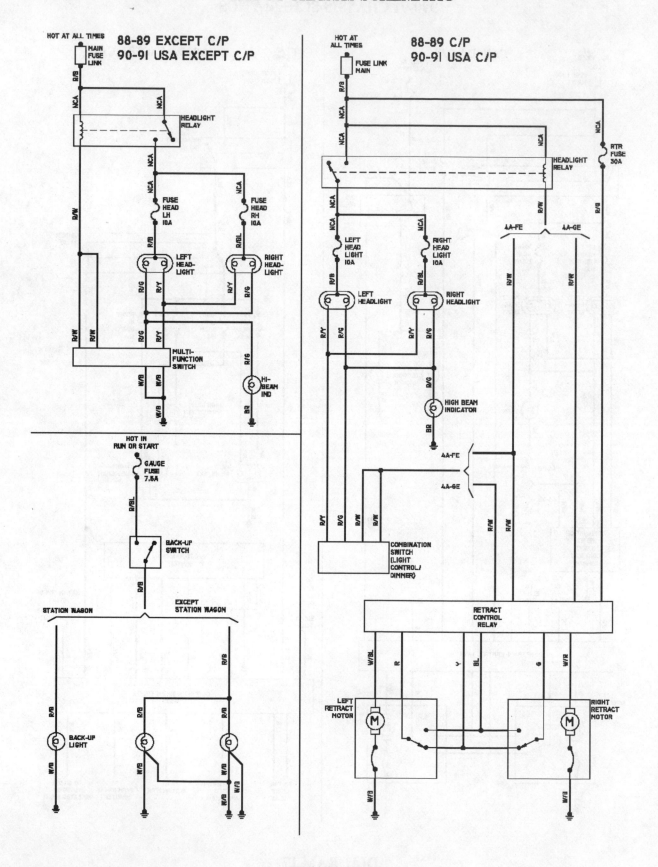

DIAGRAM 18

88276B07

1990-91 CHASSIS SCHEMATICS

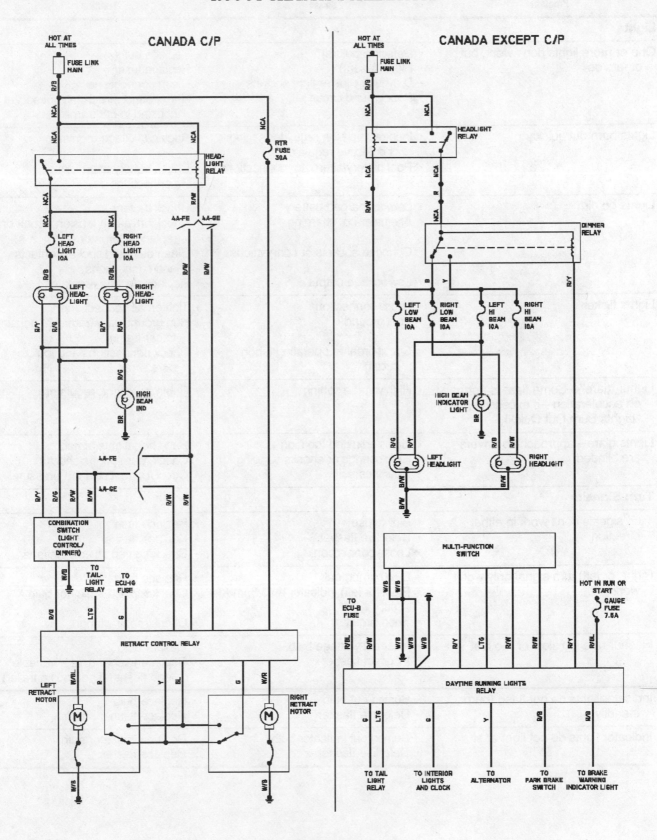

DIAGRAM 19

88276B09

Troubleshooting Basic Lighting Problems

Problem	Cause	Solution
Lights		
One or more lights don't work, but others do	• Defective bulb(s) • Blown fuse(s) • Dirty fuse clips or light sockets • Poor ground circuit	• Replace bulb(s) • Replace fuse(s) • Clean connections • Run ground wire from light socket housing to car frame
Lights burn out quickly	• Incorrect voltage regulator setting or defective regulator • Poor battery/alternator connections	• Replace voltage regulator • Check battery/alternator connections
Lights go dim	• Low/discharged battery • Alternator not charging • Corroded sockets or connections • Low voltage output	• Check battery • Check drive belt tension; repair or replace alternator • Clean bulb and socket contacts and connections • Replace voltage regulator
Lights flicker	• Loose connection • Poor ground • Circuit breaker operating (short circuit)	• Tighten all connections • Run ground wire from light housing to car frame • Check connections and look for bare wires
Lights "flare"—Some flare is normal on acceleration—if excessive, see "Lights Burn Out Quickly"	• High voltage setting	• Replace voltage regulator
Lights glare—approaching drivers are blinded	• Lights adjusted too high • Rear springs or shocks sagging • Rear tires soft	• Have headlights aimed • Check rear springs/shocks • Check/correct rear tire pressure
Turn Signals		
Turn signals don't work in either direction	• Blown fuse • Defective flasher • Loose connection	• Replace fuse • Replace flasher • Check/tighten all connections
Right (or left) turn signal only won't work	• Bulb burned out • Right (or left) indicator bulb burned out • Short circuit	• Replace bulb • Check/replace indicator bulb • Check/repair wiring
Flasher rate too slow or too fast	• Incorrect wattage bulb • Incorrect flasher	• Flasher bulb • Replace flasher (use a variable load flasher if you pull a trailer)
Indicator lights do not flash (burn steadily)	• Burned out bulb • Defective flasher	• Replace bulb • Replace flasher
Indicator lights do not light at all	• Burned out indicator bulb • Defective flasher	• Replace indicator bulb • Replace flasher

90696C00

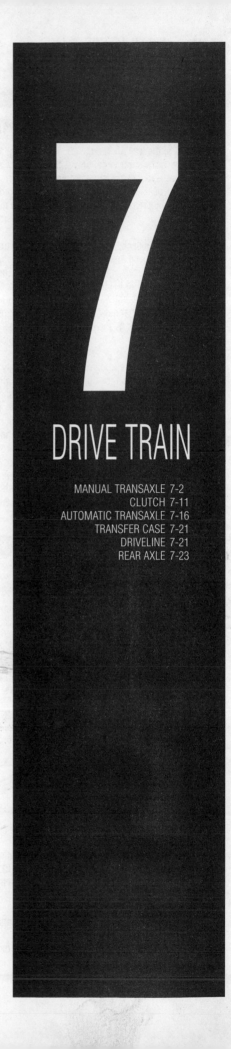

7

DRIVE TRAIN

MANUAL TRANSAXLE

Understanding the Manual Transaxle

Because of the way an internal combustion engine breathes, it can produce torque, or twisting force, only within a narrow speed range. Most modern, overhead valve pushrod engines must turn at about 2500 rpm to produce their peak torque. By 4500 rpm they are producing so little torque that continued increases in engine speed produce no power increases. The torque peak on overhead camshaft engines is generally much higher, but much narrower.

The manual transaxle and clutch are employed to vary the relationship between engine speed and the speed of the wheels so that adequate engine power can be produced under all circumstances. The clutch allows engine torque to be applied to the transaxle input shaft gradually, due to mechanical slippage. Consequently, the vehicle may be started smoothly from a full stop. The transaxle changes the ratio between the rotating speeds of the engine and the wheels by the use of gears. The gear ratios allow full engine power to be applied to the wheels during acceleration at low speeds and at highway/passing speeds.

In a front wheel drive transaxle, power is usually transmitted from the input shaft to a mainshaft or output shaft located slightly beneath and to the side of the input shaft. The gears of the mainshaft mesh with gears on the input shaft, allowing power to be carried from one to the other. All forward gears are in constant mesh and are free from rotating with the shaft unless the synchronizer and clutch is engaged. Shifting from one gear to the next causes one of the gears to be freed from rotating with the shaft and locks another to it. Gears are locked and unlocked by internal dog clutches which slide between the center of the gear and the shaft. The forward gears employ synchronizers; friction members which smoothly bring gear and shaft to the same speed before the toothed dog clutches are engaged.

Back-up Light Switch

REMOVAL & INSTALLATION

The reverse light or back-up light switch is mounted in the top area of the manual transaxle housing. Its removal and replacement is easily accomplished by disconnecting the wiring harness from the switch and unscrewing the switch from the case (always replace the mounting gasket below it). Install the new switch and tighten it 30 ft. lbs. Reinstall the electrical connector. Turn key to the **ON** position, depress clutch pedal and place shifter in R position. Check operation of back-up lights.

Adjustments

SHIFT LEVER FREE-PLAY

▶ See Figure 1

Only the 1988–92 models can be adjusted.
1. Remove the console.
2. Disconnect the shift control cables from the control shift lever assembly.
3. Using a dial indicator, measure the up and down movement of the shift lever; maximum play should be 0.0059 inch (0.15mm).
4. If necessary to adjust the free-play, perform the following procedures:
   a. Remove the shift lever cover-to-housing screws and the cover.
   b. Remove the snapring, the shift lever, the shift lever ball seat and the bushing.
   c. Install a new shift lever bushing and reverse the removal procedures.
5. Recheck the shift lever movement.

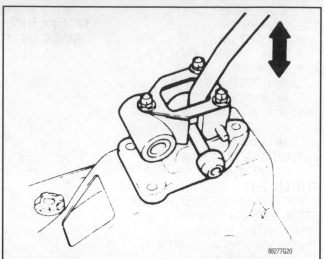

Fig. 1 Check the shift lever vertical play, then replace the bushing if necessary

CLUTCH SWITCH

Only the 1988–92 models can be adjusted.
1. Check that the engine DOES NOT start when the clutch pedal is released.
2. Check that the engine DOES start when the clutch pedal is depress
3. If necessary, adjust or replace the clutch start switch.
4. Adjust the switch as follows:
   a. Loosen the clutch switch locknut and adjust the switch to the proper clearance (2.0–6.0mm) with a feeler gauge set.
   b. Check that the engine does not start with the clutch pedal released.

Transaxle Assembly

REMOVAL & INSTALLATION

2WD Models

▶ See Figures 2 thru 17

✳✳ CAUTION

On models with an airbag, wait at least 90 seconds from the time that the ignition switch is turned to the LOCK position and the battery is disconnected before performing any further work.

1. Disconnect the negative battery cable.
2. Remove the air cleaner case assembly with hose. Remove the coolant reservoir tank.
3. Remove release cylinder tube bracket and cylinder assembly.
4. Disconnect the back-up light switch harness.
5. Remove the ground cable. Disconnect shift cables from the transaxle.
6. Disconnect vehicle speed sensor harness or speedometer cable.
7. Remove the starter set bolt from the transaxle upper side.
8. Remove the transaxle upper mounting bolts.
9. Remove the engine left mounting stay.
10. Remove the set both of the engine left mounting insulator from the transaxle upper side.
11. Install engine support fixture. Raise and safely support the vehicle.

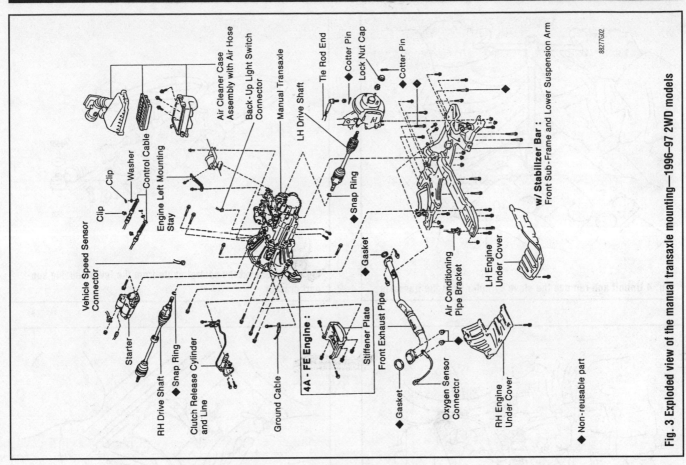

Fig. 3 Exploded view of the manual transaxle mounting—1996-97 2WD models

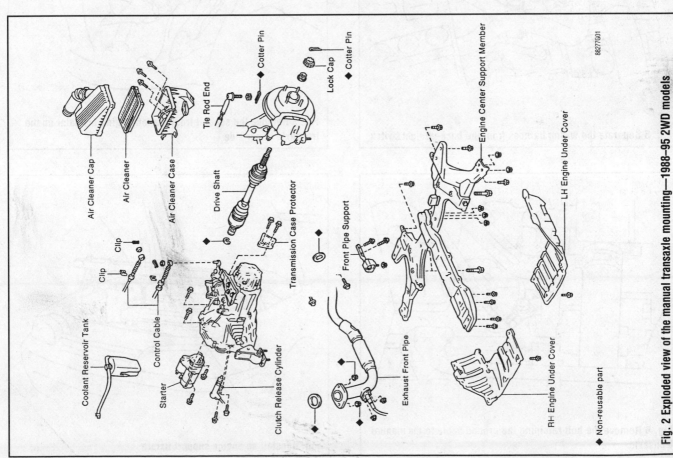

Fig. 2 Exploded view of the manual transaxle mounting—1988-95 2WD models

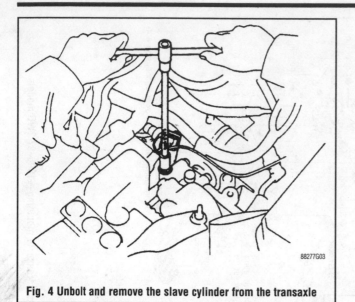

Fig. 4 Unbolt and remove the slave cylinder from the transaxle

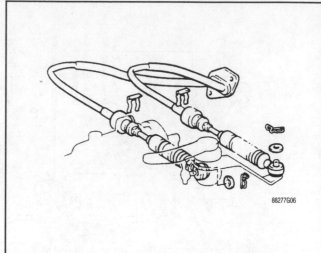

Fig. 7 Disconnect the control cable from the lever housing support bracket

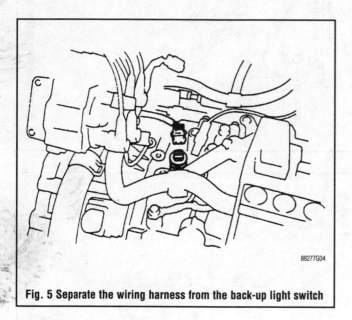

Fig. 5 Separate the wiring harness from the back-up light switch

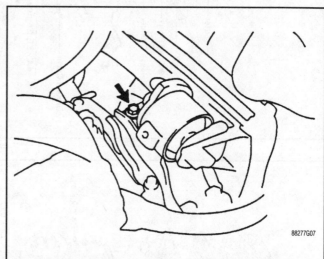

Fig. 8 Remove the set bolt from the left engine insulator on the transaxle upper side

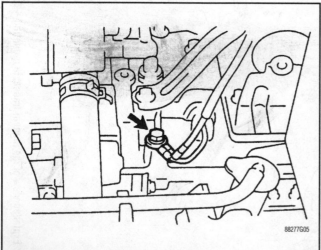

Fig. 6 Remove the bolt retaining the ground cable to the manual transaxle

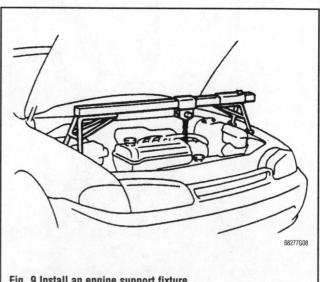

Fig. 9 Install an engine support fixture

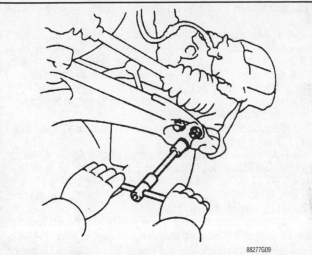

Fig. 10 Remove the bolt and nuts securing the lower control arm to the ball joint

12. Remove the front wheels. Remove the engine under covers.
13. Drain the transaxle oil.
14. Disconnect the lower ball joint from the lower arm.
15. Remove the halfshafts-refer to the necessary service procedures.
16. Remove the front exhaust pipe.
17. On 1988–95 models, remove the hole cover for the engine front mounting bolts. Remove the engine front mounting set bolts.
18. Disconnect engine rear mounting on the 1988–95 models.
19. On the 1996–97 models with a stabilizer bar, remove the 2 set bolts retaining the bar bushing bracket.
20. Remove the front sub frame (engine center support) and lower suspension arm. On 1988–95 models there are 8 bolts retaining the sub frame, on 1996–97 models there are 14 bolts and 3 nuts. Refer to the appropriate illustration.
21. Remove the starter.
22. On the 4A-FE engines, remove stiffener plate if so equipped.
23. Raise the transaxle and engine slightly with a jack. Remove the engine left mounting set bolts from the front side.
24. Remove the transaxle mounting bolts from the engine front side. Remove the transaxle mounting bolts from the engine rear side. Lower the engine left side and remove the transaxle from the engine.

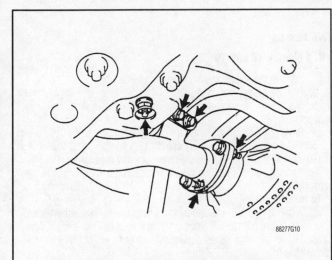

Fig. 11 Separate the front exhaust pipe to the exhaust manifold and catalyst

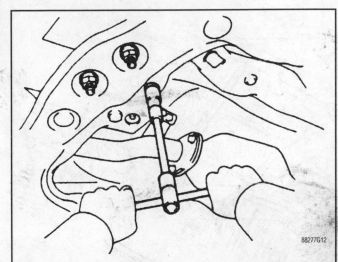

Fig. 13 Unbolt the rear engine mounting bolts—1988–95 2WD models

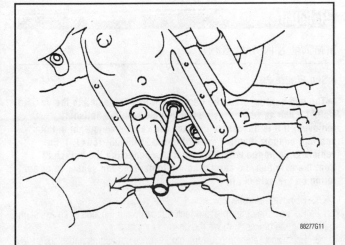

Fig. 12 Unbolt the engine front mounting, the bolts are behind a cover—1988–95 2WD models

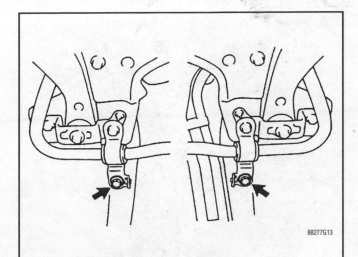

Fig. 14 On the 1996–97 models remove the stabilizer bar brackets

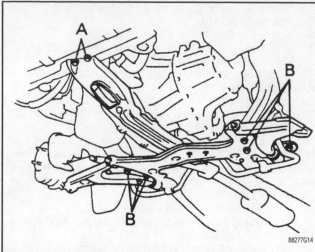

88277G14

Fig. 15 View of the engine center support bolt locations—1988–95 2WD models

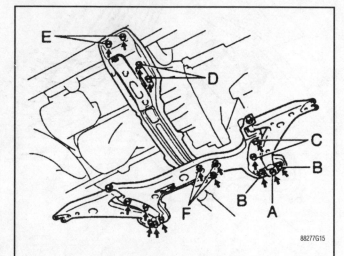

88277G15

Fig. 16 View of the sub-frame and lower suspension arm bolt locations—1996–97 models

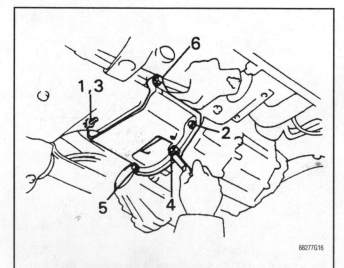

88277G16

Fig. 17 Tighten the 4A-FE stiffener plate bolts in this order

25. Installation is the reverse of removal procedure. Please note the following:
• Align the input shaft with the clutch disc and install the transaxle to the engine and torque the engine-to-transaxle bolts on 1988–95 models to 47 ft. lbs. (64 Nm) for 12mm bolts and 34 ft. lbs. (46 Nm) for 10mm bolts. On 1996–97 models tighten the 7A-FE lower side mounting bolts (A) to 17 ft. lbs. (23 Nm) and (B) to 34 ft. lbs. (46 Nm). On the 1996–97 4A-FE engine tighten the transaxle lower side bolts to 34 ft. lbs. (46 Nm) and the stiffener plate bolts to 17 ft. lbs. (23 Nm).
• Tighten the left engine mounting bracket insulator to 41 ft. lbs. (56 Nm).

26. Tighten the engine center support member on 1988–95 models to; small bolts to 45 ft. lbs. (61 Nm) and larger bolts to 152 ft. lbs. (206 Nm). On the 1996–97 models; bolt (A) to 129 ft. lbs. (175 Nm), (B) to 109 ft. lbs. (147 Nm), (C) to 167 ft. lbs. (225 Nm), (D) to 47 ft. lbs. (64 Nm), (E) to 45 ft. lbs. (61 Nm) and (F) to 42 ft. lbs. (57 Nm).0
• Tighten engine rear mounting torque bolts to 35 ft. lbs. (48 Nm). Install the engine front mounting and tighten the bolts 47 ft. lbs. (64 Nm).
• Tighten the engine left mounting set bolt to rear side to 41 ft. lbs. (56 Nm).

27. Fill the transaxle with the correct amount and type of fluid. Refer to Section 1. Connect the negative battery cable. Check front wheel alignment.

28. Road test the vehicle and check for abnormal noise and smooth shifting.

4WD Models

▶ **See Figures 18 and 19**

1. Remove the engine and transaxle as an assembly.
2. Remove the rear end plate.
3. Disconnect the vacuum lines and then remove the transfer case vacuum actuator.
4. Remove the right and center transfer case stiffener plate.
5. Pull the transaxle out slowly until there is approximately 2.36–3.15 in. (60–80mm) clearance between the transaxle and the engine.
6. Turn the output shaft in a clockwise direction and then remove the transaxle.

To install:

7. Install the transaxle assembly to the engine and tighten the 10mm bolts to 34 ft. lbs. (46 Nm). Tighten the 12mm bolts to 47 ft. lbs. (64 Nm).
8. Tighten the 8mm stiffener plate bolts to 14 ft. lbs. (20 Nm) and the 10mm bolts to 27 ft. lbs. (37 Nm).
9. Tighten the rear end plate mounting bolts to 17 ft. lbs. (23 Nm).
10. Install the engine/transaxle assembly.
11. Road test the vehicle and check for abnormal noise and smooth shifting.

Halfshafts

REMOVAL & INSTALLATION

▶ **See Figure 20**

➡**The hub bearing could be damaged if it is subjected to the vehicle weight, such as when moving the vehicle with the halfshaft removed. If it is necessary to place the vehicle weight on the hub bearing, support it with a special tool SST 09608–16041. If the vehicle is equipped with ABS, after disconnecting the half shaft from the axle hub, be careful so not to damage the sensor rotor serration on the axle shaft.**

1. Remove the wheel cover.
2. Remove the cotter pin and lock nut cap. With the aide of an assistant depressing the brakes, remove the bearing lock nut.
3. Raise and safely support the car. Remove the engine under covers and drain gear oil or transaxle fluid.
4. Remove the wheel.
5. On ABS models, unbolt and remove the ABS sensor from the vehicle.

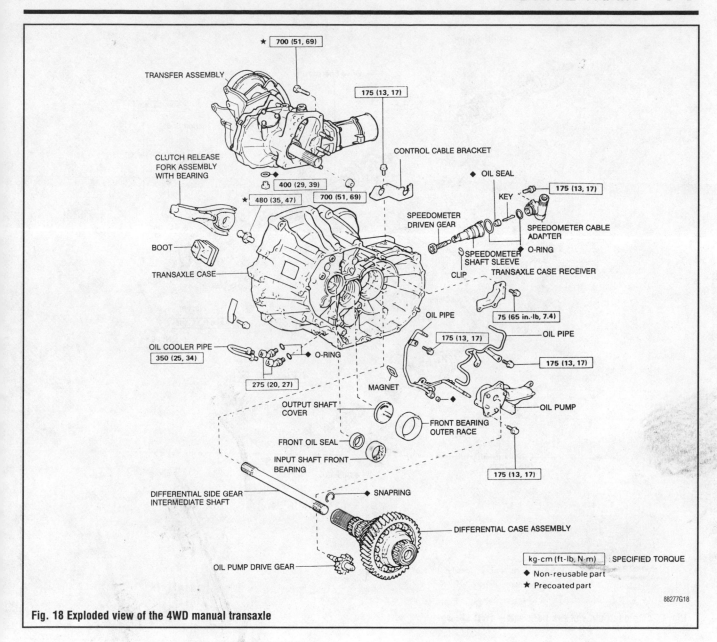

Fig. 18 Exploded view of the 4WD manual transaxle

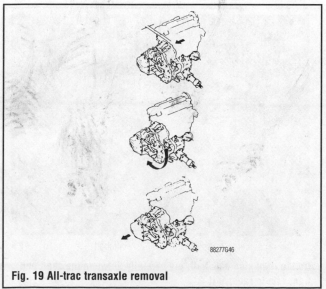

Fig. 19 All-trac transaxle removal

6. Disconnect the lower control arm to steering knuckle attaching nuts and bolts.

7. Use a ball joint separator or equivalent to remove the tie rod ball joint from the steering knuckle.

8. Remove the bolts holding the brake caliper bracket to the steering knuckle. Use stiff wire to suspend the caliper out of the way; do not let the caliper hang by its hose. Remove the brake disc.

9. Using a puller or equivalent, push the axle from the hub.

➡The axle can be separated from the hub using a brass or plastic hammer some others may require the use of a puller.

10. Use a slide hammer and hub nut wrench pull the halfshaft from the transaxle. Remove the halfshaft from the car. Be careful no to damage the dust cover and oil seal during removal.

11. Using a flat bladed tool, remove the snapring from the inboard joint spline.

To install:

12. Coat the seal lip with multi-purpose grease. Install halfshaft into transaxle. If necessary, use a long brass drift and a hammer to drive the housing ribs onto the inner joint.

➡Before installing the halfshaft, position the snapring opening side facing downward.

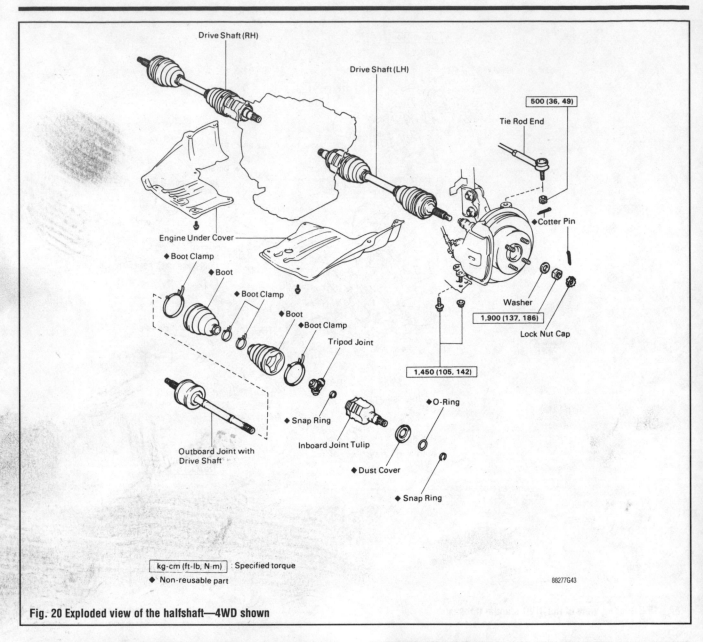

Fig. 20 Exploded view of the halfshaft—4WD shown

Use a large breaker bar to remove the axle nut

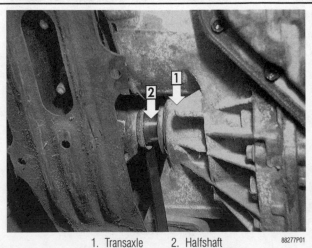

1. Transaxle   2. Halfshaft

On the right side halfshaft, pry carefully between the shaft and transaxle to remove it

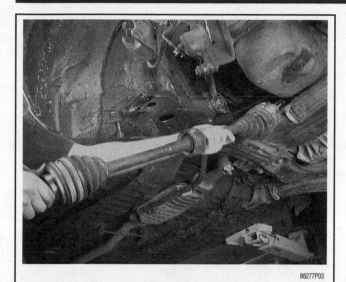

Pull the assembly out from under the vehicle

88277P03

Fig. 21 Check the CV-boot for wear

TCCS7030

13. Install the halfshaft into the wheel hub. Check that the halfshaft can not be pulled out by hand.

14. Install the lower control arm to the steering knuckle. Tighten the nuts and bolts to 105 ft. lbs. (142 Nm).

15. Install the tie rod end to the steering knuckle and tighten the nut to 36 ft. lbs. (49 Nm).

16. Install the brake disc and caliper, then tighten the bolts.

17. Install the wheel.

18. Install the hub nut and washer.

19. Lower the vehicle to the ground.

20. Tighten the wheel lugs to 76 ft. lbs. (103 Nm). Tighten the hub nut while depressing the brake pedal to 137 ft. lbs. (186 Nm). on 1988–91 models and 152 ft. lbs. (206 Nm) on 1992–97 models.

21. Install the lock nut cap and NEW cotter pin. Fill transaxle with gear oil or transaxle fluid if necessary.

22. Install the ABS sensor and tighten the retaining bolts to 71 inch lbs. (8 Nm).

23. Install engine cover. Check front wheel alignment.

CV-JOINT OVERHAUL

♦ **See Figures 21 thru 27**

The halfshaft assembly is a flexible unit consisting of an inner and outer Constant Velocity (CV) joint joined by an axle shaft. Care must be taken not to over-extend the joint assembly during repairs or handling. When either end of the shaft is disconnected from the car, any over-extension could result in separation of the internal components and possible joint failure.

The CV joints are protected by rubber boots or seals, designed to keep the high-temperature grease in and the road grime and water out. The most common cause of joint failure is a ripped boot (tow hooks on halfshaft when car is being towed) which allows the lubricant to leave the joint, thus causing heavy wear. The boots are exposed to road hazards all the time and should be inspected frequently. Any time a boot is found to be damaged or slit, it should be replaced immediately.

➡Whenever the halfshaft is held in a vise, use pieces of wood in the jaws to protect the components from damage or deformation.

1. Mount the driveshaft in a vise and check that there is no play in the inboard and outboard joint.

2. Make sure that the inboard joint slides smoothly in the thrust direction.

3. Make sure that there is no excessive play in the radial direction of the inboard joint.

4. Inspect the boots for damage (rips, punctures and cracks).

Fig. 22 Removing the outer band from the CV-boot

TCCS7031

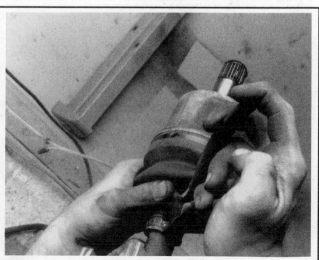

Fig. 23 Removing the inner band from the CV-boot

TCCS7032

Fig. 24 Clean the CV-joint housing prior to removing boot

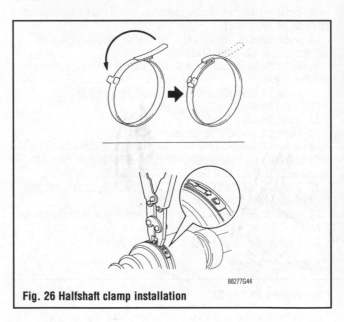

If equipped, be careful not to damage the ABS speed sensor rotor.

To assemble:

17. Using the SST and a press, install a new No. 2 dust deflector.

18. Using a press, install the inboard joint tulip into a new dust cover.

➡ **Before installing the boot, wrap the spline end of the shaft with masking tape to prevent damage to the boot. On the right side, fix the clamp position in line with the groove of the halfshaft.**

19. Install the tripod, on Toyota types:
   a. Place the beveled side of the tripod axial spline toward the outboard joint.
   b. Align the matchmarks placed before removal.
   c. Using a brass bar and hammer, tap in the tripod to the halfshaft. Do not tap the roller.
   d. Using a snapring expander, install a new snapring.

20. Pack the outboard tulip joint and the outboard boot with about 4.2–4.6 ounces of grease on Toyota types (black) and 5.8–6.4 ounces on Saginaw types (green) that was supplied with the boot kit.

21. Install the boot onto the outboard joint.

22. Pack the inboard tulip joint and boot with grease that was supplied with the boot kit.

Fig. 26 Halfshaft clamp installation

5. On Toyota type:
   a. Remove the inboard joint boot clips.
   b. Slide the inboard joint toward the outboard joint.
6. On Saginaw type:
   a. Using pliers, remove the boot clamps.
   b. Using a side cutter, cut a small boot clamp and remove it.
7. With chalk or paint, matchmark the inboard joint tulip and tripod. DO NOT use a punch.
8. Remove the inboard joint tulip from the driveshaft.
9. Using a snap ring expander, remove the snapring from the tripod.
10. Place matchmarks on the drive shaft and tripod.
11. Using a brass rod and hammer, evenly drive the tripod joint off the driveshaft without hitting the joint roller.
12. Remove the inboard joint boot.
13. On the right side, using a screw driver, remove the clamp and dynamic damper.
14. Remove the clamps and the outboard drive boot. DO NOT disassemble the outboard joint.
15. Remove the dust cover from the inboard joint using a press and SST 09950–00020 or equivalent.
16. Mount the outboard joint shaft in a soft jaw vise. Using a screws driver and hammer, remove the No. 2 dust deflector.

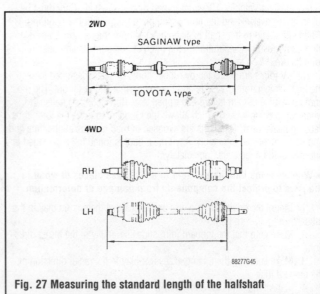

Fig. 27 Measuring the standard length of the halfshaft

Fig. 25 Removing the CV-joint outer snapring

23. Align the matchmarks on the tulip joint and tripod.
24. Install the inboard tulip joint onto the halfshaft.
25. Install the boot onto the halfshaft.
26. Make sure that the boot is properly installed on the halfshaft.
27. Before checking the standard length, bend the band and lock it.
28. Make sure that the boot is not stretched or squashed when the driveshaft is at standard length.
Standard driveshaft length:
- 1988–91 Toyota type:LH—20.598–20.992 inch (523.2–533.2mm)
- 1988–91 Toyota type:RH—32.980–33.374 inch (837.7–847.7mm)
- 1988–91 2WD Saginaw type:LH—24.551 inch (623.6mm)
- 1988–91 2WD Saginaw type:RH—36.933 inch (938.1mm)
- 1988–91 4WD type: LH—19.724–20.118 inch (501.0–511.0mm)

- 1988–91 4WD type: RH—19.850–20.244 inch (504.2–514.2mm)
- 1992—95 Toyota type: LH—20.795 inch (528.8mm)
- 1992—95 Toyota type: RH—33.177 inch (842.7mm)
- 1992 2WD Saginaw type: LH—20.795 inch (528.2mm)
- 1992 2WD Saginaw type: RH—33.177 inch (842.7mm)
- 1992 4WD type: LH—19.921 inch (506.0mm)
- 1992 4WD type: RH—20.047 inch (509.2mm)
- 1993—97 Saginaw type: LH—21.268 inch (540.2mm)
- 1993—97 Saginaw type: RH—33.756 inch (857.4mm)
- 1993—95 Toyota type: LH—20.799 inch (528.3mm)
- 1993—95 Toyota type : RH—33.177 inch (842.7mm)
- 1996—97 Toyota type: LH—21.311 inch (541.3mm)
- 1996—97 Toyota type: RH—33.693 inch (855.8mm)

CLUTCH

Understanding the Clutch

❊❊ CAUTION

The clutch driven disc may contain asbestos, which has been determined to be a cancer causing agent. Never clean clutch surfaces with compressed air! Avoid inhaling any dust from any clutch surface! When cleaning clutch surfaces, use a commercially available brake cleaning fluid.

The purpose of the clutch is to disconnect and connect engine power at the transaxle. A vehicle at rest requires a lot of engine torque to get all that weight moving. An internal combustion engine does not develop a high starting torque (unlike steam engines) so it must be allowed to operate without any load until it builds up enough torque to move the vehicle. Torque increases with engine rpm. The clutch allows the engine to build up torque by physically disconnecting the engine from the transaxle, relieving the engine of any load or resistance.

The transfer of engine power to the transaxle (the load) must be smooth and gradual; if it weren't, drive line components would wear out or break quickly. This gradual power transfer is made possible by gradually releasing the clutch pedal. The clutch disc and pressure plate are the connecting link between the engine and transaxle. When the clutch pedal is released, the disc and plate contact each other (the clutch is engaged) physically joining the engine and transaxle. When the pedal is pushed inward, the disc and plate separate (the clutch is disengaged) disconnecting the engine from the transaxle.

Most clutches utilize a single plate, dry friction disc with a diaphragm-style spring pressure plate. The clutch disc has a splined hub which attaches the disc to the input shaft. The disc has friction material where it contacts the flywheel and pressure plate. Torsion springs on the disc help absorb engine torque pulses. The pressure plate applies pressure to the clutch disc, holding it tight against the surface of the flywheel. The clutch operating mechanism consists of a release bearing, fork and cylinder assembly.

The release fork and actuating linkage transfer pedal motion to the release bearing. In the engaged position (pedal released) the diaphragm spring holds the pressure plate against the clutch disc, so engine torque is transmitted to the input shaft. When the clutch pedal is depressed, the release bearing pushes the diaphragm spring center toward the flywheel. The diaphragm spring pivots the fulcrum, relieving the load on the pressure plate. Steel spring straps riveted to the clutch cover lift the pressure plate from the clutch disc, disengaging the engine drive from the transaxle and enabling the gears to be changed.

The clutch is operating properly if:
1. It will stall the engine when released with the vehicle held stationary.
2. The shift lever can be moved freely between 1st and reverse gears when the vehicle is stationary and the clutch disengaged.

Driven Disc and Pressure Plate

REMOVAL & INSTALLATION

◗ **See Figures 28 thru 40**

1. Remove the transaxle from the vehicle.
2. Matchmark the flywheel and the clutch cover with paint or chalk.
3. Loosen each set bolt one at a time until the spring tension is relieve.
4. Remove the set bolts completely and pull off the clutch cover with the clutch disc.

➡**Do not drop the clutch disc. Do not allow grease or oil to get on any of the disc, pressure plate, or flywheel surfaces.**

5. Unfasten the release fork bearing clips. Withdraw the release bearing assembly with the fork and then separate them.
6. Remove the release fork boot.
7. Using calipers, measure the rivet head depth. Minimum depth is 0.012 inch (0.30mm). If not within the limit, replace the clutch disc.
8. Using a dial indicator and V-blocks, measure the clutch disc runout. Maximum allowable runout is 0.031 inch (0.8mm). If the runout is excessive, replace the clutch disc.
9. Using a dial indicator, measure the flywheel runout. Maximum runout is 0.004 inch (0.10mm). If the runout is excessive, machine or replace the flywheel.
10. Using calipers, measure the diaphragm spring for depth and width and wear. Maximum depth is 0.024 inch (0.60mm) and maximum width is 0.020 inch (5mm). Replace the clutch cover as necessary.

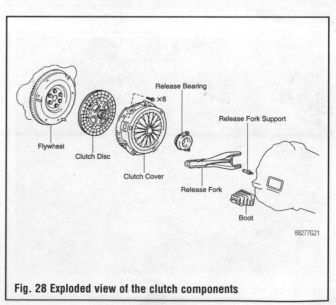

Fig. 28 Exploded view of the clutch components

11. Grasp the release bearing and turn it while applying force in the axial direction. Replace the bearing and hub as required.

To install the clutch:

12. Insert proper alignment tool into the clutch disc and set them and the clutch cover in position.

13. Install the clutch disc bolts and tighten them evenly and gradually in a criss-cross pattern in several passes around the cover until they are snug.

14. Once the bolts are snug, tighten them in sequence to 14 ft. lbs. (19 Nm).

15. Using a dial indicator with a roller attachment, measure the diaphragm spring tip alignment. Maximum non-alignment is 0.020 inch (0.05mm). Adjust the alignment as necessary using SST No. 09333–00013 or equivalent.

16. Apply molybdenum disulphide lithium base grease (NLGI No.2) to the following parts:

    a. Release fork and hub contact point.
    b. Release fork and push rod contact point.
    c. Release fork pivot point.
    d. Clutch disc spline.
    e. Inside groove of the release bearing hub.

17. Install the bearing assembly on the fork and then install them to the transaxle.

18. Install the boot.

19. Install the transaxle to the engine.

Fig. 31 . . . then carefully remove the clutch and pressure plate assembly from the flywheel

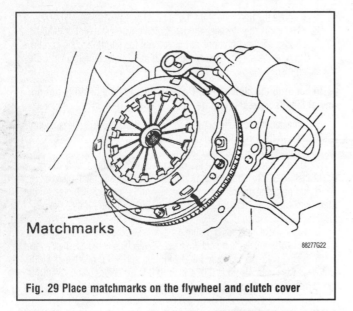

Fig. 29 Place matchmarks on the flywheel and clutch cover

Fig. 32 Check across the flywheel surface, it should be flat

Fig. 30 Loosen and remove the clutch and pressure plate bolts evenly, a little at a time . . .

Fig. 33 If necessary, lock the flywheel in place and remove the retaining bolts . . .

Fig. 34 . . . then remove the flywheel from the crankshaft in order replace it or have it machined

TCCS7122

Fig. 35 Upon installation, it is usually a good idea to apply a thread-locking compound to the flywheel bolts

TCCS7123

Fig. 36 Be sure that the flywheel surface is clean, before installing the clutch

TCCS7124

Fig. 37 Install a clutch alignment arbor, to align the clutch assembly during installation

TCCS7127

Fig. 38 You may want to use a thread locking compound on the clutch assembly bolts

TCCS7131

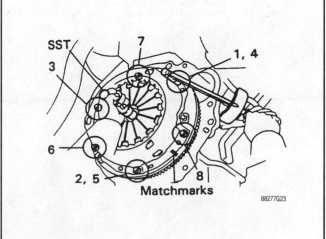

Fig. 39 Tighten the bolts on the clutch cover in this order

88277G23

Fig. 40 Be sure to use a torque wrench to tighten all bolts

TCCS7133

ADJUSTMENTS

Pedal Height

◆ See Figure 41

1. Check that the height of the clutch pedal is correct by measuring from the top of the pedal to the asphalt sheet on the kick panel. The pedal height should be within these specifications:
- 1988–93: 5.71–6.10 inch (145–155mm)
- 1993–94: 5.61–6.00 inch (142.5–152.5mm)
- 1995: 5.65–6.06 inch (138.5–148.5mm)
- 1996–97: 5.449–5.843 inch (138.4–148.4mm)

2. Loosen the lock nut and turn the stopper bolt until the pedal height is correct and tighten the lock nut.

3. After the pedal height is adjusted, check the pedal free play and pushrod play.

Pedal Free-Play

◆ See Figure 42

Measure the clutch pedal free play and pushrod play by pressing on the clutch pedal with your finger and until resistance is felt. The clutch free play

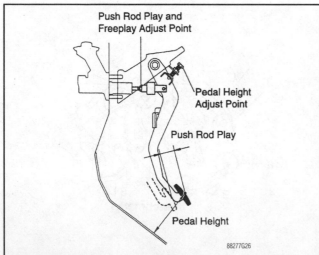

Fig. 41 Pedal height is the distance between the pedal and the floor board

88277G26

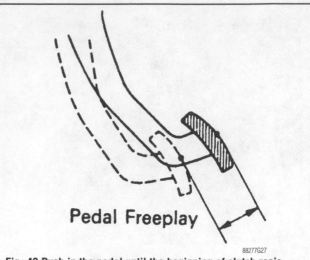

Fig. 42 Push in the pedal until the beginning of clutch resistance is felt

88277G27

should be between 0.197–0.591 inch (5–15mm). Inadequate free play wears all parts of the clutch releasing mechanisms and may cause slippage. Excessive free play may cause inadequate release and hard shifting of gears.

If necessary, adjust the free play and pushrod play as follows:

1. Loosen the lock nut and turn the master cylinder push rod while depressing the clutch pedal lightly with your finger until the free play and pushrod play is correct.
2. Tighten the lock nut.
3. Check the pedal height.

Pushrod Play

Push in on the pedal with a finger softly until the resistance begins to increase somewhat. The push rod play at the pedal top should be: 0.039–0.197 inch (1.0–5.0mm).

Clutch Master Cylinder

➡When inspecting the clutch hydraulic system for leakage or impaired function, check the inside of the firewall (under the carpet) below the clutch master cylinder. A master cylinder leak may not show up under the cylinder on the engine side of the firewall.

REMOVAL & INSTALLATION

◆ See Figure 43

1. Drain or siphon the fluid from the master cylinder. On some models the brake booster will need to be removed.
2. Disconnect the hydraulic line to the clutch from the master cylinder.

➡Do not spill brake fluid on the painted surfaced of the vehicle.

3. Inside the car, remove the underdash panel and the air duct.
4. Remove the pedal return spring.
5. Remove the spring clip and clevis pin.
6. Unfasten the bolts which secure the master cylinder to the firewall. Withdraw the assembly from the firewall side.

To install:

7. Install the master cylinder with its retaining nuts to the firewall, tighten to 9 ft. lbs. (12 Nm).
8. Connect the line from the clutch to the master cylinder and tighten to 11 ft. lbs. (15 Nm).
9. Connect the clevis and install the clevis pin and spring clip.
10. Install the pedal return spring.
11. Fill the reservoir with clean, fresh brake fluid and bleed the system.

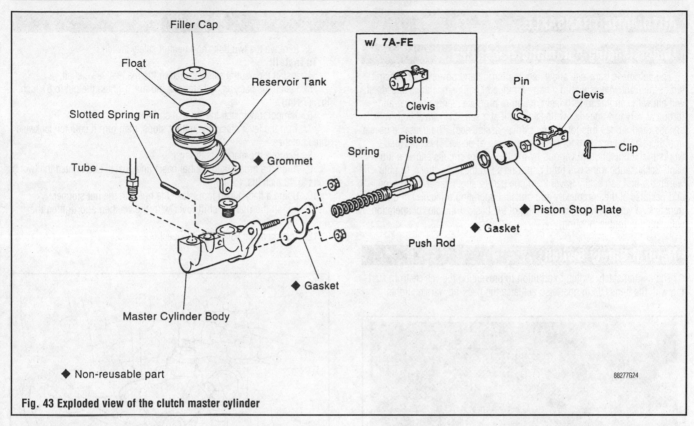

◆ Non-reusable part

88277G24

Fig. 43 Exploded view of the clutch master cylinder

12. Check the cylinder and the hose connection for leaks. Install brake booster if necessary.
13. Bleed and adjust the clutch pedal.
14. Reinstall the air duct and underdash cover panel.

Clutch Release (Slave) Cylinder

REMOVAL & INSTALLATION

▶ **See Figure 44**

➡ **Do not spill brake fluid on the painted surface of the vehicle.**

1. Raise the vehicle and safely support it with jackstands or equivalent.

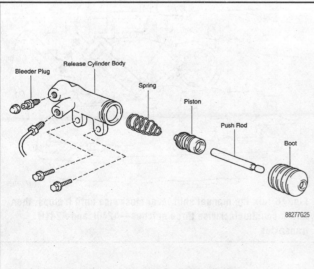

88277G25

Fig. 44 Exploded view of the clutch slave cylinder

2. If necessary, remove the under covers to gain access to the release cylinder.
3. Remove the clutch fork return spring.
4. Unfasten the hydraulic line from the release cylinder by removing its retaining nut.
5. Remove the release cylinder retaining nuts and remove the cylinder.
To install:
6. Reinstall the cylinder to the clutch housing and tighten the bolts to 9 ft. lbs. (12 Nm).
7. Connect the hydraulic line and tighten it to 11 ft. lbs. (15 Nm).
8. Install the clutch release spring.
9. Bleed the system and remember to top up the fluid in the master cylinder when finished.
10. Install the under covers as necessary. Lower the car to the ground.

HYDRAULIC SYSTEM BLEEDING

➡ **If any maintenance on the clutch system was performed or the system is suspected of containing air, bleed the system. Brake fluid will remove the paint from any surface. If the brake fluid spills onto any painted surface, wash it off immediately with soap and water.**

1. Fill the clutch reservoir with brake fluid. Check the reservoir level frequently and add fluid as needed.
2. Connect one end of a vinyl tube to the clutch release cylinder bleeder plug and submerge the other end into a container half-filled with brake fluid.
3. Slowly pump the clutch pedal several times.
4. Have an assistant hold the clutch pedal down and loosen the bleeder plug until fluid starts to run out of the bleeder plug. You will notice air bubbles mixed in with the fluid.
5. Repeat the last two steps until all the air bubbles are removed from the system.
6. Tighten the bleeder plug when all the air is gone.
7. Refill the master cylinder to the proper level as required.
8. Check the system for leaks.

AUTOMATIC TRANSAXLE

Understanding Automatic Transaxles

The automatic transaxle allows engine torque and power to be transmitted to the front wheels within a narrow range of engine operating speeds. It will allow the engine to turn fast enough to produce plenty of power and torque at very low speeds, while keeping it at a sensible rpm at high vehicle speeds (and it does this job without driver assistance). The transaxle uses a light fluid as the medium for the transmission of power. This fluid also works in the operation of various hydraulic control circuits and as a lubricant. Because the transaxle fluid performs all of these functions, trouble within the unit can easily travel from one part to another. For this reason, and because of the complexity and unusual operating principles of the transaxle, a very sound understanding of the basic principles of operation will simplify troubleshooting.

Neutral Safety Switch

The neutral safety switch in addition to preventing the vehicle from starting with the transaxle in gear also actuates the back-up warning lights.

The neutral safety switch is mounted on the transaxle

REMOVAL & INSTALLATION

A131 Transaxle

1. Disconnect the transaxle control cable from the control shaft lever.
2. Remove the transaxle control shift lever.
3. Unbolt and remove the neutral safety switch.
To install:
4. Install the neutral safety switch.
5. Adjust the switch.
6. Install the transaxle control shaft lever.
7. Connect the transaxle control cable.
8. Test drive the vehicle for operation.

A240L and A241H Transaxles

▶ **See Figures 45, 46, 47 and 48**

1. Using a flat bladed tool, unstake the nut stopper.
2. Remove the nut, nut stopper and packing.

3. Remove the two bolts and neutral safety switch.
To install:
4. Install the neutral safety switch to the manual valve shaft.
5. Install the packing, nut stopper and nut. Tighten the nut to 61 inch lbs. (7 Nm).
6. Temporarily install the manual shift lever.
7. Turn the lever clockwise until it stops, then turn it counterclockwise three notches.
8. Remove the manual shift lever.
9. Align the groove and neutral basic line. Install and tighten the two bolts to 48 inch lbs. (5 Nm).
10. Using a flatbladed tool, stake the nut with the nut stopper.
11. Install the manual shift lever with the washer, and tighten the nut.
12. Test drive the vehicle and inspect operation.

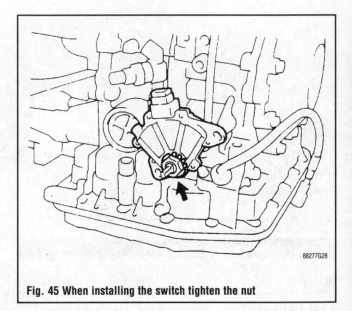

Fig. 45 When installing the switch tighten the nut

Fig. 46 Turn the manual shift lever clockwise until it stops, then turn it counterclockwise three notches—A240L and A241H transaxles

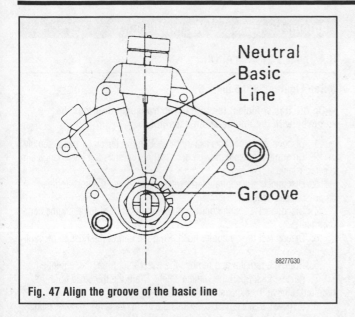

Fig. 47 Align the groove of the basic line

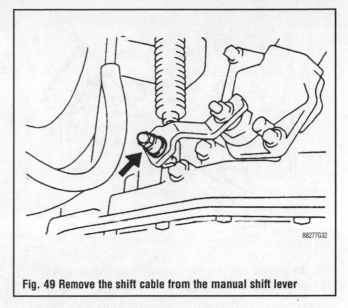

Fig. 49 Remove the shift cable from the manual shift lever

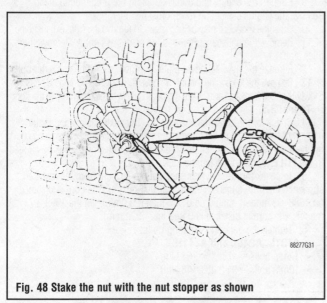

Fig. 48 Stake the nut with the nut stopper as shown

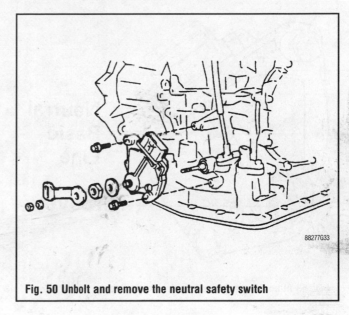

Fig. 50 Unbolt and remove the neutral safety switch

A245E Transaxle

▶ See Figures 49, 50, 51, 52 and 53

1. Raise and safely support the vehicle. If necessary, remove the No. 2 engine under cover.
2. Disconnect the neutral start switch harness.
3. Disconnect the shift cable from the manual shift lever.
4. Unstake the lock nut and remove the manual shift lever.
5. Remove the neutral start switch with the seal gasket.

To install:

6. Install the neutral start switch making sure that the lip of the seal gasket is facing inward.
7. Install the locknut and tighten to 61–108 inch lbs. (7–12 Nm). Stake the nut with the locking plate.
8. Temporarily install the manual shift lever.
9. Turn the lever counterclockwise until it stops, then turn it clockwise 2 notches.
10. Remove the manual shift lever.
11. Adjust the neutral start switch. Align the groove of the neutral basic line. Install and tighten the 2 bolts to 48 inch lbs. (5 Nm).
12. Install the manuals shift lever. Attach the electrical wiring.

Fig. 51 Attach the switch to the manual valve shaft, then install the nut and lockplate

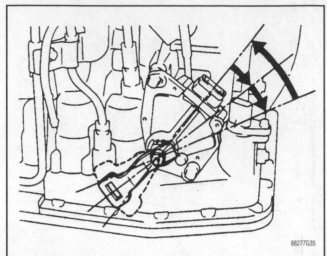

Fig. 52 Turn the lever counterclockwise until it stops, then turn it clockwise 2 notches

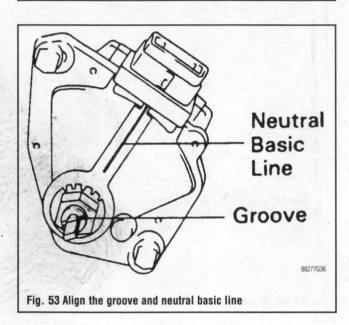

Fig. 53 Align the groove and neutral basic line

13. Connect the transaxle shift cable and install the clip.
14. Adjust the transaxle shift cable.
15. Check the operation of the switch and adjust as necessary.
16. Install the No. 2 engine under cover if removed.

ADJUSTMENT

If the engine starts with the shift selector in any position except Park or Neutral, adjust the switch as follows:
1. Loosen the two neutral start switch retaining bolts and move the shift selector to the Neutral range.
2. Align the groove and the neutral basic line. Maintain the alignment and tighten the bolts to 4–9 ft. lbs. (5–12 Nm).

Back-up Light Switch

The neutral safety switch functions as the back-up light switch. See removal, installation and adjustment procedures for the neutral safety switch as previously detailed in this section.

Automatic Transaxle Assembly

REMOVAL & INSTALLATION

▶ **See Figures 54, 55 and 56**

➡ **On All-Trac vehicles, the automatic transaxle unit must be removed with the engine as an assembly.**

1. Disconnect the negative battery cable. Remove the air cleaner assembly.
2. On some models it may be necessary to remove the level gauge and reservoir tank.
3. Disconnect the neutral start switch. Disconnect the speedometer cable or speed sensor.
4. Disconnect the shift control cable and throttle cable (at engine compartment).
5. Disconnect the oil cooler hose. Plug the end of the hose to prevent leakage.
6. Drain the radiator and remove the water inlet pipe if so equipped.
7. Raise and support the vehicle safely. Drain the transaxle fluid. As required remove the exhaust front pipe.
8. Remove the engine undercover. Remove the front and rear transaxle mounts.
9. Support the engine and transaxle using the proper equipment. Remove the engine center and lower crossmember.
10. On some models it may be necessary to remove the front exhaust pipe.
11. Remove the halfshafts. Remove the starter assembly. Remove the filler pipe.
12. Remove the flywheel cover plate. Remove the torque converter bolts.
13. Remove the left engine mount. Remove the transaxle-to-engine bolts. Slowly back the transaxle away from the engine. Lower the assembly to the floor.
To install:
14. Check torque converter installation. Transaxle installation is the reverse of the removal procedure. When installing the automatic transaxle on the 4WD All-Trac vehicles, be sure the mode selector lever is positioned in the **FREE** mode and attach the lock bolt.
15. To check torque converter installation measure from the installed surface to the front surface of the transaxle housing. The correct distance on 1988–92 models should be 0.906 inch (23.0mm). On the 1993–97 models, the correct distance is 0.898 inch (22.8mm).
16. Tighten the transaxle retaining bolts:
- **A131L, A240L and A241H:**
- 12mm bolts—47 ft. lbs. (64 Nm)
- 10mm bolts—34 ft. lbs. (46 Nm)

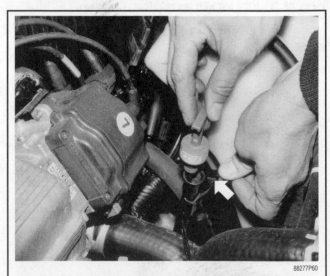

A clamp on the side of the stick retains the unit in the tube

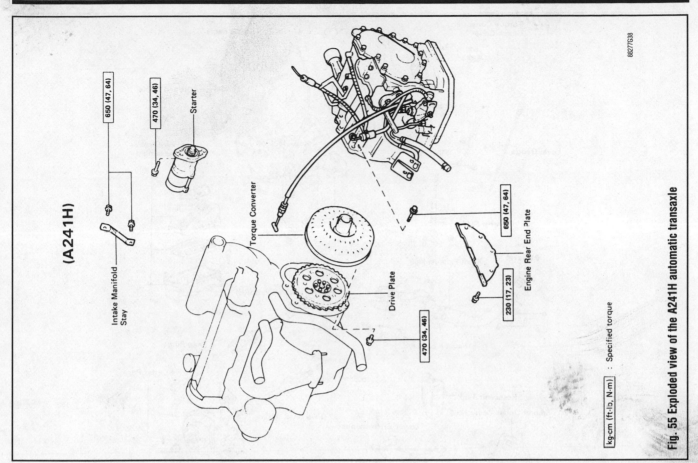

(A241H)

Intake Manifold Stay

Starter

Torque Converter

Drive Plate

Engine Rear End Plate

650 (47, 64)

470 (34, 46)

650 (47, 64)

230 (17, 23)

470 (34, 46)

88277G38

kg-cm (ft-lb, N·m) : Specified torque

Fig. 55 Exploded view of the A241H automatic transaxle

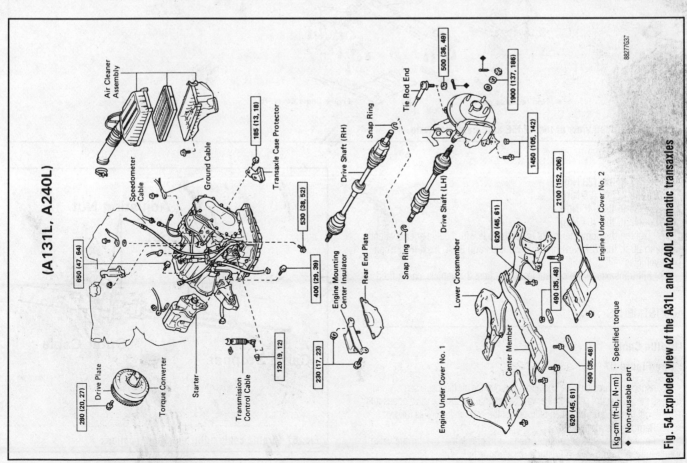

(A131L, A240L)

Air Cleaner Assembly

Speedometer Cable

Ground Cable

Transaxle Case Protector

Drive Shaft (RH)

Snap Ring

Tie Rod End

Drive Shaft (LH)

Snap Ring

Engine Mounting Center Insulator

Rear End Plate

Lower Crossmember

Center Member

Engine Under Cover No. 1

Engine Under Cover No. 2

Drive Plate

Torque Converter

Starter

Transmission Control Cable

650 (47, 64)

185 (13, 18)

530 (38, 52)

400 (29, 39)

230 (17, 23)

120 (9, 12)

280 (20, 27)

500 (36, 49)

1900 (137, 186)

1450 (105, 142)

2100 (152, 206)

620 (45, 61)

490 (35, 48)

490 (35, 48)

620 (45, 61)

88277G37

kg-cm (ft-lb, N·m) : Specified torque

◆ Non-reusable part

Fig. 54 Exploded view of the A31L and A240L automatic transaxles

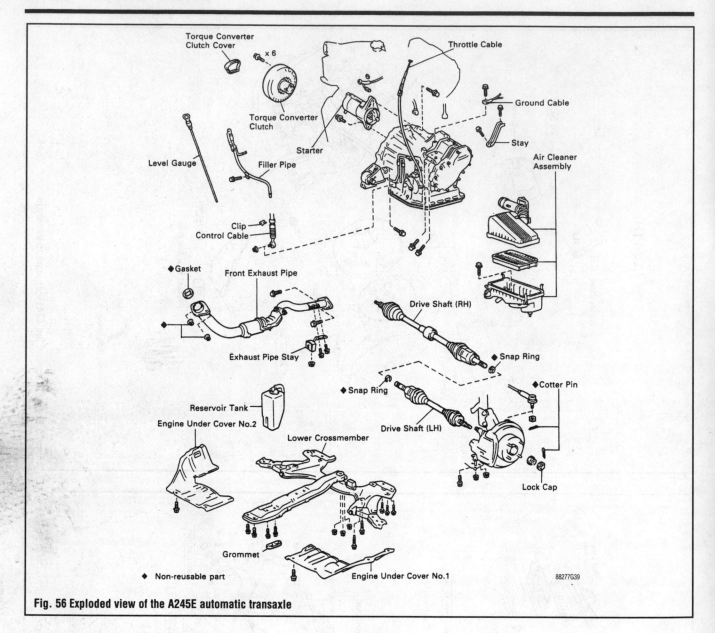

Fig. 56 Exploded view of the A245E automatic transaxle

- **A245E:**
- A—17 ft. lbs. (23 Nm)
- B—18 ft. lbs. (25 Nm)
- C—34 ft. lbs. (46 Nm)
- D—47 ft. lbs. (64 Nm)

17. Tighten the converter bolts (coat threads with Loctite or equivalent) evenly to 20 ft. lbs. (27 Nm) on 2WD vehicles and 34 ft. lbs. (46 Nm) on 4WD vehicles.

18. Fill transaxle to the correct level, roadtest the vehicle, check fluid level.

ADJUSTMENTS

Throttle Cable

▶ See Figure 57

To inspect the throttle cable operation, remove the air cleaner assembly and depress the accelerator cable all the way. Check that the throttle valve opens fully. If the throttle valve does not open fully, adjust the accelerator link as follows:

1. Remove the air cleaner.
2. Fully depress the accelerator pedal and check that the throttle valve opens fully. If it does not, adjust the accelerator link.

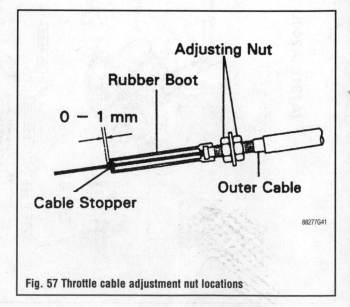

Fig. 57 Throttle cable adjustment nut locations

3. Fully depress the accelerator. Loosen the adjustment nuts.
4. Adjust the cable housing so that the distance between the end of boot and the stopper is 0–0.04 inch (0–1mm).
5. Tighten the adjusting nuts.
6. Recheck the adjustments.

Shift Control Cable

◆ See Figure 58

1. Remove the engine under cover.
2. Loosen the control cable lever swivel nut.
3. Push the control lever to the right as far as it will go.
4. Bring the lever back two notches to the Neutral position.
5. Place the shift lever in Neutral.
6. Hold the lever, lightly, toward the **R** range side and tighten the swivel nut.

Halfshafts

Refer to the Halfshaft procedures for manual transaxles in this section.

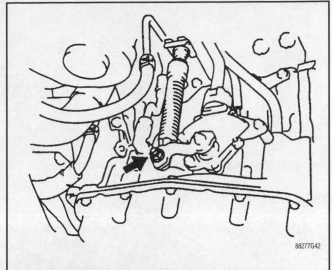

Fig. 58 Tighten the swivel nut on the shift control cable

TRANSFER CASE

Transfer Vacuum Actuator

REMOVAL & INSTALLATION

Only the All-Trac models are equipped with a transfer case.
1. Remove and tag the 4 vacuum hoses from the actuator.
2. Remove the stiffener center plate and the actuator bracket bolts and then remove the actuator.
To install:
3. Install the transfer vacuum actuator, tightening the 3 bolts, then install the stiffener center plate and actuator bracket bolts and tighten to 27 ft. lbs. (37 Nm).
4. Reinstall the vacuum hoses in their proper positions.

Rear Output Shaft Seal

REMOVAL & INSTALLATION

The following procedure can be accomplished while the transfer case is in the vehicle.
1. Drain the transaxle oil.
2. Remove the propeller shaft.
3. Drive out the output shaft oil seal using SST 09308–00010.
To install:
4. Drive in a new seal using SST 09325–20010 to a depth of 0.043–0.075 inch (1–2mm).

5. Install the propeller shaft and fill the transaxle with the proper lubricant.

Transfer Case

REMOVAL & INSTALLATION

Only the All-Trac models are equipped with a transfer case. For ease of removal, the entire transaxle assembly should be removed first.
1. Remove the transaxle assembly with the transfer case attached from the vehicle. Refer to the previous procedures for automatic or manual transaxles.
2. On manual transaxles, remove the 3 bolts and the 5 nuts.
On automatic transaxles, remove the six nuts.
3. Using a plastic hammer, remove the transfer assembly from the transaxle.
To install:
4. Make sure that the contact surfaces are clean and oil-free.
5. Apply seal packing (part No. 08826–00090 or equivalent) to the transfer and install the transfer as soon as the packing is applied.

➡**On manual transaxles, shift into 4th gear, and install the transfer assembly while turning the input shaft of the transaxle.**

6. Apply sealant (part No. 08833–00080) to the bolt threads.
7. Tighten all bolts and nuts to 51 ft. lbs. (69 Nm).

DRIVELINE

Driveshaft

REMOVAL & INSTALLATION

◆ See Figure 59

Only the All-Trac models are equipped with a driveshaft. The U-joints are not replaceable.
1. Matchmark the both front driveshaft flanges.
2. Remove the four bolts, nuts and washers and disconnect the front driveshaft.

3. Withdraw the yoke from the transfer.
4. Insert SST No. 09325–20010 or equivalent into the transfer to prevent oil leaks.
5. Have an assistant depress the brake pedal and hold.
6. Place a piece of cloth into the inside of the universal joint cover.
7. Using SST No. 09325–20010 or equivalent, loosen the cross groove joint set bolts ½ turn.
8. Matchmark the intermediate and rear driveshaft.
9. Remove the four bolts, nuts and washers.
10. Remove the two bolts from the front center support bearing and remove the bearing and the washer.

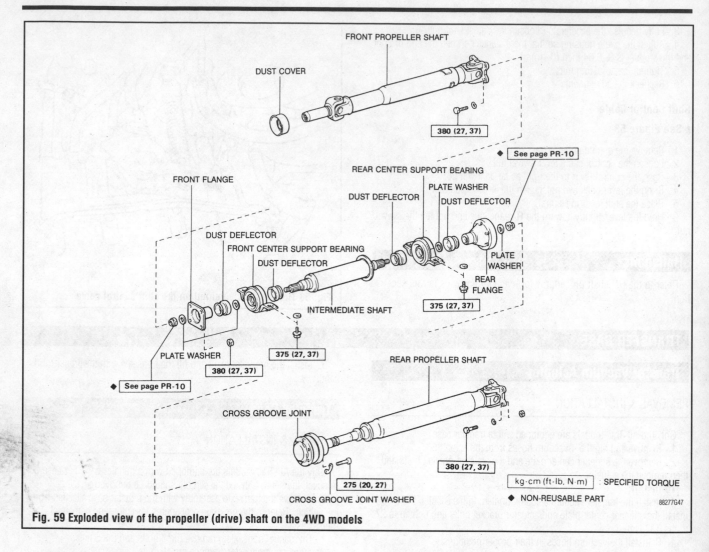

DUST COVER

FRONT PROPELLER SHAFT

380 (27, 37)

◆ See page PR-10

FRONT FLANGE

DUST DEFLECTOR

FRONT CENTER SUPPORT BEARING

DUST DEFLECTOR

INTERMEDIATE SHAFT

REAR CENTER SUPPORT BEARING

DUST DEFLECTOR

PLATE WASHER

DUST DEFLECTOR

PLATE WASHER

REAR FLANGE

375 (27, 37)

375 (27, 37)

PLATE WASHER

380 (27, 37)

◆ See page PR-10

CROSS GROOVE JOINT

REAR PROPELLER SHAFT

380 (27, 37)

275 (20, 27)

CROSS GROOVE JOINT WASHER

kg·cm (ft-lb, N·m) : SPECIFIED TORQUE

◆ NON-REUSABLE PART

88277G47

Fig. 59 Exploded view of the propeller (drive) shaft on the 4WD models

11. Remove the rear front center support bearing and washers.

To install:

12. Install the center support bearing temporarily with the two bolts.

13. Align the matchmarks on the rear and intermediate flanges and connect the shafts with the four nuts, bolts and washers. Tighten the bolts to 27 ft. lbs. (37 Nm).

14. Remove the special tool from the transfer and insert the yoke.

15. Align the matchmarks on both flanges. Install the bolts, nuts and washers and tighten to 27 ft. lbs. (37 Nm).

16. Have an assistant depress the brake pedal and hold it.

17. Using the removal tool, tighten the cross groove joint set bolts to 20 ft. lbs. (27 Nm).

18. Make sure that the vehicle is unloaded, and adjust the distance between the rear side of the boot cover and the shaft.

19. Under the same unloaded conditions, adjust the distance between the rear side of the center bearing housing of the cushion to 0.453–0.531 inch (11.5–13.5mm) and tighten the bolts to 27 ft. lbs. (37 Nm).

20. Ensure that the center line of the bracket is at right angles at the shaft axial direction.

INSPECTION

▶ **See Figure 60**

1. Matchmark the intermediate and rear shaft flanges. Use paint, chalk or a scribe. DO NOT use a punch to matchmark.

2. Using SST No. 09313–30021 or equivalent, remove the intermediate and rear flange bolts and separate the two shafts.

3. Place the propeller and intermediate shafts on V-blocks and check the run out with a dial indicator. If the run out exceeds 0.031 inch (0.08mm) replace the shaft.

4. Measure the run out of the face of the intermediate shaft flange. If the runout exceeds 0.004 inch (0.1mm), replace the shaft.

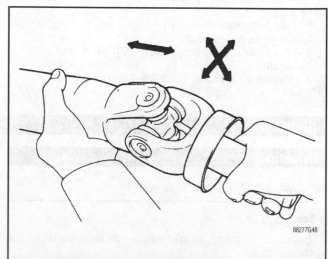

88277G48

Fig. 60 Check the front shaft spider bearings for axial play by turning the flange while holding the shaft tightly

5. Measure the run out of the rear face of the intermediate flange in the vertical direction.

6. Check the front shaft spider bearings for axial play by turning the flange while holding the shaft tightly.

7. Mount the rear propeller shaft in a vise and check the cross groove joint play. Check the joint for damage or signs of grease leakage around the boot. If damaged, replace the joint.

OVERHAUL

1. Using a ball-peen hammer and a small cold chisel, loosen the staked part of the locking nut located on the rear center support bearing front flange.

2. Using SST No. 09330–00021 or equivalent, hold the front flange and remove the nut and plate washer.

3. Match mark the rear flange and the front shaft.

4. Using SST No. 09950–20017 or equivalent, remove the rear flange.

5. Remove the rear center support bearing (note front and back location for correct installation) and plate washer.

6. Repeat the first 5 steps to remove the front center support bearing (note front and back location for correct installation).

7. Turn the center support bearing by hand while applying force in the direction of rotation. Check the bearing smooth play.

8. Inspect both support seals for cracks and damage.

To assemble:

9. Set the front center support bearing onto the intermediate shaft.

10. Install the plate washer.

11. Align the matchmark and install the bearing flange onto the shaft.

12. Using SST No. 09330–00021 or equivalent to hold the flange, press the bearing into place by tightening the new locking nut and washer to 134 ft. lbs. (181 Nm).

13. Loosen the locking nut.

14. Torque the nut again to 51 ft. lbs. (69 Nm) and stake the nut with a ball-peen hammer and small cold chisel.

15. Repeat the first 6 steps to install the rear center support bearing.

16. Mount the rear propeller shaft in a vise and check the cross groove joint play.

17. Using SST No. 09313–30021 or equivalent, temporarily tighten the six bolts and three washers using a piece of cloth on the inside of the joint cover.

Center Support Bearings

REMOVAL & INSTALLATION

Two center support bearings are used on All-Trac 4-Wheel Drive vehicles to control driveshaft noise and vibration and as a means of support for the intermediate driveshaft assembly. Refer to the service procedures under the Driveshaft.

REAR AXLE

Axle Shaft, Bearing and Seal

REMOVAL & INSTALLATION

This procedure applies to the All-Trac models only.

➤This service procedures requires use of special tools-machine shop press and oil bath or equivalent-it is best to remove axle shaft and send it out to a machine shop to replace the axle bearing assembly.

1. Raise and safely support the vehicle.

2. Remove the wheel cover, unfasten the lug nuts, and remove the wheel.

3. Punch matchmarks on the brake drum and the axle shaft to maintain rotational balance.

4. Remove the brake drum or disc brake caliper, disc rotor and related component.

5. Remove the backing plate attachment nuts through the access holes in the rear axle shaft flange.

6. Use a slide hammer with a suitable adapter to withdraw the axle shaft from its housing. Use care not to damage the oil seal when removing the axle shaft.

7. Disconnect the brake line, remove the backing plate and remove the end gasket from the axle housing.

To install:

8. To replace the axle bearing, cut the axle bearing retainer and press the bearing off the axle shaft.

9. Position bearing outer retainer and new bearing on shaft using a press install it to the correct location.

10. Heat the inner bearing retainer to about 302°F (150°C) in an oil bath-press the inner retainer on the axle shaft. Face the non-beveled side of the inner retainer toward the bearing.

11. Remove the oil seal from the axle housing.

➤The oil seal can be removed from the axle housing by using the end of the rear axle shaft for a puller by placing the outmost lip of the axle shaft against the oil seal inner lip and prying it downward.

12. Install the oil seal in the axle housing. Drive the oil seal into the axle housing to a depth of 0.220 inch (5.6mm) using the proper tools.

13. Clean flange of the axle housing and backing plate. Apply sealer to the end gasket and retainer gasket as necessary.

14. Place end gasket onto end of axle housing with the notch of gasket facing downward. Align the notches of the 2 gaskets and bearing outer retainer with the oil hole of the backing plate.

15. Install the backing plate to the axle housing and all necessary components.

16. Install the retainer gasket on the axle shaft. Install the rear axle shaft with 4 NEW SELF-LOCKING NUTS tighten to 48 ft. lbs. (66 Nm).

17. Install all other necessary parts in reverse order of removal.

18. Bleed brake system, install wheel and roadtest for proper operation.

Differential Carrier

REMOVAL & INSTALLATION

This procedure applies to the All-Trac models only.

1. Raise and safely support the vehicle. Remove drain plug and drain differential oil.

2. Remove the rear axle shafts as outlined in this section.

3. Disconnect the propeller shaft or driveshaft (matchmark flange for correct installation) form the differential assembly.

4. Remove the differential carrier assembly retaining bolts. Remove the carrier assembly.

5. Installation is the reverse of the removal procedures. Torque the differential carrier retaining bolts to 23 ft. lbs. (31 Nm) the driveshaft flange bolts 27 ft. lbs. (36 Nm). Refill the unit with 1–1.2 qts. as necessary of API GL-5 gear oil and install drain plug.

Pinion Seal

REMOVAL & INSTALLATION

This procedure applies to the All-Trac models only.

1. Matchmark the differential and driveshaft flanges.

2. Remove the four flange bolts, nuts and washers.

3. Disconnect the driveshaft from the differential.

4. With a hammer and a cold chisel, loosen the staked part of the locking nut.

5. Using SST No. 09330–00021 or equivalent to hold the flange, remove the locking nut.

6. Remove the plate washer.

7. Using SST No. 09557–22022 or equivalent, remove the companion flange.

8. Using SST No. 09308–10010 or equivalent seal puller, remove the front oil seal and then remove the oil slinger.

9. Using SST No. 09556–22010 or equivalent bearing puller, remove the front bearing.

10. Remove the front bearing spacer.

To install the front seal and bearing

11. Install a new bearing spacer and bearing onto the shaft.

12. Install the oil slinger onto the shaft.

13. Using SST No. 09554–22010 or equivalent, drive in the new oil seal to a depth of 0.157 inch (4mm).

14. Coat the lip of the new oil seal with multi-purpose grease.

15. Using the removal tool, install the companion flange.

16. Install the plate washer.

17. Coat the threads of the new nut with gear oil.

18. Using the removal tool to hold the flange, tighten the companion flange to 80 ft. lbs. (108 Nm).

19. Check and adjust the drive pinion preload as follows:

a. Using a inch lb. torque wrench, measure the preload of the backlash between the drive pinion and the ring gear. Preload for a new bearing is 8–14 inch lbs. (0.9–1.5mm) and 4–7 inch lbs. (0.4–0.7mm) for a used bearing.

b. If the preload is greater that the specified limit, replace the bearing spacer.

c. If the preload is less than specification, re-tighten the nut in 9 ft. lbs. (12 Nm) increments until the specified preload is reached. Do not exceed a maximum torque of 174 ft. lbs. (235 Nm).

d. If the maximum torque is exceeded, replace the bearing spacer and repeat the bearing preload procedure. Preload CANNOT be reduced by simply backing off on the pinion nut.

20. Stake the drive pinion nut.

21. Align the driveshaft and differential flange matchmarks.

22. Install the flange bolts and tighten to 27 ft. lbs. (36 Nm).

23. Remove the differential FILL plug and check the oil level. Fill the differential to the proper level (about 1.2 quarts) with new API GL-5 hypoid gear oil.

24. Install and tighten the fill plug with a new gasket if so equipped.

Axle Housing

REMOVAL & INSTALLATION

This procedure applies to the All-Trac models only.

1. Raise and safely support the vehicle. Remove drain plug and drain differential oil.

2. Remove the rear axle shafts as outlined in this section. Disconnect and reposition all lines or vacuum hoses that are necessary to remove the axle housing assembly from the vehicle.

3. Disconnect the propeller shaft or driveshaft (matchmark flange for correct installation) form the differential assembly.

4. Support the rear axle assembly with proper equipment. Disconnect the rear shock absorbers, upper and lower control arms, rear stabilizer bar.

5. Slowly lower the rear axle assembly, remove the rear coil springs. Remove the axle assembly from the vehicle.

6. Installation is the reverse of the removal procedure. Refill the unit (refill to the proper level) with 1–1.2 qts. as necessary of API GL-5 gear oil. Install the drain plug.

TORQUE SPECIFICATIONS

	US	METRIC
C50 and C52 Manual Transaxles:		
Back-up light switch	30 ft. lbs.	40 Nm
Drain plug	29 ft. lbs.	39 Nm
Filler plug	29 ft. lbs.	39 Nm
Transaxle case	22 ft. lbs.	29 Nm
Transaxle case cover	13 ft. lbs.	18 Nm
Transaxle case protector	9 ft. lbs.	13 Nm
Transaxle-to-engine		
12mm	47 ft. lbs.	64 Nm
10mm	34 ft. lbs.	46 Nm
Transaxle-to-rear end plate		
10mm	17 ft. lbs.	24 Nm
8mm	8 ft. lbs.	11 Nm
Transaxle-to-starter	29 ft. lbs.	39 Nm
Release cylinder-to-transaxle	9 ft. lbs.	12 Nm
E57F5 and E57F Manual Transaxles:		
Back-up light switch-to-case	30 ft. lbs.	40 Nm
Bellcrank-to-case	14 ft. lbs.	20 Nm
Drain plug	36 ft. lbs.	49 Nm
Filler plug	36 ft. lbs.	49 Nm
Oil pump-to-cover	8 ft. lbs.	10 Nm
Shift lever shaft-to-case	14 ft. lbs.	20 Nm
Transaxle case-to-case	22 ft. lbs.	29 Nm
Transaxle case-to-cover	22 ft. lbs.	29 Nm
Transaxle-to-transfer	51 ft. lbs.	69 Nm
Transfer case-to-inspection hole cover	12 ft. lbs.	16 Nm
Transaxle case-to-engine		
12mm	47 ft. lbs.	64 Nm
10mm	34 ft. lbs.	46 Nm
Starter-to-transaxle	29 ft. lbs.	39 Nm
Transaxle-to-stiffener plate		
10mm	27 ft. lbs.	37 Nm
8mm	14 ft. lbs.	20 Nm
A131L Automatic Transaxle:		
Transaxle case-to-engine		
12mm	47 ft. lbs.	64 Nm
10mm	34 ft. lbs.	46 Nm
Torque converter-to-drive plate	20 ft. lbs.	27 Nm
Neutral safety switch nut	61 inch lbs.	7 Nm
Neutral safety switch-to-case bolt	48 inch lbs.	5 Nm
Oil pan	43 inch lbs.	5 Nm
Oil pan drain plug	36 ft. lbs.	49 Nm
Oil strainer	7 ft. lbs.	10 Nm
Stiffener plate	17 ft. lbs.	23 Nm
Vehicle speed sensor	12 ft. lbs.	16 Nm

88277C20

TORQUE SPECIFICATIONS

	US	METRIC
A240L Automatic Transaxle:		
Neutral safety switch nut	61 inch lbs.	7 Nm
Neutral safety switch-to-case bolt	48 inch lbs.	5 Nm
Oil pan	43 inch lbs.	5 Nm
Oil pan drain plug	13 ft. lbs.	17 Nm
Oil strainer	7 ft. lbs.	10 Nm
Torque converter-to-drive plate	20 ft. lbs.	37 Nm
Transaxle housing-to-engine		
12mm	47 ft. lbs.	64 Nm
10mm	34 ft. lbs.	46 Nm
A241H Automatic Transaxle:		
Neutral safety switch nut	61 inch lbs.	7 Nm
Neutral safety switch-to-case bolt	48 inch lbs.	5 Nm
Oil pan	43 inch lbs.	5 Nm
Oil pan drain plug	13 ft. lbs.	17 Nm
Torque converter-to-drive plate	20 ft. lbs.	37 Nm
Transaxle housing-to-engine		
12mm	47 ft. lbs.	64 Nm
10mm	34 ft. lbs.	46 Nm
A245E Automatic Transaxle:		
Drain plug	13 ft. lbs.	17 Nm
Neutral safety switch nut	61 inch lbs.	7 Nm
Neutral safety switch-to-case bolt	48 inch lbs.	5 Nm
Oil pan-to-transaxle case	48 inch lbs.	5 Nm
Torque converter-to-drive plate	18 ft. lbs.	25 Nm
Transaxle housing-to-engine	47 ft. lbs.	64 Nm
Valve body-to-transaxle case	7 ft. lbs.	10 Nm
Vehicle speed sensor	12 ft. lbs.	16 Nm
Clutch:		
Clutch line union	11 ft. lbs.	15 Nm
Master cylinder installation nut	9 ft. lbs.	12 Nm
Bleeder plug	74 inch lbs.	8 Nm
Slave cylinder bolt	9 ft. lbs.	12 Nm
Clutch cover-to-flywheel	14 ft. lbs.	19 Nm
Flywheel set bolt	58 ft. lbs.	78 Nm
Clutch pedal setting nut	18 ft. lbs.	25 Nm
Release fork support		
2WD	27 ft. lbs.	37 Nm
4WD	35 ft. lbs.	47 Nm
Driveshaft:		
Driveshaft-to-differential	27 ft. lbs.	37 Nm
Intermediate shaft-to-driveshaft	27 ft. lbs.	37 Nm
Center support bearing-to-body	27 ft. lbs.	37 Nm
Cross groove joint set bolt	20 ft. lbs.	27 Nm

88277C21

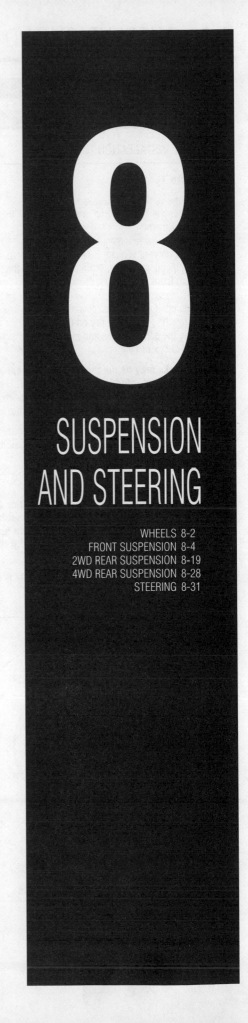

8

SUSPENSION AND STEERING

WHEELS

Wheel Assembly

REMOVAL & INSTALLATION

▶ **See Figure 1**

1. Park the vehicle on a level surface.
2. Remove the jack, tire iron and, if necessary, the spare tire from their storage compartments.
3. Check the owner's manual or refer to Section 1 of this manual for the jacking points on your vehicle. Then, place the jack in the proper position.
4. If equipped with lug nut trim caps, remove them by either unscrewing or pulling them off the lug nuts, as appropriate. Consult the owner's manual, if necessary.
5. If equipped with a wheel cover or hub cap, insert the tapered end of the tire iron in the groove and pry off the cover.
6. Apply the parking brake and block the diagonally opposite wheel with a wheel chock or two.

➡**Wheel chocks may be purchased at your local auto parts store, or a block of wood cut into wedges may be used. If possible, keep one or two of the chocks in your tire storage compartment, in case any of the tires has to be removed on the side of the road.**

7. If equipped with an automatic transmission/transaxle, place the selector lever in **P** or Park; with a manual transmission/transaxle, place the shifter in Reverse.
8. With the tires still on the ground, use the tire iron/wrench to break the lug nuts loose.

➡**If a nut is stuck, never use heat to loosen it or damage to the wheel and bearings may occur. If the nuts are seized, one or two heavy hammer blows directly on the end of the bolt usually loosens the rust. Be careful, as continued pounding will likely damage the brake drum or rotor.**

9. Using the jack, raise the vehicle until the tire is clear of the ground. Support the vehicle safely using jackstands.

10. Remove the lug nuts, then remove the tire and wheel assembly.
To install:
11. Make sure the wheel and hub mating surfaces, as well as the wheel lug studs, are clean and free of all foreign material. Always remove rust from the wheel mounting surface and the brake rotor or drum. Failure to do so may cause the lug nuts to loosen in service.
12. Install the tire and wheel assembly and hand-tighten the lug nuts.
13. Using the tire wrench, tighten all the lug nuts, in a criss-cross pattern, until they are snug.
14. Raise the vehicle and withdraw the jackstand, then lower the vehicle.
15. Using a torque wrench, tighten the lug nuts in a criss-cross pattern to 76 ft. lbs. (103 Nm). Check your owner's manual or refer to Section 1 of this manual for the proper tightening sequence.

✳✳ WARNING

Do not overtighten the lug nuts, as this may cause the wheel studs to stretch or the brake disc (rotor) to warp.

16. If so equipped, install the wheel cover or hub cap. Make sure the valve stem protrudes through the proper opening before tapping the wheel cover into position.
17. If equipped, install the lug nut trim caps by pushing them or screwing them on, as applicable.
18. Remove the jack from under the vehicle, and place the jack and tire iron/wrench in their storage compartments. Remove the wheel chock(s).
19. If you have removed a flat or damaged tire, place it in the storage compartment of the vehicle and take it to your local repair station to have it fixed or replaced as soon as possible.

INSPECTION

Inspect the tires for lacerations, puncture marks, nails and other sharp objects. Repair or replace as necessary. Also check the tires for treadwear and air pressure as outlined in Section 1 of this manual.

Check the wheel assemblies for dents, cracks, rust and metal fatigue. Repair or replace as necessary.

Wheel Lug Studs

REMOVAL & INSTALLATION

With Disc Brakes

▶ **See Figures 2, 3 and 4**

1. Raise and support the appropriate end of the vehicle safely using jackstands, then remove the wheel.
2. Remove the brake pads and caliper. Support the caliper aside using wire or a coat hanger. For details, please refer to Section 9 of this manual.
3. Remove the outer wheel bearing and lift off the rotor. For details on wheel bearing removal, installation and adjustment, please refer to Section 1 of this manual.
4. Properly support the rotor using press bars, then drive the stud out using an arbor press.

➡**If a press is not available, CAREFULLY drive the old stud out using a blunt drift. MAKE SURE the rotor is properly and evenly supported or it may be damaged.**

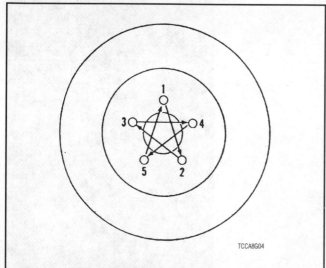

TCCA8G04

Fig. 1 Typical wheel lug tightening sequence

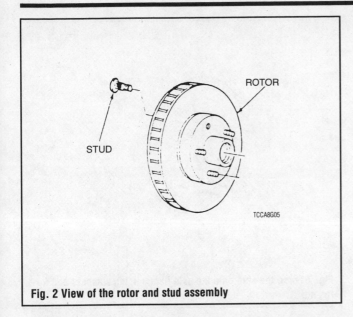

Fig. 2 View of the rotor and stud assembly

To install:

5. Clean the stud hole with a wire brush and start the new stud with a hammer and drift pin. Do not use any lubricant or thread sealer.

6. Finish installing the stud with the press.

➡ If a press is not available, start the lug stud through the bore in the hub, then position about 4 flat washers over the stud and thread the lug nut. Hold the hub/rotor while tightening the lug nut, and the stud should be drawn into position. **MAKE SURE THE STUD IS FULLY SEATED,** then remove the lug nut and washers.

7. Install the rotor and adjust the wheel bearings.
8. Install the brake caliper and pads.
9. Install the wheel, then remove the jackstands and carefully lower the vehicle.
10. Tighten the lug nuts to the proper torque.

With Drum Brakes

▶ **See Figures 5, 6 and 7**

1. Raise the vehicle and safely support it with jackstands, then remove the wheel.
2. Remove the brake drum.

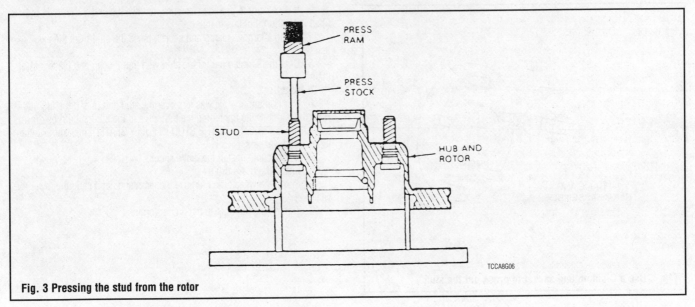

Fig. 3 Pressing the stud from the rotor

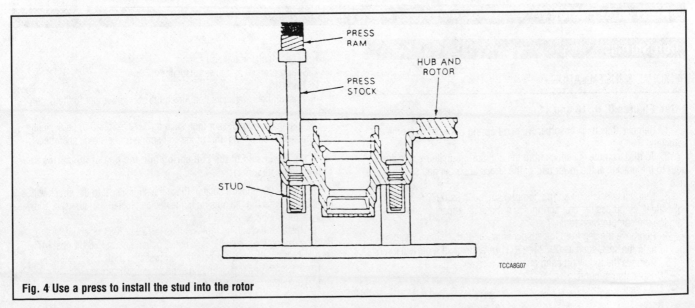

Fig. 4 Use a press to install the stud into the rotor

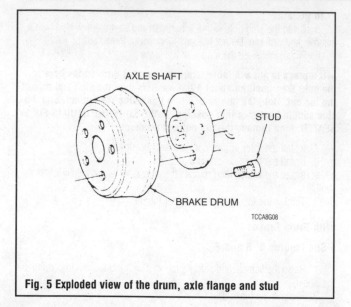

Fig. 5 Exploded view of the drum, axle flange and stud

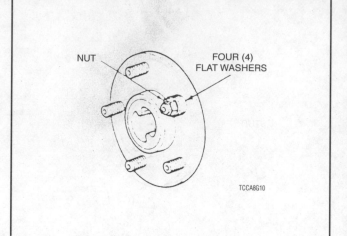

Fig. 7 Force the stud onto the axle flange using washers and a lug nut

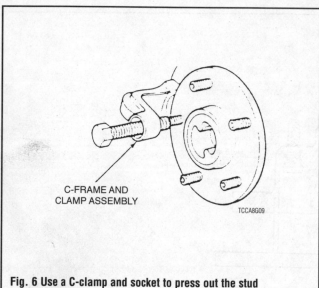

Fig. 6 Use a C-clamp and socket to press out the stud

3. If necessary to provide clearance, remove the brake shoes, as outlined in Section 9 of this manual.

4. Using a large C-clamp and socket, press the stud from the axle flange.

5. Coat the serrated part of the stud with liquid soap and place it into the hole.

To install:

6. Position about 4 flat washers over the stud and thread the lug nut. Hold the flange while tightening the lug nut, and the stud should be drawn into position. MAKE SURE THE STUD IS FULLY SEATED, then remove the lug nut and washers.

7. If applicable, install the brake shoes.

8. Install the brake drum.

9. Install the wheel, then remove the jackstands and carefully lower the vehicle.

10. Tighten the lug nuts to the proper torque.

FRONT SUSPENSION

Coil Springs

REMOVAL & INSTALLATION

♦ See Figures 8, 9, 10 and 11

1. Remove the shock absorber with coil spring out from under the vehicle.

2. To disassemble the shock from the coil spring, install 2 nuts and a both to the bracket at the lower part of the shock absorber and secure it in a vice.

3. Using a special coil spring compressor, such as 09727–30020 or equivalent, compress the coil spring. Do not use an impact wrench, it will damage the compression tool.

4. Renmove the cap from the suspension support. Using a retaining tool to hold the seat, such as 09729–22031 or equivalent remove the nut.

5. Remove the following components:
• Suspension support
• Dust seal
• Spring seat
• Upper insulator and coil spring
• Spring bumper and lower insulator

To install:

6. Install the lower insulator. Attach the spring bumper to the piston rod.

7. Using the compressor tool, such as 09727–30020 or equivalent, compress the coil spring. Install the coil spring to the shock absorber.

➡️**Fit the lower end of the coil spring into the gap of the spring seat of the shock absorber.**

8. Install the upper insulator. Place the spring seat to the shock with the OUT mark facing the outside of the vehicle. Install the dust seal and suspension support.

9. Install the retaining tool, such as 09729–22031 or equivalent to hold the spring seat, install a new nut. Tighten the nut to 34 ft. lbs. (47 Nm). Install the cap and remove the compression tool.

10. Pack the upper suspension support with MP grease.

11. Install the coil and strut assembly into the vehicle.

FRONT SUSPENSION COMPONENT LOCATIONS

1. Lower control arm
2. Ball joint
3. Wheel
4. Strut
5. Coil spring
6. Suspension crossmember
7. Halfshaft

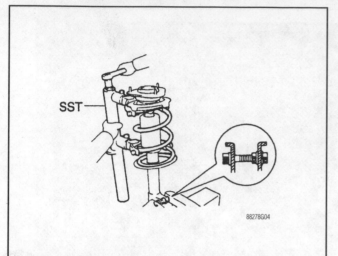

Fig. 8 Place a bolt and 2 nuts on the bracket at the lower portion of the shock and secure in a vise

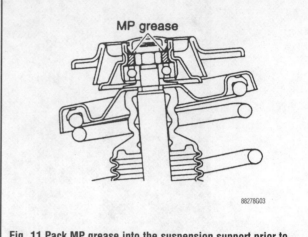

Fig. 11 Pack MP grease into the suspension support prior to installation

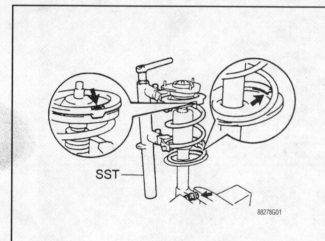

Fig. 9 A spring compressor must be used to remove and install the spring

MacPherson Struts

REMOVAL & INSTALLATION

▶ **See Figure 12**

1. Raise and support the vehicle safely. Remove the front wheel.
2. Matchmark the strut and knuckle mounting.
3. Disconnect brake hose from the shock absorber.
4. Disconnect the ABS sensor wire from the shock absorber if so equipped.
5. Loosen the two nuts on the lower side of the shock absorber.

➡ **Do not remove the 2 nuts and bolts.**

6. Remove the three nuts on the upper side of the shock absorber. Next remove the 2 nuts and bolts from the lower side of the shock absorber.
7. Remove the strut and coil spring assembly out through the wheel well.

To install:

8. Install the shock absorber with coil spring to the vehicle. Install the three nuts and tighten to 29 ft. lbs. (39 Nm).

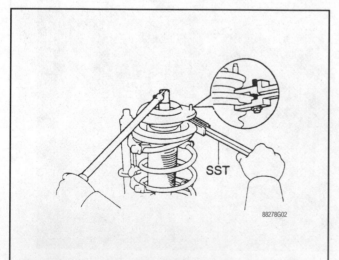

Fig. 10 Using a retaining tool, hold the spring seat and install a new nut

Mark the mating area of the strut and knuckle

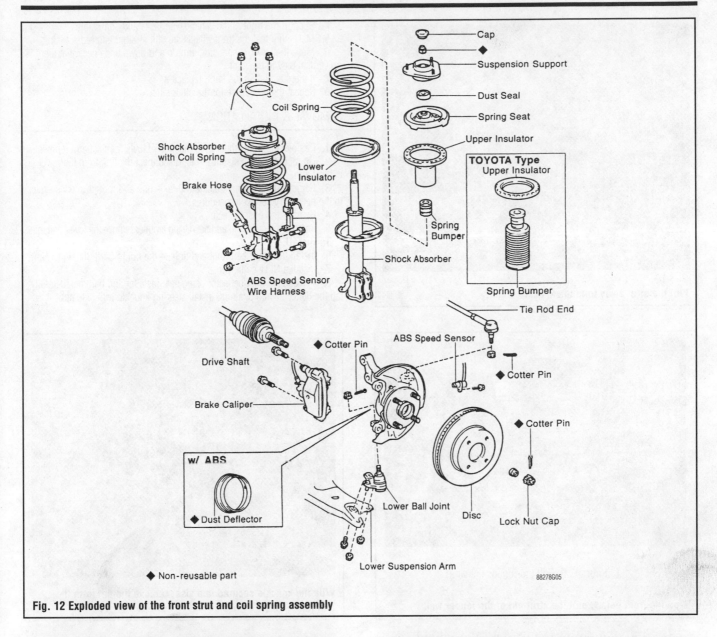

Fig. 12 Exploded view of the front strut and coil spring assembly

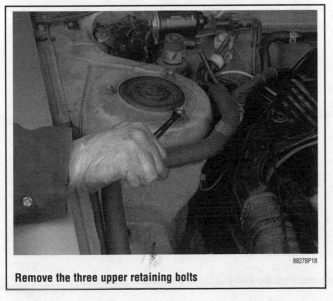

Remove the three upper retaining bolts

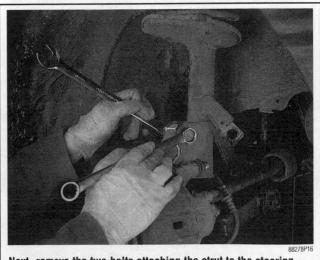

Next, remove the two bolts attaching the strut to the steering knuckle. Be sure to matchmark it first

Pull the strut away from the knuckle slightly

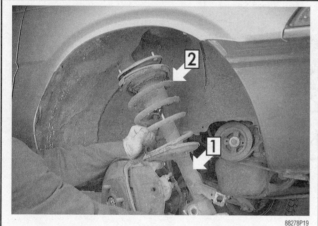

1. Strut 2. Coil (surrounds the strut)

Working from below, pull the strut out of the fender well

9. Attach the shock absorber assembly to the steering knuckle. Install the two bolts with the bolt heads to the rear of the vehicle, then tighten to 203 ft. lbs. (275 Nm).

10. Connect the ABS sensor wire to the shock absorber if so equipped.

11. Reconnect the brake hose to the shock absorber, tighten the retaining bolt to 22 ft. lbs. (29 Nm).

12. Install front wheel and lower the vehicle. Check the front wheel alignment.

OVERHAUL

The strut assembly cannot be overhauled. In order to remove the coil spring, refer to Coil Spring Removal and Installation in this section.

Lower Ball Joint

INSPECTION

1. Make the front wheels straight and jack up the front of the vehicle.

2. Place an 7.09–7.87 in. (180–200mm) wooden block under one front tire.

3. Slowly lower the jack until there is about half a load on the front coil spring.

4. Support the front of the vehicle with jackstands for safety.

5. Make sure that the front wheels are still straight and block them.

6. Move the lower suspension arm up and down and check that there is no vertical play in the joint.

7. If there is play in the joint, replace it.

8. Repeat the procedure for the other side.

REMOVAL & INSTALLATION

1. Remove the front wheel from the side of lower control arm removal.

2. On models with a stabilizer bar, disconnect the link from the lower control arm.

3. Remove the steering knuckle with axle hub and mount in a vise-refer to the necessary service procedures.

4. Remove the dust deflector.

5. Remove the cotter pin and nut. Using a puller remove the lower ball joint.

To install:

6. Install the lower ball joint and tighten the nut to 87 ft. lbs. (118 Nm).

7. Install a NEW cotter pin.

8. Replace the dust deflector using seal installer and hammer. carefully tap the deflector into position. Install steering knuckle with axle hub.

With the knuckle secured in a vise, remove the nut from the ball joint

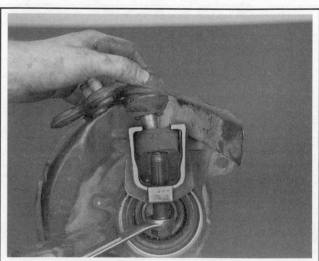

Separate the ball joint from the knuckle using a puller

Stabilizer Bar

REMOVAL & INSTALLATION

▶ **See Figures 13, 14 and 15**

Some models are not equipped with a front stabilizer bar.
1. Raise and support the vehicle safely. Remove the front wheels.
2. Disconnect the exhaust system or center pipe (2WD vehicles) or driveshaft assembly (4WD vehicles) as necessary.

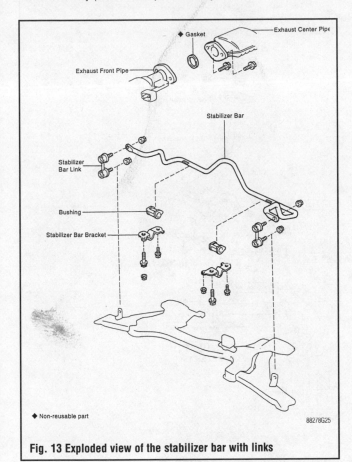

◆ Non-reusable part

Fig. 13 Exploded view of the stabilizer bar with links

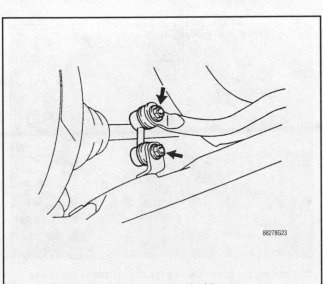

Fig. 14 Stabilizer bar links are secured with nuts

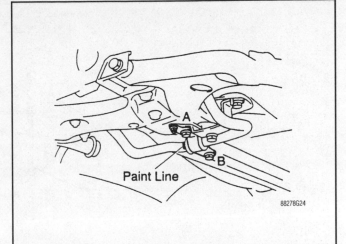

Fig. 15 Mark the positions of the brackets and bushings on the stabilizer bar

3. Disconnect stabilizer links from stabilizer bar by removing the 2 nuts and links.

➡**If the ball joint turns together with the nut, use a hexagon wrench to hold the stud.**

4. Mark the positions of the bushing before removal. Disconnect the stabilizer bar brackets from the bolt.
5. On some models it will be necessary to disconnect the center exhaust pipe. Discard the old gaskets.
6. Remove the stabilizer bar from the vehicle. Examine the insulators (bushings) carefully for any sign of wear and replace them if necessary.

➡**Check the bushings inside the brackets for wear or deformation. A worn bushing can cause a distinct noise as the bar twists during cornering operation.**

To install:
7. Place the bar in position. Place the stabilizer bar bushings in the correct position.
8. Temporarily install stabilizer bar brackets. Install both stabilizer bar links tighten link nuts to 33 ft. lbs. (44 Nm).
9. Stabilize the suspension. Bounce the vehicle up and down several times to stabilize.
10. Tighten the stabilizer bar bracket bolts and nuts; bolt (A) to 108 ft. lbs. (147 Nm), bolt (B) to 37 ft. lbs. (50 (Nm) and tighten nut (C) to 14 ft. lbs. (19 Nm).
11. If removed, install the center exhaust pipe, front pipe and driveshaft. Make sure on the exhaust pipes new gaskets are installed.
12. Install front wheels and lower the vehicle.
13. Check front wheel alignment.

Lower Control Arm

REMOVAL & INSTALLATION

1988–92 Models

EXCEPT AUTOMATIC LEFT SIDE

▶ **See Figure 16**

1. Remove the front wheel. Place a floor jack under the suspension crossmember. Use a broad piece of wood between the jack and crossmember to evenly distribute the loading.
2. On 4A-GE engines, remove the stabilizer link.

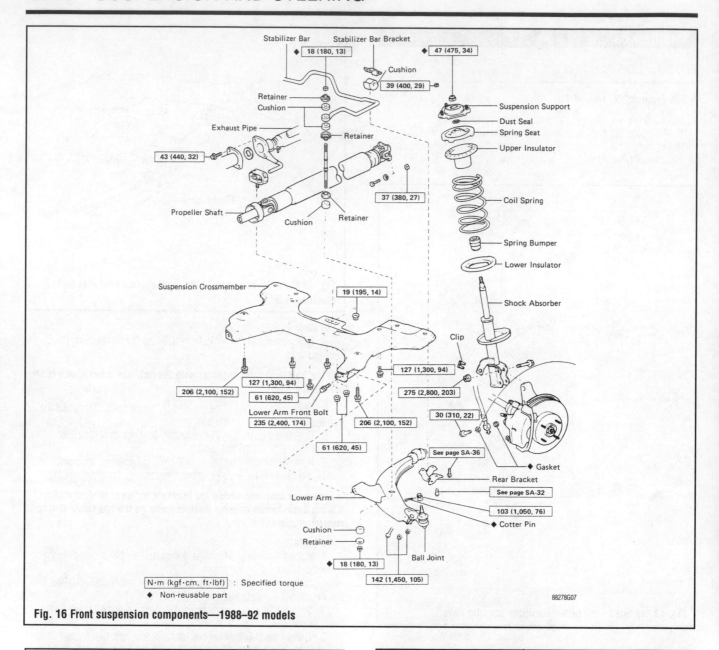

Fig. 16 Front suspension components—1988–92 models

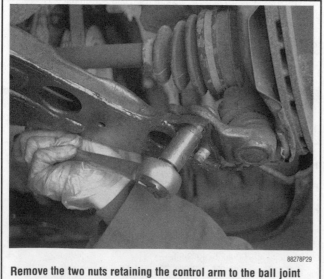

Remove the two nuts retaining the control arm to the ball joint

Now remove the bolts retaining the control arm to the engine crossmember

3. On all other models, remove the stabilizer bar nut holding the bar to the lower control arm and separate the unit form the vehicle.

4. Loosen the lower control arm front bolt.

5. Remove the rear bracket bolts and nuts. Remove the rear bracket and stabilizer bar bracket. Remove the lower arm front bolt and lower the control arm from the vehicle.

To install:

6. Install the lower control arm to the body.

7. Move the stabilizer bar into position.

8. Temporarily install and tighten the lower control arm front bolt.

9. Install the stabilizer bar bracket and rear bracket, then temporarily tighten the bolts and nut.

10. Install and tighten the bolt and two nuts to 105 ft. lbs. (142 Nm).

11. Connect the stabilizer bar to the lower control arm with the bolt and nut. If needed, connect the other side also. Tighten to 13 ft. lbs. (18 Nm).

12. Remove the stands and bounce the vehicle up and down to stabilize the suspension. Tighten the lower arm bolt, rear bracket bolts and nut.

- Lower arm front bolt—174 ft. lbs. (235 Nm)
- Rear bracket lower arm side—94 ft. lbs. (127 Nm)
- Rear bracket stabilizer bar side—37 ft. lbs. (50 Nm)
- Rear bracket bolt and nut—14 ft. lbs. (19 Nm)

13. Check the front end wheel alignment.

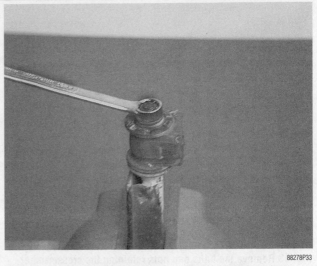

When replacing the bushing, remove the nut first

AUTOMATIC LEFT SIDE

▶ See Figures 17, 18 and 19

1. Remove the front wheel. Place a floor jack under the suspension crossmember. Use a broad piece of wood between the jack and crossmember to evenly distribute the loading.

2. Disconnect the left and right lower control arms from the steering knuckles.

3. Remove the left and right stabilizer bar nuts holding the bar to the lower control arms and disconnect the stabilizer bar.

4. Remove the left and right lower arm rear brackets.

5. Move the stabilizer bar toward the rear side, then remove the stabilizer bar bracket.

6. Remove the six bolts and two nuts, then remove the suspension crossmemeber with lower control arms.

7. Remove the lower control arm from the crossmember. Inspect and replace any bushing necessary.

To install:

8. Temporarily install the lower control arm to the crossmemeber with a bolt.

9. Install the suspension crossmember with the lower control arm to the body.

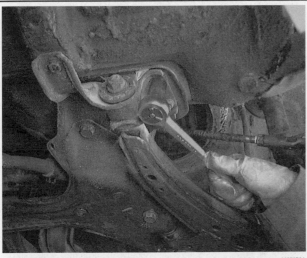

Remove the bolts and nut holding the bracket to the frame

Pull the arm out from under the vehicle

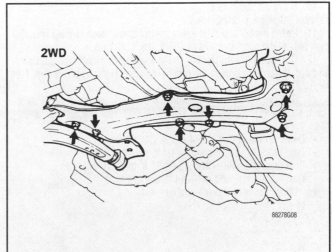

Fig. 17 Remove the bolts and nuts retaining the crossmember and lower control arms—2WD models

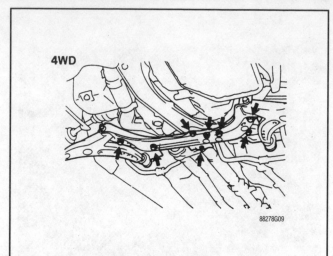

Fig. 18 Remove the bolts and nuts retaining the crossmember and lower control arms—4WD models

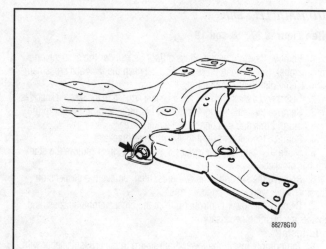

Fig. 19 Remove the remaining bolt retaining the lower control arm to the crossmember

10. Move the stabilizer bar in position and temporarily install the stabilizer bar bracket and rear bracket.

11. Install the left and right lower control arm to each steering knuckle, then tighten the bolts and nuts to 105 ft. lbs. (142 Nm).

12. Connect the stabilizer bar to the lower control arm with the bolt and nut. If needed, connect the other side also. Tighten to 13 ft. lbs. (18 Nm).

13. Remove the stands and bounce the vehicle up and down to stabilize the suspension. Tighten the lower arm bolt, rear bracket bolts and nut.

- Lower arm front bolt—174 ft. lbs. (235 Nm)
- Rear bracket lower arm side—94 ft. lbs. (127 Nm)
- Rear bracket stabilizer bar side—37 ft. lbs. (50 Nm)
- Rear bracket bolt and nut—14 ft. lbs. (19 Nm)

14. Check the front end wheel alignment.

1993–95 Models

EXCEPT AUTOMATIC LEFT SIDE

♦ See Figures 20, 21 and 22

1. Remove the front wheel. Place a floor jack under the suspension crossmember. Use a broad piece of wood between the jack and crossmember to evenly distribute the loading.

2. On models with a stabilizer bar, disconnect the bar link from the lower control arm.

3. Remove the ball joint form the lower control arm.

4. Remove the nut, 3 bolts and stabilizer bar bracket with bar.

5. Remove the bolt and lower control arm.

To install:

6. Install the lower control arm to the body.

7. Move the stabilizer bar into position.

8. Temporarily install and tighten the lower control arm front bolt.

9. Install the stabilizer bar bracket and rear bracket, then temporarily tighten the bolts and nut.

10. Connect the stabilizer bar to the lower control arm with the bolt and nut. If needed, connect the other side also.

11. Install the wheel.

12. Remove the stands and bounce the vehicle up and down to stabilize the suspension. Tighten the lower arm bolt, rear bracket bolts and nut.

- Bolt A—108 ft. lbs. (147 Nm)
- Bolt B—37 ft. lbs. (50 Nm)
- Nut C—14 ft. lbs. (19 Nm)

13. Check the front end wheel alignment.

AUTOMATIC LEFT SIDE

♦ See Figures 23 thru 28

1. Remove the front wheel. Place a floor jack under the suspension crossmember. Use a broad piece of wood between the jack and crossmember to evenly distribute the loading.

2. On models with a stabilizer bar, disconnect the bar link from the lower control arm.

3. Remove the ball joint form the lower control arm.

4. Remove the nut, 3 bolts and stabilizer bar bracket with bar.

5. Disconnect the front pipe from the center pipe and discard the gasket.

6. On the stabilizer bar, remove the nut obtained through a hole in the crossmember. Lower the stabilizer bar. Remove the grommet, 4 nuts and bolt.

7. Support the suspension crossmember with a jack.

8. Remove the 6 bolts and suspension crossmemeber with the control arms attached. Remove the bolt retaining the control arm to the crossmember.

9. Remove the nut, control arm bracket and cushion retainer.

To install:

10. Attach the lower control arm retainer and tighten the nut hand tight for now.

11. Attach the lower control arm to the crossmember.

12. Place the crossmember with control arms into the vehicle, tighten the retaining bolts to 152 ft. lbs. (206 Nm).

13. Install the 4 nuts and bolt, tighten to the following:

- Nut A—35 ft. lbs. (48 Nm)
- Bolt B—45 ft. lbs. (61 Nm)
- Nut C—45 ft. lbs. (61 Nm)
- Control arm bracket retainer nut—101 ft. lbs. (137 Nm)

14. Attach the stabilizer bar, install the nut and tighten to 14 ft. lbs. (19 Nm).

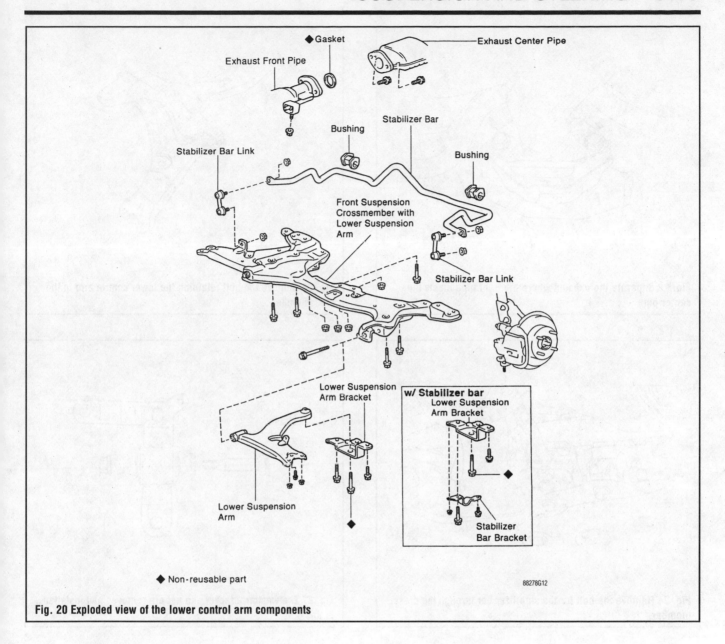

Fig. 20 Exploded view of the lower control arm components

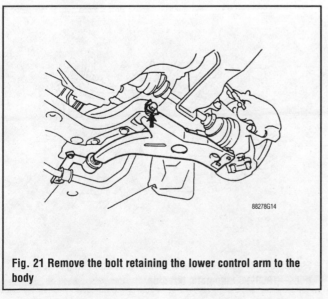

Fig. 21 Remove the bolt retaining the lower control arm to the body

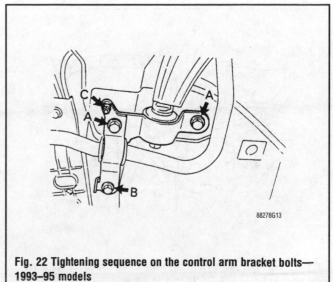

Fig. 22 Tightening sequence on the control arm bracket bolts—1993–95 models

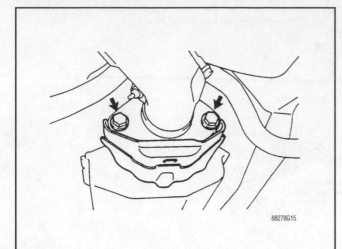

Fig. 23 Separate the exhaust where the front pipe meets the center pipe

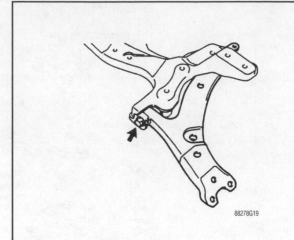

Fig. 26 Remove the bolt retaining the lower control arm to the crossmember

Fig. 24 Remove the bolt for the stabilizer bar through the cross-member

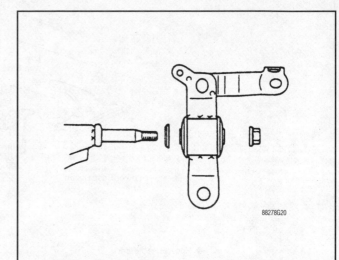

Fig. 27 The washer, bracket and nut are removed and installed in this order

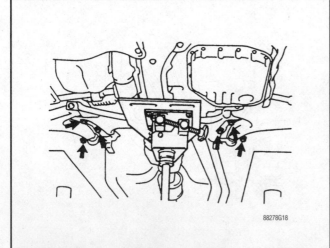

Fig. 25 With the suspension supported, remove these six cross-member bolts—1993–95 automatic left side

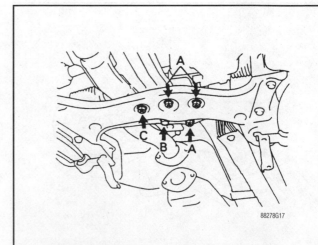

Fig. 28 Center bolt and nuts crossmember tightening locations—1993–95 automatic left side

15. Place a new gasket into position and attach the front pipe to the center pipe. Tighten the retaining nuts to 32 ft. lbs. (43 Nm).

16. Install the remaining components in the reverse order.

17. Remove the stands and bounce the vehicle up and down to stabilize the suspension. Tighten the lower arm bolt, rear bracket bolts and nut.
- Bolt A—108 ft. lbs. (147 Nm)
- Bolt B—37 ft. lbs. (50 Nm)
- Nut C—14 ft. lbs. (19 Nm)

18. Check the front end wheel alignment.

1996–97 Models

◆ See Figures 29 and 30

1. Remove the front wheel. Place a floor jack under the suspension crossmember. Use a broad piece of wood between the jack and crossmember to evenly distribute the loading.

2. Remove the stabilizer bar on vehicles equipped.

3. Remove the bolt and 2 nuts retaining the ball joint to the lower control arm.

4. When working on manual transaxles and right side automatics, remove the 4 bolts and lower control arm.

5. If working on the left side on automatics, remove the 10 bolts, 4 nuts

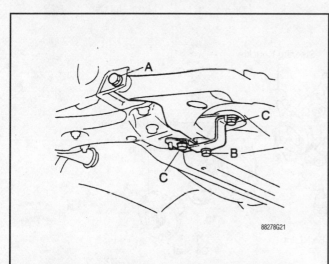

88278G21

Fig. 29 Tightening identification for the control arm bracket bolts—1996–97 models

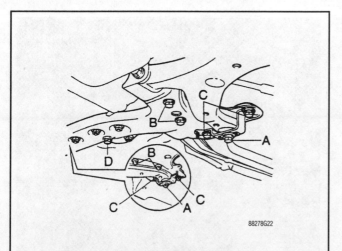

88278G22

Fig. 30 Tightening bolt identification for the crossmember bolts—1996–97 models

and crossmember with the lower control arms attached. Remove the lower control arm from the crossmember once removed from the vehicle.

To install:

6. To install the left side automatics, attach the lower control arm to the crossmember and place the assembly into the vehicle. Support the crossmember securely.

  a. Install all of the crossmember retaining bolts. Do not tighten them at this tome. Lower the vehicle and stabilize the suspension by bouncing it up and down a few times. Raise and support the vehicle.

  b. Once the suspension is stabilized, tighten the lower control arm bolt to 161 ft. lbs. (218 Nm) and tighten the crossmember bolts A, B and C.
- Bolt A—129 ft. lbs. (175 Nm)
- Bolt B—167 ft. lbs. (225 Nm)
- Bolt C—109 ft. lbs. (147 Nm)
- Bolt D—45 ft. lbs. (60 Nm)
- Nut—45 ft. lbs. (60 Nm)

  c. Tighten the remaining bolts and nuts.

7. Install the ball joint and tighten to 105 ft. lbs. (142 Nm).

8. Install the stabilizer bar and front wheel.

9. Check the front end wheel alignment.

CONTROL ARM BUSHING REPLACEMENT

If lower control arm bushings are worn or damaged, replace the complete assembly.

Steering Knuckle, Hub and Bearing

REMOVAL & INSTALLATION

◆ See Figures 31 and 32

1. Loosen the wheel nuts and the center axle nut.

2. Raise the vehicle and safely support it.

3. Remove the wheel. Remove the ABS speed sensor if so equipped.

4. Unclamp the brake hose from the shock absorber, but do not disconnect the line.

5. Remove the brake caliper and hang it out of the way on a piece of stiff wire. Do not disconnect the brake line; do not allow the caliper to hang by the hose.

6. Remove the brake disc.

7. Place a dial indicator near the center of the axle hub, and check the backlash in the bearing shaft direction. Maximum is 0.0020 inch (0.05mm). If the backlash exceeds the maximum, replace the bearing.

  a. Using a dial; indicator, check the deviation at the surface of the axle hub outside the hub bolt. Maximum is 0.0028 inch (0.07mm). If the deviation exceeds the maximum, replace the axle hub.

  b. Install the disc and caliper. Tighten to 65 ft. lbs. (88 Nm).

8. Remove the cotter pin and install the wheel. Lower the vehicle to the ground.

9. Remove the lock nut cap. While depressing the brake pedal, remove the center axle nut.

10. Raise and support the vehicle again and remove the wheel, caliper and disc.

11. Loosen the 2 nuts on the lower side of the shock absorber. Do not remove the 2 nuts and bolts.

12. Remove the cotter pin and nut from the tie rod end.

13. Remove the tie rod end from the knuckle using a joint separator or equivalent.

14. Remove the bolt and 2 nuts holding the bottom of the ball joint to the control arm and separate the arm from the knuckle.

15. Remove the 2 nuts from the steering knuckle. Place a protective cover or shield over the CV boot on the driveshaft.

16. Using a plastic mallet, tap the driveshaft free of the hub assembly.

17. Remove the bolts and remove the axle hub assembly.

18. Clamp the knuckle in a vise with protected jaws.

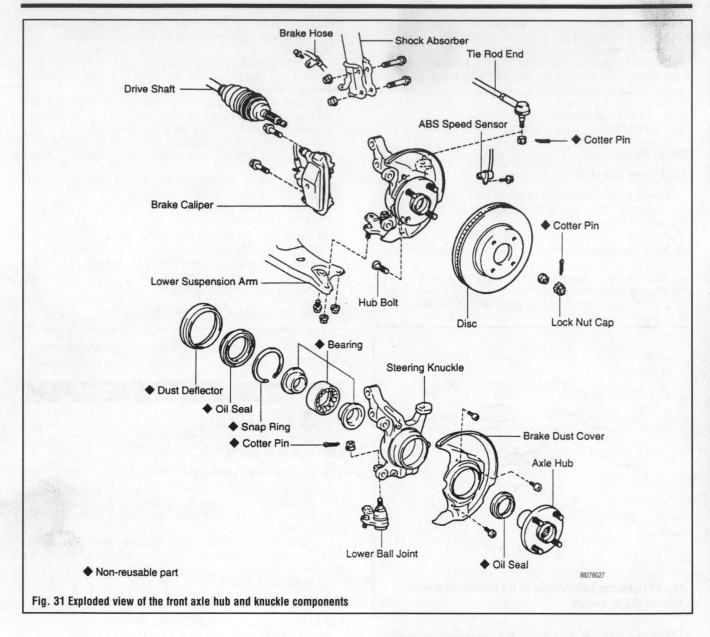

Brake Hose

Shock Absorber

Tie Rod End

Drive Shaft

ABS Speed Sensor

◆ Cotter Pin

Brake Caliper

◆ Cotter Pin

Lower Suspension Arm

Hub Bolt

Disc

Lock Nut Cap

◆ Bearing

Steering Knuckle

◆ Dust Deflector

◆ Oil Seal

Brake Dust Cover

Axle Hub

◆ Snap Ring

◆ Cotter Pin

Lower Ball Joint

◆ Oil Seal

◆ Non-reusable part

88278G27

Fig. 31 Exploded view of the front axle hub and knuckle components

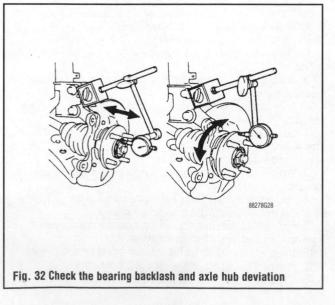

88278G28

Fig. 32 Check the bearing backlash and axle hub deviation

88278P35

Pull off the nut and washer holding the rotor to the shaft

Remove the cotter pin from the front hub

Remove the castleated nut

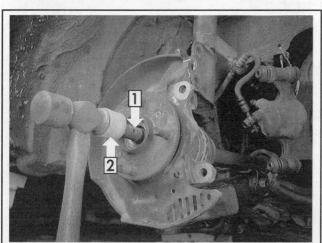

1. Driveshaft   2. Plastic mallet   88278P36
Gently tap the end of the driveshaft to allow the hub and knuckle to come off

Remove the hub and knuckle as an assembly

19. Remove the dust deflector. Loosen the nut holding the ball joint to the knuckle. Use a ball joint separator tool or equivalent to loosen and remove the joint

20. Use a slide hammer/extractor to remove the outer oil seal.

21. Remove the snapring.

22. Using a hub puller and pilot tools or equivalents, pull the axle hub from the knuckle.

23. Remove the brake splash shield (3 bolts).

24. Use a split plate bearing remover, puller pilot and a shop press, remove the inner bearing race from the hub.

25. Remove the inner oil seal with the same tools used to remove the outer seal.

To install:

26. Place the inner race in the bearing. Support the knuckle and use an axle hub remover with a plastic mallet to drive out the bearing.

27. Clean and inspect all parts but do not wash or clean the wheel bearing; it cannot be repacked. If the bearing is damaged or noisy, it must be replaced.

28. Press a new bearing race into the steering knuckle using a bearing driver of the correct size.

29. Place a new bearing inner race on the hub bearing.

30. Insert the side lip of a new oil seal into the seal installer and drive the oil seal into the steering knuckle.

31. Apply multi-purpose grease to the oil seal lip.

32. Apply sealer to the brake splash shield and install the shield.

33. Use a hub installer to press the hub into the steering knuckle.

34. Install a new snapring into the hub.

35. Using a seal installer of the correct size, install a new outer oil seal into the steering knuckle.

36. Apply multi-purpose grease to the seal surfaces which will contact the driveshaft.

37. Support the knuckle and drive in a new dust deflector.

38. Install the ball joint into the knuckle and tighten the nut to 105 ft. lbs. (142). Install NEW cotter pin.

39. Temporarily install the hub assembly to the lower control arm and fit the driveaxle into the hub.

40. Install the knuckle to strut bolts, then attach the tie rod end to the knuckle.

41. Tighten the strut bracket nuts to 203 ft. lbs. (275 Nm) and tighten the tie rod end nut to 36 ft. lbs. (49 Nm). Install the NEW cotter pin.

42. Connect the ball joint to the lower control arm and tighten the nuts to 105 ft. lbs. (142 Nm).

43. Install the brake disc.

44. Attach the brake caliper to the knuckle and tighten the bolts to 65 ft. lbs. (88 Nm).

45. Install the center nut and washer on the drive axle.
46. Install the ABS speed sensor if so equipped. Install the wheel
47. Lower the car to the ground.
48. Tighten the wheel nuts to 76 ft. lbs. (103 Nm). Tighten the hub nut while depressing the brake pedal to 137 ft. lbs. (186 Nm) on 1988–91 models and 152 ft. lbs. (206 Nm) on 1992–97 models. Install the cap and cotter pin.
49. Remove the protective cover from the CV boot. Check front wheel alignment.

Wheel Alignment

If the tires are worn unevenly, if the vehicle is not stable on the highway or if the handling seems uneven in spirited driving, the wheel alignment should be checked. If an alignment problem is suspected, first check for improper tire inflation and other possible causes. These can be worn suspension or steering components, accident damage or even unmatched tires. If any worn or damaged components are found, they must be replaced before the wheels can be properly aligned.

Wheel alignment requires very expensive equipment and involves minute adjustments which must be accurate; it should only be performed by a trained technician. Take your vehicle to a properly equipped shop.

Following is a description of the alignment angles which are adjustable on most vehicles and how they affect vehicle handling. Although these angles can apply to both the front and rear wheels, usually only the front suspension is adjustable.

CASTER

◆ See Figure 33

Looking at a vehicle from the side, caster angle describes the steering axis rather than a wheel angle. The steering knuckle is attached to a control arm or strut at the top and a control arm at the bottom. The wheel pivots around the line between these points to steer the vehicle. When the upper point is tilted back, this is described as positive caster. Having a positive caster tends to make the wheels self-centering, increasing directional stability. Excessive positive caster makes the wheels hard to steer, while an uneven caster will cause a pull to one side. Overloading the vehicle or sagging rear springs will affect caster, as will raising the rear of the vehicle. If the rear of the vehicle is lower than normal, the caster becomes more positive.

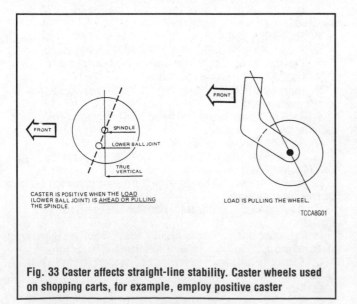

Fig. 33 Caster affects straight-line stability. Caster wheels used on shopping carts, for example, employ positive caster

CAMBER

◆ See Figure 34

Looking from the front of the vehicle, camber is the inward or outward tilt of the top of wheels. When the tops of the wheels are tilted in, this is negative camber; if they are tilted out, it is positive. In a turn, a slight amount of negative camber helps maximize contact of the tire with the road. However, too much negative camber compromises straight-line stability, increases bump steer and torque steer.

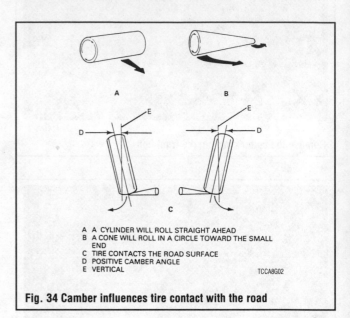

A   A CYLINDER WILL ROLL STRAIGHT AHEAD
B   A CONE WILL ROLL IN A CIRCLE TOWARD THE SMALL END
C   TIRE CONTACTS THE ROAD SURFACE
D   POSITIVE CAMBER ANGLE
E   VERTICAL

Fig. 34 Camber influences tire contact with the road

TOE

◆ See Figure 35

Looking down at the wheels from above the vehicle, toe angle is the distance between the front of the wheels, relative to the distance between the back of the wheels. If the wheels are closer at the front, they are said to be toed-in or to have negative toe. A small amount of negative toe enhances directional stability and provides a smoother ride on the highway.

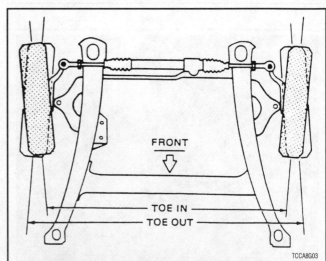

Fig. 35 With toe-in, the distance between the wheels is closer at the front than at the rear

2WD REAR SUSPENSION

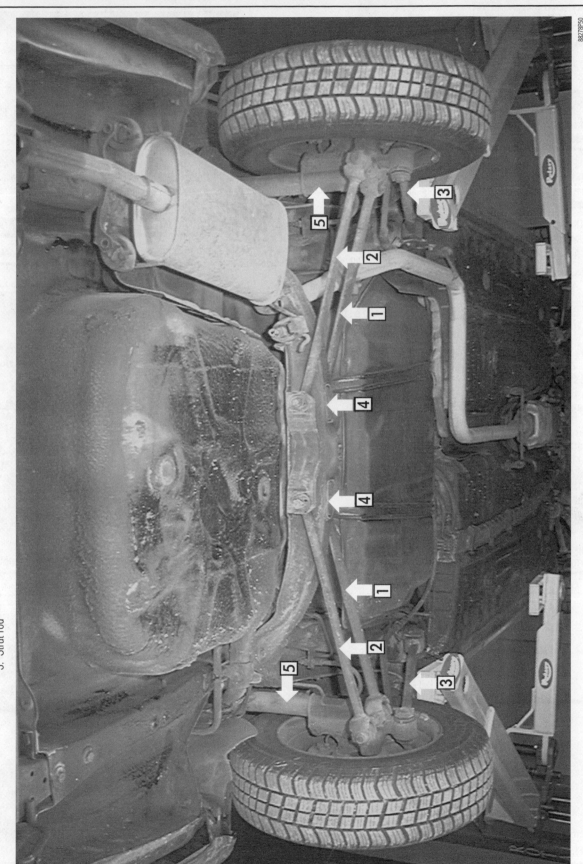

2WD REAR SUSPENSION COMPONENT LOCATIONS

1. No. 1 suspension arm
2. No. 2 suspension arm
3. Strut rod
4. No. 2 arm access cover
5. Strut assembly

Coil Springs

REMOVAL & INSTALLATION

◆ See Figure 36

1. Remove the 3 upper strut mounting nuts and carefully remove the strut assembly.

✳✳ WARNING

Do not loosen the center nut on the top of the shock absorber piston.

2. Place the strut assembly in vise. Position a bolt and two nuts between the bracket at the lower portion of the shock absorber shell and clamp shock absorber in a vise. The bolt acts as a spacer to allow for clamping without crushing the bracket.

➥**Do not attempt to clamp the strut assembly in a flat jaw vise as this will result in damage to the strut tube.**

3. Attach a spring compressor and compress the spring until the upper suspension support is free of any spring tension. Do not over-compress the spring.

4. Hold the upper support and then remove the nut on the end of the shock piston rod.

5. Remove the support, coil spring, insulator and bumper.

To install:

6. Loosely assemble all components onto the strut assembly. Make sure the spring end aligns with the hollow in the lower seat.

7. Align the upper suspension support with the piston rod and install the support.

8. Align the suspension support with the strut lower bracket. This assures the spring will be properly seated top and bottom.

9. Compress the spring slightly by pushing on the suspension support with one hand to expose the strut piston rod threads.

10. Install a new strut piston nut and tighten it to 36 ft. lbs. (49 Nm).

11. Place the complete strut assembly into the lower mount and mount it in position with the bolts.

12. Use a floor jack to gently raise the suspension and guide the upper strut mount into position.

✳✳ CAUTION

The car is on jackstands. Elevate the floor jack only enough to swing the strut into position; do not raise the car.

![Fig. 36 Correct position of the upper and lower mounts]

1. SUSPENSION SUPPORT
2. STRUT LOWER BRACKET

5°   5°

88278G37

Fig. 36 Correct position of the upper and lower mounts when reassembling the rear strut

13. Install all remaining components. Refer to McPherson Struts (2WD Models) later in this section.

MacPherson Struts

REMOVAL & INSTALLATION

1. Remove the seat back side cushion or the rear sill side panel to gain access to the upper strut mount.

2. Raise the rear of the vehicle and support it with jackstands (do not place stands under suspension arms). Remove the wheel.

3. Disconnect the brake hose from the shock absorber. Disconnect the ABS wire harnesses if so equipped.

4. Disconnect the stabilizer bar link from the strut assembly as necessary. Remove the 2 lower bolts holding the strut to the axle carriage.

5. Remove the 3 upper strut mounting nuts and carefully remove the strut assembly.

✳✳ WARNING

Do not loosen the center nut on the top of the shock absorber piston.

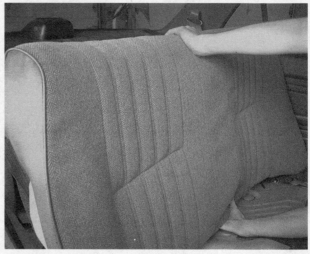

88278P46

Remove the rear seat back to access the upper strut mounting

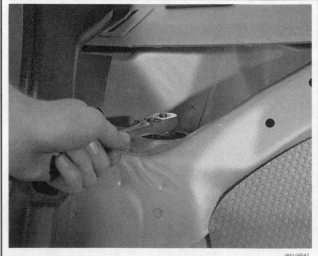

88278P47

Remove the upper strut nut from the tower in the trunk

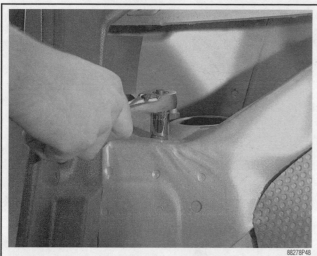

Next remove the three upper strut mounting nuts on the outer portion of the tower

Check the shock absorber by moving the piston shaft through its full range of travel. It should move smoothly and evenly throughout its entire travel without any trace of binding or notching. Use a small straightedge to check the piston shaft for any bending or deformation. If a shock absorber is replaced, the old one should be drilled at the center to vent the internal gas. Wear safety goggles and drill a small hole (2–3mm) into the center of the shock absorber. The gas within the strut is colorless, odorless and non-toxic, but should be vented to make the unit safe for disposal.

To install:

6. Use a floor jack to gently raise the suspension and guide the upper strut mount into position.

✸✸ CAUTION

The car is on jackstands. Elevate the floor jack only enough to swing the strut into position; do not raise the car.

7. Tighten the lower strut retaining nuts and bolts to 105 ft. lbs. (142 Nm).
8. Tighten the 3 upper retaining bolts to 29 ft. lbs. (39 Nm).
9. Attach the stabilizer bar link to the strut assembly and tighten the nut to 33 ft. lbs. (44 Nm).
10. Reconnect the brake hose to the shock absorber. Connect the ABS wire harnesses if so equipped.
11. Install the wheel. Lower the vehicle to the ground.
12. Reinstall the interior components as necessary.

Lower Suspension Arm and Strut Rod

REMOVAL & INSTALLATION

▶ See Figure 37

These vehicles use two control arms on each rear wheel. To avoid the obvious confusion they are referred to as No. 1 and No. 2, with arm No.1 being the closest to the front of the car. The strut rod is the bar going from front to rear of the vehicle.

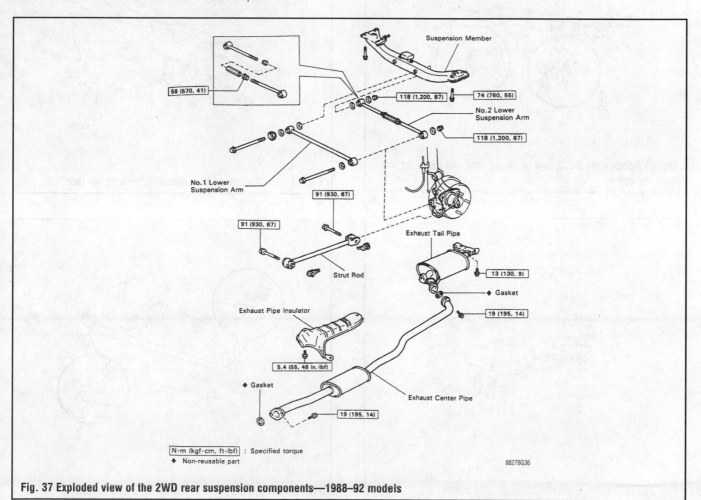

Fig. 37 Exploded view of the 2WD rear suspension components—1988–92 models

No. 1 Arm

◆ **See Figures 38, 39, 40, 41 and 42**

➡**Always matchmark all components prior to removal.**

1. Raise and safely support the vehicle.
2. If necessary, remove the exhaust system.
3. Disconnect the strut rod.
4. Remove the No. 2 lower suspension arm.
5. Support the rear crossmember with a jack. Remove the bolts retaining the crossmember and lower.
6. Remove the bolt and washer, then disconnect the No. 1 arm from the axle carrier.
7. Lower the crossmember, remove the bolt, washer and No.1 arm.

To install:

8. Install the No. 1 arm with the washers and bolts. Face the paint mark to the inside.
9. Attach the rear crossmember, tighten the retaining bolts to 55 ft. lbs. (74 Nm).
10. Install the exhaust system. Always replace the gaskets prior to installation.
11. Install the No. 2 arm, hand tighten the two lock nuts.

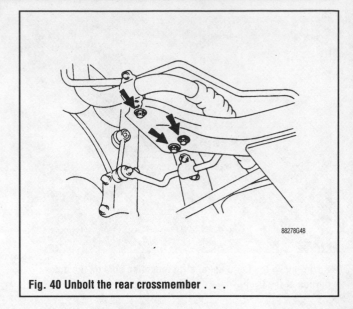

Fig. 40 Unbolt the rear crossmember . . .

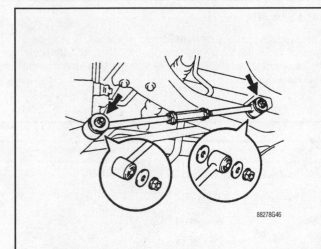

Fig. 38 Remove the No. 2 arm retaining nuts and lower the arm from the car

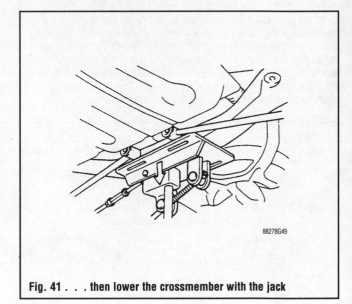

Fig. 41 . . . then lower the crossmember with the jack

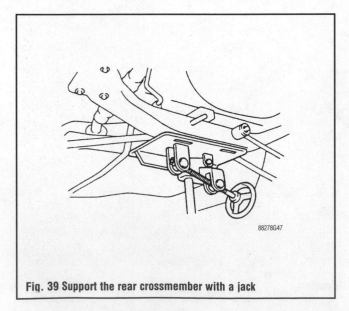

Fig. 39 Support the rear crossmember with a jack

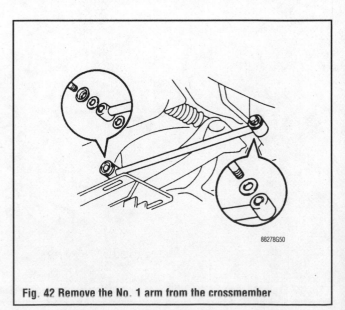

Fig. 42 Remove the No. 1 arm from the crossmember

12. Install the strut rod and hand tighten the nuts till later.
13. Install the rear wheels. Lower the vehicle.
14. Bounce the car up and down several times to stabilize the suspension.
15. Jack up the vehicle again and support the body with stands.
16. Remove the rear wheel. Support the rear axle carrier with a jack. Tighten the nuts of the No. 2 arm to 87 ft. lbs. (118 Nm) and the strut rod bolt to 67 ft. lbs. (91 Nm).
17. Install the rear wheels and lower the vehicle.
18. Inspect and adjust the rear wheel alignment.
19. Tighten the No. 2 arm lock nuts to 41 ft. lbs. (56 Nm).

No. 2 Arm

▶ See Figures 43 and 44

➡Always matchmark all components prior to removal.

1. Raise and safely support the vehicle.
2. Observe and matchmark the position of the adjusting cam at the body mount.
3. Remove the cover under the rear crossmember as shown in the illustration to access the rear arm mounting.

Once removed, be sure not to loose the adjusting cam

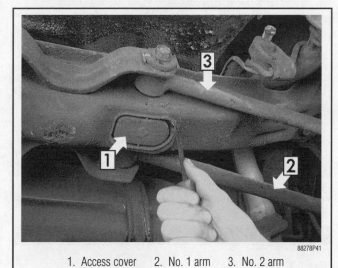
1. Access cover   2. No. 1 arm   3. No. 2 arm
No. 2 arm mounting access cover

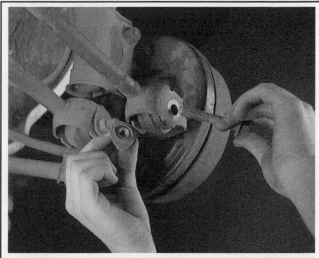
Remove the arm mounting bolt from the other side

While retaining the nut from the inside, remove the bolt on the outside

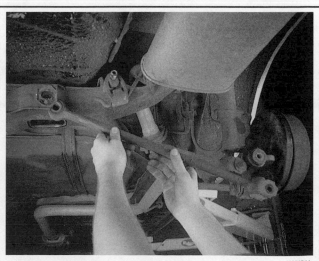
Pull the arm from the under the vehicle

4. Disconnect the bolt holding the arm to the suspension knuckle.
5. Disconnect the bolt holding the arm to the body.
6. Remove the arm.
7. Inspect the arms for any bending or cracking. If the arm is not true in all dimensions, it must be replaced. Any attempt to straighten a bent arm will damage it. Also check the bushings within the ends of the arms and replace any which are deformed or too spongy. If a bushing must be replaced, do not grease it before installation.
8. When installing the No. 2 arm, place the washers and hand tighten the nuts.
9. Install the strut rod and hand tighten the nuts till later.
10. Install the rear wheels. Lower the vehicle.
11. Bounce the car up and down several times to stabilize the suspension.
12. Jack up the vehicle again and support the body with stands.
13. Remove the rear wheel. Support the rear axle carrier with a jack. Tighten the nuts of the No. 2 arm to 87 ft. lbs. (118 Nm) and the strut rod bolt to 67 ft. lbs. (91 Nm).
14. Install the rear wheels and lower the vehicle.
15. Inspect and adjust the rear wheel alignment.
16. Tighten the No. 2 arm lock nuts to 41 ft. lbs. (56 Nm).

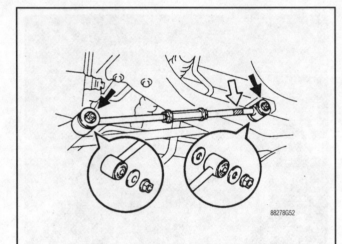

Fig. 43 Place the washers and nuts on the No. 2 arm in this order

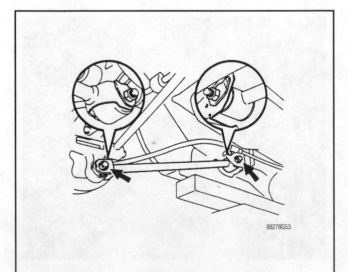

Fig. 44 Attach the strut rod and hand-tighten the nuts

Strut Rod

▶ **See Figure 45**

➡**Always matchmark all components prior to removal.**

1. Loosen the lug nuts and raise and support the vehicle.
2. Remove the rear wheel.
3. On some models it may be necessary to remove the exhaust system.
4. Remove the 2 bolts, nuts and strut rod.
To install:
5. Attach the strut rod and hand tighten the nuts.
6. Install the exhaust system if removed.
7. Install the rear wheels and lower the vehicle.
8. Tighten the lugs nuts to 76 ft. lbs. (103 Nm).
9. Inspect and adjust the rear wheel alignment.

Fig. 45 Remove the bolts and nuts retaining the strut rod to the vehicle

Rear Stabilizer Bar

REMOVAL & INSTALLATION

▶ **See Figures 46 thru 51**

1. Jack up vehicle and remove the rear wheel.
2. Disconnect the brake hose from the shock absorber. Have a container handy to catch any spilt fluid.
3. Remove the left and right stabilizer bar bushing brackets.
4. Remove the clip from the shock absorber. Remove the nuts and bolts, then disconnect the shock absorber from the steering knuckle.
5. Remove the 4 nuts retaining the left and right stabilizer links.

➡**If the ball joint turns with the nut, use a hexagon wrench to hold the stud.**

6. Matchmark the bushing and brackets to the stabilizer. Remove the 4 bolts, 2 brackets and bushings from the stabilizer bar.
7. On some models you may need to remove the exhaust system.
8. On all models, support the fuel tank with a jack. On 1988–95 models, remove only the right tank band. On the 1996–97 models, remove both tank bands.
9. On the 1993–95 models, support the rear crossmember with a jack. Remove the six bolts and lower the member. Remove the rear stabilizer bar.
To install:
10. Install the stabilizer bar.
11. On the 1993–95 models, jack up the crossmember, install the bolts, then tighten them to 55 ft lbs. (74 Nm).

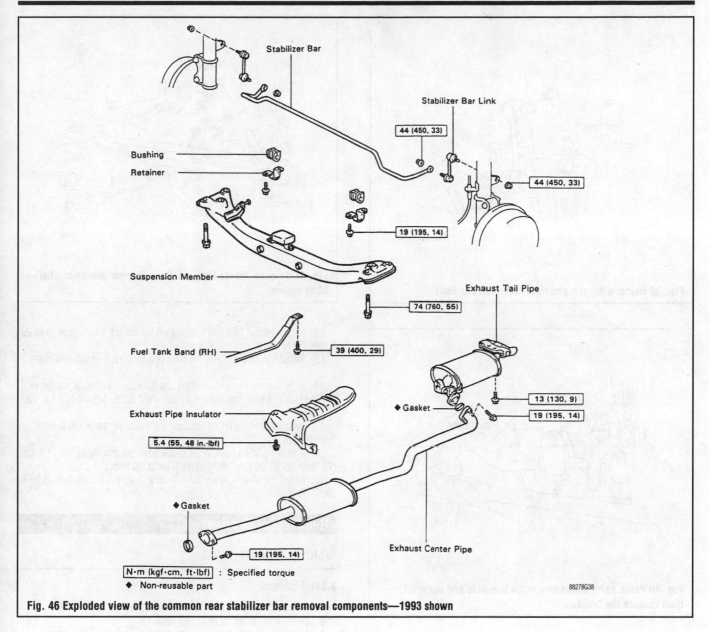

N·m (kgf·cm, ft·lbf) : Specified torque
♦ Non-reusable part

88278G38

Fig. 46 Exploded view of the common rear stabilizer bar removal components—1993 shown

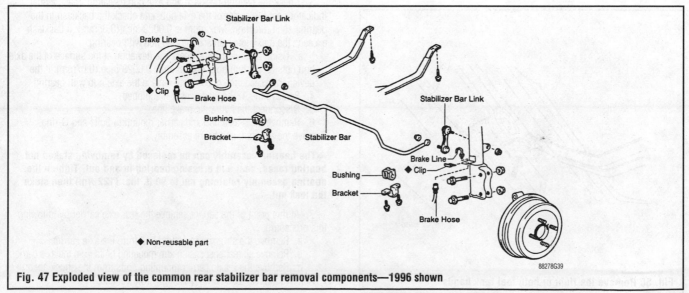

♦ Non-reusable part

88278G39

Fig. 47 Exploded view of the common rear stabilizer bar removal components—1996 shown

88278G40

Fig. 48 Remove the left and right stabilizer bar links

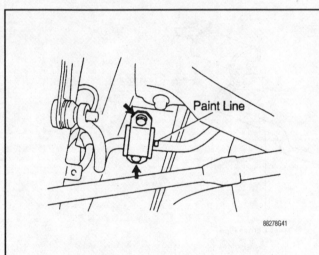

Paint Line

88278G41

Fig. 49 Place paint marks where the brackets and bar meet, then remove the brackets

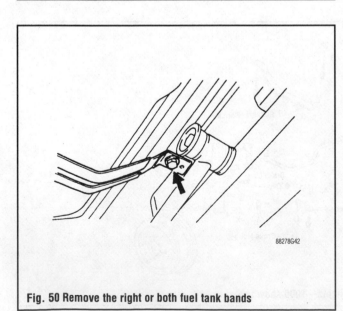

88278G42

Fig. 50 Remove the right or both fuel tank bands

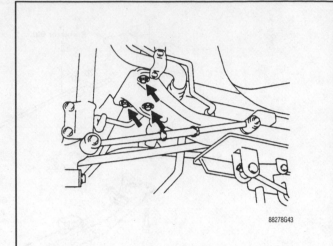

88278G43

Fig. 51 Remove the six bolts retaining the rear crossmemeber— 1996 shown

12. Install the fuel tank and bands, then tighten the retaining bolts to 29 ft. lbs. (39 Nm). Remove the jack.

13. Install the exhaust system if removed. Be sure to install new gaskets.

14. Align the marks and install the stabilizer bar bushing as shown in the illustration. Install the bushing brackets and bolts. Tighten to 14 ft. lbs. (19 Nm).

15. Install the left and right stabilizer bar links. Tighten them to 33 ft. lbs. (44 Nm).

16. Attach the brake hose to the shock absorber and tighten to 11 ft. lbs. (15 Nm). Install the clip retaining the hose to the shock.

17. Install the wheels, lower the vehicle and tighten the lug nuts to 76 ft. lbs. (103 Nm).

Rear Wheel Bearings

REMOVAL & INSTALLATION

◆ See Figure 52

1. Raise and safely support the vehicle.
2. Remove the brake drum or disc rotor.
3. Check the bearing backlash and axle hub deviation. Place a dual indicator near the center of the axle hub, and check the backlash in the bearing shaft direction. Maximum is 0.0020 inch (0.05mm). If backlash exceeds the maximum, replace the axle hub with bearing.
   a. Using a dial indicator, check the deviation at the surface of the axle hub outside the hub bolt. Maximum is 0.0028 inch (0.07mm). If the deviation exceeds the maximum., replace the axle hub with bearing.
4. Remove the ABS speed sensor if equipped.
5. Disconnect the hydraulic brake line.
6. Remove the 4 axle hub and carrier mounting bolts and O-ring. Remove the axle hub and brake assembly.

➡The bearing assembly can be replaced by removing staked nut, bearing races, seal and pressing bearing in and out. Tighten the bearing assembly retaining nut to 90 ft. lbs. (122 Nm) then stake the lock nut.

7. At this point of the service remove the rear axle carrier by following this procedure:
   a. Remove the strut rod mounting bolt from the axle carrier.
   b. Remove all rear suspension arm mounting bolts from the axle carrier.
   c. Remove the 2 axle carrier mounting bolts from the shock absorber. Remove the rear axle carrier assembly from vehicle.

8. Installation is the reverse of the removal procedure. Install new O-ring in axle carrier. Torque the rear axle carrier to shock absorber to 105 ft. lbs. (142 Nm) and the 4 axle hub retaining bolts to 59 ft. lbs. (80 Nm). Attach the speed sensor, tighten the bolt to 69 inch lbs. (8 Nm).

9. Bounce the car rear and front several times to position the suspension. Tighten the strut rod-to-axle carrier to 67 ft. lbs. (91 Nm) and the No. 1 and No. 2 arm-to-axle carrier to 92 ft. lbs. (125 Nm). Check rear wheel alignment.

Rear Wheel Alignment

The proper alignment of the rear wheels is as important as the alignment of the front wheels and should be checked periodically. If the rear wheels are misaligned the car will exhibit unpredictable handling characteristics. This behavior is particularly hazardous on slick surfaces; the back wheels of the car may attempt to go in directions unrelated to the front during braking or turning maneuvers. Refer to the front suspension alignment section for information on alignment angles.

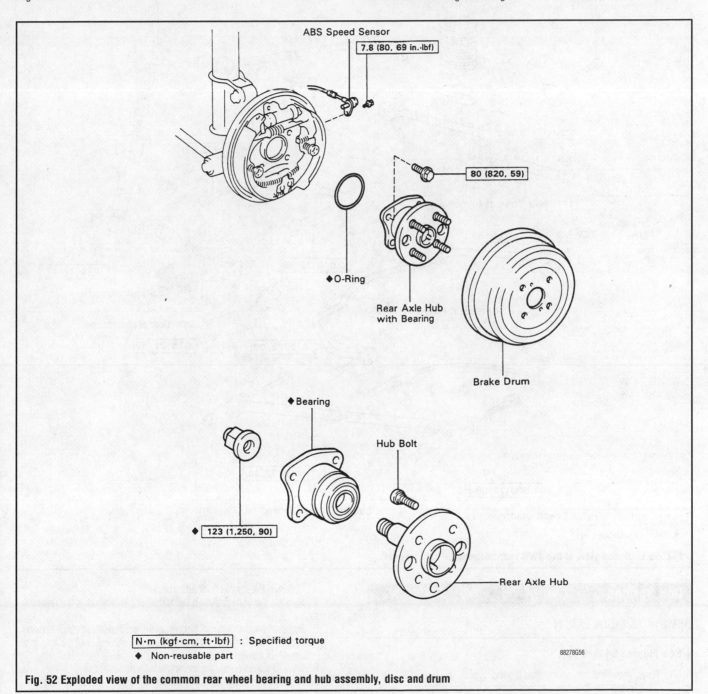

ABS Speed Sensor

7.8 (80, 69 in.·lbf)

80 (820, 59)

◆O-Ring

Rear Axle Hub with Bearing

Brake Drum

◆Bearing

Hub Bolt

◆ 123 (1,250, 90)

Rear Axle Hub

N·m (kgf·cm, ft·lbf) : Specified torque
◆   Non-reusable part

88278G56

Fig. 52 Exploded view of the common rear wheel bearing and hub assembly, disc and drum

4WD REAR SUSPENSION

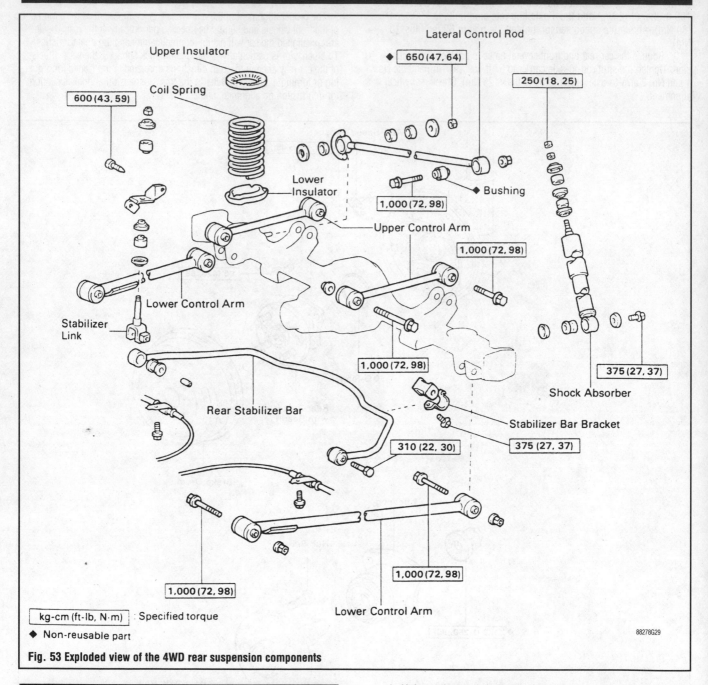

Upper Insulator

Lateral Control Rod

◆ 650 (47, 64)

250 (18, 25)

600 (43, 59)

Coil Spring

Lower Insulator

◆ Bushing

1,000 (72, 98)

Upper Control Arm

1,000 (72, 98)

Lower Control Arm

Stabilizer Link

375 (27, 37)

Shock Absorber

1,000 (72, 98)

Rear Stabilizer Bar

Stabilizer Bar Bracket

375 (27, 37)

310 (22, 30)

1,000 (72, 98)

1,000 (72, 98)

Lower Control Arm

kg-cm (ft-lb, N·m) : Specified torque

◆ Non-reusable part

88278G29

Fig. 53 Exploded view of the 4WD rear suspension components

Coil Springs

REMOVAL & INSTALLATION

▶ **See Figures 54 thru 59**

1. Remove the hubcap and loosen the lug nuts.
2. Jack up the rear axle housing and support the frame (not rear axle housing) with jackstands. Leave the jack in place under the rear axle housing.

✳✳ CAUTION

Support the car securely. Remember; you will be working underneath it.

3. Remove the lug nuts and wheel.

4. Unfasten the lower shock absorber end.
5. Remove the bolts retaining the stabilizer bar bracket to the rear axle housing.
6. Remove lateral control rod, disconnect the rod from the rear axle housing.
7. Slowly lower the jack under the rear axle housing until the axle is at the bottom of its travel.
8. Withdraw the coil spring, complete with its insulator.
9. Inspect the coil spring and insulator for wear and cracks, or weakness; replace either or both as necessary.
10. Installation is performed in the reverse order of removal procedure (install the lower insulator or spring seat in the correct position). Tighten shock absorber mounting nut to 27 ft. lbs. (36 Nm). When reconnecting the lateral control rod, tighten the bolt finger tight. Install the stabilizer brackets to the rear axle housing. Install the wheels, then lower the vehicle. Bounce it a few times to stabilize the rear suspension. Raise the rear axle housing until the body is free and then tighten the nut to 47 ft. lbs. (64 Nm).

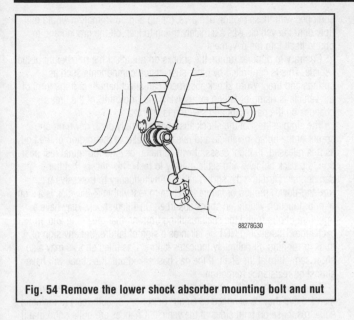

Fig. 54 Remove the lower shock absorber mounting bolt and nut

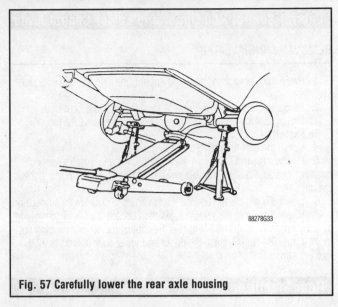

Fig. 57 Carefully lower the rear axle housing

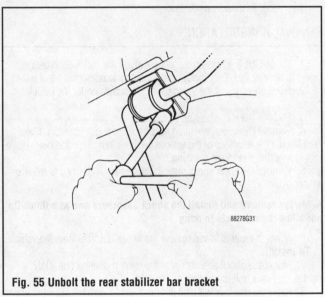

Fig. 55 Unbolt the rear stabilizer bar bracket

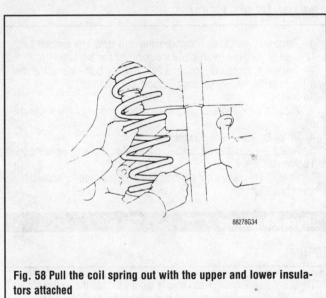

Fig. 58 Pull the coil spring out with the upper and lower insulators attached

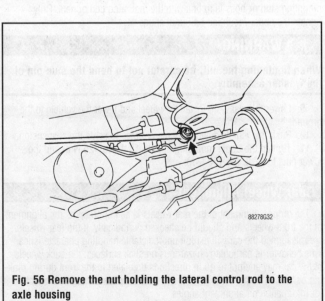

Fig. 56 Remove the nut holding the lateral control rod to the axle housing

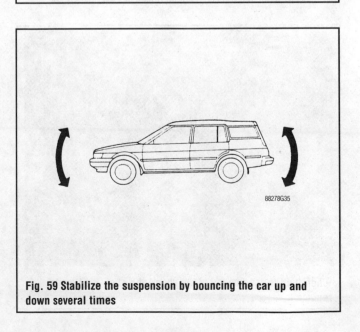

Fig. 59 Stabilize the suspension by bouncing the car up and down several times

Lateral Control Rod Upper and Lower Control Arms

REMOVAL & INSTALLATION

1. Raise the rear of the vehicle and support the axle housing with jack-stands.
2. Disconnect the lateral rod or arm from the rear axle housing.
3. Disconnect the lateral rod from the body and remove the rod.
To install:
4. Install the arm-to-body nut and finger tighten it.
5. Position the rod or arm on the axle housing and install a washer, bushing, spacer, the arm, bushing, washer and then the nut. Finger tighten the nut.
6. Lower the vehicle and bounce it a few times to stabilize the suspension.
7. Raise the rear of the vehicle again then tighten the lateral control rod-to-body nut to 72 ft. lbs. (97 Nm) and the control rod-to-axle housing nut to 47 ft. lbs. (64 Nm). Tighten the upper and lower control arms to 72 ft. lbs. (97 Nm).

Rear Stabilizer Bar

REMOVAL & INSTALLATION

1. Remove all necessary components to gain access for removal and installation of stabilizer bar. Remove the stabilizer bar brackets.
2. Remove the nuts, cushions and links holding both sides of the stabilizer bar from the suspension arms. Remove the stabilizer bar.
To install:
3. Assemble the stabilizer link sub-assembly and attach the link to the arm.
4. Install the stabilizer bar to the link.
5. Attach the stabilizer bar bracket to the differential support member and tighten to 27 ft. lbs.
6. Install all necessary components that were removed for removal access of stabilizer bar.

Shock Absorbers

TESTING

The purpose of the shock absorber is simply to limit the motion of the spring during compression and rebound cycles. If the vehicle is not equipped with these motion dampers, the up and down motion would multiply until the vehicle was alternately trying to leap off the ground and to pound itself into the pavement.

Contrary to popular rumor, the shocks do not affect the ride height of the vehicle. This is controlled by other suspension components such as springs and tires. Worn shock absorbers can affect handling; if the front of the vehicle is rising or falling excessively, the "footprint" of the tires changes on the pavement and steering is affected.

The simplest test of the shock absorber is simply push down on one corner of the unladen vehicle and release it. Observe the motion of the body as it is released. In most cases, it will come up beyond it original rest position, dip back below it and settle quickly to rest. This shows that the damper is controlling the spring action. Any tendency to excessive pitch (up-and-down) motion or failure to return to rest within 2-3 cycles is a sign of poor function within the shock absorber. Oil-filled shocks may have a light film of oil around the seal, resulting from normal breathing and air exchange. This should NOT be taken as a sign of failure, but any sign of thick or running oil definitely indicates failure. Gas filled shocks may also show some film at the shaft; if the gas has leaked out, the shock will have almost no resistance to motion.

While each shock absorber can be replaced individually, it is recommended that they be changed as a pair (both front or both rear) to maintain equal response on both sides of the vehicle. Chances are quite good that if one has failed, its mate is weak also.

REMOVAL & INSTALLATION

1. Loosen the lug nuts on the wheels where the shock absorbers are going to be removed. Only loosen the lug nuts a maximum of ½ of a turn.
2. Raise and support the vehicle with jackstands under the vehicle's frame.
3. Remove the rear wheel(s).
4. Remove the upper mounting nuts from the shock absorber. Make sure to note the locations of the various washers, bushings and nuts. Use a tool to keep the shaft from spinning.
5. Remove the lower shock retaining nut where it attaches to the rear axle housing.

➡**Always remove and install the shock absorbers one at a time. Do not allow the rear axle to hang.**

6. Lower the rear axle and remove the shock absorber from the vehicle.
To install:
7. Mount the shock absorber with the lower mounting bolt. Only tighten the lower bolt until snug.
8. Raise the rear axle with the floor jack until the shock absorber upper mounting stud or boss is in line with the mounting component. Only tighten the upper mounting bolt until snug.

❊❊❊ WARNING

When tightening the nut, be careful not to bend the stud pin of the washer assembly.

9. Lower the rear axle, install the wheel and lower the vehicle to the ground.
10. Push the vehicle down a couple of times to settle the suspension.
11. Tighten the upper mounting nuts to 18 ft. lbs. (25 Nm) and the lower nuts to 37 ft. lbs. (50 Nm).

Rear Wheel Alignment

The proper alignment of the rear wheels is as important as the alignment of the front wheels and should be checked periodically. If the rear wheels are misaligned the car will exhibit unpredictable handling characteristics. This behavior is particularly hazardous on slick surfaces; the back wheels of the car may attempt to go in directions unrelated to the front during braking or turning maneuvers. Refer to the front suspension alignment section for information on alignment angles.

TCCA8P73

When fluid is seeping out of the shock absorber, it's time to replace it

STEERING

Steering Wheel

REMOVAL & INSTALLATION

▶ **See Figures 60 and 61**

➡Do not attempt to remove or install the steering wheel by hammering on it. Damage to the energy-absorbing steering column could result.

✳✳ CAUTION

On models with an airbag, wait at least 90 seconds from the time that the ignition switch is turned to the LOCK position and the battery is disconnected before performing any further work.

1. Disconnect the negative battery cable.
2. Loosen the trim pad retaining screws from the back side of the steering wheel. Some models use torx head screws.

3. Lift the trim pad and horn button assembly straight off the wheel. Be careful not to pull on the SRS wire if equipped.

➡**If equipped with SRS, place the air bag pad with the upper surface facing up. Refer to the illustration.**

4. Matchmark the nut and steering shaft mating points. This will allow the steering wheel to be placed exactly in the same position as removed.
5. Remove the steering wheel hub retaining nut and washer. Some models are not equipped with the washer.
6. Screw the two bolts of a steering wheel puller into the wheel. Turn the bolt at the center of the puller to force the wheel off the steering shaft. Do not pound on the wheel to remove it, or the collapsible steering shaft may be damaged.
7. Install the wheel and push it onto the shaft splines by hand far enough to start the retaining nut.
8. Install the retaining nut and tighten to 25 ft. lbs. (34 Nm).
9. Connect the horn and SRS wires then reinstall the horn pad. If it is the snap-on type, make sure all the clips are engaged.
10. Connect the negative cable to the battery.

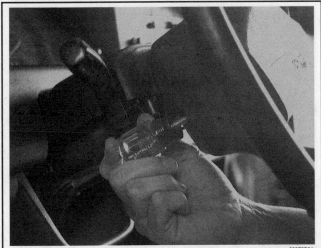

From behind the steering wheel, remove the horn pad retaining screws

With two hands pull the horn pad off the front of the steering wheel

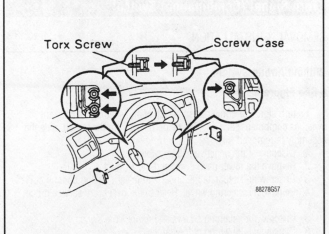

Fig. 60 Use a Torx® bit to loosen the screws until the groove along the screws circumference is on the screw case

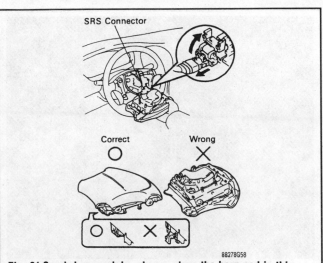

Fig. 61 On air bag models, always place the horn pad in this position when storing it

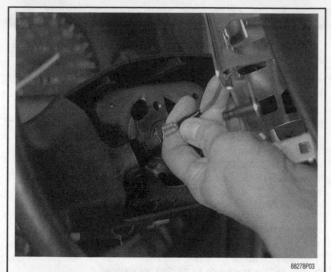

Disconnect the horn wiring from the back of the pad

88278P03

Use a steering wheel puller to separate the steering wheel from the shaft

88278P06

Matchmark the nut and steering shaft with paint or a marker

88278P04

Pull the steering wheel off the shaft once loosened by the puller

88278P07

Remove the nut retaining the steering wheel to the shaft

88278P05

Turn Signal (Combination) Switch

REMOVAL & INSTALLATION

Without Airbag System

▶ **See Figure 62**

The turn signal or combination switch is an assembly of different switches combined. Each one can be detached from the switch once the assembly is removed.

1. Disconnect the negative battery cable.
2. Remove the lower dash cover and the air duct.
3. Unscrew and separate the upper and lower steering column covers.
4. Remove the steering wheel. Refer to the necessary service procedure.
5. Unscrew the retaining screws and remove the switch.
6. Disconnect the wiring at the harness.

To install:

7. Place the switch in correct position and tighten the bolts.
8. Connect the wiring harness and reinstall the steering wheel.

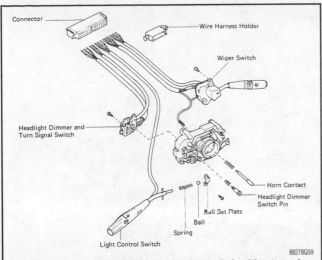

Fig. 62 Exploded view of the combination switch without an air bag

Remove the screws retaining the combination switch to the steering column

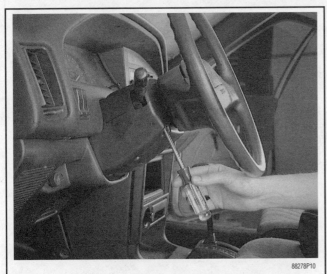

Remove the screws from under the steering column covers . . .

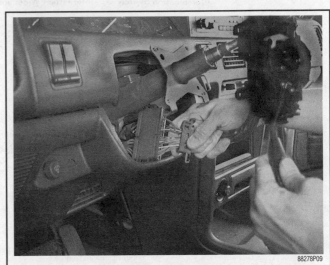

Slide the switch off the shaft and pull the wires from the back of the dash

. . . this will allow the two covers to separate

9. Reinstall the and attach column cover(s).
10. Install the lower dash trim panel.
11. Connect the negative battery cable. Check system for proper operation.

With Airbag System

▶ See Figure 63

1. Disconnect the negative battery cable. Wait at least 90 seconds before working on the vehicle.

✷✷ CAUTION

On models with an airbag, wait at least 90 seconds from the time that the ignition switch is turned to the LOCK position and the battery is disconnected before performing any further work.

2. Remove (matchmark before removal) the steering wheel, as outlined in this Section.
3. Remove the instrument lower finish panel (as required), air duct and upper and lower column covers.
4. Disconnect the combination switch harness.

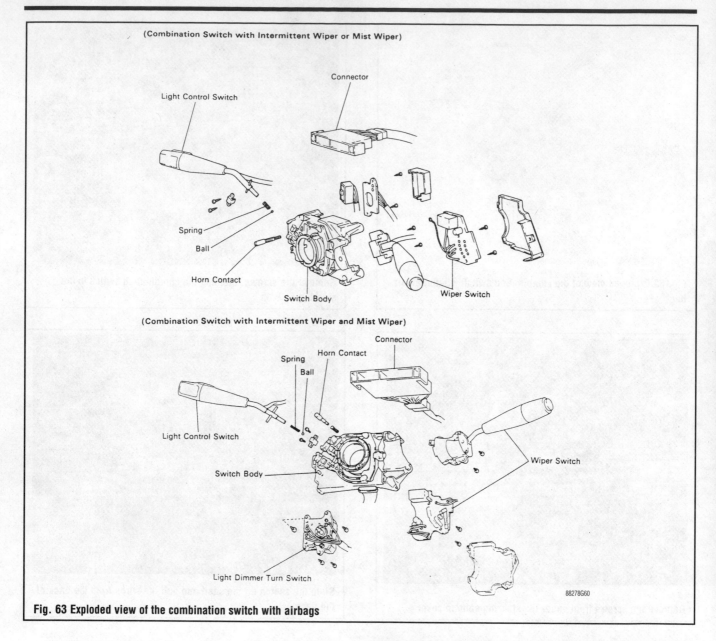

(Combination Switch with Intermittent Wiper or Mist Wiper)

Connector

Light Control Switch

Spring

Ball

Horn Contact

Switch Body

Wiper Switch

(Combination Switch with Intermittent Wiper and Mist Wiper)

Connector

Spring   Horn Contact

Ball

Light Control Switch

Switch Body

Wiper Switch

Light Dimmer Turn Switch

88278G60

Fig. 63 Exploded view of the combination switch with airbags

5. Disconnect the cable harness, remove the spiral cable housing attaching screws and slide the cable assembly from the front of the combination switch.

6. Remove the screws that attach the combination switch to its mounting brackets and remove the combination switch from the vehicle.

To install:

7. Position the combination switch onto the mounting bracket and install the retaining screws.

8. Connect the electrical harness.

9. Install the upper/lower column covers, air duct and instrument lower finish panel.

10. Turn the spiral cable on the combination switch counterclockwise by hand until it becomes harder to turn. Then rotate the cable clockwise about 3 turns to align the alignment mark. The connector should be straight up.

11. Install the steering wheel (align matchmarks) onto the shaft and tighten the nut to 26 ft. lbs. (35 Nm).

12. Connect the air bag wiring and install the steering pad.

13. Connect the battery cable, check operation and the steering wheel center point.

14. Connect the negative battery cable. Check all combination switch functions for proper operation. Check the steering wheel center point.

Ignition Switch/Ignition Lock Cylinder

REMOVAL & INSTALLATION

▶ See Figures 64 and 65

1. Disconnect the negative battery cable.

✳✳ CAUTION

On models with an airbag, wait at least 90 seconds from the time that the ignition switch is turned to the LOCK position and the battery is disconnected before performing any further work.

2. Unscrew the retaining screws and remove the upper and lower steering column covers.

3. Remove the 2 retaining screws and remove the steering column trim.

4. Turn the ignition key to the **ACC** position.

5. Push the lock cylinder stop in with a small, round object (cotter pin, punch, etc.) and pull out the ignition key and the lock cylinder.

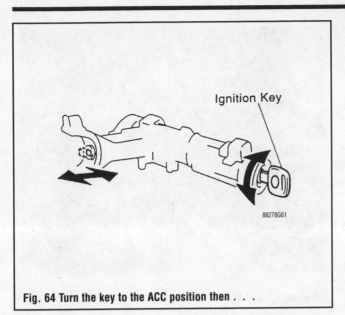

Fig. 64 Turn the key to the ACC position then . . .

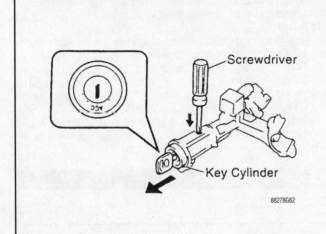

Fig. 65 . . . push down on the stop pin with a round ended tool to pull out the lock cylinder

➡ **You may find that removing the steering wheel and the combination switch makes the job easier.**

6. Loosen the mounting screw and withdraw the ignition switch from the lock housing.

7. Remove the wiring harness bands or clips. Disconnect the ignition switch harness.

To install:

8. Position the ignition switch so that the recess and the bracket tab are properly aligned. Install the retaining screw.

9. Make sure that both the lock cylinder and the column lock are in the **ACC** position. Slide the cylinder into the lock housing until the stop tab engages the hole in the lock.

10. Make certain the stop tab is firmly seated in the slot. Turn the key to each switch position, checking for smoothness of motions and a positive feel. Remove and insert the key a few times, each time turning the key to each switch position.

11. Connect the switch if it was removed from the lock assembly.

12. Connect the wiring harness and check the assembly for proper operation.

13. Reinstall or connect any wiring bands, clips or retainers which were loosened. It is important that the wiring be correctly contained and out of the way of any moving parts.

14. Reinstall the combination switch and the steering wheel if they were removed.

15. Install the steering column trim and the upper and lower column covers.

16. Connect the negative battery cable.

Steering Linkage

REMOVAL & INSTALLATION

Tie Rod Ends

1. Raise the front of the vehicle and support it safely. Remove the wheel.

2. Matchmark the inner end of the tie rod to the end of the steering rack.

3. Remove the cotter pin and nut holding the tie rod to the steering knuckle.

4. Using a tie rod separator, press the tie rod out of the knuckle.

➡ **Use only the correct tool to separate the tie rod joint. Replace the joint if the rubber boot is cracked or ripped.**

Always matchmark the tie rod end for installation purposes

Remove and discard the cotter pin, NEVER reuse the old one

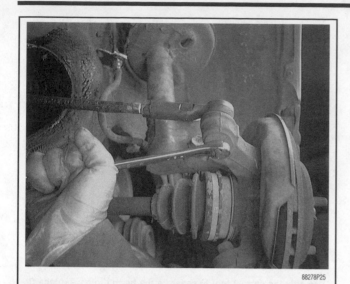

Remove the tie rod end retaining nut

Using a separating tool, press the tie rod from the knuckle

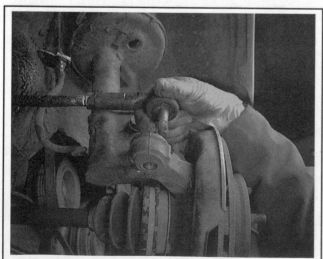

Pull the tie rod out of the knuckle using your hands

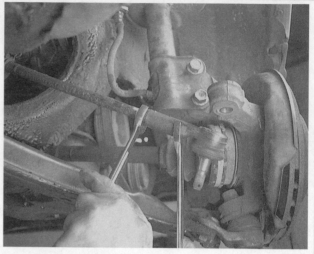

Unscrew the end from the steering rack

5. Loosen the locknut and remove the tie rod (count the number turns out to remove the tie rod) from the steering rack.

To install:

6. Install the tie rod end (count the same amount of turns in for correct installation) onto the rack ends and align the matchmarks made earlier.

7. Tighten the locknut to 41 ft. lbs. (55 Nm).

8. Connect the tie rod to the knuckle. Tighten the tie rod to steering knuckle nut to 36 ft. lbs. (49 Nm) and install a NEW cotter pin. Wrap the prongs of the cotter pin firmly around the flats of the nut.

9. Install the wheel and lower the vehicle to the ground. Have the alignment checked at a reputable repair facility. The toe adjustment may have to be reset.

Manual Steering Gear

REMOVAL & INSTALLATION

2WD Models

⬥ See Figure 66

➡ If vehicle is equipped with an air bag system, after repair is complete remove the steering wheel and make sure that the spiral cable is aligned properly. Refer to the necessary service procedures in this section.

1. Disconnect the negative battery cable. Remove the upper and lower steering column covers.

✳✳ CAUTION

On models with an airbag, wait at least 90 seconds from the time that the ignition switch is turned to the LOCK position and the battery is disconnected before performing any further work.

2. Disconnect universal joint from the gear housing. Place matchmarks before removing set bolts.

3. Raise and safely support the vehicle.

4. Remove both front wheels.

5. Remove the cotter pins from both tie rod joints and remove the nuts.

6. Using a tie rod separator, remove both tie rod joints from the steering knuckles.

7. Support the engine assembly and remove the engine mounting, lower the engine if necessary.

8. Remove the nuts and bolts attaching the steering rack to the body.

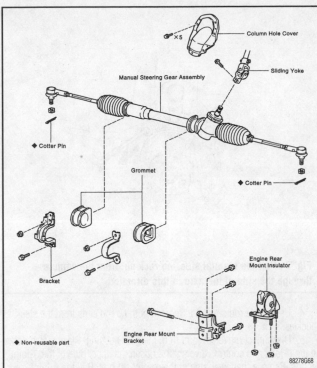

Fig. 66 Exploded view of the 2WD manual steering gear assembly

9. Remove any other necessary component to gain working access (if possible slide assembly out the wheel well opening) to remove the rack and pinion assembly from the vehicle. Remove the rack assembly.

To install:

10. Install the rack assembly. Secure it with the retaining bolts and nuts and tighten them EVENLY to 43 ft. lbs. (58 Nm).

11. Connect the tie rods to each steering knuckle. Tighten the nuts to 36 ft. lbs. (48 Nm) and install NEW cotter pins. Wrap the prongs of the cotter pin firmly around the flats of the nuts.

12. Install the front wheels.

13. Lower the car to the ground.

14. Align matchmarks and connect universal joint to the steering gear housing. Tighten the upper and lower set bolts to 26 ft. lbs. (35 Nm).

15. Install the steering column cover. Reconnect the negative battery cable. Check front wheel alignment.

4WD Models

▶ See Figures 67, 68, 69, 70 and 71

1. Disconnect the negative battery cable. Remove the steering column cover.

✻✻ CAUTION

On models with an airbag, wait at least 90 seconds from the time that the ignition switch is turned to the LOCK position and the battery is disconnected before performing any further work.

2. Raise and safely support the vehicle.

3. Remove the cotter pins from both tie rod ends and remove the nuts.

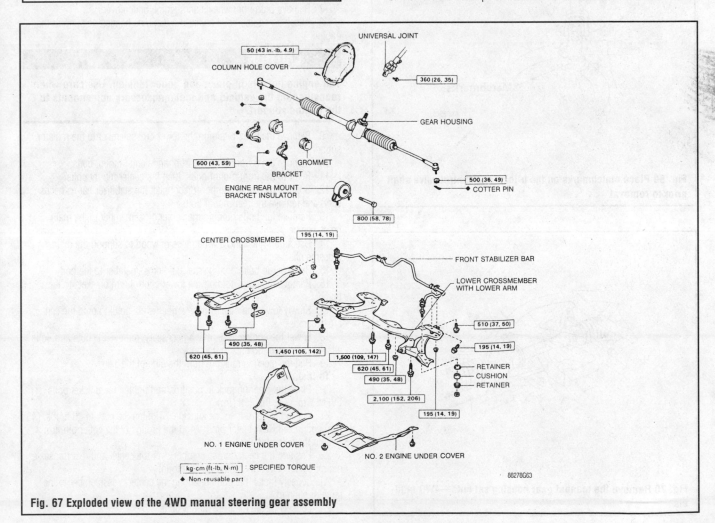

Fig. 67 Exploded view of the 4WD manual steering gear assembly

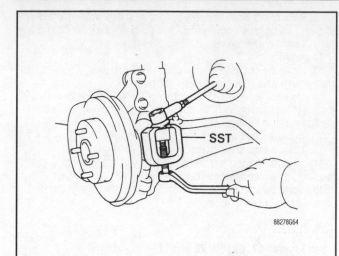

Fig. 68 Using a tie rod puller, separate the ends from the steering knuckle arms

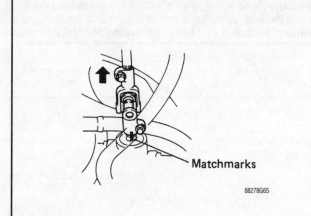

Fig. 69 Place matchmarks on the u-joint and control valve shaft prior to removal

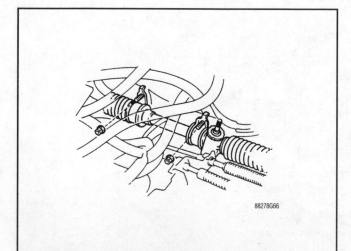

Fig. 70 Remove the manual gear housing set nuts—4WD models

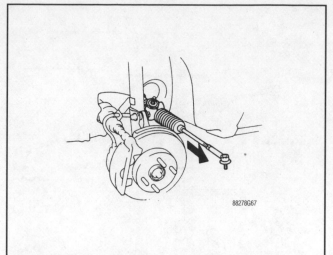

Fig. 71 Pull the manual steering rack out from the vehicle through the side of the axle in this direction

4. Using a tie rod separator, remove both tie rod ends from the steering knuckles.

5. Disconnect universal joint from the gear housing. Place matchmarks on the u-joint and control valve shaft. Loosen the upper side of the u-joint set bolt. Remove the lower side of the u-joint set bolt. Pull the u-joint upward from the control valve shaft.

6. Remove the gear housing set nuts.

7. Remove both front wheels and engine undercovers.

8. Attach an engine hoist chain to the engine hangers to support the engine.

✳✳ CAUTION

The engine hoist is in place and under tension. Use care when repositioning the vehicle and make necessary adjustments to the engine support.

9. Remove the bolts retaining the lower crossmember to the radiator support.

10. Remove the covers from the front and center mount bolts.

11. Remove the front mount bolts, then the center mount bolts.

12. Support the crossmember (disconnect the stabilizer bar as necessary) and remove the rear mount bolts.

13. Remove the bolts holding the center crossmember to the main crossmember.

14. Use a floor jack and a wide piece of wood to support the main crossmember.

15. Remove the bolts holding the main crossmember to the body.

16. Remove the bolts holding the lower control arm brackets to the body.

17. Slowly lower the main crossmember while holding onto the center crossmember.

18. Lower the engine assembly if necessary, remove the nuts and bolts attaching the steering rack to the body.

19. Pull the steering rack out from the side of the axle.

To install:

20. Place the steering rack in position and tighten the bracket bolts EVENLY to 43 ft. lbs. (58 Nm).

21. Attach the tie rods to the knuckles. Tighten the nuts to 36 ft. lbs. (48 Nm) and install NEW cotter pins. Wrap the prongs of the cotter pin firmly around the flats of the nut.

22. Position the center crossmember over the center and rear transaxle mount studs; start nuts on the center mount.

23. Loosely install the bolts retaining the center crossmember to the radiator support.

24. Loosely install the front mount bolts.

25. Raise the main crossmember into position over the rear mount studs and align all underbody bolts. Install the rear mount nuts loosely.

26. Install the main crossmember to underbody bolts loosely.

27. Install the lower control arm bracket bolts loosely.

28. Loosely install the bolts holding the center crossmember to the main crossmember.

29. The crossmembers, bolts and brackets should now all be in place and held loosely by their nuts and bolts. If any repositioning is necessary, do so now.

30. Tighten the components below in the order listed to the correct torque specification:

- Main crossmember to underbody bolts—152 ft. lbs. (206 Nm).
- Lower control arm bolts—105 ft. lbs. (142 Nm)
- Center crossmember to radiator support bolts—45 ft. lbs. (61 Nm)
- Front, center and rear mount bolts—58 ft. lbs. (78 Nm).

31. Reconnect the stabilizer bar as necessary. Install the covers on the front and center mount bolts.

32. Install the front wheels and engine undercovers.

33. Lower the vehicle to the ground.

34. Align matchmarks and connect universal joint to the steering gear housing. Tighten the upper and lower set bolts to 26 ft. lbs. (35 Nm).

35. Install the steering column cover. Reconnect the negative battery cable. Check front wheel alignment.

Power Steering Gear

REMOVAL & INSTALLATION

2WD Models

▶ See Figures 72, 73 and 74

➡If vehicle is equipped with an air bag system, after repair is complete remove the steering wheel and make sure that the spiral cable is aligned properly. Refer to the necessary service procedures in this section.

1. Place the front wheels in the straight ahead position.

2. Disconnect the negative battery cable. Remove the steering wheel pad and wheel. Refer to Steering Wheel Removal and Installation in this section.

3. Raise and safely support the vehicle. If necessary, remove both front wheels.

4. Remove the 2 engine under covers.

5. Remove the cotter pins and nuts from both tie rod joints. Separate the joints from the knuckle using a tie rod joint separator.

6. Remove the column hole cover retaining bolts, then pull the cover off.

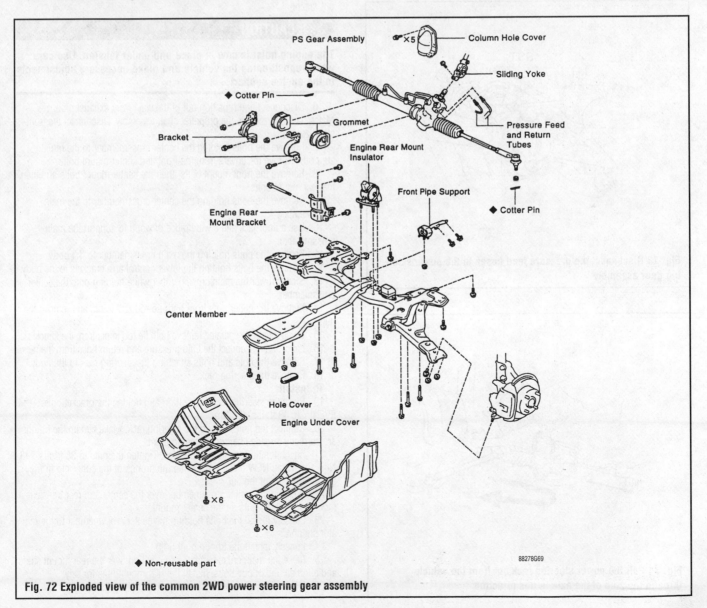

◆ Non-reusable part

88278G69

Fig. 72 Exploded view of the common 2WD power steering gear assembly

7. On some models it may be necessary to remove the left and right lower control arms.

8. Disconnect universal joint from the gear housing. Place matchmarks before removing set bolts.

9. Place a drain pan below the power steering rack assembly. Clean the area around the line fittings on the rack.

10. Support the transaxle with a jack.

11. Remove the engine crossmember. Remove the front pipe support.

12. Remove the rear engine mount and bracket.

13. Label and disconnect the fluid pressure and return lines at the steering rack.

14. Remove the bolts and nuts holding the rack brackets to the body. It will be necessary to slightly raise and lower the rear of the transaxle to gain access to the bolts.

15. Remove the steering rack through the access hole. Slide the gear assembly to the right, then slide the assembly to the left and pull it out.

To install:

16. Place the steering rack in position through the access hole and install the retaining brackets to the body. Tighten the nuts and bolts EVENLY to 43 ft. lbs. (78 Nm).

17. Connect the fluid lines (always start the threads by hand before using a tool) to the steering rack.

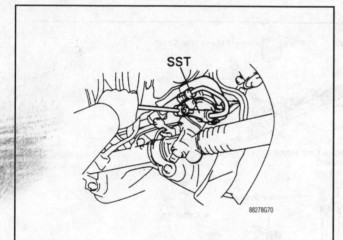

Fig. 73 Disconnect the pressure feed hoses to the power steering gear assembly

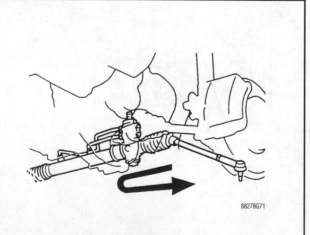

Fig. 74 Pull the power steering rack out from the vehicle through the side of the axle in this direction

18. Install the nut and bolt holding the rear engine mount to the mount bracket.

19. Reinstall the engine crossmember bolts and tighten.

20. Remove the jack from the transaxle.

21. Connect the tie rod ends to the knuckles. Tighten the nuts to 36 ft. lbs. (48 Nm) and install NEW cotter pins. Wrap the prongs of the cotter pin firmly around the flats of the nut.

22. Install the wheels and lower the vehicle to the ground.

23. Align matchmarks and connect universal joint to the steering gear housing. Tighten the upper and lower set bolts to 26 ft. lbs. (35 Nm).

24. Install the steering column cover. Add fluid and bleed the system.

25. Reconnect the negative battery cable. Check front wheel alignment.

4WD Models

▶ See Figure 75

1. Disconnect the negative battery cable. Remove the steering column cover.

2. Disconnect universal joint from the gear housing. Place matchmarks before removing set bolts.

3. Raise and safely support the vehicle.

4. Remove both front wheels and engine undercovers.

5. Install an engine support and tension it to support the engine without raising it.

✳✳ CAUTION

The engine hoist is now in place and under tension. Use care when repositioning the vehicle and make necessary adjustments to the engine support.

6. Disconnect and (position out of the way) front exhaust pipe. Matchmark and remove the propeller shaft assembly. Disconnect the front stabilizer bar.

7. Remove the bolts holding the center crossmember to the radiator support. Remove the covers from the front and center mount bolts.

8. Remove the front mount bolts, then the center mount bolts and then the rear mount bolts.

9. Remove the bolts holding the center crossmember to the main crossmember.

10. Use a floor jack and a wide piece of wood to support the main crossmember.

11. Remove the bolts holding the main crossmember to the body.

12. Remove the bolts holding the lower control arm brackets to the body.

13. Slowly lower the main crossmember while holding onto the center crossmember.

14. Remove the cotter pins from both tie rod ball joints and remove the nuts.

15. Using a tie rod separator, remove both tie rod joints from the knuckles.

16. Label and disconnect the fluid pressure and return lines from the rack.

17. Remove the nuts and bolts attaching the steering rack to the body.

18. Remove the steering rack.

To install:

19. Place the steering rack in position and tighten the bracket bolts EVENLY to 43 ft. lbs. (58 Nm).

20. Connect the fluid lines to the steering rack. Make certain the fittings are correctly threaded before tightening them.

21. Attach the tie rods to the knuckles. Tighten the nuts to 36 ft. lbs. (48 Nm) and install NEW cotter pins. Wrap the prongs of the cotter pin firmly around the flats of the nut.

22. Position the center crossmember over the center and rear transaxle mount studs; start nuts on the center mount.

23. Loosely install the bolts holding the center crossmember to the radiator support.

24. Loosely install the front mount bolts.

25. Raise the main crossmember into position over the rear mount studs and align all underbody bolts. Install the rear mount nuts loosely.

26. Install the main crossmember to underbody bolts loosely.

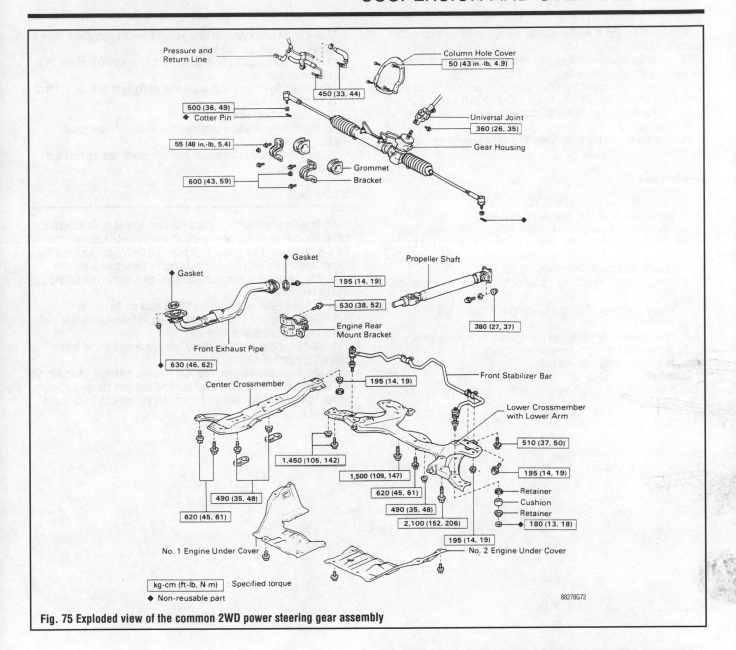

Fig. 75 Exploded view of the common 2WD power steering gear assembly

27. Install the lower control arm bracket bolts loosely.

28. Loosely install the bolts holding the center crossmember to the main crossmember.

29. The crossmembers, bolts and brackets should now all be in place and held loosely by their nuts and bolts. If any repositioning is necessary, do so now.

30. Tighten the components below in the order listed to the correct torque specification:
- Main crossmember to underbody bolts—152 ft. lbs. (206 Nm).
- Lower control arm bolts—105 ft. lbs. (142 Nm).
- Center crossmember to radiator support bolts—45 ft. lbs. (61 Nm).
- Front, center and rear mount bolts—45 ft. lbs. (61 Nm).

31. Install the covers on the front and center mount bolts. Install the propeller (align matchmarks) shaft assembly. Reconnect front exhaust pipe. Connect the front stabilizer bar.

32. Install the front wheels and engine undercovers.

33. Lower the vehicle to the ground. Align matchmarks and connect universal joint to the steering gear housing. Tighten the upper and lower set bolts to 26 ft. lbs.

34. Install the steering column cover. Add fluid and bleed the system.

35. Reconnect the negative battery cable. Check front wheel alignment.

Power Steering Pump

REMOVAL & INSTALLATION

4A-FE And 7A-FE Engines

1. Place a drain pan below the power steering pump.

2. Remove the clamp from the fluid return hose. Disconnect the pressure and return hoses at the pump. Plug the hoses and suspend them with the ends upward to prevent leakage.

3. Remove the adjusting bolt.

4. Remove the pivot bolt and remove the drive belt.

5. Remove the pump assembly.

6. Remove the pump bracket if necessary.

7. Remove the pulley if necessary. Be careful not to lose the small woodruff key (if so equipped) between the pulley and the shaft.

To install:

8. Install the pump pulley and the woodruff key. Tighten the pulley nut to 32 ft. lbs. (43 Nm).

9. Install the pump bracket and tighten the bolts to 29 ft. lbs. (39 Nm).

10. Place the pump in position and temporarily install the mounting bolts and adjusting bolt.

11. Install the drive belt. Adjust the belt to the proper tension. Tighten all mounting and adjusting bolts.

12. Connect the pressure and return lines to the pump. Tighten the banjo fitting to 40 ft. lbs. (54 Nm). Install the clamp on the return hose.

13. Fill the reservoir to the proper level with power steering fluid and bleed the system.

14. After the vehicle has been driven for about an hour, double check the belt adjustment.

4A-GE Engine

1. Place a drain pan below the pump.

2. Remove the air cleaner assembly if necessary.

3. Disconnect the return hose from the pump, then disconnect the pressure hose. Plug the lines immediately to prevent fluid loss and contamination.

4. Remove the splash shield under the engine.

5. Remove the pulley nut. Push down on the drive belt to prevent the pulley from turning.

6. Loosen the idler pulley nut an loosen the adjusting bolt.

7. Remove the drive belt.

8. Remove the pump pulley and the woodruff key if so equipped.

9. Remove the upper and lower mounting bolts.

10. Remove the power steering pump.

To install:

11. Install the pump onto the engine. Tighten the mounting bolts to 29 ft. lbs. (39 Nm).

12. Install the pump pulley and the woodruff key if so equipped. Tighten the pulley nut to 28 ft. lbs. (38 Nm).

13. Install the idler pulley bracket; tighten the 3 mounting bolts to 29 ft. lbs. (39 Nm) if necessary

14. Connect the pressure hose and tighten the fitting to 33 ft. lbs. (44 Nm).

15. Connect the return hose.

16. Adjust the belt to the proper tension.

17. Install the air cleaner if necessary and install the lower splash shield.

18. Fill the reservoir to the proper level with power steering fluid and bleed the system.

BLEEDING

Any time the power steering system has been opened or disassembled, the system must be bled to remove any air which may be trapped in the lines. Air will prevent the system from providing the correct pressures. The correct fluid level reading will not be obtained if the system is not bled.

1. With the engine running, turn the wheel all the way to the left and shut off the engine.

2. Add power steering fluid to the **COLD** mark on the indicator.

3. Start the engine and run. Stop the engine and recheck the fluid level. Add to the correct mark as needed.

4. Start the engine and bleed the system by turning the wheels fully from left to right 3 or 4 times.

5. Stop the engine and check the fluid level and condition. Fluid with air in it is a light tan color. This air must be eliminated from the system before normal operation can be obtained. Repeat until the correct fluid color and fluid level is obtained.

TORQUE SPECIFICATIONS

		US	METRIC
Front suspension			
1988-92:			
Ball joint-to-knuckle		94 ft. lbs.	127 Nm
Ball joint-to-lower control arm		105 ft. lbs.	142 Nm
Caliper-to-knuckle		65 ft. lbs.	88 Nm
Hub bearing lock nut		137 ft. lbs.	186 Nm
Shock absorber-to-knuckle		194 ft. lbs.	263 Nm
Suspension support nut	4A-GE	27 ft. lbs.	36 Nm
Suspension support-to-body		29 ft. lbs.	39 Nm
Tie rod end lock nut		41 ft. lbs.	56 Nm
Tie rod end-to-knuckle		36 ft. lbs.	49 Nm
Crossmember-to-body			
center bolts and nuts		45 ft. lbs.	61 Nm
front lower bolts		132 ft. lbs.	206 Nm
rear bolts		94 ft. lbs.	127 Nm
Stabilizer bar-to-lower arm			
	4A-F, 4A-FE	13 ft. lbs.	18 Nm
	4A-GE	26 ft. lbs.	35 Nm
Lower arm bushing nut		101 ft. lbs.	137 Nm
Lower arm-to-suspension crossmemeber (front)		174 ft. lbs.	235 Nm
Lower arm rear bracket-to-body			
lower arm side		94 ft. lbs.	127 Nm
small bolt and nut		14 ft. lbs.	19 Nm
stabilizer side		37 ft. lbs.	50 Nm
Wheel nut		76 ft. lbs.	103 Nm
1993-95:			
ABS harness-to-shock		49 inch lbs.	5 Nm
ABS sensor-to-axle carrier		71 inch lbs.	8 Nm
Axle hub nut		159 ft. lbs.	216 Nm
Ball joint-to-knuckle		87 ft. lbs.	118 Nm
Ball joint-to-lower control arm		105 ft. lbs.	142 Nm
Brake hose-to-shock absorber		22 ft. lbs.	29 Nm
Engine mount bracket-to-suspension crossmember		35 ft. lbs.	48 Nm
Knuckle-to-caliper		65 ft. lbs.	88 Nm
Knuckle-to-dust cover		74 inch lbs.	8 Nm
Lower arm bracket-to-body front side		108 ft. lbs.	147 Nm
Lower arm bracket-to-body nut		14 ft. lbs.	19 Nm
Lower arm bracket-to-body rear side		37 ft. lbs.	50 Nm
Lower arm front bolt		161 ft. lbs.	218 Nm
Shock absorber-to-knuckle		203 ft. lbs.	275 Nm
Stabilizer bar link set		33 ft. lbs.	44 Nm
Suspension crossmemember-to-body		152 ft. lbs.	206 Nm
Suspension crossmemember-to-suspension center member		45 ft. lbs.	61 Nm
Suspension upper support-to-body		29 ft. lbs.	39 Nm
Tie rod end lock nut		41 ft. lbs.	56 Nm
Tie rod end-to-knuckle		36 ft. lbs.	49 Nm

88278C20

TORQUE SPECIFICATIONS

Front suspension	US	METRIC
1996-97:		
ABS sensor-to-axle carrier	71 inch lbs.	8 Nm
Ball joint-to-lower arm	105 ft. lbs.	142 Nm
Brake hose-to-shock absorber	22 ft. lbs.	29 Nm
Ball joint-to-knuckle	87 ft. lbs.	118 Nm
Hub nut	76 ft. lbs.	103 Nm
Knuckle-to-dust cover	74 inch lbs.	8 Nm
Knuckle-to-shock absorber	203 ft. lbs.	275 Nm
Knuckle-to-tie rod end	36 ft. lbs.	49 Nm
Knuckle-to-caliper	65 ft. lbs.	88 Nm
Lower arm bracket-to-suspension crossmember	109 ft. lbs.	147 Nm
Lower arm front bolt	161 ft. lbs.	218 Nm
Lower arm rear bolt	129 ft. lbs.	175 Nm
Lower arm-to-stabilizer bar link	33 ft. lbs.	44 Nm
Stabilizer bar link-to-bar	33 ft. lbs.	44 Nm
Suspension center member-to-suspension crossmember	45 ft. lbs.	60 Nm
Suspension crossmember-to-body	167 ft. lbs.	225 Nm
Suspension crossmember-to-engine rear mounting	45 ft. lbs.	60 Nm
Suspension support-to-body	29 ft. lbs.	39 Nm
Tie rod end lock nut	41 ft. lbs.	56 Nm

Rear Suspension	US	METRIC
1988-91: 2WD		
Axle bearing lock nut	90 ft. lbs.	123 Nm
Axle carrier-to-shock	105 ft. lbs.	142 Nm
Axle hub-to-axle carrier	59 ft. lbs.	80 Nm
Strut rod-to-axle carrier	65 ft. lbs.	88 Nm
No. 1 and No. 2 arms-to-axle carrier	65 ft. lbs.	88 Nm
No. 1 arm-to-body	65 ft. lbs.	88 Nm
No. 2 arm-to-body	80 ft. lbs.	108 Nm
Strut rod-to-body	65 ft. lbs.	88 Nm
Stabilizer bar-to-stabilizer link	26 ft. lbs.	35 Nm
Stabilizer bar link-to-shock	26 ft. lbs.	35 Nm
Stabilizer bar bracket-to-body	14 ft. lbs.	19 Nm
Hub nut	76 ft. lbs.	103 Nm
1988-91: 4WD		
Differential carier-0to-axole housing	23 ft lbs.	31 Nm
Driveshaft-to-companion flange	27 ft. lbs.	37 Nm
Lateral control rod-to-body	72 ft. lbs.	98 Nm
Lower control arm-to-axle housing	72 ft. lbs.	98 Nm
Lower control arm-to-body	72 ft. lbs.	98 Nm
Rear axle shaft bearing retainer-to-backing plate	48 ft. lbs.	66 Nm
Shock absorber-to-0axle housing	27 ft. lbs.	37 Nm
Shock absorber-to-body	18 ft. lbs.	25 Nm
Upper control arm-to-body	72 ft. lbs.	98 Nm
Upper control arm-to-rear axle housing	72 ft. lbs.	98 Nm
Hub nut	76 ft. lbs.	103 Nm
Stabilizer bar bracket-to-axle housing	27 ft. lbs.	37 Nm
Stabilizer bar link-to-stabilizer bar	22 ft. lbs.	30 Nm

88278C21

TORQUE SPECIFICATIONS

Rear Suspension	US	METRIC
1992-97:		
ABS speed sensor-to-carrier	71 inch lbs.	8 Nm
Axle hub set bolt	59 ft. lbs.	80 Nm
Brace-to-body	29 ft. lbs.	39 Nm
Brake line	11 ft. lbs.	15 Nm
Hub nut	76 ft. lbs.	103 Nm
Lower control arm-to-axle carrier	92 ft. lbs.	125 Nm
Lower control arm-to-suspension member	92 ft. lbs.	125 Nm
No. 2 lower suspension arm lock nut	41 ft. lbs.	56 Nm
Shock-to-rear axle carrier	105 ft. lbs.	142 Nm
Stabilizer bar bracket-to-body	14 ft. lbs.	19 Nm
Stabilizer bar link-to-bar	33 ft. lbs.	44 Nm
Stabilizer bar link-to-shock	33 ft. lbs.	44 Nm
Strut rod-to-body	67 ft. lbs.	91 Nm
Suspension support-to-body	29 ft. lbs.	39 Nm

88278C22

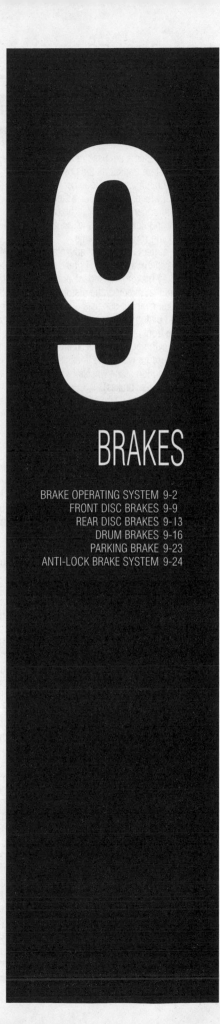

9

BRAKES

BRAKE OPERATING SYSTEM

Basic Operating Principles

Hydraulic systems are used to actuate the brakes of all modern automobiles. The system transports the power required to force the frictional surfaces of the braking system together from the pedal to the individual brake units at each wheel. A hydraulic system is used for two reasons.

First, fluid under pressure can be carried to all parts of an automobile by small pipes and flexible hoses without taking up a significant amount of room or posing routing problems.

Second, a great mechanical advantage can be given to the brake pedal end of the system, and the foot pressure required to actuate the brakes can be reduced by making the surface area of the master cylinder pistons smaller than that of any of the pistons in the wheel cylinders or calipers.

The master cylinder consists of a fluid reservoir along with a double cylinder and piston assembly. Double type master cylinders are designed to separate the front and rear braking systems hydraulically in case of a leak. The master cylinder coverts mechanical motion from the pedal into hydraulic pressure within the lines. This pressure is translated back into mechanical motion at the wheels by either the wheel cylinder (drum brakes) or the caliper (disc brakes).

Steel lines carry the brake fluid to a point on the vehicle's frame near each of the vehicle's wheels. The fluid is then carried to the calipers and wheel cylinders by flexible tubes in order to allow for suspension and steering movements.

In drum brake systems, each wheel cylinder contains two pistons, one at either end, which push outward in opposite directions and force the brake shoe into contact with the drum.

In disc brake systems, the cylinders are part of the calipers. At least one cylinder in each caliper is used to force the brake pads against the disc.

All pistons employ some type of seal, usually made of rubber, to minimize fluid leakage. A rubber dust boot seals the outer end of the cylinder against dust and dirt. The boot fits around the outer end of the piston on disc brake calipers, and around the brake actuating rod on wheel cylinders.

The hydraulic system operates as follows: When at rest, the entire system, from the piston(s) in the master cylinder to those in the wheel cylinders or calipers, is full of brake fluid. Upon application of the brake pedal, fluid trapped in front of the master cylinder piston(s) is forced through the lines to the wheel cylinders. Here, it forces the pistons outward, in the case of drum brakes, and inward toward the disc, in the case of disc brakes. The motion of the pistons is opposed by return springs mounted outside the cylinders in drum brakes, and by spring seals, in disc brakes.

Upon release of the brake pedal, a spring located inside the master cylinder immediately returns the master cylinder pistons to the normal position. The pistons contain check valves and the master cylinder has compensating ports drilled in it. These are uncovered as the pistons reach their normal position. The piston check valves allow fluid to flow toward the wheel cylinders or calipers as the pistons withdraw. Then, as the return springs force the brake pads or shoes into the released position, the excess fluid reservoir through the compensating ports. It is during the time the pedal is in the released position that any fluid that has leaked out of the system will be replaced through the compensating ports.

Dual circuit master cylinders employ two pistons, located one behind the other, in the same cylinder. The primary piston is actuated directly by mechanical linkage from the brake pedal through the power booster. The secondary piston is actuated by fluid trapped between the two pistons. If a leak develops in front of the secondary piston, it moves forward until it bottoms against the front of the master cylinder, and the fluid trapped between the pistons will operate the rear brakes. If the rear brakes develop a leak, the primary piston will move forward until direct contact with the secondary piston takes place, and it will force the secondary piston to actuate the front brakes. In either case, the brake pedal moves farther when the brakes are applied, and less braking power is available.

All dual circuit systems use a switch to warn the driver when only half of the brake system is operational. This switch is usually located in a valve body which is mounted on the firewall or the frame below the master cylinder. A hydraulic piston receives pressure from both circuits, each circuit's pressure being applied to one end of the piston. When the pressures are in balance, the piston remains stationary. When one circuit has a leak, however, the greater pressure in that circuit during application of the brakes will push the piston to one side, closing the switch and activating the brake warning light.

In disc brake systems, this valve body also contains a metering valve and, in some cases, a proportioning valve. The metering valve keeps pressure from traveling to the disc brakes on the front wheels until the brake shoes on the rear wheels have contacted the drums, ensuring that the front brakes will never be used alone. The proportioning valve controls the pressure to the rear brakes to lessen the chance of rear wheel lock-up during very hard braking.

Warning lights may be tested by depressing the brake pedal and holding it while opening one of the wheel cylinder bleeder screws. If this does not cause the light to go on, substitute a new lamp, make continuity checks, and, finally, replace the switch as necessary.

The hydraulic system may be checked for leaks by applying pressure to the pedal gradually and steadily. If the pedal sinks very slowly to the floor, the system has a leak. This is not to be confused with a springy or spongy feel due to the compression of air within the lines. If the system leaks, there will be a gradual change in the position of the pedal with a constant pressure.

Check for leaks along all lines and at wheel cylinders. If no external leaks are apparent, the problem is inside the master cylinder.

DISC BRAKES

Instead of the traditional expanding brakes that press outward against a circular drum, disc brake systems utilize a disc (rotor) with brake pads positioned on either side of it. An easily-seen analogy is the hand brake arrangement on a bicycle. The pads squeeze onto the rim of the bike wheel, slowing its motion. Automobile disc brakes use the identical principle but apply the braking effort to a separate disc instead of the wheel.

The disc (rotor) is a casting, usually equipped with cooling fins between the two braking surfaces. This enables air to circulate between the braking surfaces making them less sensitive to heat buildup and more resistant to fade. Dirt and water do not drastically affect braking action since contaminants are thrown off by the centrifugal action of the rotor or scraped off the by the pads. Also, the equal clamping action of the two brake pads tends to ensure uniform, straight line stops. Disc brakes are inherently self-adjusting. There are three general types of disc brake:

1. A fixed caliper.
2. A floating caliper.
3. A sliding caliper.

The fixed caliper design uses two pistons mounted on either side of the rotor (in each side of the caliper). The caliper is mounted rigidly and does not move.

The sliding and floating designs are quite similar. In fact, these two types are often lumped together. In both designs, the pad on the inside of the rotor is moved into contact with the rotor by hydraulic force. The caliper, which is not held in a fixed position, moves slightly, bringing the outside pad into contact with the rotor. There are various methods of attaching floating calipers. Some pivot at the bottom or top, and some slide on mounting bolts. In any event, the end result is the same.

DRUM BRAKES

Drum brakes employ two brake shoes mounted on a stationary backing plate. These shoes are positioned inside a circular drum which rotates with the wheel assembly. The shoes are held in place by springs. This allows them to slide toward the drums (when they are applied) while keeping the linings and drums in alignment. The shoes are actuated by a wheel cylinder which is mounted at the top of the backing plate. When the brakes are applied, hydraulic pressure forces the wheel cylinder's actuating links outward. Since these links bear directly against the top of the brake shoes, the tops of the shoes are then forced against the inner side of the drum. This action forces the bottoms of the two shoes to contact the brake drum by rotating the entire assembly slightly (known as servo action). When pressure within the wheel cylinder is relaxed, return springs pull the shoes back away from the drum.

Most modern drum brakes are designed to self-adjust themselves during application when the vehicle is moving in reverse. This motion causes both shoes to rotate very slightly with the drum, rocking an adjusting lever, thereby causing rotation of the adjusting screw. Some drum brake systems are designed to self-adjust during application whenever the brakes are applied. This on-board adjustment system reduces the need for maintenance adjustments and keeps both the brake function and pedal feel satisfactory.

POWER BOOSTERS

Virtually all modern vehicles use a vacuum assisted power brake system to multiply the braking force and reduce pedal effort. Since vacuum is always available when the engine is operating, the system is simple and efficient. A vacuum diaphragm is located on the front of the master cylinder and assists the driver in applying the brakes, reducing both the effort and travel he must put into moving the brake pedal.

The vacuum diaphragm housing is normally connected to the intake manifold by a vacuum hose. A check valve is placed at the point where the hose enters the diaphragm housing, so that during periods of low manifold vacuum brakes assist will not be lost.

Depressing the brake pedal closes off the vacuum source and allows atmospheric pressure to enter on one side of the diaphragm. This causes the master cylinder pistons to move and apply the brakes. When the brake pedal is released, vacuum is applied to both sides of the diaphragm and springs return the diaphragm and master cylinder pistons to the released position.

If the vacuum supply fails, the brake pedal rod will contact the end of the master cylinder actuator rod and the system will apply the brakes without any power assistance. The driver will notice that much higher pedal effort is needed to stop the car and that the pedal feels harder than usual.

Vacuum Leak Test

1. Operate the engine at idle without touching the brake pedal for at least one minute.
2. Turn off the engine and wait one minute.
3. Test for the presence of assist vacuum by depressing the brake pedal and releasing it several times. If vacuum is present in the system, light application will produce less and less pedal travel. If there is no vacuum, air is leaking into the system.

System Operation Test

1. With the engine **OFF**, pump the brake pedal until the supply vacuum is entirely gone.
2. Put light, steady pressure on the brake pedal.
3. Start the engine and let it idle. If the system is operating correctly, the brake pedal should fall toward the floor if the constant pressure is maintained.

Power brake systems may be tested for hydraulic leaks just as ordinary systems are tested.

Brake Light Switch

REMOVAL & INSTALLATION

The brake light switch is located in the driver's compartment behind the brake pedal.
1. Disconnect the negative battery cable.
2. Remove the instrument lower finish panel and the air duct if required to gain access to the stoplight switch.

3. Disconnect the stoplight switch wiring
4. Remove the switch mounting nut, then slide the switch from the mounting bracket on the pedal.
To install:
5. Install the switch into the mounting bracket and adjust.
6. Attach the switch wiring and connect the negative battery cable.
7. Depress the brake pedal and verify that the brake lights illuminate.
8. Install the air duct and the lower finish panel, if removed.

Master Cylinder

REMOVAL & INSTALLATION

▶ **See Figure 1**

The brake master cylinder is located in the engine compartment and usually attached to a brake booster on the driver's side of the vehicle.

➡**Before the master cylinder is reinstalled, the brake booster pushrod must be adjusted. This adjustment requires the use of factory special tool SST No. 09737–00010 or its equivalent.**

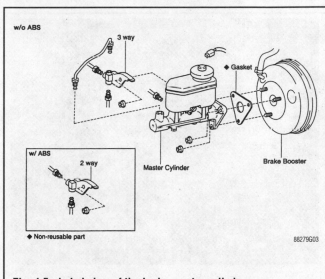

Fig. 1 Exploded view of the brake master cylinder

Disconnect the level sensor wiring from the cap, then remove the cap

1. Open the hood and disconnect the level warning switch wiring.
2. Disconnect the negative battery cable.
3. Remove the cap from the master cylinder and drain the fluid out with a syringe. Deposit the fluid into a container.

✳✳ WARNING

Do not allow the fluid to touch the painted surface of your vehicle, if so wash off the fluid immediately.

4. Disconnect the brake tubes from the master cylinder. Drain the fluid from the lines into the container. Plug the lines to prevent fluid from leaking onto and damaging painted surfaces or the entry of moisture into the brake system.
5. Remove the three nuts that attach the master cylinder and 3-way union to the brake booster.
6. Remove the master cylinder from the booster studs. Remove and discard the old gasket. The 2-way (w/ABS) or 3-way (wo/ABS) should come off with the cylinder.

To install:
7. Clean the brake booster gasket and the master cylinder flange surfaces. Install a new gasket for the master cylinder onto the brake booster.

88279P30

Using an extension, loosen and remove the cylinder retaining bolts

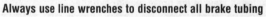

88279P27

Always use line wrenches to disconnect all brake tubing

88279P31

Carefully move aside the union to allow enough room to pull the master cylinder from the brake booster

88279P28

Carefully, without bending the line move it to the side of the cylinder

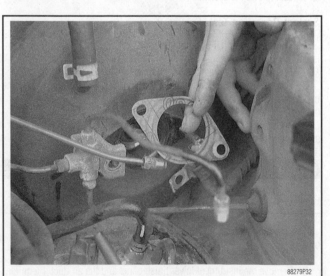

88279P32

Discard the old gasket and install a new one prior to installation

8. Adjust the length of the brake booster push rod as follows:

a. Set the special tool on the master cylinder with the gasket and lower the pin of the tool until it lightly contacts the piston.

b. Turn the special tool upside-down and position it onto the booster.

c. Measure the clearance between the booster push rod and the pin head of the tool. There must be zero clearance. To obtain zero clearance, adjust the push rod length until the push rod just contacts the head of the pin.

9. Before installing the master cylinder, make sure that the **UP** mark is in the correct position. Install the master cylinder over the mounting studs and tighten the three nuts to 9 ft. lbs. (13 Nm).

10. Connect the tubes to the master cylinder outlet plugs and tighten the union nuts to 11 ft. lbs. (15 Nm).

11. Connect the level warning switch wiring.

12. Fill the brake fluid reservoir to the proper level with clean brake fluid and bleed the brake system as described in this Section.

✳✳ WARNING

Clean, high quality brake fluid is essential to the safe and proper operation of the brake system. You should always buy the highest quality brake fluid that is available. If the brake fluid becomes contaminated, drain and flush the system, then refill the master cylinder with new fluid. Never reuse any brake fluid. Any brake fluid that is removed from the system should be discarded.

13. Check for leaks. Check and/or adjust the brake pedal.

Power Brake Booster

REMOVAL & INSTALLATION

◆ See Figures 2 and 3

The brake booster is located on the driver's side of the vehicle attached to the firewall.

➡ Before the brake booster is reinstalled, the brake booster pushrod must be adjusted so that there is zero clearance between it and the master cylinder. This adjustment requires the use of factory special tool SST No. 09737–00010 or its equivalent.

1. If necessary, remove the instrument lower finish panel, air duct and floor mats to gain access to the brake booster linkage.

2. Remove the master cylinder from the vehicle.

3. Loosen the hose clamp and disconnect the vacuum hose from the booster.

4. From inside the passenger compartment, remove the pedal return spring, clip and the clevis pin with the locknut. Remove the four mounting nuts and the clevis.

5. Remove the resonator from the air hose.

6. On some models it may be necessary to remove the charcoal canister.

7. Remove the brake booster, clevis and discard the gasket.

To install:

8. Connect the clevis pin with locknut to the booster and install the brake booster with a new gasket.

9. If removed, install the charcoal canister. Install the resonator to the air hose.

10. Install the mounting nuts and tighten them to 9 ft. lbs. (13 Nm).

11. Insert the clevis pin through the clevis and the brake pedal. Secure the pin with the retaining clip.

12. Install the pedal return spring.

13. Adjust the length of the brake booster push rod as follows: set the special tool on the master cylinder with the gasket and lower the pin of the tool until it lightly contacts the position. Turn the special tool upside-down and position it onto the booster. Measure the clearance between the booster

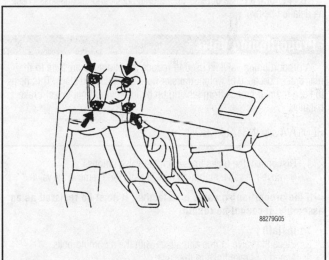

Fig. 3 Remove the 4 nuts and clevis pin retaining the brake booster to the inner panel

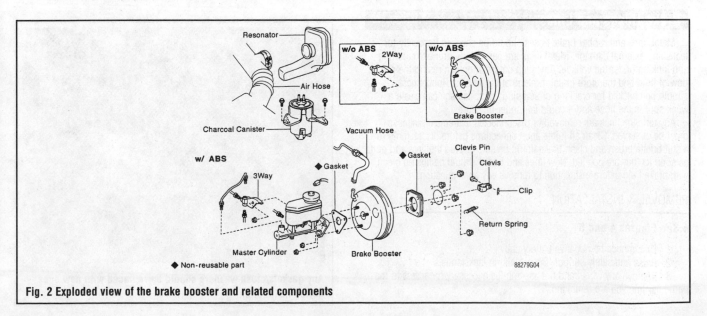

Fig. 2 Exploded view of the brake booster and related components

push rod and the pin head of the tool. There must be zero clearance. To obtain zero clearance, adjust the push rod length until the pushrod light contacts the head of the pin.

➡When adjusting the pushrod, depress the brake pedal enough so that the push rod sticks out.

14. Install the instrument lower finish panel and air duct.
15. Install the master cylinder and connect the vacuum hose to the brake booster.
16. Fill the brake fluid reservoir to the proper level with clean brake fluid and bleed the master cylinder and brake system as described in this Section.

✳✳ WARNING

Clean, high quality brake fluid is essential to the safe and proper operation of the brake system. You should always buy the highest quality brake fluid that is available. If the brake fluid becomes contaminated, drain and flush the system, then refill the master cylinder with new fluid. Never reuse any brake fluid. Any brake fluid that is removed from the system should be discarded.

17. Check for leaks. Check and/or adjust the brake pedal, then tighten the clevis lock nut to 19 ft. lbs. (25 Nm).
18. Perform a brake booster operational check and air tightness check as detailed below.

Proportioning Valve

A proportioning valve is used to reduce the hydraulic pressure to the rear brakes because of weight transfer during high speed stops. This helps to keep the rear brakes from locking up by improving front to rear brake balance.

REMOVAL & INSTALLATION

1. Disconnect the brake lines from the valve unions.
2. Remove the valve mounting bolt, if used, and remove the valve.

➡If the proportioning valve is defective, it must be replaced as an assembly; it cannot be rebuilt.

To install:
3. Place the valve in line and attach with the mounting bolts.
4. Attach all brake lines to the valve.
5. Bleed the brake system.
6. Test drive the vehicle for proper operation.

Brake Hoses and Lines

Metal lines and rubber brake hoses should be checked frequently for leaks and external damage. Metal lines are particularly prone to crushing and kinking under the vehicle. Any such deformation can restrict the proper flow of fluid and therefore impair braking at the wheels. Rubber hoses should be checked for cracking or scraping; such damage can create a weak spot in the hose and it could fail under pressure.

Any time the lines are removed or disconnected, extreme cleanliness must be observed. Clean all joints and connections before disassembly (use a stiff bristle brush and clean brake fluid); be sure to plug the lines and ports as soon as they are opened. New lines and hoses should be flushed clean with brake fluid before installation to remove any contamination.

REMOVAL & INSTALLATION

▸ See Figures 4 and 5

1. Disconnect the negative battery cable.
2. Raise and safely support the vehicle on jackstands.
3. Remove any wheel and tire assemblies necessary for access to the particular line you are removing.

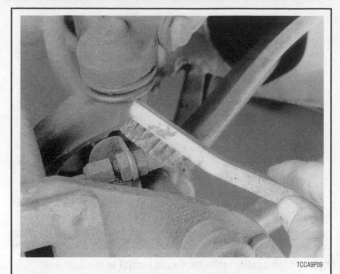
Use a brush to clean the fittings of any debris

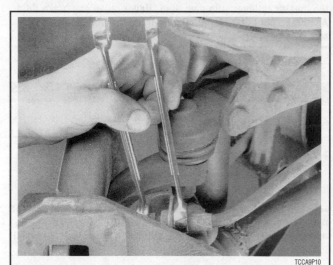
Use two wrenches to loosen the fitting. If available, use flare nut type wrenches

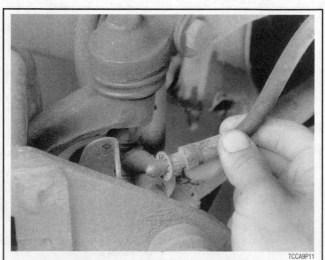
Any gaskets/crush washers should be replaced with new ones during installation

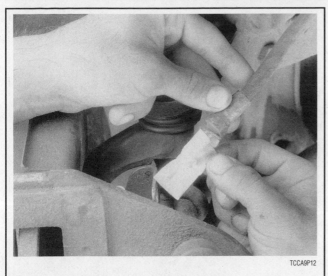

TCCA9P12

Tape or plug the line to prevent contamination

4. Thoroughly clean the surrounding area at the joints to be disconnected.

5. Place a suitable catch pan under the joint to be disconnected.

6. Using two wrenches (one to hold the joint and one to turn the fitting), disconnect the hose or line to be replaced.

7. Disconnect the other end of the line or hose, moving the drain pan if necessary. Always use a back-up wrench to avoid damaging the fitting.

8. Disconnect any retaining clips or brackets holding the line and remove the line from the vehicle.

➡ If the brake system is to remain open for more time than it takes to swap lines, tape or plug each remaining clip and port to keep contaminants out and fluid in.

To install:

9. Install the new line or hose, starting with the end farthest from the master cylinder. Connect the other end, then confirm that both fittings are correctly threaded and turn smoothly using finger pressure. Make sure the new line will not rub against any other part. Brake lines must be at least 1/2 in. (13mm) from the steering column and other moving parts. Any protective shielding or insulators must be reinstalled in the original location.

❊❊ WARNING

Make sure the hose is NOT kinked or touching any part of the frame or suspension after installation. These conditions may cause the hose to fail prematurely.

10. Using two wrenches as before, tighten each fitting.

11. Install any retaining clips or brackets on the lines.

12. If removed, install the wheel and tire assemblies, then carefully lower the vehicle to the ground.

13. Refill the brake master cylinder reservoir with clean, fresh brake fluid, meeting DOT 3 specifications. Properly bleed the brake system.

14. Connect the negative battery cable.

Bleeding the Brake System

❊❊ WARNING

Clean, high quality brake fluid is essential to the safe and proper operation of the brake system. You should always buy the highest quality brake fluid that is available. If the brake fluid becomes contaminated, drain and flush the system, then refill the master cylinder with new fluid. Never reuse any brake fluid. Any brake fluid that is removed from the system should be discarded.

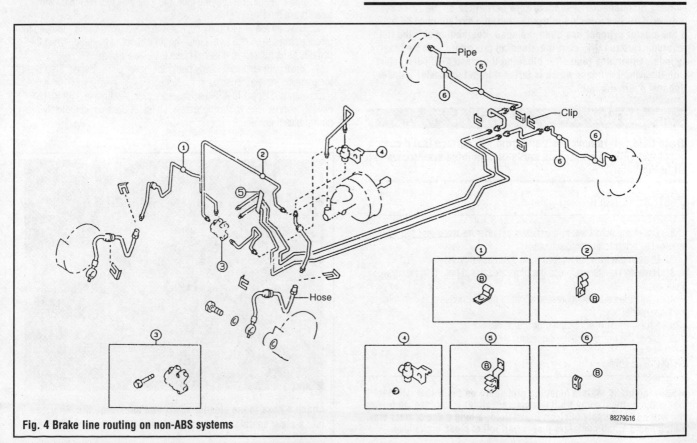

88279G16

Fig. 4 Brake line routing on non-ABS systems

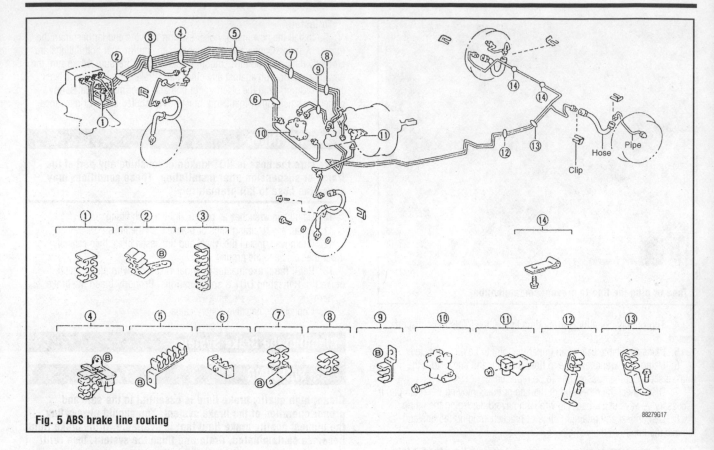

Fig. 5 ABS brake line routing

On vehicles equipped with anti-lock brakes (ABS), please refer to the appropriate procedure, later in this section.

➡**If any maintenance or repairs were performed on the brake system, or if air is suspected in the system, the system must be bled. If the master cylinder has been replaced, overhauled or if the fluid reservoir was run dry, start the bleeding procedure with the master cylinder. Otherwise (and after bleeding the master cylinder), start with the wheel cylinder which is farthest from the master cylinder (longest hydraulic line).**

✳✳ CAUTION

Brake fluid will remove the paint from any surface that it comes in contact with. If brake fluid spills on a painted surface, wash it off immediately.

MASTER CYLINDER

1. Check the fluid level in the master cylinder reservoir and add fluid as required to bring to the proper level.
2. Loosen the two brake tubes from the master cylinder.
3. Have an assistant depress the brake pedal and hold it in the down position.
4. While the pedal is depressed, tighten the fluid lines and then release the brake pedal.
5. Repeat the procedure three or four times.
6. Bleed the brake system, if needed.

BRAKE SYSTEM

➡**Start the brake system bleeding procedure on the wheel cylinder that is the furthest away from the master cylinder. To bleed the brakes you will need a supply of clean brake fluid, a long piece of clear vinyl tubing and a small container that is half full of clean brake fluid.**

1. Clean all the dirt and grease from the bleeder plugs and remove the protective caps. Connect one end of a clear vinyl tube to the fitting.
2. Insert the other end of the tube into a jar which is half filled with clean brake fluid.
3. Have an assistant slowly depress the brake pedal while you open the bleeder plug ⅓–½ of a turn. Fluid should run out of the tube. When the pedal is at its full range of travel, close the bleeder plug.
4. Have your assistant slowly pump the brake pedal. Repeat Step 3 until there are no more air bubbles in the fluid.
5. Repeat Steps 1 to 4 for each bleeder plug. Add brake fluid to the master cylinder reservoir as necessary, so that it does not completely drain during bleeding.

Attach a hose to the bleeder screw and submerge the other end into a clear container to catch the brake fluid

FRONT DISC BRAKES

❄❄ CAUTION

Brake pads may contain asbestos, which has been determined to be a cancer causing agent. Never clean the brake surfaces with compressed air! Avoid inhaling any dust from any brake surfaces. When cleaning brake surfaces, use a commercially available brake cleaning fluid.

Brake Pads

REMOVAL & INSTALLATION

▶ **See Figure 6**

1. Raise and support the vehicle safely.
2. Remove the wheels.
3. Siphon a sufficient quantity of brake fluid from the master cylinder reservoir to prevent any brake fluid from overflowing the master cylinder when removing or installing new pads. This is necessary as the piston must be forced into the caliper bore to provide sufficient clearance when installing the new pads.
4. Grasp the caliper from behind and carefully pull it to seat the piston in its bolt.
5. Loosen and remove the 2 caliper mounting pins (bolts) and then remove the caliper assembly. Position it aside. Do not disconnect the brake line.
6. Slide out the old brake pads along with any anti-squeal shims, springs, pad wear indicators and pad support plates. Make sure to note the position of all assorted pad hardware.

To install:

7. Check the brake disc (rotor) for thickness and run-out. Inspect the caliper and piston assembly for breaks, cracks, fluid seepage or other damage. Overhaul or replace as necessary.
8. Install the 4 pad support plates into the torque plate.
9. Install the pad wear indicators onto the pads. Be sure the arrow on the indicator plate is pointing in the direction of rotation.

88279P01

Remove the two upper and lower caliper mounting bolts

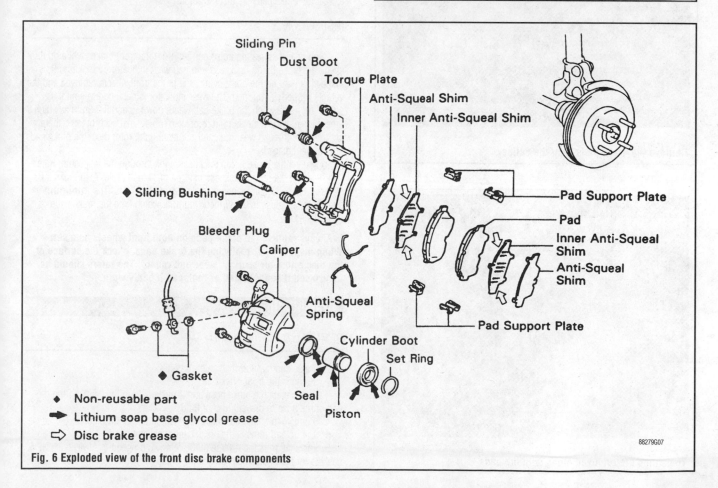

- ◆ Non-reusable part
- ➜ Lithium soap base glycol grease
- ➪ Disc brake grease

88279G07

Fig. 6 Exploded view of the front disc brake components

Pull the caliper away from the rotor

88279P02

Remove the brake pads from the caliper

88279P03

The shims are removed along with the pads

88279P04

Using pliers, remove the spring clips

88279P05

10. Install the anti-squeal shims on the outside of each pad. Do not allow oil or grease to get on the rubbing face of the pads, then install the pad assemblies into the torque plate. Install 2 anti-squeal springs.

11. Position the caliper back down over the pads. If it won't fit, use a C-clamp or a special tool and carefully force the piston into its bore.

12. Install and tighten the caliper mounting bolts to 18 ft. lbs. (25 Nm) on 1988–92 models and 25 ft. lbs. (34 Nm) on the 1993–97 models.

13. Install the wheels and lower the vehicle. Check the brake fluid level. Before moving the vehicle, make sure to pump the brake pedal a few times to seat the brake pads against the rotors.

INSPECTION

If you hear a squealing noise coming from the front brakes while driving, check the brake lining thickness and pad wear indicator by looking into the inspection hole on the brake cylinder with the front wheels removed and the vehicle properly supported. The wear indicator is designed to emit the squealing noise when the brake pad wears down to about 2.5mm at which time the pad wear plate and the rotor disc rub against each other. If there are traces of the pad wear indicator contacting the rotor disc, the brake pads should be replaced.

To inspect the brake lining thickness, look through the inspection hole and measure the lining thickness using a machinists rule. Also looks for signs of uneven wear. Standard thickness is 10–12mm. The **minimum** allowable thickness is 0.039 inch (1mm) at which time the brake pads must be replaced.

➡️**Always replace the brake pads on both front wheels as a set. When inspecting or replacing the brake pads, check the surface of the disc rotors for scoring, wear and runout. The rotors should be resurfaced if badly scored or replaced if badly worn.**

Brake Caliper

REMOVAL & INSTALLATION

1. Raise and support the vehicle safely.
2. Remove the front wheels.
3. Disconnect the brake hose and 2 gaskets from the caliper. Plug the end of the hose to prevent loss of fluid.
4. Remove the bolts that attach the caliper to the torque plate.
5. Lift up and remove the brake caliper assembly.
6. Installation is the reverse of the removal procedure. Always use NEW gaskets for the brake hose. Grease the brake caliper slides and bolts with

Lithium grease or equivalent. Install and tighten the caliper mounting bolts to 18 ft. lbs. (25 Nm) on 1990–92 vehicles and 25 ft. lbs. (34 Nm) on the 1993 vehicle. Fill and bleed the system. Before moving the vehicle, make sure to pump the brake pedal a few times to seat the pads against the rotors.

OVERHAUL

▶ See Figures 7 thru 14

➡Some vehicles may be equipped dual piston calipers. The procedure to overhaul the caliper is essentially the same with the exception of multiple pistons, O-rings and dust boots.

1. Remove the caliper from the vehicle and place on a clean workbench.

✳✳ CAUTION

NEVER place your fingers in front of the pistons in an attempt to catch or protect the pistons when applying compressed air. This could result in personal injury!

➡Depending upon the vehicle, there are two different ways to remove the piston from the caliper. Refer to the brake pad replacement procedure to make sure you have the correct procedure for your vehicle.

2. The first method is as follows:
   a. Stuff a shop towel or a block of wood into the caliper to catch the piston.
   b. Remove the caliper piston using compressed air applied into the caliper inlet hole. Inspect the piston for scoring, nicks, corrosion and/or worn or damaged chrome plating. The piston must be replaced if any of these conditions are found.
3. For the second method, you must rotate the piston to retract it from the caliper.
4. If equipped, remove the anti-rattle clip.
5. Use a prytool to remove the caliper boot, being careful not to scratch the housing bore.
6. Remove the piston seals from the groove in the caliper bore.
7. Carefully loosen the brake bleeder valve cap and valve from the caliper housing.
8. Inspect the caliper bores, pistons and mounting threads for scoring or excessive wear.

Fig. 7 For some types of calipers, use compressed air to drive the piston out of the caliper, but make sure to keep your fingers clear

Fig. 9 On some vehicles, you must remove the anti-rattle clip

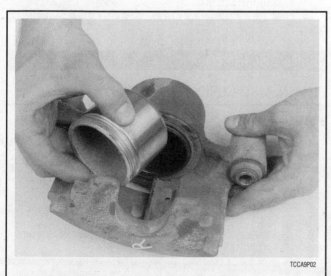
Fig. 8 Withdraw the piston from the caliper bore

Fig. 10 Use a prytool to carefully pry around the edge of the boot . . .

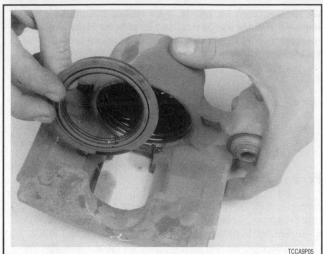

Fig. 11 . . . then remove the boot from the caliper housing, taking care not to score or damage the bore

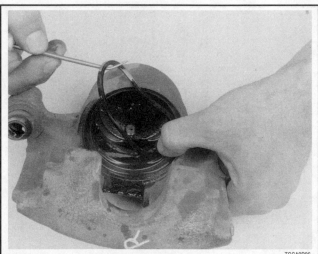

Fig. 12 Use extreme caution when removing the piston seal; DO NOT scratch the caliper bore

Fig. 13 Use the proper size driving tool and a mallet to properly seal the boots in the caliper housing

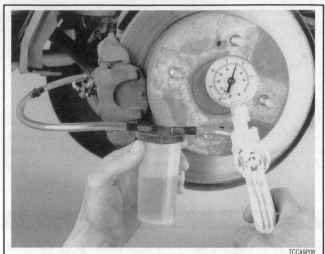

Fig. 14 There are tools, such as this Mighty-Vac, available to assist in proper brake system bleeding

9. Use crocus cloth to polish out light corrosion from the piston and bore.
10. Clean all parts with denatured alcohol and dry with compressed air.

To assemble:

11. Lubricate and install the bleeder valve and cap.
12. Install the new seals into the caliper bore grooves, making sure they are not twisted.
13. Lubricate the piston bore.
14. Install the pistons and boots into the bores of the calipers and push to the bottom of the bores.
15. Use a suitable driving tool to seat the boots in the housing.
16. Install the caliper in the vehicle.
17. Install the wheel and tire assembly, then carefully lower the vehicle.

❊❊ WARNING

Clean, high quality brake fluid is essential to the safe and proper operation of the brake system. You should always buy the highest quality brake fluid that is available. If the brake fluid becomes contaminated, drain and flush the system, then refill the master cylinder with new fluid. Never reuse any brake fluid. Any brake fluid that is removed from the system should be discarded.

18. Properly bleed the brake system.
19. Pump the brake pedal a few times, and check the brake system for leaks.

Brake Disc (Rotor)

REMOVAL & INSTALLATION

▶ **See Figure 15**

1. Loosen the front wheel lugs slightly, then raise and safely support the front of the vehicle. Remove the front wheel(s) and temporarily attach the rotor disc with two of the wheel lug nuts.
2. Remove and position aside the brake caliper. Unbolt and remove the torque plate from the steering knuckle.
3. Remove the two wheel nuts and pull the brake disc from the axle hub.

To install:

4. Position the new rotor disc onto the axle hub and reinstall the two wheel nuts temporarily.
5. Install the torque plate onto the steering knuckle. Tighten the plate bolts to 65 ft. lbs. (88 Nm). Install the brake caliper assembly-refer to the necessary service procedure.

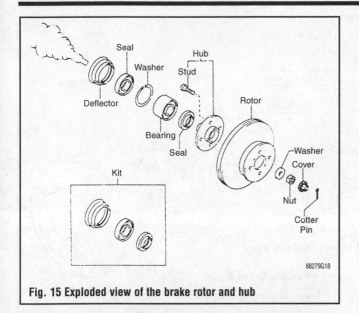

Fig. 15 Exploded view of the brake rotor and hub

Next, pull the disc off the hub

Insert bolts into the disc and evenly tighten them to allow the rotor to come off the hub

6. Remove the wheel lug nuts and install the front wheels. Secure the wheel lugs. Before moving the vehicle, make sure to pump the brake pedal a few times to seat the brake pads against the rotors.

INSPECTION

➡**The brake disc rotors should be refinished on a brake lathe, when replacing the front brake pads for the brake pads to wear properly.**

Examine the brake disc. If It Is worn, warped or scored, it must be replaced. Check the thickness of the brake disc against the specifications given in the Brake Specifications Chart. If it is below specifications, replace it. Use a micrometer to measure the thickness.

The disc run-out should be measured before the disc is removed and again, after the disc is installed. Use a dial indicator mounted on a magnet type stand to determine runout. Position the dial so the stylus is 0.039 inch (10mm) from the outer edge of the rotor disc. Check the run-out specification of brake disc against the specifications given in the Brake Specifications Chart. If run-out exceeds the specification, replace the brake disc.

➡**Be sure that the front hub bearing play is with specifications. If it is not, an inaccurate run-out reading may be obtained.**

REAR DISC BRAKES

✳✳ CAUTION

Brake pads may contain asbestos, which has been determined to be a cancer causing agent. Never clean the brake surfaces with compressed air! Avoid inhaling any dust from any brake surface. When cleaning brake surfaces, use a commercially available brake cleaning fluid.

Brake Pads

REMOVAL & INSTALLATION

◗ **See Figure 16**

1. Raise and safely support the rear of the vehicle on jackstands. Block the front wheels.
2. Siphon a sufficient quantity of brake fluid from the master cylinder reservoir to prevent the brake fluid from overflowing the master cylinder

when removing or installing the brake pads. This is necessary as the piston must be forced into the cylinder bore to provide sufficient clearance to install the new brake pads.

3. Remove the wheel, then reinstall 2 lug nuts finger tight to hold the disc in place.

➡**Disassemble brakes one wheel at a time. This will prevent parts confusion and also prevent the opposite caliper piston from popping out during pad installation.**

4. Remove the mounting (lower) bolt from the torque plate. Do not remove the caliper from the main (upper) pin. Do not disconnect the brake hose.
5. Lift the caliper from the bottom so that it hinges upward on the upper pin. Use a piece of wire to hold the caliper up. Do not allow the brake hose to become twisted or kinked during this operation.
6. Remove the brake pads with their shims, springs and support plates.
To install:
7. Check the rotor thickness and run-out. Refer to the Specifications Chart at the end of this section.
8. Install pad support plates to the lower sides of the torque plate.

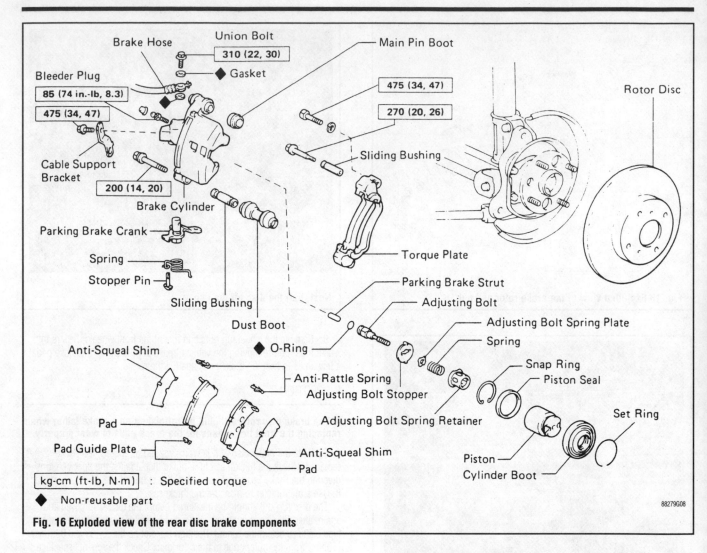

Fig. 16 Exploded view of the rear disc brake components

9. Install anti-rattle springs to the upper side of the torque plate.
10. Install a new anti-squeal shim to the back of each pad and install the pads on the torque plate. Install the pads so that the wear indicator is at the top side.
11. Using a special tool SST 09719–14020 or its equivalent to slowly turn the caliper piston clockwise while pressing it into the bore until it locks.
12. Lower the caliper so that the pad protrusion fits into the piston stopper groove. Insert the cylinder carefully so the boot is not wedged.
13. Install the mounting bolt and tighten it to 14 ft. lbs. (20 Nm).
14. Install the rear wheels.
15. Adjust the parking brake automatic adjuster by depressing brake pedal several times. Refer to rear caliper removal and installation service procedures.
16. Lower the car to the ground and fill the master cylinder reservoir to the correct level. Road test the vehicle for proper operation.

INSPECTION

If you hear a squealing noise coming from the rear brakes while driving, check the brake lining thickness and pad wear indicator by looking into the inspection hole on the brake cylinder with the rear wheels removed and the vehicle properly supported. The wear indicator is designed to emit the squealing noise when the brake pad wears down to 2.5mm at which time the brake pad wear plate and the rotor disc rub against each other. If there are traces of the pad wear indicator contacting the rotor disc, the brake pads should be replaced.

To inspect the brake lining thickness, look through the inspection hole and measure the lining thickness using a machinists rule. Also looks for signs of uneven wear. Standard thickness is 10mm. The **minimum** allowable thickness is 0.039 inch (1.0mm), at which time the brake pads must be replaced.

→**Always replace the brake pads on both rear wheels as a set. The brake disc rotors should be refinished on a brake lathe, when replacing the rear brake pads for the brake pads to wear properly.**

Brake Caliper

REMOVAL & INSTALLATION

1. Raise and safely support the rear of the vehicle on jackstands. Block the front wheels. Remove the rear wheels and install two lug nuts hand tight to hold the rotor in place.
2. Place a container under the caliper assembly to catch spillage. Disconnect the union bolt (and remove gaskets) holding the brake hose to the caliper. Plug or tape the hose immediately.
3. Disconnect parking brake cable from the caliper assembly.
4. Remove the caliper mounting bolts. Remove the brake caliper.
To install:
5. Install brake pads in the caliper if necessary.
6. Connect the parking brake cable.
7. Install the caliper so that the pad protrusion fits into the piston stopper groove. Insert the cylinder carefully so the boot is not wedged.
8. Install the mounting bolts and tighten it to 14 ft. lbs. (20 Nm).
9. Install the parking brake clip.
10. Connect the brake hose to the caliper, install new gaskets. Tighten the union bolt to 22 ft. lbs. (29 Nm).
11. Install the rear wheels.
12. Fill the brake reservoir with brake fluid and bleed brake system.

Clean, high quality brake fluid is essential to the safe and proper operation of the brake system. You should always buy the highest quality brake fluid that is available. If the brake fluid becomes contaminated, drain and flush the system, then refill the master cylinder with new fluid. Never reuse any brake fluid. Any brake fluid that is removed from the system should be discarded.

13. Adjust the parking brake lever travel as follows:
   a. Pull the parking brake lever a few times.
   b. Release the parking brake lever.
   c. Depress the brake pedal several times and adjust the rear brakes automatically.
   d. Check that the parking brake crank touches the stopper pin.
   e. Pull the parking brake lever all the way up and count the number of clicks. The correct specification for parking brake lever travel is at 44.1 lbs. of pull 5–8 clicks. If necessary adjust the parking brake lever travel at the parking brake lever assembly.

OVERHAUL

➡ **The use of the correct special tools or their equivalent is REQUIRED for this procedure.**

1. Remove the slide bushings and dust boots.
2. Remove the set ring and dust boot from the caliper piston.
3. Remove the caliper piston (turn piston counterclockwise and remove) from the bolt.
4. Remove the seal from the inside of the caliper bolt.
5. Install a special tool SST 09756-00010 or its equivalent onto the adjusting bolt and lightly tighten it with a 14mm socket. Do not overtighten the tool; damage to the spring may result.

❋❋ WARNING

Always use this tool during disassembly. The spring may fly out, causing personal injury and/or damage to the caliper bore.

6. Remove the snapring from the caliper bore.
7. Carefully remove the adjusting bolt and disassemble it.
8. Remove the parking brake strut.
9. Remove the cable support bracket, then remove the torsion spring from the parking brake crank.
10. Remove the parking brake crank from the caliper.
11. Remove the parking brake crank boot by tapping it lightly on the metal portion of the boot. Do not remove the boot unless it is to be replaced.
12. Use a pin punch to tap out the stopper pin.
13. Check all the parts for wear, scoring, deterioration, cracking or other abnormal conditions. Corrosion—generally caused by water in the system —will appear as white deposits on the metal. Pay close attention to the condition of the inside of the caliper bore and the outside of the piston. Any sign of corrosion or scoring requires new parts; do not attempt to clean or resurface either face.
14. The caliper overhaul kit will, at minimum, contain new seals and dust boots. A good kit will contain a new piston as well, but you may have to buy the piston separately. Any time the caliper is disassembled, a new piston is highly recommended in addition to the new seals.
15. Clean all the components to be reused with an aerosol brake solvent and dry them thoroughly. Take any steps necessary to eliminate moisture or water vapor from the parts.
16. Coat all the caliper components with fresh brake fluid from a new can.

➡ **Some repair kits come with special assembly lubricant for the piston and seal. Use this lubricant according to directions with the kit.**

17. Install the stopper pin into the caliper until the pin extends 1 inch (25mm).
18. Install the parking brake crank boot. Use a 24mm socket to tap the boot to the caliper.

19. Install the parking brake crank onto the caliper. Make certain the crank boot is securely matched to the groove of the crank seal.
20. Install the cable support bracket. Press the surface of the bracket flush against the wall of the caliper and tighten the bolt to 34 ft. lbs. (46 Nm).
21. Check that the clearance between the parking brake crank and the cable support is 6mm.
22. Install the torsion spring.
23. Inspect the crank sub-assembly, making sure it touches the stopper pin.
24. Install the parking brake strut. Before adjusting the strut, adjust the rollers of the needle roller bearing so they do not catch on the caliper bore.
25. Install a new O-ring on the adjusting bolt.
26. Install the stopper, plate, spring, and spring retainer onto the adjusting bolt. Using a special tool or equivalent hand tighten the assembly. Make certain the inscribed portion of the stopper faces upward. Align the notches of the spring retainer with the notches of the stopper.
27. Install the adjusting bolt assembly into the cylinder.
28. Install snapring into the bore. Make certain the gap in the ring faces toward the bleeder side.
29. Pull up on the adjusting bolt by hand to make certain it does not move.
30. Move the parking brake crank by hand and make certain adjusting bolt moves smoothly.
31. Install a new piston seal in the caliper bore.
32. Install the piston into the caliper bore. Using a special tool or its equivalent, slowly screw the piston clockwise until it will not descend any further.
33. Align the center of the piston stopper groove with the positioning marks of the caliper bore.
34. Install the piston dust boot and its set ring.
35. Install a new boot on the main (upper) caliper pin. Use a 21mm socket to press in the new boot.
36. Install the slide bushings and boots onto the caliper.

Brake Disc (Rotor)

REMOVAL & INSTALLATION

1. Loosen the rear wheel lugs slightly, then raise and safely support the rear of the vehicle. Remove the rear wheel(s) and temporarily attach the rotor disc with two of the wheel lug nuts.
2. Remove and position aside the brake caliper. Unbolt and remove the torque plate from the axle carrier.
3. Remove the two wheel nuts and pull the brake disc from the axle hub.
To install:
4. Position the new rotor disc onto the axle hub and reinstall the two wheel nuts temporarily.
5. Install the torque plate onto the axle carrier. Tighten the plate bolts to 34 ft. lbs. (46 Nm). Install the brake caliper assembly-refer to the necessary service procedure.
6. Remove the wheel lug nuts and install the rear wheels. Secure the wheel lugs. Before moving the vehicle, make sure to pump the brake pedal a few times to seat the brake pads against the rotors.

➡ **The brake disc rotors should be refinished on a brake lathe, when replacing the rear brake pads for the brake pads to wear properly.**

INSPECTION

Examine the brake disc. If it is worn, warped or scored, it must be replaced. Check the thickness of the brake disc against the specifications given in the Brake Specifications Chart. If it is below specifications, replace it. Use a micrometer to measure the thickness.

The disc run-out should be measured before the disc is removed and again, after the disc is installed. Use a dial indicator mounted on a magnet type stand to determine runout. Position the dial so the stylus is 0.039 inch (10mm) from the outer edge of the rotor disc. Check the run-out specification of brake disc against the specifications given in the Brake Specifications Chart. If run-out exceeds the specification, replace the brake disc.

DRUM BRAKES

REAR BRAKE DRUM COMPONENTS

1. Wheel cylinder
2. Pin
3. Cup

4. Hold-down spring
5. Front shoe
6. Rear shoe

7. Anchor spring
8. Adjuster

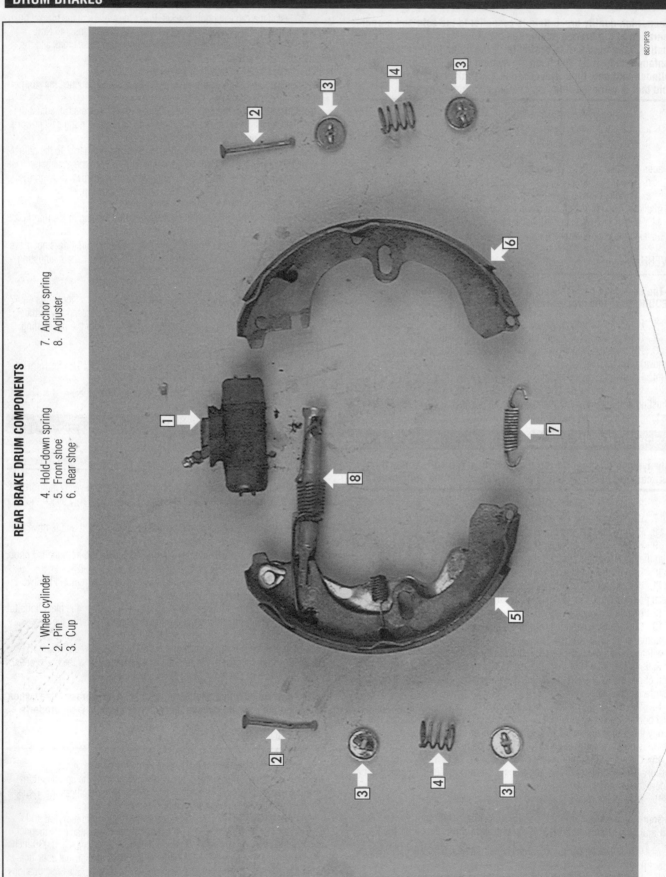

Brake shoes may contain asbestos, which has been determined to be a cancer causing agent. Never clean the brake surfaces with compressed air! Avoid inhaling any dust from any brake surface. When cleaning brake surfaces, use a commercially available brake cleaning fluid.

Brake Drums

REMOVAL & INSTALLATION

1. Loosen the rear wheel lug nuts slightly. Release the parking brake.
2. Block the front wheels, raise the rear of the vehicle, and safely support it with jackstands.
3. Remove the wheel lug nuts and the wheel.
4. Tap the brake drum lightly with a rubber mallet to free the drum if resistance is felt. Sometimes brake drums are stubborn. If the drum is difficult to remove, perform the following: Insert the end of a bent wire (a coat hanger will do nicely) through the hole in the brake drum and hold the automatic adjusting lever away from the adjuster. Reduce the brake shoe adjustment by turning the adjuster bolt with a brake tool. The drum should now be loose enough to remove without much effort.

88279P08

The brake drum can be accessed after removing the wheel

To install:
5. Clean the drum and inspect it as detailed in this section.
6. If the adjuster was loosened to remove the brake drum, turn the adjuster bolt to adjust the length to the shortest possible amount.
7. Hold the brake drum so that the hole on the drum is aligned with the large hole on the axle carrier and install the drum.
8. Pull the parking lever all the way up until a clicking sound can no longer be heard. Check the clearance between brake shoes and brake drum if necessary.
9. Install the rear wheels, tighten the wheel lug nuts and lower the vehicle.
10. Retighten the wheel lug nuts and pump the brake pedal a few times before moving the vehicle.

INSPECTION

1. Remove the inspection hole plug from the backing plate, and with the aide of a flashlight, check the lining thickness. The minimum brake lining thickness is 0.039 inch (1.0mm). If the brake lining does not meet the minimum specification, replace the brake shoes as a set.
2. Remove the brake drum and clean it thoroughly.
3. Inspect the drum for scoring, cracks, grooves and out-of-roundness. Replace or refinish the brake drum, as required. Light scoring may be removed by dressing the drum with fine grit emery cloth. Heavy scoring will require the use of a brake drum lathe to turn or refinish the brake drum.
4. Using inside calipers or equivalent, measure the inside diameter of the brake drum. The standard inside diameter is 7.874 inch (200mm). The maximum inside diameter is 7.913 inch (201mm). If the brake drum exceeds the maximum diameter, replace it.

Brake Shoes

INSPECTION

1. Inspect all brake parts and springs for rust, wear and damage.
2. Measure the brake lining thickness. The minimum allowable thickness is 0.039 inch (1.0mm). If the lining does not meet the minimum specification, replace it.

➡**If one of the brake shoes needs to be replaced, replace all the rear shoes in order to maintain even braking.**

3. Measure inside diameter of the drum as detailed in this section.
4. Place the shoe into the brake drum and check that the lining is in proper contact with the drum's surface. If the contact is improper, repair the lining with a brake shoe grinder or replace the shoe.
5. To measure the clearance between brake shoe and parking brake lever, temporarily install the parking brake and automatic adjusting levers onto the rear shoe, using a new C-washer. With a feeler gauge, measure the clearance between the shoe and the lever. The clearance should be within 0.0138 inch (0-0.35mm). If the clearance is not as specified, use a shim to adjust it. When the clearance is correct, stake the C-washer with pliers.

REMOVAL & INSTALLATION

◗ **See Figures 17, 18 and 19**

The brake shoes are located behind the brake drum in the shape of a half moon. There are two brake shoes on each rear wheel.

➡**The brake drums should be refinished on a brake lathe, when replacing the rear brake shoes for the brake shoes to wear properly.**

1. Raise and support the vehicle safely. Remove the wheels.
2. Perform the brake drum removal procedure as previously detailed. Do one set of shoes at a time. Note the position and direction of each component part so that they may be reinstalled in the correct order.

➡**Do not depress the brake pedal once the brake drum has been removed.**

3. Carefully unhook the return spring from the leading (front) brake shoe. Grasp the hold-down spring pin with pliers and turn it until its in line with the slot in the hold-down spring. Remove the hold-down spring and the pin. Pull out the brake shoe and unhook the anchor spring from the lower edge.
4. Remove the hold-down spring from the trailing (rear) shoe. Pull the shoe out with the adjuster strut, automatic adjuster assembly and springs attached and disconnect the parking brake cable. Unhook the return spring and then remove the adjusting strut. Remove the anchor spring.
5. Remove the adjusting strut. Unhook the adjusting lever spring from the rear shoe and then remove the automatic adjuster assembly by popping out the C-clip.
To install:
6. Inspect the shoes for signs of unusual wear or scoring.
7. Check the wheel cylinder for any sign of fluid seepage or frozen pistons.

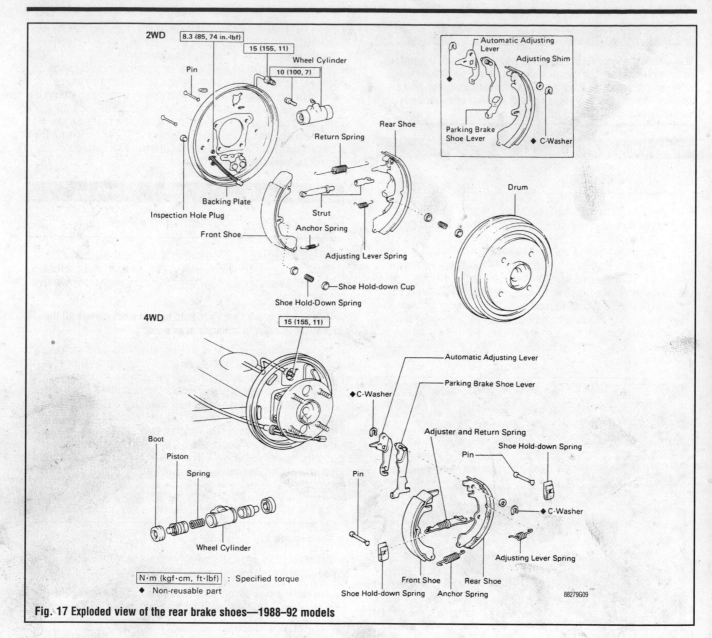

Fig. 17 Exploded view of the rear brake shoes—1988–92 models

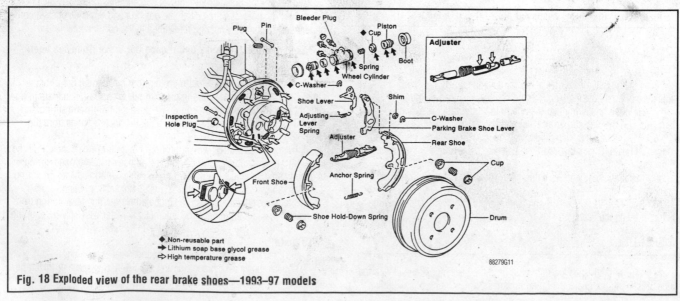

Fig. 18 Exploded view of the rear brake shoes—1993–97 models

Press the drum off the hub by using two bolts

Pull on both shoes and remove the assembly from the backing plate

While pushing in and turning, remove the hold-down springs

Disconnect the parking cable from the shoe

Remove the return spring. This can be done with pliers

8. Clean and inspect the brake backing plate and all other components. Check that the brake drum inner diameter is within specified limits. Lubricate the backing plate bosses and the anchor plate.

9. Mount the automatic adjuster assembly onto a new rear brake shoe. Make sure the C-clip fits properly. Connect the adjusting strut/return spring and then install the adjusting spring.

10. Connect the parking brake cable to the rear shoe and then position the shoe so the lower end rides in the anchor plate and the upper end is against the boot in the wheel cylinder. Install the pin and the hold-down spring. Rotate the pin so the crimped edge is held by the retainer.

11. Install the anchor spring between the front and rear shoes and then stretch the spring enough so the front shoe will fit as the rear did in Step 10. Install the hold-down spring and pin. Connect the return spring/adjusting strut between the 2 shoes and connect it so it rides freely.

12. Check that the automatic adjuster is operating properly; the adjusting bolt should turn when the parking brake lever (in the brake assembly) is moved. Adjust the strut as short as possible and then install the brake drum. Set and release the parking brake fully several times.

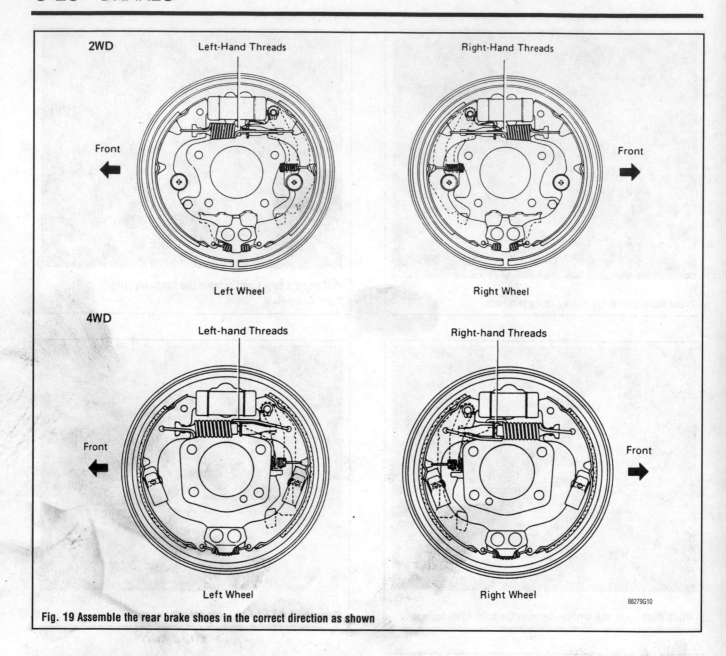

Fig. 19 Assemble the rear brake shoes in the correct direction as shown

13. Check clearance between brake shoes and drum if necessary by measuring the brake drum inside diameter and diameter of the brake shoes. Check that the difference between the diameters is the correct rear brake shoe clearance. The rear brake shoe clearance specification is 0.024 inch (0.6mm) for all vehicles.

14. Install the wheel and lower the vehicle. Bleed brake system if necessary. Check the level of brake fluid in the master cylinder. Road test the vehicle for proper operation.

ADJUSTMENTS

Most models are equipped with self-adjusting rear drum brakes. Under normal conditions, adjustment of the rear brake shoes should not be necessary. However, if an initial adjustment is required insert the blade of a brake adjuster tool or a screw driver into the hole in the brake drum and turn the adjuster slowly. The tension is set correctly if the tire and wheel assembly will rotate approximately 3 times when spun with moderate force. Do not over adjust the brake shoes. Before adjusting the rear drum brake shoes, make sure emergency brake is in the OFF position, and all cables are free.

Wheel Cylinder

REMOVAL & INSTALLATION

The wheel cylinder is located on the upper portion of the brake unit. The brake shoes attach on either side of it.

1. Raise and safely support the vehicle.
2. Remove the brake drums and brake shoes-refer to the necessary service procedures.
3. Working from behind the backing plate, disconnect the hydraulic line from the wheel cylinder, use a line wrench or equivalent.
4. Remove the bolts retaining the wheel cylinder and withdraw the cylinder.

To install:

5. Attach the wheel cylinder to the backing plate. Torque the bolts to 7 ft. lbs.
6. Connect the hydraulic line to the wheel cylinder and tighten it.
7. Install the brake shoes and drums. Make all the necessary adjustments.

From behind the backing plate, unsecure the hydraulic line with a brake tool

Pull the line away from the back of the wheel cylinder

Remove the wheel cylinder mounting bolts and withdraw it from the vehicle

Clean, high quality brake fluid is essential to the safe and proper operation of the brake system. You should always buy the highest quality brake fluid that is available. If the brake fluid becomes contaminated, drain and flush the system, then refill the master cylinder with new fluid. Never reuse any brake fluid. Any brake fluid that is removed from the system should be discarded.

8. Fill the master cylinder to the proper level with clean brake fluid bleed the brake system. Check the brake system for leaks.

OVERHAUL

Wheel cylinder overhaul kits may be available, but often at little or no savings over a reconditioned wheel cylinder. It often makes sense with these components to substitute a new or reconditioned part instead of attempting an overhaul.

If no replacement is available, or you would prefer to overhaul your wheel cylinders, the following procedure may be used. When rebuilding

Remove the outer boots from the wheel cylinder

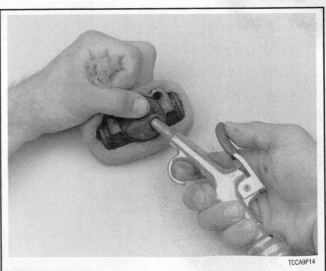

Compressed air can be used to remove the pistons and seals

TCCA9P15

Remove the pistons, cup seals and spring from the cylinder

TCCA9P18

Once cleaned and inspected, the wheel cylinder is ready for assembly

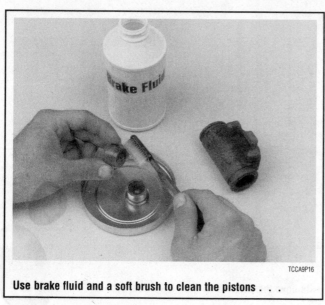

TCCA9P16

Use brake fluid and a soft brush to clean the pistons . . .

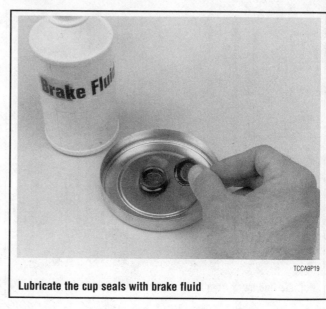

TCCA9P19

Lubricate the cup seals with brake fluid

TCCA9P17

. . . and the bore of the wheel cylinder

TCCA9P20

Install the spring, then the cup seals in the bore

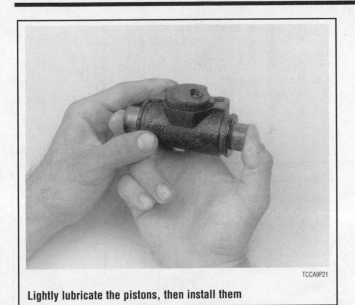

Lightly lubricate the pistons, then install them

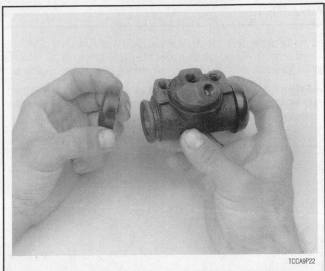

The boots can now be installed over the wheel cylinder ends

and installing wheel cylinders, avoid getting any contaminants into the system. Always use clean, new, high quality brake fluid. If dirty or improper fluid has been used, it will be necessary to drain the entire system, flush the system with proper brake fluid, replace all rubber components, then refill and bleed the system.

1. Remove the wheel cylinder from the vehicle and place on a clean workbench.
2. First remove and discard the old rubber boots, then withdraw the pistons. Piston cylinders are equipped with seals and a spring assembly, all located behind the pistons in the cylinder bore.
3. Remove the remaining inner components, seals and spring assembly. Compressed air may be useful in removing these components. If no compressed air is available, be VERY careful not to score the wheel cylinder bore when removing parts from it. Discard all components for which replacements were supplied in the rebuild kit.
4. Wash the cylinder and metal parts in denatured alcohol or clean brake fluid.

PARKING BRAKE

Cables

REMOVAL & INSTALLATION

♦ **See Figure 20**

➡**This procedure is general service procedure (no factory service procedure are given). Modify the service steps as required.**

1. Elevate and safely support the car. If only the rear wheels are elevated, block the front wheels. Release the parking brake after the car is supported.
2. Remove the rear wheel(s).
3. If equipped with drum brakes, remove the brake drum and remove the brake shoes.
4. If equipped with disc brakes, remove the clip from the parking brake cable and remove the cable from the caliper assembly.
5. If equipped with drum brakes, remove the parking brake retaining bolts at the backing plate.
6. Remove any exhaust heat shields which interfere with the removal of the cable.

※※ WARNING

Never use a mineral-based solvent such as gasoline, kerosene or paint thinner for cleaning purposes. These solvents will swell rubber components and quickly deteriorate them.

5. Allow the parts to air dry or use compressed air. Do not use rags for cleaning, since lint will remain in the cylinder bore.
6. Inspect the piston and replace it if it shows scratches.
7. Lubricate the cylinder bore and seals using clean brake fluid.
8. Position the spring assembly.
9. Install the inner seals, then the pistons.
10. Insert the new boots into the counterbores by hand. Do not lubricate the boots.
11. Install the wheel cylinder.

7. Remove the 2 cable clamps.
8. Disconnect the cable retainer.
9. Remove the cable from the equalizer (yoke).
To install:
10. Fit the end of the new cable into the equalizer and make certain it is properly seated.
11. Install the cable retainer, and, working along the length of the cable, install the clamps.

➡**Make certain the cable is properly routed and does not contain any sharp bends or kinks.**

12. Feed the cable through the backing plate and install the retaining bolts.
13. If equipped with disc brakes, connect the cable to the arm and install the clip.
14. If equipped with drum brakes, re-install the shoes. The cable will be connected to the shoes during the installation process.
15. Reinstall the wheel(s) and lower the car to the ground. Adjust the parking brake.

ADJUSTMENT

Pull the parking brake lever all the way up and count the number of clicks. The correct range is 4–7 clicks rear drum brake type and 5–8 clicks rear disc brake type for full application. A system which is too tight or too loose requires adjustment.

➡**Before adjusting the parking brake cable, make certain that the rear brake shoe or rear brake pad clearance is correct. Refer to the necessary service procedures.**

1. Remove the center console box.
2. At the rear of the handbrake lever, loosen the locknut on the brake cable.
3. Turn the adjusting nut until the parking brake travel is correct.
4. Tighten the locknut.
5. Reinstall the console.

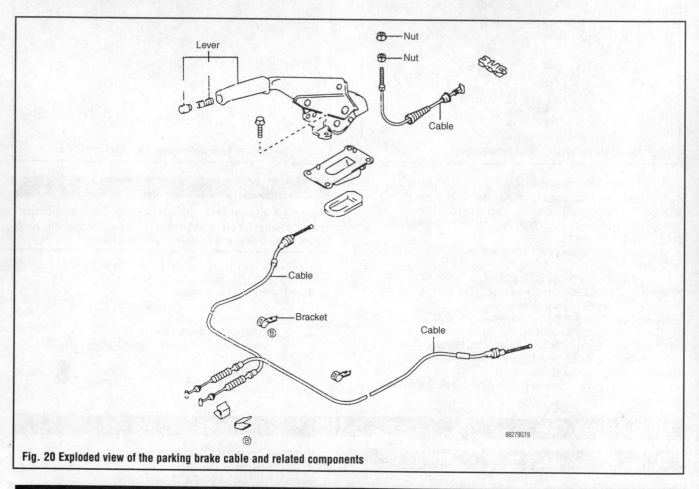

Fig. 20 Exploded view of the parking brake cable and related components

88279G19

ANTI-LOCK BRAKE SYSTEM

General Information

▶ **See Figure 21**

The system is designed to prevent wheel lock-up during hard or emergency braking. By preventing wheel lock-up, maximum braking effort is maintained while preventing loss of directional control. Additionally, some steering capability is maintained during the stop. The ABS system will operate regardless of road surface conditions.

There are conditions for which the ABS system provides no benefit. Hydroplaning is possible when the tires ride on a film of water, losing contact with the paved surface. This renders the vehicle totally uncontrollable until road contact is regained. Extreme steering maneuvers at high speed or cornering beyond the limits of tire adhesion can result in skidding which is independent of vehicle braking. For this reason, the system is named anti–lock rather than anti–skid.

Under normal braking conditions, the ABS system functions in the same manner as a standard brake system. The system is a combination of electrical and hydraulic components, working together to control the flow of brake fluid to the wheels when necessary.

The Anti-lock Brake System Computer (ABSC) is the electronic brain of the system, receiving and interpreting speed signals from the speed sensors. The ABSC will enter anti-lock mode when it senses impending wheel lock at any wheel and immediately controls the brake line pressure(s) to the affected wheel(s). The actuator assembly is separate from the master cylinder and booster. It contains the wheel circuit valves used to control the brake fluid pressure to each wheel circuit.

During anti-lock braking, line pressures are controlled or modulated by the rapid cycling of electronic valves within the actuator. These valves can allow pressures within the system to increase, remain constant or decrease depending on the needs of the moment as registered by the ABSC.

The operator may hear a popping or clicking sound as the pump and/or control valves cycle on and off during normal operation. The sounds are due to normal operation and are not indicative of a system problem. Under most conditions, the sounds are only faintly audible. If ABS is engaged, the operator may notice some pulsation in the body of the vehicle during a hard stop; this is generally due to suspension shudder as the brake pressures are altered rapidly and the forces transfer to the vehicle.

Although the ABS system prevents wheel lock–up under hard braking,

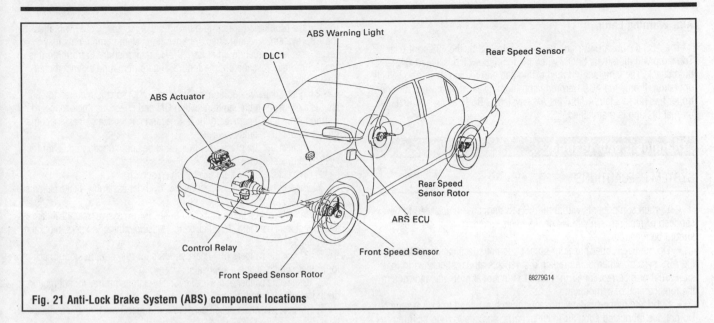

Fig. 21 Anti-Lock Brake System (ABS) component locations

as brake pressure increases, wheel slip is allowed to increase as well. This slip will result in some tire chirp during ABS operation. The sound should not be interpreted as lock–up but rather than as indication of the system holding the wheel(s) just outside the point of lock–up. Additionally, the final few feet of an ABS–engaged stop may be completed with the wheels locked; the system does not operate below 4 mph.

SYSTEM COMPONENTS

Wheel Speed Sensors

◆ See Figures 22 and 23

The speed of each wheel is monitored by a sensor. A toothed wheel (sensor rotor) rotates in front of the sensor, generating a small AC voltage which is transmitted to the ABS controller. The ABS computer compares the signals and reacts to rapid loss of wheel speed at a particular wheel by engaging the ABS system. Each speed sensor is individually removable. In most cases, the toothed wheels may be replaced if damaged, but disassembly of other components such as hub and knuckle, constant velocity joints or axles may be required.

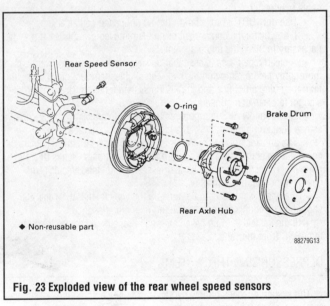

Fig. 23 Exploded view of the rear wheel speed sensors

ABS Controller

This computer-based unit interprets inputs from the speed sensors, the brake lights and the brake warning lamp circuit. After processing the inputs, the unit controls output electrical signals to the hydraulic control solenoids, causing them to increase, decrease or hold brake line pressures. Additionally, the controller oversees operation of the pump motor and the ABS warning lamp.

Additionally, the controller constantly monitors system signals, performs a system actuation test immediately after engine start-up and can assign and store diagnostic fault codes if any errors are noted.

ABS Actuator

Also called the hydraulic unit, the actuator contains the control solenoids for each brake circuit. The pump which maintains the system pressure during ABS braking is also within this unit. The control relay is mounted externally near the actuator. The ABS actuator can only be replaced as a unit; with the exception of the relay, individual components cannot be replaced.

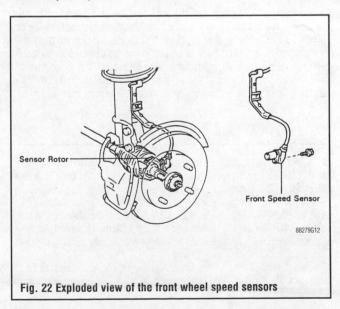

Fig. 22 Exploded view of the front wheel speed sensors

ABS Warning Lamp

The ABS dashboard warning lamp is controlled by the ABS controller. The lamp will illuminate briefly when the ignition switch is turned **ON** as a bulb check. The lamp should then extinguish and remain out during vehicle operation. If only the ABS warning lamp illuminates while driving, the controller has noted a fault within the ABS system. ABS function is halted, but normal braking is maintained.

Diagnosis and Testing

SYSTEM PRECAUTIONS

- Certain components within the ABS system are not intended to be serviced or repaired. Only those components with service procedures should be repaired.
- Do not use rubber hoses or other parts not specifically specified for the ABS system. When using repair kits, replace all parts included in the kit. Partial or incorrect repair may lead to functional problems and require the replacement of components.
- Lubricate rubber parts with clean, fresh brake fluid to ease assembly. Do not use lubricated shop air to clean parts; damage to rubber components may result.
- Use only DOT 3 brake fluid from an unopened container.
- If any hydraulic component or line is removed or replaced, it may be necessary to bleed the entire system.
- A clean repair area is essential. Always clean the reservoir and cap thoroughly before removing the cap. The slightest amount of dirt in the fluid may plug an orifice and impair the system function. Use denatured alcohol to clean components.
- Do not allow ABS components to come into contact with any substance containing mineral oil; this includes used shop rags.
- The anti-lock brake controller is a microprocessor similar to other computer units in the vehicle. Ensure that the ignition switch is **OFF** before removing or installing controller harnesses. Avoid static electricity discharge at or near the controller.
- If any arc welding is to be done on the vehicle, the ABS controller should be disconnected before welding operations begin.
- If the vehicle is to be baked after paint repairs, disconnect and remove the ABSC from the vehicle.

DEPRESSURIZING THE SYSTEM

The system operates on low hydraulic pressure and requires no special system depressurization prior to the opening of hydraulic lines or other system repairs. Simply verify the ignition switch is **OFF** and pump/motor is not running.

DIAGNOSTIC CODES

If a malfunction occurs, the system will identify the problem and the computer will assign and store a fault code for the fault(s). The dashboard warning lamp will be illuminated to inform the driver that a fault has been found.

During diagnostics, the system will transmit the stored code(s) by flashing the dashboard warning lamp. If two or more codes are stored, they will be displayed from lowest number to highest, regardless of the order of occurrence. The system does not display the diagnostic codes while the vehicle is running.

INITIAL CHECKS

Visual Inspection

Before diagnosing an apparent ABS problem, make absolutely certain that the normal braking system is in correct working order. Many common brake problems (dragging parking brake, seepage, etc.) will affect the ABS system. A visual check of specific system components may reveal problems creating an apparent ABS malfunction. Performing this inspection may reveal a simple failure, thus eliminating extended diagnostic time.

Also check battery condition; approximately 12 volts is required to operate the system. Turn the ignition switch **ON** and check that the dashboard warning lamp (ABS) comes on for 3-4 seconds. If the lamp does not come on, repair the fuse, bulb or wiring.

1. Inspect the tire pressures; they must be approximately equal for the system to operate correctly.
2. Inspect the brake fluid level in the reservoir.
3. Inspect brake lines, hoses, master cylinder assembly, brake calipers and cylinders for leakage.
4. Visually check brake lines and hoses for excessive wear, heat damage, punctures, contact with other parts, missing clips or holders, blockage or crimped.
5. Check the calipers or wheel cylinders for rust or corrosion. Check for proper sliding action if applicable.
6. Check the caliper and wheel cylinder pistons for freedom of motion during application and release.
7. Inspect the wheel speed sensors for proper mounting and connections.
8. Inspect the sensor wheels for broken teeth or poor mounting.
9. Inspect the wheels and tires on the vehicle. They must be of the same size and type to generate accurate speed signals.
10. Confirm the fault occurrence with the operator. Certain driver induced faults, such as not releasing the parking brake fully, will set a fault code and trigger the dash warning light(s). Excessive wheel spin on low-traction surfaces, high speed acceleration or riding the brake pedal may also set fault codes and trigger a warning lamp. These induced faults are not system failures but examples of vehicle performance outside the parameters of the control unit.
11. Many system shut-downs are due to loss of sensor signals to or from the controller. The most common cause is not a failed sensor but a loose, corroded or dirty connector. Incorrect adjustment of the wheel speed sensor will cause a loss of wheel speed signal. Check harness and component connectors carefully.

READING CODES

Turn the ignition **ON**, use a jumper wire to connect terminals Tc and E1 of the check connector or DLC1. Remove the short pin from the terminals of the DLC1.

If a fault code has been set, the dashboard warning lamp will begin to blink 4 seconds later. The number of flashes corresponds to the first digit of a 2-digit code; after a 1.5 second pause, the second digit is transmitted. If a second code is stored, it will be displayed after a 2.5 second pause. Once all codes have been displayed, the entire series will repeat after a 4 second pause. If no codes have been stored, the warning lamp will flash continuously every ½ second with no variation.

CLEARING DIAGNOSTIC CODES

With the system set to read codes (short pin disconnected and jumper wire in place), turn the ignition switch **ON**. Apply the brake pedal 8 or more times within 3 seconds.

After the rapid pedal application, the dash warning lamp should display constant flashing, indicating a normal system. If codes are still displayed, make certain the repairs made to the system are correct. Also inspect the brake light switch at the brake pedal for any binding or sticking.

Once the codes are cleared, disconnect the jumper wire. Reinstall the short pin. The dash warning lamp should go out.

DTC CHART

HINT: Using SST 09843-18020, connect the terminals Tc and E1, and remove the short pin.

If a malfunction code is displayed during the DTC check, check the circuit listed for that code.

DTC No.	Detection Item	Trouble area
11	Open circuit in ABS control (solenoid) relay circuit	• ABS control (solenoid) relay • Open or short in ABS control (solenoid) relay circuit • ECU
12	Short circuit in ABS control (solenoid) relay circuit	• ABS control (solenoid) relay • B+ short in ABS control (solenoid) relay circuit • ECU
13	Open circuit in ABS control (motor) relay circuit	• ABS control (motor) relay • Open or short in ABS control (motor) relay circuit • ECU
14	Short circuit in ABS control (motor) relay circuit	• ABS control (motor) relay • B+ short in ABS control (motor) relay circuit • ECU
21	Open or short circuit in 3-position solenoid circuit for right front wheel	• ABS actuator • Open or short in SFR circuit • ECU
22	Open or short circuit in 3-position solenoid circuit for left front wheel	• ABS actuator • Open or short in SFL circuit • ECU
23	Open or short circuit in 3-position solenoid circuit for right rear wheel	• ABS actuator • Open or short in SRR circuit • ECU
24	Open or short circuit in 3-position solenoid circuit for left rear wheel	• ABS actuator • Open or short in SRL circuit • ECU
31	Right front wheel speed sensor signal malfunction	• Right front, left front, right rear and left rear speed sensor • Open or short in each speed sensor circuit • ECU
32	Left front wheel speed sensor signal malfunction	
33	Right rear wheel speed sensor signal malfunction	
34	Left rear wheel speed sensor signal malfunction	
35	Open circuit in left front or right rear speed sensor circuit	• Open in left front or right rear speed sensor circuit • ECU
36	Open circuit in right front or left rear speed sensor circuit	• Open in right front or left rear speed sensor circuit • ECU
37	Faulty rear speed sensor rotor	• Rear axle hub • Right rear, left rear speed sensor • Wire harness for rear sensor system • ECU
41	Lower battery positive voltage or abnormally high battery positive voltage	• Battery • IC regulator • Open or short in power source circuit • ECU
51	Pump motor is locked Open in pump motor ground	• ABS pump motor
Always ON	Malfunction in ECU	• ECU

88279C20

DTC of Speed Sensor Check Function

Code No.	Diagnosis	Trouble area
71	Low output voltage of right front speed sensor	• Right front speed sensor • Sensor installation
72	Low output voltage of left front speed sensor	• Left front speed sensor • Sensor installation
73	Low output voltage of right rear speed sensor	• Right rear speed sensor • Sensor installation
74	Low output voltage of left rear speed sensor	• Left rear speed sensor • Sensor installation
75	Abnormal change in output voltage of right front speed sensor	• Right front speed sensor rotor
76	Abnormal change in output voltage of left front speed sensor	• Left front speed sensor rotor
77	Abnormal change in output voltage of right rear speed sensor	• Right rear speed sensor rotor
78	Abnormal change in output voltage of left rear speed sensor	• Left rear speed sensor rotor

88279C21

ABS Actuator

REMOVAL & INSTALLATION

▶ **See Figure 24**

1. Using a syringe or similar device, remove as much fluid as possible from the master cylinder reservoir.
2. Remove the washer tank and wheel well housing.

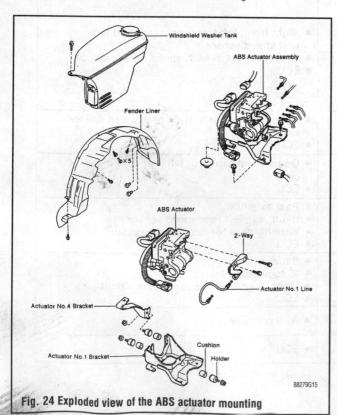

Fig. 24 Exploded view of the ABS actuator mounting

88279G15

3. Disconnect the electrical connectors at the actuator.
4. Using special tool 09751-36011 or equivalent, disconnect each brake line from the actuator assembly. Disconnect the brake line clamp from the strut tower.
5. Remove the nuts and bolts holding the actuator and bracket to the vehicle.
6. Remove the actuator unit with the bracket attached.

To install:

7. Install the bracket if removed and tighten the nuts to 48 inch lbs. (5.4 Nm).
8. Place the actuator into position. Tighten the retaining nuts to 48 inch lbs. (5.4 Nm). If the unit is held by bolts, tighten them to 14 ft. lbs. (19 Nm).
9. Connect the brake lines to the actuator, tightening them to 11 ft. lbs. (15 Nm). Install the brake line clamp at the strut tower.
10. Connect the wiring connectors. Install the washer tank and inner wheel well.
11. Fill the reservoir with brake fluid. Bleed the system.
12. Inspect the system for leakage, particularly at any line fitting which was loosened or disconnected.

Front Wheel Speed Sensors

REMOVAL & INSTALLATION

▶ **See Figure 22**

1. Raise and safely support the front of the vehicle.
2. Remove the tire and wheel. Remove the fender liner.
3. Disconnect the wheel speed sensor lead from the ABS harness. Remove any retaining bolts or clips holding the harness in place.

➡**Clips and retainers must be reinstalled in their exact original location. Take careful note of the position of each retainer and of the correct harness routing during removal.**

4. Remove the single bolt holding the speed sensor.
5. Carefully remove the sensor straight out of its mount. Do not subject the sensor to shock or vibration; protect the tip of the sensor at all times.

To install:

6. Fit the sensor into position. Make certain the sensor sits flush against the mounting surface; it must not be crooked.

7. Install the retaining bolt and tighten to 71 inch lbs. (8 Nm).

8. Route the sensor cable correctly and install the harness clips and retainers. Secure the harness clamp bolts to 49 inch lbs. (5 Nm). The cable must be in its original position and completely clear of moving components.

9. Connect the sensor cable to the ABS harness.

10. Install the wheel and tire. Attach and secure the fender liner.

11. Lower the vehicle to the ground.

Rear Wheel Speed Sensors

REMOVAL & INSTALLATION

▸ See Figure 23

1. Disconnect the negative battery cable. Remove the rear seat cushion, seat sideback and quarter trim, as required to gain access to the sensor harness connector.

2. Raise and safely support the rear of the vehicle. Remove the tire and wheel.

3. Disconnect the wheel speed sensor lead from the ABS harness. Remove any retaining bolts or clips holding the harness in place.

➡**Clips and retainers must be reinstalled in their exact original location. Take careful note of the position of each retainer and of the correct harness routing during removal.**

4. Remove the bolt(s) holding the speed sensor.

5. Carefully remove the sensor straight out of its mount. Do not subject the sensor to shock or vibration; protect the tip of the sensor at all times.

6. If necessary remove the rear axle hub.

To install:

7. Install the rear axle hub if removed and tighten to 59 ft. lbs. (80 Nm).

8. Before installation, make certain all traces of paint are removed from the hub carrier surface. A clean metal-to-metal contact is required. Fit the sensor into position. Make certain the sensor sits flush against the mounting surface; it must not be crooked.

9. Install the retaining bolt. Tighten the bolt to 71 inch lbs. (8 Nm).

10. Route the sensor cable correctly and install the harness clips and retainers. The cable must be in its original position and completely clear of moving components.

11. Connect the sensor cable to the ABS harness and secure the mounting bolts to 49 inch lbs. (5 Nm).

12. Install the wheel and tire.

13. Lower the vehicle to the ground.

Sensor Rotor Wheels

REMOVAL & INSTALLATION

All sensor rotor wheels are integral parts of either the driveshaft or the axle hub; if the ring is damaged, the axle hub or driveshaft must be replaced. Components are not interchangeable. Ring diameter and tooth spacing are critical to the correct operation of the system. Use only exact specified components when replacement is necessary.

Filling The System

The brake fluid reservoir is located on top of the master cylinder. While no special procedures are needed to fill the fluid, the reservoir cap and surrounding area must be wiped clean of all dirt and debris before removing the cap. The slightest dirt in the fluid can cause a system malfunction. Use only DOT 3 fluid from an unopened container. Use of old, polluted or non-approved fluid can seriously impair the function of the system.

BLEEDING THE SYSTEM

❄❄ WARNING

Clean, high quality brake fluid is essential to the safe and proper operation of the brake system. You should always buy the highest quality brake fluid that is available. If the brake fluid becomes contaminated, drain and flush the system, then refill the master cylinder with new fluid. Never reuse any brake fluid. Any brake fluid that is removed from the system should be discarded.

Bleeding is performed in the usual manner, using either a pressure bleeder or the 2-person manual method. If a pressure bleeder is used, it must be of the diaphragm type with an internal diaphragm separating the air chamber from the fluid. Tighten each bleeder plug to 74 inch lbs. (8 Nm).

Always begin the bleeding with the longest brake line, then the next longest, and so on. If the master cylinder has been repaired or if the reservoir has been emptied, the master cylinder will need to be bled before the individual lines and calipers. During any bleeding procedure, make certain to maintain the fluid level above the MIN line on the reservoir. When the bleeding procedure is complete, fill the reservoir to the MAX line before reinstalling the cap.

BRAKE SPECIFICATIONS
All measurements in inches unless noted

Year	Model	Master Cylinder Bore	Brake Disc Original Thickness	Brake Disc Minimum Thickness	Brake Disc Maximum Runout	Brake Drum Diameter Original Inside Diameter	Brake Drum Diameter Max. Wear Limit	Brake Drum Diameter Maximum Machine Diameter	Minimum Lining Thickness Front	Minimum Lining Thickness Rear
1988	Corolla	NA	0.709	0.669	0.0035	7.874	7.913	NA	0.039	0.039
	Corolla GT-S	NA	0.866 ①	0.827 ②	0.0035 ③	NA	NA	NA	NA	NA
1989	Corolla	NA	0.709	0.669	0.0035	7.874	7.913	NA	0.039	0.039
	Corolla GT-S	NA	0.866 ①	0.827 ②	0.0035 ③	NA	NA	NA	NA	NA
1990	Corolla	NA	0.709	0.669	0.0035	7.874	7.913	NA	0.039	0.039
	Corolla GT-S	NA	0.866 ①	0.827 ②	0.0035 ③	NA	NA	NA	NA	NA
1991	Corolla	NA	0.709	0.669	0.0035	7.874	7.913	NA	0.039	0.039
	Corolla GT-S	NA	0.866 ①	0.827 ②	0.0035 ③	NA	NA	NA	NA	NA
1992	Corolla	NA	0.709	0.787	0.0020	7.874	7.913	NA	0.039	0.039
1993	Corolla	NA	0.866	0.787	0.0020	7.874	7.913	NA	0.039	0.039
1994	Corolla	NA	0.866	0.787	0.0020	7.874	7.913	NA	0.039	0.039
1995	Corolla	NA	0.866	0.787	0.0020	7.874	7.913	NA	0.039	0.039
1996	Corolla	NA	0.866	0.787	0.0020	7.874	7.913	NA	0.039	0.039
1997	Corolla	NA	0.866	0.787	0.0020	7.874	7.913	NA	0.039	0.039

① Rear disc STD: 0.354 inch
② Rear disc Limit: 0.315 inch
③ Rear disc runout: 0.0039 inch

88279C01

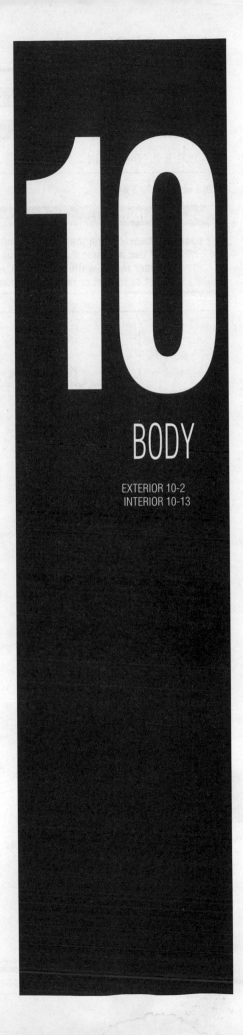

10

BODY

EXTERIOR

Doors

REMOVAL & INSTALLATION

♦ **See Figures 1, 2 and 3**

✷✷ WARNING

The doors are heavier than they appear. Support the door from the bottom and use a helper during removal and installation. Do not allow the door to sag while partially attached and do not subject the door to impact or twisting motions.

1. Disconnect the negative battery terminal.
2. If equipped with power door locks, windows or any other power option located on the door, remove the inner door panel and disconnect the electrical component.
3. Remove the wire harness retainers and extract the harness from the door.
4. Use a floor jack padded with rags or soft lumber to support the door at its lower midpoint. Use a felt tip marker to outline the hinge position on the door.
5. Disconnect the door check rod. To prevent the rod from falling inside the door, install the retainer into the hole in the end of the check rod.
6. Have a helper support the door, keeping it upright at all times. Remove the bolts holding the upper and lower hinge to the door.

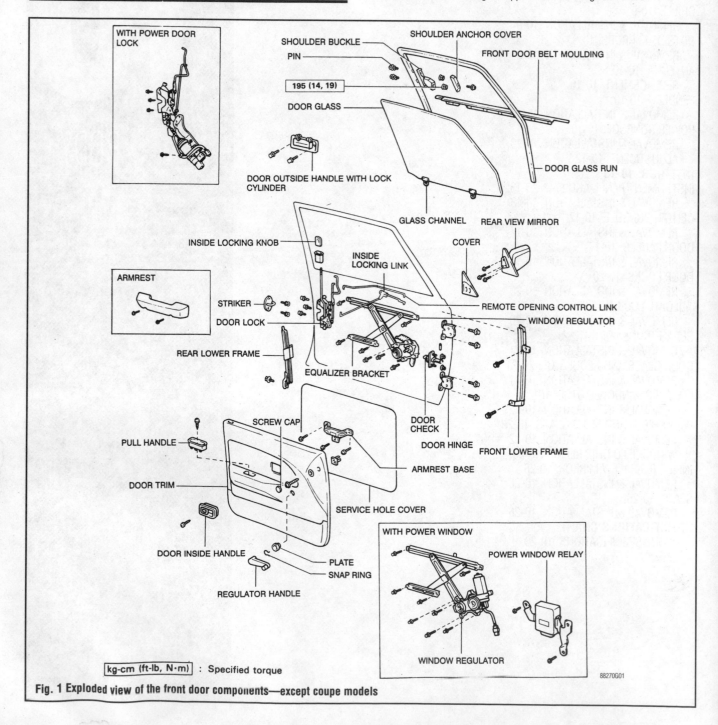

WITH POWER DOOR LOCK

SHOULDER BUCKLE
PIN
195 (14, 19)
DOOR GLASS

SHOULDER ANCHOR COVER
FRONT DOOR BELT MOULDING

DOOR GLASS RUN

DOOR OUTSIDE HANDLE WITH LOCK CYLINDER

GLASS CHANNEL
REAR VIEW MIRROR
COVER

INSIDE LOCKING KNOB

ARMREST

INSIDE LOCKING LINK

STRIKER
DOOR LOCK

REMOTE OPENING CONTROL LINK
WINDOW REGULATOR

REAR LOWER FRAME

EQUALIZER BRACKET

DOOR CHECK
DOOR HINGE
FRONT LOWER FRAME

SCREW CAP

PULL HANDLE

DOOR TRIM

ARMREST BASE

SERVICE HOLE COVER

DOOR INSIDE HANDLE

PLATE
SNAP RING

REGULATOR HANDLE

WITH POWER WINDOW

POWER WINDOW RELAY

WINDOW REGULATOR

88270G01

| kg-cm (ft-lb, N·m) | : Specified torque

Fig. 1 Exploded view of the front door components—except coupe models

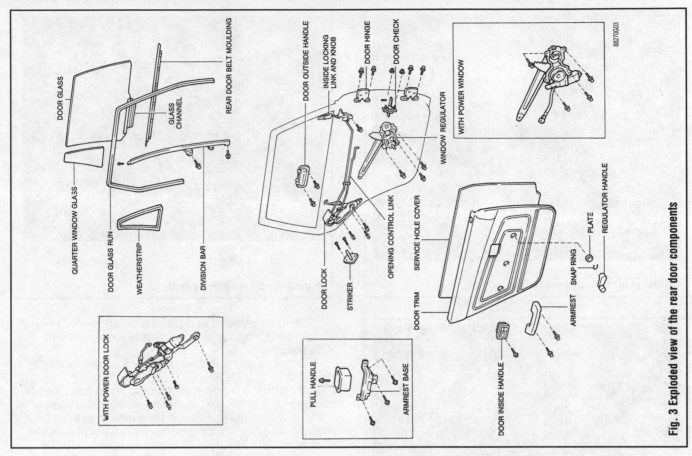

Fig. 3 Exploded view of the rear door components

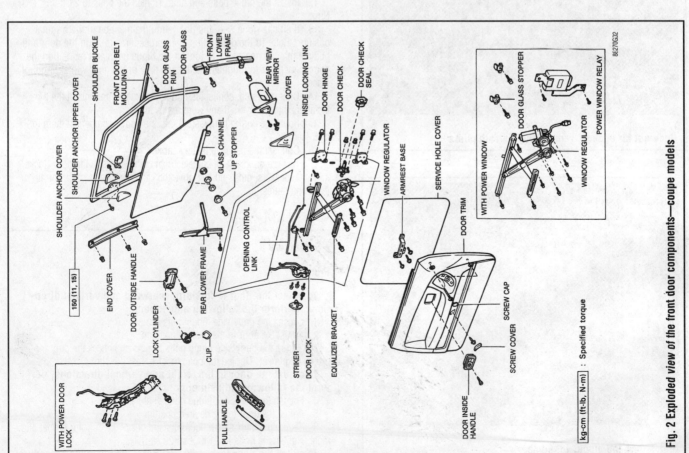

Fig. 2 Exploded view of the front door components—coupe models

Carefully tap the door check pin out

88270P12

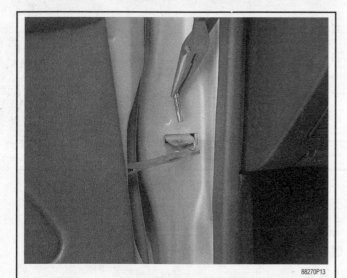

Once out far enough, remove the pin with pliers

88270P13

Matchmark the hinges to the door

88270P14

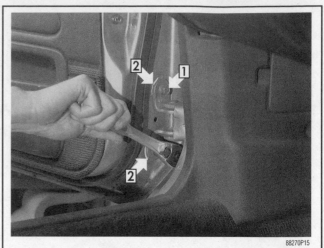

88270P15

1. Retaining bolts   2. Hinge matchmarks

Remove the hinge retaining bolts

7. Using two people, lift the door clear of the car.

8. The door hinge may be removed from the body if necessary.

To install:

9. If the door hinge is removed from the body, reinstall it and tighten the bolts to 21 ft. lbs. (28 Nm).

10. Place the door in position and support it. Use the jack to fine tune the position until the bolt holes and matchmark (hinge outline) align.

11. Apply an appropriate amount of multipurpose grease to the lower hinge and cam sliding area. Using engine oil, lubricate between the lower hinge pin and the roller.

12. Install the hinge bolts and nuts. Tighten the bolts to 21 ft. lbs. (28 Nm).

13. If all has gone well, the door should almost be in the original position. Refer to the door adjustment procedures to align the door and body. It may be necessary to loosen the hinge bolts and reposition the door; remember to retighten them each time or the door will shift out of place.

14. Once adjusted, connect the door check lever and install the pin. Install the hinge covers if any were removed.

15. Route the wiring harness(es) into the body and connect them to their leads.

16. Connect the negative battery cable.

17. Test the operation of any electrical components in the door (locks, mirrors, speakers, etc.) and test drive the car, checking the door for air leaks and rattles.

ADJUSTMENT

▶ See Figure 4

Front

To adjust the door in forward, rearward and vertical directions, perform the following adjustment:

1. Loosen the body side hinge bolts or nuts.

2. Adjust the door to the desired position.

3. Secure the body side hinge bolts or nuts and check the door for proper alignment. Tighten the bolts to 21 ft. lbs. (28 Nm).

To adjust the door in left, right and vertical directions, perform the following adjustments:

4. Loosen the door side hinge bolts slightly.

5. Adjust the door to the desired position.

6. Secure the door side hinge bolts and check the door for proper alignment. Tighten the bolts to 21 ft. lbs. (28 Nm).

To adjust the door lock striker, perform the following procedure:

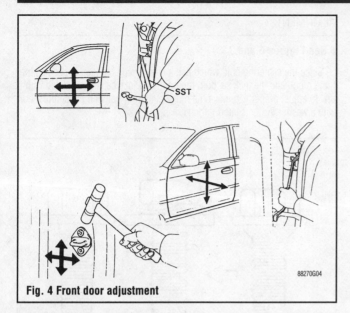

Fig. 4 Front door adjustment

7. Check that the door fit and the door lock linkages are adjusted properly.

8. Slightly loosen the striker mounting screws and tap striker with a hammer until the desired position is obtained.

9. Tighten the striker mounting screws.

Rear

♦ **See Figure 5**

To adjust the door in the forward/rearward and vertical directions perform the following:

1. Remove the rear seat cushion and rear seat back.
2. Remove the roof side inner garnish.
3. Remove the rear seat side garnish.
4. Unscrew and remove the front door scuff plate.
5. Remove the center pillar lower garnish.
6. Loosen the body side hinge nuts to adjust. Tighten them to 21 ft. lbs. 928 Nm).
7. Install the center pillar lower garnish.
8. Secure the front door scuff plate.
9. Install the rear seat side garnish.

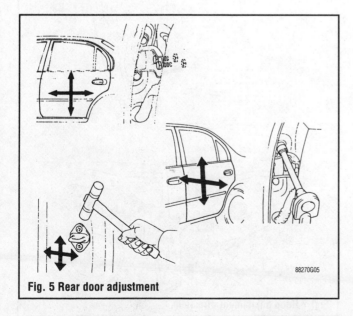

Fig. 5 Rear door adjustment

10. Attach the roof side inner garnish.
11. Install the rear seatback and rear seat cushion. Tighten the bolts to 14 ft. lbs. (19 Nm).

To adjust the door in the left/right and vertical positions perform the following:

12. Loosen the door side hinge bolts to adjust.
13. Substitue the standard bolt for the centering the bolt. Tighten to 21 ft. lbs. (28 Nm).

To adjust the door lock striker, perform the following procedure:

14. Check that the door fit and the door lock linkages are adjusted properly.
15. Slightly loosen the striker mounting screws and tap striker with a hammer until the desired position is obtained.
16. Tighten the striker mounting screws.

Hood

REMOVAL & INSTALLATION

➡**It is advisable to use two people while removing the hood from the vehicle. The hood is lightweight and can be easily damaged by twisting or dropping it.**

1. Open the hood and support it with the aid of a helper.
2. Use a felt tip marker or grease pencil to mark the hinge location on the hood.
3. Remove the bolts attaching the hood to the hood hinges. Have a helper support the rear of the hood as the bolts are removed. Without support, the hood will slide off the hinges and hit the upper bodywork.
4. Remove the hood assembly. Place the hood out of the work area, resting on its side on a protected surface.

To install:

5. Reinstall the hood by carefully placing it in position and installing the hinge bolts finger-tight. Install the hood prop immediately. Move the hood around on the hinges until the matchmarks (felt tip marker) align.

✳✳ WARNING

Take great care to prevent the hood from bumping the windshield. Not only will the hood be damaged, the windshield can be broken by careless installation.

6. Adjust the hood. When the hood is in final alignment, tighten the hinge bolts to 10 ft. lbs. (14 Nm).

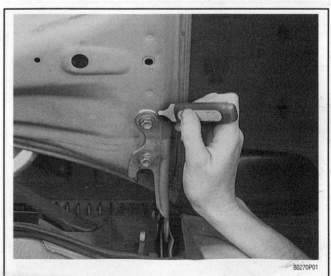

Make a mark on the hood where the hinge edges meet

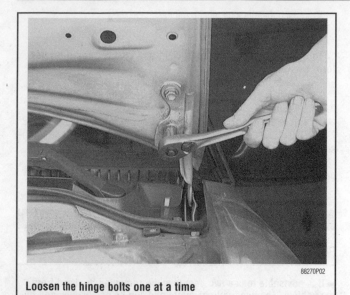

Loosen the hinge bolts one at a time

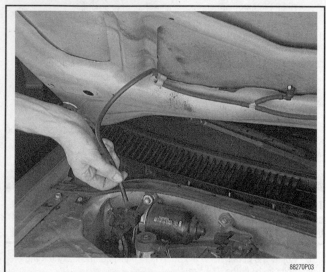

Don't forget to disconnect the wiper hose from the hood

While supporting the hood with the aid of a helper, remove the retaining bolts

ALIGNMENT

▶ **See Figures 6 and 7**

Since the centering bolt, which has a chamfered shoulder, is used as the hood hinge and the lock set bolt, the hood and lock can't be adjusted with it on. To adjust properly, remove the hinge centering bolt and substitute a bolt with a washer for the centering bolt.

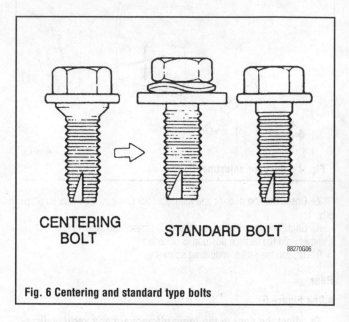

CENTERING BOLT **STANDARD BOLT**

Fig. 6 Centering and standard type bolts

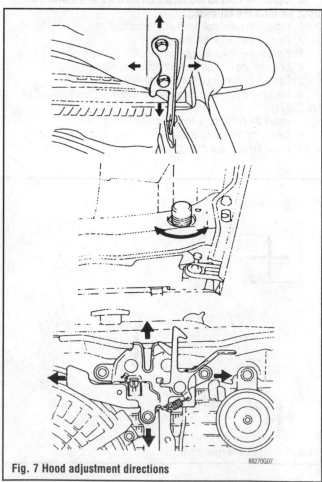

Fig. 7 Hood adjustment directions

To adjust the hood forward or rearward and left or right directions, adjust the hood by loosening the side hinge bolts and moving the hood to the desired position. Secure the hinge bolts to 10 ft. lbs. (14 Nm) tighten.

To adjust the front edge of the hood in a vertical direction, turn the cushions as required.

To adjust the hood lock, loosen the lock retainer bolts and move the lock to the desired position. Torque the hood lock mounting bolts to 74 inch lbs. (8 Nm).

Tailgate

REMOVAL & INSTALLATION

▶ See Figure 8

1. Open the tailgate completely.
2. Remove the inner trim panel.
3. Disconnect all electrical wiring. Remove the harness and position out of the way.
4. Scribe the hinge location on the tailgate to aid in installation.
5. Disconnect the damper stays from the tailgate and position out of the way. Disconnect the rear defroster wiring, if equipped.
6. Remove the tailgate-to-hinge bolts and remove the tailgate from the vehicle.

To install:

7. Position the tailgate on the vehicle and align the scribe marks.
8. Install the tailgate-to-hinge bolts and secure tightly.

9. Attach the damper stays to the tailgate assembly.
10. Install the electrical harness and reattach all connections.
11. Install the interior trim panel.
12. Close the tailgate slowly to check for proper alignment, and adjust as required.

ALIGNMENT

▶ See Figures 9, 10 and 11

To adjust the door in forward/rearward and left/right directions, loosen the body side hinge bolts and position the tailgate as required. tighten the bolts to 9 ft. lbs. (13 Nm).

To adjust the tailgate lock striker, loosen the mounting bolts and using a plastic hammer, tap the striker to the desired position. Removing of the lower trim panel is normally required to access the striker.

Vertical adjustment of the door edge is made by removing or adding shims under the hinges.

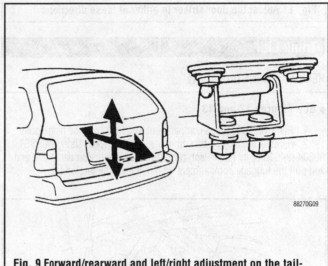

Fig. 9 Forward/rearward and left/right adjustment on the tailgate

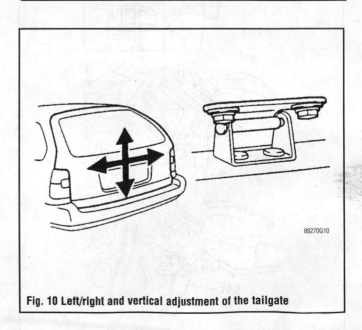

Fig. 10 Left/right and vertical adjustment of the tailgate

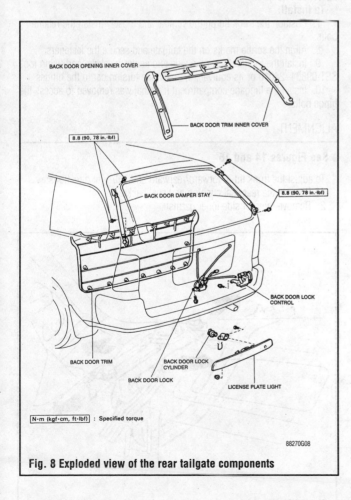

Fig. 8 Exploded view of the rear tailgate components

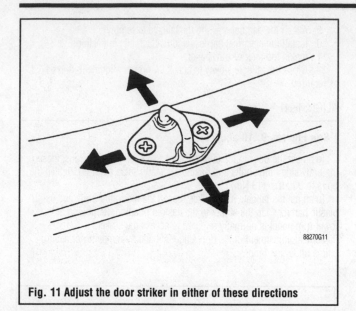

Fig. 11 Adjust the door striker in either of these directions

Trunk Lid

REMOVAL & INSTALLATION

▶ See Figures 12 and 13

1. Remove the luggage compartment trim to access the hinge bolts.
2. Remove the torsion bars from the center bracket. Using tool SST 09804–24010 or its equivalent, push down on the torsion bar at one end and pull the luggage compartment lid hinge from the torsion bar.

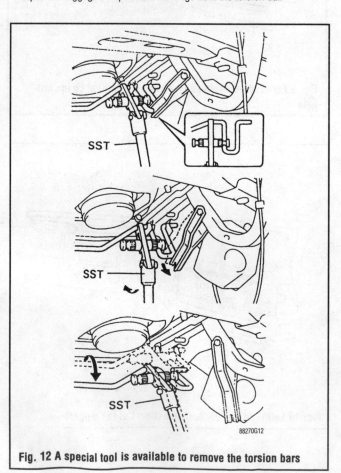

Fig. 12 A special tool is available to remove the torsion bars

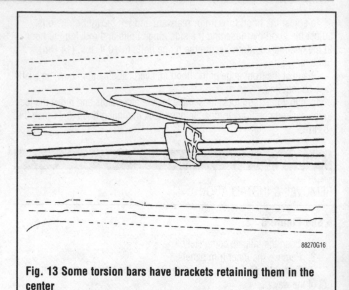

Fig. 13 Some torsion bars have brackets retaining them in the center

3. Slowly lift the tool and remove the torsion bar from the bracket.
4. Repeat steps 2 and 3 on the other side of the trunk lid to remove that torsion bar.
5. Prop the hood in the upright position and scribe the hinge locations in the trunk.
6. Remove the hinge-to-trunk lid mounting bolts and remove the trunk lid from the vehicle.

To install:

7. Position the trunk lid on the vehicle and loosely install the retainer bolts.
8. Align the scribe marks on the tailgate and secure the fasteners.
9. Install the torsion bar to the side and center brackets, and using tool SST 09804–24010 or its equivalent, install the torsion bar to the hinges.
10. Install the luggage compartment trim that was removed to access the hinge bolts.

ALIGNMENT

▶ See Figures 14 and 15

To adjust the trunk lid in forward/rearward and left/right directions:
1. Remove the rear seat cushion and seat back.
2. Remove the roof side inner garnish.

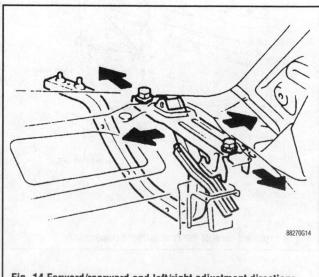

Fig. 14 Forward/rearward and left/right adjustment directions

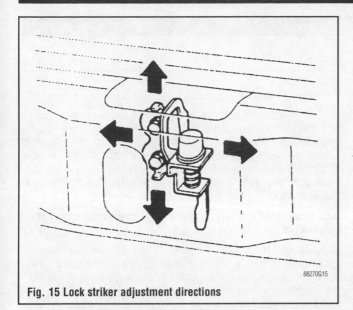

Fig. 15 Lock striker adjustment directions

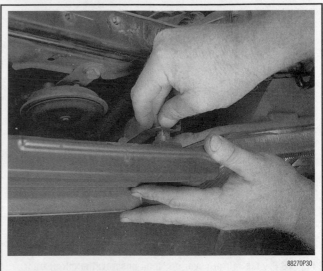

Pull the grille away from the retaining clips . . .

3. Remove the rear seat side garnish and package tray trim.
4. Loosen the hinge bolts and position the trunk lid as required. Tighten the hinge bolts to 48 inch lbs. (5 Nm).
To adjust the trunk lid lock striker:
5. Remove the rear floor finish plate by pulling.
6. Remove the clips and the rear luggage trim.
7. Loosen the bolts and adjust. Install the necessary trim panels.

Grille
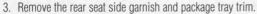

REMOVAL & INSTALLATION

The grille can be separated without removing any other parts. The grille is held on by a number of fasteners. Raise the hood and look for screws placed vertically in front of the metalwork. Remove the retainer screws and lift the grille from the vehicle.

On installation, make sure that all the retainers are installed in their original locations.

. . . then remove the grille from the vehicle

Unscrew all of the retaining screws on the grille

Outside Mirrors

REMOVAL & INSTALLATION

The mirrors on these models can be removed from the door without disassembling the door liner or other components. Both left and right outside mirrors may be either manual, manual remote (small lever on the inside to adjust the mirror) or electric remote. If the mirror glass is damaged, replacements may be available through your dealer or a reputable glass shop in your area. If the plastic housing is damaged or cracked, the entire unit will need to be replaced.

Manual

▶ See Figure 16

1. Remove the set screw and the adjustment knob, if equipped.
2. Remove the delta cover; that's the triangular black inner cover. It can

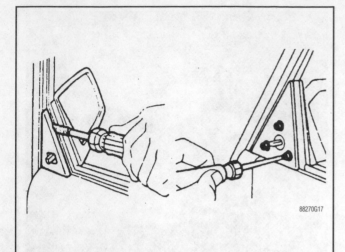

88270G17

Fig. 16 Pry the mirror cover off, then unscrew the mirror from the door

be removed with a blunt plastic or wooden tool. Don't use a metal prytool; the plastic will be marred.

3. Depending on the style of mirror, there may be concealment plugs or other minor parts under the delta cover—remove them.

4. Support the mirror housing from the outside and remove the three bolts or nuts holding the mirror to the door.

5. Remove the mirror assembly.

To install:

6. Fit the mirror to the door and install the nuts and bolts to hold it. Pay particular attention to the placement and alignment of any gaskets or weatherstrips around the mirror; serious wind noises may result from careless work.

7. Install any concealment plugs, dust boots or seals which were removed.

8. Install the delta cover and install the adjustment knob, if it was removed.

9. Cycle the mirror several times to make sure that it works properly.

Power

▶ See Figure 16

1. Disconnect the negative battery cable.

2. Remove the delta cover; that's the triangular black inner cover. It can be removed with a blunt plastic or wooden tool. Don't use a metal prytool; the plastic will be marred.

3. Depending on the style of mirror, there may be concealment plugs or other minor parts under the delta cover—remove them. Unplug all electric connectors.

4. Support the mirror housing from the outside and remove the three bolts or nuts holding the mirror to the door.

5. If the wiring to the electric mirror was not disconnected previously, detach it now. Some connectors can only be reached after the mirror is free of the door. Remove the mirror assembly.

To install:

6. Fit the mirror to the door and install the nuts and bolts to hold it. Connect the wiring harnesses if they are on the outside of the door. Pay particular attention to the placement and alignment of any gaskets or weatherstrips around the mirror; serious wind noises may result from careless work.

7. If the wiring connectors are on the inside of the door, plug them back together and install any concealment plugs, dust boots or seals which were removed.

8. Install the delta cover and install the control lever, if it was removed.

9. Connect the negative battery cable.

10. Cycle the mirror several times to make sure that it works properly.

Antenna

REPLACEMENT

Manual

If your antenna mast is the type where you can unscrew the mast from the fender, simply do so with a pair of pliers. Most damaged antennas are simply the result of a car wash or similar mishap, in which the mast is bent.

Disconnect the antenna cable at the radio by pulling it straight out of the set. Depending on access, this may require loosening the radio and pulling it out of the dash. Working under the instrument panel, disengage the cable from its retainers.

➡**On some models, it may be necessary to remove the instrument panel pad to get at the cable.**

Outside, unsnap the cap from the antenna base. Remove the screw(s) and lift off the antenna base, pulling the cable with it, carefully. When reinstalling, make certain the antenna mount area is clean and free of rust and dirt. The antenna must make a proper ground contact through its base to work properly. Install the screws and route the cable into the interior. Make certain the cable is retained in the clips, etc. Attach the cable to the radio; reinstall the radio if it was removed.

Power

Some models are equipped with a power antenna located in the trunk. Disconnect the negative battery cable first before working on any electrical components. To access the antenna, simply remove the trim panel from the interior of the vehicle. Detach the electrical wiring harness from the component. Unbolt the unit. The antenna may have a mounting nut retaining it to the outside of the quarter panel. Remove this nut and retainer to slip the unit out from inside the car. Pull the unit out from the vehicle.

Installation is the reverse to install. Connect the negative battery cable and check component operation.

Fenders

REMOVAL & INSTALLATION

1. Remove the inner fender liner from the fender to be removed.

2. Remove of disconnect all electrical items attached to the fender.

3. If necessary, remove the front bumper assembly.

4. Remove all bolts attaching the fender and the brace to the firewall and the radiator/grille panel.

5. Remove the rear attaching bolts through the pillar opening and remove the fender from the vehicle.

To install:

6. Attach the fender to the vehicle with the mounting bolts and tighten securely. Make sure the fender is aligned correctly with all other panels.

7. If removed, attach the front bumper.

8. Install and connect all electrical components removed.

9. Attach the inner fender liner.

Power Sunroof

REMOVAL & INSTALLATION

▶ See Figures 17 thru 22

If there is ever an emergency, and the sunroof is stuck in the open position, do the following. On 4WD All-track wagons: remove the map light lens, on all models except 4WD All-tracks; remove the control switch cover. Then, remove the large screw inside. Manually operate the sun roof by inserting a special crank-shaped tool into the hole and turning the driveshaft.

→ **Be careful not to loose the spring washer and shim.**

1. Disconnect the negative battery cable.

2. Using a screwdriver (with a taped tip), remove the cover and the power roof switch. Separate the switch wiring from the harness.

3. Remove the inner rear view mirror, sun visors and holders, assist grips and interior light.

4. Remove the front pillar garnishes and the side garnishes. It may be necessary to remove the upper and the lower side garnishes to allow enough clearance for the removal of the headliner.

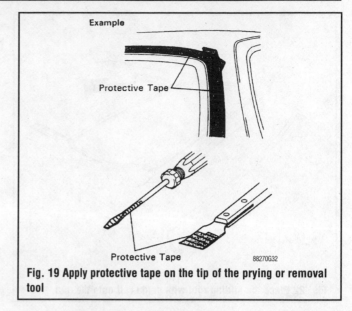

Fig. 19 Apply protective tape on the tip of the prying or removal tool

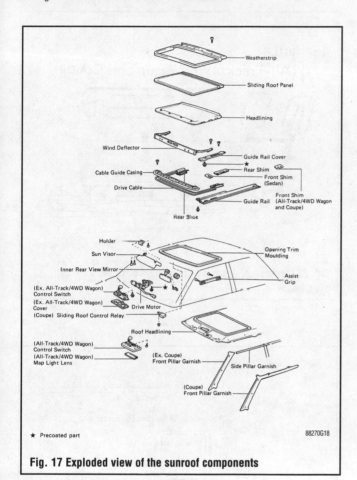

Fig. 17 Exploded view of the sunroof components

★ Precoated part

88270G18

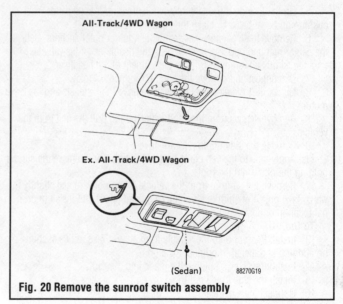

Fig. 20 Remove the sunroof switch assembly

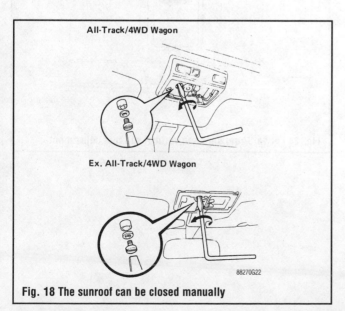

Fig. 18 The sunroof can be closed manually

Fig. 21 Unbolt and disconnect the wiring remove the motor

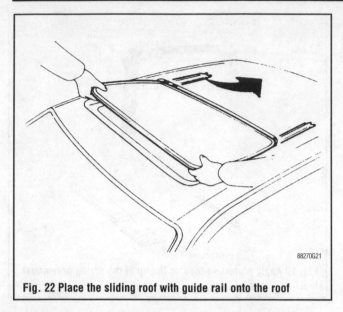

Fig. 22 Place the sliding roof with guide rail onto the roof

5. On the four door models, remove the rear door scuff plates, seat cushion and seat back. Unclasp the headliner rear trim.

6. Remove the front and rear seat belt shoulder outer anchors. Detach the center rear and upper garnishes. Pull the headliner off the vehicle. Make sure the trim is all removed prior to detachment of the headliner.

7. Disconnect and remove the sliding roof control relay.

8. Disconnect the electrical harness, remove the fasteners and the drive motor.

9. Remove screws from the wind deflector and pull the unit from the vehicle.

10. Remove the side guide rail trim cover.

11. Apply tape to the vehicle to protect the finish and remove the screws holding the glass into the roof.

12. Remove the sunroof from the vehicle lifting outward and slightly forward. Take notice of shim positioning (if so equipped) and install in original location on installation.

To install:

13. Install the roof onto the vehicle from above. Take notice of shim positioning and install in original location.

14. Install the screws holding the glass into the roof.

15. Install the side guide rail trim covers.

16. Connect the electrical harness, then install the drive motor and fasteners.

17. Position the sliding roof control relay and secure, attach the wiring.

18. Install the wind deflector and secure on the vehicle with the retaining screws.

19. Install the front side of the headliner and front pillar garnishes. Attach the upper and the lower side garnishes, if removed. Attach the seat belt shoulder anchors, tighten the mounting bolts to 32 ft. lbs. (43 Nm).

20. Install the inner rear view mirror, sun visors and holders, assist grips and interior light.

21. Install the roof switch and cover.

22. Connect the negative battery cable. Check sliding roof for proper operation.

ADJUSTMENT

◆ See Figures 23 and 24

1. Adjust sliding roof level difference—by increasing or decreasing the number of shims between the bracket and sliding roof.

2. Adjust sliding roof in forward/rearward and vertical directions—loosen the sliding roof installation bolts to adjust.

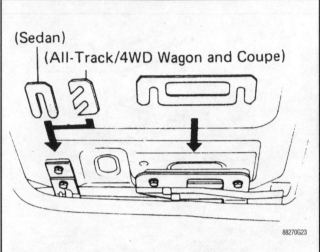

Fig. 23 Increase or decrease the amount of shims for level adjustment

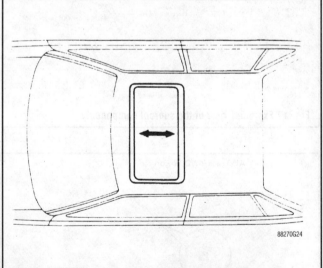

Fig. 24 Forward/rearward and vertical sun roof adjustment

INTERIOR

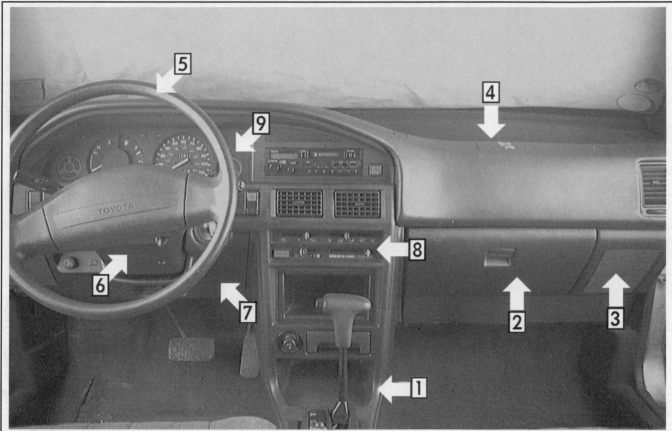

1. Center console
2. Glove box
3. Speaker grille
4. Dash pad
5. Steering wheel
6. Steering wheel cover
7. Lower dash panel
8. Center trim panel
9. Combination meter

88270P07

View of the dashboard components

Instrument Panel and Pad

REMOVAL & INSTALLATION

1988–92 Models

▶ **See Figures 25 and 26**

1. Disconnect the negative battery cable.
2. Remove the steering wheel. Disarm air bag system if so equipped.
3. Unbolt and remove the right and left front pillar garnish trim.
4. Remove the rear then front floor console boxes. Disconnect the wiring.
5. Remove the engine hood release lever.
6. Next, detach the lower finish No. 1 trim panel. Remove the No. 1 speaker panel. Pry out the two panel hole covers. Pull pout the lower finish panel No. 1, then disconnect the speaker wires. On models with A/C, disconnect the No. 5 heater register duct.
7. Remove the steering column cover.
8. Remove the center cluster finish panel. Disconnect the wiring and remove the switches.

9. Remove the cluster finish panel and detach the wiring to the unit.
10. Remove the radio and disconnect the antenna wire and harness from behind the unit..
11. Remove the stereo opening cover or center differential control switch if so equipped. Remove any wiring from components.
12. Remove the combination meter assembly. Disconnect the wiring.
13. Remove the lower finish No. 2 panel with glove compartment door.
14. Separate the heater control assembly from the safety pad and hang it.
15. Remove the lower center finish panel.
16. Remove the No. 1 and No. 2 side defroster nozzles. Be sure to tape the end of the removal tool to avoid scratching the dash components.
17. Remove the safety pad assembly from the vehicle. Disconnect the wiring.

➡**The defroster nozzle has a boss on the reverse side for clamping onto the clip on the body side. When removing, pull upward at an angle.**

18. Installation is the reverse of the removal procedure.

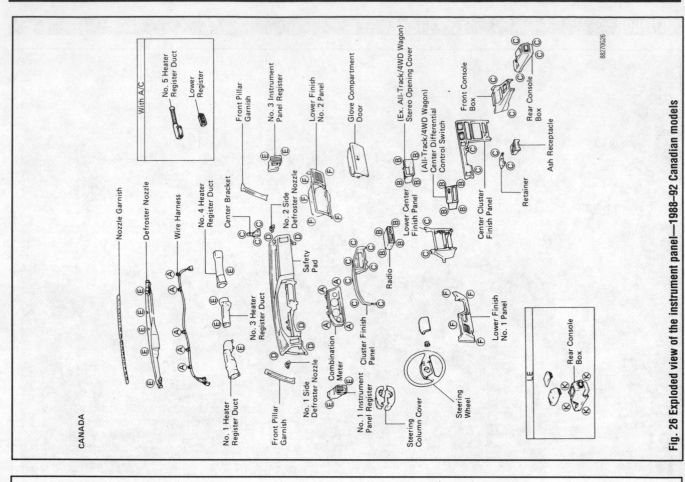

Fig. 26 Exploded view of the instrument panel—1988–92 Canadian models

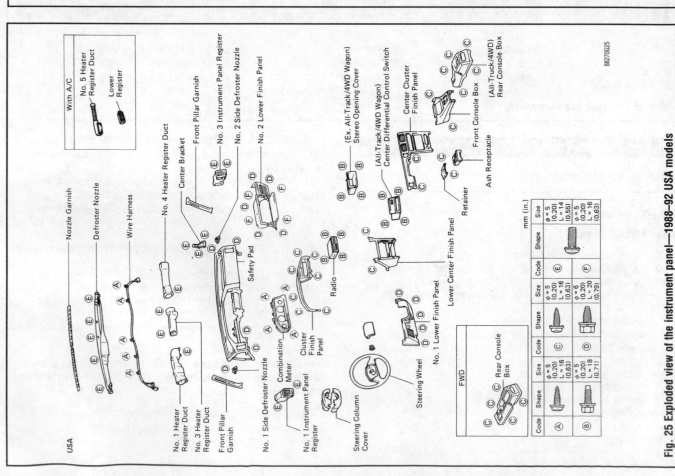

Fig. 25 Exploded view of the instrument panel—1988–92 USA models

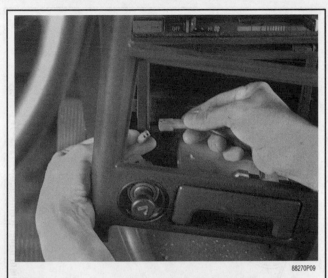

Pull the center trim out and disconnect any wiring

With everything disconnected, pull the trim panel out from the dash

Remove the screws retaining the upper trim panel

1993–97 Models

▶ See Figures 27, 28 and 29

⁂ WARNING

This procedure requires the drivers and passengers air bags are to be removed from the vehicle. Refer to Section 7 for warnings and information concerning this matter.

⁂ CAUTION

On models with an airbag, wait at least 90 seconds from the time that the ignition switch is turned to the LOCK position and the battery is disconnected before performing any further work. Refer to Section 7 for all air bag warnings.

1. Disconnect the negative battery cable.
2. Remove the following components:
- Front door lower garnishes
- Front door scuff plates
- Front pillar garnishes
3. Remove the steering wheel. Refer to Section 8.

⁂ CAUTION

The Supplemental Restraint System (SRS) must be disarmed before removing the steering wheel. Failure to do so may cause accidental deployment of the air bag, resulting in injury. In addition, the fasteners, screws and bolts originally used or the air bag components have a special coating on them specifically designed for use in this system. They must never e replaced with any substitutes. Anytime new fasteners are needed, replace them with the correct fasteners.

4. Remove the following components:
- Steering column cover
- Shifting hole bezel
- Rear console box
- Hood lock release lever
- Lower finish panel
- Combination switch
- Lower panel
5. Remove the glove box compartment door. Detach the connector cover from the compartment door.
   a. Remove the wiring from the connector cover.
   b. Detch the wiring from the harness.
   c. Remove the screws and bolts from the compartment.
   d. Remove the glove box door.

➡ When handling the airbag connector, take care not to damage the air bag wire harness.

6. Remove the center cluster finish lower panel. Disconnect the wiring from the panel cluster. Remove the stereo opening cover.
7. Remove the heater knobs, then remove the center cluster finish panel. Unbolt and detach the radio. Remove the heater control.
8. Remove the cluster finish panel and combination meter.
9. Remove the following components:
- Finish lower center panel
- Cluster finish panel sub assembly
- Duct heater to register No. 2
- Side defroster nozzle No. 2
10. Remove the passenger air bag assembly. Disconnect the wiring harness to the assembly. Remove the 4 bolts and 2 clips. Pull the air bag assembly from the dash.

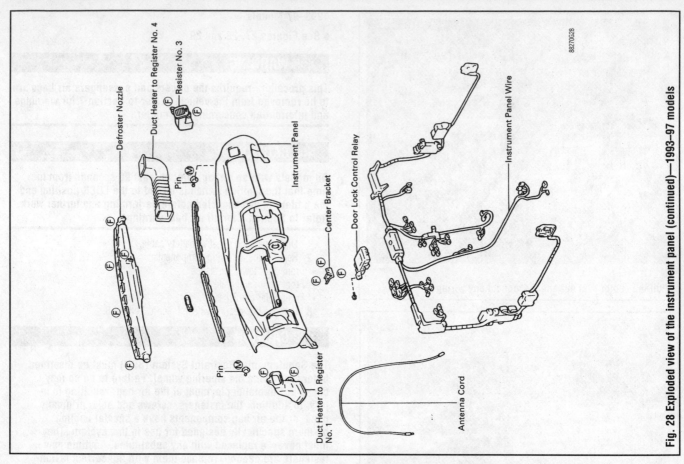

Fig. 28 Exploded view of the instrument panel (continued)—1993–97 models

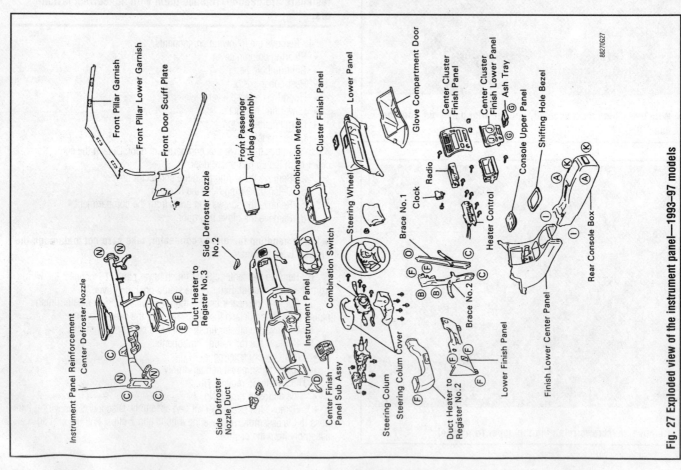

Fig. 27 Exploded view of the instrument panel—1993–97 models

11. To remove the instrument panel, detach the wiring from the components. Remove the 5 bolts retaining the panel. Unbolt the junction block No. 1 and No. 4.

12. Remove the screw, 8 bolts and instrument panel.

13. Remove the instrument panel reinforcement.

14. Installation is the reverse of the removal procedure.

Center Console

REMOVAL & INSTALLATION

To remove the center console on most models, refer to the Instrument Panel Removal and Installation. In some cases, the center console can be separated by simply removing the shift lever (manual transaxles), unbolting the console pieces and removing them from the floor.

Door Panels

REMOVAL & INSTALLATION

▶ **See Figures 30 and 31**

➡**This is a general procedure. Depending on vehicle and model, the order of steps may need to be changed slightly.**

1. Remove the inner mirror control knob (if manual remote) and remove the inner triangular cover from the mirror mount.

2. Remove the screws holding the armrest and remove the armrest. The armrest screws may be concealed behind plastic caps which may be popped out with a non-marring tool.

3. Remove the surround or cover for the inside door handle. Again, seek the hidden screw; remove it and slide the cover off over the handle.

4. If not equipped with electric windows, remove the window winder handle. This can be tricky, but not difficult. Install a piece of tape on the door pad to show the position of the handle before removal. The handle is held onto the winder axle by a spring clip shaped like the Greek letter Ω. The clip is located between the back of the winder handle and the door pad. It is correctly installed with the legs pointing along the length of the winder handle. There are three common ways of removing the clip:

   a. Use a door handle removal tool. This inexpensive slotted and toothed tool can be fitted between the winder and the panel and used to push the spring clip free.

   b. Use a rag or piece of cloth and work it back and forth between the winder and door panel. If constant upward tension is kept, the clip will be forced free. Keep watch on the clip as it pops out; it may get lost.

   c. Straighten a common paper clip and bend a very small J-hook at the end of it. Work the hook down from the top of the winder and engage the loop of the spring clip. As you pull the clip free, keep your other hand over the area. If this is not done, the clip may vanish to an undisclosed location, never to be seen again.

5. In general, power door lock and window switches mounted on the door pad (not the armrest) may remain in place until the pad is removed. Some cannot be removed until the doorpad is off the door.

6. If the car has manual vertical door locks, remove the lock knob by unscrewing it. If this is impossible (because they're in square housings), wait until the pad is lifted free.

7. Using a broad, flat-bladed tool, (not a screwdriver) begin to gently pry the door pad away from the door. You are releasing plastic inserts from plastic seats. There will be 6–12 of them around the door. With care, the plastic inserts can be reused several times.

8. When all the clips are loose, lift up on the panel to release the lip at the top of the door. This may require a bit of jiggling to loosen the panel; do so gently and don't damage the panel. The upper edge (at the window sill) is attached by a series of retaining clips.

9. Once the panel is free, keep it close to the door and check behind it. Disconnect any wiring for switches, lights or speakers which may be attached.

➡**Behind the panel is a plastic sheet taped or glued to the door. This is a watershield and must be intact to prevent water entry into the car. It must be securely attached at its edges and not be ripped or damaged. Small holes or tears can be patched with waterproof tape applied to both sides of the liner.**

Code	Shape	Size	Code	Shape	Size	Code	Shape	Size
Ⓐ		ϕ = 8 (0.31) L = 20 (0.79)	Ⓑ		ϕ = 8 (0.31) L = 17 (0.67)	Ⓒ		ϕ = 8 (0.31) L = 15 (0.59)
Ⓓ		ϕ = 6 (0.24) L = 20 (0.79)	Ⓔ		ϕ = 6 (0.24) L = 20 (0.79)	Ⓕ		ϕ = 5.22 (0.2055) L = 14 (0.55)
Ⓖ		ϕ = 5.22 (0.2055) L = 14 (0.55)	Ⓗ		ϕ = 5.22 (0.2055) L = 12 (0.47)	Ⓘ		ϕ 5 (0.20) L = 16 (0.63)
Ⓙ		ϕ = 5 (0.20) L = 16 (0.63)	Ⓚ		ϕ = 5 (0.20) L = 14 (0.55)	Ⓛ		ϕ = 4.5 (0.177) L = 14 (0.55)
Ⓜ		ϕ = 4.5 (0.177) L = 12 (0.47)	Ⓝ		—	Ⓞ		—

88270G29

Fig. 29 Fasteners used to secure the instrument panel and its components

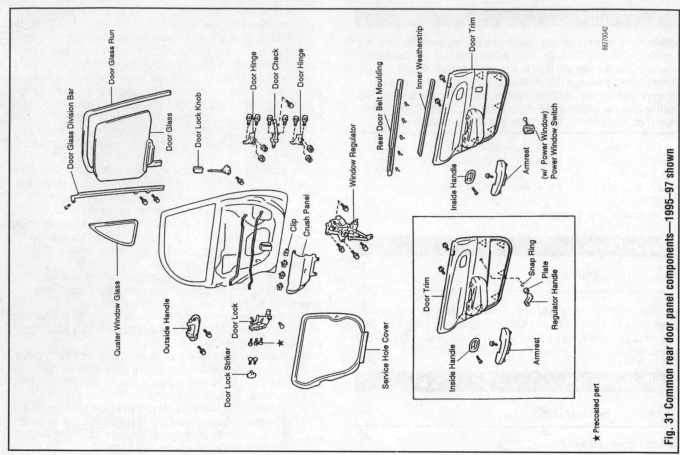

Fig. 31 Common rear door panel components—1995–97 shown

★ Precoated part

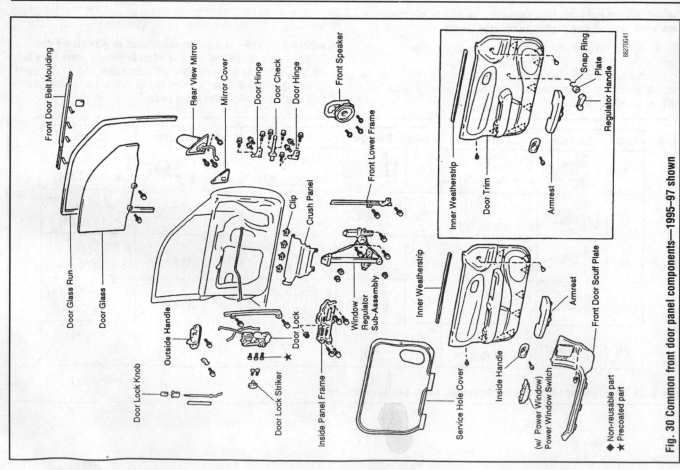

Fig. 30 Common front door panel components—1995–97 shown

◆ Non-reusable part
★ Precoated part

Remove the window crank from the door panel

Remove the door handle screw . . .

Remove the armrest securing screws. . .

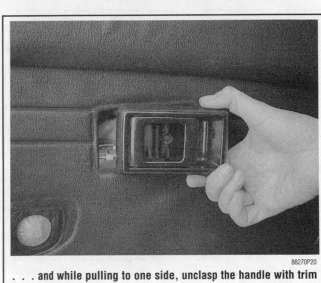

. . . and while pulling to one side, unclasp the handle with trim from the panel

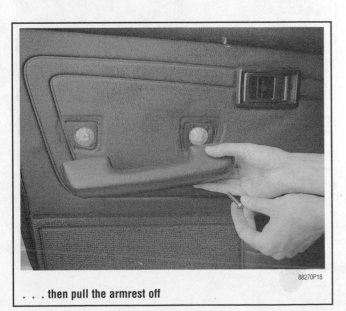

. . . then pull the armrest off

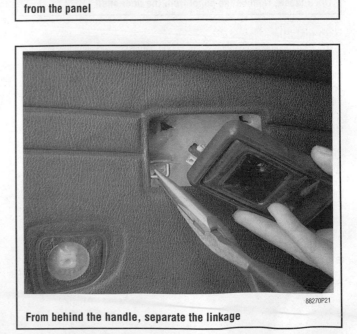

From behind the handle, separate the linkage

Carefully pry from behind the door panel to disengage the clips

88270P22

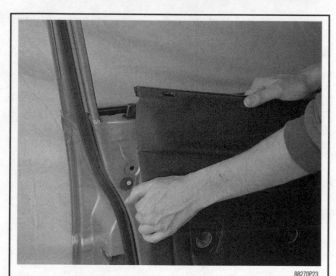
Once loose, remove the panel from the door shell

88270P23

To install:

10. When reinstalling, connect any wiring harnesses and align the upper edge of the panel along the top of the door first. Make sure the left-right alignment is correct; tap the top of the panel into place with the heel of your hand.

11. Make sure the plastic clips align with their holes; pop each retainer into place with gentle pressure.

12. Install the armrest and door handle bezel, remembering to install any caps or covers over the screws.

13. Install the window winder handle on vehicles with manual windows. Place the spring clip into the slot on the handle, remembering that the legs should point along the long dimension of the handle. Align the handle with the tape mark made earlier and put the winder over the end of the axle. Use the heel of your hand to give the center of the winder a short, sharp blow. This will cause the winder to move inward and the spring will engage its locking groove. The secret to this trick is to push the winder straight on; if it's crooked, it won't engage and you may end up looking for the spring clip.

14. Install any remaining parts or trim pieces which may have been removed earlier. (Map pockets, speaker grilles, etc.)

15. Install the triangle cover and the remote mirror handle if they were removed.

Door Locks

REMOVAL & INSTALLATION

▶ **See Figure 32**

1. Disconnect the negative battery cable.
2. Remove the door panel and watershield. Remove the service hole cover.
3. Disconnect the door outside opening linkage. Remove the two mounting bolts and remove the door handle if in need of replacement.
4. Disconnect the lock cylinder control linkage.
5. Remove the lock knob and the child protector lock lever knob.
6. Remove the lock assembly retaining screws and remove the door lock. If equipped with power locks, disconnect the electrical harness.
7. To remove the lock cylinder, remove the lock cylinder retaining clip and pull the cylinder from the door.

To install:

8. Coat all the door lock sliding surfaces with multi-purpose grease.
9. Install the outside handle with the two retaining bolts, if removed.
10. Install the door lock solenoid linkage to the door lock.
11. Connect the link to the outside handle.
12. Install the lock knob and the child protector lock lever knob.
13. Install the door opening control link tighten the mounting bolts to 48 inch lbs. (5 Nm).
14. Install the door lock cylinder control linkage.
15. Install the door panel and watershield.
16. Reconnect the negative battery cable.

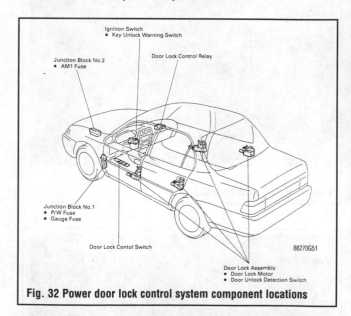
Fig. 32 Power door lock control system component locations

Tailgate Lock

REMOVAL & INSTALLATION

▶ **See Figure 33**

1. Disconnect the negative battery cable.
2. Remove the back door inside garnish trim.
3. Remove the trim panel.
4. Disconnect the links from the door control and door lock cylinder.

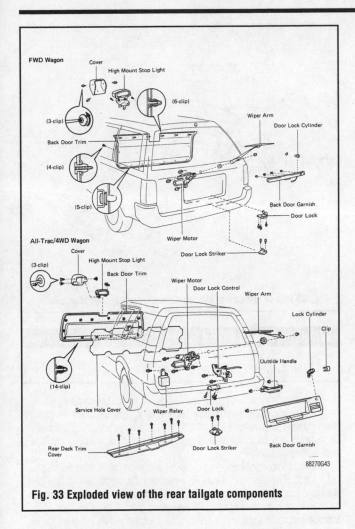

Fig. 33 Exploded view of the rear tailgate components

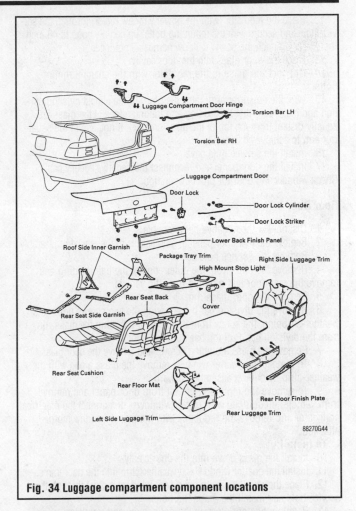

Fig. 34 Luggage compartment component locations

5. Remove the bolts and the door lock control with solenoid.
6. Remove the cylinder retaining screws, then the cylinder.

To install:

7. Install the door lock cylinder and secure with the retaining screws.
8. Install the bolts and the door lock control with the solenoid.
9. Connect the links to the door control and door lock cylinder.
10. Install the trim panel.
11. Install the back door inner garnish trim.
12. Connect the negative battery cable.

Sedan Trunk Lock

REMOVAL & INSTALLATION

▶ **See Figure 34**

1. Disconnect the negative battery cable.
2. Remove the inside trunk garnish trim.
3. Remove the bolts and the door lock assembly.

To install:

4. Attach the trunk lock with the securing bolts and tighten.
5. Secure the inside garnish trim.
6. Connect the negative battery cable.

Door Glass and Regulator

REMOVAL & INSTALLATION

Front Door

1. Disconnect the negative battery cable.
2. Remove the front door panel to gain access to the regulator assembly.
3. Remove the service hole cover.
4. Lower the regulator until the door glass is in the fully open position.
5. Remove the two glass channel mount bolts.
6. Pull the glass up and out of the door.
7. Unbolt and remove the inside door panel frame if so equipped.
8. If equipped with power windows, disconnect the electrical connector.
9. Remove the equalizer arm bracket mounting bolts.
10. Remove the window regulator mounting bolts and the regulator (with the power window motor attached) through the service hole.

To install:

11. Coat all the window regulator sliding surfaces with multi-purpose grease.

12. Place the regulator (with the power window motor) through the service hole and secure with the mounting bolts. tighten the bolts to 48 inch lbs. (5 Nm). Attach the power window harness if equipped.

13. Place the door glass into the door cavity.

14. Connect the glass to the regulator with the channel mount bolts.

15. With the equalizer arm, raise the glass to the almost closed position and make sure that the leading and trailing edges of the glass are equally distant from the top of the glass channel. If not, adjust the equalizer arm to achieve an even fit.

16. Install the service hole cover.

17. Install the door panel and reconnect the negative battery cable. Check window and door for proper operation.

Rear Door

1. Disconnect the negative battery cable.

2. Remove the rear door panel to gain access to the regulator assembly.

3. Remove the service hole cover.

4. Remove the clips from the outer edge of the belt molding and remove the rear door belt molding from the vehicle.

5. Remove the door glass run.

6. Remove the division bar by removing the two screws under the weather-stripping, the screw from the panel and pulling the glass run from the division bar. Pull the bar from the door.

7. Remove the glass mounting screws and remove the door glass.

8. To remove the quarter window, remove the glass along with the weather-strip by pulling assembly forward.

9. To remove the regulator, unbolt from door panel and remove from vehicle. If equipped with power windows, disconnect the electrical connector and remove the regulator with the power window motor attached.

To install:

10. Install the glass down into the door cavity.

11. Install the quarter window and weather-strip into the door frame.

12. Place the regulator (with the power window motor) through the service hole and install the mounting bolts.

13. Position the door glass in the door cavity and regulator.

14. Connect the glass to the regulator with the channel mount bolts.

15. Install the rear door belt molding, division bar and the door glass run.

16. With the equalizer arm, raise the glass to the almost closed position and make sure that the leading and trailing edges of the glass are equidistant from the top of the glass channel. If not, adjust the equalizer arm to achieve an even fit.

17. With the door glass fully closed, adjust the door glass stopper so it lightly makes contact with the glass plate.

18. Install the service hole cover.

19. Install the door panel and connect the negative battery cable. Check window and door for proper operation.

Electric Window Motor

REMOVAL & INSTALLATION

♦ See Figure 35

The power window motor, if equipped, is attached to the window regulator. If service is required, remove the window regulator from the inside of the door panel and detach the motor from the regulator. Removal and installation of the window regulator is described in this section.

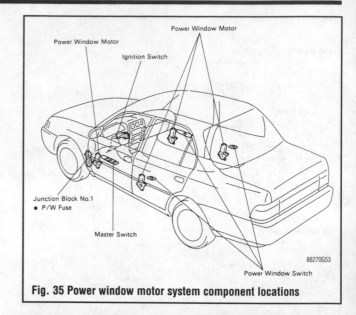

Fig. 35 Power window motor system component locations

Windshield and Fixed Glass

REMOVAL & INSTALLATION

If your windshield, or other fixed window, is cracked or chipped, you may decide to replace it with a new one yourself. However, there are two main reasons why replacement windshields and other window glass should be installed only by a professional automotive glass technician: safety and cost.

The most important reason a professional should install automotive glass is for safety. The glass in the vehicle, especially the windshield, is designed with safety in mind in case of a collision. The windshield is specially manufactured from two panes of specially-tempered glass with a thin layer of transparent plastic between them. This construction allows the glass to "give" in the event that a part of your body hits the windshield during the collision, and prevents the glass from shattering, which could cause lacerations, blinding and other harm to passengers of the vehicle. The other fixed windows are designed to be tempered so that if they break during a collision, they shatter in such a way that there are no large pointed glass pieces. The professional automotive glass technician knows how to install the glass in a vehicle so that it will function optimally during a collision. Without the proper experience, knowledge and tools, installing a piece of automotive glass yourself could lead to additional harm if an accident should ever occur.

Cost is also a factor when deciding to install automotive glass yourself. Performing this could cost you much more than a professional may charge for the same job. Since the windshield is designed to break under stress, an often life saving characteristic, windshields tend to break VERY easily when an inexperienced person attempts to install one. Do-it-yourselfers buying two, three or even four windshields from a salvage yard because they have broken them during installation are common stories. Also, since the automotive glass is designed to prevent the outside elements from entering your vehicle, improper installation can lead to water and air leaks. Annoying whining noises at highway speeds from air leaks or inside body panel rusting from water leaks can add to your stress level and subtract from your wallet. After buying two or three windshields, installing them and ending up with a leak that produces a noise while driving and water damage during rainstorms, the cost of having a professional do it correctly the first time may be much more alluring. We here at Chilton, therefore, advise that you have a professional automotive glass technician service any broken glass on your vehicle.

WINDSHIELD CHIP REPAIR

▶ **See Figures 36 thru 50**

➡**Check with your state and local authorities on the laws for state safety inspection. Some states or municipalities may not allow chip repair as a viable option for correcting stone damage to your windshield.**

Although severely cracked or damaged windshields must be replaced, there is something that you can do to prolong or even prevent the need for replacement of a chipped windshield. There are many companies which offer windshield chip repair products, such as Loctite's® Bullseye™ windshield repair kit. These kits usually consist of a syringe, pedestal and a sealing adhesive. The syringe is mounted on the pedestal and is used to create a vacuum which pulls the plastic layer against the glass. This helps make the chip transparent. The adhesive is then injected which seals the chip and helps to prevent further stress cracks from developing. Refer to the sequence of photos to get a general idea of what windshield chip repair involves.

➡**Always follow the specific manufacturer's instructions.**

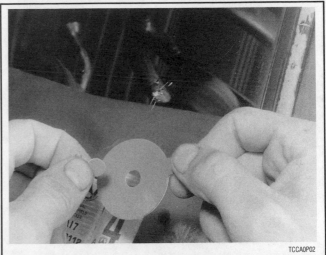
Fig. 38 Remove the center from the adhesive disc and peel off the backing from one side of the disc . . .

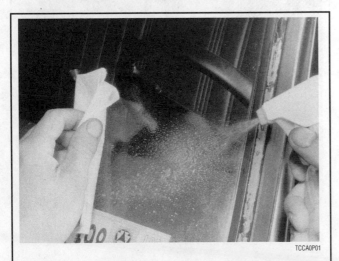
Fig. 36 Small chips on your windshield can be fixed with an aftermarket repair kit, such as the one from Loctite®

Fig. 39 . . . then press it on the windshield so that the chip is centered in the hole

Fig. 37 To repair a chip, clean the windshield with glass cleaner and dry it completely

Fig. 40 Be sure that the tab points upward on the windshield

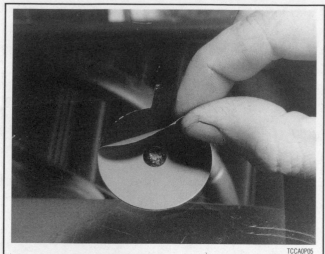

Fig. 41 Peel the backing off the exposed side of the adhesive disc . . .

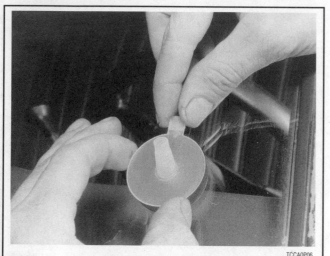

Fig. 42 . . . then position the plastic pedestal on the adhesive disc, ensuring that the tabs are aligned

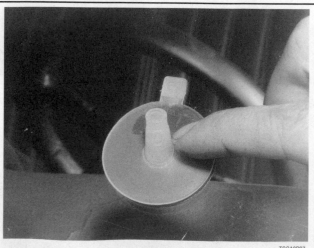

Fig. 43 Press the pedestal firmly on the adhesive disc to create an adequate seal . . .

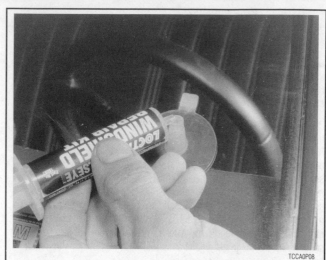

Fig. 44 . . . then install the applicator syringe nipple in the pedestal's hole

Fig. 45 Hold the syringe with one hand while pulling the plunger back with the other hand

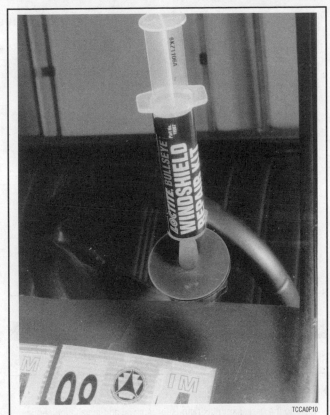

TCCA0P10

Fig. 46 After applying the solution, allow the entire assembly to sit until it has set completely

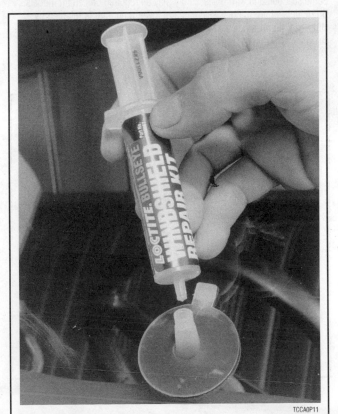

TCCA0P11

Fig. 47 After the solution has set, remove the syringe from the pedestal . . .

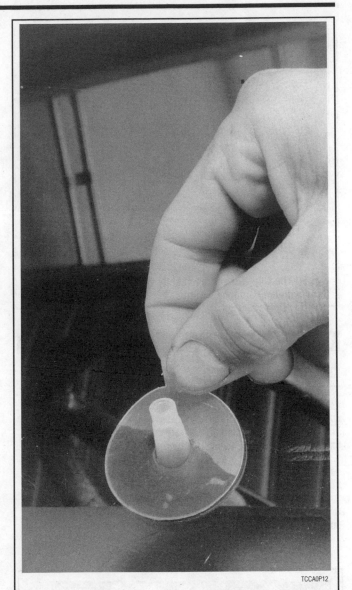

TCCA0P12

Fig. 48 . . . then peel the pedestal off of the adhesive disc . . .

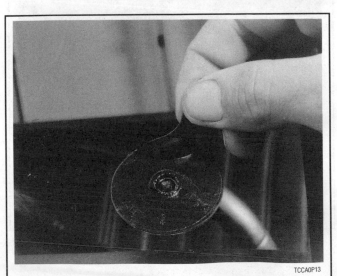

TCCA0P13

Fig. 49 . . . and peel the adhesive disc off of the windshield

TCCA0P14

Fig. 50 The chip will still be slightly visible, but it should be filled with the hardened solution

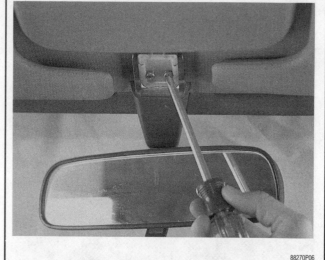

88270P06

Remove the retaining screws, then lower the mirror

Inside Rear View Mirror

REMOVAL & INSTALLATION

The inside mirror is held to its bracket by screws. Usually these are covered by a colored plastic housing which must be removed for access. These covers can be stubborn; take care not to gouge the plastic during removal.

Once exposed, the screws are easily removed. The mirror mounts are designed to break away under impact, thus protecting your head and face from serious injury in an accident.

Reassembly requires only common sense (which means you can do it wrong—pay attention); make sure everything fits without being forced and don't overtighten any screws or bolts.

Seats

REMOVAL & INSTALLATION

♦ See Figures 51 thru 56

Refer to the necessary illustrations for removal and installation service procedures of the seat for your vehicle. Most front seats are mounted by seat track retaining bolts. Remove the bolts and lift the seats out of the vehicle. Tighten the front seat retaining bolts to 22–32 ft. lbs. (29–43 Nm). Some seat belt and trim disassembly may be required on certain models. On models where the rear seat cushion lower mounting is retained by clips, pull the front left and right levers forward and pull up the rear seat cushion.

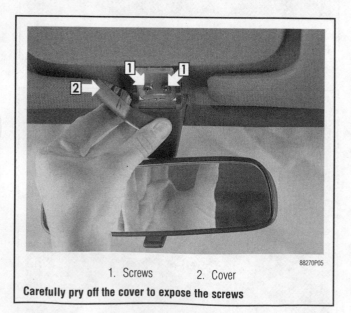

88270P05

1. Screws   2. Cover

Carefully pry off the cover to expose the screws

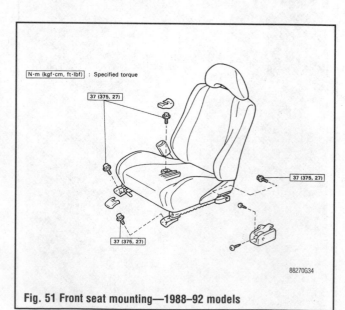

N·m (kgf·cm, ft·lbf) : Specified torque

37 (375, 27)

37 (375, 27)

37 (375, 27)

88270G34

Fig. 51 Front seat mounting—1988–92 models

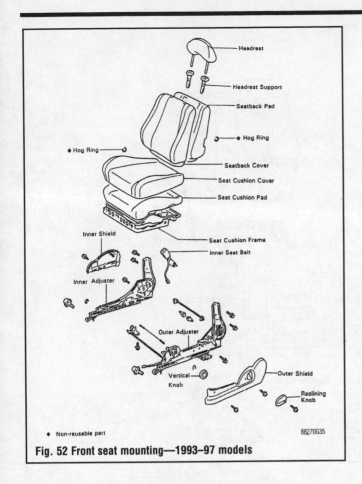

Fig. 52 Front seat mounting—1993–97 models

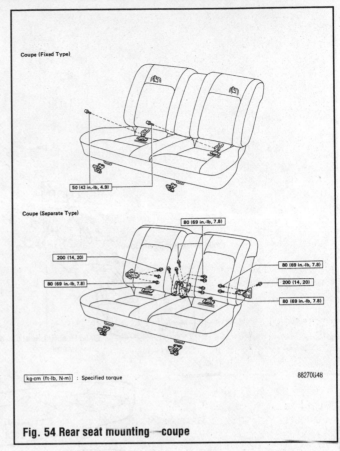

Fig. 54 Rear seat mounting—coupe

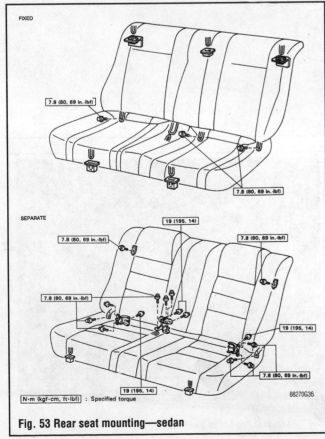

Fig. 53 Rear seat mounting—sedan

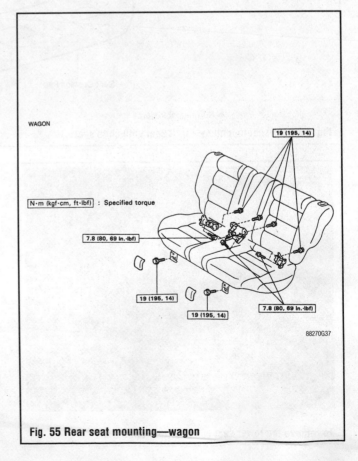

Fig. 55 Rear seat mounting—wagon

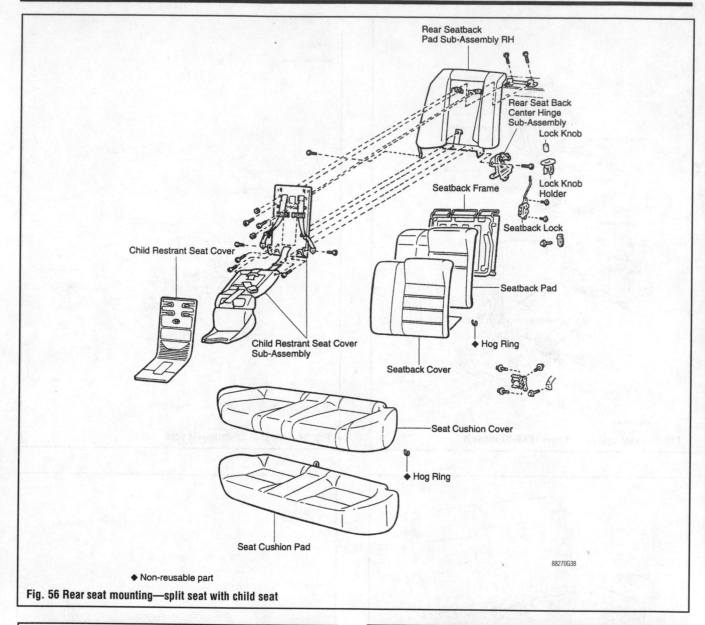

Fig. 56 Rear seat mounting—split seat with child seat

◆ Non-reusable part

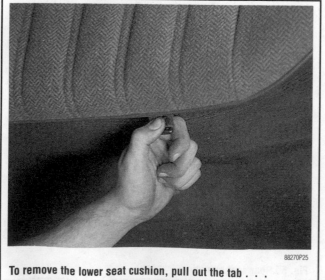

To remove the lower seat cushion, pull out the tab . . .

. . . then pull the lower seat out

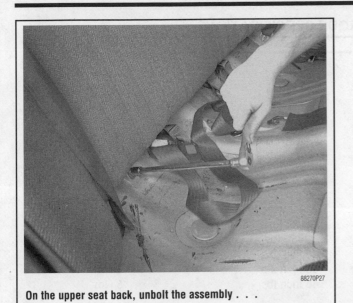

On the upper seat back, unbolt the assembly . . .

88270P27

. . . and remove the upper seat back

88270P28

TORQUE SPECIFICATIONS

Component	U.S.	Metric
1988-92 Models:		
Front seat-normal		
seat back-to-adjuster	27 ft. lbs.	37 Nm
seat cushion-to-adjuster	13 ft. lbs.	18 Nm
seat adjuster-to-body	27 ft. lbs.	37 Nm
Front seat-sport		
seat back-to-adjuster	13 ft. lbs.	18 Nm
seat cushion-to-adjuster	13 ft. lbs.	18 Nm
seat adjuster-to-body	27 ft. lbs.	37 Nm
Rear seat sedan-fixed type		
seat back-to-body	48 inch lbs.	5 Nm
Rear seat sedan-separate type		
seat back-to-body	13 ft. lbs.	18 Nm
seat back side hinge-to-seat back	13 ft. lbs.	18 Nm
seat back side hinge-to-body	69 inch lbs.	8 Nm
seat back center hinge-to-seat back	69 inch lbs.	8 Nm
seat back center hinge-to-body	69 inch lbs.	8 Nm
side seat back-to-body	69 inch lbs.	8 Nm
Rear seat coupe-fixed type		
seat back-to-body	43 inch lbs.	5 Nm
Rear seat coupe-separate type		
seat back side hinge-to-seat back	14 ft. lbs	20 Nm
seat back side hinge-to-body	69 inch lbs.	8 Nm
seat back center hinge-to-seat back	69 inch lbs.	8 Nm
seat back center hinge-to-body	69 inch lbs.	8 Nm
Rear seat FWD wagon		
seat back side hinge-to-seat back	13 ft. lbs.	18 Nm
seat back side hinge-to-body	69 inch lbs.	8 Nm
seat back center hinge-to-seat back	69 inch lbs.	8 Nm
seat back center hinge-to-body	69 inch lbs.	8 Nm
seat lock striker-to-body	13 ft. lbs.	18 Nm
seat cushion-to-body	13 ft. lbs.	18 Nm
Rear seat 4WD/All-Track wagon		
seat back side hinge-to-seat back	13 ft. lbs.	18 Nm
seat back side hinge-to-body	69 inch lbs.	8 Nm
seat back center hinge-to-seat back	69 inch lbs.	8 Nm
seat back center hinge-to-body	69 inch lbs.	8 Nm
Front seat belt		
shoulder belt anchor-to-body	32 ft. lbs.	43 Nm
shoulder belt lower side-to-body	32 ft. lbs.	43 Nm
ELR lower side-to-body	32 ft. lbs.	43 Nm
inner belt-to-body	32 ft. lbs.	43 Nm
Rear seat belt		
ELR-to-body	32 ft. lbs.	43 Nm
center rear seat belt-to-body	32 ft. lbs.	43 Nm
outer belt shoulder anchor-to-body-upper	48 inch lbs.	5 Nm
outer belt shoulder anchor-to-body-lower	32 ft. lbs.	43 Nm
outer belt lower anchor-to-body-upper	48 inch lbs.	5 Nm

88270C01

TORQUE SPECIFICATIONS

Component	U.S.	Metric
Rear seat belt continued		
outer belt lower anchor-to-body-lower	32 ft. lbs.	43 Nm
inner belt-to-body	32 ft. lbs.	43 Nm
CRS tether anchor-to-body	15 ft. lbs.	21 Nm
1993-97 Models:		
Hood		
hood hinge	10 ft. lbs.	14 Nm
hood lock	74 inch lbs.	8 Nm
Front door		
door hinge-to-body	21 ft. lbs.	28 Nm
door hinge-to-panel	21 ft. lbs.	28 Nm
door check-to-body	25 ft. lbs	33 Nm
door lock-to-panel	48 inch lbs.	5 Nm
window regulator-to-inside panel frame	48 inch lbs.	5 Nm
window regulator-to-door panel	48 inch lbs.	5 Nm
Rear door		
door hinge-to-body	21 ft. lbs.	28 Nm
door hinge-to-panel	21 ft. lbs.	28 Nm
door check-to-body	25 ft. lbs	33 Nm
door lock-to-panel	48 inch lbs.	5 Nm
window regulator-to-door panel	48 inch lbs.	5 Nm
Back door		
back door hinge-to-body	9 ft. lbs.	13 Nm
back door hinge-to-back door	9 ft. lbs.	13 Nm
back door damper stay-to-body	78 inch lbs.	9 Nm
back door damper stay-to-back door	78 inch lbs.	9 Nm
Luggage compartment		
luggage door hinge-to-body	48 inch lbs.	5 Nm
luggage door hinge-to-compartment door	74 inch lbs.	8 Nm
Front seat		
seat adjuster-to-body	27 ft. lbs.	37 Nm
seat track-to-body	27 ft. lbs.	37 Nm
seat adjuster-to-seat back	27 ft. lbs.	37 Nm
seat adjuster-to-cushion frame	13 ft. lbs.	18 Nm
seat track-to-cushion frame	13 ft. lbs.	18 Nm
Back seat		
seat back-to-body	69 inch lbs.	8 Nm
seat side cushion-to-body	69 inch lbs.	8 Nm
seatback hinge-to-seatback	14 Nm	19 Nm
seatback hinge-to-body	69 inch lbs.	8 Nm
seat cushion hinge-to-sea cushion	48 inch lbs.	5 Nm
seat cushion hinge-to-body	14 Nm	19 Nm
seat back lock-to-seatback	14 Nm	19 Nm
seat back-to-center armrest hinge	69 inch lbs.	8 Nm
Seat belt-front		
shoulder anchor-to-adjustable anchor	32 ft. lbs.	43 Nm
outer belt anchor-to-body	32 ft. lbs.	43 Nm
ELR-to-body upper side	48 inch lbs.	5 Nm
ELR-to-body lower side	32 ft. lbs.	43 Nm
adjustable anchor-to-body	32 ft. lbs.	43 Nm
inner belt-to-seat	32 ft. lbs.	43 Nm
Seat belt-rear		
shoulder anchor-to-body	32 ft. lbs.	43 Nm
outer belt anchor-to-body	32 ft. lbs.	43 Nm
ELR-to-body	32 ft. lbs.	43 Nm
center belt-to-body	32 ft. lbs.	43 Nm

GLOSSARY

AIR/FUEL RATIO: The ratio of air-to-gasoline by weight in the fuel mixture drawn into the engine.

AIR INJECTION: One method of reducing harmful exhaust emissions by injecting air into each of the exhaust ports of an engine. The fresh air entering the hot exhaust manifold causes any remaining fuel to be burned before it can exit the tailpipe.

ALTERNATOR: A device used for converting mechanical energy into electrical energy.

AMMETER: An instrument, calibrated in amperes, used to measure the flow of an electrical current in a circuit. Ammeters are always connected in series with the circuit being tested.

AMPERE: The rate of flow of electrical current present when one volt of electrical pressure is applied against one ohm of electrical resistance.

ANALOG COMPUTER: Any microprocessor that uses similar (analogous) electrical signals to make its calculations.

ARMATURE: A laminated, soft iron core wrapped by a wire that converts electrical energy to mechanical energy as in a motor or relay. When rotated in a magnetic field, it changes mechanical energy into electrical energy as in a generator.

ATMOSPHERIC PRESSURE: The pressure on the Earth's surface caused by the weight of the air in the atmosphere. At sea level, this pressure is 14.7 psi at 32°F (101 kPa at 0°C).

ATOMIZATION: The breaking down of a liquid into a fine mist that can be suspended in air.

AXIAL PLAY: Movement parallel to a shaft or bearing bore.

BACKFIRE: The sudden combustion of gases in the intake or exhaust system that results in a loud explosion.

BACKLASH: The clearance or play between two parts, such as meshed gears.

BACKPRESSURE: Restrictions in the exhaust system that slow the exit of exhaust gases from the combustion chamber.

BAKELITE: A heat resistant, plastic insulator material commonly used in printed circuit boards and transistorized components.

BALL BEARING: A bearing made up of hardened inner and outer races between which hardened steel balls roll.

BALLAST RESISTOR: A resistor in the primary ignition circuit that lowers voltage after the engine is started to reduce wear on ignition components.

BEARING: A friction reducing, supportive device usually located between a stationary part and a moving part.

BIMETAL TEMPERATURE SENSOR: Any sensor or switch made of two dissimilar types of metal that bend when heated or cooled due to the different expansion rates of the alloys. These types of sensors usually function as an on/off switch.

BLOWBY: Combustion gases, composed of water vapor and unburned fuel, that leak past the piston rings into the crankcase during normal engine operation. These gases are removed by the PCV system to prevent the buildup of harmful acids in the crankcase.

BRAKE PAD: A brake shoe and lining assembly used with disc brakes.

BRAKE SHOE: The backing for the brake lining. The term is, however, usually applied to the assembly of the brake backing and lining.

BUSHING: A liner, usually removable, for a bearing; an anti-friction liner used in place of a bearing.

CALIPER: A hydraulically activated device in a disc brake system, which is mounted straddling the brake rotor (disc). The caliper contains at least one piston and two brake pads. Hydraulic pressure on the piston(s) forces the pads against the rotor.

CAMSHAFT: A shaft in the engine on which are the lobes (cams) which operate the valves. The camshaft is driven by the crankshaft, via a belt, chain or gears, at one half the crankshaft speed.

CAPACITOR: A device which stores an electrical charge.

CARBON MONOXIDE (CO): A colorless, odorless gas given off as a normal byproduct of combustion. It is poisonous and extremely dangerous in confined areas, building up slowly to toxic levels without warning if adequate ventilation is not available.

CARBURETOR: A device, usually mounted on the intake manifold of an engine, which mixes the air and fuel in the proper proportion to allow even combustion.

CATALYTIC CONVERTER: A device installed in the exhaust system, like a muffler, that converts harmful byproducts of combustion into carbon dioxide and water vapor by means of a heat-producing chemical reaction.

CENTRIFUGAL ADVANCE: A mechanical method of advancing the spark timing by using flyweights in the distributor that react to centrifugal force generated by the distributor shaft rotation.

CHECK VALVE: Any one-way valve installed to permit the flow of air, fuel or vacuum in one direction only.

CHOKE: A device, usually a moveable valve, placed in the intake path of a carburetor to restrict the flow of air.

CIRCUIT: Any unbroken path through which an electrical current can flow. Also used to describe fuel flow in some instances.

CIRCUIT BREAKER: A switch which protects an electrical circuit from overload by opening the circuit when the current flow exceeds a predetermined level. Some circuit breakers must be reset manually, while most reset automatically.

COIL (IGNITION): A transformer in the ignition circuit which steps up the voltage provided to the spark plugs.

COMBINATION MANIFOLD: An assembly which includes both the intake and exhaust manifolds in one casting.

COMBINATION VALVE: A device used in some fuel systems that routes fuel vapors to a charcoal storage canister instead of venting them into the atmosphere. The valve relieves fuel tank pressure and allows fresh air into the tank as the fuel level drops to prevent a vapor lock situation.

COMPRESSION RATIO: The comparison of the total volume of the cylinder and combustion chamber with the piston at BDC and the piston at TDC.

CONDENSER: 1. An electrical device which acts to store an electrical charge, preventing voltage surges. 2. A radiator-like device in the air conditioning system in which refrigerant gas condenses into a liquid, giving off heat.

CONDUCTOR: Any material through which an electrical current can be transmitted easily.

CONTINUITY: Continuous or complete circuit. Can be checked with an ohmmeter.

COUNTERSHAFT: An intermediate shaft which is rotated by a mainshaft and transmits, in turn, that rotation to a working part.

CRANKCASE: The lower part of an engine in which the crankshaft and related parts operate.

CRANKSHAFT: The main driving shaft of an engine which receives reciprocating motion from the pistons and converts it to rotary motion.

CYLINDER: In an engine, the round hole in the engine block in which the piston(s) ride.

CYLINDER BLOCK: The main structural member of an engine in which is found the cylinders, crankshaft and other principal parts.

CYLINDER HEAD: The detachable portion of the engine, usually fastened to the top of the cylinder block and containing all or most of the combustion chambers. On overhead valve engines, it contains the valves and their operating parts. On overhead cam engines, it contains the camshaft as well.

DEAD CENTER: The extreme top or bottom of the piston stroke.

DETONATION: An unwanted explosion of the air/fuel mixture in the combustion chamber caused by excess heat and compression, advanced timing, or an overly lean mixture. Also referred to as "ping".

DIAPHRAGM: A thin, flexible wall separating two cavities, such as in a vacuum advance unit.

DIESELING: A condition in which hot spots in the combustion chamber cause the engine to run on after the key is turned off.

DIFFERENTIAL: A geared assembly which allows the transmission of motion between drive axles, giving one axle the ability to turn faster than the other.

DIODE: An electrical device that will allow current to flow in one direction only.

DISC BRAKE: A hydraulic braking assembly consisting of a brake disc, or rotor, mounted on an axle, and a caliper assembly containing, usually two brake pads which are activated by hydraulic pressure. The pads are forced against the sides of the disc, creating friction which slows the vehicle.

DISTRIBUTOR: A mechanically driven device on an engine which is responsible for electrically firing the spark plug at a predetermined point of the piston stroke.

DOWEL PIN: A pin, inserted in mating holes in two different parts allowing those parts to maintain a fixed relationship.

DRUM BRAKE: A braking system which consists of two brake shoes and one or two wheel cylinders, mounted on a fixed backing plate, and a brake drum, mounted on an axle, which revolves around the assembly.

DWELL: The rate, measured in degrees of shaft rotation, at which an electrical circuit cycles on and off.

ELECTRONIC CONTROL UNIT (ECU): Ignition module, module, amplifier or igniter. See Module for definition.

ELECTRONIC IGNITION: A system in which the timing and firing of the spark plugs is controlled by an electronic control unit, usually called a module. These systems have no points or condenser.

END-PLAY: The measured amount of axial movement in a shaft.

ENGINE: A device that converts heat into mechanical energy.

EXHAUST MANIFOLD: A set of cast passages or pipes which conduct exhaust gases from the engine.

FEELER GAUGE: A blade, usually metal, or precisely predetermined thickness, used to measure the clearance between two parts.

FIRING ORDER: The order in which combustion occurs in the cylinders of an engine. Also the order in which spark is distributed to the plugs by the distributor.

FLOODING: The presence of too much fuel in the intake manifold and combustion chamber which prevents the air/fuel mixture from firing, thereby causing a no-start situation.

FLYWHEEL: A disc shaped part bolted to the rear end of the crankshaft. Around the outer perimeter is affixed the ring gear. The starter drive engages the ring gear, turning the flywheel, which rotates the crankshaft, imparting the initial starting motion to the engine.

FOOT POUND (ft. lbs. or sometimes, ft.lb.): The amount of energy or work needed to raise an item weighing one pound, a distance of one foot.

FUSE: A protective device in a circuit which prevents circuit overload by breaking the circuit when a specific amperage is present. The device is constructed around a strip or wire of a lower amperage rating than the circuit it is designed to protect. When an amperage higher than that stamped on the fuse is present in the circuit, the strip or wire melts, opening the circuit.

GEAR RATIO: The ratio between the number of teeth on meshing gears.

GENERATOR: A device which converts mechanical energy into electrical energy.

HEAT RANGE: The measure of a spark plug's ability to dissipate heat from its firing end. The higher the heat range, the hotter the plug fires.

HUB: The center part of a wheel or gear.

HYDROCARBON (HC): Any chemical compound made up of hydrogen and carbon. A major pollutant formed by the engine as a byproduct of combustion.

HYDROMETER: An instrument used to measure the specific gravity of a solution.

INCH POUND (inch lbs.; sometimes in.lb. or in. lbs.): One twelfth of a foot pound.

INDUCTION: A means of transferring electrical energy in the form of a magnetic field. Principle used in the ignition coil to increase voltage.

INJECTOR: A device which receives metered fuel under relatively low pressure and is activated to inject the fuel into the engine under relatively high pressure at a predetermined time.

INPUT SHAFT: The shaft to which torque is applied, usually carrying the driving gear or gears.

INTAKE MANIFOLD: A casting of passages or pipes used to conduct air or a fuel/air mixture to the cylinders.

JOURNAL: The bearing surface within which a shaft operates.

KEY: A small block usually fitted in a notch between a shaft and a hub to prevent slippage of the two parts.

MANIFOLD: A casting of passages or set of pipes which connect the cylinders to an inlet or outlet source.

MANIFOLD VACUUM: Low pressure in an engine intake manifold formed just below the throttle plates. Manifold vacuum is highest at idle and drops under acceleration.

MASTER CYLINDER: The primary fluid pressurizing device in a hydraulic system. In automotive use, it is found in brake and hydraulic clutch systems and is pedal activated, either directly or, in a power brake system, through the power booster.

MODULE: Electronic control unit, amplifier or igniter of solid state or integrated design which controls the current flow in the ignition primary circuit based on input from the pick-up coil. When the module opens the primary circuit, high secondary voltage is induced in the coil.

NEEDLE BEARING: A bearing which consists of a number (usually a large number) of long, thin rollers.

OHM: (Ω) The unit used to measure the resistance of conductor-to-electrical flow. One ohm is the amount of resistance that limits current flow to one ampere in a circuit with one volt of pressure.

OHMMETER: An instrument used for measuring the resistance, in ohms, in an electrical circuit.

OUTPUT SHAFT: The shaft which transmits torque from a device, such as a transmission.

OVERDRIVE: A gear assembly which produces more shaft revolutions than that transmitted to it.

OVERHEAD CAMSHAFT (OHC): An engine configuration in which the camshaft is mounted on top of the cylinder head and operates the valve either directly or by means of rocker arms.

OVERHEAD VALVE (OHV): An engine configuration in which all of the valves are located in the cylinder head and the camshaft is located in the cylinder block. The camshaft operates the valves via lifters and pushrods.

OXIDES OF NITROGEN (NOx): Chemical compounds of nitrogen produced as a byproduct of combustion. They combine with hydrocarbons to produce smog.

OXYGEN SENSOR: Use with the feedback system to sense the presence of oxygen in the exhaust gas and signal the computer which can reference the voltage signal to an air/fuel ratio.

PINION: The smaller of two meshing gears.

PISTON RING: An open-ended ring with fits into a groove on the outer diameter of the piston. Its chief function is to form a seal between the piston and cylinder wall. Most automotive pistons have three rings: two for compression sealing; one for oil sealing.

PRELOAD: A predetermined load placed on a bearing during assembly or by adjustment.

PRIMARY CIRCUIT: the low voltage side of the ignition system which consists of the ignition switch, ballast resistor or resistance wire, bypass, coil, electronic control unit and pick-up coil as well as the connecting wires and harnesses.

PRESS FIT: The mating of two parts under pressure, due to the inner diameter of one being smaller than the outer diameter of the other, or vice versa; an interference fit.

RACE: The surface on the inner or outer ring of a bearing on which the balls, needles or rollers move.

REGULATOR: A device which maintains the amperage and/or voltage levels of a circuit at predetermined values.

RELAY: A switch which automatically opens and/or closes a circuit.

RESISTANCE: The opposition to the flow of current through a circuit or electrical device, and is measured in ohms. Resistance is equal to the voltage divided by the amperage.

RESISTOR: A device, usually made of wire, which offers a preset amount of resistance in an electrical circuit.

RING GEAR: The name given to a ring-shaped gear attached to a differential case, or affixed to a flywheel or as part of a planetary gear set.

ROLLER BEARING: A bearing made up of hardened inner and outer races between which hardened steel rollers move.

ROTOR: 1. The disc-shaped part of a disc brake assembly, upon which the brake pads bear; also called, brake disc. 2. The device mounted atop the distributor shaft, which passes current to the distributor cap tower contacts.

SECONDARY CIRCUIT: The high voltage side of the ignition system, usually above 20,000 volts. The secondary includes the ignition coil, coil wire, distributor cap and rotor, spark plug wires and spark plugs.

SENDING UNIT: A mechanical, electrical, hydraulic or electro-magnetic device which transmits information to a gauge.

SENSOR: Any device designed to measure engine operating conditions or ambient pressures and temperatures. Usually electronic in nature and designed to send a voltage signal to an on-board computer, some sensors may operate as a simple on/off switch or they may provide a variable voltage signal (like a potentiometer) as conditions or measured parameters change.

SHIM: Spacers of precise, predetermined thickness used between parts to establish a proper working relationship.

SLAVE CYLINDER: In automotive use, a device in the hydraulic clutch system which is activated by hydraulic force, disengaging the clutch.

SOLENOID: A coil used to produce a magnetic field, the effect of which is to produce work.

SPARK PLUG: A device screwed into the combustion chamber of a spark ignition engine. The basic construction is a conductive core inside of a ceramic insulator, mounted in an outer conductive base. An electrical charge from the spark plug wire travels along the conductive core and jumps a preset air gap to a grounding point or points at the end of the conductive base. The resultant spark ignites the fuel/air mixture in the combustion chamber.

SPLINES: Ridges machined or cast onto the outer diameter of a shaft or inner diameter of a bore to enable parts to mate without rotation.

TACHOMETER: A device used to measure the rotary speed of an engine, shaft, gear, etc., usually in rotations per minute.

THERMOSTAT: A valve, located in the cooling system of an engine, which is closed when cold and opens gradually in response to engine heating, controlling the temperature of the coolant and rate of coolant flow.

TOP DEAD CENTER (TDC): The point at which the piston reaches the top of its travel on the compression stroke.

TORQUE: The twisting force applied to an object.

TORQUE CONVERTER: A turbine used to transmit power from a driving member to a driven member via hydraulic action, providing changes in drive ratio and torque. In automotive use, it links the driveplate at the rear of the engine to the automatic transmission.

TRANSDUCER: A device used to change a force into an electrical signal.

TRANSISTOR: A semi-conductor component which can be actuated by a small voltage to perform an electrical switching function.

TUNE-UP: A regular maintenance function, usually associated with the replacement and adjustment of parts and components in the electrical and fuel systems of a vehicle for the purpose of attaining optimum performance.

TURBOCHARGER: An exhaust driven pump which compresses intake air and forces it into the combustion chambers at higher than atmospheric pressures. The increased air pressure allows more fuel to be burned and results in increased horsepower being produced.

VACUUM ADVANCE: A device which advances the ignition timing in response to increased engine vacuum.

VACUUM GAUGE: An instrument used to measure the presence of vacuum in a chamber.

VALVE: A device which control the pressure, direction of flow or rate of flow of a liquid or gas.

VALVE CLEARANCE: The measured gap between the end of the valve stem and the rocker arm, cam lobe or follower that activates the valve.

VISCOSITY: The rating of a liquid's internal resistance to flow.

VOLTMETER: An instrument used for measuring electrical force in units called volts. Voltmeters are always connected parallel with the circuit being tested.

WHEEL CYLINDER: Found in the automotive drum brake assembly, it is a device, actuated by hydraulic pressure, which, through internal pistons, pushes the brake shoes outward against the drums.

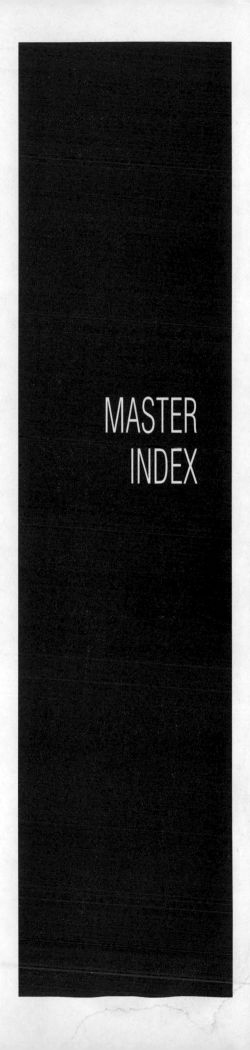

MASTER
INDEX